Douglas R. McGaughey
Strangers and Pilgrims

Theologische Bibliothek Töpelmann

Herausgegeben von
O. Bayer · W. Härle · H.-P. Müller

Band 81

Walter de Gruyter · Berlin · New York
1997

Douglas R. McGaughey

Strangers and Pilgrims

On the Role of Aporiai in Theology

Walter de Gruyter · Berlin · New York
1997

∞ Printed on acid-free paper which falls within the guidelines of the ANSI to ensure permanence and durability.

Die Deutsche Bibliothek — Cataloging-in-Publication Data

McGaughey, Douglas R.:
Strangers and pilgrims : on the role of aporiai theology / Douglas R. McGaughey. — Berlin ; New York : de Gruyter, 1997
(Theologische Bibliothek Töpelmann ; Bd. 81)
ISBN 3-11-015493-5

© Copyright 1997 by Walter de Gruyter & Co., D-10785 Berlin

All rights reserved, including those of translation into foreign languages. No part of this book may be reproduced or transmitted in any form or by any means, electronic or mechanical, including photocopy, recording or any information storage and retrieval system, without permission in writing from the publisher.

Printed in Germany
Printing: Werner Hildebrand, Berlin
Binding: Lüderitz & Bauer-GmbH, Berlin

Preface

The present project is indebted consciously and unconsciously to many. Any attempt to speak only demonstrates that one is a mere midget standing on the shoulders of the giants of a tradition that has gone before. I have been blessed with rigorous conversation partners. Many of them I have not had the pleasure of meeting in person, but their presence permeates what follows and can be found documented in the footnotes. Others, such as those constituting the breakfast sessions (which often lasted from 6:00 a.m. to 12:00 noon) in graduate school, the circle of friends in Tübingen from 1980 to 1983, colleagues, friends, and students at Greensboro College and Willamette University, have more personally influenced the content of this project - although I hasten to add that none of them is to be held accountable for my foibles. They are only responsible for whatever valuable insights are found here. To all of these persons I express my deep gratitude and highest respect.

Willamette University funded several summers of research through Atkinson foundation grants, a faculty seminar on Ricoeur's *Time and Narrative*, computers, and secretarial assistance without which this project would still be a mere possibility. It was also assisted by a 1991 summer grant from the Oregon Council for the Humanities and a year in Germany made possible by a Fulbright research grant.

Above all, I express my appreciation to Margit, Sarah, Hanna, and Kerstin. They not only tolerated my disappearance early in the evening, but they kept tugging me back to the real world, and have provided the experiential richness that no words on a page can ever grasp.

Table of Contents

Preface V

Introduction 1
   Why Aporiai? 1
   Two Agendas 10
   On the Crisis in Theology 16
   An Experiential Faith 34

PART I: THE CONTEXT OF POST-METAPHYSICAL THEOLOGY

1. What is Theology? 43

   On Paradox 45
   Precedents for Paradox in Theology 51
      Hegel's Double Negation Denying History 51
      Tillich's One Absolute Paradox 54
      Kierkegaard's Thought that Thought Cannot Think 55
   Beyond Metaphysics 67
      Materialism 69
      Idealism 70
      A Common Substance 73
      Conditions of Possibility 73
      Beyond Metaphysics to Faith 74
   A Finite God? 78
      Theology Alone Has No Object 79
   Is Theology a Method? 83
   Is the Focus of Theology the Call to Decision? 97
   Theology and the Aporetic 104

2. Theology and Aporiai 105

   Not Mere Astonishment 108
   Contingent Necessity and More 110
   Retrieval of Spirituality 112
   Dialogue and Application: Listening 113
   Dialogue and Application: Speaking 121
   Dialogue and Application: Humility 125
   Theology as the "Fusion of Horizons 126

3. After Heidegger and Derrida 129

   Heidegger: On the Meaning of Being 129
   On the Copula 131
   Heidegger: Being as "World" 139

	Derrida and Binary Thought	148
	Derrida and Vulgar Skepticism	151
4.	David Tracy: Theology as Correlation	157
	Contingent versus Metaphysical Necessity	159
	On the Role of Concealment in What is Manifest	161
5.	On George Lindbeck's Cultural-Linguistic Theological Model	172
	Reality and Religion as a Social Construct: Truth as Pragmatic Usage	175
	Our Debt to Language: Rules Prior to Paradigms?	178
	Faith Precedes Language: But Certainty is the Pre-Condition of Doubt	187
	A New Heteronomy	189
6.	Theology as Inquiry into Paradox: Strangers and Pilgrims	195
	Augustine?	196
	Beyond Dualism	197
	Unknowing is not Ignorance	199
	Faith Seeking Understanding	201
	Ogden's Reflective Faith	204
	Second Naiveté and Praxis	205
	Beyond Reductionism	206
	Theology as a Subversive Enterprise	208

PART II: ON THE ROLE OF APORIAI IN THEOLOGY

7.	The Aporia of Spirit and Matter	213
	The Aporia of Spirit and Matter	214
	Matter in Contrast to Spirit	216
	The Problem of Definition	219
	Simile of the Sun	221
	Simile of the Line	222
	Everydayness and the Real	229
	On Universals	233
	The Aporia of Universals and Particulars	239
8.	The Aporia of Logic and Praxis	241
	Two Kinds of Paradigms	242
	Sociological Paradigms and Understanding	244
	The Subversion of Coherence as the Consequence of Coherence	249

	The Non-Cumulative Character of Human Knowledge	250
	Paradigm Revolutions and the Aporia of Logic and Praxis	253
	Religious Language and the Aporia of Logic and Praxis	256
	Conclusion	259
9.	The Aporiai of Language	263
	Reality as Vitally Metaphoric	263
	I.A. Richards: From Analogy to Tenor and Vehicle	266
	Wheelwright: Metaphor and Tensive Reality	270
	Metaphorical Tension at the Heart of Language	286
	Metaphorical Tension at the Heart of Reality	297
	Conclusion	324
10.	The Aporiai of Truth	328
	Truth as Correspondence: Verification and Falsification	331
	Truth as Disclosure: Metaphorical Truth	338
	On the Open-endedness of Understanding	346
	On the Historicality of Understanding	352
	Language as the Mediator of Possibility	357
	Aletheia and Symbolic Reality	372
	Conclusion	376
11.	The Aporiai of Temporality	379
	Clock Time and Eternity	379
	Cosmological Time	384
	Plato	384
	Aristotle	387
	Plotinus	391
	Time and Not-Being	393
	Anthropological Time	393
	Augustine	393
	Kant	395
	Husserl	397
	Ontological Time	401
	Heidegger	403
	Being as Time Unites the Unchanging and the Temporal	407
	Conclusion	409
12.	The Aporia of Self and Other	412
	Defining the Self?	412
	The Self: Beyond Actuality to the Dynamic Tension	417
	of Possibilities Between Intellect and World	
	Beyond Heidegger's Logos to Nous	423
	On the Unique and Unrepeatable Character	426
	of Individual Consciousness	

Lévinas and Ricoeur on the Self 434
The Self as Ambiguous Dialectic: The "Structure of Selfhood" .. 438
Conclusion 441

13. Conclusion: Faith in a Post-Metaphysical Context 443

The Crisis of Reason: Two Kinds of Rationality 450
Beyond Critical Realism and Heidegger 453
Non-epistemic Faith and the Priority of Spirit 459
Beyond Self and Actuality to Concealed Possibility 461
The Correspondence Theory of Truth and ἀλήθεια 463
Sola scriptura and Protestant Theology 467
Beyond Plurivocity to Spirit and Faith 471
Two Models of the Faith 476
Faith in a Post-metaphysical Context 480
From Vulgar to Refined Skepticism: 483
Faith Seeking Understanding

Appendix: Division of the Task of Theology 490

Theology's Threefold Division 495
Philosophical Theology: The Aporetic 497
Systematic Theology: Diachronic and Synchronic 503
   Diachronic and Synchronic 503
   Descriptive Phenomenology 505
Practical Theology: Institutional Religion 507
   Procedural Practical Theology 507
   Instructional Practical Theology 508
   Prophetic Practical Theology 509
   Pastoral Practical Theology 509
   Parenetic Practical Theology 510
   Practical Theology 510

Works Cited 511

Index 531

On Pragmatism and the Limits to Reason:

"... if a man (sic) has accustomed himself to skeptical considerations on the uncertainty and narrow limits of reason, he will not entirely forget them when he turns his reflection on other subjects; but in all his philosophical principles and reasoning, I dare not say, in his common conduct, he will be found different from those who either never formed any opinions in the case or have entertained sentiments more favorable to human reason.

To whatever length anyone may push his speculative principles of skepticism, he must act, I own, and live, and converse like other men; and for this conduct he is not obliged to give any other reason than the absolute necessity he lies under of so doing. If he ever carries his speculations farther than this necessity constrains him, and philosophizes either on natural or moral subjects, he is allured by a certain pleasure and satisfaction which he finds in employing himself after that manner. He considers, besides, that everyone, even in common life, is constrained to have more or less of this philosophy; that from our earliest infancy we make continual advances in forming more general principles of conduct and reasoning; that the larger experience we acquire, and the stronger reason we are endued with, we always render our principles the more general and comprehensive; and that what we call *philosophy* is nothing but a more regular and methodical operation of the same kind. To philosophize on such subjects is nothing essentially different from reasoning on common life, and *we may only expect greater stability, if not greater truth*, from our philosophy on account of its exacter and more scrupulous method of proceeding."

    Philo in David Hume, *Dialogues Concerning Natural Religion*, pp. 6-7. (emphasis added)

On the Existence or Non-existence of a Deity:

"About the gods I am unable to affirm either how they exist or how they do not exist."
    Protagoras quoted by Cicero in *De nat. deor.*, I.XXIII, 62, 63; LCL p. 60; found in Egil Grislis, "Calvin's Use of Cicero in the Institutes I:1-5 - A Case Study in Theological Method" in *Archiv für Reformationsgeschichte* 62/1 (1971), p. 19.

On Critical Reflection and Faith:

"Don't you remember, said *Philo*, the excellent saying of *Lord Bacon* on this head? That a little philosophy, replied *Cleanthes*, makes a man an atheist; a great deal converts him to religion. That is a very judicious remark, too, said *Philo*. But what I have in my eye is another passage, where, having mentioned *David's* fool, who said in his heart there is no God, this great philosopher observes that the atheists nowadays have a double share of folly. For they are not contented to say in their hearts there is no God, but they also utter that impiety with their lips, and are thereby guilty of multiplied indiscretion and imprudence."
David Hume, *Dialogues Concerning Natural Religion*, p. 11.

"To be a philosophical skeptic is ... the first and most essential step towards being a sound, believing *Christian* ..."
David Hume, *Dialogues Concerning Natural Religion*, p. 89.

On the Emergence of Spiritual Understanding:

"... the same thing happens in the spiritual life as with many plants--the main shoot comes last."
Kierkegaard, *Repetition*, p. 154.

Introduction

Why Aporiai?

In viewing the human situation and its limits in the last third of the 20th century, this project maintains that the central concern for Christian theology at this point is neither God, nor Christ, nor biblicism, but the aporiai[1] of the spirit. Rather than theology commencing with God, the Christ, or the Scriptures, it must start today with human experience and the spiritual character of that experience to understand the constitutive aporiai or paradoxes shaping experience before it can turn to the task of inquiring after an understanding of God, Christ, and the scriptures. This is neither to argue that natural theology is to replace revealed theology nor to elevate the human above the divine by appealing to human reason as an ultimate arbiter of truth claims. The dichotomy of natural and revealed theology and human reason are placed into question by the aporiai of the human condition.[2] Hence, the

---

[1] Literally the Greek work aporia means "no crossing," "no ford," or "no way through or over," but its meaning is more adequately expressed with something like "being on the way, but not knowing the way ahead." One may think of its meaning in the sense of being fogged in on a mountain pass and not knowing the way either ahead or back yet having to go on, somehow. Gottfried Martin says of aporia: "Im griechischen Verbum ist das griechische Substantiv *Poros* enthalten. *Poros* bedeutet den Weg durch ein schwieriges Gelände, den Pfad durch ein Gebirge, die Furt durch einen Fluß, den Weg über das Meer. *Aporein* [the present infinitive of ἀπορέω from the same root as "aporia"] bedeutet also keinen Weg mehr wissen ..." (in *Grundprobleme der großen Philosophen*. *Philosophie des Altertums und des Mittelalters* (Göttingen: Vandenhoeck & Ruprecht, 1978, p. 10). This project prefers the term "aporia" and its plural "aporiai" to paradox, because aporia preserves the praxis side of knowing (or more appropriately, unknowing) - unlike the term paradox which suggests merely a logical conundrum. The limits to knowledge are no plaidoyer for simple observation and passive inactivity. That the human condition is one of radical unknowing does not mean that we cannot not act. In our unknowing we must always act. This is both the source of human greatness and the reason humanity is so dangerous.

[2] The dichotomy between natural and revealed theology is a consequence of Aquinas and the subsequent school of Nominalism, and it presupposes a "separationist" model of the Christian faith, i.e., that fundamental to the human condition is its radical separation from God because of sin requiring one to accept in faith the atoning sacrificial death and conquering victory of resurrection as the means for accomplishing a reconciliation with the divine in the next life. Since humanity is corrupted by original sin (a notion introduced into the tradition by Augustine through a misreading of Romans 5:12), there is no human capacity in its natural state capable of instructing one about God. Knowledge of God can only be acquired through revelation, i.e., through the divine Word all too fre-

present project is not elevating reason (natural theology) above revelation (revealed theology). Both natural and revealed theology presuppose a kind of knowledge that the human cannot possess. In contrast, what follows is attempting to indicate the radical aporetic limits to reason that require speaking of the human condition as faith seeking understanding. At the same time the aporetic character of the human condition enables a retrieval (but not a mere repetition) of the classical spirituality informing the Christian tradition through its first four centuries. This may no longer be a retrieval, though, of the *metaphysics* associated with that classical spirituality. Rather, it is a retrieval that acknowledges the spiritual (non-material) character of human experience rooted in its historical circumstances. The structure of what follows is shaped by the need to establish the circumstances requiring a turn to aporiai in theology (Part I) and to clarify what the aporiai are which limit humans and the theological task (Part II). Hence, the project is divided into two parts. Part I seeks to define what the tasks of theology are by dialoguing with key individuals and responding to central issues confronting the theologian today. Part II turns explicitly to describe six aporiai shaping the task of

---

quently identified with the words of the scriptures, and one quarreled over the extent to which revealed theology must be in conformity with reason. This separationist model stands in contrast to the "unification" model of the Christian faith, i.e., that constitutive of the human condition is a unification with the divine in spirit ($νοῦς$, $θεωρία$, $λόγος$, and/or $νόμος$) already if incomplete in this life requiring the refocusing of attention to enhance that which one has in common with the divine. This latter unification model of the Christian faith informed every representative of Christian theology down to the 5th century.

The present discussion of the relationship between natural and revealed theology today continues to overlook the radical difference between these two over-arching models of the Christian faith. See, for example, Michael Kappes, "'Natürliche Theologie' als innerprotestantisches und ökumenisches Problem?: Die Kontroverse zwischen Eberhard Jüngel und Wolfhart Pannenberg und ihr ökumenischer Ertrag" in *Catholica: Vierteljahresschrift für ökumenische Theologie* 49/4 (1995), pp. 276-309. Kappes suggests, following distinctions made by Pannenberg and Kraus, that the term "natural theology" in the sense of the conditions necessary for the human reception of a possible revelation but in no way prescriptive of the content of that revelation should be replaced by either "philosophical theology" or "verifiable (verifikative) theology". See, in addition, *ibid.*, pp. 302-303. I suggest that the term "philosophical theology" be used for that theological agenda concerned with contingency, non-epistemic faith, and historical spirituality. Hence, the more appropriate term to substitute for "natural theology" here would be the term which expresses what these theologians are claiming, i.e., verifiable theology in the sense of those insights gleaned from the human condition which could be confirmed by revelation. Since there is no possibility of absolute verification, however, verifiable theology presupposes philosophical theology.

theology. An appendix suggests the division of theology into three disciplines: philosophical, systematic, and practical theology.

After an overview of the individual chapters and a discussion of the two agendas shaping the entire project, this introduction identifies the crisis confronting the theologian in our age in terms of her/his alienation from the community s/he is meant to serve as well as in terms of the loss of credibility for Christian theology that Sallie McFague speaks of as theology's irrelevancy and idolatry.[3] Theology has become irrelevant for many, she argues, because of the ease with which one can dismiss a tradition which has supported racism, sexism, classism, xenophobia, the raping of the environment, and the slaughtering of millions in the name of God. Theology has become idolatrous to the extent that it has insisted that its language is literal rather than figurative. No matter what one's judgment with respect to McFague's description of Christianity, theology has become irrelevant both for institutions and for individuals in our age. This present project seeks a retrieval of faith and the role of an experienced spirituality at the core of the human condition in order to respond to the alienation, irrelevancy and idolatry of theology today.

This task is accomplished by maintaining that such a theology of spirit rests upon six aporiai shaping the human condition. These allow a retrieval (but not a mere repetition) of a classic notion of human spirituality shaping the Western theological tradition and the situating of aporetic theology within the discipline of theology as a historical discipline.

Chapter one addresses more explicitly what this project understands theology to be concerned with, i.e., the aporiai or paradoxes shaping the human condition. It looks at previous discussions of paradox by theologians, and finds them too narrow and insensitive to the dynamic of aporetic tensions at work in human experience. The chapter looks at more frequent approaches to theology, e.g., as metaphysics, as method, and as a call to decision, and argues that these, too, misrepresent the aporetic character of experience and understanding.

Chapter two continues the investigation of the meaning of theology as a discipline suggesting that it perhaps commences with astonishment, or an awareness of dependence, but that such astonishment leads to a necessary acknowledgment of the limits to reason requiring judicious review of any and all speculation. Aporetic theology recognizes that, although there is a radical

---

[3] See Sallie McFague, *Metaphorical Theology: Models of God in Religious Language* (Philadelphia: Fortress Press, 1988), pp. 4-10.

contingency to both our existence and our knowledge, there is nevertheless no choice about the necessity to act. Everything hinges, however, upon what "grounds" one makes one's decisions. The search for criteria requires that one be vigilant with both a hermeneutics of restoration and a hermeneutics of suspicion.

Although pragmatic action in the material world is a necessary condition of human experience, this projects argues emphatically for a retrieval of the historical character of the "*spiritual*" by proposing that the theologian stands in the tension between an inheritance (the acting and suffering of others as Paul Ricoeur calls it in *Time and Narrative*) and the call to responsible *action* in the world. Acknowledging the uniqueness and unrepeatability of individual experience inaccessible to the senses, it is nevertheless impossible for us to begin to make sense out of our present experience without the "linguistic" inheritance,[4] of our cultural and family heritage. This context requires both a "hermeneutics of restoration" and a "hermeneutics of suspicion" as we actualize the possibilities enabled by our heritage (restore the tradition ever anew) but recognize that restoration involves concealing, suppression, and the danger of systematic distortion[5] (the need for suspicion).

All understanding leads to application of one kind or other, Hans-Georg Gadamer reminds us,[6] and it is crucial that we take ownership of that process of understanding and application to the extent that we are able. Nevertheless, there are limits to that process, and these limits are aporetic limits. Therefore, although this project maintains that essential for a rebirth

---

[4] Ricoeur speaks of language as "... the great institution, the institution of institutions, that has preceded each and every one of us. And by language we must here understand not just the system of *langue* in each natural language, but the things already said, understood, and received." *Time and Narrative*, vol. 3, trans. by Kathleen Blamey and David Pellauer (Chicago: The University of Chicago Press, 1988), p. 221. This does not mean to suggest that our inheritance is only a matter of a specific language of cultural range, i.e., our "mother" tongue. Rather, it acknowledges that all of our experience is mediated and depends upon some kind of "symbol system" to accomplish that mediation. In the words of Thomas Kuhn, there is no immediate access to stimuli. We experience sensations filtered by a host of quasi-metaphysical commitments constituting a cognitive, coherent, normative and communal representation of the way we take reality and its causality to be.

[5] See Jürgen Habermas, "On Systematically Distorted Communication" in *Inquiry* 13 (1970), pp. 205-218, and "Towards a Theory of Communicative Competence" in *Inquiry* 13 (1970), pp. 360-375

[6] See, for example, "The Hermeneutic Problem of Application" in Hans-Georg Gadamer, *Truth and Method*, trans. by Garret Barden and John Cumming (New York: The Seabury Press/Continuum, 1975), pp. 274-278.

of experiential faith is a retrieval of a classic understanding of spirituality, this does not involve a call out of the world of pragmatic action. Rather, it is a call into the world as spiritual agents of reconciliation and transformation. Foremost in such a task, however, is not merely a call to action, but a learning to listen to the broad spectrum of voices of the tradition offering models for engagement in the world. Such a careful listening can empower theology by serving as the basis for critically reflective application and action concerned, above all, with preserving the conditions of possibility of experience in a posture of humility. Finally, this chapter concludes with the appropriation of Gadamer's notion of the "fusion of horizons" for trying to point to the dynamic and the depths of aporetic theology as an open-ended odyssey of accountable understanding and action.

Chapter three suggests that, although theology must move beyond Heidegger and Deconstructionism, there are valuable lessons to be learned from both. This project is indebted particularly to Heidegger's analysis of the human as always and already embedded in a world. What is found wanting in Heidegger is an adequate appreciation of the spiritual dimension of that embededness in the world. In addition, what follows is indebted to Derrida's analysis of deferment and différance, which reminds us that human experience and understanding is always symbolically mediated and never absolute or complete. Nevertheless, binarity is defended not as a route to absolutes but precisely as a way of describing the dynamic tensions informing and demanding accountability to them in experience. In addition, by embracing what Hume calls "vulgar skepticism," Derrida has thrown the baby out with bath water. While it is true that we can give no logical argument within the mind to prove the independent existence of anything "outside" of the mind, pragmatic action demands that we be accountable to both an empirical world "without" and universals "within" which are beyond the logical proof of the mind. Hume calls such an accountability "refined skepticism." The necessity of refined skepticism is confirmation of the role of faith in experience.

Chapter four investigates David Tracy's understanding of theology as correlation, but observes that his project is attempting to reconcile two contradictory components: Process metaphysics and hermeneutics. The analysis leads to the conclusion that at best Process thought can speak of contingently but not metaphysically necessary conditions of possibility. If such a claim is appropriate, then the project of Process thought collapses into hermeneutics, and one must surrender any and all notions of metaphysical explanation and turn to some kind of aporetic theology of faith seeking understanding but without sacrificing critical reflection and accountability.

Chapter five turns to George Lindbeck's "cultural-linguistic" theological model which dismisses liberal theologies as "experience-expressivist" turning theology into mere aesthetics. The chapter proposes that Lindbeck's analysis of so-called "experience-expressivist" theologies inadequately appreciates the historical context of religious experience, understanding, and action. At the same time, his "cultural-linguistic" model, while employing the notion of paradigm from Kuhn, has failed to follow Kuhn's insistence that rules are not prior to paradigms but subsequent to them. Furthermore, his "cultural-linguistic" model can offer no defense against possible systematic distortion in a community. Once again, theology requires a hermeneutics of suspicion as much as it involves a hermeneutics of restoration. Without a hermeneutics of suspicion, his "cultural-linguistic" model is simply another form of heteronomy.

Chapter six seeks to develop what this project means by "faith seeking understanding." It returns to Augustine of Hippo by way of Anselm of Canterbury to enquire about the meaning of this aphorism. Although one can find echoes, as well, of this project's title ("Strangers and Pilgrims") in Augustine's writings, the meaning attributed to these terms in Augustine fails to grasp the aporetic richness that this project wants to underscore. On the other hand, "faith" here is not George Santayana's or Schubert Ogden's "animal faith" in the basic trust or confidence in the worthwhileness of our lives. Once again, such a formulation fails to appreciate the aporetic depths of the human condition. Therefore, the project turns to the identification of six fundamental aporiai at the core of the human condition that require the acknowledgment that the path we are on is ambiguous, driven by irreconcilable tensions, and demanding of vigilance, accountability, and responsible action.

Part II turns to the explicit investigation of these six aporiai which are unavoidable for theology and which insist that theology can be no other than faith seeking understanding. Part II, also, is divided into six chapters.

Chapter seven employs the similes of the sun and of the line from Book VI of Plato's *Republic* to gain access to a radically experiential grasp of the human condition as shaped by the aporia of spirit and matter. Furthermore, it indicates the limits to reason by its acknowledging with Socrates that definition (the establishing of both identity and difference) is impossible. Hence, an examination of the human condition establishes the centrality of non-epistemic faith at the very heart of human experience: neither the spiritual nor the material dimensions of life provide the human with epistemic absolutes.

Chapter eight is concerned with what this project describes as the aporia of logic and praxis. Employing primarily the analysis of Thomas Kuhn in *The Structure of Scientific Revolutions*, it seeks not to establish a distinct epistemic place for theology over against science but to indicate how both science and religion/theology are dependent upon mediation and an internal coherence to their "sociological" (i.e., socially constructed) models of reality. Nevertheless, Kuhn's analysis makes it clear that acknowledgment of the socially constructed character of reality, including judgments with respect to causality, does not mean that one can ignore the claims of an exogenous world. Once again, one cannot *not* act, and the anomalous does challenge the coherence of the community's paradigm even if one cannot have direct access to the world in which one is acting and by which one is being challenged. The aporia here calls us to accountability to both the "spiritual" paradigm and the "material" world of action and accountability.

Chapter nine addresses what can be described as the aporia of figurative and literal language. The everyday assumption is that figurative language is secondary to literal language. The metaphorical and symbolic are taken to be grounded in a univocal, literal meaning that is then somehow "stretched" or "distorted" to figurative language as a form of ornamentation and embellishment upon the world of factuality. As such, the figurative is taken to be dispensable. One uses, or has used, figurative language because one wanted to sound erudite, did not have the time, or was too lazy to speak literally. The analysis of this chapter indicates that the relationship between the figurative and the literal, however, is just the reverse. Having established in chapter seven the "spiritual" and non-epistemic character of human experience, i.e., that the human is faith seeking understanding, and having established in chapter eight the mediated character of all reality including notions of causal explanation by means of sociological paradigms, chapter nine addresses the indispensable task performed by consciousness of establishing identity in the midst of difference by indicating how this task is a radically figurative process. Univocity of meaning is a sedimentation arrived at *after* an experience of sometimes disjointed, but always different, phenomena within which we identify similarity and with luck a judgment of identity. Seeking similarity in difference is the key to metaphor and symbol, i.e., the figurative. Such an a posteriori dis-covering of identity (universals) indicates, as well, the unavoidable role of concealment (of selectivity requiring ignoring and suppressing of some aspects) in the search for understanding. Understanding can only occur where there is a judgment of identification. But there is no direct and immediate access to the referent of the judgment.

Hence, identification is an activity accomplished by consciousness out of the diversity of its experienced images of the referent. That "jump" from diversity to identity, from different to identical, is the result of the figurative nature of consciousness. The *judgment* of identification is always accompanied with the *fact* of difference. Ricoeur labels this the radical "is"/"is not" level of tension in-forming the metaphorical and elevating it above the univocal and literal. Here one encounters, as well, the limits reigning in metaphysical claims regarding the univocity of Being as either a common substance or common element uniting everything that "is."[7] The aporia here is reflected in the difference in emphasis between Plato and Aristotle with respect to universals. Leaving aside whether or not Plato taught that universals are independent of a world of sense perception, he did take them to be ontologically prior to sense perception. Aristotle, however, is concerned with epistemology, and he speaks of the human experience of universals as first in sense perception, that is, as form in matter. If universals are constituted in consciousness a posteriori, they are inherited at least in language as a priori, but this does not exhaust the aporia with respect to the "is"/"is not" of metaphysical claims. It is not simply that universals are experienced by humans as the a posteriori consequence of mediation in consciousness of particulars ("is not") judged to have something in common ("is"), but Being itself is equally a tension between an "is" and an "is not." When Being is understood as the concealed possibilities of all that is actually manifest, then Being is a "sameness" shared by all that "is" as a sameness of *general* possibility, but that "sameness" is always limited by the *particular* actual circumstances of the individual and her/his community, i.e., a radical difference in sameness emerges within the dynamic of the revealing and concealing of Being. This aporia of an "is"/"is not," characterizing Being not merely in the sense of the ontological difference between "things" and "to be-ness" but in the sense of general and circumstantially limited possibilities, requires the surrendering of the notion that there is or can be some "intropathic fusion that precedes ... subject object duality."[8] It calls radically into question any quest

---

[7] This is the metaphysical move made by Karl Rahner in *Hearer of the Word. Laying the Foundations for a Philosophy of Religion*, trans. by Joseph Donceel (New York: Continum, 1994) where the philosophy of religion is defined as the investigation of the common unity or ground serving as the condition of possibility of all things. See particularly his discussion of the "one ground of all reality" and the "luminosity of being" in Chapter 3.

[8] Paul Ricoeur, *The Rule of Metaphor*, trans. by Robert Czerny et al. (Toronto: University of Toronto Press, 1977), p. 246.

for a mystical unity that ignores the "is not" in an attempt to experience some pure "is."

Chapter ten addresses the aporia of the revealing and concealing nature of truth. It is not simply that every experience that one has and every judgment that one forms involves the suppression or concealing of a background. What is called the correspondence theory of truth (truth in terms of the correspondence of our judgments with the state of affairs to which the judgment refers) focuses attention on actuality at the expense of possibility. However, what is true about an experience or an object is inseparable from the concealed possibilities of that experience and that object. Hence, truth may not be reserved to the merely factual. Truth is inseparable from the possible. Truth, therefore, requires concealment. Such an insight into the nature of truth permits the retrieval of the Greek notion of truth as ἀλήθεια based on the root λανθάνω meaning to cover over or to escape notice. ἀ-λήθεια (truth) means what is both manifest and simultaneously covered over; with the covered over escaping all notice. Truth depends upon the concealed. This understanding of truth radically escalates the non-epistemic character of human understanding and confirms that the human condition is, once again, a radical form of non-epistemic faith seeking understanding.

Chapter eleven addresses the aporiai of temporality shaping the human condition. It undertakes a survey of the discussions of time in the Western tradition from Plato and Aristotle over Plotinus and Augustine to Kant, Husserl, and Heidegger to point out the manner in which the very temporality of our experience is paradoxical. Three kinds of paradox emerge here. First, time is both linear and simultaneous. Second, according to Aristotle, the individual experiences time as a sequence of moments that are surely something, but dependent upon a present "gap" of nothing uniting those moments. Third, cosmologically the individual and her/his moment (i.e., phenomenological time) is meaningless, but the phenomenological time of the individual is the key to the meaning of cosmological time.

Chapter twelve seeks to describe the aporia of self and other/Other. These terms "other" and "Other" are applied to the world of experience in this project, and they do not presuppose (nor do they deny) a relationship to some otherness beyond that world of experience. Hence, "other" applies in this project to the phenomenal world of things, and "Other" applies to persons. Employing the work of Lévinas and Ricoeur, it commences with Kant's insight that the self is not accessible to itself.[9] The self knows itself

---

[9] See Immanuel Kant, *Critique of Pure Reason*, trans. by Norman Kemp Smith (New York: St. Martin's Press, 1965), B152-3, pp. 165-166.

only as it appears to itself - not as it really is. Once again, we encounter the necessary role of concealment in experience, because our understanding of who we are as selves involves in the present moment the "suppression" of who we were, the concealing of much if not most of what we are in that moment, and the inaccessibility to us in the moment of what we are yet to become. The aporia here, however, is that discovery of the possibilities of the self, unknowable as the self is to itself, is inseparable from our encounter with the Other both as other selves and as world. An appropriate understanding of the self, then, involves acknowledgment of the radically nonepistemic nature of that understanding. Not only is there no literal meaning to the world and the Other as Other self, but there is no literal meaning to the self. The self's understanding of itself and the Other is radically figurative involving both manifestation and concealment.

Part II concludes with a summary of the entire project and a discussion of applications. Its intent is to move from $\theta\epsilon\omega\rho\eta\tau\iota\kappa\acute{o}\varsigma$ to $\pi\rho\hat{\alpha}\xi\iota\varsigma$ to suggest what difference a theology, which commences with an investigation of the fundamental aporiai of experience, can make for one's own and for the community's life. Given that we cannot not act is central to the human condition, it will be suggested that critical reflection about those conditions enabling and informing one's acting in the world are essential for a life that seeks understanding, tolerance, justice, and peace.

Two Agendas

In addition to these six aporiai, two agendas shape the project. The first seeks to retrieve an experiential sense of a classic kind of spirituality while the second attempts to engage theology in a post-metaphysical context.

The notion of spirituality pursued here is one informing the Christian tradition since its origins, but increasingly lost with the rise of empiricism and the mathematization of reality beginning in the 14th century. This is not meant to suggest that as of the 14th century theologians ceased to work out of this understanding of spirituality. The writings of such disparate theologians as Jonathan Edwards, William Ellery Channing, Ralph Waldo Emerson, Theodore Parker, Horace Bushnell, Charles S. Peirce and the Niebuhrs (H. Richard and Reinhold), to mention only a few of just the American 18th to 20th centuries tradition, are shaped by the framework of a Christian spirituality inaccessible to the senses but constitutive of all our experience.

What is claimed here, however, is that the greater the dominance of empirical sense experience as *the* criterion for what constitutes reality and a valid truth claim, the greater the loss of the spiritual dimension of our lives in terms of the real "life of the intellect."[10] But what follows does not wish to simply retrieve the "internal" realm of spiritual experience at the expense of the "external" realm of material experience. Instead, it argues that any reductionism is as costly to our understanding of who we are in the order of things as is the ignoring of the contradictory and irreconcilable constitutive elements of human experience. Nor does what follows seek to retrieve a two substance ontology of spirit and matter. This issue leads to the second agenda of the present project.

Just what does "post-metaphysical" mean, and how can one do theology in a post-metaphysical context? Post-metaphysical thought acknowledges that we have lost all absolute grounding of the human condition in any enduring reality. Jean-Francois Lyotard describes this situation as the loss of any meta-narrative. In addition to pointing out the failures of the meta-narratives of Hegel, Dilthey, Marx and Capitalism, Lyotard concludes:

> ... [I]t must be clear that it is our business not to supply reality but to invent allusions to the conceivable which cannot be presented. And it is not to be expected that

---

[10] This is precisely the claim made by Lawrence S. Stepelevich in "From Tübingen to Rome: The First Catholic Response to Hegel" in *The Heythrop Journal*, 32/4 (1991), 477-492. He documents the predominance of the "Principle of Positivity" in the Catholic response to Hegel "... that philosophy must begin with the acceptance of an objective reality that exists *per se* and exists with all of its qualifications independently of subjective mind ... [T]he world of objects is taken as substantial reality, and the knowing mind understood to be merely a mirror-image of that reality" (*ibid.*, 481) He then observes (*ibid.*, 487-488): "The principle of positivity degrades thought into an epiphenomenon. Such a principle not only sunders human thought from reality, the rational from the real, but, *in so far as it also asserts the physically given as the true objectivity, it has a debilitating effect upon spiritual life. In the practical order it cannot but make the believer less concerned about the mind and more concerned about the body ...*" (emphasis added). I have no difficulty going this far with Stepelevich, but, as will be made clear shortly in the discussion of post-metaphysics, this project cannot embrace his Hegelian meta-narrative or totalization project. In addition, it is simply a mis-reading of Hume to suggest that his "pluralistic viewpoint" resting upon "empiricism" "... logically leads to both scepticism and atheism" (*ibid.*, 487) A careful reading of Hume's *Dialogues Concerning Natural Religion* will make clear that Philo in these dialogues is not a "vulgar" but a "refined skeptic" dedicated to the preservation of true religion and only an enemy of "vulgar superstitions." Philo does, indeed, challenge the notion maintained by Stepelevich (*ibid.*, 489) that reason "links man and God" (this is the position taken by Cleanthes in the *Dialogues*), but not unequivocally. Philo is concerned to indicate the limits to reason and affirm where true faith commences.

this task will effect the last reconciliation between language games ... [O]nly the transcendental illusion (that of Hegel) can hope to totalize them into a real unity. But Kant also knew that the price to pay for such an illusion is terror. The nineteenth and twentieth centuries have given us as much terror as we can take. *We have paid a high enough price for the nostalgia of the whole and the one, for the reconciliation of the concept and the sensible, of the transparent and the communicable experience.* Under the general demand for slackening and for appeasement, we can hear the mutterings of the desire for a return of terror, for the realization of the fantasy to seize reality. The answer is: *let us wage a war on totality; let us be witnesses to the unpresentable; let us activate the differences and save the honor of the name*.[11] (emphasis added)

This does not deny our dependence upon conditions and circumstances that we have not created ourselves. We are dependent upon a life-world and a range of possibilities not of our own creation. The loss of any absolute grounding of reality means, rather, that there is no logical proof (from within the intellect) possible for any dimension (either as empirical or idealist) independent of finite and contingent consciousness much less a logical proof for something that is eternal. Yet even the self is a fiction. In post-metaphysical thought the self is spoken of as decentered, because there is no permanent center or ego that integrates the self. We know our selves no differently than we know the objects of sense perception, i.e., in terms of the way the self appears to us.

There is no logical argument for a world existing independent of the individual's conscious life, because everything s/he knows and does is experienced by her/him exclusively in the intellect. If we cannot give a logical

---

[11] Jean-Francois Lyotard, *The Postmodern Condition*, trans. by Geoff Bennington and Brian Massumi (Minneapolis: University of Minnesota Press, 1984), pp. 81-82. See, as well, *ibid.*, pp. xxiii-xxiv.

Paul Ricoeur rejects the temptation of totalization, as well. See *Time and Narrative*, vol. 3, chapter 9, "Should We Renounce Hegel?," pp. 193-206, particularly p. 206 (emphasis added): "Despite the seduction of the idea, the cunning of reason is not the peripeteia that can encompass all the reversals of history, because the realization of freedom cannot be taken as the plot behind every plot. In other words, the leaving behind of Hegelianism signifies renouncing the attempt to decipher the supreme plot ... To admit that the self-understanding of the historical consciousness can be so affected by events that ... we cannot say whether we produced them or they simply happened, is to admit the finitude of the philosophical act that makes up the self-understanding of the historical consciousness. This finitude in interpretation signifies that *all thought about thought has presuppositions that it can never master*, which in their turn become the situations beginning from which we think, without our being able to think them through in themselves ... For what readers of Hegel, once they have been seduced by the power of Hegel's thought as I have, do not feel the abandoning of this philosophy as a wound, a wound that ... will not be healed? For such readers if they are not to give into the weaknesses of nostalgia, we must wish the courage of the work of mourning."

argument for the independent existence of the empirical world and our experience is radically non-material and inaccessible to the senses, then we might conclude that the ultimate order to reality comes from universals deeper "within" and structuring of consciousness. Why? Because they are obviously experienced in the intellect, they are incapable of being objects of sense, and the intellect cannot begin to function in an orderly fashion without them. But Socrates demonstrated that there are no absolute definitions for these universals. As constant as they appear to consciousness to be, they are indefinable and are only experienced to the extent that they are accessible to consciousness.

There are, to be sure, pragmatic proofs demonstrating that we are dependent upon conditions and circumstances not of our own making. Try ignoring a speeding train heading toward the crossing where you're car is stalled. But exactly the same pragmatic argument can be applied for a dimension of experience exactly opposite of the empirical world of speeding trains. For it is just as pragmatically impossible for us to ignore "universals" or "ideas" as it is for us to ignore "objects" of sense perception. One can argue that without access to universals there would be no order or coherence to experience, and it would be impossible to identify similarities, much less identity, among the flow of differences that would be the phantasm of experience. Without dependence upon universals, language would be meaningless and communication impossible.

But these kinds of pragmatic arguments do not demonstrate the existence of anything absolute or eternal. Any argument dependent upon action is at best a contingent argument, not an absolute argument, for the presupposition of all action is that an individual exist. But no individual exists absolutely necessarily. We exist contingently, so that any pragmatic knowledge dependent upon our contingent existence must itself be contingent. It is this insight that characterizes our current context and situation as post-metaphysical. Such pragmatic arguments establish two opposite, yet contingently necessary, dimensions to experience: 1) the dimension of the objects of sense perception and 2) the dimension of the intellect inaccessible to sense perception. Neither can be avoided nor ignored, and it is a central thesis of this project that neither can be reduced to the other. In the midst of secular materialism a dimension of experienced spirituality can and must be affirmed as equally constitutive of the human condition.

In the absence of an absolute metaphysical foundation or metanarrative, are we left merely with trust in a communal truth in the sense developed by George Lindbeck and Stanley Hauerwas? Or must we have confidence in the truth of a revelation in which history is ultimately denied as with Mircea Eliade, Kurt Hübner, Karl Barth, and Wolfhart Pannenberg? Or must we insist on an unmediated truth in no way dependent upon the mediation of a process of interpretation as with biblical literalists? Or must we opt for either a spiritual explanation (a form of Gnosticism) or a material explanation (a positivist explanation) of experience which would exclude the possibility of the other? These options are inadequate not because they can be demonstrated to be false, but because they fail either to perceive or sufficiently grapple with the aporiai at the core of their individual claims.

Sensitivity to the role of the aporetic in the human condition teaches one to appreciate the aphorism of Clement of Alexandria: simple faith is always sufficient, but reasoned knowledge is a higher possession.[12] Yet, one does not need to be a trained theologian or biblical scholar to be a person of faith.[13] To be in the world is to live out of faith and not simply in terms of commitment to the teachings of the church or confidence in the trustworthiness and worthwhileness of our lives. The life of faith rests on our necessary dependence upon both what is seen and unseen in our lives. The "unseen," however, is more than what is simply outside of the horizon of our physical range of vision. The unseen includes what necessarily must be either concealed or negated in order for us to experience the world as we do. Yet the "unseen" involves not only that which is not available to the sense organs in any moment. It includes our entire life of the intellect which is completely inaccessible to the senses. We cannot see, hear, touch, smell, or taste our minds/consciousness. Further, our entire affective life is equally inaccessible to the senses. Yet, even with this, the role of concealment and negation in experience is not exhausted. The universals upon which our experience of order and our communication depend, the possibilities upon which our actualized lives depend, as well as the non-observable "I," that gives a decentered identity to our experience, are all inaccessible to our senses.

Martin Heidegger spoke of the "nullity" (or a fundamental negativity not entirely unlike the negativity of Hegel, but without the regulating Concept that explains that negativity in light of the cunning of reason) at the center of the dynamic process of actualization. All movement to actuality requires the necessary denial and suppression of possibilities, which can never

---

[12] From Williston Walker, *A History of the Christian Church*, 3rd ed. (New York: Charles Scribner's sons, 1970), p. 73.

[13] Max Pohlenz quotes from Seneca: "... die Weisheit liege nicht in der Schrift und sei darum auch dem nicht verschlossen, der nicht lesen und schreiben könne." From Max Pohlenz, *Die Stoa. Geschichte einer geistigen Bewegung* (Göttingen: Vandenhoeck & Ruprecht, 1992 <1947>), p. 292.

again be retrieved in the same way.[14] By definition, then, unactualized possibilities remain "unseen." We may regret not having actualized them, or they may even initiate a dynamic which will eventually return to influence us at some later point; nevertheless, they remain forever inaccessible to us as they originally were, once we enter on a path of actualization. However, to focus our attention simply upon "what actually happened" severs understanding from possibility and conceals the irretrievable, yet undeniable, dynamic of what might have been and what could be to merely focus on "what is." It is to sever understanding from the sea of possibility (the ontological "is"/"is not") that "unites" spirit and matter.

This project seeks to investigate precisely these kinds of aporetic necessities that operate at the heart of the human condition. In one sense there is nothing new in what is to be discussed. If the Western tradition was shaped by a classic dualism between spirit and flesh (intellect and matter), then this project is "simply" a retrieval of that dualism (to be sure, the dualism is retrieved for the sake of distinction, but this retrieval is not a mere repetition of an absolute dualism: spirit and matter are inseparable as they are united in concealed possibility). There is a fundamental difference between the dualist models of the tradition and this present project. The Western tradition has consistently absolutized one side of the dualism over against the other.[15]

One can witness the swing of the pendulum from spirit to flesh, or from intellect to matter, in the Western tradition with the transition point commencing with the work of Aquinas on the writings of Aristotle which resulted in the subsequent Nominalism of Occam. As historically accurate as such a description might be, this project rejects such absolutes as metaphysical fictions. Here both dimensions of spirit and flesh are understood to rest

---

[14] See Heidegger, *Being and Time*, trans. by John Macquarrie and Edward Robinson (New York: Harper & Row, 1962), pp. 329-331.

[15] This is the charge made by Derrida against the Western tradition. See Barbara Johnson's introduction to Jacques Derrida, *Dissemination*, trans. by Barbara Johnson (Chicago: The University of Chicago Press, 1981), p. viii: "Western thought, says Derrida, has always been structured in terms of dichotomies or polarities: good vs. evil, being vs. nothingness, presence vs. absence, truth vs. error, identity vs. difference, mind vs. matter, man vs. woman, soul vs. body, life vs. death, nature vs. culture, speech vs. writing. These polar opposites do not, however, stand as independent and equal entities. The second term in each pair is considered the negative, corrupt, undesirable version of the first, a fall away from it ... the two terms are not simply opposed in their meanings, but are arranged in a hierarchical order which gives the first term *priority*, in both the temporal and the qualitative sense of the word."

on wagers of faith, on presuppositions or assumptions, and at best we can offer only pragmatic arguments for their independent status. Therefore, for this project, both of these dimensions (both spirit and flesh, intellect and matter, possibility and actuality, the abstract and the concrete) must be held in dynamic tension for us to adequately understand our experience.[16] They constitute a necessarily aporetic tension that does not permit either "side" to serve as the explanation of the other. To be human is to experience these "dualisms" (and all other aporetic tensions) as inextricably interrelated and irreducible one to the other within the concealed unity in diversity of possibility.

Even if one can observe such thematic echoes in the Western tradition, that cannot detract from the attempt at a new formulation stressing the limits to reason and the role of faith which are constitutive of what it means to be human. At the same time, perhaps one can retrieve an experiential dimension to the claims of the past that is otherwise lost as humanity has so radically embraced materialism (the world of the senses) in the "secular" world. In short, it is just as "reasonable" (pragmatically reasonable, not logically reasonable) to believe in the Logos as a system of universals or ideas independent of our consciousness, as it is to believe in the existence of an empirical world independent of our consciousness. As contradictory as these two beliefs are, they belong irreducibly together in a tension of possibility with one another, coupled with the role of concealment in all that is manifest, if we are to come to anything like an adequate understanding of our human condition.

On the Crisis in Theology

The discipline of Christian theology is in a state of crisis. It simply no longer plays any significant role in either public or private life. With the rise

---

[16] In this respect I share the intent, but not the vocabulary of metaphysics or the pejorative understanding of myth, of Douglas Berggren's "The Use and Abuse of Metaphor, I" in *The Review of Metaphysics*, XVI/2 (December 1962), 237-258, and "The Use and Abuse of Metaphor, II" in *The Review of Metaphysics*, XVI/3 (March 1963), 450-472. Berggren concludes his project with a defense of metaphysics. He warns, however, against the "abuse" of metaphysics which forgets that it rests upon metaphorical tension and "stereoscopic vision" (Stanford) resulting in what Berggren calls "myth" (*ibid.*, 471-2). I wish to completely give up the dream of metaphysics. It is not simply that we risk distortion when metaphysics is improperly understood. Rather, we perpetuate the illusion of totality and the dream of absoluteness, which has brought such terror to humanity and the environment, that must be surrendered once and for all.

of critical scholarship on the Bible at the end of the 18th century, Christian scholars have become increasingly detached and isolated from the institutions they once served and not simply because of the training and expertise required for one to engage in anything like a competent theological discourse. It is true to be sure that theologians play the game of the academy preparing papers for national, regional, and area meetings of the American Academy of Religion/Society of Biblical Literature (AAR/SBL) and other such professional groups. This game is both cognitively and existentially meaningful to the small circle of professionals, but incomprehensible to the everyday Christian. But even the trained theologian is hard pressed to keep up with important currents in the theological debates, e.g., Neo-Orthodoxy, Death of God, Process Theology, Hermeneutics, Deconstructionism, Postmodernism, Post-liberalism, Narrative Theology and the end of metaphysics. For the laity the jargon and issues are even more incomprehensible, because they, for the most part, have not been introduced to, much less grasped the significance of, the importance of historical, form, redaction, and literary criticism essential to the study of scripture.[17] This is particularly

---

[17] The reader will note here, that a distinction is being drawn between Christian theological "schools" (Neo-Orthodoxy, Process Theology, Deconstructionism, etc.) and biblical theology. Such a distinguishing between theology and the Bible is an illusion, for Christian theology has always been rooted in the biblical tradition though it *never* is limited to that textual tradition. For even when theologians have claimed to be exclusively "biblical," their questions, reflections, and writings have always been shaped by their historical context and never been limited to the biblical text. No theologian can jump out of her/his "skin" into another context/situation. What is observed here is that the discussion of the "schools" presupposes awareness of textual criticism, and one cannot begin to understand the "schools" without understanding the issues at issue in textual criticism.

There has always been an ambiguous relationship between theology and its scriptures. The patristic scholar Jean Daniélou acknowledged the determining influence of culture (and not merely of the text) on Christian theology when he observed: "'Three worlds went to the making of the Christian Church, three cultures, three visions and expressions of truth - the Jewish, the Hellenistic and the Latin; and each of them produced its own distinctive theology.'" (In *The Theology of Jewish Christianity* (Chicago: Regenery, 1974), p. 1, from Bernard McGinn, *The Foundations of Mysticism. vol. I: The Presence of God: A History of Western Christian Mysticism* (New York: The Crossroad Publishing Co., 1992), p. 189.)

Theology as a distinct "discipline," that is, as distinct from other scholarly disciplines outside of the church as well as distinct from metaphysics and the study of the scriptures, did not develop until the founding of the new institution of the university and the development of the new church orders in the 13th century, according to Ulrich Köpf (see, for example, *Die Anfänge der theologischen Wissenschaftstheorie im 13. Jahrhundert*. Tübingen: J.C.B. Mohr (Paul Siebeck), 1974, pp. 27-8). Central to the development of theology as a "science" was its growing awareness of, and insistence upon,

crucial for the Protestant laity whose tradition is based on "sola scriptura," that is, on the biblical text alone.[18] Professional theology appears to the church to be an esoteric game of abstraction without any rootedness in practical experience whatsoever.

But the crisis in theology extends beyond theological esotericism. Many if not most of the laity ultimately meant to be served by theology are either so alienated from an authoritative church hierarchy, so alienated from the racism, sexism, and classism of the Christian tradition, and/or so

alienated from a senselessly fragmented church squabbling over doctrine and dogma, that they have chosen to simply ignore their religious heritage. Those remaining often cling to an empty theological shell participating in institutional religion out of a traditional cultural or familial loyalty, and/or recognition of the necessity of a pastoral ministry responding to the personal needs of individuals, and/or recognition of the necessity of a value system as a guide to moral behavior, and/or acknowledgment that this institution is the only one in society which in any way offers a critique of cultural and individual values (even though more often than not even the institutional church fosters blind conformity to the predominate mind set), and/or the wish to participate in one institution in their culture acting out of compassion for the welfare of others. Severed from the intellectual currents

---

its distinctiveness from metaphysics and scriptural studies (*ibid.*, pp. 26, 261, 269). Above all, it was Lombards *Sentences* that contributed to the separation of theology from biblical studies (*ibid.*, pp. 78, 126, 169). However, Köpf observes that this separation was "nicht sauber und endgültig" (*ibid.*, p. 262) in the 13th century primarily because the special status of theological principles over against the principles of other disciplines was dependent upon the revelation of theology's principles in the scriptures (*ibid.*, pp. 142-3).

This project understands the relationship between theology and its scriptures to be shaped by what Hans-Georg Gadamer calls *Wirkungsgeschichte*. The texts of the entire tradition, and not merely the scriptures, serve as one source of theological reflection along with the novel experience of the theologian in her/his situation. The understanding of those texts is always shaped by the "intervening historical distance" between the text and its reader(s). Hence, experience and understanding are radically historical in contrast to those metaphysical claims of the tradition that have sought to ground, and explain, experience and understanding in terms of some ahistorical dimension (whether that be what the Greeks called the First Principle and "universals," or Positivism's "empiricism," or Process thought's "primordial nature" of God).

[18] The biblical theology out of which the present project emerges was initially articulated in my doctoral dissertation "On the Soteriological Significance of the Symbol of the Kingdom of God in the Language of the Historical Jesus" (Ph.D. diss., University of Chicago, 1983).

of their religious heritage, and severed from any experiential notion of spirituality except for some variety of emotionalism or some superstitious belief in a power externally related to the self, the laity are theologically rudderless in a sea of religious and commercial consumerism. One simply cannot say that theology plays a significant motivating role in institutional or private religious life.[19]

Numbers crunching has become the measure of success both for the Christian church and for judging the worth of a theological project. Not only is the success of a church ministry gauged by persons flocking like sheep to the church in their community (or on their television) that is able to generate the most excitement at the moment. But even in theological circles, the work of a theologian is evaluated not merely in terms of the number of books s/he has sold, but in terms of the value of her/his work for evaluating statistically the state of Christianity. At a recent meeting of the AAR/SBL Andrew Greeley, perhaps the leading sociologist of religion today, had a standing room only audience as he reported on his latest international survey on Christianity employing the categories of the analogical and dialectical imagination as descriptive of Roman Catholic and Protestant sensibilities, respectively, taken from the work of the pre-eminent Roman Catholic theologian, David Tracy.[20] Tracy's work was applauded because of its applicability for evaluating the "empirical" statistical data - an accomplishment "shared by no other theologian." It was not the subtlety, breadth, or depth of Tracy's theological reflection, but rather the descriptive power of his categories, enabling an empirical evaluation of what was currently going on in Roman Catholic and Protestant religious communities, that was applauded. In other words, Christian theology is appreciated most where it is empirically descriptive. As a spiritually descriptive, prescriptive, normative, and speculative discipline, theology has lost all credibility and accessibility certainly for the lay person and one suspects for many theologians, as well.

---

[19] The church and private life constitute two of the three publics for theology according to David Tracy. See *The Analogical Imagination: Christian Theology and the Culture of Pluralism* (New York: Crossroad Press, (1981) 1989), pp. 30, 47, 80-82, where he suggests that theology is not primarily concerned with the tension between "private" vs. "public" but is rather constituted out of three disciplines (Fundamental, Systematic, and Practical Theology) attempting to speak to three publics (Academy, Church, Society). This project maintains that there is a crisis in theology in all three publics.

[20] Though one must acknowledge that Tracy recognizes that even the "great" dialectical theologians of Protestant Neo-Orthodoxy in their maturity turn to the analogical imagination as at the least a complement to dialectical proclamation if not as a substitution for the dialectical imagination. See *The Analogical Imagination*, pp. 417-421.

Christian theology was once rooted in a world view or paradigm shared to a great extent by society at large.[21] This shared world view shaped theology's reflections and pronouncements, and it gave theology an audience among the laity. For the first 1,300 years of its tradition, Christianity was rooted in the "dualism" of the Greek world, particularly Platonism but shared by Aristotelians and Stoics[22], that both experientially and not merely intellectually affirmed the human condition as rooted in an eternal, spiritual reality of the infinite even as humans were viewed as sojourners in the transient, material reality of the finite. This dualism permeates the language of the New Testament from speaking, for example, of God as the invisible enabling the visible (Romans 1:20), of humanity as constituted out of a tension between spirit and flesh (Romans 8:4-10), and of things as shadow whose substance is the invisible Christ yet to come (Colossians 2:16-17); for humans are to set their minds on the things that are above, not on the things that are on earth (Colossians 3:2), since it is through Christ (the Logos, John 1:1-5) as the image of the invisible God that all things visible and invisible were created and are held together (Colossians 1:15-17).[23]

Some have argued that this classical spirituality was the preserve only of the educated elite. This is the position taken by Adolf von Harnack who blames Gnosticism for the "acute hellenization" of Christianity arguing that the Gnostics were primarily from the educated upper class.[24] Speaking of

---

[21] This is not to argue for a "golden age" of Christian spirituality where all Christians shared the same spiritual understanding. I do mean to suggest that the predominant paradigm for reality was rooted in what one must now call a classical spirituality that distinguished between the material world accessible through the senses and experience itself that occurs exclusively in the intellect and is not accessible to the senses.

[22] See Pohlenz, *Die Stoa*, p. 32-36, 255-256. Pohlenz maintains that Stoics reigned in the courtyard; Cynics in the alleyways. Both shared the same "Hellenic" world view of spirit having experiential priority over matter (νοῦς over αἰσθήσισ).

[23] This imagery is not limited to the so-called canonical texts. See, for example, the discussion of the "inner" and the "outer" and the "two becoming one" in the Gospel of Thomas (Logion 20), 2 Clement 12:2, and the Gospel according to the Egyptians quoted by Clement in *Miscellanies* 3.92.2. I am indebted to Robert Grant's article "Neither Male nor Female" in *Biblical Research*, 37 (1992), p. 13, for these references. Grant is concerned to develop the notion of the generic that is higher than species and/or individuals in order to shed some light on such passages as Paul's in Galatians 3:28: "There is neither Jew nor Greek, there is neither slave nor free, there is neither male nor female; for you are all one in Christ Jesus." This would suggest, however, that the oneness is a matter of logic, but I would claim that higher than νομός, even higher than λόγος, is the oneness not of ἑνός but of νοῦς - the illimitable, indivisible oneness of spirit/mind/Geist - experienced and shared by humanity as that dimension in which all experience transpires.

[24] See Adolf v. Harnack, *Lehrbuch der Dogmengeschichte*, vol. 1 (Tübingen: 1909) (Nachdruck Darmstadt: Wissenschaftliche Buchgesellschaft, 1964), pp. 243-292. I am in-

"clichés" as "... common thoughts and images ... which constantly shape the statements and the actions of ... societies and distinguish them, to a certain extent, from other societies,"[25] Robert Brentano claims that

> [o]f these clichés the most central for understanding the things people said in this five hundred years [500 - 1000 C.E.], perhaps because it was, *among the literate*, the most intensely felt, was the primacy of the ideal and the spiritual and the internal over the actual and the physical and the external.[26] (emphasis added)

I agree to this extent with A.H. Armstrong that: "[t]he educated and articulate people, the only ones to whose thoughts and feelings we can possibly have any kind of direct access [even here, do we really have "direct" access?], were throughout the history of that [old Mediterranean] world a tiny minority..."[27] However, does the fact that the educated and articulate to whom we can possibly have access is a tiny minority, justify the conclusion: "... even in what is generally supposed to be the most 'spiritual' period of that history, the first centuries of the Christian era and the last centuries of the Roman Empire, those who could in any way be called deeply spiritual were a small minority of that minority?"[28]

The "dualism" suggested here was more widely grasped than among a few intellectuals. Max Pohlenz observes that by the time of Augustus and through the second half of the third century[29] Stoicism, the intellectual heir of the Athenian world view, dominated Roman philosophy and theology, but not simply among the educated. Stoicism was at home both at the seats of power and in the alleyways.[30] Pohlenz reports that Stoicism's only competitor was Cynicism, which was most appealing to the lower classes, but then he quickly adds that the Cynic philosophy that was popularized was nothing other than a "crude" Stoicism.[31] Klaus Koschorke observes that so-

---

debted to Klaus Koschorke, "Gnosis, Montanismus, Mönchtum. Zur Frage emanzipatorischer Bewegungen im Raum der Alten Kirche" in *Evangelische Theologie* 53/2,3 (1993), p. 217, for this citation. Koschorke refers to Kippenberg's thesis, as well, that Gnosticism emerged particularly among the hellenized intellectuals who were marginalized politically. See, *ibid.*, p. 218, and particularly n. 4 for a discussion of the sociological conditions in which Gnosticism emerged.

[25] Robert Brentano, *Sources in Western Civilization - The Middle Ages*, (New York: The Free Press of Glencoe, 1964), p. 6.
[26] Brentano, *Sources in Western Civilization - The Middle Ages*, p. 6.
[27] A.H. Armstrong in his "Introduction" to *Classical Mediterranean Spirituality: Egyptian, Greek, Roman* (New York: Crossroad Press, 1986), p. xiv.
[28] Armstrong, *Classical Mediterranean Spirituality*, p. xiv.
[29] See Max Pohlenz, *Die Stoa*, pp. 276, 290.
[30] Pohlenz, *Die Stoa*, p. 276.
[31] Pohlenz, *Die Stoa*, p. 279.

called hellenized Gnostic Christianity was best received among the "little, unassuming, oppressed" people of society.[32] It was the preserve of the "little man and the little woman on the street."[33] This is not surprising, for one does not have to reflect very deeply, i.e., one does not have to be an intellectual, to notice a difference between one's mental (spiritual) life and the physical (material) world. That the laity did not necessarily *reflect* or *write* about the full implication of their spirituality does not by any means prove that they did not *live* out of an experientially informed understanding of their spirituality.

As much as my own position is subject to the charge of anachronism, so, too, is Armstrong's when he maintains:

> When it was said above that the archaic piety [of the majority] was one of worship, not of belief, this did not, of course, mean that the worshipers had no beliefs. It means that it was common worship - with the implicit and unformulated faith that all genuine worship requires - which united them, not a common profession of a formulated faith in the sense in which we often use the word.[34]

It could be maintained that precisely the spiritual and theological vacuity of present ritualized activity in churches across the Christian world is being read back into the ritualized behavior of the old Mediterranean world. Theologians in any age tend to reflect the paradigm for reality shared by the community at large. One can argue that few lay persons today *reflect* about their paradigm but they *live* a pragmatic empiricism. Is it any wonder that theological discussions in the 20th century, then, are concerned with verification, falsification, and pragmatism? An analogy can easily be constructed that maintains that theologians of the first 1,300 years of the tradition were concerned with a spiritual paradigm for reality precisely because that was the unreflected commonplace of the community at large.

The great debates of Christian theology rest upon this experiential dualism. For example, the debates of the first 500 years of Christianity over Christology (Did the Logos have a beginning or was "He" eternal?; or How can the Christ be both God and man?) and the Trinity (How can God be both three and one?) presuppose the "dualism" of the Greek world as their horizon of intelligibility. Without that dualism (which, it must be underscored, was an experiential dualism and not a mere head trip), all of the debates of

---

[32] See Koschorke, "Gnosis, Montanismus, Mönchtum," pp. 218-219.
[33] Koschorke, "Gnosis, Montanismus, Mönchtum," p. 218.
[34] Armstrong, *Classical Mediterranean Spirituality*, p. xvii.

the Christian community, beginning with matyriology, the role of the monarchical bishop, Gnosticism, Montanism, and Marcionism, and ending in the great theological systems of the pre-Protestant Reformation era, all of these debates are simply incomprehensible.

This dualism, which is not necessarily an absolute dualism demanding choice between one "side" or the other, is not only understandable by the intellectually sophisticated Christian theologians. It is the experienced world of the laity. Particularly in the pre-20th century world, given the suffering and tragedies of experience, given the established hierarchies of the social and church order, and, above all, given the shortness of life, the fact of one's already having at least partial access to an invisible and eternal realm is existentially real, because this invisible and eternal realm is the realm of experience accessible to, and of, mental experience. One's own mental life can, and was, understood to give one a proleptic taste of a promised fullness and a perfect harmony (when was the last time that the most contradictory ideas beat up on one another in the mind?) in a spiritual realm beyond the life of the flesh. One could surrender the flesh (or the world of sense experience) to the animals in the arena like the martyrs; one could claim that a loving and perfect God could not have created the world as did Marcionism and the Gnostics; one could speak of the power and presence of the Paraclete as did the Montanists; one could withdraw to the hermitage or the cloister of the desert; one could debate the issue of whether or not there was a time when the Son was not as at Nicaea;[35] and one could argue over whether or not the church had the power to forgive sins;[36] all on the basis of the experienced

---

[35] This debate did not center on the question of the virgin birth, but was addressed in terms of the Logos as the eternal thoughts of God. Did the Logos have a beginning in time? If so, then the Logos was a creature and not co-eternal with the Father.

The notion that the Father is more than the Logos is analogous to the recognition that the individual is more than her/his thoughts. Hence, this debate was over the question of the relationship of thoughts to the individual as the primary analogate (i.e., the known or experienced proportionality of the analogy) as the basis for speaking about a secondary analogate (i.e., the unknown proportionality of the analogy - in this case God in relation to "His" thoughts/Logos).

[36] It is not anachronistic to read this debate in light of the dualism of spirit and flesh. Although one cannot ignore motivation, one can sin only in the flesh, for one can only act in the flesh. (See, e.g., Romans 7:13-25) The question, then, is what effect do the actions in the flesh have on the spirit? If they are only "accidental" and not "essential," then, they have no "real" significance, and the contrite, who truly regret their transgressions, can hope to have them forgotten in the spiritual realm. Proper spiritual understanding means that particulars are not "really real," and it is only what is in the spirit that is enduringly real. Taken as "accidental," the only question is who has the power to forgive them? By the mid-third century it had become the universal teaching of the

24   Introduction

"dualism" of spirit and flesh which was comprehensible, precisely because it is experiential - even to the laity.

Robert Markus has suggested that a dramatic change occurred in the period between Augustine and Gregory the Great. It was precisely this interval which witnessed the loss of "pagan" pluralism to leave the religious and intellectual field occupied solely by Christianity.[37] This hegemony made it

---

church that not merely God but "Confessors" (i.e., those who had experienced persecution in the name of the faith) had the power to forgive sins. Matthew 16:18-19 was generally read to provide the warrant from the Christ for this practice.

The issue over the church's power to forgive sins was essentially a debate between North Africa and Rome in two stages roughly a half century apart. See W.H.C. Frend *The Rise of Christianity* (Philadelphia: Fortress Press, 1984), pp. 345-357, and Peter Kaufman, *Church, Book, and Bishop: Conflict and Authority in Early Latin Christianity* (Boulder: Westview Press, Inc., 1996), especially chapters two, "Tertullian," and three, "Leadership: Bishops, Councils, and Emperors."

The first stage (early third century) is represented in North Africa by the strict moralist, Tertullian, and in Rome by Callistus. Tertullian in Carthage reserved the forgiveness of sins exclusively to God, and he insisted that there were three "capital sins" unpardonable in any event, i.e., idolatry, adultery, and bloodshed (Frend, *ibid.*, p. 351). Callistus, responding in Rome to the demand for ethical rigor by Hippolytus, argued that the church was to be a "mixed body" "containing unworthy as well as worthy members" in which "the church might absolve any sin" (Frend, *ibid.*, p. 346). Such an attitude was in strong contrast to Tertullian's position in North Africa as well as to Hippolytus, and it represented the emerging contrast between Rome and North Africa regarding church discipline. Rome increasingly came to view the church as the "school for sinners," and North Africa viewed the church as "God's elect on earth" (Frend, *ibid.*, p. 346).

The second stage followed the Decian persecutions in North Africa. Cyprian now argued in Carthage that the church had the power to forgive the sins of believers with the exception of the clergy's sins, because the clergy were the conduit for the passage of grace to the recipient. The conduit must be clean for grace to be effective. (Frend, *ibid.*, pp. 323-4) However, Stephen in Rome argued that the efficacy of the mass rested on the faith of the believer not on the purity of the officiant, and so defended the forgiveness of sins for the clergy, as well. (Frend, *ibid.*, pp. 353-4)

One might see this conflict represented in the alternative understandings of miracles between the three synoptic gospels and John. The synoptic gospels represent the efficacy of the miracle as depending upon the faith of the recipient. John's gospel, to the contrary, portrays miracles as evoking the faith of the recipient. With respect to the efficacy of the "miracle" of the sacrament and the church's ability to forgive sins, Rome, with its defense of the clergy as imperfect, tends to follow the synoptic gospels by focussing on the recipient of the sacrament; North Africa, with its insistence on the purity of the clergy, tends to follow John's gospel by focussing on the clergy as the conduit for the Holy Spirit communicated by the sacrament evoking the faith of the recipient.

[37] See Robert Markus, *The End of Ancient Christianity* (Cambridge: Cambridge University Press, 1994).

easier for Christianity in the West to lose the world view of Greek culture, which had shaped it for five hundred years, because there were no alternatives left (with the exception of the esoteric monastic traditions) to challenge the adequacy of the Latin world view.

A case could be made that, once Aristotle's corpus,[38] as it is known today, was finally available to the West in the 13th century, classical Christianity began to lose its existential rootedness. Theology increasingly lost its experiential echo in the life of the laity (and theologians?). In the 13th century Aquinas was able to follow the example of Boethius in the 6th century. He sought a great theological synthesis between Plato and Aristotle. But the subsequent Nominalist movement effectively destroyed human experiential connectedness to an eternal, spiritual realm by arguing that ideas are ectypal (arising out of our experience of things as mere abstractions) rather than archetypal (eternally existing independent of our consciousness of them). By the time we get to the Copernican Revolution of the 17th century, challenging the geocentric universe with a heliocentric universe, the wedge between the world view of the theologians and that of the laity had split them in two. The laity were left with nothing but pragmatics. Both theology and knowledge were increasingly the preserves of an educated elite.

The Copernican Revolution wedded a Platonic physics (mathematical description) to an Aristotelian metaphysics (the world of things is what exists independent of our consciousness rather than a realm of ideas).[39] But Galileo

---

[38] David Knowles, speaking of the transmission of classical Greek texts by medieval monks in *Christian Monasticism* (New York: McGraw-Hill Book Co., 1977), p. 46, reports: "... through no fault of their own, they [the monks] did nothing to transmit the Greek classics. The text of almost all of the works of Plato was unknown; Aristotle's scientific and philosophical works, and some of the Greek medical and astronomical writers, came to Paris from the Arabs [13th century], while classical Greek literature arrived only in the fifteenth century."

[39] See Alexander Koyré, "Galileo and Plato," *Journal of the History of Ideas*, IV (1943), 400-428. Koyré suggests that Galileo's mathematization of reality is a form of Platonism (*ibid.*, p. 424). One finds a strange hybrid in the Enlightenment: what one can witness is a Platonic physics (based on mathematization of the realm of sense perception) that rejects Platonic metaphysics (consisting of a realm of ideas/universals existing as a perfect, harmonious order independent of the world of the senses and which serves as the model of which the physical world is mere copy and shadow). Rather than a Platonic metaphysics one finds an Aristotelian metaphysics (arguing that form in matter precedes our knowing of form without matter, see *Metaphysics* 1077b) that rejects Aristotelian physics (the notion that physics is based on common sense perception emphasizing the category of motion as always leading to a natural state of rest). In other words, the Enlightenment is the result of a hybrid of Platonic physics and Aristotelian metaphysics. The laity were left with the pragmatic consequences of this revolution, but they were severed from the mathematical physics explaining their new reality.

"won" in terms of popular consciousness (although he "lost" with respect to the Roman Catholic Church[40]) because of the pragmatic consequences of his work (e.g., navigation was made easier) and surely not because the average lay person was able to grasp his mathematical physics.[41] Sense perception confirms the judgments not of Platonic mathematical physics but of Aristotelian physics, which is based upon the notion that all motion is moving toward rest. Galileo's work depends upon grasping the power of non-sense (mathematics) to explain physical, or sensed, phenomena. Once the connection was made between the applicability of mathematics for explaining physical phenomena (by identifying the Laws of Planetary Motion, for example, as was accomplished by Kepler and his students), the door was open for the experts (and closed to the lay person) to be set loose calculating, predicting, manipulating, and controlling the material world to the (at least hoped for) pragmatic benefit of the human species (with the consequence that the environment and non-human species have had to suffer like never imagined).

One may mark the spiritual demise of popular consciousness (the world view of the Christian laity) with the rise of Galilean science. Eternal laws were perhaps only grasped by the mathematical mind, but the eternal was now found in the material world. The subsequent rise of Deism removed the spiritual from the material world.[42] God, viewed as the great clock maker who created and set the universe in motion, remains aloof from the functioning of the universe except to intervene occasionally to "repair" it. The so-called Argument from Design for the existence of God, once employed in the context of Platonic dualism,[43] became an argument from

---

[40] The history of Galileo and the church is often distorted. For a description of Galileo's case, see Owen Gingerich, "Hypothesis, Proof, and Censorship or How Galileo Changed the Rules of Science" in *Colloquium: The Australian and New Zealand Theological Review* 25/2 (1993), 54-66.

[41] See Edmund Husserl, *The Crisis of European Sciences and Transcendental Phenomenology: An Introduction to Phenomenological Philosophy*, trans & intro by David Carr (Evanston: Northwestern University Press, 1970).

[42] This is what was "lost" in the Enlightenment. It is not, as Karl Barth maintained, that the Copernican Revolution resulted in anthropomorphism - placing humanity rather than God at the center of reality. (See Karl Barth, *Die protestantische Theologie im 19. Jahrhundert. Ihre Vorgeschichte und ihre Geschichte*, 5. Aufl. (Zürich: Theologischer Verlag Zürich, 1981), pp. 19-20, 503, 509.) Instead, human spiritual experience has been impoverished by the rise of empiricism.

[43] Things in the world are imperfect copies of perfect counterparts in the realm of ideas. Human creativity is based upon making an external copy of an idea (or system of ideas) had first in the mind. Since the design of human artifacts always points to a human designer, it was argued that the design found in nature points to a divine designer.

mechanics. Rather than see the natural order as analogous to all human creativity, the natural order was seen as analogous to the creative activity of the few geniuses who created the new mechanical wonders.

Although philosophically undermined by the work of Hume in the 18th century, the Argument from Design was not popularly surrendered (witness the success of Paley's *Natural Theology* in 1802 or the eight *Bridgewater Treatises* published between 1833 and 1836[44]); even though the geologists and paleontologists (particularly the result of the work of William Smith between 1791 and 1799[45]) had made indefensible the Biblical notion that the world was only 6,000 years old. The extension of the age of the earth almost indefinitely, coupled with the Uniformitarian school's conclusion that the laws of nature are uniform throughout all time, paved the way for Darwin's argument against the "special creation" of species (special creation was based on the Argument from Design).[46] These two anomalies to the Biblical paradigm (unlimited time and uniformity of natural law) gave credibility to Darwin's theories of natural and sexual selection where other proponents of similar theories prior to Darwin had failed. Those prior to Darwin had demanded acceptance of incredulities from their audience equally miraculous as God's creating complete species *ex nihilo*.[47]

Although theologically Darwin's exclusive concern for secondary and not primary causes left several other arguments for God unscathed (e.g., Aristotle's Cosmological, Anselm's Ontological, Descartes' Causal, and Kant's Moral arguments), and Darwin left room for great mystery and wonder before nature (for example, whence initial species and subsequent

---

[44] For a review of some of the literature from the first half of 19th century England addressing the relationship between God and nature, see Charles Coulston Gillispie, *Genesis and Geology: A Study in the Relations of Scientific Thought, Natural Theology, and Social Opinion in Great Britain, 1790-1850* (New York: Harper Torchbooks, 1959), pp. 243-247.

[45] See Gillispie, *Genesis and Geology*, p. 84.

[46] For a more thorough discussion of the issues involved here, see Douglas R. Mcgaughey, "Coming to Terms with Darwin and the 19th Century Paradigm Revolution" in *The Willamette Journal of the Liberal Arts*, 6 (Fall 1991), 65-90.

[47] See John Angus Campbell, "Scientific Revolution and the Grammar of Culture: The Case of Darwin's *Origin*" in *The Quarterly Journal of Speech*, 72/4 (November 1986), p. 365. In later editions of *The Origin* Darwin acknowledged some 30 predecessors to his work. See the "Editor's Introduction" to Charles Darwin, *The Origin of Species by Means of Natural Selection or the Preservation of Favoured Races in the Struggle for Life* (London: Penguin Books, 1985 (1859)), p. 27.

variation?), his work remained a decisive blow against popular Christianity and Christian theology by placing both on the defensive in terms of the common everyday experience of the popular world view. Not only can one identify the eternal in experience as the merely material "eternal Laws of Nature," but one can at least hope to account for all of life, even spiritual or mental life, from out of the material order with it all happening "blindly," i.e., without divine providence guiding it,[48] and surely with a loss of any and all notions of human spirituality with the exception, perhaps, of the Spirit as some kind of "material" force.

Ironically, conservative religious groups, believing themselves to be defenders of the faith by adhering to the literal words of the text, have contributed to the undermining of human spirituality and faith. They have totally embraced the empiricism of their opponents. All that distinguishes them from the agnostic physicist is the question: which empirical data counts as authoritative? The physicist chooses the sense data "from nature." The biblicist chooses the sense data "from *the* text." Both are materialists. Both have totally discounted their own spiritual or mental experience. Both fail to grasp the necessary role of concealment making possible our experience of what is actually manifest.

This has not meant to be an exhaustive survey of Western intellectual history from the 13th to the 19th century.[49] It does indicate that clearly the pendulum of popular consciousness swung 180° in this period of Western history. Whereas Hellenistic thought *experienced* the "real" as the invisible and unchanging realm of ideas (according to which the world is mere copy and shadow accounting for its constant change), popular consciousness since the Copernican Revolution has increasingly *experienced* the "real" as the visible material world. It is this material order (according to which, ideas

---

[48] There did remain nomothetic creation, championed by Robert Chambers' anonymously (Gillispie, p. 282, n. 1) published *Vestiges of the Natural History of Creation* of 1844 prior to Darwin's *Origin of the Species*. The theory of nomothetic creation argues that God creates precisely by having established the Laws of Nature. Donald Wiebe writes in "An Unholy Alliance? The Creationists' Quest for Scientific Legitimation" in *The Toronto Journal of Theology*, 4/2 (1988), p. 170: "Non-miraculous nomothetic creationism presupposes a body of laws, established by God from the beginning of the world, through the operation of which new species evolved. In such a view, new species are seen to be 'divinely created' but without involving any *special intervention* by God." God's creative activity is nevertheless far removed from daily life.

[49] For a more complete, yet accessible, survey see John N. Deely's essay "Situating Semiotic" in John Poinsot, *Tractatus de Signis: The Semiotic of John Poinsot*, trans. by John Deeley (Berkeley: University of California Press, 1985), pp. 490-514.

are mere impermanent and constantly changing copies or abstractions) which endures through all change.

Platonism[50] maintains that ideas are archetypal remaining the same yesterday, today, and tomorrow. According to Platonism, the material world is grounded in the invisible Logos of archetypes, since the world is understood to be created analogously to objects derived from human creativity (first the idea, then the externalization of the created object modeled after the enduring idea). The created objects come into and pass out of existence in the realm of becoming, but the invisible ideas constitute a dimension of eternal being. Here the intellect or spiritual dimension of experience has priority over the perceptible or material dimension of experience.

One can trace the transition from ideas as archetypes to ectypes in the discussion of the status of "universals" in early scholasticism.[51] The options ranged from Extreme and Moderate Realism to Nominalism. The key difference between Realists and Nominalists rested on the question of the status of universals independent of human consciousness. The Realists insisted that universals indeed existed independent of human consciousness though in two radically different senses. Extreme Realists argued that universals were a priori of any and all experience. They argued that universals are archetypal in the Neo-Platonic sense of constituting a pure spiritual realm independent of all materiality. Moderate Realists argued that universals first occurred as form in matter, i.e., a posteriori. They argued that universals are first found in materiality as form in matter and only secondarily thought as form without matter (they are focussing, however, on how human beings come to experience universals not on the ultimate ontological status of universals). The Nominalists denied any independent status to universals arguing that we experience only particulars. So-called "universals," they argued, are mere abstractions or names, i.e., ideas or universals are ectypal or mere names for abstractions drawn a posteriori from the experience of particulars - not a priori and archetypal.

The theological consequences of these distinctions are profound. Extreme Realists and Moderate Realists argued that even God conforms to rationality. What distinguishes them is the role of human reason in approaching God. Extreme Realists claim an intimate, internal connection between

---

[50] The term "Platonism" should not be read as narrowly applying to the official schools growing out of the Academy in Athens. One would be equally correct to speak generically of "Hellenism" were it not for exceptions such as the Epicurians.

[51] See Walker, *A History of the Christian Church*, pp. 238f, and Edward B. Davis, "God, Man and Nature: the Problem of Creation in Cartesian Thought" in *The Scottish Journal of Theology*, 44/3 (1991) 325-349.

human reason and the divine, for we are following/employing the very thoughts of God to the extent that we are thinking universals. Moderate Realists insist that reason is limited to grasping the natural order, but that the divine is only fully grasped through revelation - although this revelation must conform to reason, i.e., the rational order of nature, since God created the natural order according to "His" reason and cannot violate "His" own order. Hence, although affirming human reason's ability to grasp divine reason in part through the natural order, Moderate Realists initiated the separation between human reason and the divine where Extreme Realists take human and divine reason to be one and the same.

The Nominalists, to the contrary, emphasize the priority of the divine will over rationality arguing that reason is limited to nature. God is not limited to human understanding (or reason), hence, God is not bound by our rationality and can will whatever "He" wishes.[52] Given the Nomalists' victory both among theologians and in popular consciousness, Extreme Realism has lost all of its champions. Here the separation of reason and divinity is complete as the imageo dei has shifted from reason to will.[53]

---

[52] Following the Copernican revolution in the 17th century, one can observe a reverse image of these schools in the theological discussion. The Rationalists and Neologians of the late 18th and mid-19th centuries argue that God must conform to the laws of nature and reason, because these laws and rationality constitute the eternal order behind all phenomena. Neo-orthodoxy in the late 19th and 20th centuries argues that God is beyond reason, accessible only through revelation, and in principle, if not in fact, not required to conform to either the laws of nature or reason.

[53] This is nowhere more clear than in Descartes' discussion of the will as the grounds for the imageo dei in his *Meditations*, "Meditation Four." The notion of the human will as "unlimited by anything else," which is that capability shared by humanity with divinity according to Descartes, is clearly taken by Descartes to be distinguished from the understanding. He argues that humanity would not make any mistakes were it to withhold engaging of the will until it had perfect understanding. Since God has given us two capacities, the will and the understanding, which in and of themselves are perfect, error occurs only by our misapplying these two capacities. We are responsible for our errors, according to Descartes theodicy. God has not created anything imperfect.

Max Pohlenz argues in *Die Stoa*, p. 124, that such a notion of the will as an independent capacity unlimited by anything else is foreign to the Greek tradition. For the Greeks, the will was understood to have been subordinate to the understanding. The will is no independent capacity; we are only able to will what we understand. This led Stoicism to defend the absolute sovereignty of the Logos reigning over all of reality by means of the "Heimarmene" or the uninterruptible chain of cause and effect. See *ibid.*, p. 102. The pragmatic consequence was their defense of astrology and divination as means for leaning the divine plan for the present and future. See *ibid.*, pp. 106-108.

Paul Barth maintains in "Die stoische Theodizee bei Philo" in *Philosophische Abhandlungen* (Berlin: Ernst Siegfried Mittler und Sohn, 1906), pp. 30-31, that the notion of an unlimited freedom of the human will comes from Judaism. Philo shared this judg-

Over 500 years, then, the relationship between what is permanent and impermanent in experience has completely reversed. According to the "new science" based on Aristotelian metaphysics, it is the material world that is permanent. Consciousness or the intellect is merely a passing phenomenon, and consciousness is what is dependent, i.e., it is grounded in the material order with ideas being mere abstractions (or ectypes) of material objects. Hence, ideas come into and pass out of existence, constituting the realm of becoming, whereas material objects constitute the dimension of eternal being. Here the perceptible or material dimension of experience has priority over the intellect or spiritual dimension. The consequence is the victory of materialism over spirituality.

Yet we are currently witnessing the crumbling of reality as it is understood by popular consciousness. Not only has the Newtonian Universe collapsed as a consequence of Einsteinian and, more importantly, post-Einsteinian physics, but *experientially* the human community is confronted with an invisible dynamic of ecological catastrophe set loose by our confidence in the mathematization of the world. The calculation, prediction, manipulation, and control of our technological world view increasingly are seen to conceal as much, if not more, than they make manifest and accessible. What was once perceived as a means opening the door to unlimited progress has brought not merely the massive human destruction of modern warfare since the American Civil War, but the power to destroy the entire world. The material order is precariously impermanent creating a threatening anomaly for a world view based on the material rather than the spiritual as permanent. The consequence is that all permanence is threatening to crumble, and popular consciousness is increasingly aware that it is adrift without orientation. Its grasp on reality is slipping.

It is no longer substance but appearance that governs all aspects of life from the shopping mall to the electoral urn. Success in the marketplace, at the centers of political power, and in the academy is dependent upon

---

ment with his tradition arguing that Adam and Eve were created perfect but that their descendents have fallen into evil. Philo continues to argue, again in contrast to Stoic teaching, that repentance is what liberates humanity from its sickness of the soul. "Only for God is repentance something foreign" (*Ibid.*, p. 31).

Barth points out, however, that the implicit contradiction between an all-powerful deity and an unlimited freedom of the human will was not reconciled by Philo. Even Philo maintained that "... evil persons are created by the anger of God while good persons are created out of the grace of God" (*Ibid.*, p. 31)

manipulating perceptions and not upon truth. Life in all of its dimensions (from personal relationships to workplace, social groups, and national patriotism) is increasingly exposed to rest exclusively upon superficialities and effervescence.

Theology must stop playing the fiddle while Rome burns. Theology must, of course, live up to the rigorous demands of its descriptive task, but it must also become once again normative. Make no mistake, however, this is no call for fideism or blind allegiance to dogmatism. Theology cannot retreat either to the metaphysics of Platonism or to the metaphysics of Aristotelianism/Nominalism. What theology can do is retrieve an *experiential* awareness of the human condition as unavoidably one of faith seeking understanding.

The descriptive task of theology indicates the inescapable role of paradox at the core of human experience. But the retrieval of faith in human experience is not merely descriptive. It is also a retrieval of what Jonathan Edwards called the "heart."[54] In other words, it has normative consequences that are of tremendous magnitude. The retrieval of experiential faith just might check hubris and reign in human destruction of both Others and the

---

[54] I take the distinction between the head and the heart (or will) from Jonathan Edwards, *Religious Affections*, ed. by John E. Smith (New Haven: Yale University Press, 1959), p. 272: "There is a distinction to be made between a mere notional understanding, wherein the mind only beholds things in the exercise of a speculative faculty; and the sense of the heart, wherein the mind don't only speculate and behold, but relishes and feels. That sort of knowledge, by which a man has a sensible perception of amiableness and loathsomeness, or of sweetness and nauseousness, is not just the same sort of knowledge with that, by which he knows what a triangle is, and what a square is. The one is mere speculative knowledge; the other sensible knowledge, in which more than the mere intellect is concerned; the heart is the proper subject of it, or the soul as a being that not only beholds, but has inclination, and is pleased or displeased." To be sure, Edwards clearly distinguishes between his notion of the heart and "all kinds and forms of enthusiasm." See, *ibid.*, pp. 285-291, especially, p. 291: "But there is a great difference between these two things, viz. lively imaginations [which are directed "outward" in the classic Platonic sense, see pp. 210-212, rather than "inward" in spiritual understanding] arising from strong affections [= the heart], and strong affections arising from lively imaginations. The former may be, and doubtless often is, in case of truly gracious affections. The affections don't arise from the imagination, nor have any dependence upon it; but on the contrary, the imagination is only the accidental effect, or consequent of the affection, through the infirmity of human nature. But when the latter is the case, as it often is, that the affection arises from imagination, and is built upon it as its foundation, instead of a spiritual illumination or discovery; then is the affection however elevated, worthless and vain." The "Fifth Sign" argues that the heart is subordinate to the head. See, *ibid.*, p. 298.

environment by insisting on compassion and responsibility for all Others and otherness to whom and to which we are intimately connected, for we cannot be without Others and otherness.[55]

Granted, one might argue that precisely the loss of absolutes and of meta-narratives results in the loss of any and all limits to egocentric and self-serving behavior. This situation, however, is analogous to Socrates' in "The Apology." Having established that wisdom consists in knowing that one does not know what one thinks one knows, Socrates nevertheless maintains that he always taught the pursuit of virtue and the general welfare above individual self-interest. How so? How can one pursue virtue when one cannot know what virtue is? The least one can do in a situation of unknowing is to preserve the conditions of possibility with the minimum of impact on others and the environment. Ironically, Socrates' fellow citizens believed they "knew" that he was guilty and they killed him. Their knowledge led to the destruction of Socrates' conditions of possibility (i.e., murder). Socrates knows he does not know, and calls for the pursuit of virtue. Socrates' lack of knowledge leads to the defense of virtue. It's in this spirit that the loss of absolutes and of metanarratives may be the vehicle for checking human hubris and reigning in human destructiveness. The norm announced by the "is" of experience (in other words, the "ought" of Being) is the demand to maintain the contingent conditions of possibility requisite for humanity to become what it is. Properly understood, those conditions include preservation of all otherness, i.e., the world and persons.

Theology must reclaim the call of truth but not in terms of a particular comforting narrative read literally and, therefore, superficially (for example, that Christ died for human sin promising all believers eternal life in the next world). Rather, the call of truth exposing human faith must be seen in all of its danger foremost and only then as a balm (however, *not* the danger of the threat of eternal damnation). The real danger is that one always must risk the possibility of distortion in understanding, although one nevertheless has to

---

[55] One can find such a standpoint in Hugh of St. Victor who spoke of the human having "three" sets of eyes: physical eyes, the eyes of mental understanding of sense experience, and the eyes of mental contemplation of the "eternal spiritual order." Given humanity's unique location in the order of the spiritual and the material, humanity, Hugh claims, has a "human providential" responsibility for the physical order analogous to the "divine providential" responsibility for history. See Eckard Wolz-Gottwald, "Oculus Triplex - Das dreifache Auge der Erkenntnis" in *Internationale Katholische Zeitschrift Communio* 23, no. 3 (1994): 248-60; and "Die Transzendentale Phänomenologie und die philosophische Mystik" in *Philosophisches Jahrbuch* 101, no. 1 (1994): 98-115.

act on the basis of that finite understanding. This is the character of paradoxical truth as concealed possibilities in the midst of manifest actuality which takes us to the core of emerging reality. More than the future of merely the human species, then, is dependent upon our learning to listen within both theology and popular consciousness to the paradoxical nature of reality.

An Experiential Faith

It is time that theology cease talking either about God or for God.[56] Theology needs to take a breather from such absolute claims and re-examine first, and foremost, the meaning of experiential faith. Faith is not belief in the sense of a belief in something particular. Faith is a form of unknowing that is constitutive of the human condition. Yet it is a form of unknowing that "leans into mystery rather than runs from it."[57] Hence, what is required is a careful examination of human experience itself for an adequate understanding of the unknowing and mystery informing it.

Our epoch has become so materialistic that it has come to define experience only in terms of material categories. In what follows, it will be argued that experience rests, rather, on an aporetic mix of the spiritual and

---

[56] This does not mean that this project embraces Radical Theology's claim that God is dead. God can only be declared dead from a position of absoluteness, e.g., the absolute claim that empirical, historical reality exhausts the truth of experience which is the argument of Radical Theology. Not only will it be shown that such a position is patently absurd, but this project commences with the presupposition that there simply is no metaphysical absolute indubitably accessible to us. Neither the empirical world of sense perception nor the spiritual world of universals (nor a combination of both as with the abstract and concrete poles of Process metaphysics) serve as an absolute ground explaining either itself or the presence of its contrary in experience. In the absence of indubitable metaphysical claims, we are simply not in the position to ground in any absolute sense our talk about God. Our experience of ultimacy is always and already an experience of faith not of absolute knowledge.

A future project intends to explore the implications for God talk that emerge as a consequence of the notion of "possibility" in this text. Although one might want to see a hidden metaphysical agenda in the notion of "possibility," it will be argued here that "possibility" is "no-thing" and it is not "univocal." There is a radical "tensiveness" to "possibility" that is the consequence of an "is"/"is not" at the core of any and all experience. At the least, the notion of "possibility" here would require the surrendering of the mystical notion of direct and immediate experience of an absolute Oneness (ἑνός), since "possibility" is simultaneously "one" and "many."

[57] Taken from notes shared by Peter Kaufman on an earlier version of this manuscript which he gracefully read.

the material. This will require that the theological task commence with a retrieval of the spiritual dimension of everyday experience. To do so, it is helpful to reexamine Platonic metaphysics in order to obtain a sense of the experiential, spiritual dimension of our lives, but not in order to obtain a metaphysical explanation for life on the basis of some claim that "ideas" exist independent of our consciousness of them. Our post-metaphysical situation denies any such metaphysical explanation, whether it be Platonic, Aristotelian, or some variation based on them,[58] and reinforces the judgment that the human condition is one of individual and communal faith seeking understanding.

This does not mean, however, that theology is merely descriptive and not prescriptive or speculative. But theology must first be descriptive of the aporetic basis upon which our lives are dependent, before it can be prescriptive and speculative. What must first be described is not *what* experience is all about, but rather *how*, and upon what paradoxical foundation, experience transpires. Hence, human *experience* always establishes the horizon of the theological task. Even the speculative moment of theology must be rooted in, and *speak from*, human experience.[59] When theology claims to *speak for*

---

[58] A case could be made that in the 20th century Aristotle has dominated Western thought across the spectrum from Process metaphysics to Heidegger and Hermeneutics.

[59] The insistence on the rootedness of theology in experience will be seen by students of George Lindbeck as situating this project in the "experience-expressivist" model of theology. For a description of Lindbeck's *four* theological models of the cognitive propositional, the experiential-expressive, the hybrid of these two, and his preferred cultural linguistic, see George A. Lindbeck, *The Nature of Doctrine: Religion and Theology in a Postliberal Age* (Philadelphia: The Westminster Press, 1984), p. 16. However, this insistence on the priority of experience in the theological task is not based upon making a claim for any specific content of human experience which would then serve as the source for the religious, linguistic expression of that experience. One could agree with Lindbeck that something of this form has been the claim of the major non-Orthodox theologies since the Enlightenment (e.g., Schleiermacher's absolute dependence, Otto's idea of the holy, Lonergan's dynamic state of being in love without restrictions and without an object, Ogden's animal faith, Tracy's trustworthiness and worthwhileness to our lives, or Tillich's notion of the priority of Being over non-being), but reject Lindbeck's claim that all of these are representatives of liberal theology (see David Tracy's analysis of the five models of theology, e.g., orthodox, liberal, neo-orthodox, radical, and revisionist, in chapter 2 of *Blessed Rage for Order: The New Pluralism in Theology* (New York: The Seabury Press, 1975). Lindbeck argues that such an experiential claim is taken by "experience-expressivists" as the underlying unity behind all religious traditions which thereby negates either a distinctiveness or a priority of one tradition over another. See *ibid.*, pp. 23 and 127.

Acknowledgment of the aporiai at the core of experience, however, denies that there is any one content to experience that serves as the religious content of our lives which humans subsequently express in the liturgy and theology of a particular tradition.

a dimension beyond the horizon of human experience, it is engaged in an illegitimate speculative task.

The claim that human experience establishes the horizon of the theological task does not mean, as Karl Barth maintained with respect to the liberal theologies of the 19th century,[60] that humanity is being substituted here for God. All that is maintained is that the human condition is characterized by a radical unknowing whose full implications have not yet been adequately investigated and embraced. Once those consequences are made clear, then one must see the human condition as necessarily rooted in faith. This faith, however, is not simply some other kind of knowledge accessible by means of an auxiliary capacity in addition to the knowledge arrived at by "reason." On the contrary, faith, as it is meant here, is to be underscored as an "unknowing" characterizing both the material and spiritual dimensions of human experience. Far from experiential faith establishing the human as the absolute anchor for all that is, experiential faith places human hubris radically in question.[61]

That theology is at first a descriptive or phenomenological discipline does not mean, however, that it is concerned merely with the present moment of sense perception. To limit the descriptive task to the present would not only be a denial of human historicality or of our debt to the acting and suffering by both others and ourselves retained in collective and individual memory, nor would it not only be to fail to appreciate the role of future anticipation in shaping the human condition. Far more, it would mean a denial of all of our experience.

The aporiai of experience undermine any simple dichotomy between "inside" and "outside," experience and expression. The conditions for the possibility of experience are aporetic which denies the privileging of any particular experience as the explanation or root of the whole of experience (including any community).

Aporetic theology's emphasis on experience focuses not on any "what" or specific content of experience but rather on the "how" of experience. Such a focus permits and even insists upon acknowledging the unique and unrepeatable character of experience while simultaneously (paradoxically) affirming the universal character of experience. Denial of either the particular or the universal or reducing either down to the other is a violation of what we are as human beings. Our experience is constituted out of both.

For a further discussion of Lindbeck's theological project, see Chapter 5.

[60] See Karl Barth, *Die Protestantische Theologie im 19. Jahrhundert*, pp. 19-20, 503, 509; see, also, Barth's critique of Pietism, p. 589.

[61] Where Barth argued that the heliocentric shift of the Copernican revolution resulted in a shift to anthropocentrism, his dialectical theology claims to know more than it is possible to know (it is a form of Gnosticism). Dialectical theology displaces general human experience with an elitist "insider" experience reigned over by the gurus of revelation.

It has become a commonplace, when the present is taken as the standard or exclusive source for describing the human condition, to limit experience to sense perception. But humans are hardly understood if we describe ourselves only in terms of what is available to the senses. In fact, that God is not experienced with the senses is nothing censurable or lamentable. For all of experience occurs in a dimension completely inaccessible to the senses. Experience occurs exclusively in the intellect which one can not see, touch, hear, taste, or smell.[62] To limit the descriptive task to the present moment of sense perception would mean to eliminate precisely that dimension of experience that is our primary concern as human beings and theologians. In short, it would mean a denial of all that is concealed to the senses but which is necessary for us to be who and what we are in the order of things.

Theology, however, is concerned with more than mere description. Theology is also normative; its "is" immediately contains an "ought." Why? Because the removal or loss of the constitutive descriptive ingredients of theology would mean the impossibility of any experience. At the least, the "ought" discovered in theological analysis is concerned with preservation of those conditions that are necessary for our experience.[63] Implicit in the des-

---

[62] It is curious that Tracy's discussion of the importance of "non-sensuous experience" in *Blessed Rage for Order*, e.g., pp. 64-5, 71, does not develop the dimension of the intellect which is the exclusive dimension of experience even of "sensuous experience." The risk that one takes in emphasizing the intellect is that one will be written off as trapped in Cartesianism which "everyone knows" is no longer defensible today. What one does not want to do, however, is throw the baby out with the bath water. The critique of Cartesianism is not simply that we can no longer speak of two "substances" (e.g., mental and material) constituting human experience. What is to be rejected in Cartesianism is that "substance-ontology, which sees being in terms of what is present and actual" (Hans-Georg Gadamer, *Truth and Method*, p. 239). This requires suspicion about any discussion of either the "sensuous" or the "non-sensuous" that is understood exclusively in terms of what is "present and actual." Perhaps the explanation for Tracy's failure to address the intellect as constitutive of the "non-sensuous" is that the metaphysics of Process thought rests upon an ontology of "presence." In other words, it fails to appreciate both the presence, and necessity of, concealment and suppression active in everything present and actual. Once one overcomes a metaphysics of presence, however, one is justified, nevertheless, in distinguishing between (but not separating) possibility and actuality, universal and particular, abstract and concrete, or mental and physical differences. The life of the mind, i.e., the intellect, is radically different from the objects of sense, but that in no way forces one to argue for two different substances based on what is present and actual.

[63] It must be noted, however, that the necessary conditions of possibility of experience are not metaphysically necessary conditions. Given the contingency of experience, the best that can be said is that the necessary conditions of that experience involve contingent necessity. In other words, given the fact of our experience, there are conditions that are necessary in order for us to experience as we do. But it is not absolutely necessary that

criptive activity of theology, then, is a prescriptive moment which serves as the key to ethics. To be sure, this does not remove all ambiguity, nor does it provide one with the cornerstone of an exhaustive casuistry. Human experience can only occur in radical dependence upon conditions of possibility over which it has ultimately limited control and which can never be entirely transparent, and human experience will always include a fundamental mystery of concealment with respect to what is manifest. Theology must, at the very least, insist on an ethic which preserves those conditions of possibility and requires acknowledgment of that mystery.

It is only *after* one has engaged in the descriptive and prescriptive moments of theological analysis and reflection that one is able to approach the speculative task that takes one beyond the phenomenological and the ethical to speak of the nature of this mystery and radical dependence of the human condition.

By emphasizing the priority of the descriptive and prescriptive over the speculative, one acknowledges that both "the head and the heart" must be engaged in order to reign in unbridled speculation. By the head, I mean the careful exercise of description, prescription, and critical evaluation of the ultimate causal explanation of one's socially constructed paradigm. Yet the heart is equally requisite, for the heart is one's conviction with respect to, and profession of, the insights gained by the head. But this project argues that it is only once the aporiai of the human condition are open before us, that one can adequately engage the heart. There is no experience without conviction (the heart), but not all conviction engages the head.

Central to this theological project, then, is the claim that the descriptive or phenomenological moment of the theological task leads one to a number of aporiai or paradoxes at the core of the human condition.[64] Aporiai is

---

any individual is. We exist contingently, not absolutely. Hence, the conditions of possibility for us to experience are themselves contingently necessary not metaphysically or absolutely necessary. It is precisely because the description of these conditions of possibility involves contingent necessity, however, that the description contains an "ought." These conditions of possibility ought to be preserved or else there could be no experience whatsoever.

[64] Paul Ricoeur calls for a move beyond "Phenomenology" to "speculation." Ricoeur concludes Section 1 of volume 3 of *Time and Narrative* by observing the aporetic relationship between the phenomenological and the speculative rooted as both are in time: "... we have undertaken a process that is no longer that of phenomenology, the process the reader may have expected to find here, but rather a process that is one of reflective, speculative thought as a whole in its search for a coherent answer to the question: what is time? If, in stating an aporia, we emphasized the phenomenology of time, what emerges at the end ... is a broader and more balanced insight - namely, that we cannot

used in the title of this work, rather than paradoxes, because the term aporia includes etymologically the notion of "being underway" or, more accurately, "not knowing the way." Raising the spectre of paradox does *not* mean, however, that theology simply surrenders intellectual rigor and accountability in the face of the inexplicable and incomprehensible. Paradox is constituted out of a tension between components that are irreconcilable and incommensurable yet both necessarily indispensable.[65] Aporiai or paradoxes

---

think about cosmological time (the instant) without surreptitiously appealing to phenomenological time and vice versa. If the statement of this aporia outruns phenomenology, this aporia thereby has the great merit of resituating phenomenology within the great current of reflective and speculative thought. This is why I did not title this first section of this volume "The Aporias of the Phenomenology of Time," but rather "The Aporetics of Temporality" (*Ibid.*, p. 96).

[65] David Tracy warns against "premature announcements of paradox" (see *Blessed Rage for Order*, p. 249) and mystification (see *ibid.*, pp. 4-10). He equates the functioning of "paradox" and "scandal" in Protestant theology with "mystery" in Roman Catholic theology (see *ibid.*, p. 198. 66).

This project understands the role of aporiai and paradox in theology quite differently from the usual usage of paradox by such theologians as Kierkegaard or Tillich and particularly the usage of scandal by Karl Barth. It will be argued that acknowledgment of the functioning of aporiai in human experience does not shut down critical reflection but awakens us to critical accountability and awareness.

Tracy argues that the critical moment, or the issue of truth claims in theology, is dependent upon a move to metaphysics. See *ibid.*, pp. 68, 160, and 175-187. He suggests that "... the choice is not really between metaphysics or no metaphysics; the only real choice is between a self-conscious and explicit metaphysics or an unconscious yet operative one" (*ibid.*, p. 68). I would formulate what is at issue here by substituting "presuppositions" for "metaphysics." Clarification of the presuppositions enabling experience discloses that metaphysical explanation is an illusion. Tracy acknowledges this when he writes: "Both the modern and contemporary reformulations of the philosophical task continue to involve themselves in the central aim of classical metaphysics: what are the basic *a priori* conditions of all human living and thinking? That task alone is properly transcendental - or, if one prefers, metaphysical. The accomplishment of that task will always remain 'problematic' in the exact sense that it can no more be indubitably 'proved' than it can be avoided by any serious philosophical thinking" (*ibid.*, p. 68). The very lack of "proof" indicates that metaphysical options are wagers of faith, and should be acknowledged to be necessary presuppositions rather than establishing metaphysical necessity. While I applaud the move by Tracy "... away from the secondary phenomenon of the world constituted by the experience of our senses to the primal phenomenon of a social and temporal self ..." (*ibid.*, p. 173), I understand the "non-sensuous" character of experience of the self not only in terms of our "moving, feeling, sensing, thinking, acting, and deciding" (*ibid.*, p. 173), but in terms of the aporetic dependence of our moving, feeling, sensing, etc., on indefinable universals and mind in aporetic interface with an "objective" reality.

This aporetic interaction is described by Ernst Cassirer, for example, in *Philosophie der symbolischen Formen, Erster Teil: Die Sprache*, 4 Aufl. (Darmstadt: Wissen-

involve a dialectical interaction between irreducible yet contradictory components. Hence, understanding of a paradox requires an accountability to both sides or constituent moments of the paradoxical tension. Once again, the limits to the theological task are seen as *furthering the critical* engagement of the head prior to one's commitment of the heart rather than being destructive of reason and surrendering to emotionalism. Just as the descriptive moment leads to the prescriptive, the aporetic moment leads to the critical and responsible task of accountability to the constitutive components of the paradox.

By focussing on the role of aporiai in the descriptive task of theology, this project denies that reason is sovereign over the whole of experience. The Hegelian temptation to insist that all of history conforms to the dictates of reason is analogous to the more classical claim that the Logos is the explanation of all that is. Both of these options, while always attractive to the intellectual, are seductive forms of reductionism. They both are a denial of the aporiai of experience and maintain an illusory priority of explanation over understanding. All reason rests upon both presuppositions and concealment which are necessary for arriving at clarity and distinctness in understanding. In short, theology is foremost a discipline not of reason but of faith.

---

schaftliche Buchgesellschaft, 1964), pp. 26, 41, 47, 149 and in "Was ist 'Subjektivismus'?," *Theoria: A Swedish Journal of Philosophy and Psychology*, V (1939), pp. 126, 127, and 131-2.

PART I:
THE CONTEXT OF POST-METAPHYSICAL THEOLOGY

Chapter 1
What is Theology?

Theology is the living out of and reflecting upon the aporetic character of human experience. Since theology is concerned with the fundamental aporiai shaping the human condition, it addresses the dimension of faith that is at the core of all understanding and action. Hence, in order to enter into the theological task as it is understood here, it is necessary to turn initially to ask what the aporetic is and what it suggests for the life of faith before addressing what the constitutive paradoxes of the human condition are.

Contrary to the etymological construction of the term "theology," then, theology as it is understood here does not have the object "God" as its terminus.[1] Rather, faith is the focus of theology. Because theology is con-

---

[1] It is with respect to the role of God in theological reflection that I have a fundamental problem with David Tracy's otherwise insightful and extremely valuable work. In *The Analogical Imagination*, Tracy maintains in contradiction to his important call for appreciating pluralism in theology (based on the fundamental hermeneutical character of human understanding as an open-ended process as a consequence of the necessarily inherent tension between inherited texts/traditions and the always novel experience of the particular individual/community) that there is only one appropriate object for theology. Tracy's entire theological project is torn between hermeneutical pluralism and metaphysical absolutes. This is nowhere more clearly articulated than in his insistence that: "Theology in all its forms is finally nothing else but the attempt to reflect deliberately and critically upon . . . God. Theology is *logos* on *theos*." (*ibid.*, p. 51) Or, again: ". . . any theological discourse which loses its anchorage to the doctrine of God is no longer theological." (*ibid.*, p. 52) It is because Tracy roots fundamental theology in metaphysics (see, e.g., *ibid.*, pp. 85, n. 31; 86, n. 34; 90-91, n. 63; 97-98, n. 114; and 159), specifically Process metaphysics, that he can insist that the proper object of theological concern is "God" while simultaneously insisting that any particular articulation with respect to God is (and by necessity must be) less than absolute (i.e., pluralistic). Just as an individual person must necessarily be as the "object" of any statements about who that individual is, nevertheless, no statement about the individual is adequate for articulating who that individual "in fact" is. So Process metaphysics argues, God is the necessary condition of possibility for any and all experience, though no statement about experience can exhaust what God is.

What is overlooked with respect to both usages of necessity here is that they are contingent necessities. Neither is an absolute necessity. Rather than making "God" the object of theology, the present project argues that it is "faith" that is at the center of the theological task of reflecting upon human experience. The radically pluralistic character of theology is rooted in the tentativeness of faith at the very core of our experience rather than in the ambiguity of human expression concerning God as the ultimate ground of (or condition of possibility for) experience.

cerned with faith, and not because human reason can unlock the doors to all of reality, human experience establishes the parameters of theological understanding and discourse. In other words, the recognition, that we are dependent upon contingent conditions of possibility that are not of our creation, always and only takes place from the side of the effects of those conditions and never from our immediate access to the side of some absolute cause of those conditions. What is at stake in theology, then, is human experience. The value of a theological project rests entirely upon how adequately it engages human experience both in its details and in terms of its limits.[2]

Ulrich Köpf suggests that the insistence, that "God" is the proper object of theology, comes from the struggles in the 13th century to define theology as a science among other sciences in the new institution of the university and given the rise of the new orders in the church (see Köpf, *Die Anfänge der theologischen Wissenschaftstheorie*, pp. 27-8). Following Aristotle (e.g., *Aristoteles* Met. 1074b34 f.; EE 1216b11-15, from Köpf, *ibid.*, p. 80, n. 7), that all knowledge or science has an object, theologians for the most part, in agreement with the Dominicans (*ibid.*, p. 103) concluded that God was the proper object of its science. Köpf observes: "Jede Wissenschaft ist - wie jede Erkenntnis überhaupt - auf Gegenstände gerichtet. Ihre Eigenart ist durch den Kreis ihrer Gegenstände mitbestimmt, dessen Abgrenzung daher immer einen wichtigen Teil der Wissenschaftstheorie ausmacht." (*ibid.*, p. 79) Given the metaphysical presuppositions of the 13th century, however, more rigorous theologians recognized that God cannot be the "object" of a science, because we cannot know anything directly about God (see *ibid.*, p. 98). Rather, the object of theology was understood by Bonaventura, for example, to be *credible* (see *ibid.*, pp. 107-8). In contrast to those who wished to make some "object" (ein Seiendes) the determining locus of theology, Thomas Aquinas and Bonaventure argued, "[die] Sache der Theologie ist nicht ein Seiendes ansich, sondern insofern es in seiner Beziehung zum erkennenden Subjekt betrachtet wird." (*ibid.*, p. 111) In short, Thomas and Bonaventure place the locus of theology in the receptive individual, i.e., concerned with how God is perceived by us (to the extent that God is perceived through faith, *ibid.*, p. 103) and not how God is in itself. To be sure, here Tracy has two important compatriots corroborating his insistence that appearance or reception dominates Christological reflection (see, e.g., *op.cit.*, pp. 236, 238, 239, 295, n. 68) rather than access to God as He is in Himself. What they equally have in common is a confidence in metaphysics as providing us at least a hint about who God is behind the appearance/reception.

Once one grasps the aporetic and historical character of all human understanding, however, one must acknowledge that the theological task is more appropriately understood as an odyssey of faith seeking understanding given the speculative nature of all judgments of causality and the limits of the human condition. Faith is not concerned with a particular object, cause, or condition of possibility, because they are all contingent rather than absolute. Hence, they give us no warrants for making judgments about God. Faith is concerned with the paradox of our "unknowing knowing."

[2] For a discussion of George Lindbeck's work critiquing experience-based theology, see Chapter 5.

On the other hand, the primary concern of theology is not to offer answers to the questions generated by experience.[3] Theology is not a form of medicine healing our illnesses when all other cures are exhausted and have failed. Nor is theology a form of psychology helping us to adjust and be happy. Theology is a sober and demanding examination of the source of human questions: core aporiai or paradoxes structuring human experience. It is, therefore, an open-ended process of faith seeking understanding of the human condition as individuals in community and in relationship to the world. Only as such can theology empower responsible action or praxis in life.

On Paradox

The word paradox etymologically comes from two Greek roots: *para* (πα-ρα, meaning "contrary to" or "beyond") and *doxa* (δόξα, meaning "opinion" or "mere opinion"). Simply juxtaposing the two Greek roots suggests that paradox means "contrary to" or "beyond opinion." That would imply that paradox is concerned with the "really real" as opposed to "mere opinion." The implication of such a distinction between real and opinion is that paradox is concerned with some foundational level of experience free of the arbitrary perspectives of opinion. But just what is the "real" and how is it related to opinion?

What has been meant by "reality" in the Western tradition can be represented by a spectrum with two radically opposed extremes. At one end of the spectrum is our current understanding defined by the material and the perceptible. At the other end of the spectrum is the Greek understanding defined by the spiritual and the imperceptible.

If we follow Webster's definitions for "reality" and "opinion" today, we find that we are far removed indeed from the Greek world that gives us the etymological roots to the word paradox. Reality, according to Webster, is concerned with fact and fidelity to nature (objectivity). Opinion, according to Webster, means belief, and is related to personal judgment (subjectivity).

In his analysis of the simile of the line at the end of Book VI in *The Republic* (509d-511e), however, Plato defines *doxa* (opinion) to be that

---

[3] This is Paul Tillich's understanding of theology. He suggests that the "method of correlation" involves theological answers to existential questions. See Paul Tillich, *Systematic Theology*, vol. 1, p. 62. David Tracy calls Tillich's project, however, not a correlation but a juxtaposition: "... it juxtaposes questions from the 'situation' with answers from the 'message.'" Tracy, *Blessed Rage for Order*, p. 46.

region of experience accessible to the senses (sight, touch, smell, hearing, and taste). He concludes that all judgments made about the realm or region of sense experience are matters of *doxa* (opinion), because such judgments of sense perception rest foremost upon change and are experienced as mere products of the imagination (we "image" the world in the intellect). In addition, such judgments are formulated by means of hypotheses or assumptions that are themselves inaccessible to the senses and indefinable.

A definition has two moments: α) It must establish what all elements in a group have in common, allowing their identification as members of the same group (identity); and β) it must establish what distinguishes the group from all other groups (difference). The problem, Socrates discovered, is that it is impossible to establish both identity and difference for even the most basic components of everyday experience. Nothing that we could identify as common to all "chairs" (identity), for example, is uniquely restricted to chairs (difference). In order to demonstrate the role of hypotheses in what we call "sense perception," Plato uses an example from Euclidian geometry in which he discusses the three kinds of angles ("right" or 90°, "acute" or less than 90°, and "obtuse" greater than 90°). He first stresses that what one is really concerned with in discussing angles is not the angle that one can draw (and is accessible to the senses), but rather the angle that one thinks. Okay, so angles, since they are really thought not seen, are inaccessible to the senses, but, surely, the judgments of mathematics rest upon clear and precise definitions? If there is anything that is "beyond opinion" or more than a mere matter of opinion, it is mathematics. But no! The point, line, and plane, upon which Euclidian geometry depend, are indistinguishable from one another *by definition*. A point with any extension is not a point but a line. A line with any width is not a line but a plane. Points and lines must be presupposed, they are hypotheses. Assume that they are, and one can go on to calculate, predict, manipulate and control the things of the realm of sense. But, in terms of what can be established by human reason, it all rests upon assumptions or hypotheses. Is this a foundation of sand? Ironically (paradoxically?), in his simile of the line Plato uses a line divided by three sets of right angles to represent our experience to us, and these lines, points, and angles cannot "be" by definition. Just what *is* "real" in human experience?

To be accurate with respect to Plato's simile of the line, the dimension of human experience concerned with hypotheses and focussed "down" the line to the realm of sense perception is called "understanding," for understanding is the activity of employing hypotheses (assumptions) to make sense of the "imaged" world of opinion. The priority of understanding over opinion is that the understanding is aware of its presuppositions and of its activity of "making sense" out of the realm of sense perception, i.e., out of the realm of opinion. Opinion is placed on the line between the "understanding" of the intellect (that is, inaccessible to the senses) and "shadows/reflections" at the bottom end of the line with shadows and reflections constituting the second of the two divisions in the realm of sense perception. In other words, Plato calls "opinion" precisely the dimension of our experience that we today call objects and things of fact with their shadows and reflections.

Not only are objects not "real," according to Plato, because they are impermanent, but they are accessible to the intellect only by means of the power of "imaging." It is not the "object" that we experience, it is an image created by means of the imagination that we experience in the human intellect. Hence, the dividing "line" between the realm of sense perception and the intellect is the imagination (not to be confused with fantasy). Again, the very simile of the line is using a construct of the imagination to represent human experience to us. Just what is "real" according to Plato?

The criterion for identifying what is real, according to Plato and the Greeks in general, is "that which endures." The realm of sense perception, then, is not real because it is constantly changing, i.e., it does not endure. In contrast, the intellect has access to ideas that are the same yesterday, today, and tomorrow. The intellect, then, has access to what endures.

This does not mean that there is no change in the intellect. We may change our mind from one moment to the next, but in order to do so we must employ ideas. These ideas themselves do not increase or decrease, they are always in principle accessible to the intellect, and they remain always what they "are" (unlike physical objects, which can be other than the way they appear to be).

The realm of *doxa*, in short, is not real, because it is constantly changing. The realm of the intellect is real, because it rests upon what is the same yesterday, today, and tomorrow. In addition, the realm of the intellect is "necessary," since it cannot be other than what it is in contrast to what is accessible to the senses which can be other than the way it appears to be. Further, the realm of the intellect constitutes a perfect harmony. When was the last time that even the most contrary ideas beat up on one another (here as in Isaiah 65 the lamb *always and already* lays down with the lion). Foremost, the intellect *is* experience. All that we experience, including all that we understand, claim to know, and do, is experienced in the intellect. In this sense, then, reality, according to Plato, is a matter of non-sense, since the realm of ideas is inaccessible, by both definition and experience, to the senses. We cannot see, touch, smell, hear, or taste our ideas or our experience. They are "beyond sense" (beyond opinion) or "non-sense." Reality, according to Plato, is beyond opinion or para-doxical.

Such definitions of reality and opinion are exactly the opposite of Webster's definitions with which we started. When we turn to Webster's definition of paradox we see how far we today now are from the Greek paradoxa. Webster defines paradox as "a statement that seems contradictory, unbelievable, or absurd but that may actually be true in fact." The terms "seems," "actually," and "fact" can now be seen to be thoroughly ambiguous (without beginning to touch the correspondence notion of truth operative in their definitions). If as with Plato the realm of sense perception is the region of opinion, then what are facts, what constitutes actuality, and what is the basis upon which one concludes that something "seems" to be such and such but in "fact" or "actually" it is not?

The dilemmas increase, however, once one focuses on the notion of truth in Webster's definition. "Actually" is an adverb built from the noun actual. It is interchangeable in our day with "true." What is actual is true. Equating actuality and truth, though, means that we have already wagered for sense experience at the expense of the intellect in our definition of the real. What we mean for the most part by "actual" is the material world. *Things* are actual, i.e., real. Hence, truth has, above all, to do with material things, and this relationship to material things establishes the criterion for the clarity and distinctness of truth. For thoughts are less real, according to materialists, because thoughts are subjective. Nonetheless, thoughts are also understood to be actual to the extent that at any particular moment the thought I am having is my "actual" mental state. The entire tradition of the West since Plato has defined truth as the correspondence of an actual mental judgment with the actual thing to which it refers. For example, it is true, that there is a tree outside my study window only if the actual mental judgment ("there is a tree outside my study window") in "fact" *corresponds* to something that is materially and actually the case (a tree outside my study window).

The very criterion of reference, that was thought to protect us from arbitrary mental judgments, however, must now be seen as providing us with the most arbitrary form of truth for two reasons. One, it is riddled with dependence upon assumptions. All judgments, built upon assumptions or presuppositions, Plato labels "understanding," and, analogous to our inability to define point, line, and plane, Socrates had demonstrated that we cannot define the universals employed by the understanding (although they are obviously "known" by everyone and they remain the same yesterday, today, and tomorrow).[4] Second, the criterion or touchstone of truth here is grounded in that which is by definition not part of experience, that is, the sensed, material world, and our experience is neither sensed nor material.

When one is completely precise about it, I never experience the tree outside my study window as it actually is. I only experience an "image" of that tree in my intellect. How can I ever be certain that my mental judgment in fact corresponds to something materially existing independent of my judgment when I can *never* experience anything of the actual material "thing" except as a product of the imagination?

We must return later to a discussion of "truth." We have encountered enough of the dilemma of truth to observe that calling the "actual world" true is to call true what Plato called opinion (*doxa*). The tradition of the West has turned reality upside down from Plato's point of view.

What we want to acquire at this point, though, is an understanding of what paradox is all about. If we remain correct (in the popular sense of truth as "correspondence") to the etymological roots of the term paradox, which take us back into the Greek terms *para* and *doxa*, then Webster's definition leads us in a direction completely opposite to what paradox is all about. Webster's definition encourages us to judge the validity of "non-sense" from the standpoint of "sense." But we have now learned from Plato that experience is by definition "non-sense." How can we judge the validity of our experience by means of something (the sensed object) that we cannot experience except as a product of the imagination? To do so would be analogous to Aesop's dog dropping the bone to grasp for the reflection in the water. In short, Webster's definition conceals that which "goes beyond" (*para*) the realm of "opinion" (*doxa*), because it privileges what is accessible to the senses (the material, factual world) over what is inaccessible to the senses (the immaterial, intellectual world).

The privileging of sense experience over "non-sense" in Webster's definition is clearly announced in the concluding word of the definition: "fact." The term fact originally meant "deed" or "act." It is not until the mid-18th century, we are told by Christian Hartlich,[5] that the term takes on its current meaning of "*things* as they are; reality; actuality; truth." Once

---

[4] See Plato's *Apology* and Book VI of *The Republic*.
[5] See Christian Hartlich, "Historisch-kritische Methode in ihrer Anwendung auf Geschehnisaussagen der Hl. Schrift" in *Zeitschrift für Theologie und Kirche*, 75/4 (November 1978), 479, especially n. 9.

again, the dictionary commences from a presumption of what constitutes reality which is exactly opposite to the original Greek roots of the term paradox. The consequence is that the necessary tension serving as the core of paradox is lost, for Webster's "common-sense" assumption with respect to "reality" discredits any "beyond" that could possibly stand in tension with "the actual." The tension or dialectic constituting the fundamental meaning of paradox is completely lost. Paradox, according to Webster's definition, is a form of illusion or a logical conundrum. Such a definition suppresses all of the tension of the aporetic at the heart of the paradoxical.

Returning to the exegesis of paradox based upon Plato's simile of the line, the paradoxical ("going beyond") is radically dependent upon that which it goes beyond. This dependence is expressed in Hegel's German by the verb *aufheben* which, among other things, in Schwäbisch means "to take or pick up" or "to preserve" something. The "going beyond" of paradox takes up or preserves that which it goes beyond, and paradox does so by maintaining a dialectical tension with what has been superseded. Paradox, then, involves a *necessary inter relatedness* of "opinion" (the realm of sense perception) and "that which goes beyond opinion" (the intellect inaccessible to sense perception). The paradoxical keeps these components of tension in play. In other words, one cannot simply suppress *doxa* to arrive at that which is beyond, i.e., to arrive at *para-(doxa)*. Rather, both dimensions always and already depend upon one another. The later-Plato recognized this, for he writes in *The Sophist*:

> ... only one course is open to the philosopher who values knowledge and the rest above all else. He (sic) must refuse to accept from the champions either of the one or of the many forms the doctrine that all reality is changeless, and he must turn a deaf ear to the other party who represent reality as everywhere changing. Like a child begging for 'both,' he must declare that reality or the sum of things is both at once - all that is unchangeable and all that is in change.[6]

Reality is paradoxical. Now it is possible to suggest a definition of paradox. Paradox involves a necessary contradiction and incommensurability between its constitutive moments that requires that they be held in a dialectical tension with one another. In other words, neither component of the paradoxical tension is reducible to, or explainable by, the other. This is the meaning of the aporetic which is defined by Paul Ricoeur in terms of the tension between two concepts where "... neither concept, considered separately, proposes a satisfying solution to their unresolvable disagreement."[7]

---

[6] Plato, *The Sophist*, 249c-d.
[7] Paul Ricoeur, *Time and Narrative*, vol. 3, p. 12.

Precedents for Paradox in Theology

There is ample precedent for taking paradox (or the aporetic) to be the center of the theological task. However, previous uses of paradox in Christian theology have emphasized one key paradox as the focus of the Christian faith. That key paradox has consistently been the Christ as either the ultimate criterion for speaking of the positive conquest by negativity of its own negativity (Hegel and Tillich) or as absolute likeness in absolute unlikeness[8] (Kirkegaard). Only a brief sketch of these three usages of paradox in theology is possible here. Broad strokes must suffice to contextualize this key element in the work of these three individuals.

Hegel and Tillich's central paradox is concerned with negation. Negation both confirms its dependence upon what it negates and is the condition of possibility for the emergence of a "more" to experience which couldn't surface except by negation. The difference between Hegel and Tillich is that Hegel calls humanity out of history where Tillich anchors humanity in history.

Hegel's Double Negation Denying History

Hegel is the first "God is dead" theologian.[9] The God/Man had to die in order to represent to all consciousness its own capability. According to Hegel the relationship between the world of sensed objects and the invisible intellect is articulated historically as a consequence of a process of double negation. Being in its Oneness first negates itself into the manyness of the physical order. It only slowly and developmentally moves through the different stages of the physical order to reach the level of the human where the developmental stages of consciousness are ultimately capped by the second negation where Oneness is thought in the Concept (*der Begriff*). Uniting the whole course of history, as well as uniting subject and object, is the Oneness of Being. All that is, despite appearances to the contrary, is the consequence of the "cunning of reason" moving toward the second negation from whose perspective the individual can grasp the totality of what was, is, and will be.

The key moment in history, according to Hegel, is the event of the God/Man, i.e., the Christ. Although still only a "representation" for con-

---

[8] This is the paradox of Kierkegaard and Kenotic Christology. See the discussion of Kenotic Christology in Claude Welch, ed. and trans., *God and Incarnation in Mid-Nineteenth Century German Theology* (New York: Oxford University Press, 1965), pp. 295-307.

[9] See, G.W.F. Hegel, *The Phenomenology of Mind*, trans. by J.B.Baillie (New York: Harper Torchbooks, 1967), pp. 752-3.

sciousness of the unity of God and humanity in the Spirit, the Christ, nevertheless, announces the goal of history. That goal is for the entire species to experience the One-ness of God in the Spirit/Mind. One-ness cannot experience itself, because experience requires being able to distinguish something from something else. In other words, experience requires at least two-ness. Hence, for God to experience "Himself," He had to negate His own One-ness and spill out into multiplicity. But that very multiplicity established the conditions for One-ness to eventually experience Itself, because multiplicity when combined with consciousness makes for experience. The goal of history, then, has been to establish the material conditions for consciousness to emerge. The cultural development of consciousness in history has served to establish the stages for the development of consciousness to engage in abstraction. Abstraction is the ability to think the "one" in the "many," and, ultimately, this can lead to the insight that one can think the "One" (God) by means of the "Many." This thought (*Begriff*) can only occur in consciousness. In other words, God can experience itself, God can be thought, only in human consciousness. This is why Christology is so important to Hegel, for with the Christ, who is claimed to be the God/Man, the Idea came into history that humanity can experience God intimately and directly.

Hegel's understanding of history and Christology, then, involves the paradox of a "double negation." God had to negate Himself into multiplicity. The Christ event represents the universal possibility of a "second" negation from multiplicity back to the One. The paradox of the Christ event, however, is that it is only by means of death (negation of the physical or material conditions of life) that one can experience the spiritual One, who is true Life. But the Christ event presents this paradoxical negativity to humanity only as a representation (*Vorstellung*). Consciousness cannot take up the material world and another's consciousness directly into itself. Consciousness can only image the material world and another's consciousness to itself (i.e., the individual can only re-present the material world and another's consciousness to itself in the individual's immaterial mind/Spirit). The first stage of abstract thought for humanity is to dis-cover one-ness (the universal) by means of its experience of many-ness (physical objects). This is the stage of re-presentation; thinking a "one" (universal) on the basis of experience of "many" images of some-thing or other person. But this stage establishes the condition for consciousness to think One-ness by means of the many "ones" of universals entirely independent of the many-ness of the physical world. Such a Thought or Concept (*Begriff*), according to Hegel, constitutes the self-experience of God as the original One having negated itself out into history in the first place. Spirit grasps Spirit directly and immediately through the ultimate Concept of synthesis "above" all one-ness and many-ness. According to Hegel, this is the goal of history (i.e., the elevation of all consciousness above history in the "second negation"). The "first" negation is God's Oneness spilling itself out into manyness. The "second" negation can occur exclusively in human consciousness as it grasps the ultimate Concept in negating all multiplicity to think Oneness. But the second negation remains only a possibility for humanity to the extent that the second negation remains a re-presentation (*Vorstellung*) by means of the "image" of the Christ. It is not until each individual moves from representation (*Vorstellung*) to the personal experience of the Concept (*Begriff*) of the One in the many that history will be fulfilled.

> Conceptual comprehension [of the Christ event or any event] ... does not mean for it [self-consciousness] a grasping of this conception (*Begriff*) which knows natural existence when canceled and transcended to be universal and thus reconciled with itself; but rather a grasping of the imaginative idea (*Vorstellung*) that the Divine Being is reconciled with its existence through an event, - the event of God's emptying Himself of His Divine Being through His factual Incarnation and His Death. The grasping of this idea now expresses more specifically what was formerly called in figurative thinking spiritual resurrection, or the process by which God's individual self-consciousness [the Christ] becomes the universal, becomes the religious communion. The death of the Divine Man, *qua* death, is abstract negativity ... In spiritual self-consciousness death loses this natural significance ... Death ... ceases to signify what it means directly - the non-existence of *this* individual - and becomes transfigured into the universality of the spirit, which lives in its own communion, dies there daily, and daily rises again.[10]

What is merely represented (*vorgestellt*) by the paradox of religious consciousness is, of course, only absolutely realized by each individual where all "objectivity" of representation is overcome in "Absolute Knowledge or Spirit knowing itself as Spirit."[11]

This paradox of negativity, that is, that God can only experience Himself by means of two stages of negation which gives history its goal and humanity its status in the divine plan, provides Hegel with a meta-narrative encompassing all mini-narratives of human history. Ultimately, however, this meta-narrative is a denial of the significance of all mini-narratives, for the drama of history is ultimately only God experiencing Himself. The suffering of humanity is meaningless, because it is not preserved. It is acknowledged

---

[10] Hegel, *The Phenomenology of Mind*, p. 780.
[11] Hegel, *The Phenomenology of Mind*, p. 808. See, in addition, Michael Theunissen, *Hegels Lehre vom absoluten Geist als theologisch-politischer Traktat* (Berlin: Walter de Gruyter & Co., 1970).

only in the first level of conscious abstraction, but that level must be negated in order for the One to be Thought.

Tillich's One Absolute Paradox

Paul Tillich's work is representative of the role of paradox in 20th century theology. Tillich defines paradox as "'against opinion,' namely, the opinion of finite reason."[12] He then claims that "[t]here is, in the last analysis, only *one* genuine paradox in the Christian message - the appearance of that which conquers existence under the conditions of existence."[13]

Paradox, however, is central to all experience, Tillich claims in *The Courage to Be*, because all experience involves negativity and ultimately the negativity of death. But:

> The paradox of every radical negativity, as long as it is an active negativity, is that it must affirm itself in order to be able to negate itself. No actual negation can be without an implicit affirmation ... The negative lives from the positive it negates.[14]

According to Tillich, it is this paradox of negativity that empowers human beings with the "courage to be" even in light of the apparent victory of death. Death itself is dependent upon life. Hence, Tillich is a "philosopher/theologian of life," because all negation in life is an affirmation of the priority of life.[15] A theologian of life affirms not simply by arbitrary conviction, but out of necessity,[16] the priority of life over death.

Nevertheless, Tillich insists that there is only one place in history where the victory over negativity is ultimately announced. This is the paradox of the Christ. He writes in "The Theologian (Part III)" in *The Shaking of the Foundations*:

> We must not distort, by ecclesiastical and theological arrogance, that great cosmic paradox that there is victory over death within the world of death itself. We must not impose the heavy burden of wrong stumbling-blocks upon those who ask us questions. But neither must we empty the true paradox of its power. For true theological

---

[12] Paul Tillich, *Systematic Theology*, vol. I (Chicago: The University of Chicago Press, 1971), p. 57.

[13] Tillich, *Systematic Theology*, vol. I, p. 57.

[14] Paul Tillich, *The Courage to Be* (New Haven: Yale University Press, 1969), p. 176.

[15] See "The Courage to Be as the Key to Being-Itself: Nonbeing Opening Up Being" in Tillich, *The Courage to Be*, pp. 178-181.

[16] Though, just as in the case of the necessity of the conditions of possibility spoken of in Process thought and the priority of the universal/eternal over the individual/temporal spoken of by Kierkegaard, this necessity proves to be a contingent necessity rather than an absolute or metaphysical necessity.

existence is the witnessing to Him Whose yoke is easy and Whose burden is light, to Him Who is the true paradox.[17]

He had written earlier in "The Theologian (Part I):"

> ... no one can say 'Jesus is Lord' except in the Holy Spirit. He who accepts Jesus as the Christ proves by that very acceptance that he has received the Spirit of God. For the spirit of man alone is not capable of making the statement: 'I accept Jesus as the Christ'. That statement is the mystery of the foundation of the Christian Church, the paradox and the stumbling-block, which produce curses against Christianity. It is the depth and the power which create a new Being in the world, in history, and in man.[18]

Speaking of the "exclusivity" of the Christ, then, Tillich writes in the *Systematic Theology*:

> What, then, is the peculiar character of the healing through the New Being in Jesus as the Christ? ... The answer cannot be that there is no saving power apart from him but that he is the ultimate criterion of every healing and saving process ... [I]n him the healing quality is complete and unlimited. The Christian remains in the state of relativity with respect to salvation; the New Being in the Christ transcends every relativity in its quality and power of healing. It is just this that makes him the Christ. Therefore, wherever there is saving power in mankind, it must be judged by the saving power in Jesus as the Christ.[19]

Although it is the paradox of negativity (that the negative always and already presupposes the positive that it negates indicating the "priority" of the positive over the negative) that is at the heart of Tillich's theology, this paradox finds its ultimate criterion in the victory of life over death in the Christ.

This notion of "ultimate criterion" must be seen as the weak link in Tillich's systematic theology. Christological claims on the basis of the victory of Being over non-Being are hard pressed to indicate just why a particular, individual event of that victory of Being over non-Being should serve as the criterion for all events which, in fact, are all victories of Being over non-Being. The one, individual paradox is a universal.

Kierkegaard's Thought that Thought Cannot Think

If Tillich is representative of a 20th century theological position grounded in paradox, the focus on the role of paradox in human experience

---

[17] Paul Tillich, *The Shaking of the Foundations* (New York: Charles Scribner's Sons, 1948), p. 129.

[18] Paul Tillich, *The Shaking of the Foundations*, pp. 119-120.

[19] Paul Tillich, *Systematic Theology*, vol. II (Chicago: The University of Chicago Press, 1971), pp. 167-8. This is a classic case of an "inclusive Christology," which sees the Christ event as unsurpassable by any other saving power, instead of an "exclusive Christology," which sees the Christ alone as saving power.

in general and in Christian theology in particular (with its "one Absolute Paradox" as both the key to, and foundation for, the universal claim of Christianity) is found already in the 19th century in the writings of Søren Kierkegaard.

Kierkegaard describes the human condition as riddled with paradox, so it is no surprise that he finds the resolution to the paradoxes of experience in an "Absolute Paradox."[20] Kierkegaard's paradoxical human situation is that of an existing idealist.[21] Since the best that one can accomplish with respect to objective truth is an "approximation,"[22] the meaning of Christianity can only rest in a radical inwardness. But that inwardness does not take one to a mere speculative system which from "within" explains all that is both "within" and "without" to which one gives mere intellectual assent. Hegel's project represents such a system, but its achilles heel, according to Kierkegaard, is that it has forgotten "faith" or the "infinite interest" in "personal eternal happiness."[23]

---

[20] See Johannes Climacus, *Philosophical Fragments or A Fragment of Philosophy*, responsible for publication Søren Kierkegaard, trans. by David Swenson (Princeton: Princeton University Press, 1969), p. 46: "The supreme paradox of all thought is the attempt to discover something that thought cannot think."

[21] This is the meaning of the individual as the "idea in motion" mentioned frequently in *Repetition*. See, for example, the importance of the theme of motion in Kierkegaard (Constantin Constantius), *Repetition: A Venture in Experimenting Psychology*, ed. and trans. by Howard V. Hong and Edna H. Hong in *Fear and Trembling/Repetition* (Princeton: Princeton University Press, 1983), p. 131 (the opening sentence), 179, 180, 185, 204, 218, and 221. In addition, Kierkegaard writes: "... the accidental is second only to the ideal" (From *ibid.*, p. 162); "The moment it becomes a matter of actuality, all is lost, then it is too late. The actuality in which she is supposed to have her meaning remains but a shadow for me, a shadow that trots alongside my essential spiritual actuality ..." (*ibid.*, p. 201). Spiritual actuality is what enables objective actuality. See, *ibid.*, p. 149: "The dialectic of repetition is easy, for that which is repeated has been - otherwise it could not be repeated - but the very fact that it has been makes the repetition into something new. When the Greeks said that all knowing is recollecting, they said that all existence, which is, has been; when one says that life is a repetition, one says: actuality [spiritual actuality], which has been, now comes into existence. *If one does not have the category of recollection or of repetition, all life dissolves into an empty, meaningless noise.* Recollection is the ethnical ... view of life, repetition the modern; repetition is the *interest* ... of metaphysics, as also the interest upon which metaphysics comes to grief; repetition is the watchword ... in every ethical view; repetition is *conditio sine qua non* ... for every issue of dogmatics." (partial emphasis added)

[22] See Søren Kierkegaard (Johannes Climacus), *Concluding Unscientific Postscript to the Philosophical Fragments*, trans. by David f. Swenson (Princeton: Princeton University Press, 1968), pp. 24-47.

[23] See, Kierkegaard, *Concluding Unscientific Postscript*, pp. 49-55.

Nevertheless, according to Kierkegaard the *existing* idealist, humanity is constituted out of two irreconcilable dimensions: the essential/eternal and the accidental/temporal. Most human beings are unaware of their rootedness in the essential/ eternal, for they live their lives absorbed in, and chasing after, the accidental/temporal. Kierkegaard, however, seeks an unrealizable reconciliation with the essential (or actual), because the "exceptional" or actual individual presupposes the universal/eternal essential which means that experientially the universal/essential/eternal has a priority over the accidental temporal. The individual (the non-repetitive[24]) "thinks the universal with intense passion,"[25] for "... although he is in conflict with the universal still [the exceptional or particular individual] is an offshoot of it [the universal][26] (the repetitive[27]).

The highest expression of the human, according to Kierkegaard is to live the infinite in the finite: "To have one's daily life in the decisive dialectic of the infinite, and yet continue to live: this is both the art of life and its difficulty."[28] As will be described below in terms of Kierkegaard's description of stages on life's way, one neither discovers this dialectic nor achieves its content without an existential struggle, for, as Kierkegaard observed, "... the same thing happens in the spiritual life as with many plants - the main shot comes last."[29]

The existential experience of the infinite in the finite Kierkegaard calls the "Moment."[30] In the *Philosophical Fragments*, Kierkegaard had described the Moment as a paradox:

---

[24] Kierkegaard or Constantinus reports that in his search for repetition he returned to the Königstädter Theater in Berlin through which he learned that "[t]he only repetition was the impossibility of repetition" (*Repetition*, p. 170), "... for I had discovered that there simply is no repetition and had verified it by having it repeated in every possible way (*ibid.*, p. 171)."

[25] Constantin Constantius, *Repetition*, p. 227.

[26] Constantinus, *Repetition*, p. 227. Further: "The exception ... thinks the universal in that he thinks himself through; he works for the universal in that he works himself through; he explains the universal in that he explains himself" (*ibid.*, p. 227).

[27] See Constantinus, *Repetition*, p. 221: "Here only repetition of the spirit is possible, even though it is never so perfect in time as in eternity, which is the true repetition."

[28] Kierkegaard, *Concluding Unscientific Postscript*, p. 79n.

[29] Kierkegaard, *Repetition*, p. 154.

[30] See, for example, Kierkegaard, *Concluding Unscientific Postscript*, p. 176: "It is only momentarily that the particular individual is able to realize existentially a unity of the infinite and the finite which transcends existence. This unity is realized in the moment of passion."

Heidegger speaks of a "moment of vision" in terms of authentic resolution which rethinks Kierkegaard's notion of the "Moment". See *Being and Time*, p. 376: "When resolute, Dasein has brought itself back from falling [into the inauthenticity of the public

> Here ... we have the Moment, on which everything depends. Let us recapitulate. If we do not posit the Moment we return to Socrates; but it was precisely from him that we departed, in order to discover something. If we posit the Moment the Paradox is there; for the Moment is the Paradox in its most abbreviated form. Because of the Moment the learner is in Error [because the learner recognizes her/his unknowing and her/his unlikeness from the infinite]; and man, who had before possessed self-knowledge [of the accidental, finite and temporal], now becomes bewildered with respect to himself; instead of self-knowledge he receives the consciousness of sin [the awareness of absolute unlikeness between the self and the essential, infinite, or God[31]], and so forth; for as soon as we posit the Moment everything follows of itself.[32]

This notion of the "Moment" allows Kierkgaard to distinguish between "essential" and "accidental" knowledge:

> All essential knowledge relates to existence, or only such knowledge as has an essential relationship to existence is essential knowledge. All knowledge which does not inwardly relate itself to existence, in the reflection of inwardness, is, essentially viewed, accidental knowledge; its degree and scope is essentially indifferent. That essential knowledge is essentially related to existence does not mean the above-mentioned identity which abstract thought postulates between thought and being;[33]

"they" world], and has done so precisely in order to be more authentically 'there' in the 'moment of *vision*' as regards the Situation which has been disclosed." He echoes Kierkegaard's temporal interpretation of the Moment, to be sure not in terms of the Eternal and the Temporal but as the moment of individualization in which Dasein appropriates its own authentic possibilities, when he writes, *ibid.*, p. 387: "That *Present* which is held in authentic temporality and which thus is *authentic* itself, we call the '*moment of vision*'. This term must be understood in the active sense as an ecstasis. It means the resolute rapture with which Dasein is carried away to whatever possibilities and circumstances are encountered in the Situation as possible objects of concern, but a rapture which is *held* in resoluteness." See, as well, *ibid.*, p. 463.

[31] See Kierkegaard, *Philosophical Fragments*, p. 59.

[32] Kierkegaard, *Philosophical Fragments*, p. 64.

[33] Kierkegaard had just described truth as "subjective" or existential truth in contrast to the mere correspondence of an abstract judgment with an objective being: "Not for a single moment is it forgotten that the subject is an existing individual, and that existence is a process of becoming, and that therefore the notion of the truth as identity of thought and being is a chimera of abstraction, in its truth only an expectation of the creature; not because the truth is not such an identity, but because the knower is an existing individual for whom the truth cannot be such an identity as long as he lives in time. Unless we hold fast to this, speculative philosophy will immediately transport us into the fantastic realism of the I-am-I, which modern speculative thought has not hesitated to use without explaining how a particular individual is related to it ... In passion the existing subject is rendered infinite in the eternity of the imaginative representation, and yet he (sic) is at the same time most definitely himself." Kierkegaard, *Concluding Unscientific Postscript*, p. 176.

nor does it signify, objectively, that knowledge corresponds to something existent as its object. But it means that knowledge has a relationship to the knower, who is essentially an existing individual, and that for this reason all essential knowledge is essentially related to existence. Only ethical-religious knowledge[34] has an essential relationship to the existence of the knower.[35]

By distinguishing between essential and accidental knowledge, Kierkegaard underscores what he calls the paradox of "truth," for truth is infinite but existentially experienced only in radical inwardness by the finite individual.[36] This paradox of the inward, existing individual is viewed by Kierkegaard to disclose a radical fault (error/sin) which can neither be escaped nor overcome by one's own efforts, because it is a fault in one's existential conditions of possibility. One can discover the fault only by confirming it: in order for one to experience the eternal/infinite one must be temporal/finite, and one's temporal/finite world of experience is impossible without the eternal/infinite which is necessary for one to experience and understand the temporal/finite while simultaneously confirming one's separation from the eternal/infinite.

The key, according to Kierkegaard, to any hoped for "repetition" (or restitution) of an original, pristine unity with the infinite unlikeness of God, the repetition which overcomes all forms of human estrangement, is the Absolute Paradox[37] of the Teacher/Christ as the objective answer to the irresolvable contradictions of radical human inwardness. However, there are two elements in Kierkegaard's project announcing its limitations as a theological project of paradox. First, although there is a recognition of the two irreconcilable components of the eternal and the temporal constitutive of the human condition, the notion of "double reflection" described above in terms of the twoness of 1) the abstract thought of the eternal and 2) the existing individual's relation to that eternal thought,[38] there is an exclusive priority given to radical inwardness with respect to the individual's relationship to "eternal happiness" which excludes any real significance for the historical

---

[34] See the discussion below of the existential "stages" of the aesthetic, ethical, religiousness A and religiousness B.
[35] Kierkegaard, *Concluding Unscientific Postcript*, pp. 176-7.
[36] See, Kierkegaard, *Concluding Unscientific Postscript*, pp. 177-8.
[37] Kierkegaard (Johannes Climacus) writes in *Philosophical Fragments or a Fragment of Philosophy*, p. 46: "... one should not think slightingly of the paradoxical; for the paradox is the source of the thinker's passion, and the thinker without a paradox is like a lover without feeling: a paltry mediocrity ... The supreme paradox of all thought is the attempt to discover something that thought cannot think."
[38] See Kierkegaard, *Concluding Unscientific Postscript*, pp. 68-71.

"accidents" of the particularities of the individual's life. Second, this focus on the individual's inward relationship to the promise of eternal happiness is dependent upon confidence in a meta-narrative inherited from the tradition,[39] i.e., the "true" Christian narrative of redemption which is not to be confused with the tranquilizing self-satisfying practices of "domesticated Christianity." Kierkegaard appropriates from the Christian meta-narrative, for example, that God is a subject,[40] that human radical unlikeness from the infinite constitutes sin,[41] and that the reconciler of humanity with absolute unlikeness is the Teacher or the Christ.[42] It is a meta-narrative rather than human experience which fundamentally shapes Kierkgaard's reflections. Above all, the categories of sin and guilt (both ethical guilt and the guilt of separation of "religiousness A") surface foremost because of the Christian meta-narrative rather than because they are an adequate description of the human condition. It is not that an adequate description of human experience would deny that human beings are estranged from themselves, others, or their conditions of possibility. It is not that human beings don't err by commission and omission, or that they don't commit grievous atrocities both individually and as

---

[39] Kierkegaard writes in the *Concluding Unscientific Postscript*, pp. 18-19: "... is is at once necessary to recall that our treatment of the problem does *not* raise the question of *the truth of Christianity*. It *merely* deals with *the question of the individual's relationship to Christianity*. It has nothing whatever to do with the systematic zeal of the personally indifferent individual to arrange the truths of Christianity in paragraphs; it deals with the concern of the infinitely interested individual for his own relationship to such a doctrine. To put it as simply as possible, using myself by way of illustration: I, Johannes Climacus, born in this city and now thirty years old a common ordinary human being like most people, *assume* that there awaits me a highest good, an eternal happiness, in the same sense that such a good awaits a servant-girl or a professor. *I have heard that Christianity proposes itself as a condition for the acquirement of this good, and now I ask how I may establish a proper relationship to this doctrine.*" (emphasis added) Kierkegaard chides "the System" for failing to understand that it has concealed its presupposition, that is, the givenness of an existing individual with an infinite passion for the truth. Kierkegaard acknowledges he has a presupposition, but it is not merely the presupposition of an eternal truth. It is the presupposition of a meta-narrative concerning truth. If we presume an "eternal happiness," what is it that we are presuming? Does it need ben an eternal happiness independent from history? And why limit the "how" of our experience of "eternal happiness" to one paradox, that is, the Christ?

The significance of Kierkegaard's presupposition is acknowledged by Emanuel Hirsch in his *Geschichte der neuern evangelischen Theologie im Zusammenhang mit den allgemeinen Bewegungen des europäischen Denkens*, vol. 5 (Gütersloh: C. Bertelsmann Verlag, 1954), pp. 482-3.

[40] See Kierkegaard, *Concluding Unscientific Postscript*, p. 178.
[41] See Kierkegaard, *Philosophical Fragments*, 57f.
[42] See Kierkegaard, *Philosophical Fragments*, pp. 68f.

social groups. The point here is not that Kierkegaard has misrepresented the potential for and actually of evil in the human condition. Rather, it is that he has treated as a fault what is necessary and unavoidable, and has taken unlikeness to constitute radical separation and grounds for condemnation. This is the consequence of his employing "*a*" (not to be confused with *the*) Christian meta-narrative to explain the human condition rather than remaining rigorously true to that human experience. It is "*a*" Christian meta-narrative that teaches that humanity is estranged from and condemned by God, if not sentenced to eternal damnation, because of its sin. Foremost, it is "*a*" Christian meta-narrative that maintains that there ever was a pristine unity with God, violated by humanity's hubris, which humans would desire to repeat (restore). In short, the aporiai of human existence are taken by Kierkegaard to be an expression of radical rupture, brokenness, estrangement, and separation.[43] Life is to be lamented, and the individual is distressingly isolated and lonely in her/his absolute inwardness.

Kierkegaard is the Christian theologian par excellence of inwardness. Human experience is radically unique and internal which in itself is the ground for a paradoxical dilemma for communication. The individual is an internal unity constituting a complete totality inaccessible to another. Therefore, communication can only be indirect, since there can be no direct transference from one inaccessible self to another. Kierkegaard writes of the individual

> ...who exists in the isolation of his inwardness, and who desires through this inwardness to express the life of eternity, where sociality and fellowship is unthinkable, because the existential category of movement, and with it also all essential communication, is here unthinkable, since everyone must be assumed essentially to possess all, nevertheless wishes to impart himself; and hence desires at one and the same time to have his thinking in the inwardness of his subjective existence, and yet also to put himself into communication with others. This contradiction cannot possibly ... find expression in a direct form.[44]

To be sure, the focus on human inwardness is not an original theme with Kierkegaard. Not only is it central to Reformation theology in general, but inwardness is the key to Stoic thought which heavily influenced Christianity.[45]

---

[43] Reminiscent of Karl Barth's severing of all human relatedness to God with the one exception of a possible relationship through the Christ.

[44] Søren Kierkegaard, *Concluding Unscientific Postscript to the Philosophical Fragments* (Princeton, N.J.: Princeton University Press, 1968), p. 68n.

[45] This influence can be seen not the least in Calvin whose first publication was a treatise on the Stoic philosopher Seneca (4 B.C.E. - 65 C.E.). See Brian Gerrish, *Grace and Gratitude: The Eucharistic Theology of John Calvin* (Minneapolis: Fortress Press,

If the concern with inwardness was not new with Kierkegaard, neither is the notion of developmental stages on life's way. Both themes are central already to Kant. True religion, according to Kant, has to do with the inward disposition of the individual and not with external appearance.[46] Hence, the transcendentalist distinction between appearance and thing-in-itself, which applies to our perception of objects, others, the self, and God (the noumena), applies, as well, to the religious individual. Only the individual knows in her/his inwardness what her/his inward disposition is. In *Religion within the Limits of Reason Alone* Kant distinguished among three levels or stages of human development: animality, humanity, and personality.[47] At the level of animality one is concerned exclusively with self-satisfaction and satiation. The level of humanity finds one focussed on pleasing, i.e., attempting to live up to the expectations of, others. Here one's life is completely shaped by one's social milieu in an attempt to achieve esteem in the eyes of others. The highest level of humanity, according to Kant, is personality. This individual is no longer merely motivated by social expectations although they are not simply ignored. Rather, here the individual's inward disposition is shaped by the "moral law" within. In short, such a focus on the moral law within shifted the motivation for one's actions away from pleasing either the Other (person) or the crowd to taking personal responsibility for one's decisions and actions. Such responsibility acknowledges that one cannot not act and that every action is accompanied by a moral evaluation of the appropriateness of the action. Kant, as did Fichte as well, presumed that the moral criteria, employed for the evaluation of human action, were absolute and rooted in the fundamental structure and order enabling all experience.[48] According to Kant, then, the highest level of human

---

1993), p. 33 and, as well, p. 38. The classic history of Stoicism is Max Pohlenz, *Die Stoa. Geschichte einer geistigen Bewegung* (Göttingen: Vandenhoeck & Ruprecht, 1992 <1943/1947>).

[46] See Immanuel Kant, *Religion within the Limits of Reason Alone*, trans. by Theodore M. Greene and Hoyt H. Hudson (New York: Harper Torchbooks, 1960), pp. 17, 23, 99, 102, 107-8, and 123.

[47] See Kant, *Religion within the Limits of Reason Alone*, pp. 21-23.

[48] See J.G. Fichte, *Versuch einer Critik aller Offenbarung* in *J.G. Fichte-Gesamtausgabe*, I, 1, hrsg. von Reinhard Lauth und Hans Jacob (Stuttgart-Bad-Cannstatt: Friedrich Fromann Verlag (Günther Holzboog), 1964 <1792>), pp. 122-123. See, further, Fichte, "Drittes Buch: Glaube" in *Die Bestimmung des Menschen* in *J.G. Fichte-Gesamtausgabe*, I, 6, hrsg. von Reinhard Lauth und Hans Gliwitzky (Stuttgart-Bad-Cannstatt: Friedrich Fromann Verlag (Günther Holzboog), 1981 <1800>), pp. 253f. Neither Kant nor Fichte were concerned with the possible cultural relativity of the moral order, however. For both, the "fact" of the presence of a moral standard, announced with every need to act, was sufficient confirmation of a divine moral order.

development is achieved when one embraces the inward moral order as the motivation of one's inward disposition. All evil in the world is the consequence of humanity making what is external, the transitory or sensuous, the key to one's life rather than the moral order within.[49] Regeneration, according to Kant, occurs when one's inward disposition is transformed by embracing the eternal moral order enabling one to reach the stage of personality. Hence, what motivates religiousness for Kant is not fear of damnation, but an inward transformation that leads to the up building of the moral kingdom on earth overcoming the focus on externality shaping the inward disposition at the levels of animality and humanity. Therefore, Kant could say that all that one needs is astonishment at the heavens without and knowledge of the moral order within for the emergence of true religiousness, i.e., the transformation of one's inward disposition.

If Kierkegaard was not the first to focus on human inwardness and stages of development, nevertheless, he was the first to emphasize the paradoxical nature of that inwardness and those stages. He divided human developmental stages into the aesthetic, the ethical, religiousness A, and religiousness B.[50] All four levels, according to Kierkegaard, are characterized

---

[49] Harald Schützeichel asks: "Warum ... hat der erste Mensch das moralische Gesetz übertreten, den Sündenfall verursacht und so den Hang zum Bösen begründet? Kant kann hierauf keine Antwort geben, weil einerseits zwar das Böse nur dem moralisch Bösen entspringen kann, d.h. die Annehmung einer bösen Maxime erfordert, andererseits aber eben die ursprüngliche Anlage des Menschen eine Anlage zum Guten ist. Also, so Kant, ist 'kein begreiflicher Grund da, woher das moralische Böse in uns zuerst gekommen sein könne.'" From Schützeichel, "Kants Auffassung vom Ursprung des Bösen. In seiner Schrift 'Die Religion innerhalb der Grenzen der bloßen Vernunft'" in *Renovatio*, 46/1 (1990), p. 35.

[50] Kierkegaard discusses the stages of the aesthetic and ethical in "Guilty?/Not Guilty?" particularly in the "Epistle to the Reader" from Frater Taciturnus in *Stages on Life's Way*, trans. by Walter Lowrie (New York: Schocken Books, 1967). The additional stages of "religiousness A" and "religiousness B" are introduced in Kierkegaard's *Concluding Unscientific Postscript*, pp. 226-227 and 261. The most succinct summary of the stages is found in *ibid.*, p. 507: "If the individual is in himself undialectical and has his dialectic outside himself, then we have the *aesthetic interpretation*. If the individual is dialectical in himself inwardly in self-assertion, hence in such a way that the ultimate basis is not dialectic in itself, inasmuch as the self which is at the basis is used to overcome and assert itself, then we have the *ethical interpretation*. If the individual is inwardly defined by self-annihilation before God, the we have *religiousness A*. If the individual is paradoxically dialectic, every vestige of original immanence being annihilated and all connection cut off, the individual being brought to the utmost verge of existence, then we have the *paradoxical religiousness* [of religiousness B]. This paradoxical inwardness is the greatest possible ..."

by paradoxes which motivate the individual in her/his quest for true happiness to move "higher" and to embrace, eventually, thorough faith the Absolute Paradox of the Christ as the key to ultimate happiness.

Kierkegaard's stages on life's way are not reducible to Kant's even if, at points, they are comparable. Kierkegaard collapses Kant's animality and humanity stages into the aesthetic stage. What characterizes the aesthetic stage, above all, is concern with the external as the key to human happiness. This concern with the external can either take the form of self-gratification and satiation or of seeking to win the approval of others. In both cases, the focus of attention is on the sensuous, external world. What one eventually learns at this level of living is that the happiness one seeks by pursuing the external is transitory, at best, and illusory, in fact. Paradoxically, one's concern to consume or to please others leads to disillusionment and depression, because that, which one has sought, happiness through the external, has denied and concealed the inwardness that is the key to all happiness. "... [T]he age has forgotten what it means to exist, and what inwardness is. It has lost faith in the truth that inwardness makes the apparently scanty content richer, while a change in externals is merely a diversion sought by the life-weary and the life-empty."[51]

Kierkegaard's ethical stage corresponds with Kant's level of personality. Here one has decided not only that one is capable of personal decision but to decide, in fact, for oneself, and one has acknowledged that true happiness comes from individual inwardness where concern for continuity in movement brings one to make a personal decision.

> In so far as existence consists in movement there must be something which can give continuity to the movement and hold it together, for otherwise there is no movement. Just as the assertion that everything is true means that nothing is true, so the assertion that everything is in motion means that there is no motion ... Now while pure thought either abrogates motion altogether, or meaninglessly imports it into logic, the difficulty facing an existing individual is how to give his existence the continuity without which everything simply vanishes. An abstract continuity is no continuity, and the very existence of the existing individual is sufficient to prevent his continuity from having essential stability; while passion gives him a momentary continuity, a continuity which at one and the same time is a restraining influence and a moving impulse. The goal of movement for an existing individual is to arrive at a decision, and to renew it. The eternal is the factor of continuity; but an abstract eternity is extraneous to the movement of life, and a concrete eternity within the existing individual is the maximum degree of passion.[52]

---

[51] Kierkegaard, *Concluding Unscientific Postscript*, p. 255.
[52] Kierkegaard, *Concluding Unscientific Postscript*, p. 277.

One embraces in decision the concrete eternal, moral standard as the real key to personal choice, action, and happiness, but here, too, the paradoxical emerges to thwart one's acquisition of happiness. First, one's inward happiness turns out to be inseparably linked to the very external, sensuous world from which one seeks autonomy. Furthermore, one learns that one cannot live up to the standards of the moral order. That which was to guarantee one's happiness, adherence to the moral order, increasingly enhances one's estrangement not only from the external world and but from the self as well, for it results in the birth of guilt. Guilt emerges both because of one's failure to live up to the expectations of the inward moral order one wishes to fulfill and because of chagrin about one's actions prior to one's having embraced the inward moral order.

What one gains at the ethical stage is the awareness of one's inwardness. What is able to emerge at this point is the awareness of the paradox that one's striving to live in finite time according to one's personal, autonomous standard is rooted in the infinite and eternal. Kierkegaard's religiousness A, then, is equivalent to Schleiermacher's piety that is deeper than reason and action, i.e., that feeling of one's absolute dependence upon the eternal conditions of existence.[53] For the individual of religiousness A, the "exister," "... reposes in the consciousness of eternity."[54] What becomes increasingly clear at the level of religiousness A, however, is not merely the paradox that the temporal presupposes the eternal, but that there is an unfathomable and absolute difference between the existing individual and its eternal ground. This absolute unlikeness leads to the Absolute Paradox of religiousness B in which one discovers that one's true inward happiness is dependent upon an external redeemer figure, the Teacher. Kirkegaard wrote in *The Philosophical Fragments*:

> In Order to be man's Teacher, the God proposed to make himself like the individual man, so that he might understand him fully. Thus our paradox is rendered still more appalling, or the same paradox has the double aspect which proclaims it as the Absolute Paradox; negatively by revealing the absolute unlikeness of sin, positively by proposing to do away with the absolute unlikeness in absolute likeness.[55]

---

[53] See Schleiermacher's "Second Speech" in *On Religion: Speeches to Its Cultured Despisers*, trans. by John Oman (New York: Harper Torchbooks, 1958), pp. 26-118.

[54] Kierkegaard, *Concluding Unscientific Postscript*, p. 512.

[55] Kierkegaard, *Philosophical Fragments*, pp. 58-9. Kierkegaard distinguishes between "religiousness A" and "religiousness B" precisely on the basis of the paradox of Christology. See, for example, Kierkegaard, *Concluding Unscientific Postscript*, pp. 506-507, 512-513, 516-519.

Or in his *Concluding Unscientific Postscript*: "In the fantasy medium of possibility God can perfectly well for the imagination be fused with a man, but that this should occur in reality with an individual man, this precisely is the paradox."[56]

There is perhaps no other theologian in the tradition who has grasped more extensively the pervasive presence of paradox in the human situation than Kierkegaard. Yet he has misrepresented the paradoxes. His paradox of the eternal and the temporal is ultimately not an irreducible paradox but a mere juxtaposition of two irreconcilable dimensions over which the spiritual has ultimate priority. Furthermore, how eternal is Kierkegaard's eternity? He has presupposed the eternality of the essential (of the universal) affirming as a metaphysical necessity what is in fact a contingent necessity. There is no more a logical argument for the existence of an eternal realm independent of individual consciousness than there is for the existence of an external, temporal realm. Nevertheless, that which remains the same yesterday, today, and tomorrow, i.e., universals or essences, are necessary for the human to make sense out of the flow of perceptual phenomena. But the conditions of possibility for the experience of a contingent being, i.e., the individual, are no more metaphysically or absolutely necessary than the individual her/himself.

Not only has Kierkegaard unjustifiably embraced a metaphysical necessity, he has equally unjustifiably embraced a meta-narrative as the source for the ultimate resolution of the irresolvable paradoxical dilemma confronting the existing individual who is unable autonomously and from within to overcome her/his unlikeness with the eternal in existence. Where Kierkegaard spoke of "two worlds" rooted in a "third factor" which moves and transforms the individual,[57] one must speak of one world constituted out of the aporetic tensions of spirit and matter which are "rooted" in the non-substantial no-thingness of possibility in general and limited possibility in particular. Yet Kierkegaard has appropriated a personal deity, a concept of sin, and a Christology from a narrative that does not arise out of the paradoxical experience of the existing individual but rather is appropriated from out of the tradition, precisely because of its absurdity, in order to restore what Kierkegaard judges to be unrepeatable.

In contrast to this use of paradox by Kierkegaard, the present project does not see the paradoxical or aporetic character of human experience to be

---

[56] Kierkegaard, *Concluding Unscientific Postscript*, p. 515.
[57] Kierkegaard, *Repetition*, p. 202.

the announcement of a fault or sin, rupturing our original unity with God, as is the case for Kierkegaard. Nor does this project limit the discussion of paradox in theology to Christology as does Tillich. In an attempt to come to grips with the uncanniness of the contemporary world, where we find ourselves afloat without a foundational grounding in either the spiritual or the material realms. Nor is this project satisfied with the call out of history announced by the central paradox in Hegel's system. This project suggests that we can best understand our circumstance of faith by seeking to understand the "how" of paradox in history. A cluster of paradoxes are identified at the very core of human experience. These paradoxes are what make all of our experience and "knowledge" both possible and suspect. They are what force us to be ever vigilant about the adequacy of our understanding, and require that we acknowledge a leap of faith prior to any and all experience, understanding, knowledge, and action. In fact, our experience, understanding, knowledge, and action ultimately depend upon our experience *of a world*, which we cannot experience as it is in itself, *and upon universals*, which we cannot absolutely define but must necessarily presuppose.

Beyond Metaphysics

What this approach to the theological task as a study of aporetics means, then, is that theology is not reflecting about or speaking for God. Theology is concerned with all of life.[58] In other words, theology is not simply a special kind of knowledge among other kinds of knowledge nor is it limited to some region of experience.

Both the title, "theology," and the practice of theologians have led to the belief that theology is the study of a specific subject matter, God. Theology is taken to be a discipline like biology, sociology, or anthropology. But theology is not the "science of God" like biology is the "science of life" or sociology the "science of society" or anthropology the "science of humans." Theology, unlike any other discipline, has no specific object or circumscribed region of experience as its concern.[59] Theology, as will be fur-

---

[58] Theology as a discipline can be divided into Philosophical Theology, Systematic Theology, and Practical Theology (see Appendix A).

[59] In short, this project rejects Martin Heidegger's definition of theology in "Section 7" of *Being and Time*, and in "Phänomenologie und Theologie" in *Wegmarken* (Frankfurt a.M.: Klostermanns, 1978), pp. 45-67, a lecture delivered in 1927, the same year as the publication of *Being and Time*, but not published until 1970. Heidegger writes in *Being and Time*, p. 50: "Taken superficially, the term 'phenomenology' is formed like 'theology', 'biology', 'sociology' - names which may be translated as 'science of God', 'science of life', 'science of society'." He argues in "Phänomenologie und Theologie"

ther discussed below,[60] has *all experience* both universal and particular as its focus.

If theology is not to be defined by an "object" (i.e., God), then neither is theology to be defined by metaphysics. Metaphysics is understood by the present project to be concerned with that which exists independent of our consciousness of it. In other words, metaphysics is the belief that there can be a presuppositionless standpoint[61] that explains or grounds all experience. The usual metaphysical options are 1) that the material world of sense per-

---

that theology is to be defined in terms of its "object." Theology, according to Heidegger, is an ontic science concerned with a specific object, whereas only philosophy as phenomenology is ontological (i.e., concerned with the fundamental conditions of possibility as well as the particular content of all experience). See, in addition, Alfred Jäger, *Gott. Nochmals Martin Heidegger* (Tübingen: J.C.B. Mohr (Paul Siebeck), 1978), especially pp. 63f.

[60] See below "A Finite God?"

[61] Walter Schweidler argues in *Die Überwindung der Metaphysik: Zu einem Ende der neuzeitlichen Philosophie* (Stuttgart: Ernst Klett Verlag - J.G. Cotta'sche Buchhandlung, 1987) that metaphysics is the belief in a "presuppositionless standpoint" (*ibid.*, p. 183). He goes further to suggest that as soon as philosophy believes it has something to say it is being metaphysical (*ibid.*, p. 183). "Having something to say" here means going beyond description to establishing foundations. As soon as one maintains that one can say something philosophical, beyond describing what one is doing when one is being philosophical, one is trapped in metaphysics (*ibid.*, p. 183), Philosophy as metaphysics begins, then, in "questioning" and ends with "having something to say" (*ibid.*, p. 184). The "overcoming of metaphysics" can only commence where one recognizes that the "drive [to question] prior to every beginning" cannot be grounded. "Der Prozess, den wir den philosophischen nannten, hat uns gezeigt, in welchem Verhältnis wir zur Sache unseres Denkens stehen. Ihr Wert erschließt sich, wenn wir sie übernehmen. Übernehmen aber können wir von ihr alles außer einem: dem Anstoß, uns zu ihr zu führen, mit ihr zu verbinden, ihre Existenz vor uns hintreten zu lassen. *Alles an ihr kann uns gehören; nur daß wir ihr gehören, liegt nicht in unserer Macht*. Solange wir nach einer letzten Begründung suchen, durch die wir sie uns verfügbar machen wollen, haben wir sie nicht verstanden. Sobald wir aber darauf verzichten, sie zu uns zu zwingen, schenkt sie sich uns und wir besitzen sie ganz" (*ibid.*, p. 207). Such an overcoming of metaphysics is described by Schweidler as "the remembering of spiritual power" (Erinnerung an geistige Macht) (See, p. 209). This situates the human as a recollection of that which is given to us without being able to establish any grounding or foundation for "that which gives" what is to be re-collected.

Wilhelm Weischedel speaks of our post-metaphysical situation as one of thinking "das Vonwoher der Fraglichkeit" (thinking "the origin - or source - of questioning) fully aware that that is not to make the human the criterion (because we are the questioner) but rather to express the questionableness of the giving that is the factually necessary condition of possibility for us to question. See Wilhelm Weischedel, *Der Gott der Philosophen: Grundlegung einer philosophischen Theologie im Zeitalter des Nihilismus*, 2 vols. (München: Deutscher Taschenbuch Verlag, 1985), especially vol. 2, 206f.

ception exists independent of our consciousness of it, and all experience can be explained by means of "materialism" (or "empiricism"); 2) that the world of the intellect, inaccessible to sense perception, rests upon universals that exist independent of our consciousness of them, and all experience can be explained by means of "realism" or "idealism;" 3) that there is either some kind of common substance; or 4) there are structural or necessary conditions of possibility that ground(s) both materialism and realism. In light of the discussion of paradox above, however, all of these metaphysical claims are suspect, for, while they are pragmatically arguable, they remain logically unprovable. Furthermore, as pragmatic judgments they can point to only contingent necessity, at best, and not metaphysical necessity.

Materialism

With respect to the first metaphysical claim about the world of objects: we never have direct and immediate access to those objects. Our experience of the world of objects is by means of the imagination and remains an experience exclusively in the intellect. Logically or from the side of the intellect, then, we can offer no proof for the existence of a world of objects known by the senses and independent of our consciousness of it. Pragmatically or from the side of our actions, however, we *necessarily* must assume the "existence" of a world of objects known by the senses, for not to do so would be to get us into serious trouble. The alternatives here are either the solipsistic option that the world is solely my invention (such as the notion of Maya in Eastern philosophy or the vulgar skepticism of Deconstructionism) or that there is something logically inexplicable yet experientially repeatable about our encounters with objects in the world that we pragmatically cannot ignore.

The Bhagavad-Gita argues for the former option, that my experience of the world is simply analogous to a dream. But that is contradicted by the repeatability of my experience of the world of sense which is precisely the criterion that distinguishes being awake from being asleep. A consistent realist/idealist would have to argue that this repeatability is simply a function of heightened memory alone, and that memory is diminished, or not as acute, in the sleeping state. Such an argument, however, would be contradicted by the surprise character of experience, because experience of the world of objects of sense continually shocks the memory with new phenomena. Furthermore, the solipsistic argument is contradicted by the very phenomena of language. Whatever one's theory of language, it is the vehicle of communication. But why would one communicate, or even want to, if the world is solely one's own intricate invention of the imagination? Here we arrive at the same dilemma, but at the level of the human, that we encounter in the notion that God created the world/universe, according to an absolute divine plan, in order to love and be loved. If this were the case, then the entire process of the world would be a chimera of self-delusion and a horrible, even terrorizing, lie created by an author merely playing with him-/her-/it-self.

With respect to the second option, if the world is the creation of my imagination and if I have control over my imagination, obviously I am not concerned with the tragedy and suffering of other human beings much less in nature. For I would simply have to change my mind, and I could author a world of peace, harmony, and justice.

The result of such reflection is clearly: we cannot logically prove the existence of a material world independent of our consciousness nor can we ignore it. As Hume observed in the *Dialogues Concerning Natural Religion*,[62] we never experience consciousness separate from a body although we possess no absolute certainty concerning either consciousness or the body.

Idealism

Exactly the same conclusions must be drawn with respect to the second metaphysical claim, i.e., that there exists a realm of universals independent of any individual's consciousness of them. Logically or from the side of the intellect, we can offer no proof of the independent existence of a realm of universals. We cannot even define them. Just as is the case of our experience of the world of objects known by the senses, we are "on this side" of the universals, i.e., they are a given and are not logically provable. Pragmatically or from the side of our experience and actions, we *necessarily* must assume the "existence" of a world of universals employable by the intellect, for not to do so would be to get us into serious trouble. We would not be able to recognize even similarity among different phenomena much less identity, nor would we be able to experience shared understanding with an other.

The alternatives here are that universals are either ectypal, generalizations constituted by each individual as a consequence of repeated encounters with identical phenomena, or archetypal, existing independently of individual consciousness and in principle accessible to all. This is the key to the medieval debate between the *via moderna* and the *via antiqua*, or between the Aristotelian nominalists and the Platonic realists.

---

[62] David Hume, *Dialogues Concerning Natural Religion and the Posthumous Essays of the Immortality of the Soul and On Suicide*, ed. by Richard H. Popkin (Indianapolis: Hackett Pub., Co., 1982), pp. 40-46.

On the one hand, if we conclude that universals are ectypal, then we must also conclude that the identical nature of universals from one individual to the next depends upon the existence of a world of sensed objects independent of individual consciousness, for ectypal universals are by definition a posteriori (after the encounter with things in the world of sensed objects). The consistency among persons with respect to universals could only be explained by the independent existence of a world of sensed objects. To the extent that we can doubt the independent existence of a world of sensed objects, we must doubt that universals are ectypal.

The fact that the physical order can be grasped mentally and corresponds to universals suggests that any ectypal argument for the existence of universals is merely pushing the problem back one step. For one might want to argue that an individual consciousness comes to awareness of universals ectypally, but how is it that the order of the empirical world corresponds to a non-empirical order of universals? Since one is concerned here with two radically contrasting dimensions of experience and cause can only be a relationship between similarities not between what is radically different, a case could be made that universals are at least equally primordial as the empirical, material order, i.e., neither is the copy of the other. There are physicists and philosophers today, who are suggesting that such observations indicate that the empirical order is "rooted" in a "sea of information", which provides the order for empirical reality. They call this "sea of information" "meta-realism."[63]

On the other hand, if we conclude that universals are archetypal, then we must also acknowledge that they constitute some kind of Logos independent of our consciousness of them. The notion of the Logos would be the ultimate explanation of the origin of the universe and individual intellects on the basis of an analogy to human creativity (i.e., idea - copy). In other words, humans create by first formulating a mental idea and then shaping materials to make a more or less adequate copy of the idea. The Logos would provide the mental idea both for the shaping of the universe by God and the creation of artifacts by individuals. This is the classic teleological or Argument from Design originating from Anaxagoras and found in Plato's

---

[63] See Jean Guitton, Grichka Bogdanov and Igor Bogdanov, *Gott und die Wissenschaft. Auf dem Weg zum Metarealismus*, trans. by Eva Modenhauer (Münich: Artemis & Winkler Verlag, 1993). Though this "meta-realism" is simply a retrieval of a central teaching of Stoicism over against the skepticism of the Academy (not driven out of the Academy until the leadership of Antiochos in the middle of the 80's). See Max Pohlenz, *Die Stoa*, pp. 252. See, as well, *ibid.*, 174, 227, 230.

Timaeus 69b f. The classic critique of this argument, though to be sure no outright rejection of it, is made by Philo in Hume's *Dialogues Concerning Natural Religion*. Hume points out that analogies are appropriate only where the analogates are similar (Part II). An analogy drawn between humanity and God involves analogates which could not be more dissimilar. Further, Hume warns that one must beware of using parts to explain wholes (Part II); he observes that ideas in and of themselves offer no causal explanation for the way the world is, since all the chimera and fantasies of the mind would be equally empirically actual (Part II); he observes, further, that we never experience mind independent of body where there is at least a reciprocal action between them (Part IV); and, finally, experience teaches that mind is dependent upon generation or vegetation not vice versa (Part VII). Nevertheless, Philo does not completely dismiss the Argument from Design. He maintains that, if one is to avoid blind or vulgar superstition, one must acknowledge the limits to reason and such analogies, but those limits are grounds enough to indicate the radical faith character of the human condition (Parts I, XII).

Yet, there is order to our experience that permits us to recognize not mere similarity but identity in the flux of phenomena constituting our mental lives. If understood as archtypal, this order is dependent upon universals that are imperceptible, immaterial, indivisible, immeasurable, unchanging, and the same for all consciousness, but, since we cannot define them and we only have mediated access to them in consciousness, we are forced to the acceptance of universals as archtypal only on the basis of faith not demonstrated proof. An account for our experience of universals ectypally, on the other hand, depends upon the existence of a world of sensed objects independent of our consciousness of it. Such a world of sensed objects can only be demonstrated pragmatically not logically. Hence, since we must accept such a world of sensed objects on faith, we are forced as with archtypal universals to the acceptance of universals as ectypal on the basis of faith not demonstrated proof.

I would propose the analogy that the ectypal is to the archetypal as phenomena are to things-in-themselves. The important point here, however, is that the acceptance of either archetypal universals or of the existence of things-in-themselves is a speculative judgment perhaps pragmatically justified but illogical, i.e., logically unprovable. Human experience is always on this side of the archetypal and of things-in-themselves, i.e., human experience is a radical wager of faith. Denial of universals, however, would be the denial of order and coherence in our experience. We have a degree of choice about our experience of the world of sensed objects, we have no choice about our experience of universals. They are necessary for our experience. There is no conscious experience without universals. They remain the same yesterday, today, and tomorrow, and they are accessible, if only indirectly, in principle to all. Yet, to the extent that they are taken to be archetypal, one can speak, on the one hand, of universals as constitutive of the language we each have inherited. To the extent that they are experienced as ectypal, on the other hand, one can speak of universals as the consequence of the metaphorical activity of the mind able to incessantly "see" similarity (even identity) in difference as will be discussed in chapter 9 below.

Important here, however, is that if there is any difference in pragmatic significance between our experience of the world of sensed objects and imperceptible universals, since ignoring either would lead to disastrous consequences, it is that we may or may not choose to ignore the world of sensed objects, but it is impossible for us to ignore universals.

A Common Substance

The third kind of metaphysical claim argues that there is some kind of common substance uniting the world of sensed objects and the invisible intellect. If first proposed by Parmenides, it is extensively developed by Plato in Book VI of the *Republic* in his notion of the Good that is not an idea among other ideas, but is the First Principle of the whole analogous in the intellect to the sun in the realm of sense perception. Where the sun provides the "third thing" or light in addition to the eye and the object which is necessary for us to see, the Good is the "third thing" or Being in addition to our ability to distinguish between two (or among many) ideas (even though we are unable to say where one idea stops and the other begins) which is necessary for us to reason (to distinguish which is the presupposition of all dialectic). The Good, then, is the light of the mind that is ultimately what unites all of the segments of Plato's simile of the line: from reason, through understanding, opinion or objects/things, to shadows and reflections. If the Good is taken to be a common substance or univocity prior to all multiplicity (e.g., as it is by Karl Rahner), then the Good explains metaphysically all multiplicity.

Conditions of Possibility

The most recent metaphysical claim of this century is that made by Process thought which argues that there are fundamental structures, which remain permanent and which serve as the necessary conditions of possibility for any and all experience. Process thought describes these fundamental structures in light of the "reformed subjectivist principle." Although there are great variations among proponents of this metaphysical option, they all draw an analogy between our human experience as constituted out of personal identity amidst change to suggest that fundamental to all events is such a tension between a primordial (that which remains identical) and a consequent nature (that which changes).[64] This serves as the framework for speaking of a dipolar theism, i.e., that God has both a primordial (abstract) and consequent (concrete) nature that enables the avoidance of such dilemmas raised by classical theism with respect to how an unchanging God can truly love, since to love involves being affected by the object of one's love. To be affected, however, means to change. Dipolar theism enables an understanding of deity that can change (the consequent nature) but as the permanent identity of the universe it is unsurpassable by all that is yet surpassable by itself as it includes change.

Beyond Metaphysics to Faith

All of these metaphysical options, however attractive, are inadequate not because there is another metaphysical position that is more adequate, but because they all hold out the false hope of ultimate explanation or of a metanarrative. They all fail to recognize the paradoxical nature of human experience, and as a consequence they turn too quickly to a speculative moment to account for the whole of experience. Each metaphysical option in its own way reduces experience ultimately down to some dimension that is taken to be independent of our consciousness of it, and uses this dimension to explain the whole. These dimensions are a) the world of sensed objects, b) the dimension of imperceptible universals, c) Being which is beyond beings, or d) a structure resting upon metaphysically necessary conditions of possibility arrived at analogously from human experience.

Option "a" fails, because there is no logical argument to demonstrate its indubitability. Option "b" fails, for exactly the same reason. Just as the experience of objects in the world of sense experience is limited to the constructs of the imagination based upon phenomena rather than the things-in-themselves, so the experience of universals in the imperceptible world of the intellect is limited to ectypal constructs. While the ectypal rests, as well, upon the imagination and phenomena, the intellect has the priority over the world of sensed objects in that all experience transpires within it. Since uni-

---

[64] Perhaps there is no greater challenge to this metaphysics based on the reformed subjectivist principle then the denial by post-modern thinkers (though already present in Kant - *Critique of Pure Reason*, B152-153; see Ricoeur, *Time and Narrative*, vol. 3, pp. 54-55) of the classical notion of the self as some kind of permanent substrate of experience from which we "go out" and "return."

versals are essential to that experience and phenomena are accidental, there is every reason to pragmatically believe that universals exist independent of consciousness just as it is pragmatic to believe that the world of sensed objects exists independent of consciousness. But a pragmatic argument is not a necessary, logical argument. A pragmatic argument is no absolute explanation, but an argument based on contingent necessity. In other words, it appeals to experience, but experience is never absolutely necessary. Although by doubting one "proves" that the self exists, the self, obviously, does not absolutely necessarily exist - the conditions that enable that existence, then, are at best contingently necessary. One takes a speculative leap when one makes either option "a" or "b" the grounds for a metaphysical "explanation" of the whole of what is. One always and already remains on this side of the "things-in-themselves" and of absolute "universals." The independent existence of either is a matter of pragmatic or speculative wager, i.e., faith, and not something indubitably demonstrable. Experience, then, is constituted out of the paradoxical interaction between the ectypal and the phenomenal which is rooted in, and leads to the enrichment of, language where the ectypal is inherited as archetypal and the phenomenal is grasped only in terms of actuality.

With respect to metaphysical option "c," explaining experience in terms of the Being beyond beings in either the Platonic or the Hegelian sense, Being is made the ultimate principle to reality. In the case of Plato's Good, he himself admits that it cannot be spoken of directly, because it is not another entity (or idea) among entities. It can only be arrived at analogically. An analogy, however, is an imaginative construct that establishes relation not explanation. Plato's Good remains an assumption, equally as necessary to experience (though only contingently necessary) as are the assumptions or hypotheses at the level of the understanding, and equally indefinable. Here one can employ only metaphors, e.g., light of light, ineffable name, "immortal, invisible, God only wise." For Plato the First Principle of the whole establishes a whole grounded in reason, for everything in the visible realm of sense perception is a copy or shadow of the universals. Reason is what soars above understanding, according to Plato, engaging in a dialectic that distinguishes between indistinguishable ideas (we cannot say where one idea stops and the next starts) to arrive at a synthesis that paradoxically compromises neither of the components of the dialectic yet suggests or points in the direction of their ultimate unity, Being. If we think this dialectic as a dialectic between Being as "to be" and Being as "entity" or "thing," then the dialectic of reason can be thought in terms of a distinguishing between at least two entities that both must "be" in order for us to distinguish between them. They both participate in Being in this sense of "to be." Yet "to be" as a verb is not an entity or thing, it is beyond entities but their necessary "ground." It would be a mistake to read this as some kind of static reality, however. Being, or the First Principle, is what unites all the segments of Plato's line, and it is what permits the "soul" to move up and down the line. Being, then, includes becoming; Being includes history. It does so on the basis of reason. History or becoming, according to Plato, is radically dependent upon participation in the universals, for that accounts for the order of the universe and the coherence of events. Yet this entire hierarchical order (and that alone today is sufficient grounds for rejecting its legitimacy!?) rests upon an analogy and a metaphorical construction based upon points, lines, and angles that by definition cannot exist. It can serve as a valuable heuristic model for speculative thinking, that has first engaged in rigorous description, but it is illegitimate as a metaphysical explanation. Analogies establish relations not explanations. The metaphorical empowers judgment of similarity (the ectypal), but identity (the universal) is a speculative moment based upon habit, i.e., repetition. There are no primary or ultimate building blocks to the universe of experience. Experience is paradoxical, that is, it is aporetic.

The Hegelian system is more obviously speculative. It, too, rests upon the privileging of reason as the ultimate explanation of all of history. Hegel's system knows in advance the alpha and the omega. This does not make history any less necessary, for history is the very condition of possibility for the alpha and omega (Being) to come to significance. History is under the sovereignty of the Concept (*der Begriff*). Paul Ricoeur identifies Hegel's originality as the effort to make the tragic and the logical correspond.[65] Negativity is acknowledged by Hegel as the necessary condition of possibility for the Concept to be realized, i.e., the key to history is the double negation. Ricoeur also identifies the central problem in Hegel: "The very notion of history is abolished by philosophy as soon as the present, equated with what is real, abolished its differences from the past. The self-understanding that goes with historical awareness is born precisely from the unescapable fact of this difference."[66] Ricoeur points out that the loss of this difference results in the collapse of the project of totalization.

> ... all the components that come together in the concept of the cunning of reason - particular interests, the passions of great historical men, the higher interests of the

---

[65] See Ricoeur, *Time and Narrative*, vol. 3, p. 199. Chapter 9 of this text is entitled "Should We Renounce Hegel?"
[66] Ricoeur, *Time and Narrative*, vol. 3, p. 204.

state, the spirit of a nation, and the world spirit - come apart and appear to us today like the *membra disjecta* of an impossible totalization. Even the expression "cunning of reason"[67] no longer intrigues us. Instead we find it repugnant, almost like a magician's trick that does not work.[68]

Ricoeur concludes that "... the leaving behind of Hegelianism signifies renouncing the attempt to decipher the supreme plot."[69] The human is always on this side of the alpha and the omega in a historical process that always and already remains an open-ended process of faith seeking understanding. Ricoeur teaches us that this is because of the cosmological paradox in which cosmic time, for which each moment is an indistinguishable instant and for which *the individual, then, is totally insignificant*, is dependent upon phenomenological time, for which the moment is a present because the present is necessarily related to an individual, in order *that cosmic time have any significance*.[70] The human is condemned to significance, and this is the source of our lament and our joy.

Finally, metaphysical option "d" also fails, because it, too, rests upon analogy, and a structure arrived at analogously cannot explain. It can at best establish an aporetic relationship among the four terms, and identify contingent necessity - but not metaphysical necessity. In other words, we can say what the conditions of possibility are for our present experience, i.e., what must necessarily be in order for us (as a contingent necessity) to experience and act in the world as we do now. But there is nothing about our experience and action that forces us to conclude that those conditions of possibility (either as transcendental structures or as universals) are eternally necessary (in the sense of metaphysical necessity).

The discussion of metaphysically necessary conditions of possibility is one of two ways of talking about "that which cannot be other than the way it

---

[67] Hegel had spoken of the "cunning of reason" (*List der Vernunft*) in the *Lectures on the Philosophy of World History: Introduction - Reason in History*, trans. by H.B. Nisbet (Cambridge: Cambridge University Press, 1975), p. 89. Ricoeur observes that Hegel writes of this "cunning of reason" in a context "... that has been made precise through the double stamp of evil and unhappiness - on the condition, first, that a particular interest animated by a great passion unknowingly serves freedom's self-production; on the condition, second, that the particular be destroyed in order that the universal be saved. The 'cunning' here consists simply in the fact that reason 'sets the passions to work in its service' ... Hence the thesis of the cunning of reason comes to occupy exactly the place that theodicy assigns to evil when it protests that evil is not in vain." *Time and Narrative*, Vol. 3, p. 198.
[68] Ricoeur, *Time and Narrative*, vol. 3, p. 205.
[69] Ricoeur, *Time and Narrative*, vol. 3, p. 206.
[70] See Ricoeur, *Time and Narrative*, vol. 3, p. 90.

is" in contrast to "that which can be other than the way it appears to be". The first way is to talk about what conditions must necessarily be satisfied in order for something to be. The second way of talking about "that which cannot be other than what it is" is the realist or idealist position that universals (or the foundation of the intellect) and even the transient content of mental experience are "necessary," because they cannot be other than what they are in contrast to objects in the sensed world which always in principle can be other than they way they appear to be as a consequence of their composite nature. The things of the sensed world are made up of parts where universals are simple. But there is a second sense of "necessity," as well, which applies to the transient element of mental experience in contrast to the spatial, physical world. Although there is no necessity that I experience a particular flow of mental data, as long as I am *I must* necessarily experience some flow of mental data. Furthermore, what I am actually experiencing in that flow of mental data is precisely what I am experiencing - even if it is not "correct" with respect to its source. I may be mis-representing physical objects, but that is how I am representing them in the moment and I can't represent them *in that moment* in any other way than the way I am representing them. Both of these ways of talking about "that which cannot be other than the way it is," however, apply to factual or contingent necessities and not metaphysical necessities.

To draw conclusions about metaphysical necessity denies the paradoxical conditions of human experience and substitutes some form of Gnosis (or knowledge) for faith. Of course, the bane of metaphysics as Gnosis is that it makes theology the preserve and prerogative of the elite few who can grasp it, that is, professional theologians and those pastors especially learned in these schools of "theological metaphysics." This project argues that it is not just the professionals who are theologians. Every person is a theologian, because *theology is concerned with all experience and with all of the profound questions of life*. At stake, then, is not whether one is a theologian, but what kind of theologian one is? How comprehensive and rigorous has one engaged in understanding one's experience, and at what level of awareness one has with respect to the fundamental questions of life? We turn to "professional" theologians not to gain answers but to assist us in clarifying the questions truly worth asking.

A Finite God?

If theology, unlike any other discipline, has no specific object or region of experience as its concern, one immediately asks, what is a discipline without an object or region of experience of investigation?[71] The very question betrays how pervasive our contemporary, dominate system of rationality is. We are conditioned to commence all experience and thought with things rooted in the world of sensed objects. An investigation that does not commence with some-*thing* must be concerned with no-*thing* which is absurd. How can one investigate and think nothing? As will be seen below, negation, concealment, and no-thing (which can be understood as either possibility or the verb "to be") are necessary constitutive elements of human experience. They are in paradoxical tension in experience with what is positive, manifest, actual, and some-thing (which can be understood as either actualized possibility or something particular - a being).

Were theology to be defined as that discipline which has "God" as its object, then whatever this "God" was taken to be, God would be some thing (even if the highest or greatest thing) among other things. This would make God something finite by definition, that is, distinguishable from other things. We do not have to limit our focus to some physical thing. One could distinguish God from physical things by saying that God is an idea, even *the* Idea. But, as an idea among other ideas, God would be distinguishable from other ideas, hence, finite.[72]

Theology Alone Has No Object

Theology has erroneously insisted that it has some object or region of experience as its focus. Paul Tillich, for example, defines theology as concerned with "ultimates."[73] This is simply another way of defining theology in terms

---

[71] To reject this definition of a discipline is, of course, to reject the Aristotelian notion (see, for example, Met 1074b34 f.) that has shaped theology since the 13th century.

[72] For this very reason Plato, for example, refuses to speak of the Good as an idea among other ideas. Plato writes: "... the objects of knowledge not only receive from the presence of the good their being known, but their very existence and essence is derived to them from it, though the good itself is not essence [idea] but still transcends essence in dignity and surpassing power." Plato, *Republic*, trans. by Paul Shorey in *The Collected Dialogues of Plato* (Princeton: Princeton University Press, 1973), p. 744.

One might conclude as did Philo and later the Neo-Platonists that this "Good" of Plato's is the true "object" of theology (see Plotinus, and Porphyry). But then "object" must be meant metaphorically, for this "object" is precisely not an object. Even were we to conclude, as Ernst Cassirer does (see his analysis of Plato's *The Sophist* 259e - look at 249d-3, as well - in "Zur Logik des Symbolbegriffs" in *Wesen und Wirkung des Symbolbegriffs* (Darmstadt: Wissenschaftliche Buchgesellschaft, 1965), pp. 206-7, and *Philosophie der symbolischen Formen*, Erster Teil: *Die Sprache* (Darmstadt: Wissenschaftliche Buchgesellschaft, 1964), pp. 28 and 296), that Plato's system rests upon a paradox, placing Plato's later work at least in the province of theology, theology is not concerned with just one paradox but with paradox in general, i.e., the life of faith.

[73] See Tillich, *Systematic Theology*, vol. 1, p. 211.

of its object. Rather than be concerned with plants, chemicals, or fiscal ledgers as are botany, chemistry, and accounting, theology is defined by Tillich in terms of another "region" of experience, ultimates. Theology is then a discipline among other disciplines distinguished from the others in terms of the things it investigates.

Tillich's presupposition, and what is at stake in his definition of theology, is what he calls the "method of correlation."[74] Defining theology in terms of an object requires developing a method appropriate to the investigation of the object. Tillich's method of correlation is based upon a correlation between questions and answers. In the case of theology, the correlation is between questions, arising out of our situation as existing beings, and answers provided by theology.

> The method of correlation requires that every part of the system should include one section in which the question is developed by an analysis of human existence and existence generally, and one section in which the theological answer is given on the basis of the sources, the medium, and the norm of systematic theology. This division must be maintained. It is the backbone of the structure of the present system.[75]

He acknowledges the circularity of his definition of the theological task when he writes: "*... no method can be developed without a prior knowledge of the object to which it is applied.*"[76]

This is an attractive definition of theology, particularly for theologians. It presupposes knowledge possessed by the theologian that is not available to other disciplines. All other disciplines or regions of human experience, according to Tillich, are question marks whose answers are found in theology. This makes the theologian a true "scientist," for s/he is in the possession of both a region of investigation (in Tillich's case, that of ultimate concerns) and answers (to the troubling questions of humanity) analogous to every other "scientific" discipline which has a specific region of investigation in which answers are discovered. David Tracy has pointed out, however, that Tillich's method of correlation is not a method of correlation but of juxtaposition.[77] It juxtaposes one answer, Tillich's answer of what constitutes the true Christian message, with the human situation without critically evaluating either other Christian messages or other answers from alternative religious traditions.

---

[74] See Tillich, *Systematic Theology*, vol. 1, pp. 59-66.
[75] Tillich, *Systematic Theology*, vol. 1, p. 66.
[76] Tillich, *Systematic Theology*, vol. 1, p. 60.
[77] See David Tracy, *Blessed Rage for Order*, p. 46.

Perhaps in the end we might want to conclude that God is a thing, or that God is finite, somehow distinguishable from other things in order to both give theologians some-thing to do and to avoid pantheism (the notion that the divine is everything). But this cannot be the starting point of theological reflection for two reasons.

First, whatever the legitimacy of the claim, the tradition has always insisted that God is infinite not finite. For example, there is the tradition that the Tetragrammaton (YHWH) of the Hebrew Scriptures (or of the Christian Old Testament) is not to be pronounced.[78] Even the Christian "Lord's Prayer" begins with the qualification "hallowed be thy name." Why this reverence for the name? Because giving God a name is to make God a thing among things, and that would not only make God finite, but the dominion of humanity over the earth is expressed in the scriptures in terms of humanity's giving names to everything (Genesis 1:26; 2:19-20). The human cannot have dominion over YHWH. Giving God a name has two consequences. First, it makes God just another thing among things, which could then be either simply ignored or made the focus of our attention arbitrarily (either out of fear, or the exercising of our will, or by demanding our attention). Second, it makes God into an object manipulable by us just as are other objects (the intent of most ritual and worship which seeks God's attention in the hope of influencing HIS decisions with respect to our lives). Theology is then a form of techné (the Greek root of technology). That is, theology becomes an art or skill whereby something is gained (be it "knowledge" of God or some other benefit). But this makes theology a form of "method" which will be challenged below.

There is a second reason why we must hesitate to make the starting point of theology some unique, finite object or region of experience. Regardless of what the tradition has maintained with respect to God's in-

---

[78] This tradition is rooted in Exodus 3:12-14 where Moses asks for the name of God. It is clear that the Mosaic tradition is here introducing a new name (YHWH) as opposed to the more traditional El Shaddai used by the Patriarchs. Exodus 3:12-14 is obviously an attempt to justify the new name YHWH, because it expresses the reality of God for the Hebrews and is not simply a label for an object. Despite all warnings to the contrary about employing philosophical speculation on this text, it cannot be denied that, even if among other agendas, there is clearly a concern here to articulate the reality of God in terms of the verb "to be." God is not a thing, but is, was, and will be as potentiality/possibility. A similar reading of this passage from Exodus 3 can be found in Gabriel Motzkin, "'Ehyeh' and the Future: 'God' and Heidegger's Concept of 'Becoming'" in *Ocular Desire/Sehnsucht des Auges*, ed. by Aharon R.E. Agus and Jan Assmann (Berlin: Akademie Verlag, 1994), pp. 173-182.

finite nature, we would not want to commence our study of theology with such an arbitrary and suspect presupposition that God is finite. To treat God as a thing among other things right from the very beginning of our study of theology would run the too obvious risk of defining God in terms of our finite self-image.[79] To do so would require that we either deprecate the human in the sense described by Feuerbach or elevate the human to be the measure of what constitutes divinity. In either event, it would be to define the divine as finite at the beginning of the theological enterprise eliminating other possibilities for thinking about God and the nature of the theological task. Both options in and of themselves should give us pause.

The question of what is a discipline without an object of investigation applies to every other discipline except theology. Theology is concerned not merely with the contingent conditions necessary for any and all experience but with all of experience and not simply some object or region of experience. This project rejects any suggestion that God be some thing among things serving as the cause or explanation of all other things. Rather theology is precisely that discipline which is concerned with non-sense and nothing just as much as with sense and some-thing. Theology is that discipline concerned with aporiai.

---

[79] This is the charge made by Ludwig Feuerbach that all God talk is really the projection of "predicates" upon an "infinite subject" when those predicates have the human as their appropriate subject. A predicate is something affirmed or denied about the subject of a proposition. Feuerbach suggests that such predicates as "Person," "Law-giver," "Father of mankind," the "Holy One," the "Just," the "Good," the "Merciful," etc., are all predicates that apply to a human subject. Humans love. To apply such a predicate to God by saying "God is love," is to project a human predicate onto an infinite subject. See Feuerbach's *Essence of Christianity* in Bernard M.G. Reardon, *Religious Thought in the Nineteenth Century* (Cambridge: Cambridge University Press, 1966), p. 103. Feuerbach's insight is that, by projecting these human predicates onto an infinite subject, we are abnegating our responsibility for the predicate. For example, it is God's task to love appropriately, we can only love inappropriately. Such is the message of John 21 with its play on agape (unconditional love) and philia (familial love or love of those closest to us). Peter rejects the predicate agape limiting himself to philia. Feuerbach writes: "... in proportion as the divine subject is in reality human, the greater is the apparent difference between God and man; that is, the more, by reflexion on religion, by theology, is the identity of the divine and human denied, and the human, considered as such, is depreciated ... To enrich God, man must become poor; that God may be all, man must be nothing." *Ibid.*, p. 107.

Is Theology a Method?

To the extent that method must already know in advance what the object of its investigation is, theology is not a method. As much as theology is an intellectual discipline, as much as theology is a task of distinguishing and conceptually clarifying, theology is not reducible to critical reflection as Schubert Ogden suggests.[80] Above all, the theologian is existentially in the midst of that which needs cognitive clarification. There is neither indifference/disinterest or distanciation, but all cognitive clarification rests upon both presuppositions and concealment as its very condition of possibility.

This is easy to say, but extremely difficult to describe, much less defend. Both Paul Ricoeur in "The hermeneutical function of distanciation"[81]

---

[80] Schubert Ogden defines theology as critical reflection. He defines theology as "second order" reflection upon "first order" experience. See Schubert Ogden, "The Task of Philosophical Theology" in *The Future of Philosophical Theology*, ed. by Robert Evans (Philadelphia: The Westminster Press, 1971), pp. 48-84. However, this distinction concerning first- and second-order questions was earlier formulated by Mortimer J. Adler. See Mortimer J. Adler and Charles Van Doren, *How to Read a Book* (New York: Simon and Schuster, 1972 <1940>), p. 276.

Ogden sees the crisis of our secular age not in terms of a loss of the reality of God, but the "demise of a 'cast of thought'" with respect to faith. Schubert Ogden, *The Reality of God and Other Essays* (New York: Harper & Row, 1966), p. 19. Although initially formulated in terms of a crisis of "faith," in the end the crisis is a crisis with respect to the "reality" of God, however. Building on the two-fold structure of experience and reflection, Ogden defines theology as the critical articulation (re-presentation) of a faith in "an original confidence in the meaning and worth of life, through which not simply all our religious answers, but even our religious questions first become possible or have any sense..." (*ibid.*, p. 34). Characteristic of the so-called "third stage of linguistic analysis" with respect to religious claims (see David Tracy, *Blessed Rage for Order*, p. 120), Ogden moves beyond the first two stages of "verification" and "falsification" of religious statements to argue that "God *is* radically different from everything else we experience, and one of the implications of this difference is the peculiar character of the question for God itself." *The Reality of God*, p. 21. Two observations are relevant here: 1) theology is a certain kind of inquiry for Ogden, i.e., a method of critical reflection and cognitive claims; and 2) theology, according to Ogden, has a specific object of reference for its re-presentative language, i.e., God. Ogden writes: "Faith in God of a certain kind is not merely an element in Christian faith along with several others; it simply *is* Christian faith, the heart of the matter itself" (*ibid.*, p. 14). Later Ogden adds: "I hold that the primary use or function of 'God' is to refer to the objective ground in reality itself of our ineradicable confidence in the final worth of our existence" (*Ibid.*, p. 37). See Frank Burch Brown, "Transfiguration: Poetic Metaphor and Theological Reflection" in *The Journal of Religion*, 62/1 (January 1982), 39-56, for a discussion of Ogden's critical methodology.

[81] See Ricoeur, "The hermeneutical function of distanciation" in *Hermeneutics and the human sciences: Essays on language, action and interpretation*, trans. by John B. Thompson (Cambridge: Cambridge University Press, 1981), pp. 131-144.

and David Tracy, affirming Ricoeur's "correction" of Heidegger and Gadamer in *The Analogical Imagination*,[82] wish to stress a positive function to "distanciation" in the production of a text (which can be generalized to include all "expression,"[83]). Ricoeur points to three kinds of "distanciation" in the production of a text as a result of the objectification of discourse in the work[84]: 1) distanciation from the author,[85] 2) distanciation from the original life-world of the author to open up a world "in front of" the text[86]; and 3) what Ricoeur calls "a new sort of distanciation which could be called a distanciation of the real from itself"[87] opening up imaginative variations of possibility for the reader. These three forms of distanciation involved in the production of a work have their correlate in the process of "appropriation" by the reader/hearer or the discovering of the reader's "ownmost possibilities."[88]

These three components, shaping the production of a work, are so common-sensical that it seems ridiculous to quarrel with them. Yet this discussion of distanciation preserves a remnant of a naiveté with respect to the world as something "out there," serving as the "place" of deposit for human expression, which is then appropriated "within" by the reader/hearer.

The issues at issue here are twofold: 1) First, "what does it mean to be "in" the world?" Are we "next" to the world; does the world "contain us" like a liquid in a bottle? Do we put "things" out into the world from some location of the self "outside" of the world? 2) Second, "is there such a thing as pre-predicative experience?" Do we experience a world "out there" without any mediation either of a "public language" or a "private" symbol system of representation?

Nowhere do these issues find a more complex instantiation than with respect to "texts" or human "products." It is one thing to describe "experi-

---

[82] See Tracy, *The Analogical Imagination*, p. 127.
[83] See Tracy, *The Analogical Imagination*, pp. 150, n. 103; 175; and 210.
[84] See Ricoeur, "The Hermeneutical Function of Distanciation," p. 138.
[85] See Ricoeur, "The Hermeneutical Function of Distanciation," p. 139.
[86] See Ricoeur, "The Hermeneutical Function of Distanciation," p. 141.
[87] See Ricoeur, "The Hermeneutical Function of Distanciation," p. 142.
[88] See Ricoeur, "The Hermeneutical Function of Distanciation," p. 142, e.g., "... we understand ourselves only by the long detour of the signs of humanity deposited in cultural works" (*Ibid.*, p. 143). Note, to the contrary, that Tracy identifies the three kinds of distanciation in the production of the work in terms of "... a distancing from the author, from the original situation and from the original audience" (Tracy, *The Analogical Imagination*, p. 128). Ricoeur emphasizes in his third notion of distanciation more the role of the imagination in the production of the work than does Tracy.

ence" of objects; it is quite another to describe our experience of the activity of another consciousness available to us through human productivity. In play in the latter case are at least Ricoeur's three levels of filtering as a consequence of our experience consisting of a re-presentation of "what is" rather than as an immediate presentation of "what is," i.e., 1) the pre-filtering of language and experience symbolically mediated to the author over which the author her/himself is not master, 2) the filtering re-presentation of the "author" her/himself in the generating of a text, and 3) our own filtering re-presentation as reader/hearer. Ricoeur calls this "filtering" "a distanciation of the real from itself."[89]

But just what is "the real?" The present project calls into question any notion of "the real" as something "out there" to which we have immediate access. All experience is shaped by presuppositions (universals or principles which cannot be defined), inherited by language (though appropriated out of the horizon of our historicality and generated out of novel experience), and shaped by the dynamic process of concealing possibility in the events of actuality mediated to consciousness through re-presentation.

Without embracing the entire Heideggerian project, one must concur that one irreversible achievement of *Being and Time* is its portrayal of the human condition as always and already in a world that is far more than an actual world "out there" but rather a world of possibility from which we are precisely not "distanced." This is what is meant by our "facticity."[90]

---

[89] See Ricoeur, "The Hermeneutical Function of Distanciation," p. 142. Note that Ricoeur speaks here of "everyday reality". In *Time and Narrative*, Ricoeur speaks of this pre-filtering in terms of the author's engagement of the "pre-figured" of $mimesis_1$ (see Ricoeur *Time and Narrative*, vol. 1, 54-64) and of narrative re-presentation by the author as a "con-figuring" or $mimesis_2$ (see Ricoeur, *Time and Narrative*, vol. 1, 64-70 for $mimesis_2$). Finally, though, he speaks of the re-presentation by the reader in terms of a "refiguring" or $mimesis_3$ of application as the event which completes the narrative (see Ricoeur, *Time and Narrative*, vol. 1, pp. 70-71 and vol. 2, pp. 27 and 164, n. 20)

[90] Theodore Kisiel calls this notion of "facticity" Heidegger's "ontological breakthrough." See Theodore Kisiel, "Das Kriegsnotsemester 1919: Heideggers Durchbruch zur hermeneutischen Phänomenologie" in *Philosophisches Jahrbuch*, 99/1 (1992), 116. See, as well, Kisiel, "Das Entstehen des Begriffsfeldes 'Faktizität' im Frühwerk Heideggers" in *Dilthey-Jahrbuch*, vol. 4 (1986-7), p. 97: "Im Erleben 'weltet es' mich. Es soll nicht, es existiert nicht, wertet nicht, gibt eigentlich nicht, sondern ... es weltet. [Hier finden wir bereits die erste Anzeige der Urdimension des Faktischen.]" This "ontological breakthrough" is already conceptually present in das Kriegsnotsemester 1919 and first called "facticity" in the following summer semester of 1920 (see *ibid.*, p. 107), i.e., some 7 years before the publication of *Being and Time* (see Martin Heidegger, "Die Idee der Philosophie und das Weltanschauungsproblem. Kriegsnotsemester 1919" in *Gesamtausgabe. II. Abteilung: Vorlesungen*. vol. 56/7 (Frankfurt a. M.: Vittorio Klostermann, 1987)).

Ricoeur seems to be sensitive to Heidegger's analysis of facticity, for his discussion of "distanciation" recognizes that "*Verstehen*" (understanding) is rooted in "*Befindlichkeit*" (state-of-mind) in Heidegger's analysis.[91] The activity of what Ricoeur calls the emplotment or the configuring of the "prefigured," is on the other side of understanding from state-of-mind. Dasein is first radically rooted in a world of possibility by its thrownness into an unavoidable and inescapable situation (*Befindlichkeit* or state-of-mind), and Dasein is always and already engaged in a projecting of possibilities (understanding) prior to any author's production (on the basis of the "prefigured"), prior to the reading of that production (the reader's "configuration" of the author's production), or prior to the appropriation by the reader of the author's production (what Ricoeur calls "re-figuration") in terms of imaginative variations for a possible lived world in front of the text.

Paradoxically, however, this always and already rootedness in the world from which we are in no way distanced, involves the role of the "other" (as both the "other" of things/texts and the "Other" of persons) in the dynamic of experience. If not, the hermeneutical circle would be the vicious circle of solipsism,[92] and we would have entirely missed the "circle"

Was this "ontological breakthrough" inspired by Carl Braig, the Roman Catholic theologian in Freiburg who influenced Heidegger in his early years as a theology student? Hugo Ott writes in "Engelbert Krebs und Martin Heidegger 1915." Freiburger Diözesan - Archiv 113 (1993): 239-48), p. 247: "Die meisten Professoren der Theologischen Fakultät standen mit dem jungen Privatdozenten Heidegger in enger Beziehung. Hinzuweisen wäre z.B. auf Josef Sauer, an dessen Zeitschrift 'Literarische Rundschau' Heidegger seit 1911 mitarbeitete. Zu erinnern ist auch in diesem Zusammenhang, wieviel Heidegger dem Freiburger Dogmatiker Carl Braig verdankte. Auch wenn eine bestimmte Richtung der Heidegger-Forschung nicht zur Kenntnis nimmt, aus welchen Quellen der Philosoph geschöpft hat - wohl zeitlebens - , sei es hier erneut erwähnt: Man lese Braigs 'Vom Sein. Abriß der Ontologie' ... - etwa die Darlegungen zu Zeit und Raum - , um leicht zu sehen, daß Aristoteles, Augustinus (Confessiones, Buch XI) und Kant samt den einschlägigen Quellenbelegen als die maßgebenden Führer vermittelt wurden ..."

[91] See Ricoeur, "The Hermeneutical Function of Distanciation," 142.

[92] Gadamer surely acknowledges this when he writes in *Wahrheit und Methode*, 4th ed. (Tübingen, J.C.B. Mohr (Paul Siebeck), 1975), p. 252: "Man wird sagen müssen, daß es im allgemeinen erst die Erfahrung des Anstoßes ist, den wir an einem Text nehmen - sei es, daß er keinen Sinn ergibt, sei es, daß sein Sinn mit unserer Erwartung unvereinbar ist - , die uns einhalten und auf das mögliche Anderssein des Sprachgebrauchs achten läßt." He then adds: "Wer einen Text verstehen will, ist vielmehr bereit, sich von ihm etwas sagen zu lassen. Daher muß ein hermeneutisch geschultes Bewußtsein für die Andersheit des Textes von vornherein empfänglich sein. Solche Empfänglichkeit setzt aber weder sachliche 'Neutralität' noch gar Selbstauslöschung voraus, sondern schließt die abhebende Aneignung der eigenen Vormeinungen und Vorurteile ein" (*ibid.*, 253). Here, at least, it is clear that the "other" is not a mere "Gegenstand" approachable as an

of possibility that has us already intimately related to the text prior to, and shaping of, any conscious reading. "Distanciation" is only possible because of our always and already "belonging" at the level of possibilities to the world of the text (even when we are "distanced" from the original horizon of actuality of the text) as a consequence of *Befindlichkeit* and understanding, which in turn function as the filters in play in every reading/experience.

Befindlichkeit, translated by Macquarrie and Robinson as "state-of-mind," includes the notion of "finding oneself." We always and already find ourselves in a world, and that dis-covery is foremost as possibility. Mood or state-of-mind, the brute "situation that we are and cannot not be," is always a matter of actuality and concealed possibility, and included in the situation, of course, are the things and Others of one's world.[93]

Ricoeur is fully aware of this. His discussion of narrative in terms of a threefold mimesis recognizes the role of the pre-figured or pre-understanding[94] in the process of production as precisely the activity of mimesis$_1$.[95]

Hence, contrary to Tracy's judgment, I find it hard to identify any "correction" of Heidegger and Gadamer by Ricoeur here. All three are thoroughly aware of the ambiguity, even paradox, of the relationship of the "other" to the "self" as a relationship not between an "external world" and

---

object "out there" by a neutral and distanced subject "in here." The "shock" of the "other" is always and already a shock of intimacy. But understanding is no mere "private" process, according to Gadamer. It involves public agreement, and Gadamer can speak of the goal of interpretation to be our agreement concerning the "object" (Sache) (see *ibid.*, 260 (German, 276)) without reducing "agreement" to truth as correspondence between our "internal" judgments with respect to the text and the text "out there" as it "really" is. The text is foremost possibility, as Gadamer well knew.

On the other hand, although we are intimately connected as a "horizon of possibility," the reading of a text gives the appearance of the text as "distanced" by and from our "horizon of actuality." It is this interplay between possibility and actuality that is the key to the hermeneutical role of temporal distance for Gadamer. See "Die hermeneutische Bedeutung des Zeitenabstandes" in *ibid.*, 275f.

[93] Heidegger's discussion of space as "distantiality" is developed both in terms of our relatedness to "things" as "ready-to-hand" in de-severance rather than as "present-at-hand," i.e., in terms of a relationship of possibility (see *Being and Time*, 98-100, 141-3) and to the "public they-world" (see *ibid.*, 163-5). Distantiality is not concerned with space in a neutral Newtonian sense. Rather space is existentially encountered in terms of possibilities of engagement. Hence, what is "measurably" distant from one, i.e., a loved one or a project, is in fact "closer" than the chair one is sitting in, and that "closeness" is not merely one of emotional attachment. The closeness has to do with the Other or the project in terms of their possibilities.

[94] See Ricoeur, *Time and Narrative*, vol. 1, 81.

[95] See Ricoeur, *Time and Narrative*, vol. 1, 53-64, 182.

an "internal world," but precisely as they are both rooted in one world of possibility that is always a possibility for some-one in community. Hence, we are intimately connected to, rather than distanced from, the actions and sufferings of others/Others and their actions and sufferings have meaning and matter because of the fundamental historicality of any and all experience.

If we affirm the priority of *Befindlichkeit* (state-of-mind) and *Verstehen* (understanding) before Auslegung (interpretation) in Heidegger's terminology, if we agree that there is no neutrality with respect to the "shock" (Anstoß) of the other in Gadamer's terminology, if we acknowledge the "pre-figured" as the condition of possibility for the "con-figured" and the "re-figured" in Ricoeur's terminology, if we give a priority to "reception" in Tracy's terminology, then we must acknowledge that there is no real "dis tanciation." There is only a paradoxical moment where the "Other/other" in its actuality is experienced in terms of her/his/its possibilities for a self intimately connected and rooted in a shared "world" of possibility. If we were to speak of "distance," it would be solely a matter of a difference in range of possibility.

With respect to the reading of a text, the situation, as intimated above, is most complex, because reading is possible, to use Ricoeur's language, only because of the interplay of the pre-figured possibilities (mimesis$_1$) of the author's always and already rootedness in a world, filtered through the con-figuring possibilities generated by the author (mimesis$_2$), which are available to the reader/hearer only through the understood possibilities (the re-figured possibilities of mimesis$_3$) available to the life-world of that reader/hearer. What has happened to our so-called "objective reality"? Here "everyday reality" is always and already a reality of projecting possibilities according to the pre-formed understanding of the self in a shared world of projecting understanding.

Observed from any notion of "actuality," then, the actual must be seen as provisional and transient even if it is experienced as an enduring repeatability over time. Agreement about the actual is only agreement about an empty shell. Foremost, however, is not actuality but possibility. There is no distanciation from possibility. There is (and can be) no disinterestedness at the level of possibility.

Therefore, to define theology either in terms of its having a specific, actual object of its reflection (as does Paul Tillich) or as a method of critical self-appropriation of a prior existential faith with respect to God's actual reality (as does Schubert Ogden) is to reduce theology down to the investigation of an actual object to the neglect of the horizon of possibility and to fail

Theology as Method   89

to recognize the paradoxical moments at the core of the human condition. Foremost among the paradoxical moments in experience is the necessary recognition that even critical reflection rests upon concealed possibilities and undefinable universals together constituting a concealment of possibilities which by necessity must be assumed before critical evaluation can even commence.

All universals are assumptions (hypotheses in the Socratic sense[96]). Without these assumptions there is no rationality or critical reflection. Hence, every form of rationality not only conceals its irrational foundation on assumptions (irrational in the sense that these assumptions cannot be logically demonstrated or proved), but every form of rationality is selective.[97] That is, all forms of rationality allow us access to only certain phenomena or other mental data while concealing all that is not immediately accessible in our experience of those phenomena or mental data.

Hence, the judgment that theology cannot be defined as method does not rest simply on the conclusion that all methodologies know in advance what the object under investigation is or ought to be.[98] The limits to method

---

[96] See, once again, the analysis of the simile of the line in Book VI of Plato's *Republic*.

[97] I have in mind here Paul Ricoeur's understanding of language and reference born out of his analysis of metaphor. Metaphors are "an 'instance of discourse' *par excellence*" (Ricoeur, *The Rule of Metaphor*, p. 97). For Ricoeur, this means that metaphors are not mere semiotic events internal to language, but rather metaphors are the heart of semantics or the actual use of language in a world. Two principles are at stake in the actual use of language: selection and plenitude (*ibid.*, p. 96). Both the semiotic and semantic contexts of the metaphor suppress and enable focussing attention upon a certain range of meanings, but above all the metaphorical functions precisely because of a "blockage of any literal interpretation of the statement." On the basis of this radical selectivity a new "semantic pertinence" is generated "obtained through the 'twist' of the literal meaning" (*ibid.*, p. 230). At the core of all discourse then is a process of suppression and selectivity that conceals in order to reveal meaning. Theology must always be suspect of such concealment just as it is eager to point out what is "revealed."

Ricoeur's tension theory of metaphor distinguishes between an ontic revealing and concealing of metaphor and the more radical revealing and concealing at the level of the copula at the core of the metaphorical. See *The Rule of Metaphor*, pp. 247f.

[98] There is an understanding of "method" that is not restricted to the notion of technique or way of approaching a thing or region of experience, but is concerned with the "how" that is prior to all technique, i.e., the way in which things are manifest at all in order for us to "methodologically" manipulate them.

An extremely helpful and carefully developed paper by Thomas Sheehan ("Heidegger's 'Introduction to the Phenomenology of Religion,' 1920-21" in *The Personalist* not only documents the rootedness of Heidegger's thought in Christianity as well as Greece (see, for example, p. 315: "The difference between the two experiences [Christian and Greek] is in this nuance: In early Christianity this primordial pres-absential [presence-absence or revealing-concealing] movement is understood in terms of

in theology are not merely dependent upon a judgment that God is not a finite thing or an object. The limits to method in theology are far more radical. Method conceals its presuppositions, its selectivity, and all that is not phenomenally or ontically accessible to the human in the moment of application of the method.

A variant of Ogden's definition of theology in terms of second order critical reflection is the position taken by David Tracy with respect to "fundamental theology."[99] Rather than define theology as a Tillichian "method of correlation," correlating questions arising out of our common human situation with answers found in theology, Tracy suggests that theology is not concerned with answers but with "limit questions."[100] But in *Blessed Rage for*

---

temporality, whereas in early Greek experience, the pres-ab-sential movement is thematized in terms of *disclosure* or 'truth.' Temporality and truth - the two ways of looking at Heidegger's one and only topic - are rooted respectively in his readings of early Christianity and of archaic Greece."). But Sheehan identifies Heidegger's "Phenomenology" to be a "method" in a peculiar sense of the term. Quoting Heidegger, Sheehan observes: "'All questions in philosophy are basically questions about the 'how' (*Wie*) or, strictly understood, questions about method.' And 'method' here is to be taken in the Aristotelian sense of *methodos*, 'pursuit' of a subject matter (cf. *Physics*, G,1,200b 12f) and not in the sense of a 'technique.' It appears that for Heidegger this *methodos* is ultimately nothing other than temporality." The "how" of Heidegger's method, then, is not a way of approaching a task, but this "how" is the how of "coming to be." The how of coming to be is usually understood ontically (i.e., as a sequence of efficient causality connecting things and their properties), but Heidegger's concern for the how of coming to be addresses the event that is *prior to* that sequence of efficient causality by means of which one thing causes another thing to have certain predicates. The originating event of the presence of something is a simultaneous event of making manifest and concealment. This event of making manifest while simultaneously concealing, or the how of coming to be, is prior to efficient causality and constitutes the "how" of coming "to be."

99 Tracy in *Blessed Rage for Order* defines "fundamental theology," to be concerned with metaphysics and the doctrine of God (see *The Analogical Imagination*, pp. 22; 58; 89, n. 47; 159; 183, n. 26; 95-6, n. 104) as distinct from the task of *The Analogical Imagination* concerned as it is with "systematic theology" which is confessional (*ibid.*, 76), phenomenological (*ibid.*, 160), metaphysical (though distinguished from fundamental theology in that here in systematic theology one starts with the event of Jesus Christ rather than the abstract questions concerning "religion," "God," and the "reasonableness of the Christ event," *ibid.*, 241-2, n. 1), and, above all, hermeneutical (*ibid.*, 104; 131; 183, n. 26) and centered in a "paradigmatic focal meaning" (*ibid.*, 428) that, at its best, serves as a "classic" (*ibid.*, 68, 108) that continues to illuminate the human condition far beyond the horizon of its initial formulation. Both "fundamental" and "systematic" theology are distinguished from "practical" theology concerned with praxis (*ibid.*, 97, n. 114).

100 See Tracy, *Blessed Rage for Order*, chapter 5.

Order Tracy, too, is a victim of defining theology in terms of clarity and coherence with respect to its object or region of investigation.

Not content with identifying the "religious dimension" as the limit question at the core of both our contemporary human experience[101] and the scriptures of the Christian tradition,[102] Tracy insists that theology must take the further step and demand conceptual clarity about its limit claims.[103] It is simply not enough, he insists, to identify the language of the New Testament as figurative language (for example, if taken literally, e.g., Matthew 5:29-30, that language is absurd). Such figurative language, Tracy suggests, is designed to wrench our everyday perceptions forcing us to look beyond our notions of normalcy to see the role of presuppositions that serve as the "limit-of" our experience.[104] Important as this insight is with respect to the originating texts of the Christian tradition, Tracy goes the step further, however, to argue that the truth status of that religious dimension, found both in experience and in the scriptural tradition, can only be critically evaluated by employing metaphysics (specifically Process Thought) to adjudicate the adequacy of our understanding of that figurative language.

Taking the notion of "God is love" as the key to his analysis of the central Christian claim, Tracy argues that "classical theism" simply is inadequate for understanding such a claim. Classical theism argues that God is both eternal and unchanging. Yet everything we know and experience about love is that love involves being affected or changed by the object of one's love. If God is understood to be unchanging, then our individual or particular experience of joy, suffering, and tragedy is meaningless for such an unchanging being. Rejecting both Karl Rahner and Bernard Lonergan, because of "their unwillingness to break with the classical theistic concepts of Aquinas,"[105] Tracy argues that the truth claim of the Christian message of "God is love" is most adequately articulated by the dipolar character of neoclassical theism.[106] Such a dipolar theism understands God to be unchanging

---

[101] See Tracy, *Blessed Rage for Order*, chapter 5.
[102] See Tracy, *Blessed Rage for Order*, chapter 6.
[103] See Tracy, *Blessed Rage for Order*, chapter 8.
[104] Tracy distinguishes two kinds of limits: First, what he calls "... 'limits-to' ordinary experience (e.g., finitude, contingency, or radical transience)" (*Blessed Rage for Order*, p. 93). Second, what he calls "limits-of" human experience which constitute the horizon or ground as "the implicitly disclosed dimension which functions as limit-of or ground to (e.g., *fundamental* faith or trust) our more ordinary ways of being-in-the-world" (*ibid.*, p. 93).
[105] Tracy, *Blessed Rage for Order*, p. 172.
[106] Tracy, *Blessed Rage for Order*, p. 178.

in one aspect (analogous to that aspect of the human that remains the same throughout all the changes of life) and changing in a second aspect (again, analogous to that concrete and particular aspect of change in the human that enriches or impoverishes us).

Hence, this metaphysical analysis, arrived at through the methodological concern with limit-questions, leads one to draw certain critical conclusions about the truth of God which remains the ultimate focus or object of Christian theology. Tracy writes: "To many contemporary analysts of Christian experience and language ... the central, indeed the constitutive cognitive claim of that religion is its articulation of the Christian God as the sole and single objective ground of all reality. With that judgment I am in full agreement."[107] Only after one has clarified conceptually this Christian truth claim about God can and must one return to the figurative language of the Christian tradition to understand adequately the mystery and open endedness (now best described in terms of the "consequent nature" of God) which that language evokes:

> ... I do not understand the common fear that such an employment of metaphysics will eliminate the "mystery" which the religious use of metaphors are intended to disclose. The correct employment of metaphysics *can* eliminate incoherence and self-contradiction in the concepts used to explicate the "disclosure" which the "interaction" of the metaphorical statement is meant to evoke.[108]

Tracy's fundamental theology represents a definition of theology in terms of three moments: First, theology is defined by its object (i.e., "the Christian God as the sole and single objective ground of all reality"). Second, this object is arrived at by means of a theological method concerned to identify the limit-questions of experience rather than correlate theological answers to existential questions. Finally, these limit-questions require the adoption of Process metaphysics for their conceptual clarification.

There is a circularity here, that Tracy would not deny, which further justifies classifying his project in terms of defining theology as a kind of method. Once one has an object to investigate, then the discipline concerned with that object must be defined as the method for arriving at it. As Tillich said: "... no method can be developed without a prior knowledge of the object to which it is applied."[109]

I have discussed at greater length this theological option below in Chapter 4: "David Tracy: Theology as Correlation." Although Tracy quick-

---

[107] Tracy, *Blessed Rage for Order*, pp. 146-147.
[108] Tracy, *Blessed Rage for Order*, p. 161.
[109] Tillich, *Systematic Theology*, vol. 1, p. 60.

ly adds that such critical reflections must be followed by a second naiveté of application, his project clearly has little if any appreciation for the paradoxical moments of the human condition. In fact, he explicitly rejects a turn to paradox.[110] It is clear, however, that what Tracy means by paradox is Kierkegaard's and Tillich's notion of a central paradox at the core of the Christian faith playing the role in their theological reflections as "scandal" plays for Barth's neo-orthodoxy.[111]

Having commenced the theological task *on this side of the text*, i.e., the scriptures, and thoroughly appropriated the standards of rationality of the Enlightenment world for critically reflecting on human experience, he argues analogically for a dipolar deity *behind the text and experience* to claim that "the Christian God ... [is] the sole and single objective ground of all reality."[112]

Theology, however, is not to be defined by either a specific object or region of investigation as does Tillich,[113] nor is theology critical reflection or a "second order" reflection about the "objective ground in reality itself of our ineradicable confidence in the final worth of our existence"as defined by Ogden,[114] nor is theology a combination of both as the critical reflection and clarification of limit-questions by means of Process metaphysics to lead us to the Christian God who is "the sole and single objective ground of all reality" as defined by Tracy. There is no object, no psychological certainty, no metaphysical clarity grounding theology as a scientific discipline among other scientific disciplines. Philosophical theology remains the queen of the sciences not because it has a particular object or psychological state as its focus, or because it possesses a method or a metaphysical certainty that is "superior" to other disciplines. Theology remains the queen of the sciences because it alone of the disciplines addresses the paradoxes at the commencement of all "scientia," or knowledge, which establish the human condition as faith seeking understanding.

Theology is not a method in the senses meant by Tillich, Ogden, and Tracy. Method conceals, is selective, and maintains the illusion of rational transparency. Method turns theology from faith to knowledge. In the rush to guard theology against the irrationalism of emotional excesses in faith, in the rush to guard theology against blind faith, which suspends all critical judg-

---

[110] See, Tracy, *Blessed Rage for Order*, p. 249.
[111] See Tracy, *Blessed Rage for Order*, p. 198, n. 66.
[112] Tracy, *Blessed Rage for Order*, pp. 147.
[113] Tillich, *Systematic Theology*, vol. 1, p. 60.
[114] Ogden, *The Reality of God*, p. 37.

ment over against the miraculous and makes human beings subject to the most crude forms of material and spiritual exploitation, in the rush to make theology intellectually defensible among those other scientific disciplines, which have the edge on defining rationality in the moment, in the rush to make theology intellectually credible to its cultured despisers in an age of materialism, theology has had to sell its birthright to Enlightenment rationality. As necessary as these detours in theology have been,[115] in the process, theology has severed itself from its experiential roots just as has all of Enlightenment rationality.[116] That reason, which liberated us from the hegemony of Christian Platonism with its patriarchal hierarchy and its hocus pocus, has severed the tap root to our own experience.

But this is not to call theology back to emotionalism[117] above the head. Nor is the call to set the heart over against the head as did Chauncy and Channing.[118] If we take a detour over the heart, it must be in terms of

---

[115] This present project in theology and paradox would have been impossible were it not for these detours.

[116] See Gadamer's discussion of the Enlightenment and Romanticism in *Truth and Method*, pp. 239-245. Gadamer argues that Enlightenment rationality has forgotten the necessity of presuppositions in all rationality. Romanticism, on the other hand, rejects rationality as itself the product of the "cultural corruption" of tradition. Romanticism believes that it can "jump over" the tradition to return to some "natural order."

Alois Emanuel Biedermann in the 19th century spoke of the Enlightenment as having only accomplished half of its task. The negative achievement was its project of human liberation from arbitrary ecclesial and social heteronomy which it accomplished by means of autonomous rationality. The full task of the Enlightenment under his perspective is concerned, further, with the positive task of liberation of the human from "objectivity." He spoke of the Enlightenment as "... die beginnende Emancipation des subjectiven Bewusstseins von der unmittelbaren Anerkennung objectiver Autoritäten" (Biedermann, *Christliche Dogmatik* (Zürich: Verlag von Orell, Füssli & Co., 1869), p. 5). Biedermann saw the Enlightenment not in terms of the victory of absolute, autonomous, and transparent reason over arbitrary prejudice, but rather as the initiation of a process whereby the human was no longer defined in terms of an empirical, objective world accessible exclusively through the senses. In this light, the Enlightenment project was a still birth. See, in addition Alois E. Biedermann, "Die Aufklärung" in *Zeitstimmen aus der Reformierten Kirche der Schweiz*, 6 (1864), 104-112, 113-127. One need not embrace the totalization project of German Idealism to appreciate this reading of the Enlightenment as an initial attempt at challenging "positivist" claims as the route toward the exhaustive explanation of humanity and its world.

[117] It was Alfred Jules Ayer who suggested that all non-empirical (non-scientific) expressions "... are simply expressions of emotion which can be neither true nor false." From *Language Truth and Logic* (New York: Dover Publications, Inc., 1952), p. 103.

[118] See Charles Chauncy, "Enthusiasm Described and Caution'd Against" in *The Great Awakening: Documents Illustrating the Crisis and Its Consequences*, ed. by Alan Heimert and Perry Miller (Indianapolis: The Bobbs-Merrill Co., Inc., 1967), 228-256, and "Seasonable Thoughts on the State of Religion" in *ibid.*, 291-304. See William El-

Jonathan Edwards in *The Religious Affections* or in terms of Martin Heidegger's "*Befindlichkeit*" in *Being and Time*. In short, the heart is understood by Edwards as the commitment or profession of the individual to her/his faith. Intellectual assent without commitment is vacuous. But assent without intellectual understanding is dangerous.[119] For Edwards, both the head and the heart are essential for theology. However, the understanding (head) in Edwards is not the critical reflection of Ogden or Tracy. It is the understanding of a Christian Platonist.

The call of this project is not to the heart over against the head any more than it is a call to place the human at the center of reality. Faith is at the center of human reality, and it displaces all hubris as it calls to accountability. The call, then, is to the aporetic depths of the human, about which we need critical awareness and understanding. It is the paradoxical depths that establish always and already the human condition as faith seeking understanding. Having first demonstrated and clarified the dialectical tensions at the core of human experience, theology then has an evaluative framework for observing and critically reflecting about the theological claims of a particular religious tradition. In short, second order reflection (the task not of philosophical but of systematic theology in its synchronic and diachronic moments[120]) about first order religious experience of a particular religious tradition can be appropriately and adequately undertaken only after the human condition of faith as aporetic has been clarified and articulated. Such a procedure can clearly and carefully map the claims of any particular religious tradition in terms of that tradition's emphasis upon specific paradoxes or in terms of the tradition's having failed to appreciate certain paradoxical ingredients of experience.

As the following investigation will demonstrate, however, the theological task is not a simple collapsing of the focus of concern down to contemporary experience at the expense of the inherited tradition.[121] The cor-

---

lery Channing, "Unitarian Christianity Discourse at the Ordination of the Rev. Jared Sparks, Baltimore, 1819" in *William Ellery Channing: Selected Writings*, ed. by David Robinson (New York: Paulist Press, 1985, 70-102.

[119] Even Jonathan Edwards subordinates the heart to the understanding. See Edwards, *The Religious Affections*, the Fifth Sign, especially pp. 294, 295, 296, 298.

[120] See Appendix: "Division of the Task of Theology," below.

[121] This is a charge leveled against liberal theologies by conservatives. The accusation is made that totalitarianism emerged in the 20th century because of the liberal insistence that the tradition is subservient to present self- and cultural-understanding. See Leibholz's "Memoir" in Dietrich Bonhoeffer, *The Cost of Discipleship*, trans. by R.H. Fuller (New York: Touchstone Simon & Schuster Inc., 1995), p. 30: "Both modern liberal theology and secular totalitarianism hold pretty much in common that the message of

relation between tradition and experience is constitutive of one of the essential paradoxes of the human condition, for that condition simply cannot be adequately understood without both moments. Yet tradition and experience are incommensurable and absolutely irreducible one to the other. Paul Ricoeur indicates in part the dilemma of this tension when he observes from Hayden Whites' *Tropics of Discourse: Essays in Cultural Criticism* "... the paradox that an excess of information prevents understanding and an excess of understanding impoverishes information (*Tropics*, p. 102)."[122] We will return to this aporia when we examine the relationship between literal and figurative language in experience. This tension between tradition and experience serves as the framework as well for the debate between Hans-Georg Gadamer and Jürgen Habermas.[123]

---

the Bible has to be adapted, more or less, to the requirements of a secular world. No wonder, therefore, that the process of debasing Christianity as inaugurated by liberal theology led, in the long run, to a complete perversion and falsification of the essence of Christian teaching by National Socialism."

Founded in 1863 in Frankfurt am Main, the German Protestant Society (der deutsche Protestantenverein) was an attempt to organize liberal Protestants across Germany. Richard Rothe, a major leader of the movement, saw the Protestant Society as the vehicle for harmonizing Christianity with culture, and he spoke of Christianity as "the most flexible of all essences, which was in possession of an unlimited capacity for adaptation" (Walter Nigg, *Geschichte des religiösen Liberalismus. Enstehung, Blütezeit, Ausklang* (Zürich: Max Niehaus Verlag, 1937), p. 217). Although this sounds like it confirms the conservative reading of liberal theology as chameleon, the term "culture" was not simply equated with "civilization," but it referred to the entirety of humanity's mental (geistig) activity. Nigg adds: "Es ist eine Ungerechtigkeit, dem Protestantenverein blinde Kulturvergötterung vorzuwerfen. Er hat allerzeit betont, daß protestantische Kulturfreundlichkeit nicht gleichbedeutend sei mit Kulturseligkeit, und aus seiner Mitte wurde auch immer wieder Kritik an den kulturellen Auswüchsen geübt. Es war eine durchaus kritische Kulturbejahung, für die im Zeitalter der gegenwärtigen Kulturzertrümmerung [1937] wieder mehr Sinn vorhanden sein dürfte, als es noch vor einem Jahrzehnt der Fall war" (*Ibid.*, pp. 217-8).

[122] Ricoeur, *Time and Narrative*, vol. 3, p. 311, n. 37.
[123] See Karl-Otto Apel, et. al., *Hermeneutik und Ideologiekritik* (Frankfurt a.M.: Suhrkamp, 1971).

Habermas sees Gadamer's position as so dominated by listening to the tradition that liberating praxis is compromised if not impossible. See Jürgen Habermas, *Philosophische Rundschau*, Beiheft 5 (1967); "Der Universalitätsanspruch der Hermeneutik" in *Hermeneutik und Dialektik*, hrsg. von R. Bubner, u.a. (Tübingen: J.C.B. Mohr (Paul Siebeck), 1970. An English translation can be found in Josef Bleicher, *Contemporary Hermeneutics: Hermeneutics as Method, Philosophy, and Critique* (London: Routledge and Kegan Paul, 1980); and "Der hermeneutische Ansatz" in *Zur Logik der Sozialwissenschaften*, fünfte, erweiterte Auflage (Frankfurt a.M.: Suhrkamp Verlag, 1982). Gadamer's comments on the issue can be found in "Rhetorik, Hermeneutik und Ideologiekritik: Metakritische Erörterungen zu 'Wahrheit und Methode'" in *Kleine Schriften*, I (Tübingen: J.C.B. Mohr (Paul Siebeck), 113-130. English translation of

Is the Focus of Theology the Call to Decision?

Rudolf Bultmann can be credited with the establishment of the theological agenda of decision in 20th century theology. His project of demythologization rests, first, upon the insight of the 19th century's "mythic school," which observed that there is a husk - kernel structure to myth.[124] Although the titles varied, the mythic school argued that there were basically three kinds of myths: historical myths having an historical event at their core that was embellished by the imagination into the mythical narrative; poetic myths having a figurative symbol at their core; and philosophical myths having an idea at their core.[125] Second, Bultmann's project rests upon the philosophical anthropology of Heidegger's *Being and Time*, which is a call out of the public "they-world's" inauthenticity to individual authentic existence.[126] Heidegger's work in *Being and Time* challenges the individual to actualize her/his

---

Gadamer's texts can be found under the title "On the Scope and Function of Hermeneutical Reflection" in *Continuum*, 8/1 (1970), 77-133, and in *Philosophical Hermeneutics*, trans. by David E. Linge (Berkeley: University of California Press, 1976), 18-43.

[124] See Douglas R. McGaughey, "Through Myth to Imagination: On the Collapse of the Separation Between Myth and History" in *Journal of the American Academy of Religion*, LVI/1 (Spring, 1988), 51-76.

[125] See Christian Hartlich and Walter Sachs. *Der Ursprung des Mythosbegriffes in der modernen Bibelwissenschaft* (Tübingen: J.C.B. Mohr (Paul Siebeck), 1952), pp. 1-5. Instead of speaking of a "philosophical myth," as did the mythic school, when one encounters a story shaped around a philosophical or theological idea, Bultmann calls it an "ideal scene" (see Bultmann, *Die Geschichte der synoptischen Tradition*, 9. Auflage (Göttingen: Vandenhoeck & Ruprecht, 1979), p. 48, n. 3).

[126] See Heidegger, *Being and Time*, p. 68. Heidegger did not claim that "inauthentic" existence was an "inferior" form of Being (see *ibid.*, p. 68). Time and again he indicated that authenticity is dependent upon inauthenticity, i.e., there is no such thing as "pure" authenticity, for inauthenticity is the "existentiale," authenticity is an "existentiell." "*Authentic Being-one's-Self* does not rest upon an exceptional condition of the subject, a condition that has been detached from the 'they'; *it is rather an existentiell modification of the 'they' - of the 'they' as an essential existentiale*" (*ibid.*, p. 168, see, as well, pp. 312, 345-346, and 422). This is precisely why there is so much ambiguity, anxiety, and uncanniness connected with authentic existence. See *ibid.*, pp. 320-323, 393-5.

Theodore Kisiel called my attention to what appears to be a contradiction in Heidegger here. Heidegger also wrote, *ibid.*, p. 365: "It has been shown that proximally and for the most part Dasein is *not* itself but is lost in the they-self, which is an existentiell modification of the authentic Self." One could read this as a contradiction of the earlier passages, which claim that authenticity is an existentiell of the existentiale inauthenticity, or one might read this passage to mean that being "lost in the they-self" is an existentiell modification of the authentic self - placing the emphasis on "lost" rather than the "they-self" - to suggest degrees of authenticity stretching from the truly authentic projection of one's "ownmost possibilities" to having entirely "lost" the self in the fulfilling of the possibilities expected by the "they-world." Such an "ab-

ownmost possibilities rather than simply allow the public they-world to define those possibilities for her/him.

Bultmann demythologizes the call "out of the world" issued by the earliest layer of the Christian tradition to be an expression of a philosophical or theological idea. This is the central theological kernel at the heart of the mythology of the New Testament[127] of a call to authentic existence. He writes:

> ... [F]aith is *not a dualistic world-view*. It does not arise by a man's wavering in his security and getting bewildered at the world and so turning away from it to waft himself up into a world beyond by speculative thought or devout silence ... Faith is not flight from the world nor asceticism, but *desecularization* in the sense of a smashing of all human standards and evaluations. It is in this sense that the believer is no longer "of the world" ... But their not being "of the world" must not be confused with a retreat out of the world.[128]

The believer makes a decision to be no longer "of the world." This is the central act of faith and theology for Bultmann.[129]

> The membership of a person to the world of darkness [the public they-world] or to the world of light [authenticity] is determined not by his (sic) fate nor by his "nature" but by his decision. The Gnostic dualism of fate has become a dualism of decision ... And faith is neither more nor less than the *decision*, achieved in the overcoming of the offense, *against the world* for God.[130]

Bultmann argues that philosophy presents humanity with a *possibility in principle*, that is, the possibility of authentic existence. Theology, on the

---

solute" lostness, to the exclusion of any kind of authenticity, would be to make an existentiell modification of the authentic self.

[127] Bultmann wrote already in *Die Geschichte der synoptischen Tradition*, p. 396: "Der Christus, der verkündigt wird, ist nicht der historische Jesus, sondern der Christus des Glaubens und des Kultes." The opening lines of his *Theology of the New Testament* reemphasize that what we find in the New Testament is by no means a historical record of empirical facts, but the development of ideas and articulation of faith by the earliest levels of the Christian tradition: "*The message of Jesus* is a presupposition for the theology of the New Testament rather than a part of that theology itself. For New Testament theology consists in the unfolding of those ideas by means of which Christian faith makes sure of its own object, basis, and consequences" (*ibid.*, p. 3). Bultmann claims that the material attributed to the historical Jesus in the New Testament is overwhelmingly the formation of the earliest Palestinian church (see Rudolf Bultmann, *Die Geschichte der synoptischen Tradition*, , p. 49).

[128] Rudolf Bultmann, *Theology of the New Testament*, II vols. in one, trans. by Kendrick Grobel (New York: Charles Scribner's Sons, 1955), vol. II, p. 76.

[129] See Rudolf Bultmann, *Primitive Christianity In Its Contemporary Setting*, trans. by R.H. Fuller (New York: Meridian Books, 1956), pp. 175-208.

[130] Bultmann, *Theology of the New Testament*, p. 76. See, as well, *ibid.*, p. 241 and 251. In addition, see Rudolf Bultmann, "The Case for Demythologization: A Reply by

other hand, presents humanity, through the call of the Christ, with a *possibility in fact* of authentic existence which the individual can appropriate in the freedom of personal decision.[131] This constitutes the liberation of Christian salvation: "*Freedom* is promised to the possessor of this faith-knowledge. From what? From the world, from sham 'reality,' from both its seductiveness and its open enmity ..."[132] Since this freedom is already a possibility now, it constitutes what John's gospel calls the realized eschatology of the Christian faith and forms the core of faith and theology according to Bultmann.

This present project by no means discounts the importance of decision in the life of faith. Yet theology commences before one encounters any kerygma.[133] Theological thinking is constitutive of the human condition and it is what drives the human to look for a kerygma.

To be sure, it is correct to say that human beings are "hearers of the Word."[134] But this is an expression of our always and already having been

---

Rudolf Bultmann" in Karl Jaspers and Rudolf Bultmann, *Myth and Christianity: An Inquiry into the Possibility of Religion without Myth*, trans. by Norbert Guterman (New York: Noonday Press, 1971), p. 68.

[131] See Rudolf Bultmann, "The Historicity of Man and Faith" in Schubert Ogden, trans., *Existence and Faith: Shorter Writings of Rudolf Bultmann*, pp. 92-110. In addition, see the discussion and critique of Bultmann's position in Schubert Ogden, *Christ Without Myth: A Study Based on the Theology of Rudolf Bultmann* (New York: Harper and Row, 1961), pp. 111-126.

[132] Bultmann, *Theology of the New Testament*, p. 78.

[133] Bultmann wrote in *Theology of the New Testament*, p. 3: "... [T]heological thinking - the theology of the New Testament - begins with the *kerygma* of the earliest Church and not before."

[134] This is the English title of the initial translation by Michael Richards of Karl Rahner's, *Hörer des Wortes. Zur Grundlegung einer Religionsphilosophie* (München: Verlag Kösel-Pustet, 1941), which employed the massively edited German text from Johannes Baptist Metz as the basis of that translation. A second translation uses the title *Hearer of the Word*, for the German "Hörer" is both singular and plural and the translator presumably wished to distinguish this translation from the initial translation. The new edition is based on Rahner's original German text.

Rahner acknowledges that he is doing metaphysics (see *Hearer of the Word*, p. 2). His task is to describe the conditions which require the human to be understood as always and already open for an as yet not entirely complete revelation (see *ibid.*, pp. 5-6, 14, 71-73). The key for a possible revelation, according to Rahner, is that the human and its world is grounded in the unity of Being (see *ibid.*, pp. 28, 30) which is a mysterious ground (although by definition knowable, see, *ibid.*, p. 29, 72) serving as the condition of possibility for the human *Vorgriff*, i.e., our ability to go beyond the particular to the abstract (see *ibid.*, 46-47). Accompanying this *Vorgriff* is an act of the will, which is similar to Schelling's understanding of "will," i.e., as the striving (*Sehnsucht*) which characterizes all that is. Hence, co-affirmed with the will or striving of the human is the will or striving of Being (see, *ibid.*, pp. 68-70).

thrown into the linguistic system of our mother tongue which we must of necessity use in order to make sense of our experience.[135] Furthermore, we are

---

Rahner avoids a charge of natural theology by insisting that, although the human already anticipates a disclosure of Being in the "more" of the *Vorgriff*, human finitude cannot determine in advance what the content of the disclosure of Being (i.e., revelation) is going to be. It is this combination of the will (the striving) of Being and the concealedness or withholding of Being that allows Rahner to analogically speak of God as "person." According to Rahner the core of personhood is will and the ability to withhold one's self from the Other (see, *ibid.*, pp. 70-73).

Although the present project finds tremendous resonance in Rahner, grave reservations must be expressed regarding the notion of the "unity of Being" that serves as the metaphysical ground of any and all experience. Rahner is, apparently, reading the notion of the Being-of being (*das Sein des Seienden*) in terms of "to be-ness" as an ontological unity in which any and all things of metaphysical necessity must participate, i.e., for one to encounter a thing it must "be" and the self must "be" - hence, the unitary ground enabling any and all experience is "be-ness." If "be-ness" or the "is" is removed from any-*thing*, then it could not be experienced.

The present project understands *das Sein des Seienden* not as "to be-ness" but as possibility. Hence, it is inappropriate to speak of Being as merely some "unitary ground" enabling any and all experience, because what is "unitary" about possibility is only that for any-*thing* to be it must be "embedded" in possibility, but, precisely because Being is always the Being-of being, the actual situation of any particular thing circumscribes the possibilities of that thing contributing to the absolute uniqueness of the thing. No two things or persons have the same possibilities, because no two things or persons have exactly the same circumstances. In short, the Being-of being as possibility is not some univocal "is" but a tensive "is"/"is not."

[135] This tension is that of "*langue*" und "*parole*" found in Ferdinand de Saussure. See Saussure, *Course in General Linguistics* (1915), trans. by Wade Baskin (New York: McGraw-Hill, 1966). Although de Saussure's text does not acknowledge it (The book is a set of lecture notes collected and edited by two of Saussure's students.), this distinction between *langue* and *parole* is not original. Eberhard Hildenbrandt reports in *Versuch einer kritischen Analyse des Cours de linguistique generale von Ferdinand de Saussure* (Marburg: N.G. Elwert Verlag, 1972), p. 5, that Saussure wrote his dissertation in Leipzig in 1880 and that he was beyond doubt familiar with Wilhelm von Humboldt's distinction between *ergon* and *energeia* which is equivalent to the distinction between *langue* and *parole*.

However, a second central insight of Saussure's *Course in General Linguistics* in all likelihood was also appropriated across the same linguistic frontier. This is his insistence that static or synchronic linguistics is a system of oppositions with each part or linguistic unit having its place only within the horizon of the interactions of the whole. Ludwig Noire, Professor in Leipzig at the time Saussure studied there, wrote in *Die Welt als Entwicklung des Geistes: Bausteine zu einer monistischen Weltanschauung* (Leipzig: Verlag von Veit & Comp., 1874), p. 194: "Jedes Wort steht in der allergeschloßensten, allseitigsten Bedingtheit zu dem ganzen Sprachvorrath und dessen Leben, wird von den nahen und fernerliegenden Worten umgränzt, definirt und erleuchtet. Das Wort sagt also schon um deswillen etwas ungemein Bestimmtes." Noire proceeds to insist, however, that this linguistic system can only be appropriately and fully understood in terms of its relatedness to a world of reference. See *ibid.*, pp. 194-

always "on this side of the text," to quote Ricoeur, and that is what makes us "hearers of the Word." However, there is no special privileging of a particular text or set of texts[136] necessarily implied in our being "hearers of the Word." Making theology dependent upon our hearing *the* kerygma privileges a certain set of texts in the extraordinary sense that only in these texts do we encounter "salvation."

Privileging a kerygma makes the theology of decision analogous to the theologies built upon privileging the Christological moment: they both turn the a posteriori into an a priori and deny the significance of the particularity of historical experience. In other words, an original experience by an individual or group was reflected upon by her/him/them a posteriori (after the experience). Then the individual or group proclaimed that something a priori (prior to all experience) and absolute (in contrast to experience which is non-absolute and finite) transpired in the original experience. The logical error of such an a posteriori absolutizing is that all of the rest of historical experience, the particular acting and suffering of individuals and groups throughout all of time, is trivialized and relativized over against the absolute moment in time taken to be a priori. Particularly, if the kerygma is the call to authentic existence, then why privilege one individual's authentic decision over another's? This is analogous to the problem of Paul Tillich's Christology of the New Being. Being is announced in *every* moment, the victory of Being over non-Being is confirmed by *every* event, and is not restricted to one particular moment nor does it require a privileged event to confirm it.

Theology does not depend upon a privileged Word in the sense of the words in a particular set of texts or a particular kerygma calling to authentic decision. Theology does not depend upon acknowledgment of a collection of absolutized Scriptures. It does depend, paradoxically, upon a prior Word into which we are thrown as a mediated filtering of the symbolic. Once active reflection commences, this filtering of the symbolic has already been "formalized" into our mother tongue and tradition and serves as the linguistic horizon for our understanding and creative activity. Yet the filtering of the symbolic is not limited to "public" languages. It is the process of re-presentation that characterizes experience already in the womb. Hence, to privilege a particular collection of words as *the* Word is to discount both our (pre-)understanding and our creative activity. This is a paradoxical relation-

---

5. Saussure has not completely forgotten this link of language to world. See *Course in General Linguistics*, pp. 22, 80, 104, 109.

[136] This is the wish of George Lindbeck. See, for example, *The Nature of Doctrine*, p. 136, n. 5.

tionship in that it reflects the tension between the inherited words, which determine and shape us, and our new experience, which confirms the freedom, dignity, and worth of the individual in community.

As hearers of the Word, then, there is a process transpiring *prior to our making any decisions* in faith. That is the process of imagination and understanding that rests upon the paradoxical moments (e.g., of the filtering of the symbolic in dialectical tension with what the symbolic seeks to represent) that are constitutive of experience. These paradoxical moments make life an odyssey of faith rather than resting on a particular decision for a specific content of faith as either private or public. If we are to privilege a human activity in the life of faith, it is not decision but imagination. The imagination always and already precedes decision. It is the imagination along with memory that unites the paradoxical moments of the human condition which call us to accountability and decision in our historical moment.

This is not imagination in the sense of mere fantasy, however. Imagination is constitutive of our experience in that it is by means of the imagination that the individual and her/his community re-present reality by means of her/his/their corporate paradigm. Plato acknowledged the power of imaging in the line simile.[137] Kant acknowledge the central role of the imagination in the first edition of the *Critique of Pure Reason*.[138] Ricoeur emphasizes the role of the productive imagination as constitutive of life as an event consisting of both historical and fictional narratives with his theory of a three-fold mimesis bridging the gap between cosmological and phenomenological time in his three volume work *Time and Narrative*.[139] It is the power of the text to enable the projecting of imaginative variations of possible being in the world that constitutes the very notion of "reference" for the text,[140] i.e., the text does not refer merely empirically to the actual. The

---

[137] See Book VI of the Republic 510.

[138] See *The Critique of Pure Reason* A118 and A124. Heidegger's analysis of Kant's *Critique of Pure Reason* focuses on the shift "away" from the imagination (precisely, because it is pre-rational) in the second edition of the *Critique*. See Heideger, *Kant and the Problem of Metaphysics*. Translated by James S. Churchill. With a foreword by Thomas Langan. (Bloomington: Indiana University Press, 1962), pp. 166-176.

[139] See, in particular, his discussion of mimesis in volume 1, *Time and Narrative*, pp. 54-71.

[140] See Ricoeur's initial discussion of this notion as "heuristic fiction" in Study 7, "Metaphor and Reference," in *The Rule of Metaphor*. The term "imaginative variations" is first introduced in volume 2 of *Time and Narrative*, in chapter 4, "The Fictive Experience of Time." The notion resurfaces as the title and content of chapter 5 of volume 3 of *Time and Narrative*, "Fiction and Its Imaginative Variations on Time," where he explicitly makes reference to Heidegger's notion of "the projection of our ownmost possibilities," p. 141. The notion of "imaginative variations" is employed, as well, in

text refers by enabling possibilities beyond the actual. There is no point in Ricoeur's work where he is more indebted to Heidegger than here.

Focussing on decision, rather than the imagination as the central human activity in theology, would mean, once again, to perpetrate the travesty of concealing and suppressing without reflective ownership of the process of concealment in decision. By retrieving the central role of the imagination in the historical human odyssey of faith, we have the possibility of grasping the depths of faith constitutive of the human condition.

David Tracy emphasizes the priority of the imagination over the will (or decision making) lamenting that there is

> ... the tendency in much contemporary theological hermeneutics to include a "decision element" in the hermeneutical task itself and to give relatively little attention to the question of the aesthetic meanings uncovered by theological hermeneutics ... Indeed, this [revisionist] theory of interpretation [argued for by Tracy] appeals primarily to the imagination (by disclosing a possible way of being-in-the-world as a project for our imagination to envision) rather than to the will (an ethical enterprise). By means of that aesthetic differentiation, the theologian is free to develop his (sic) further tasks of the ethical and metaphysical appropriation of the meanings referred to by the text as genuinely distinct inquiries.[141]

Oswald Bayer reports that Ricoeur, too, challenges the "theology of decision." He quotes Ricoeur to say: "'A theory of interpretation, which immediately turns to the moment of decision, does so too quickly; it jumps over the moment of meaning that presents the stage of objectivity.'"[142] A theology of decision presupposes the activity of the imagination. The imagination and memory present to us what we take to be reality. This activity always and already involves selectivity and suppression which can never be simply overlooked. This activity of the imagination and memory (both individual and corporate) establishes what "reality" is. By definition, then, decision is a derivative process, for only on the basis of some notion of what is real can one make a decision. Theology, however, is concerned with the leap of faith necessary for our even commencing to encounter "reality."

Ricoeur's *Oneself as Another*, trans. by Kathleen Blamey (Chicago: The University of Chicago Press, 1992), pp. 148, 159, 288.

[141] Tracy, *Blessed Rage for Order*, pp. 78-79. Though Tracy, to be sure, does not deny entirely a role for decision. See, *ibid.*, p. 223. The present project, however, calls all metaphysical appropriation into question by emphasizing the role of aporiai at the core of human experience making our lives an odyssey of faith seeking understanding.

[142] From Oswald Bayer, "Theologie im Konflikt der Interpretationen," *Communio Viatorum* (Prague), 32/4 (1989), p. 226.

Theology and the Aporetic

The task of theology, then, is foremost that of investigating, articulating, and critically evaluating the aporetic or paradoxical depths of human experience. Theology is not defined by a "what" (either as an object, or as a specific region of experience, or as a particular action) nor is it defined by a "way" (or method of investigation). Theology, in other words, is not to be defined either in terms of an object (Tillich's method of correlation) or as critical reflection about the objective ground of experience ensuring the worthwhileness of the human odyssey (Ogden and Tracy), or as a call to decision in terms of authenticity (Bultmann). If its parameters are established by an interrogative, it is neither "what" nor "why" but "how?" In other words, how is experience at all possible? Attention to this question of "how," acknowledges the descriptive, the prescriptive, and the speculative components in theology.

Theology's first task is descriptive. In other words, it must first investigate and describe the aporiai enabling and shaping the human condition as faith seeking understanding. Once the conditions of faith have been identified, theology provides not simply an "is" but an "ought." For these conditions of faith are the necessary (if contingently necessary) constitutive elements for human life and experience, and they demand preservation and cultivation for the enrichment of all. These conditions include the world, Others, and the radically spiritual character of human experience.

Chapter 2
Theology and Aporiai

Theology is first and foremost a living out of, a listening to, and an adjudicating of aporiai in the human odyssey of faith. As classically stated by Anselm (but borrowed from Augustine), the human condition is faith seeking understanding.[1] Focussing on aporiai, however, does not turn theology into a mind-numbing event of mere awe before mystery. Although the theologian is always and already in the midst of a groundless wagering in faith, s/he can adjudicate which wager is most adequate to her/his experience as an individual in community. In other words, theology is rooted in paradox, but there are more or less adequate graspings of what is at stake in any given paradox just as there are more or less adequate articulations of what constitutes a particular paradox. Furthermore, it is not as if one could choose not to wager. Faith has as much to do with our acting as it does with our understanding, and one cannot not act.

Theology is both a form of unknowing and of knowing. It is an unknowing to the extent that it rests upon aporiai. It is a knowing to the extent that it is critically reflective about the nature of those aporiai. In other words, by emphasizing the role of paradox and unknowing in theology, I am not proposing a simple return to the tradition of Negative Theology articulated by Pseudo-Dionysius in the 6th century[2] which has shaped an almost forgotten (as far as the Protestant tradition is concerned, to be sure) trajectory of spirituality[3] over John Scotus Erigena, Thomas Aquinas, Meister

---

[1] Anselm tells us in his preface to the "Proslogion" that he originally entitled the text "Faith Seeking Understanding." See "Proslogion" in *Anselm of Canterbury*, vol. I (Toronto: Edwin Mellen Press, 1975), p. 90. Augustine, however, is the source of this aphorism. See "On the Trinity," Bk. VII.12, where Augustine employs an old Latin translation of the Septuagint's Isaiah 7:9 (from *Anselm of Canterbury*, vol. I, p. 152, n. 23).

[2] See *Pseudo-Dionysius: The Complete Works*, trans. by Colm Luibheid (New York: Paulist Press, 1987).

[3] The notion of "spirit" has suffered great abuse with the rise of the materialistic explanation of the human condition. At least in popular opinion, and even in theological circles, spirit itself has been reduced to a material force. It is taken to be either a power breaking into the "closed system of causality," for the natural order is understood to be a closed system of causality, or it is understood to be an emotional force transporting one out of one's everyday world of concerns, or it is taken to be some region or special part of one's personal being, or it is another term for "personality," i.e., an individual's pecu-

Eckhart, *The Cloud of Unknowing*, and St. John of the Cross, to mention only a few. What makes the theological situation radically new in the 20th century is that all such metaphysical explanations as Christian Platonism informing the tradition of Negative Theology have collapsed. An inadequacy of a part, however, does not justify dispensing with the whole.

The experiential dimension, for which Platonic metaphysics attempts to provide an explanation, is as legitimately real as ever. While we have no trouble accepting the credibility of our sense perceptions, we have reached the point where we give little if any credibility to our intellects as a spiritual life, although in both cases we can give no *logical argument* for any reality independent of our consciousness either of the world or of universals. On the

---

liar spirit. In short, spirit is reduced to either a force, an emotion, some substantial ingredient of one's life, where it is identified with some part of life among other parts, or personality. This materialistic understanding of spirit has a constructive role to play in a religious community as a psychological mechanism to handle tragedy or a context of oppression, exploitation, and injustice. To the extent, however, that our human spirituality is conceived fundamentally as a materialistic force or some kind of substance, it has totally lost its rootedness in the classic notion of spirituality that has shaped Christianity (in Eastern Christianity almost exclusively to this day; in Western Christianity almost universally down to the Renaissance and among monastic and mystic groups to this day). Although the metaphysics of this classic notion of spirituality can no longer be defended, human spirituality must be retrieved if both theology and culture are to be established on an adequate understanding.

The literature of classic spirituality is broad. An invaluable aid in accessing this literature is the projected four volume work by Bernard McGinn of which the first volume has just appeared under the title *The Foundations of Mysticism*, but one should not overlook Cornelia de Vogel's article "Platonism and Christianity: A Mere Antagonism or a Profound Common Ground?" in *Vigiliae Christianae* 39 (1985), pp. 1-62; Antonie Wlosok's, *Laktanz und die Philosphische Gnosis* (Heidelberg: Carl Winter, Universitätsverlag, 1960); or Egon Brandenburger's, *Fleisch und Geist. Paulus und die dualistische Weisheit* (Neukirchen-Vluyn: Neukirchener Verlag, 1968)..

One can argue that this classic spirituality is rooted in Paul and John in the New Testament, that it is the shaping element of Christian Gnosticism and Marcionisim, which dominated the mid-point of 2nd century Christianity, that it is the key to the writings of Justin Martyr in the struggle of "orthodoxy" to establish itself over against the anti-worldliness and anti-Semitism of Gnosticism and Marcionism in the last half of the 2nd century, not to mention its role in the writings of the Jewish philosopher contemporary with Jesus of Nazareth, Philo, who deeply influenced the Alexandrians and Plotinus, who shaped Pseudo-Dionysius, the inaugurator of Christian mysticism as "secret knowledge." If Christianity was defined as the pursuit of happiness by Augustine, Christian spirituality remained the profound experiential basis that informed it. In the 20th century, Christianity has been reduced to a superficial psychological gospel, dispensing advice on how to find happiness in the competitive marketplace and in the home, that is, as a survival strategy in a materialistic world, or to a social gospel totally severed from its classical experiential, spiritual foundations.

other hand, the same *pragmatic argument*, which argues for the existence of an empirical world independent of our consciousness of it (i.e., try to ignore that empirical world and see what the consequences are), applies to the spiritual realm, as well. If theology needs to engage in retrieval in this new situation, it is the retrieval of the spiritual dimension of human experience.

However, this can never be a simple retrieval of the traditional Platonic metaphysics which sought to explain the source and cause of human spirituality in terms of the Logos and the First Principle of the whole. Both the metaphysics of Christian Platonism as well as the metaphysics of empirical materialism must be bracketed as speculative wagers. This is the case not only because they lack logical proof, but because the experiential dimensions, for which these metaphysical options were meant to provide an explanation, are aporetically related rather than causally related. In other words, where the tradition has sought to explain the origin of the one side of spirituality or materiality by means of the other on the basis of the metaphysical priority of one side over the other, we must see both sides as constitutive of human experience - as inexplicable and contradictory as these dimensions of experience are.

These two metaphysical options are represented in the tradition under the rubric of "idealism" and "realism" (the latter is known today as "empiricism") though in scholastic theology "idealism" is labelled the *via antiqua* (or Platonic "realism") and "realism" is called the *via moderna* (or Aristotelian "nominalism"). Since the 13th century we can observe a swing of the metaphysical pendulum from "idealism" to "realism"/empiricism. Yet one can equally observe an increasing experiential uncanniness that the process has not only been destructive ecologically, but, more importantly, that something has been lost experientially. In other words, human experience and praxis is only in the last third of the 20th century beginning to catch up with the intellectual judgments formed both at the beginning of the century, when the death of God (or the end of Platonism[4]) was shrilly announced in the

---

[4] Nietzsche labelled Christianity "Platonism for the masses." See "Jenseits von Gut und Böse" in *Nietzsche's Werke*, vol. VII (Leipzig: Alfred Kröner Verlag, 1910), p. 5. See, as well, Martin Heidegger, *Nietzsche*, 2 vols., 2nd. ed. (Pfullingen, Verlag Günther Neske, 1961), vol. I, pp. 187, 543; vol. II, 83, 274. Hence, his declaration of the death of God was an announcement that the Platonism of the Christian world with its absolute hierarchy and absolute morality had come to an end. See Heidegger, *Nietzsche*, vol. II, pp. 33, 38, 276. Heidegger speaks of five fundamental themes in the work of Nietzsche: 1) the will to power (meaning that "becoming" rather than absolute "Being" characterizes the human condition, for, according to Heidegger's reading, Nietzsche is not speaking of the will to power in the sense of a struggle for political dominance); 2) nihilism (or the history of truth in terms of the essence of beings or mere things); 3) the eternal

writings of Nietzsche, and at mid-century, when Heidegger[5] proclaimed the end of metaphysics coupled with his critique of technology.[6]

Not Mere Astonishment

Defining theology as the living out of and reflecting upon the aporiai of experience does not mean that theology merely stands dumb before the in-

---

recurrence of the same (or the way that beings in their totality are); 4) the overman or *Übermensch* (the kind of human being that the human condition, properly understood, demands); and 5) justice (what the essence of truth as nihilistic requires, i.e., the highest effort). See Heidegger, *Nietzsche*, vol. II, pp. 259-260. He concludes, however, that Nietzsche remains a victim of the Western tradition's prioritizing of "entities" or beings i.e., the ontic, at the expense of the *Ereignis* character of the Being-of beings which constitutes a more original dynamic of ontological disclosure and concealment. See Heidegger, *Nietzsche*, vol. II, p. 335.

[5] See Martin Heidegger, *The Question Concerning Technology and Other Essays*, trans. by William Lovitt (New York: Harper & Row, Pub., 1977).

[6] Contrary to the judgment of Alan Bloom in *The Closing of the American Mind* (New York: Simon & Schuster, Inc., 1988), pp. 141-156, 207, we do not owe nihilism to Nietzsche and Heidegger. Although Ivan Turgenev claimed to have invented the term in his novel *Fathers and Sons* (1861) (see Wolfgang Müller-Lauter, "Nihilism als Konsequenz des Idealismus: F.H. Jacobis Kritik an der Transzendentalphilosophie und ihre philosophiegeschichtlichen Folgen" in *Denken im Schatten des Nihilismus: Festschrift für Wilhelm Weischedel zum 70. Geburtstag*, hrsg. von Alexander Schwan (Darmstadt: Wissenschaftliche Buchgesellschaft, 1975), p. 162, n. 112), the concept was used already in Russia in an article attacking Puschkin in 1829. See Otto Pöggeler, "'Nihilist' und 'Nihilismus'" in *Archiv für Begriffsgeschichte*, vol. XIX (Bonn: Bouvier Verlag Herbert Grundmann, 1965), p. 198. But Pöggeler also points out (*ibid.*, p. 202) that one finds in Eisler's *Handwörterbuch der Philosophie* from 1922 that Friedrich Heinrich Jacobi had used the term in his famous open letter to Fichte of March 3/6, 1799. See Hans Lindau, hrsg., *Die Schriften zu J.G. Fichtes Atheismus-Streit* (München: Georg Müller, 1912), pp. 157-195. Despite Eisler's judgment that Jacobi originated the term (Heidegger, too, attributes the first usage to Jacobi, see *Nietzsche*, vol. II, p. 31), Pöggeler points out that the term was used by Friedrich Schlegel in 1797, by Daniel Jenisch in 1796, and by J.H. Obereit as early as 1787. All of these usages were in attacks on Kantian transcendentalism. See Otto Pöggeler, "Hegel und die Anfänge der Nihilismus-Diskussion" in *Man and World: An International Philosophical Review*, 3/3 (Sept. 1970), p. 187, and "'Nihilist' und 'Nihilismus,'" p. 201.

Bloom laments the loss of Platonic metaphysics as the cause of the deterioration of the American mind. See *The Closing*, pp. 36-38. His judgment is simply too facile having been made with no appreciation for the impossibility of making a logical proof for the existence of universals independent of human consciousness. We experience universals primarily as ectypals (a posteriori). Universals are experienced as archetypals (a priori) only as an inheritance of our language. See Chapter 9 below for an analysis of language and universals.

explicable and mysterious. To be sure, theology commences with wonder and astonishment (in the sense of an encounter with the "holy" as "*mysterium fascinans et tremendum*" to borrow Rudolf Otto's phrase[7]) and with recognition of our radical dependence (or complete dependence to borrow Schleiermacher's phrase[8]), but for rigorous theology, not only are we theo-

---

[7] For Rudolf Otto's notion of the "holy," see *The Idea of the Holy*, trans. by John W. Harvey (New York: Oxford University Press, 1926).

[8] See Friedrich Schleiermacher, *The Christian Faith*, vol. 1, 2nd German ed., ed. by H. R. Mackintosh and J. S. Stewart (New York: Harper Torchbooks, 1963), Section 4 (pp. 12-18) entitled: "The Common element in all howsoever diverse expressions of piety, by which these are conjointly distinguished from all other feelings, or, in other words, the self-identical essence of piety, is this: the consciousness of being absolutely [*schlechthinig*, more appropriately translated as "completely"] dependent, or, which is the same thing, of being in relation with God." He adds (*ibid.*, pp. 19-20): "... there seems to be no objection to our distinguishing three grades of self-consciousness: the confused animal grade, in which the antithesis [of "the objective and the introversive" (*ibid.*, p. 18) or object and subject] cannot arise, as the lowest; the sensible self-consciousness, which rests entirely upon the antithesis, as the middle; and the feeling of absolute [complete] dependence, in which the antithesis again disappears and the subject unites and identifies itself with everything which, in the middle grade, was set over against it, as the highest." Note how these grades are parallel to Kierkegaard's stages of aesthetic, ethical, and Religiousness A. But the highest grade of self-consciousness, according to Schleiermacher is no simple "losing of one's self" in the other. In the second speech of *On Religion*, pp. 26-34, he argues that piety is prior to knowing and doing. He adds (*ibid.*, pp. 37-38): "Only when piety takes its place alongside of science and practice, as a necessary and an indispensable third, as their natural counterpart, not less in worth and splendor than either, will the common field be altogether occupied and human nature on this side complete." In order to explain what he means by piety here, Schleiermacher challenges us to look at how we go about becoming conscious of something (*ibid.*, pp. 41-42): "Your thought can only embrace what is sundered. Wherefore as soon as you have made any give definite activity of your soul an object of communication or of contemplation, you have already begun to separate. It is impossible, therefore, to adduce any definite example, for, as soon as anything is an example, what I wish to indicate is already past. Only the faintest trace of the original unity could then be shown ...

Consider how you delineate an object. Is there not both a stimulation and a determination by the object, at one and the same time, which for one particular moment forms your existence? The more definite your image, the more, in this way, you become the object, and the more you lose yourselves. But just because you can trace the growing preponderance of one side [the object] over the other [the self], both must have been one and equal in the first, the original moment that has escaped you."

In another passage Schleiermacher speaks of "the Whole," which is what he means by the idea of "absolute [complete] dependence:" "How now are you in the Whole? By your senses. And how are you for yourselves? By the unity of your self-consciousness, which is given chiefly in the possibility of comparing the varying degrees of sensation. How both can only rise together, if both together fashion every act of life, is easy to see. You become sense and the Whole becomes object. Sense and object

logical beings prior to wonder and astonishment, everything hinges upon what kind of holiness and what kind of dependence.⁹ This project insists that an adequate understanding of dependence (which would mean to acknowledge the limits to rational explanation and to indicate where speculation begins) can tell us nothing directly or literally about that upon which we are dependent except to argue for its aporetic character. Its holiness, then, says nothing about a specific region or sphere of experience in contrast to the secular, but is, rather, expressive of our limits and a call to humility in light of all that is (both manifest and concealed).

Contingent Necessity and More

Although not merely foundational, as that discipline which identifies the conditions of possibility - in terms of contingent not metaphysical necessity - of any and all experience, theology *is* concerned with those constitutive elements of life which we cannot deny or negate without that denial affirming them. Such a Cartesian criterion for truth[10] leads us to a faith quite unlike Descartes', however. The notion of faith operative here is that faith as an un-knowing at the core of all that we are, know, and do, and not a kind of

---

mingle and unite, then each returns to its place, and the object rent from sense is a perception, and you rent from the object are for yourselves, a feeling. It is this earlier moment I mean, which you always experience yet never experience. The phenomenon of your life is just the result of its constant departure and return" (*ibid.*, p. 43).

That all of this sounds similar to Heidegger (see the discussion of "thrownness" (*Being and Time*, p. 174) or Dasein's always and already finding itself in a world of objects present- and ready-to-hand (*ibid.*, p. 82), of "*Befindlichkeit*" (*ibid.*, pp. 172f)," of the dynamic of possibilities being projected in the "understanding" (*ibid.*, p. 188), which results in the suppression of possibility (the fundamental "nullity" of Dasein's life, e.g., *ibid.*, p. 331) and serves as the basis for authentic responsibility (*ibid.*, p. 68) for one's actualizing one's ownmost possibilities, and of the impossibility of one's returning to a past condition of possibility, which denies historicism (*ibid.*, p. 448) but affirms our "historicality" (*ibid.*, p. 442) is perhaps because of the influence of Schleiermacher on Heidegger's "protestantism." See Hugo Ott, *Martin Heidegger: Unterwegs zu seiner Biographie* (Frankfurt a.M.: Campus Verlag, 1988), pp. 110 and 112, where Ott documents the impression Schleiermacher's "second speech" made on Heidegger.

9 For example, Schleiermacher's analysis suggests that the self is some kind of permanent substrate that "goes out" and "returns" to itself, i.e., "[s]ense and object mingle and unite, then each returns to its place ... " (*On Religion*, p. 43). We have no access, however, to such a permanent substrate which might account for a "unified self."

10 See "Meditation Two" of Descartes, *Meditations on First Philosophy in Which the Existence of God and the Distinction of the Soul from the Body are Demonstrated*, trans. by Donald A. Cress (Indianapolis: Hackett Publishing Co., Inc., 1983).

epistemic faith in the Cartesian God, who is the guarantor of an exogenous world independent of our perception of it. Theology is, rather, concerned with that faith resting upon paradox. Theology is not concerned primarily with knowledge but with that faith prior to all knowledge.

Theology is mistakenly understood to be of marginal interest for humanity. However, theology is concerned with both that pre-reflective living, dependent upon aporiai *and* that conscious reflection facilitating our asking of those questions and confronting of those paradoxical depths that take us to the core of our lives as individuals thrown into a natural and social environment where one must act always on the basis of one's unknowing.

It is important to recognize that theology is both pre-reflective and reflective. Every human being is a theological being regardless of her/his personal convictions or conscious reflection. So-called "critical" theology must never forget its rootedness in the experience of everydayness, since it is concerned with the aporiai at the core of that everydayness. In other words, even critically reflective theology is a matter of faith just as is pre-reflective theology. What is won with critical reflection in theology is not absolute truth, is not a "superior" knowledge, but rather a more radical understanding of faith, of the limits or concealment of truth, and of the provisional character of all knowledge. To be sure, critical reflection in theology is preferable, but not because it gives us truth. Rather, critical reflection is the only tool the human has to reign in unbridled speculation and to assist us in acknowledging and in coming to terms with the concealment at the core of all experience. There is a warning to all not to elevate critical reflection above faith in the words of Clement of Alexandria who maintained that "simple faith is always sufficient, but reasoned knowledge is a higher possession."

Theology is radically experiential. It speaks to, and out of, the core of our human condition as a condition of faith. Once theology's issues are grasped, life can no longer be the same, because theology challenges us to examine what is accessible in the appearance of our everyday experience in light of the inaccessible and what does not appear. Humanity is the focus of theological reflection not because it has the rational capacity or the responsibility to give an explanation. Nor is humanity the focus of theological reflection at the expense of one's trying to understand the world and "transcendence" - for humanity is nothing if separated from either. Humanity is the focus of theological reflection, because humans are the beings which can know that they don't know, and can't know, but nevertheless must act.

Retrieval of Spirituality

This definition of theology will enable a retrieval of an understanding of spirituality shaping Christianity both East and West since its beginnings. This does not mean that theology is by definition Christian theology. But theology is never done outside of a context or a tradition. One may, and will, find similar discussions of aporiai and spirituality in other traditions, but one is a Jew, a Muslim, a Hindu, a Buddhist, a Christian, etc., as much, if not more, as a consequence of the accidents of one's personal history as by choice. One's language, understanding, and horizon of meaning is thoroughly shaped by one's cultural (and that means ultimately, one's religious) context even when that culture has been radically secularized.[11]

This project seeks to cultivate an appreciation of a notion of spirituality that has shaped the Christian tradition since at least its founding documents in the writings of Paul.[12] One cannot begin to either understand or appreciate the profundity of the dualism and soteriology of either Eastern or Western Christianity without an awareness of the Platonism that has so radically shaped both. What is argued here, however, is that this notion of spirituality is not simply a metaphysical head game. It is deeply experiential. A theology of the aporetic, however, must go one step further to ensure that both the spiritual and the material are recognized as in tension with one another and not engage in a metaphysical reduction of "reality" down to one side or the other. Such an erroneous reductionism can be observed as occurring again and again in the Christian tradition. This kind of reductionism is the hallmark of an inadequate theology, and is to be assiduously avoided by aporetic theology.

The retrieval of this classic notion of spirituality from within the Christian tradition is neither unequivocal nor does it offer an explanation of what Christian theology is "truly" all about. Rather, the human condition is the paradoxical place of interface between spirit and world contributing to our situation as one of faith seeking understanding as one acts and responds to the destruction, suffering, and needs of the world in solidarity with Others.

---

[11] The inseparability of religion and culture is a central theme of Paul Tillich's. See, for example, Paul Tillich, *Theology of Culture* (London: Oxford University Press, 1970) especially Chapter IV, "Aspects of a Religious Analysis of Culture," and Tillich's *Systematic Theology*, vol. I, pp. 394 and 52. It was also the central issue of Protestant Liberalism in the 19th century in German speaking countries. See Walter Nigg, *Geschichte des Religiösen Liberalismus*, pp. 216-218.

[12] Paul's First Thessalonians is the oldest document in the New Testament.

Dialogue and Application: Listening

Doing theology deliberately, rather than merely pre-reflectively, is by definition a matter of dialogue and application. A theological understanding and position is born out of listening and speaking - in that order.[13] However, the very texts that we hear and the very words that we speak are themselves selective and suppressive of what was and is not said - and at its deepest level, of what cannot be said.

First, everything hinges not just upon how well one has listened, but just as much if not more, as implied above, upon the accidents that lead one to hear certain texts rather than others. In other words, theological understanding is no different from understanding in general, i.e., it is not cumulative or necessarily progressive. Theology, then, is not a "science" if we mean by science a linear process of accumulating better and better, or more and more, insight and truth.[14] Rather, theological understanding is an open-

---

[13] No one exemplifies this more than David Tracy. See Chapter 4, "David Tracy: Theology as Correlation Beyond Absolute Necessity to Concealment."

[14] Science is placed deliberately in quotation marks here, because it is only a popular fiction that the natural sciences are linearly progressive in their accumulation of knowledge. Thomas Kuhn has convincingly demonstrated that the very notion that the natural sciences are engaged in a process of cumulatively gaining knowledge with respect to stable data is an illusion. So long as a single paradigm dominates in a research tradition, so long as the anomalous data are either unthreatening or eventually able to be integrated into that dominate paradigm, only so long can one speak of cumulative knowledge. But science (and human understanding in general) is ultimately characterized by paradigm revolutions rather than mere paradigm shifts. Hence, cumulative knowledge is a passing illusion. He writes in *The Structure of Scientific Revolutions*, 2nd ed. (Chicago: The University of Chicago Press, 1962), p. 126: "... is sensory experience fixed and neutral? Are theories simply man-made interpretations of given [fixed] data? The epistemological viewpoint that has most often guided Western philosophy for three centuries dictates an immediate and unequivocal, Yes. In the absence of a developed alternative, I find it impossible to relinquish entirely that viewpoint. Yet it no longer functions effectively, and the attempts to make it do so through the introduction of a neutral language of observations now seem to me hopeless [see Kuhn's similar judgments with respect to epistemology since Descartes, pp. 126 and 195].

The operations and measurements that a scientist undertakes in the laboratory are not 'the given' of experience ... They are not what the scientist sees ... Far more clearly than the immediate experience from which they in part derive, *operations and measurements are paradigm-determined*." (emphasis added) Kuhn reminded his reader earlier in the text (*ibid.*, p. 121) that "[w]hat occurs during a scientific revolution is not fully reducible to a reinterpretation of individual and stable data. In the first place, the data are not unequivocally stable." See, in addition, *ibid.*, pp. 135, 150, 192, 195, and 206. If the data are not unequivocally stable in the natural sciences, then we must relinquish the notion that "knowledge" is a cumulative process. Kuhn teaches us precisely this. See, *ibid.*, pp. 84., 92, 96, 108., 123, 128, 150. Perception is already pre-shaped by a

ended process of listening (both to our tradition(s) and present context of experience) and understanding. Yet, the nature of the theological situation excludes the notion that understanding and knowledge are on some evolutionary track toward completeness. Hans-Georg Gadamer reminds us:

> Neither is the mind of the interpreter in control of what words of tradition reach him (sic), nor can one suitably describe what happens here as the progressive knowledge of what exists, so that an infinite intellect would contain everything that could ever speak out of the whole tradition.[15]

---

paradigm or model that is the prerequisite for our observing anything. As we walk into the laboratory, we carry with us not only a model (a set of lenses) shaping the discipline of the particular laboratory entered, but we carry a whole world view that functions so subliminally that we are usually completely unaware of it. Perception is never neutral. There is always a set of lenses, provided by a paradigm, through which all perception passes. Hence, experience itself involves a tension of contradiction: perception is based on an illusion of stable data, which in fact are paradigm relative, but at the same time we have no other arena to appeal to for adjudicating the adequacy of our perceptions than the correspondence of our judgments coherently and non-contradictorily with this data. In addition, that which we appeal to in perception for the confirming of our judgments is itself a concealing and suppression of what necessarily cannot be present in any particular perception. Hence, the correspondence theory of truth essential to pragmatic experience rests itself on two levels of paradox: 1) our inability to unequivocally test out the truth of our judgments because a) the data do not possess the stability we believe they do and b) we have no immediate (only mediate) access to that data; and 2) the dynamic of revealing and concealing (of actuality and possibility and not merely of figure and background) that is essential to any event of experience prohibits any judgment of certainty with respect to that experience.

For a far more rigorous analysis of the epistemological problems only mentioned in passing by Kuhn, see Wolfgang Stegmüller, *Metaphysik, Skepsis, Wissenschaft*, Zweite, verbesserte Auflage (Berlin: Springer-Verlag, 1969). Two of the four quotes at the beginning of his text present succinctly the issues at issue in the discussion of epistemology today:

O, welche Flammenschrift brennt mir im Haupte?
"Nichts glauben kannst du, eh' du es nicht weißt,
Nichts wissen kannst du, eh' du es nicht glaubst."
        Ch.D. Grabbe: Don Juan und Faust.

... Nicht, daß er uns als wahr einleuchtet,
sondern, daß wir das Einleuchten gelten lassen,
macht ihn zum mathematischen Satz.
        L. Wittgenstein: Bemerkungen über die
        Grundlagen der Mathematik.

[15] Hans-Georg Gadamer, *Truth and Method*, p. 437. See *Wahrheit und Methode*, p. 437. This insight has profound theological implications, for it denies the notion that there could ever be, and not simply that we are incorrect to speculate or to believe in, an "infinite consciousness" that is accumulating the details of experience as some kind of "cosmic mind." This, then, is a denial of the model of Process Theology argued for by Charles Hartshorne, whose primary analogate for speaking of God is "mind." See

But this sounds counter intuitive to the contemporary ear. What is knowledge if not the gaining of more and more clarity about the things of the world? What does this mean that the "interpreter is not in control of what words of tradition reach" her/him? Surely, I pick and choose the texts that I read.?

Contrary to this common sense understanding, knowledge (no matter of what kind) is just not a simple cumulative process of gaining more and more information about an exogenous world of things (object, texts, or persons).[16] All of our pragmatic experience in the world, all of our activities having to do with things experienced, engaged, and manipulated either by means of the senses of sight, sound, touch, taste, and smell or on the basis

---

Charles Hartshorne, "The Subject of All Change" in *Man's Vision of God: The Logic of Theism* (Hamden, Conn.: Archon Books, 1964), especially pp. 264-5. The classic critique of the teleological argument for God (the argument employed by Plato that God is analogous to the human mind) is found in Hume, *Dialogues Concerning Natural Religion*, especially Part II, where he argues (pp. 18-19) that the greater the dissimilarity between the analogates the less appropriate the analogy. Yet there is no greater dissimilarity than between the finite human mind and an infinite mind that would be the accumulated knowledge at an omega point.

[16] Our belief in such an understanding of knowledge as cumulative and progressive serves the pragmatic interests of our paradigm which prizes one's sagacity and dexterity with respect to calculating, predicting, manipulating, and controlling the things of our world. However, so long as one is engaged in the progressive accumulation of knowledge, one is by definition a defender of the status quo. One is "filling in the blanks" in the dominant cultural or discipline paradigm rather than challenging the adequacy of the paradigm, seeking out anomalous data, or attempting new orders of intrasystematic coherence. Is this not the way we acquire security, measure success, and assess the quality of our lives? Most education and activities of a career are primarily involved in socialization.

Such cumulative knowledge is had at a dear price. It is had at the expense 1) of the only tool we have for adjudicating the adequacy of our experience, i.e., the tool of critical reflection which is not rooted simply in rational processes but in the aporetic. Human beings are an interfacing of both the logical (the intellect and spiritual) and the pragmatic (the material). Reducing experience down to one side or the other (as in this case to materialism at the expense of the spiritual) deprives us of essential aspects of our experience necessary for us to judge whether or not that experience is adequate and appropriate. 2) Such knowledge is had at the expense of our achieving any sense whatsoever of the pervasiveness of the spiritual in all experiencing, understanding, and action. 3) Such knowledge is had at the expense of what constitutes the very dignity and worth of our individual, particular, and unrepeatable experience, i.e., it is not simply what we have and can acquire, but far more the individuality of our experience that establishes human dignity. 4) Such knowledge is had at the expense of all that is concealed or covered over (including the "self") by what is manifest to us by the senses.

of them, all of that experience occurs exclusively in our intellects (the "logical" dimension of experience). Even our experience of space and time, Kant teaches us,[17] transpires exclusively in our minds - as incredible an insight as that is, it is superseded by the actual individual accomplishment. Furthermore, Hume observed that causality itself is radically a human construct, since we do not *perceive* ultimate causal relatedness in things.[18] Given these circumstances, our so-called knowledge is not only *not* simply a re-*presentation* (a mere immediate repetition in the mind) of "things out there," it is always and already a *presentation* by the intellect to the intellect filtered by the experience and understanding of the intellect. Knowledge is foremost a matter of consistency and coherence within the intellect rather than a matter of greater or less correspondence between our judgments and an external world.

This does not by any means force a surrender of all notions of an "external world." The world is not merely a private mental creation. That would be solipsism. The identification of the aporiai constitutive of our experience requires that both the "logical" and the "material" (that is, that which praxis cannot ignore) must be acknowledged and held in tension with one another. To deny either would close us off from a constitutive dimension of our experience. But the world is not a mere exogenous world "out there." It is a "life-world"[19] experienced as a consequence of the interaction between the spiritual and the material. Spirit, the human intellect, does not float above or outside of the world of history. It is radically and intimately rooted within the horizon of possibility enabled by the individual's life-world of pragmatic action.[20]

---

[17] See Immanuel Kant, "Erster Abschnitt: Von dem Raume" and "Zweiter Abschnitt: Von der Zeit" in *Kritik der reinen Vernunft* (Hamburg: Felix Meiner Verlag, 1976), pp. 66-83.

[18] See, for example, Hume, "The Treatise of Human Nature. Book I. On the Understanding" in *Hume: Selections*, ed. by Charles W. Hendel, Jr. (New York: Charles Scribner's Sons, 1955), p. 48.

[19] The notion of "life-world" is used here in the Phenomenologically technical sense from Husserl. See his discussion of life-world in *The Crisis of the European Sciences*. If there is a modification of Husserl's notion of the "life-world" occurring here, it is identifying the rootedness of the lived world within the all-encompassing horizon of possibility which eliminates any division between consciousness as a project of intentionality enclosed within itself and an exogenous world, i.e., it is to complement Husserl's project with that of Heideger's in *Being and Time*. But surely even Husserl did not mean to close consciousness in upon itself by means of the phenomenological epoché.

[20] There can be no denial of historicality to affirm the spiritual or the intellect as the "really real." We are spirit in the world radically and intimately rooted in a horizon of possibility that emphasizes equally particularity and generality. There can be no denial of his-

Precisely because the emphasis is on possibilities in the sense of a "horizon of possibility," however, *there is no division between an "internal" intellect and an "external" world. The two together constitute a seamless unity of possibility even as that common general horizon of possibility is always experienced by the individual as a specific limited range of possibilities enabled by her/his situation.* For even "pragmatic action" cannot be assigned exclusively to actions "in" the world "out there." We can no more deny our dependence upon the structures and processes of the intellect than we can deny our dependence upon a world independent of consciousness, i.e., the other/Other, the anomalous, the shock, the everydayness of the world.

Nevertheless, we cannot but acknowledge the pervasiveness of our experience as spiritual. If there is any "priority" in the interaction between the "logical" and the "pragmatic" one must give priority to the spiritual. But this is not an ontological or metaphysical priority. In the language of the tradition, it is exclusively an epistemological priority or a Phenomenological priority in the sense of Husserl's Phenomenology. It is a priority rooted in the radically non-sensuous character of experience.

This is the very point where the present theological project enables the engagement of a dialogue with the entire Christian tradition. As has already been indicated, what the Western tradition and Eastern Orthodoxy have understood to be a dualistic ontological or metaphysical alternative between spirit and flesh is taken here to be a Phenomenological, dialectical tension. Yet that does not mean that we can learn nothing from the theological debates of the tradition.

On the contrary, careful study of the theological discussions throughout the tradition (particularly of the "orthodox" Logos tradition as well as such "non-orthodox" traditions as Montanism, Gnosticism, Marcionism, but by no means limited to them, i.e., the same issues permeate the discussions of the medieval period, e.g., the mystics, the Cathari, and Protestant theology) can teach us a great deal about the relationship between spirit and matter.[21] Our culture and theology have much to retrieve.

---

toricality, the acting and suffering of Others, as constitutive of who we are in the order of things. To deny particularity is to deny the individual, and that would be to deny any meaning to the living and dying of individuals much less the suffering of the 12 to 14 million who died in the death camps of Europe during World War II. Theology is not, and dare not be, an escape from history. Theology calls humanity to accountability in history.

[21] For example, Hans Jonas identifies the absence in Gnosticism of any positive doctrine of virtue (areté; Tugendlehre). (See, *Gnosis und spätantiker Geist*, Teil 2: *Von der Mythologie zur mystischen Philosophie* (Göttingen: Vandenhoeck & Ruprecht, 1954), p. 24. This is because the material world has nothing positive to offer the enslaved pneuma in

However, full appreciation of Gadamer's claim, that we lack control over what "words of the tradition" come to us, and Kuhn's claim, that knowledge is not cumulatively progressing towards an absolute, requires acknowledgment of not only how experience is completely and exhaustively an experience and understanding re-presented by the individual intellect to itself always and already within the horizon of possibility enabled by a lifeworld. It requires, in addition, acknowledgment of *how* that very experience and understanding re-presentation by the individual intellect to itself is both a making manifest and a concealing/suppression. For any notion of knowledge as a greater or lesser approximation to the way things truly are is the consequence only of habit and mutual agreement among persons for the sake of some (commonly) shared agenda, and not because our knowledge is "correct" and progressively increasing. All *"knowledge" that is concerned with actuality conceals far more than it makes accessible.* Just as this is one of the fundamental aporiai of the human condition, it is the one aporia that is most frequently overlooked.

Only with the discussion of the role of paradigms as sociological constructs has it become possible to witness the shallowness of the belief that the way we take things to actually be is both correct and progressively increasing. Having acquired an understanding of sociological paradigms

---

the human soul (*ibid.*, 11). Where a positive doctrine of virtue emphasizes the cultivation of qualities and character traits with respect to goals (teloi) in the world (*ibid.*, 26), such a notion of praxis is absent in Gnosticism. Employing Heidegger's language of "inauthentic" and "authentic" existence, i.e., of Dasein's confrontation with the alternative of losing itself in the possibilities presented to the self by the "public they-world" or appropriating for one's self one's ownmost possibilities, Jonas indicates that for the Gnostics the world offered exclusively inauthenticity where authenticity was a possibility only of something to be anticipated in the next "world," the exclusively spiritual world of light beyond this world of darkness (*ibid.*, 28).

At stake here, of course, is the question of the role of the material world for a people of the spirit. Gnosticism and Marcionism were united in their rejection of any positive relationship between the "highest" deity and this world of darkness. The consequence was not simply an "anti-semitic" rejection to the creator God of the Jewish scriptures (see W.H.C. Frend, *The Rise of Christianity*, p. 196, 216), nor was it simply the rejection of any notion of "goodness" about the world of the senses, it was equally a rejection of any positive action (any real notion of virtue) in the world of sense by the true Gnostic. The only appropriate "action" was activity in the spirit, and even that was necessary only for the psychoi not the pneumatikoi (*ibid.*, 30) though only the latter reached the pleroma. The psychoi only could achieve the "region of the middle" (*ibid.*, 30).

Not only is this discussion understandable solely from the perspective of the tension between our spiritual nature and sense perception, but it portrays precisely the issues at stake with one's absolutizing the "alternatives" as an ontological dualism instead of approaching spirit and world as a "tension" related by dialectical interaction.

(meaning that humans create a social model for reality), one can observe over and over again in the course of Western science, for example, the crumbling of one paradigm (e.g., the Ptolemaic, the Copernican, the Newtonian, the Einsteinian, and now the open-endedness of the post-Einsteinian models of the universe) as it is supplanted by another. Thomas Kuhn reminds us, however, that this is not because each subsequent paradigm was more correct than the one before.[22] No one paradigm can be exhaustive of human experience.[23] Each paradigm has been embraced because it accounted for not merely more than any of its opponents, but in addition the new paradigm facilitated the fulfillment of both pragmatic personal and social agendas. What initially appears to be a linear progression of improved knowledge over former understandings of the universe only collapses into chaos as we move into the post-Einsteinian universe where nothing is fixed and everything is relative.[24] If the scientist's universe no longer offers immediate pragmatic gain to society in general, there is no question that it fulfills the role of establishing the pragmatic agenda for the practitioners of a particular scientific discipline. Kuhn reminds us that a primary role of a scientific paradigm is to establish the research agenda for a scientific community.[25]

Nevertheless, despite what physicists and historians of science are telling us about the instability and non-cumulative character of our knowledge,

---

[22] See Kuhn, *Structure of Scientific Revolutions*, p. 75-76.
[23] See Kuhn, *Structure of Scientific Revolutions*, pp. 75-6.
[24] See the famous debate between Albert Einstein, et al., "Can Quantum-Mechanical Description of Physical Reality be Considered Complete?" in *The Physical Review*, 47, second series (April-June 1935), 777-780, and Neils Bohr, "Can Quantum-Mechanical Description of Physical Reality be Considered Complete?" in *The Physical Review*, 48, second series (July-December 1935), 696-702. At issue here is the importance of Heisenberg's "uncertainty principles" in physics. Einstein, et. al., argue that there must be a stable order to the universe about which we are gaining improved knowledge, i.e., quantum-mechanics is not completely understood with Heisenberg's "uncertainty principles." Bohr argued, to the contrary, that there is no stable order to the universe. Hence, Heisenberg's "uncertainty principles" represent the completeness of quantum-mechanics.
[25] See Kuhn's discussion of "puzzle-solving" in "normal science" in "The Nature of Normal Science," *The Structure of Scientific Revolutions*, pp. 23-34, and "Normal Science as Puzzle-solving" in *ibid.*, pp. 35-42. He writes, p. 38: "The scientific enterprise as a whole does from time to time prove useful, open up new territory, display order, and test long-accepted belief. Nevertheless, *the individual* engaged on a normal research problem *is almost never doing any one of these things*. Once engaged, his (sic) motivation is of a rather different sort. What then challenges him (sic) is the conviction that, if only he is skillful enough, he will succeed in solving a puzzle that no one before has solved or solved so well." (emphasis in original)

our common-sense and intuitive notions of the way "things are" has us living in a Newtonian universe although that paradigm has long since lost its ontological status in physics. In other words, our common-sense and intuitive notions of the world rest upon a concealing and suppression of the way "reality" truly is in order for us to pursue individual and common cultural agendas.

The true complexity of this dynamic of making manifest and concealing must be left to later in the text. Here the apparently counter-intuitive judgments by Gadamer, that we have no control over what "words of the tradition" come to us, and by Kuhn, that our knowledge is simply not progressively commulative, indicate that we need to be very suspicious of the notion that we are gaining ever better insight into reality.[26] Our knowledge is always and already a presentation by the intellect to the intellect consisting of the experience and understanding of the intellect. Our knowledge is rendered all the more problematic by the recognition that it depends upon (not that it is, or one day will be, able to eliminate) concealing as it names what it knows. Our situation of "thrownness,"[27] of coming to find ourselves as always and already "placed" in the world at a time not of our own choosing, of thereby having no control over which tradition and what texts constitute that tradition, of having limited understanding because of the parameters of historical accident, prejudices, and lenses that shape our experience in the intellect, all this serves as the context for Gadamer's claim that the interpreter has no control over what "words of tradition" reach her/him.

---

[26] The natural sciences are, themselves, caught in the predicament that "more" knowledge is really "less." A.R. Peacocke in *Creation and the World of Science: The Bampton Lectures, 1978* (Oxford: Clarendon Press, 1979) quotes V. Weisskopf, p. 64: "'Our knowledge is an island in the infinite ocean of the unknown.'" But Peacocke immediately stresses that our situation is not one in which it is just a matter of time until the island becomes a continent and then a universe as the unknown becomes clarified: "If the world were a closed system we would expect an ultimate convergence in our knowledge as it accumulates, but nothing like this seems [Kuhn denies its possibility] to be happening. Our awareness of our ignorance grows in parallel with, indeed faster than, the growth in our knowledge" (*ibid.*, pp. 64-5).

[27] This notion of "thrownness" (*Geworfenheit*) comes from Heidegger. He writes in *Being and Time*, pp. 173-174: "... even in the most indifferent and inoffensive everydayness the Being of Dasein [= human being] can burst forth as a naked 'that it is and has to be' [als nacktes 'Das es ist und zu sein hat']. The pure 'that it is' shows itself, but the 'whence' and the 'whither' remain in darkness ... This characteristic of Dasein's Being this 'that it is' is veiled in its 'whence' and 'whither', yet disclosed in itself all the more unveiledly; we call it the '*thrownness*' of this entity into its 'there;' indeed, it is thrown in such a way that, as Being-in-the-world, it is the 'there'. The expression 'thrownness' is meant to suggest the *facticity of its being delivered over*." (emphasis in original)

We must surrender the very notion of progressive or cumulative knowledge either about our present experience or about the tradition.

Since there is no understanding that can escape historical accident, prejudice, and lenses, then any notion of absolute knowledge towards which we might be headed as a species or as "Intellect" is indefensible and both logically and pragmatically absurd and distorting. It constitutes a speculative leap out of the human situation that is justified only on the basis of wish and fantasy. The price that the human pays for such a speculative leap, as suggested above, is tremendous. For ultimately, such a leap, and belief in it, sacrifices the only tool we have for adjudicating the adequacy of our understanding (critical reflection) by seducing us away from sensitivity to the aporetic components permeating experience and understanding, by concealing from us the role of the intellect in all experience, and by costing us the dignity and worth of our individual experience by relativizing it over against an "absolute Intellect."

We must be as concerned, then, about which "words of tradition" reach us as we are concerned about how carefully we hear them. Nevertheless, we may never forget that those words (texts) that do reach us suppress and conceal words, meanings, and understanding that do *not* reach us.

It is, hopefully, obvious that cultivation of our sensitivity for what is concealed, marginalized, and suppressed, given the conditions of human experience, understanding, and knowing, serves as the vehicle for retrieving lost perspectives and voices in a tradition that has all too often taken "truth" as some form of "correctness" as its exclusive standard of worth. Though, all too often one must observe that those, who are concealed, marginalized, and suppressed, have understood themselves to be defenders of the truth over against a dominant cultural or community paradigm. The present project's articulating of the fundamental aporiai at the core of the human not only fully recognizes the problem of the concealed, marginalized, and suppressed, but offers some strategies for retrieval, as well. Above all, metaphorical tension and narrative application (praxis) can be taken as two preeminent strategies avoiding absolute truth claims by everyone.

Dialogue and Application: Speaking

Theology is not, however, simply listening. Theology is equally a speaking. Hans-Georg Gadamer reminds us, as well, that "[e]ven the most genuine and solid tradition does not persist by nature because of the inertia of what once existed. It needs to be affirmed, embraced, cultivated."[28] All understanding is an affirmation, embracing, and cultivation of an inherited tradition. Traditions never die, they go underground in consciousness to shape future generations subliminally. They can resurface, at least in part, whenever a retrieval of those lost possibilities proves beneficial to a new context of understanding. The only question involved with respect to the affirmation, embracing, and cultivation of an inherited tradition is: what level of consciousness will the affirmation, etc., occur? There is no total transparency to a tradition because of the role of both paradox and the finite limits to the breadth of understanding. There is to a certain extent a choice, however, about how much light can be shed upon the tradition and our contemporary context as an aid in understanding.

If speaking at some level is constitutive of the human condition, then the speaking at stake in theology is a deliberate speaking out - attempting to clarify the aporiai shaping its speaking while always sensitive to the concealing and suppression concomitant with it. Theology, then, is a dialogue with the pre-textual (what Paul Ricoeur calls mimesis$_1$[29] or the symbolic, "pre-figured" level of representations in which we always and already find ourselves) and texts (what Ricoeur calls mimesis$_2$ or the "con-figured" of narratives). The end result of this dialogue is either a non-critical appropriation or a critical clarity about our individual and communal assumptions and contexts in order to inform our speaking and actions (what Ricoeur calls mimesis$_3$ or "re-figured" application).

The task of theology as speaking is precisely that of critically reflective application, praxis, and action. All understanding leads to application, but theology has the responsibility to be critically reflective about both the conditions for, and the content of, action. Gadamer teaches us that understanding and interpretation always involve application.[30] Hence, dialogue with our tradition and application to our contemporary experience are inseparable components of theology, which accounts for why philosophical theology is not only indistinguishable from ethics, but also for why theology as speaking is more than mere morality.[31] What must be stressed is that the metaphor of

---

[28] Gadamer, *Truth and Method*, p. 250.
[29] See Ricoeur's "Chapter 3: 'Time and Narrative: Threefold Mimesis'" in *Time and Narrative*, vol. I, pp. 52-87.
[30] See Gadamer, "The Hermeneutic Problem of Application" in *Truth and Method*, pp. 274-278. The issue of the role of praxis in hermeneutics constitutes the debate between Gadamer and Jürgen Habermas. See Chapter 1, n. 121.
[31] Since the Enlightenment, however, religion has been defined almost exclusively as morality with a resulting loss of appreciation for the aporetic. As the Schleiermacher of *On Religion* well understood with his dialectical structure of religion, which places reli-

theology as speaking is not meant to imply that theology simply engages in abstract pronouncements. What is meant here by speaking is praxis. Speaking is to be taken in the sense that it includes both the head and the heart, or the understanding and the will, which inform one's actions.

The condition for this dialogue between the pre-textual, the textual, and human praxis is the tension that exists between our new experience as

---

gion prior to "knowing" and "doing," this concern for morality has meant cutting the tap root of religion for the sake of proper conduct. Action, or the application of understanding, is rooted completely in paradox. To focus on action, or the visible, without an appreciation of paradox in the human condition is to turn religion into simply a doing of one's duty, and to neglect the spiritual nature of the human condition.

Perhaps nowhere is this focus on religion and morality so clear as it is reflected in the character Cleanthes in Hume's *Dialogues Concerning Natural Religion*. Cleanthes says: "Religion, however corrupted, is still better than no religion at all. The doctrine of a future state is so strong and necessary a security to morals that we never ought to abandon or neglect it ... The proper office of religion is to regulate the hearts of men, humanize their conduct, infuse the spirit of temperance, order, and obedience ... " (*ibid.*, p. 82). Although Philo, Cleanthes opponent in the dialogues, quickly rebukes such an argument in defense of religion because it rests upon superstitious belief in an afterlife beyond our experience and reason now (see *ibid.*, p. 83), because such a religion in no way motivates the vulgar in need of such moral correction (see *ibid.*, p. 84), and, finally, because it tends to encourage selfishness and self-centeredness rather than true charity and benevolence (*ibid.*, p. 84), there is no question that morality remains among popular piety a primary motivator of religious practice.

Kant argues that a religion within the limits of reason alone is concerned with morality, but he emphasizes that this is not a religion focussed on actions "apparent to the senses." Immanuel Kant, *Religion within the Limits of Reason Alone*, p. 16. Rather, religion is concerned with the moral predisposition "antecedent of every act apparent to the senses" (p. 16).

The point to be stressed here is that Kant distinguishes the appearance of morality from morality in itself analogous to his distinguishing between appearance and the thing-in-itself of sense perception. True religion for Kant is concerned with an inward disposition that is manifest in one's actions, but not to be defined in terms of external action. Hence, Enlightenment religion is itself only superficially grasped when taken to be concerned with judgments concerning empirical behavior. Nevertheless, this understanding of religion by Kant has three limitations:

1) It cannot account for the origin of evil in society, central to his understanding of humanity as "by nature evil" (see *ibid.*, p. 27).

2) Nor can it account for the transformation of the individual by means of a desire for a change of predisposition (see *ibid.*, p. 46). (I am indebted for these two insights with respect to Kant to Harald Schützeichel, "Kants Auffassung vom Ursprung des Bösen," pp. 29-38.)

3) It emphasizes principle or predisposition (the universal) over action (the particular) when in fact both are equally constitutive for an adequate understanding of the human condition.

human beings in the world and our inherited metaphors, symbols, and narratives from out of our particular tradition which have sought to articulate the human condition before us. This tension marks out the historical conditions of theology. Were our situation simply one of repetition of inherited archetypes,[32] then history would be denied and there would be no dialogue between the pre-textual, the textual, and human praxis. Dialogue requires tension or incommensurability. Repetition of archetypes eliminates tension and incommensurability. But our understanding of experience acknowledges the tension that exists between inherited texts and contemporary experience.[33]

---

[32] No theologian wrestled more deeply with the notion of "repetition" than did Kierkegaard, for Kierkegaard valued the archetypal, the eternal and universal, above all particularity. He realized that our particularity prevents us from full participation in the eternal, and this contradiction fueled his understanding of religion which embraces the contradiction in faith that the resolution will occur in the life to come. See Kierkegaard, *Repetition: An Essay in Experimental Psychology*, trans. by Walter Lowrie (New York: Harper Torchbooks, 1964).

Perhaps there's no more clear indication of the influence of Kierkegaard on Heidegger than Heidegger's attempt to re-think repetition in *Being and Time*. But Heidegger shows that repetition is mis-understood from the "ground" up if it is only focussed on actuality as did Kierkegaard. Repetition in the existential sense, which is the only sense we can experience and understand, has to do with the "re-covery" of possibilities not mere actualities. Hence, repetition places us in history and does not call us out of history to the archetypal. Rather, the possibilities of the past are always and already there "ahead" of us, because they are not merely "behind" but are constantly capable of being projected by us into our future. It is because possibilities are concealed that they can be forgotten, but in resolution they can be retrieved as we consciously throw them ahead of ourselves. The desire for authentic selfhood, according to Heidegger, arises out of the encounter with our radical individualization, whereby we realize that we alone can and must live our possibilities; no one else can live them for us. If not before, an awakening from the siren call of the public "they" world, seeking to shape the individual for its collective possibilities to awareness of individualization, can occur when one recognizes that no one else can die for the self. Then one grasps that one's living towards death is not a futile negation of finitude but precisely that limit that forces us to confront her/himself as an individual inseparable from, and in tension with, the possibilities enabled by her/his concrete situation shared with Others. For the notion of "repetition," see Heidegger, *Being and Time*, 388f. For the notion of Being-towards-death and individualization, see the treatment of anxiety, *ibid.*, p. 232, and the discussion of Being-towards-death in *ibid.*, sections 48-53. To be sure, it is not merely death that individualizes possibilities. Birth and our "historicality," i.e., the thrownness into a particular temporal horizon of possibilities making for our individualized situation, is equally important in this respect as is our death. See *ibid.*, pp. 425-426 and 442-443.

[33] Heidegger develops an entirely different notion of "repetition" over against the notion of the repetition of archetypes. Rather, for Heidegger repetition means the retrieval not of actual archetypes but of concealed possibilities. See *Being and Time*, pp. 388, 437-438, 442-444. He discusses Nietzsche's three kinds of historiology, "the monumental, the

Every inherited formulation even at best is inadequate to our unique and unrepeatable experience. In order to speak the meaning of our experience we must engage in not mere repetition but correction, further clarification, and even at times rejection of the inherited texts of our tradition. However, recognition of this dialogical situation reminds us that the adequate understanding of the meaning of our own new experience requires the cultivation and preservation of even that which we reject out of our tradition. Given the dynamic of revealing and concealing at the core of the human condition, we cannot afford to destroy or lose any part of the tradition, because it may be that which we most need or it may shed light in terms of its figurative, if not literal, meaning on understanding in the future. Above all, the relationship to the tradition is dialogical not mere repetition. To the extent that it is dialogical it is historical.

In short, we have no ultimate control over the tradition out of which we are required to speak, or over the accidents which constitute our unique personal and corporate experience (in Gadamer's sense, over the accidents that determine which texts we encounter). That we have the Western tradition, and within that Western tradition a particular sub-tradition (e.g., an ethnic, gender, class, or religious tradition) as the horizon of our struggle for understanding is as much a matter of arbitrary thrownness as is our control over what texts of our tradition will reach us. The starting point of gaining personal and corporate ownership of a tradition, and of understanding at all, is to embrace the arbitrariness and along with it the concealment and suppression that is our context of experience, reflection, and action. This is what makes theology a speaking. Theology is more than listening, it is appropriation and application. That task is most informed when it rests upon an understanding of all of the paradoxical dynamics in play in the human condition. Only then can theology make a valuable contribution to liberation.

Dialogue and Application: Humility

Theology is not only listening and speaking, but above all else theology commences and ends in humility. We are recipients far more than we are

---

antiquarian, and the critical," suggesting that "... these three possibilities must be united factically and concretely in any historiology which is authentic ...

As historical, Dasein is possible only by reason of its temporality, and temporality temporalizes itself in the ecstatico-horizontal unity of its raptures. Dasein exists authentically as futural in resolutely disclosing a possibility which it has chosen. Coming back resolutely to itself, it is, by repetition, open for the 'monumental' possibilities of human existence" (*ibid.*, p. 448).

speakers/actors. Awareness of the depth and breadth of that which is given as well as that which is withheld permits one to appreciate our debt to the acting and suffering of others. Here we are again in the middle of the theological challenge of living out of and reflecting upon paradox. For the human condition is constituted out of a tension of incompleteness and incommensurability, and yet it demands a rigor of understanding.

Theology commences with astonishment as a consequence of listening. Its content must always be grounded in humility as it continually seeks to speak and act. Theology's passion is born out of the drive to understand a world of joy and tragedy, hope and despair, peace and injustice, advantage and oppression and to understand a tradition of clarity and contradiction, wonder and terror, sustenance and destruction. Theology's contribution is the preparing of individuals and communities to play an informed and responsible role on life's journey. That contribution must occur prior to any discussion of "salvation."

Theology as the "Fusion of Horizons"

The reader will have noticed a correlation implied in this description of the task of theology. The correlation implied here is that between our contemporary world of experience and our inherited tradition. It has been argued by theologians as apparently diverse as Paul Tillich, Schubert Ogden, and David Tracy[34] that theology is concerned with the correlating, or matching up, of past and present understandings of the human condition in relation to some kind of transcendent ultimacy. Chapter 4 below addresses in detail this discussion of the "method of correlation" in theology. I find Hans-Georg Gadamer's notion of the "fusion of horizons"[35] to be more appropriate than the notion of "correlation" for grasping the situation of the theologian.

---

[34] See Tillich, *Systematic Theology*, vol. I, pp. 13-28; 59-66; Schubert Ogden, "What is Theology?," *The Journal of Religion*, 52/1 (January 1972), pp. 23-24, Thesis 2: "... theology presupposes as a condition of its possibility the correlation of the Christian witness of faith and human existence, both poles of which alike have a variable as well as a constant aspect;" and David Tracy, *Blessed Rage for Order*, pp. 43-46, the first two thesis of Chapter 3 entitled "A Revisionist Model for Contemporary Theology" in which he maintains in Thesis 1: "The Two Principal Sources for Theology are Christian Texts and Common Human Experience and Language" and in Thesis 2: "The Theological Task will Involve a Critical Correlation of the Results of the Investigations of the Two Sources of Theology."

[35] For Gadamer's discussion of the "fusion of horizons," see "The Principle of Effective-History" in *Truth and Method*, pp. 267-274, particularly 269-273.

Correlation suggests an exogenous relationship between the past and the present, as if my inquiry in the present was one exercise, that I then match up with what I know in terms of an objective historical analysis of the past. It presupposes a historicist understanding of history, focussed on what is supposed to have actually occurred or been said in the past, without an appreciation for the impossibility of fulfilling such an agenda. History is not a record of what actually happened, or even of what is textually preserved of what was actually said or actually reported to have happened. It is impossible for us to reconstruct what actually happened or what actually was said, for actuality is always tied to possibility. The range of possibilities, that enabled the actuality available to us in the historicist's factual account of history, are no longer accessible. Those possibilities are no more accessible to a historical reconstruction in any complete sense than are the possibilities of this present moment. Many if not most of the range of possibilities in this moment are not consciously reflected. Yet the actuality of this moment is intimately connected with, and shaped by, those possibilities. Focussing only upon actuality at any point in time is to focus only on surfaces and to neglect the richness of life as an ongoing dynamic of possibility and actuality which is for the most part pre-reflective. How much more impoverished is a historicist's reconstruction of the past based exclusively on what actually occurred?

Gadamer's notion of the fusion of horizons articulates the relationship between our inheritance and our present as constituted out of an internal tension rather than the relationship being an external encounter with objects, events, and teachings in the past. It rests upon an appreciation of the historicality of experience with all of the dynamics of pre-reflective prejudices or presuppositions that are always and already in play as we engage our heritage. The task is not one of juxtaposition of the present and the past but of illuminating the intimate connectedness between the present and the past.

It is an illusion to believe that we encounter our individual or cultural past as a mere object somehow standing-over-against us. We are always and already pre-shaped by our individual and cultural heritage (in a manner discussed by Gadamer, though borrowed from Heidegger, as a "fore-structure of understanding"[36]).

---

[36] See Gadamer, "The Elevation of the Historicality of Understanding to the Status of Hermeneutical Principle" in *Truth and Method*, pp. 235-374, where Gadamer develops the notion of "*Wirkungsgeschichte*" or "effective history." For Heidegger's analysis of the fore-structure of understanding as a "fore-having," "fore-sight," and "for-conception," see *Being and Time*, pp. 191-195.

The most ready and obvious example of our already being pre-shaped by our individual and cultural heritage is, of course, our use of language. We tend to believe that we are sovereign over our language, and believe we have shaped it for the purpose of articulating our unique experiences. Notwithstanding, it is an illusion to believe that language is some kind of mere neutral tool that we pick up and lay down at will. To the contrary, our language pre-shapes and in-forms our cognitive, affective, and objective experience so pervasively that we are unconscious of its functioning. Such a pre-shaping or fore-understanding is in play not merely with our use of language. All that we preconsciously and consciously bring along from our individual and cultural heritage into the present situation is subject to this same dynamic of concealment and making transparent. It requires our understanding and responsible vigilance lest we be warped by what is destructive of our situation.

It is theology's task to recognize and own this contradictory character of experience and understanding. We are never sovereign over ourselves or over our tradition. Our most critical analysis and grasp of our present situation illuminates and conceals; selects and suppresses. With respect to our individual and cultural past the opaqueness increases exponentially because of the dynamic of actuality and possibility.

Theology must be seen as an open-ended dialogue that listens to the wisdom and folly of the tradition as it attempts to speak in wisdom and folly in the present. To define theology otherwise is to turn theology into a heteronomous discipline having forgotten that it commences and ends in faith. The only difference between theological positions is how rigorously do they listen and speak/act. In other words, how disclosive are they of what is essential for, or necessary to, experience and understanding? How sensitive are they to what is concealed in experience? How adequately do they enable responsible action in the world?

Chapter 3
After Heidegger and Derrida

To the extent that the present project seeks a retrieval of a notion of νοῦς (Geist), positively appropriates binary tensions as central to our understanding of the human condition, and seeks to hold humanity accountable to the profound aporiai of the human condition without sacrificing either critical reflection or responsible action, it appears to ignore the work of Martin Heidegger and Jacques Derrida. Heidegger's *Being and Time* is an attempt to overcome that traditional understanding of the human condition which focussed (at least since Descartes) on consciousness as self-encapsulated, autonomous, and only problematically related to the world. Derrida, on the other hand, critiques the motif permeating Western thought that rests upon binary oppositions (mind vs. body, good vs. evil, light vs darkness, presence vs. absence) and the privileging of the first term over the second.

Though not to be uncritically appropriated, neither Heidegger nor Derrida may be ignored. One will not find in the present project, nor can there be, a return to a transcendental consciousness "over against the world." Nor does the recognition of the role of binary oppositions, and even giving experiential and epistemological (but not ontological) priority of one term over the other, mean that one is less sensitive to the de-centering "différance" and aporetic interrelatedness of the binary terms, or that one denies the ubiquitous role of mediation in all understanding and communication. Nevertheless, one must not succumb to either ontological passivity, that merely waits on the history of Being, or to linguistic obscurity that isolates the individual in an endless play of subjective word meanings.

Heidegger: On the Meaning of Being

Being and Time is an analysis of the human condition in the world. Yet, it is not simply an anthropological project focussed exclusively on the human. The primary question of *Being and Time* is not "what is the meaning of human experience?," but rather "what is the meaning of Being?" The human occupies a privileged place with respect to this question "only" to the extent that human beings alone can ask the question of the meaning of Being.[1]

---

[1] See Heidegger, *Being and Time*, p. 32, 35.

Heidegger uses the term "Dasein" rather than "Mensch" (human being) in his analysis to express the intimate relationship between human being and Being. "Dasein" literally means "there-being," i.e., the term evokes the sense of the human as the "place" or "space" (Where? There!) in which Being is questioned and named. This particularity and individualization of "place" is central to Heidegger's analysis of the Being question. Being is not a mere abstraction for Heidegger. Being is the Being of the world, and, to the extent that Being is the focus of attention, the Being of the world is always related to the particular possibilities of a Dasein in community.

Already with his choice of terminology we find a modification of traditional understanding, for "Dasein" in the philosophical tradition prior to Heidegger means simply "object" - any object and not merely human beings. Heidegger, however, assiduously avoids the term "object" in his analysis preferring instead to use terminology for both the human and for the "things" of the world that evokes a relationship to Being. Hence, Heidegger employs the term "das Seiende" for the "things" or "objects" of the world. "Seiend" is the present participle of the verb "to be," and literally means "being" (equivalent to the English alternative for "thing"). For Heidegger "das Seiende" refers to being (thing) in general, but expresses, as well, the intimate relationship between all things and Being. "Das Seiende" in general (beings, things) is distinguished from "das Seiende" that is "Dasein" (human being) in that "das Seiende" in general simply "is" and cannot ask the question of the meaning of "Being." Dasein, on the other hand, is precisely that "Seiende" which can ask about Being, and, therefore, it is "more" than mere "Seiend" (or more than a mere thing). It is the place where Being "comes face to face with itself and is named."[2]

If *Being and Time* were a mere anthropological analysis, its fundamental manner of questioning with respect to Being would have been "what is the meaning of human being?" What is the meaning of my life as an individual human being? This is the level at which the question of the meaning of Being is usually asked: Who am I? Where did I come from? Why am I here? What is expected of me? What should I expect of myself? Where am I going? What is to become of me? Since at least the Apollo cultus at Delphi in ancient Greece, the Western tradition has placed the charge "γνῶθι

---

[2] Martin Heidegger, *An Introduction to Metaphysics*, trans. by Ralph Manheim (Garden City, N.Y.: Doubleday, 1961), p. 171. In *What is Called Thinking?*, trans. by Glenn J. Gray (New York: Harper and Row, Pub., 1972), pp. 61-2, Heidegger speaks of humans as "the *persona*" or "the mask" of Being.

σαυτόν" ("Know Thyself") at the center of wisdom. Heidegger contends that an adequate questioning of the "self" (Dasein) takes one far deeper than the "I" as a separate, unique individual with merely a particular personal history.

All of the usual questions with respect to the human condition overlook the ubiquitous, silent presence of "is" (the verb "to be"/Being) permeating all questioning and experience - in short, they overlook the question "how" "*is*" Dasein? Sometimes this "is" is even explicit in such questions as: "who *am* I?;" "why *am* I here?" which include the first person singular of the verb "to be" (Being). But even with such questions as "What will/should I do today?," the verb "to be" is implicitly included, for "were" I not "to be," I could not do anything much less hold myself (or be held) responsible for what I do today or any day. But, in addition, I cannot do anything much less hold myself (or be held) responsible for what I do if there "were" not a "world" in which I engage, and am engaged by, things. Our usual way of asking about who we are as human beings completely overlooks (even conceals) the presence and role of "Being" even when the verb "to be" is explicitly included in the formulation of the question. What "is" the meaning of this Being that is either explicitly or implicitly announced and presupposed by everything? What is this "Being" that is obviously not a thing among other things? What is this "Being," then, that is not itself mere "becoming," the coming into and passing out of Being, but is precisely what is presupposed by all becoming? This is the question of *Being and Time*.

On the Copula

The Being question has dominated Western thought since the pre-Socratics. Parmenides was the first to ponder the ubiquitous presence of the copula ("is") and its relationship to thinking. What is new with Heidegger's analysis is the consequence of the historical place of his questioning. One had drawn a line through the tradition with Descartes which resulted in the focus of reflection upon the autonomous, critically reflecting self over against a world of extension. Particularly with respect to the copula, Descartes constitutes a dividing line between Anselm (and the tradition up to him) and Kant.[3]

---

[3] Descartes employs Anselm's "ontological" argument in Meditation V, but he supplements it with a "causal" argument with two presuppositions: a) the first is "something cannot come into existence from nothing" (This is a principle as old as Xenophanes, see Johann Buhle, *Geschichte der neuern Philosophie* (Göttingen: Johann Georg Rosenbusch's Witwe, 1800), p. 44: "Der Satz: Aus Nichts wird Nichts; zeigte sich im Bewußtsein als unbezweifelbar ... Aus Nichts wird Nichts; also, schloß Xenophanes, ist

Anselm's ontological argument[4] employs the copula for "proving" the existence of God. Kant dismissed Anselm's argument with the aphorism "existence is not a predicate."[5]

Anselm did not call his "argument for God" a "proof," but rather, he spoke of a "meditation" on the meaning of God.[6] For Anselm the copula is

---

alles Vorhandene ewig." Aristotle in *Physics* 203a23-25 refers to Anaxagoras (Frg. 17) with respect to this aphorism.). According to Descartes, the cause must have as much "formal reality" (independent of its being perceived) as its effect. b) As a second presupposition Descartes maintains a distinction between "formal cause," which has exactly the same degree or amount of reality and perfection as its effect, and "eminent cause," which contains more reality and perfection than its effect. See, Descartes, *Meditations on First Philosophy*, pp. 27-28. Descartes concludes: "... if the objective reality of one of my ideas is such that I am certain that the same reality is not formally or eminently in me, and that therefore I myself cannot be the cause of the idea, then it necessarily follows that I am not alone in the world, and that something else - the cause of this idea - also exists" (*ibid.*, p. 28). The idea God, Descartes concludes, which includes the notions of infinite, independent substance, intelligent and powerful in the highest degree, and my creator, cannot be formally or eminently in me. Since something cannot come from nothing, God must be a formal reality independent of myself that is the formal cause of my idea of God. See, *ibid.*, p. 30-33.

4   Kant is the first to call Anselm's argument an "ontological argument." See *Kritik der reinen Vernunft*, p. 566.
5   Kant, *Kritik der reinen Vernunft*, p. 572-3. Of course, Kant's famous aphorism here conceals a shift in meaning with respect to the term "being" from a "quantitative" to a "locative" meaning. In short, rather than the being of something referring to the degree of participation (quantitative meaning) in being, being as existence is concerned with location in space. A being exists to the extent that it has a spatial location. For this reason, existence is no predicate increasing or decreasing the idea, since all existence is concerned with is spatial actualization. See John Nijenhuis, "'Ens' Described as 'Being or Existent'" in *American Catholic Philosophical Quarterly*, 68/1 (Winter 1994): 1-14.
6   Charles Hartshorne and George L. Goodwin have recently revived interest in Anselm's ontological argument by observing that there are, in fact, two arguments given by Anselm in the Proslogion. Hartshorne prefers the second argument that is dependent upon the relationship between "possibility" and "actuality." In short, if it can be shown that God "possibly" exists, then God must actually exist, for actuality precedes possibility. In other words, for there to be possibilities there must be a prior actuality. See George L. Goodwin, *The Ontological Argument of Charles Hartshorne* (Missoula, Montana: Scholars Press, 1978), pp. 26-28, 40-41, 64, 67, 74, where p. 123 is representative: "Possibilities must have actual antecedents; the metaphysical locus of possibility is in actuality ... Every actuality is a concrete instance of abstract individual existence (the existence of socially ordered sequences of actualities). Possibility, therefore, is a feature of existing individuals" (*ibid.*, p. 120). The entire argument from Hartshorne/Goodwin depends upon there being "something" that is unconditionally and existentially necessary. See *ibid.*, pp. 18, 21, 27-28, 44-45. "... 'something exists' is not even conceivably falsifiable, and so is a *necessary* truth. 'Something exists' denies that nothing exists, and 'nothing exists' is a literally inconceivable and nonsensical proposition. In order to illustrate or verify 'nothing exists,' one thing at least would have to

synonymous with "reality." If something can be demonstrated "to be" than it

exist, namely, the being which is illustrating or verifying. And if one thing exists, something exists" (*ibid.*, pp. 20-21). This is precisely the same logic for the priority of Being over Non-being employed by Tillich in *The Courage to Be*, pp. 34, 40, 176-177. It is equally fallacious, as Descartes well understood, for the indubitability of my present existence does not constitute an unconditional necessary truth. Rather, my present existence is only a conditionally necessary truth - I don't have to be, nor does "something" have to be.

On the surface the argument that actuality precedes possibility/potentiality sounds illuminating, but it rests upon presuppositions of an empirical world view quite foreign to Anselm's world. The difference between Anselm and Hartshorne/Goodwin is more radical than a difference in the understanding of the nature of "perfection." See *ibid.*, p. 51. An essential difference is rooted in their working out of two different notions of necessity. Yet, the primary difference hinges upon Anselm giving possibility priority over actuality where Hartshorne/Goodwin give actuality priority over possibility.

For Anselm and Greek thought in general (see, for example, Aristotle, *Posterior Analytics*, 71b8 - 12, 74b5f; *On the Heavens*, 279b22; *Metaphysics*, 1015a34; and *Nicomachean Ethics*,1139a7-10), necessity is concerned with that which cannot be other than what it is (i.e., mental experience); in contrast to the world of perception that is precisely not necessary, since it can be other than the way it appears to be. For Hartshorne/Goodwin necessary truths "... are distinguished by their complete lack of conflict with any conceivable state of affairs [i.e., spatial reality]. 'All triangles have exactly three sides' ... conflicts with no genuine possibility. Statements of this sort are *completely nonrestrictive* of existential possibilities" (*ibid.*, p. 14). In short, for Anselm necessity is defined with respect to the intellect; for Hartshorne/Goodwin necessity is defined with respect to the empirical world.

The issue of the relationship between possibility and actuality takes one back at least to Plato and Aristotle, if not before. It is precisely Aristotle's critique of Plato that Plato failed to see that actual knowledge precedes potential knowledge. (For an insightful analysis of the relationship between Aristotelian and Process thought, see Fetz, "Aristotelian and Whiteheadian Conceptions of Actuality: I" in *Process Studies* 19/1 (1990), pp. 15-27, and "Aristotelian und Whiteheadian Conceptions of Actuality: II" in *ibid.* 19/3 (1990), pp. 145-156.) Aristotle's critique is that Plato fails to explain how "ideas" are related to other "universals" as well as to "particulars," and he ridicules Plato for merely having created a mirror or duplicate world in the intellect. See Aristotle's *Metaphysics*, 987b, 992a, 1031a-b, 1033b-1034a, 1039a-b,1049b,1050b, 1059a, where 1079b is representative: "... all other things cannot come from the Forms in any of the usual senses of 'from'. And to say that they are patterns and the other things share in them is to use empty words and poetical metaphors." Aristotle attempted to explain the relationship between universals and between universals and particulars on the basis of πρὸς ἕν (reference to one) equivocity. See Joseph Owens, *The Doctrine of Being in the Aristotelian 'Metaphysics': A Study in the Greek Background of Mediaeval Thought*, 2nd Edition (Toronto, Canada: Pontifical Institute of Mediaeval Studies, 1963). Aristotle's presupposition is, precisely, that actuality precedes potentiality. Although the post-Cartesian world finds this presupposition enlightening, it cannot be overlooked that this is a presupposition. Plato's presupposition is precisely the opposite: potentiality precedes actuality. If the First Principle of the whole is thought as possibility, then possibility precedes all actuality, and universals, to the extent that they are indefinable, are never

exists in reality. This presents the post-Cartesian world with a difficulty, because we have a different notion of reality from that of Anselm's world. In the post-Cartesian world, something is said to be "real" when it can be demonstrated to be independent and "outside" of human consciousness. For example, the tree outside my office window is said to be "real," because it can be shown, at least pragmatically, to be independent of my (or anyone's) perception of it. The same cannot be said of a unicorn. A unicorn is dependent upon human consciousness for it "to be." The notion of unicorn is merely "internal" to consciousness. Hence, unicorns are not real.

With respect to Anselm's meditation on the existence of God, when the post-Cartesian world hears "real," then, it thinks immediately: "independent and 'outside' of human consciousness." However, when Anselm builds his meditation on the theme "that than which nothing greater can exist," he proceeds from a view of reality that is a coherent unity of spirit as both ground and cause of all that is. In short, what is real is not "outside" but, rather, "deeper within." Our intellect ($νοῦς$/Geist) has access to that which endures - the eternal ideas or "thoughts of God." These universals are shared with God, and the meditation on God is meant to demonstrate our dependence upon a God to whom we are intimately related rather than upon God as a reality entirely separate from us.[7]

---

entirely actual, they are presupposed possibilities. It was precisely such unknowing that resulted in the radical skepticism of Middle Platonism. See, for example, A.H. Armstrong, "Pagan and Christian Traditionalism in the First Three Centuries A.D." in *Studia Patristica* XV (1984), pp. 414-431.

There is no way to logically adjudicate between these positions. That one must agree with David Hume's pragmatic argument for the priority of matter over mind only confirms that a) the issue can only be adjudicated pragmatically, not logically, and b) that, therefore, for us to adequately understand our experience, we must presuppose both as illuminating of an aporetic tension central to that experience. See, Hume, *Dialogues Concerning Natural Religion*, Part VII, p. 47: "[Philo:] Judging by our limited and imperfect experience, generation has some privileges above reason: for we see every day the latter arise from the former, never the former from the latter." See, as well, Part VIII, pp. 52-3: "[Philo:] In all instances which we have ever seen, thought has no influence upon matter except where that matter is so conjoined with it as to have an equal reciprocal influence upon it."

[7] This is entirely contrary to Karl Barth, who is an anomaly in the tradition precisely in this respect. For Barth humanity is entirely separated from God and have even established itself autonomously over against God. See Emanuel Hirsch, "Das Ringen der idealistischen Denker um eine neue, die Aufklärung überwindende Gestalt der philosophischen Ausagen über Gott. Dargestellt nach seinem Verhältnis zur reformatorischen Gotteserkenntnis" in *Christliche Wahrheit und neuzeitliches Denken. Zu Emanuel Hirschs Leben und Werk*, ed. by Hans Martin Müller (Tübingen: Katzmann Verlag, 1984), pp. 203-4. The history of Hirsch's political relationship to Barth as well as of Hirsch's anti-Semitism is told by Heinrich Assel in "'Barth ist entlassen ...' Emanuel

"That than which nothing greater can exist" does not take us "outward" from an idea to a thing, but, rather, "inward" from ideas to that upon which all ideas are dependent although it itself is not an idea: the Being that is God. Here the copula is thought as Being in contrast to *both* the internal system of unchanging ideas and the external world of objects (the world of becoming). Here Being is seen as the necessary condition of possibility for all reality (internal being and external becoming).

The copula is thought in this context as a binding by which all reality (internal and external) is united.[8] It is not an accidental quality (predicate) among other qualities. Nor is it employed with respect to an apodictic claim for the independent existence of some "thing," e.g., as if in the assertion "the tree is" the "is" was equivalent with "exists independent of some observer." To the contrary, the dual meaning of the copula ("being" and "to be") provided a vehicle for thinking the relationship between all beings both accessible to the senses and inaccessible to the senses. Yet, it is "higher" than either the sensible or non-sensible, hence, better articulated as "greater," than either the internal world of the individual and the external world of sense perception, since it is not another being among beings nor is it limited to the individual. Again, it is the condition of possibility for all that "is" as it unites all that is unchanging with all that is becoming.

Kant's famous critique of Anselm's ontological argument is that "being" is not a predicate. In other words, to say that something (for example, a tree) "is" does not add anything to our idea "tree." In other words, to say that an idea "is" does not indicate anything "greater" than our original idea. Note, however, that Kant takes the copula to mean "existence" independent and outside of our consciousness of it. Kant used the example of the idea of "100 Thaler." The idea of 100 Thaler is neither increased nor decreased in any way by our having 100 Thaler in the hand.[9] Predicates,

---

Hirschs Rolle im Fall Barth und seine Briefe an Wilhelm Stapel." *Zeitschrift für Theologie und Kirche* 91, no. 4 (1994): 445-75.

[8] One etymological meaning for the term "religion" is "binding."

[9] This very example discredits the significance of the "mere" idea of 100 Thaler, since everyone "knows" that 100 Thaler in the hand is more valuable than a mere idea. What is already concealed here is that one cannot begin to understand the particular 100 Thaler in the hand without the idea/the universal. The pragmatic world has not only forgotten its dependence on νοῦς/Geist. Far more significantly and with far reaching consequences, the pragmatic world discredits νοῦς/Geist as mere copy and of value, when at all, only to the "experts" who have learned how to manipulate the pragmatic world on the basis of their "abstract" descriptions.

however, tell us something additional (that would "increase" our understanding of something existing independent of the self) about the subject. Predicates qualify an object in some way, or give us information that we need, in order to understand which object is under discussion. For example, saying that "the tree is a coniferous and a Douglas Fir from the Pacific Northwest qualifies which tree is meant, and enriches what the term "tree" can mean - where "merely" saying that the tree "is" in no way affects our idea of tree. Furthermore, to say that something "is" does not mean that that something exists in a world (either a material or a world of non-material ideas) independent of our thought. Our idea of a unicorn "is" or our idea of a mermaid "is" although unicorns and mermaids are merely creations of human fantasy, that is, they do not exist "outside" of the human mind that thinks of them. The copula does not help us distinguish between what is fantasy and what exists. In short, the copula (the "is") is not of any value for giving us information about actual subjects; it in no way is "greater" than the original idea - it is *not* a predicate.

Yet this entire discussion of the copula by Kant is possible only because he is in a different world from Anselm and the tradition prior to him. Descartes stands between them. Kant is in a polarized world defined by an autonomous subject over against the world. Anselm is in a unified world defined by the "eternal thoughts" of God and rooted in God's Being. Given the historical distance (not in the sense of quantity of time, but in the sense of the historical transformation of the meaning of "world") between ourselves and Anselm, we can no more return to Anselm's world than we can to Kant's. We must, however, acknowledge the different presuppositions that radically distinguish the Anselmian and the Kantian worlds.

The Kantian world we all know, since it is fundamentally the world of Newton which still shapes our "naive" everyday lives. This is the world of individual subjects who are engaged in private and corporate calculation, prediction, manipulation and control of a world independent of their status as observers. In this world objects are "absolute" and the observer is "accidental." We can substitute anyone for the observer, the observations would remain the same. Although this is a fundamental canon of our present reality, we know that it is an illusion. It is not only that Heisenberg's uncertainty principles pull the rug out from under any claim of neutral observation by demonstrating that the subject influences the object,[10] but we all

---

[10] The classic formulation of the issues here can be found in the two articles Albert Einstein, et.al. "Can Quantum-Mechanical Description of Physical Reality Be Considered Complete?" and Niels Bohr, "Can Quantum-Mechanical Description of Physical Reality Be Considered Complete?"

know that the accumulated experience of the observer determines radically what s/he is able to experience of an object. This difference in the midst of sameness is nowhere more clearly seen than in the difference of perception because of a difference in experience between a mother and a father when relating to their child.

It is simply not the case that the "world" was/is always absolutely there, and it is waiting for the individual with adequate understanding to come along to grasp it. No, the world is radically dependent upon both individual and corporate human understanding that transforms the world under observation. For example, we can no longer return to a pre-automobile world any more than we can return to a pre-agrarian world. Both individual and corporate human understanding and expectation have made automobiles and agriculture constituent of what it means to be in the world. It is not as if the automobile was merely "out there" waiting for the informed observer. The way from fire to the internal combustion engine is by no means either logically or objectively necessary. To the extent that we acknowledge a level of non-necessity along that way, we contradict the naive claim that the "world" is merely "out there" waiting to be discovered. The fundamental canon of the Enlightenment world of Kant and Newton, that the world is "absolute" and the observer is "accidental," has failed to grasp not merely the statistical character of the "laws of nature" (erroneously taken by Newton to be the *absolute* foundation of physical reality), but it fails to grasp the historical character of human understanding that has made us victims[11] as much as beneficiaries of a humanly transformed world.

---

[11] Rousseau is the name normally associated with the judgment that culture is destructive, because it undermines and destroys humanity's natural virtues. Culture begins with the emergence of technology, agriculture, and private property, and simultaneously there emerges inequality, bondage, tyranny, and slavery. Culture is a "second dimension" imposed on top of nature (the "first dimension") by humanity, and, therefore, humanity can only improve its lot by returning to the first dimension. Karl Barth reports that Rousseau commenced a life, at least from appearances, for all intents and purposes like that of a monk. He stopped wearing the normal clothes of his station in life exchanging them for a simple cloth robe. Perhaps the central symbolic act, indicating his desire to escape the corruptions of culture, was his ceasing to use his pocket watch (long before "Easy Rider"). See Barth's discussion of Rousseau in *Die protestantische Theologie im 19. Jahrhundert*, p. 159, as well as pp. 158-170, particularly p. 164: "... der Freudenschrei des Menschen, der jenseits all des Menschenwerkes, an das dieses Jahrhundert mit so ganz besonderer Inbrunst glaubte, sich selber entdeckt hat, und der Notschrei desselben Menschen, der, dem Menschenwerk nicht entrinnen können und auch nicht entrinnen wollend, auch mit sich selber nichts anzufangen weiß, gerade weil er jenseits alles Menschenwerks nun doch nur sich selber entdeckt hat. Das war die neue Héloïse. Und das war der ganze Rousseau."

Anselm's world is even more foreign to us than Kant's or Newton's - as foreign as Kant's and Newton's world has become to us. If the characteristic moment of Kant's and Newton's world is the separation or alienation of the "self" (and by Kant the very alienation of the self from itself[12]) as observer from a neutral objective world "out there," Anselm's world is rooted in a fundamental unity that connects everything (world, the human community, and God). This unified world is rooted in an "objectivity" as certain for its proponents as was the world of Newton and Kant for its defenders (though no less problematic for us). What unites all that is, then, by definition is "greater" than any part of the whole.

Anselm's reality is an eternal spiritual unity which is the ground and cause of the transient material world and the eternal world of universals. Here the copula (the "is") has an entirely different function from the role it plays in a world inhabited by alienated, interchangeable subjects situated in a world of absolute objects. In Anselm's world the "is" has nothing to do with establishing an "object" as independent of any possible "subject." Here the copula does not prove the *existence* of a reality *separated from* the thinking subject; rather, the copula confirms the rootedness of all reality in a common unity greater than any universal, individual, or thing. Rather than failing to increase our knowledge about the particularities of an "object" under consideration (as a meaningless predicate among other "real" predicates), the "is" here announces not merely the "eternal" or the universals, which are the same yesterday, today, and tomorrow, but that which both the material order and the invisible spiritual order presupposes. For Anselm (though no longer for contemporary thought) this dimension of universals as "the same yesterday, today, and tomorrow" was unequivocally absolute. The copula, however, is not itself a universal (not an idea or essence), it is "more universal"

Barth reports that Diderot, Rousseau's friend at the time, maintains that this thesis, regarding the corrupting role of culture (which was articulated by Rousseau in his prize winning essay for the Academy of Dijon and made him instantaneously famous in 1750), actually was a suggestion from Diderot. See Barth, *ibid.*, p. 158. Of course, the thesis is not original with either individual. The founder of the so-called Cynics (the name comes from the lifestyle which he led with his followers, i.e., that of a dog - in Greek the adjective κυνικός means "like a dog"), Diogenes (4th century B.C.E.) had already not only articulated the thesis that culture was the enemy, for it destructively perverts humanity's natural condition. Furthermore, he not only taught this but lived by it. See, Wilhelm Capelle, *Die griechische Philosophie II. Von den Sokratikern bis zur hellenistischen Philosophie* (Berlin: Walter de Gruyter & Co., 1971), pp. 10-14.

[12] See Kant, *Critique of Pure Reason*, B152-153.

than all universals, since all that "is" is rooted in this "reality." "That than which nothing greater can exist" is the unity of Being, and that unity is foremost spiritual (potential and eternal) not material (actual and transient), because it is presupposed by both. The spiritual is what truly "is" in contrast to the material which is *only transient* and "farthest removed" (on the basis of the analogy of copy to original) from the real reality of Being.

In our post-Cartesian world, then, we approach Anselm's meditation with a set of presuppositions that completely transform the meaning of his "argument." We are looking for an argument that proves God's existence external and independent of any observer. Anselm offers an argument that is meant to prove our connectedness to "eternal" Being in a spiritual (nonmaterial) dimension of experience.

Heidegger: Being as "World"

If Heidegger is by no means the first to ask the question of the meaning of the copula, he does ask the question at a new point in the tradition and with irreversible consequences. The Heidegger of *Being and Time* draws Being *down from the spiritual heavens into the concrete world of becoming*. The classical world presupposed there to be a fundamental dualism between being and becoming and between subject and world. Although Heidegger's project is not incompatible with an immaterial, spiritual moment of the human condition, Heidegger's analysis demonstrates the irrefutable rootedness of Dasein (human being) in the world of concrete actuality, where its real possibilities are actualized. Being is rethought as Being in the world; Being is here the Being of "world" and not of some etherized dimension of the unchanging over against a material world of Becoming.

Being in *Being and Time* means possibility.[13] "Possibility" is neither an object over against Dasein nor is it a material substance uniting all that

---

[13] I am indebted to conversations with Joseph Kockelmann for this conclusion. As early as 1922 in a programmatic essay accompanying his application for teaching positions in Göttingen and Marburg Heidegger focussed on Being in terms of facticity, possibility and movement on the basis of his reading of Aristotle. A key passage uniting these themes is the following from "Phänomenologische Interpretation zu Aristoteles (Anzeige der hermeneutischen Situation)" in *Dilthey-Jahrbuch*, 6 (1989 <1922>), pp. 244-6: "Die angezeigten konstitutiven Charaktere der Faktizität, das Sorgen, die Verfallenstendenz, das Wie des den Tod Habens, scheinen aber dem zuwider zu laufen, was als Grundeigentümlichkeit des faktischen Lebens herausgehoben wurde, daß es ein Seiendes ist, dem es in der Weise seiner Zeitigung auf sein eigenes Sein ankommt. Aber das scheint nur so. In allem Sichausdemweggehen ist das Leben faktisch für es selbst da; im 'Wegvonihm' stellt es sich gerade und jagt hinter dem Aufgehen in welthafter Besorgnis

"is." Being (or "isness") is not taken by Heidegger in any sense to mean "substance." Possibility can only occur as a process. It always involves a totality of self and world. Therefore, Being for Heidegger is not a "thing" or a collection of things, but, rather, an "event" intimately constitutive of Dasein and its entire world.

Dasein's possibilities situate Dasein in a process involving the projection and interpretation of possibilities. Approaching the human condition from this perspective of possibility, rather than mere actuality, Being is understood to be "time" by Heidegger. Possibility involves Dasein in a unitary horizon where the future is primary, the past provides the nourishment, and the present is the point of ambiguous actualization (ambiguous, because actualization always involves concealment and suppression of possibilities that were not, and cannot be, actualized). When the focus of the discussion of time is placed on possibility, then the present loses its dominance as the orientation point for the understanding of time. Time is no longer taken to be a linear sequence of present moments, but rather is the encompassing whole of possibility in the world. The copula is here understood as time and no longer as timeless Being as it was for Anselm and the tradition prior to the Cartesian turn to the subject.

---

her. Das 'Aufgehen in' hat wie jede Bewegtheit der faktischen Zeitlichkeit in ihm selbst eine mehr oder minder ausdrückliche und uneingestandene Rücksicht auf das, wovor es flieht. Das Wovor seines Fliehens ist aber das Leben selbst als die faktische Möglichkeit, ausdrücklich ergriffen zu werden, als Gegenstand der Bekümmerung ... Dieses im faktischen Leben für es selbst zugängliche Sein seiner selbst sei bezeichnet als Existenz. Das faktische Leben ist als existenzbekümmertes umwegig. Die Möglichkeit der Existenz ist immer die der konkreten Faktizität als ein Wie der Zeitigung dieser in ihrer Zeitlichkeit. Was die Existenz zeigt, kann direkt und allgemein überhaupt nicht gefragt werden. Sie wird an ihr selbst nur einsichtig im Vollzug des Fraglichmachens der Faktizität, in der jeweiligen konkreten Destruktion der Faktizität auf ihre Bewegtheitsmotive, Richtungen und willentlichen Verfügbarkeiten.

Die Gegenbewegung gegen die Verfallenstendenz darf nicht ausgelegt werden als Weltflucht ... Die Bekümmerung des faktischen Lebens um seine Existenz ist ihrerseits nicht ein Sichzergrübeln in egozentrischer Reflexion (emphasis added), sie ist, was sie ist, nur als Gegenbewegung gegen die Verfallenstendenz des Lebens, das heißt, sie ist gerade in der je konkreten Umgangs- und Besorgensbewegtheit ... Der Vollzug der Einsicht und des einsichtnehmenden Ansprechens des Lebens in Hinsicht auf seine existenzielle Möglichkeit hat den Charakter der bekümmerten Auslegung des Lebens auf seinen Seinssinn. Faktizität und Existenz besagen nicht dasselbe, und der faktische Seinscharakter des Lebens ist nicht bestimmt von der Existenz, diese ist nur eine Möglichkeit, die sich zeitigt in dem Sein des Lebens, das als faktisches bezeichnet ist. Das besagt aber: In der Faktizität zentriert die mögliche radikale Seinsproblematik des Lebens." For Heidegger's dependence upon Aristotle for his interpretation of Being as "movement," see *ibid.*, pp. 260-261, 266-267.

Possibility, however, is never possibility in some never-never land. Rather, possibility is always and already possibility in a concrete world.[14] It is for this reason that Heidegger can say that only Dasein "has a world.[15]" No other being has a relationship to possibility the way that Dasein does. Yet possibilities are never completely transparent to Dasein. Possibilities are always and already "there" constitutive of Dasein, but they are equally *concealed and only partially comprehended* by Dasein.

The question of Being is by no means, then, simply the question about human beings, although, to be sure, every questioning of the meaning of who human beings "are" includes Being, includes *our* possibilities, as part of the question. Even where the focus of Heidegger's analysis is the question of personal "authenticity" and "decision," the concern is not with any particular agenda, nor is there a defense of a particular hierarchy of virtues. The focus of "authenticity" is exclusively limited to Dasein's relationship to Being, i.e., possibilities.

> That Being which is an *issue* for this entity [Dasein] in its very Being, is in each case mine ... Because Dasein has *in each case mineness* ..., one must always use a *personal* pronoun when one addresses it. 'I am,' 'you are.'
>
> Furthermore, in each case Dasein is mine to be in one way or another. Dasein has always made some sort of decision as to the way in which it is in each case mine ... That entity which in its Being has this very Being as an issue, comports itself towards its Being as its ownmost possibility. In each case Dasein *is* its possibility, and it 'has' this possibility, but not just as a property ... And because Dasein is in each case essentially its own possibility, it *can*, in its very Being, 'choose' itself and win itself; it can also lose itself and never win itself; or only 'seem' to do so. But only in so far as it is essentially something which can be *authentic* - that is, something of its own - can it have lost itself and not yet won itself. As modes of Being, *authenticity* and *inauthenticity* (these expressions have been chosen terminologically in a strict sense) are both grounded in the fact that any Dasein whatsoever is characterized by mineness. But the inauthenticity of Dasein does not signify any 'less' Being or any 'lower' degree of Being. Rather it is the case that even in its fullest concretion Dasein can be characterized by inauthenticity ...[16]

In other words, the question for Heidegger turns our attention to the most fundamental conditions of possibility for our being *in the world*. Precisely

---

[14] Theodore Kisiel has demonstrated the centrality of the theme "world" in Heidegger's thought as early as the "Kriegsnotsemester 1919," i.e., eight years before the publication of *Being and Time*. See Theodore Kisiel, "Das Entstehen des Begriffsfeldes 'Faktizität' im Frühwerk Heideggers" and "Das Kriegsnotsemester 1919: Heideggers Durchbruch zur hermeneutischen Phänomenologie."

[15] See Heidegger, *Being and Time*, p. 417; Heidegger, *Kant and the Problem of Metaphysics*, p. 15; and Martin Heidegger, *Discourse On Thinking*, trans. by John M. Anderson and E. Hans Freund (New York: Harper Torchbooks, 1966), p. 83.

[16] Heidegger, *Being and Time*, p. 68.

because the conditions of possibility for our being in the world include the ability to think or forget Being, i.e., include a most radical form of freedom, there cannot be an absolute valuing of "authenticity" over "inauthenticity."[17] We cannot be without being inauthentic. Inauthenticity is a constitutive condition of our ability to choose our own authentic possibilities.

Given the centrality of world as the horizon of any and all possibilities in Heidegger's work, it would be simply erroneous to suggest that he ignores the place and role of the Other in his analysis of Dasein. Dasein, he suggests, is only as "Dasein-with" and as "Being-with." Dasein-with is Heidegger's way of talking about human relatedness to Others within a shared horizon of possibility. Rather than speaking of this relatedness as one of "concern" (appropriate to entities taken to be mere things), Dasein-with is spoken of as "solicitude" involving the notions of "considerateness" and "forebearance." Concretely, this solicitude can be played out in the form of "leaping in" for, or "leaping ahead" of, the Other, that is, as a taking away of the Other's possibility or as an enabling of her/his possibilities.[18]

However, Heidegger's analysis is clearly not concerned with ethical implications. The focus for Heidegger is exclusively upon Dasein's relationship to Being understood in terms of "possibility" in the world not in terms of "actuality" (science and theology are concerned with the actual). In other words, the analysis is not engaged at the level of what one must actually do in any particular situation, but, rather, on the prior conditions of possibility that enable one to actually do something. The ethical, on the other hand, is concerned with actual circumstances or what Heidegger calls the "ontic." The "ontic" has to do with treating "die Seienden" (persons and things as Others and as objects) as merely "over against" the self as "subject." The Being question, on the other hand, is concerned with the ontological conditions of possibility for a world to be experienced ontically. In other words, the ontological "level" of analysis is prior to (or "deeper than") the mere ontic "level" of our experiencing of persons and things. For this reason (though by no means is this a sufficient reason), Heidegger can engage in a radical analysis of Dasein and completely fail ethically. Furthermore, he can

---

[17] Heidegger did not claim that "inauthentic" existence was an "inferior" form of Being (see *Being and Time.*, p. 68). Time and again he indicated that authenticity is dependent upon inauthenticity, i.e., there is no such thing as "pure" authenticity. See, *ibid.*, 168, 312, 345-346, and 422.

[18] See Section 26 of Heidegger, *Being and Time*, "The Dasein-with of Others and Everyday Being-with," pp. 153-167.

sweep aside any critique of his personal ethical decisions and actions by insisting that such a discussion completely fails to grasp the more important question of the meaning of Being.[19]

Heidegger dismisses any philosophical questioning that does not acknowledge the primary (in the sense of prior) question of the meaning of Being. He writes off most of the Western tradition and all of the usual disciplines (including theology) as having "forgotten" the Being question (das Sein) to focus on "beings" (das Seiende). Even God, the "highest being" of

---

[19] The literature on Heidegger's political and ethical failures is growing daily as the result of the not uncontroversial claims made by Victor Farias in *Heidegger and Nazism* (Philadelphia: Temple University Press, 1989 (1987)). The following citations make no claim to be exhaustive (there is not enough space here). Rather, they are meant to be representative.

One can gain an orientation to the issues in English in Thomas Sheehan, "Heidegger and the Nazis," *New York Review of Books*, 16 June 1988, pp. 38-47, and in the contributions by Davidson, Gadamer, Habermas, Derrida, Blanchot, Lacoue-Labarthe, and Lévinas in *Critical Inquiry*, 15/2 (Winter 1989). Heidegger's defensive interview with *Der Spiegel* from September 23, 1966, published only on the condition that it appear after Heidegger's death *Der Spiegel*, 23 (1976), is to be found in English translation in Thomas Sheehan's *Heidegger: The Man and the Thinker* (Chicago: Precedent Publishing, Inc., 1981), pp. 45-67, along with other significant essays on Heidegger's personal life and relationship to Nazism. Heidegger's rector lecture (1933) and his reflections about his relationship to the Nazis while rector of the university in Freiburg written for the French de-Nazification committee in 1945 entitled "Das Rektorate 1933/34 Tatsachen und Gedanken" can both be found in English translation from Karsten Harries in *Review of Metaphysics*, 38 (March, 1985), pp. 467-502. To date the most extensive study in German on the topic is Hugo Ott, *Martin Heidegger: Unterwegs zu seiner Biographie*. See, as well, Ott's "Martin Heidegger als Rektor der Universität Freiburg i.Br. 1933/34," *Zeitschrift des Breisgau-Geschichtsvereins*, 102 (1983), 121-136, and *ibid.*, 103 (1984), pp. 107-130, "Martin Heidegger und die Universität Freiburg nach 1945," *Historisches Jahrbuch*, 105/1 (1985), pp. 95-128, and "Martin Heidegger und der Nationalsozialismus" in *Heidegger und die praktische Philosophie*, ed. by Annemarie Gethmann-Siefert und Otto Pöggeler (Frankfurt a. M.: Suhrkamp Taschenbuch Wissenschaft, 1988), 64-77. See, as well, Guido Schneeberger, *Nachlese zu Heidegger: Dokumente zu seinem Leben und Denken* (Bern, 1962); Karl Löwith, *Mein Leben in Deutschland vor und nach 1933* (Stuttgart: Metzler, 1986); and Herbert Marcuse's correspondence with Heidegger concerning the Holocaust in *Pflasterstrand* (Frankfurt), 109/4 (May 17, 1985), pp. 42-44.

On the question of an internal or organic relationship between Heidegger's philosophy and his personal political life, see Winfried Franzen, *Von der Existentialontologie zur Seinsgeschichte* (Meisenheim am Glan, 1975), part 3, pp. 63-101; the afterword to the second edition of Pöggeler's *Der Denkweg Martin Heideggers* (Pfullingen, 1983), pp. 319-355, and Nicolas Tertulian, "Heidegger - oder: die Bestätigung der Politik durch Seinsgeschichte. Ein Gang zu den Quellen. Was aus den Texten des Philosophen alles sprudelt" in *Frankfurter Rundschau*, 2. Februar, 1988.

theology, has been consistently understood to be a being (ein Seiende). Hence, Heidegger makes a clear distinction not only between his philosophical project and the rest of the tradition[20] but between "real" philosophy (i.e., his philosophy) and theology.[21]

Heidegger's discussion of Dasein as thrown Being-in-the-world, as a process of understanding that is a "projecting of possibilities" rooted in the present-at-hand and the ready-to-hand of things (and not rooted in an abstract, spiritual world of the unchanging), is necessary for overcoming the transcendental turn to the subject. But it is not sufficient for understanding who Dasein is in the world. It is simply not the case that the human is thrown into, and lives out of, a chaotic sea of possibility (be they mental or physical possibilities). Our possibilities are always and already ordered within the coherent structuring of mental life that itself is rooted in a world of both mental (= νοῦς, Geist, spirit) and material possibilities. In short, Heidegger's "existentiale" are no substitute for Kant's "categories" even when we cannot merely return to Kant's abstract dualism.[22] Heidegger's

---

[20] See Heidegger's analysis of Nietzsche, who represents for Heidegger the "end of the Western tradition of metaphysics," in *Nietzsche*, vol. 2 (Pfullingen: Verlag Günther Neske, 1961), p. 260: "Der folgende Versuch kann zureichend nur aus der Grunderfahrung von *Sein und Zeit* mitgedacht werden. Sie besteht in der ständig wachsenden, aber an einigen Stellen vielleicht auch sich klärenden Betroffenheit von dem einen Geschehnis, daß in der Geschichte des abendländlischen Denkens zwar von Anfang an das Sein des Seienden gedacht worden ist, daß jedoch die Wahrheit des Seins als Sein ungedacht bleibt und als mögliche Erfahrung dem Denken nicht nur verweigert ist, sondern daß das abendländische Denken als Metaphysik eigens, wenngleich nicht wissentlich, das Geschehnis dieser Verweigerung verhüllt." See, as well, *ibid.*, p. 352: "Das Sein bleibt in der Sicht von Begriffen, sogar im Scheinen des absoluten Begriffes durch die spekulative Dialektik - und bleibt dennoch *ungedacht*." (emphasis in original) Finally, see, *ibid.*, p. 353: "Inzwischen wurde ... deutlicher: Das Sein selbst west als die Unverborgenheit, in der das Seiende anwest. Die Unverborgenheit selbst jedoch bleibt als diese verborgen. An ihr selbst, der Unverborgenheit, bleibt im Bezug auf sie selbst die Unverborgenheit weg. *Es bleibt bei der Verborgenheit des Wesens der Unverborgenheit. Es bleibt bei der Verborgenheit des Seins als solchen. Das Sein selbst bleibt aus.*" (emphasis in original)

[21] See Martin Heidegger. "Phänomenologie und Theologie."

[22] See Biedermann, *Christliche Dogmatik*, 2nd ed., vol. 1, p. 148; and *ibid.*, p. 102: "Daß ... Kant das Object der metaphysischen Frage, den objectiven Grund der subjectiven Erscheinungswelt für ein bewusstseins-transcendentes, jedoch positiv zu postulirendes reines X für unser Bewusstsein erklärt, ist nur die Folge davon, dass Kant denselben, dem Grundsatze des reinen Realismus zuwider, einerseits zwar als ideell in der Erscheinungswelt mit gegeben anerkannt, andererseits aber doch zugleich dinglich jenseits der Erscheinungswelt sich vorstellt. Den Standort des Bewusstseins-subjectes hat Kant richtig fixirt; aber den seines Bewusstseins-objectes von vornherein dogmatistisch verrückt."

"existentiale" are not a substitute for, or a simple alternative to, the classic discussion of universals. It has been suggested that Heidegger's focus on the structuring of "existentiale" place his project very much in the trajectory of the Enlightenment.[23] Nevertheless, Dasein is no more a mere consciousness totally transparent to itself and "in" a world from which it is alienated than it is a mere set of material possibilities by which it is necessarily determined or in front of which it must passively wait.

Heidegger does not claim that Dasein's possibilities in the world are limited to material necessity. This is immediately clear with his linguistic turn in "Letter on Humanism."[24] Language is here called the "house of Being."[25] In "Logos (Heraklit, Fragment 50)"[26] Heidegger speaks of a concealing of Being in the very essence of language. He is concerned in this essay to make a case for thinking Logos itself as the Being-of beings,[27] though he acknowledges that, although the Greeks "lived" in this essence of language, they never "thought" Logos as the Being-of beings.[28] Nevertheless, Heidegger suggests that in this fragment[29] there was a lightning flash that thought Logos as the Being-of beings.[30] He acknowledges the function-

---

[23] See Frank Lilie, "Heideggers Forderung nach einer Destruktion der Tradition," in *Neue Zeitschrift für Systematische Theologie und Religionsphilosophie*, 34, no. 3 (1992): 322, 323.

[24] See Martin Heidegger, "Letter on Humanism" in William Barrett and Henry D. Aiken, *Philosophy in the Twentieth Century*, vol. 3 (New York: Harper & Row, 1971).

[25] See, Heidegger, "Letter on Humanism," p. 201: "Language is in its essence not utterance of an organism nor is it expression of an animal. Thus it is never thought of with exactness in its symbolical or semantic character. Language is the clearing-and-concealing advent of Being itself." See, in addition, *ibid.*, p. 205: "Man, however, is not only a living being, who besides other faculties possesses language. Language is rather the house of Being, wherein living, man ex-sists, while he (sic), guarding it, belongs to the truth of Being."

[26] Martin Heidegger, "Logos (Heraklit, Fragment 50)" in *Vorträge und Aufsätze* (Pfullingen: Verlag Günther Neske, 1959), p. 228.

[27] See Heidegger, "Logos (Heraklit, Fragment 50)", p. 227.

[28] See Heidegger, "Logos (Heraklit, Fragment 50)", p. 228.

[29] See Heidegger, "Logos (Heraklit, Fragment 50)", p. 207:
"οὐκ ἐμοῦ τοῦ Λόγου ἀκούσαντας
ὁμολογεῖν σοφόν ἐστιν Ἓν Πάντα."
Following his detailed analysis of the text, Heidegger gives the interpretive translation, pp. 225-6: "Nicht mich, den sterblichen Sprecher, hört an; aber seid horchsam der lesenden Lege; gehört ihr erst dieser, dann hört ihr damit eigentlich; solches Hören *ist*, insofern ein beisammen-vor-liegen-Lassen geschieht, dem das Gesamt, das versammelnde liegen-Lassen, die lesende Lege vorliegt; wenn ein liegen-Lassen geschieht des vor-liegen-Lassens, ereignet sich Geschickliches; denn das eigentlich Geschickliche, das Geschick allein, ist: das Einzig-Eine einend Alles."

[30] See Heidegger, "Logos (Heraklit, Fragment 50)", p. 229.

ing of a hermeneutical circle in this judgment in that we are able to see this lightning flash only if we ourselves have already begun to think the Being-of beings.[31] This way of thinking Being is difficult to accomplish, Heidegger claims, because Being has remained "forgotten" since Heraklites.[32] Being has remained forgotten in the Western tradition, he suggests, because the very notion of truth, dominating Western metaphysics and science, has been defined in terms of "representational thought" which distorts Being as it seeks to nail down what beings are.[33]

Surely, here it is clear that Heidegger's understanding of language and Logos is fundamentally concerned to pull language and Logos "down" into the world as part of the gathering and giving of the event of Being taken to be a dynamic process of possibility and actuality in the world. In this respect, Heidegger even refers to the discussion of Logos in §7 of *Being and Time* as discourse.[34] As laudable as Heidegger's project is, as a seeking to think Being in terms of the event of possibility in the world (particularly in light of the predominance of neo-Kantian transcendentalism of his historical context), λόγος in his discussion conceals far more than the gathering and giving of Being as possibility. Heidegger's discussion simply too facilely ignores the functioning of λόγος in its relation to νοῦς/Geist by writing off the entire tradition as "representational thinking."

What is true of Kant and the Neo-Kantians is not necessarily true of the entire tradition. Already in Plato there is a more radical thinking of Being that is not rooted in a superficial dualism between Being and Becoming, nor in a monism of possibility within the horizon of the present-at-hand and the ready-to-hand of world, but understands the "First Principle" or the Good (Being in the highest sense beyond essence) as the very condition of possibility for the unity of νοῦς/Geist as well as the world as an interrelated reality. Plato wrote in the *Sophist*:

> ... only one course is open to the philosopher who values knowledge and the rest above all else. He (sic) must refuse to accept from the champions of either of the one or of the many forms the doctrine that all reality is changeless, and he must turn a deaf ear to the other party who represent reality as everywhere changing. Like a child

---

[31] See Heidegger, "Logos (Heraklit, Fragment 50)", p. 229.
[32] See Heidegger, "Logos (Heraklit, Fragment 50)", p. 227.
[33] See Heidegger, "Logos (Heraklit, Fragment 50)", p. 227.
[34] See Heidegger, "Logos (Heraklit, Fragment 50)", p. 213: "Der λόγος bringt das Erscheinende, das ins Vorliegen hervor-Kommende, von ihm selbst her zum Scheinen, zum gelichteten Sichzeigen (vgl. Sein und Zeit §7 B)."

begging for 'both,' he must declare that reality or the sum of things is both at once - all that is unchangeable and all that is in change.[35]

Heidegger seems to acknowledge this in his ambiguous statements concerning spirit and spirituality with reference to Dasein in *Being and Time*. In order to avoid the trap of a subject-object split, Heidegger rejects any merely ontic description of human facticity (Dasein's thrown Being-in-the-world) that is formulated in terms of human "Being-in" the world as some kind of spiritual entity contained in a body.[36] Similarly, he rejects any notion of Dasein as an encapsulated "inside" from which one goes "outside" to the world.[37] Furthermore, he rejects any notion of there being some kind of spiritual substance, clearly in reference to Hegel, that is a synthesis of soul and body.[38] What characterizes Dasein above all is existence, which is neither rooted in any substance nor definable in terms of mere thingness, but is more radically understood as the dynamic process of actuality and possibility or revealing and concealing. Nevertheless, Heidegger can write: "... because Dasein is 'spiritual', *and only because of this*, it can be spatial in a way which remains essentially impossible for any extended corporeal thing."[39] Is this a recognition that "reality or the sum of things is both at once - all that is unchangeable and all that is in change"?[40]

---

[35] Plato, *Sophist*, 249c-d. The *Phaedo* has a passage indicating the non-absolute character of the human experience of λόγος or the so-called eternal order: "It is our duty to do one of two things either to ascertain the facts, whether by seeking instruction or by personal discovery, or, if this is impossible, to select the best and most dependable theory which human intelligence (ἀνθρωπίνων λόγων) can supply, and use it as a raft to ride the seas of life - that is, assuming that we cannot make our journey with greater confidence and security by the surer means of a divine revelation (λόγου θείου)." (85c-d)

[36] See Heidegger, *Being and Time*, pp. 73-4 and especially p. 82.

[37] See Heidegger, *Being and Time*, p. 89.

[38] See Heidegger, *Being and Time*, p. 153.

[39] See Heidegger, *Being and Time*, p. 419.

[40] Heidegger was aware (*Being and Time*, p. 446, n. xi) of the work of Eduard Spranger, "Zur Theorie des Verstehens und zur geisteswissenschaftlichen Psychologie" in *Festschrift Johannes Volkelt zum 70. Geburtstag* (München: C.H. Beck'sche Verlagsbuchhandlung Oskar Beck, 1918) wherein (p. 369) Spranger distinguished among an "epistemological subject," a "psychological subject," and a "spiritual subject." The spiritual subject unites the epistemological and psychological to account for culture. "Nennen wir das Subjekt, das dem reinen Sachzusammenhange der Erkenntnisobjekte entspricht, das *erkenntnistheoretische Subjekt*, und das andere Subjekt, das in alle Zufälligkeiten eines räumlich-zeitlich-individuell bedingten Erlebens hineingetaucht ist, kurz das Ich oder *das psychologisch-aktuelle Subjekt*, so ist *zwischen beiden ein drittes Subjekt* zu konstruieren, *das* zwar dem einzelnen Ich überlegen ist, aber doch *unter Bedingungen bestimmter Kulturverhältnisse steht und von der Ichperspektive nie ganz loskommt*. Wir nennen es *das geistige Subjekt. Im Gegensatz zum erkenntnistheoretischen Subjekt hat es einen historisch und geographisch wandelbaren Inhalt*. Aber dieser Inhalt ist doch nicht

Regardless what one concludes in this respect, one can identify as Heidegger's important contributions: a) the retrieval of the importance of "world" for the understanding of the human in the order of what is; b) the underscoring of the dynamic interrelationship of concealment and disclosure in the project of human understanding; and c) the re-focussing of attention on the question of time once one thinks Being as possibility and not as the unchanging over against the changing. If one can claim that Heidegger seeks to think the notion "world" without reduction to empiricism, this present project seeks to think the notion "νοῦς/Geist" in terms of an aporetic relationship between spirit and world without reduction to either an absolute a priori or an absolute a posteriori. At the same time, this project seeks to think possibility and "worldhood" as inclusive of νοῦς/Geist in a way that acknowledges a certain priority of the latter over materiality.

Derrida and Binary Thought

Any attempt to contemplate the human condition in terms of such binary tensions as νοῦς/Geist and materiality, and, particularly, any suggestion that one has a privileged position over the other, seems to completely ignore the work of Jacques Derrida. No one has drawn out the implications of Ferdinand de Saussure's linguistics with greater consistency than Derrida. Derrida demonstrates that Saussure's insight taken to its logical extreme, that language in its static or synchronic aspect is a system of oppositions with each part or linguistic unit having its place, and receiving its meaning, only within the horizon of the interactions of the sign system as a whole,[41] results in an endless word play where no term has a primary or "permanent" meaning.

Derrida engages Plato's reference to the *pharmakon* in the *Phaedrus* with its double meaning of "beneficent and maleficent." *Parmakon* indicates the "danger" of written language.[42] Writing is "dangerous" because it con-

---

nur für ein Ich da; er erschöpft sich auch niemals in den aktuell präsenten psychologischen Erlebnissen. Sondern er umfaßt Akte, die über das Einzel-ich hinausgreifen und in ihrem Sinn für mehrere (potentiell wohl auch für alle) Ichs zugänglich sind. *Die Art wie dieses geistige Subjekt in das individuelle Ich hineingeschlungen ist, bedeutet dann das große Problem, mit dem es das Verstehen zu tun hat.*" (emphasis added)

[41] See Saussure, *Course in General Linguistics*, p. 9, where Saussure distinguishes between "langage" as a social product and "langue" as "a self-contained whole and a principle of classification."

[42] See Jacques Derrida, "Plato's Pharmacy" in *Dissemination*, p. 70.

ceals and presupposes an ontological order that is an illusion. Plato speaks of writing (a "pharmakon") as "the going or leading astray."[43] Derrida adds:

> ... along with the account (*logos*) of the supplements ..., along with what comes above and beyond the One in the very movement through which it absents itself and becomes invisible, thus requiring that its place be supplied, along with differance and diacriticity, Socrates introduces or discovers the ever open possibility of the *kibdelon*, that which is falsified, adulterated, mendacious, deceptive, equivocal. Have a care, he says, lest I deceive you with a false reckoning of the interest (*kibdelon apodidous ton logon tou tokou*). *Kibdeleuma* is fraudulent merchandise.[44]

Quite in the spirit of Saussure, Derrida claims that

> Plato thinks of writing, and tries to comprehend it, to dominate it, on the basis of *opposition* as such. In order for these contrary values (good/evil, true/false, essence/appearance, inside/outside, etc.) to be in opposition, each of the terms must be simply *external* to the other, which means that one of these oppositions (the opposition between inside and outside) must already be accredited as the matrix of all possible opposition. And one of the elements of the system (or of the series) must also stand as the very possibility of systematicity or seriality in general.[45]

Derrida rejects this notion that one of the elements can serve as the possibility of systematicity in general. Such a claim is dependent upon a metaphysics external to the language system. Rather, Derrida sees language as entirely "metaphorical," but, since metaphor itself depends upon a "primary meaning" he prefers to speak of language as an endless "folding over." In "The Double Session" Derrida concludes: "Since everything becomes metaphorical, there is no longer any literal meaning and, hence, no longer any metaphor either ... If there is no such thing as a total or proper meaning, it is because the blank *folds over.*"[46]

Barbara Johnson's introduction to *Dissemination* offers the following interpretation that has become the standard for every discussion of binarity in Derrida:

> Western thought, says Derrida, has always been structured in terms of dichotomies or polarities: good vs. evil, being vs. nothingness, presence vs. absence, truth vs. error, identity vs difference, mind vs matter, man vs. woman, soul vs. body, life vs. death, nature vs. culture, speech vs. writing. These polar opposites do not, however, stand as independent and equal entities. The second term in each pair is considered the negative, corrupt, undesirable version of the first, a fall away from it.[47]

---

[43] Derrida, "Plato's Pharmacy," p. 71.
[44] Derrida, "Plato's Pharmacy," p. 83.
[45] See Derrida, "Plato's Pharmacy," p. 103.
[46] Derrida, "The Double Session" in *Dissemination*, p. 258.
[47] Derrida, *Dissemination*, p. viii. Philo of Alexandria identified 54 binary oppositions in *Quis rerum divinarum heres sit*, 207-214. See Paul Barth's comments on Philo's usage of binary opposition for his epistemology in "Die stoische Theodizee bei Philo," p. 33.

Johnson writes further, that Derrida

> ... attempts to show that the very possibility of opposing the two terms [speech vs. writing] on the basis of presence vs. absence or immediacy vs. representation is an illusion, since speech is *already* structured by difference and distance as much as writing is ... As soon as there is meaning, there is difference. Derrida's word for this lag inherent in any signifying act is *différance*, from the French verb *différer*, which means both "to differ" and "to defer" ... The illusion of the self-presence of meaning or of consciousness is thus produced by the repression of the differential structures from which they spring.[48]

Although one would want to question the implication that the Good or First Principle of Book VI of Plato's *Republic* is thought in terms of the binarity good vs. evil, there is no question that the First Principle for Plato, as the condition of possibility for all that is, can only be indirectly mediated through what is, since it itself is not an essence among other essences. It is another question entirely whether one then concludes that "what is" or the indirect mediator is "evil" in contrast to this Good.[49]

Nevertheless, one must agree with Derrida that deferment and différance characterize human experience, which is always and already mediated through a symbol system, and that written language compounds that deferment and différance by its distance from living speech. The dangerous tendency is for humans to absolutize their representational model constituting their "reality." Derrida reminds us that humans too readily overlook that the very capability that distinguishes them from other species (the complexity and coherence of the individual, yet always corporate, representation of reality) is also an Achilles heel. His project shakes one out of complacency and reminds one of the dangerous destruction of others, the environment, and the self that accompanies every absolutizing of a representational model.

On the other hand, the present project does not view binarity as either an evil or something to be avoided. If Derrida represents a form of Augustinian original sin (though without hope of salvation), this project is Coelestian to the extent that the ambiguity of the human condition is taken to be a virtue rather than a vice - as has proven to be the case too often in his-

---

[48] Derrida, *Dissemination*, p. ix. See, in addition, Kerry McKeever, "How to Avoid Speaking About God. Poststructuralist Philosophers and Biblical Hermeneutics" in *Literature and Theology: An Interdisciplinary Journal of Theory and Criticism*, 6/3 (1992), 233.

[49] Though this surely is the primary binarity informing martyriology and some forms of asceticism (e.g., anchoritic monasticism).

tory, a potentially dangerous virtue. Acknowledging an experiential (though not an ontological) priority of spirit over matter in no way diminishes the fact of mediation and deferment central to human experience. On the contrary, it enables a more adequate understanding of mediation and deferment. Human experience is not adequately elucidated when reduced to either a linguistic word play or a play of possibility of the present-at-hand or the ready-to-hand. These options can only lead to forms of linguistic obscurantism or ontological passivity.

Human experience in the world is representational, but it is equally pragmatically rooted in a concrete world of possibility and actuality. Furthermore, every representational construct presupposes at least ectypal (if not archetypal) universals as equally pragmatically necessary for our experience of order and meaning. Every reduction of experience to mere representation, mere empiricism, or mere linguisticality, while tempting, will always prove inadequate so long as it ignores the pragmatic dimensions of world and universals constitutive of human experience.

Derrida and Vulgar Skepticism

Ferdinand de Saussure distinguished between language and human speech by suggesting that the latter is "... both a social product of the faculty of speech and a collection of necessary conventions that have been adopted by a social body to permit individuals to exercise that faculty."[50] However, Saussure differentiates between "external linguistic phenomena" and "internal linguistics" to argue that internal linguistics, that is, the linguistic system as a system of signs without external reference, constitutes a discipline of focus entirely for itself.[51] This leads to a structuralist approach to language, for the meaning of the linguistic event is determined by the structural framework in which a sign is situated. Levi Strauß applied this insight to narrative units as a whole seeking to analyze the meaning of the narrative in terms of its "internal" structural relationships.

When the notion of "internal linguistics" is combined with Descartes' observation in the second Meditation that perception is merely a series of mental judgments, one can easily understand how the notion of language as a mere folding over onto itself becomes intriguing to Derrida.[52]

---

[50] Saussure, *General Course in Linguistics*, p. 9.
[51] See Saussure, *General Course in Linguistics*, pp. 9, 20, 22-23, 80, 112-113, 107, 114-115, 133
[52] See Jacques Derrida, "The Double Session" in *Dissemination*, pp. 270-271.

It is clearly Nietzsche who provides Derrida with the connection between the dissimulation of all perception and the mere conventional meaning (for there is no literal meaning) of words. Nietzsche articulates a classic form of what Hume in his *Dialogues Concerning Natural Religion* calls "vulgar skepticism."[53] Nietzsche combines vulgar skepticism with contempt for humanity in his essay "On Truth and Lies in a Nonmoral Sense.[54]

> ... when it is all other (sic) [over] with the human intellect, nothing will have happened. For this intellect has no additional mission which would lead it beyond human life ...
> ... [T]he intellect ... was allotted to these most unfortunate, delicate, and ephemeral beings merely as a device for detaining them a minute within existence.[55]

---

[53] Hume distinguishes between "vulgar" and "refined" skepticism. Vulgar skepticism ignores the pragmatic dimension of life, i.e., that we cannot not act. Vulgar skepticism maintains that we can doubt everything. In the *Dialogues* (see p. 5), Cleanthes challenges what he takes to be Philo's vulgar skepticism in the very first dialogue by suggesting that the vulgar skeptic is disarmed as soon as the conversation is over when the vulgar skeptic must act. As soon as one must act, one cannot maintain total skepticism. It turns out later in the *Dialogues* (see pp. 12 and 82) that Philo, in fact, defends what Hume labels "refined" skepticism which is a kind of "critical realism." Acknowledging that we cannot establish indubitable arguments, we nevertheless must employ critical reason to adjudicate the evidence as best we can.

[54] Friedrich Wilhelm Nietzsche, "On Truth and Lies in a Nonmoral Sense," in *Philosophy and Truth: Selections from Nietzsche's Notebooks of the Early 1870's*, trans. by Daniel Breazeale (Atlantic Highlands, N.J.: Humanities Press Inc., 1979), pp. 79-97. The publisher has made a consistent error (how would one know - if everything is dissimilitude?) in the heading used throughout the translation. Rather than reading "On Truth and Lies in a *Nonmoral* Sense," the heading reads "On Truth and Lies in a *Normal* Sense."

[55] Nietzsche locates the power of that intellect in memory, which makes humanity "historical" rather than merely "unhistorical" like other animals. He commences his work "Vom Nutzen und Nachteil der Historie" with an account of watching a herd of sheep on a hillside. An animal was once asked, "why don't you speak and tell of your happiness rather than only silently staring back?" The animal, Nietzsche suggests, would like to answer and say: "That's because I always immediately forget what I want to say" - but it had already forgotten this answer and, therefore, remained silent. See Nietzsche, "Vom Nutzen und Nachteil der Historie" in *Unzeitgemässe Betrachtungen*, zweites Stück, in volume 1 of *Werke* (Frankfurt a.M.: Ullstein, 1980), p. 211. Nevertheless, the "unhistorical" is equally essential for humanity's self-understanding, Nietzsche maintains: "Dies gerade ist der Satz, zu dessen Betrachtung der Leser eingeladen ist: *das Unhistorische und das Historische ist gleichermaßen für die Gesundheit eines einzelnen, eines Volkes und einer Kultur nötig*" (ibid., p. 214). Ignoring of the unhistorical is the source, if not cause, of a central illusion: "Diese historischen Menschen glauben, daß der Sinn des Daseins im Verlaufe seines *Prozesses* immer mehr ans Licht kommen werde, sie schauen nur deshalb rückwärts, um an der Betrachtung des bisherigen Prozesses die Gegenwart zu verstehen und die Zukunft heftiger begehren zu lernen; sie wissen gar nicht, wie unhistorisch sie trotz aller ihrer Historie denken und handeln, und wie auch ihre Beschäftigung mit der Geschichte nicht im Dienste der reinen Erkenntnis,

For without this addition they would have every reason to flee this existence as quickly as Lessing's son. The pride connected with knowing and sensing lies like a blinding fog over the eyes and senses of men (sic), thus deceiving them concerning the value of existence ...

As a means for the preserving of the individual, the intellect unfolds its principle powers in dissimulation, which is the means by which weaker, less robust individuals preserve themselves - since they have been denied the chance to wage the battle for existence with horns or with the sharp teeth of beasts of prey. This art of dissimulation reaches its peak in man. Deception, flattering, lying, deluding, talking behind the back, putting up a false front, living in borrowed splendor, wearing a mask, hiding behind convention, playing a role for others and for oneself - in short, a continuous fluttering around the *solitary* flame of vanity - is so much the rule and the law among men that there is almost nothing which is less comprehensible than how an honest and pure drive for truth could have arisen among them. They are deeply immersed in illusions and in dream images; their eyes merely glide over the surface of things and see "forms." Their senses nowhere lead to truth; on the contrary, they are content to receive stimuli and, as it were, to engage in a groping game on the backs of things.[56]

It is only the desire to make "peace" with others, i.e., out of a wish "to exist socially and with the herd," that

... a uniformly valid and binding designation is invented for things, and this legislation of language likewise establishes the first laws of truth. For the contrast between truth and lie arises here for the first time. The liar is a person who uses the valid designations, the words, in order to make something which is unreal appear to be real ... He (sic) misuses fixed conventions by means of arbitrary substitutions or even reversals of names ... What men avoid by excluding the liar is not so much being defrauded as it is being harmed by means of fraud ... [H]e desires the pleasant, life-preserving consequence of truth. He is indifferent toward pure knowledge which has no consequences; toward those truths which are possibly harmful and destructive he is even hostilely inclined.[57]

Hence, convention for the sake of comfort, i.e., peace, is what motivates humans to develop language, according to Nietzsche.

... [W]hat about these linguistic conventions themselves? Are they perhaps products of knowledge, that is, of the sense of truth? Are designations congruent with things? Is language the adequate expression of all realities?

It is only by means of forgetfulness that man can ever reach the point of fancying himself (sic) to possess a "truth" of the grade just indicated. If he will not be satisfied with truth in the form of tautology, that is to say, if he will not be content

---

sondern des Lebens steht" (*ibid.*, p. 217). But what this means is that "Die Historie, sofern sie im Dienst des Lebens steht, steht im Dienste einer unhistorischen Macht [der Wille zur Macht] und wird deshalb nie, in dieser Unterordnung, reine Wissenschaft, etwa wie die Mathematik es ist, werden können und sollen" (*ibid.*, p. 219).

[56] Nietzsche, "On Truth and Lies in a Nonmoral Sense," p. 80.
[57] Nietzsche, "On Truth and Lies in a Nonmoral Sense," p. 81.

with empty husks, then he will always exchange truths for illusions. What is a word? It is the copy in sound of a nerve stimulus. But the further inference from the nerve stimulus to a cause outside of us is already the result of a false and unjustifiable application of the principle of sufficient reason ... [W]ith words it is never a question of truth, never a question of adequate expression; otherwise, there would not be so many languages. The "thing in itself" ... is likewise something quite incomprehensible to the creator of language and something not in the least worth striving for. This creator only designates the relations of things to men, and for expressing these relations he lays hold of the boldest metaphors. To begin with, a nerve stimulus is transferred into an image: first metaphor. The image, in turn, is imitated in a sound: second metaphor.[58]

Metaphor, according to Nietzsche, is a form of un-truth. It is a manner of deception, for it conceals the radical dissimilitude of human experience and understanding.

It is this way with all of us concerning language: we believe that we know something about the things themselves when we speak of trees, colors, snow, and flowers; and yet we possess nothing but metaphors for things - metaphors which correspond in no way to the original entities. In the same way that the sound appears as a sand figure, so the mysterious X of the thing in itself first appears as a nerve stimulus, then as an image, and finally as a sound. Thus the genesis of language does not proceed logically in any case, and all the material within and with which the man of truth, the scientist, and the philosopher later work and build, if not derived from never-never land, is at least not derived from the essence of things.[59]

Even more explicitly, Nietzsche says: "Truths are illusions which we have forgotten are illusions; they are metaphors that have become worn out and have been drained of sensuous force, coins which have lost their embossing and are now considered as metal and no longer as coins."[60] This is

---

[58] Nietzsche, "On Truth and Lies in a Nonmoral Sense," pp. 81-2.
[59] Nietzsche, "On Truth and Lies in a Nonmoral Sense," pp. 82-3.
[60] Nietzsche, "On Truth and Lies in a Nonmoral Sense," p. 84. A case will be made later that, rather than a form of un-truth, metaphor is precisely the key to truth. Nietzsche writes in *Thus Spoke Zarathustra*, trans. by Walter Kaufmann (New York: The Viking Press, 1966), p. 16: "They do not understand me; I am not the mouth for these ears. Must one smash their ears before they learn to listen with their eyes?"), remains trapped in the metaphysical presuppositions of the tradition he despises. For Nietzsche understands experience to be exclusively concerned with actuality (things and words). If truth is to give us information exclusively about what actually is, then it is radically reductionistic. Reality is not defined by what is actual. Reality is defined equally, if not more, by what is possible. Metaphor is indispensable for suggesting the truth of reality. This is what enables Heidegger to conclude that Nietzsche represents the completion and fulfillment, and not an overcoming, of metaphysics (see, e.g., Heidegger, *Nietzsche*, vol. 2, p. 192, and the section "Nietzsches Metaphysik," pp. 257-333), because Nietzsche's nihilism does not and cannot think "Being" (= possibility) (see, e.g., *ibid.*, p. 335, 340-241, 346, 358, especially, 351: "Das Wesen des Denkens ist das Seinsverständnis in den Möglichkeiten seiner Entfaltung, die das Wesen des Seins zu vergeben hat.").

where Derrida picks up Nietzsche's analysis.[61] Derrida thinks of metaphor, as well, as a form of un-truth.[62]

It is because all literal language is ultimately dependent upon the figurative moment,[63] according to Derrida, that his claim with respect to the "untruth" of metaphor is representative of his skepticism.

> The disappearance of truth as presence, the withdrawal of the present origin of presence, is the condition of all (manifestation of) truth. Nontruth is the truth. Nonpresence is presence. Differance, the disappearance of any originary presence, is *at once* the condition of possibility *and* the condition of impossibility of truth ... What is is not what it is ...[64]

Already in *Of Grammatology*, Derrida had written, "*There is nothing outside of the text* ...[65] If this was not an explicit enough articulation of his thorough skepticism, Derrida immediately adds:

> ... there has never been anything but writing; there have never been anything but supplements, substitutive significations which could only come forth in a chain of differential references, the "real" supervening, and being added only while taking on meaning from a trace and from an invocation of the supplement, etc. And thus to infinity, for we have read, *in the text*, that the absolute present, Nature, that which words like "real mother" name, have always already escaped, have never existed; that what opens meaning and language is writing as the disappearance of natural presence.[66]

Yet this linguistic skepticism found in both Nietzsche and Derrida is just a form of "vulgar skepticism" already properly ridiculed and dismissed by Cleanthes in Part I of Hume's *Dialogues Concerning Natural Religion* (1776):

> Whether your skepticism be as absolute and sincere as you pretend, we shall learn by and by, when the company breaks up; we shall then see whether you go out at the

---

[61] See Jacque Derrida, "White Mythology: Metaphor in the Text of Philosophy" trans. by Alan Bass in *Margins of Philosophy* (Chicago: The University of Chicago Press, 1982), p. 217, n. 14, 262, n. 74. Derrida's discussion of "coinage" (see *ibid.*, p. 210, 216) comes directly from Nietzsche.

[62] "Metaphor is less in the philosophical text (and the rhetorical text coordinated with it) than the philosophical text is within metaphor. And the latter can no longer receive its name from metaphysics, except by a catachresis, if you will, that would retrace metaphor through its philosophical phantom: as 'nontrue metaphor.'" Derrida, "White Mythology," p. 258.

[63] See Derrida, "Plato's Pharmacy," p. 81.

[64] Derrida, "Plato's Pharmacy," p. 168.

[65] Jacques Derrida, "'... That Dangerous Supplement ...,'" in *Of Grammatology*, trans. by Gayatri Chakravorty Spival (Baltimore: The Johns Hopkins University Press, 1980), p. 158.

[66] Derrida, "'... That Dangerous Supplement...',", p. 159.

door or the window, and whether you really doubt if your body has gravity or can be injured by its fall, according to popular opinion derived from our fallacious senses and more fallacious experience.[67]

The very fact that Nietzsche, Derrida or any Deconstructionist shows up for a discussion, much less publishes a text or does what s/he does once the discussion is over, contradicts the assertion of the mere arbitrariness of linguistic formulations. So long as pragmatic usage is bracketed out, so long as the act of speaking[68] is eliminated from linguistic analysis, one can treat language as a self-referential and "arbitrary" system of signs. As soon as one moves from logic to pragmatics, though, one is caught up in the paradoxical ambiguities of the referential character of linguistic utterances: Language is a mediating, communal form filtering to consciousness *a world* that, if not directly accessible to consciousness, cannot be ignored any more than the very universals employed by that language (or any language) are not directly accessible to consciousness, yet cannot be ignored.

It is only by acknowledging the fundamental aporiai in experience and, refusing to treat them in a reductionistic fashion, by holding them together in all of their tension that one can appreciate adequately the binary elements of experience. Furthermore, it is only by acknowledging the pragmatic moment in all experience both physical and mental that one can avoid the absurdities of vulgar skepticism.

This project goes "beyond" Heidegger and Derrida in an attempt to recover the spiritual dimension of any and all possible Being-in-the-world as well as to preserve the non-epistemic character of faith resting on the dynamic interaction of binaries and pragmatic experience that require reason's vigilant attention lest we overlook the aporiai and the concealment necessary for us to be individuals in community in the world.

---

[67] Hume, *Dialogues Concerning Natural Religion*, p. 5.

[68] Benveniste argues that it is precisely discourse or the act of speaking that requires linguistics to move from semiotics, concerned with language as a merely self-referential system of signs, to semantics, concerned with language at the level of sentences, i.e., as an event. See the analysis of Benveniste's theory of discourse and the "six pairs of characteristics" of discourse in Ricoeur, *The Rule of Metaphor*, pp. 66-76, that indicate how language is inseparable from a world. Ricoeur is making a case for the inseparability of the human from its world on the basis of language as Heidegger does on the basis of his transcendental ontology of the "existentials of Care" in *Being and Time*.

Chapter 4
David Tracy: Theology as Correlation Beyond Absolute Necessity to Concealment

David Tracy's work represents the standard for a theology of dialogue. One only needs to undertake the most cursory reading of *Blessed Rage for Order* or *The Analogical Imagination*,[1] or just glance at the footnotes of Tracy's texts to recognize that his "revisionist theology"[2] has been hammered out on the anvil of rigorous dialogue. If the main ingredients of his "revisionist theology" come out of the transcendental questioning of Bernard Lonergan and the theological metaphysics of Schubert Ogden and Charles Hartshorne, his dialogue with Ricoeur on metaphor and narrative has taught him to be suspicious of the adequacies of a theology defined purely in terms of critical reflection.

There are many ingredients to Tracy's work that are invaluable for a theology seeking to embrace constructively the pluralism of tradition. In addition to his honest, exhaustive, and penetrating analysis of theological issues, Tracy has engaged in pioneering work on the notion of the "classic[3]" as distinguished from a "period piece"[4] for determining a text and/or event's authority as candidate for attention in illuminating the human condition. This authority rests not upon its univocal message, but upon the permanence of its ability to disclose new insight into ever new situations as it is a concrete and

---

[1] These are the first two parts of a theological trilogy. See *The Analogical Imagination*, pp. 95-96, n. 104. Tracy calls *Blessed Rage for Order* a "fundamental theology" concerned primarily with critical arguments for legitimate God talk. *The Analogical Imagination* is his "systematic theology" concerned with establishing the Christian classic and its role in shaping the historical trajectory of the Christian tradition. The third volume on "practical theology" has been sketched out in comments to be found throughout these first two volumes, but it is yet to be published.

[2] Tracy distinguishes five models of theological reflection in chapter 2 of *Blessed Rage for Order*: orthodox, liberal, neo-orthodox, radical, and revisionist.

[3] The central criterion for the determination of a "classic," according to Tracy, is not that it is the preserve of elitist classicists or an achievement of immediate commercial success (see, *The Analogical Imagination*, p. 140, n. 37) but that it discloses permanent possibilities (see, *ibid.*, p. 14) for human existence in ever new contexts of interpretation (see, *ibid.*, pp. 68, 108, and especially 150, n. 103).

[4] See, for example, Tracy, *The Analogical Imagination*, p. 116.

particular expression of a situation.⁵ Furthermore, Tracy does not equate the role of the "classic" with "classical theism." Since Tracy understands God to be the gracious event of love,⁶ he has underscored like no one else that the unchanging deity of classical theism is incapable of love: because to love means to be affected by the object of one's love and to be affected means to undergo change. In addition to the notion of the classic and his turn to "neo-classical theism" of divine love, Tracy makes a crucial contribution to theological dialogue by shifting the focus of Christology away from dependence merely upon the "historical Jesus" to the Christ event as the classic of the Christian tradition.⁷ The importance of what occurred in the Christ event, however, is not that this event is ontologically exclusive,⁸ but, rather, its challenge as a "dangerous memory" to any and all situations.⁹ In short, Christology is properly understood as inclusive in its "dangerous" transformative negativity and power rather than exclusive. Not least, by far, is Tracy's insistence that theology, precisely as the discipline concerned with this "dangerous memory," embrace the dimension of risk¹⁰ in the odyssey of human, historical understanding as a trajectory of wagering faith.

There are two aspects in particular of Tracy's work, however, which help the present project clarify the task of theology in a post-metaphysical context structured by radical aporiai. These two aspects may perhaps be formulated as critical moments in this author's encounter with Tracy's work, but even they were able to surface only because of the rigorous standard Tracy establishes for his own theological reflection. In short, whatever value the insights which follow have, they could not have been engaged (in one case it was one of Tracy's own footnotes which stimulated the reflection leading to the critique) without the exhaustive and illuminating quality of Tracy's writings.

This author has come to conclude that it is precisely the two foci of the transcendental/metaphysical and hermeneutic-phenomenological that reflect

---

[5] See, for example, Tracy, *The Analogical Imagination*, p. 106-7.

[6] See Tracy, *Blessed Rage for Order*, pp. 189-191; *The Analogical Imagination*, pp. 218, 316, 431, 438, 443, n. 30.

[7] See, for example, Tracy, *The Analogical Imagination*, pp. 238-239; 298, n. 85; 300, n. 97.

[8] See, for example, Tracy, *Blessed Rage for Order*, p. 206-7.

[9] See, for example, Tracy, *The Analogical Imagination*, pp. 235; 243, n. 12; 239; 289, n. 21; 254, 259; 298, n. 85; 317; 324; 327; 329; 330; 372; 391; 424; 427; and 443, n. 31.

[10] The call to risk is ubiquitous in Tracy's *Analogical Imagination*. See, for example, pp. 99; 100; 102-104; 113-114; 216; 130; 134; 154-156; 163; 167; 171; 173; 195; 249-250; 332; 339; 344; 356; 375; 405-407; 429, 432; 454.

two irreconcilable trajectories in Tracy's work unless they are to be seen as a paradox. 1) The first, resulting from the influence of Bernard Lonergan, Schubert Ogden, and Charles Hartshorne, is a transcendental or metaphysical focus which Tracy sees as the key to establishing the truth claims of religious language. Here the argument is that there are necessary conditions of possibility that permit any and all experience. This truth claim is Cartesian in that it is based on "the self-contradictory character which their denial involves for any intelligent and rational ('reflective') inquirer."[11]

2) The second, resulting from the influence of Paul Ricoeur, is a hermeneutical focus. It is an exercise in the "third stage" of linguistic analysis,[12] which denies any empirical grounding of religious language, and is combined with hermeneutic phenomenology stressing the open-endedness of understanding and the priority of "imagination" over the will (decision) by enabling the projection in front of the text of different possible modes of Being-in-the-world. Here truth is concerned with "adequacy," for even metaphysical claims are matters of "belief" that cannot be proved.[13] Yet this moment of Tracy's work remains unconcerned with the role of concealment crucial to any and all adequacy.

Contingent versus Metaphysical Necessity

The tensions between the two trajectories of metaphysics and hermeneutics surface in Tracy's discussion of religious language as "limit" language. Here two kinds of limits are identified: "limit-to" (contingency) and "limit-of" (grounding of experience).[14]

The character of limit for the grounding of experience (limit-of) becomes most clear in the discussion of anxiety:

> In analyzing anxiety, we may ... see that our very situation is, in fact, correctly described as a limit-situation. We are grounded or horizoned by no other thing in the universe, but rather by No-thing ... [A]t a certain point the language of conceptual analysis begins to falter. Instead, the human spirit begins to search for metaphors expressive of the experience (abyss, chasm, limit) and for narratives capable of expanding and structuring these metaphors (parables, myths, poems). Such metaphors, images, symbols, and myths seem linguistically necessary to express that literally unspoken, and perhaps unspeakable, final dimension to the end of our lives.[15]

---

[11] Tracy, *Blessed Rage for Order*, p. 159.
[12] For discussion of these stages in linguistic analysis, see below.
[13] See Tracy, *Blessed Rage for Order*, p. 68.
[14] Tracy, *Blessed Rage for Order*, p. 93.
[15] Tracy, *Blessed Rage for Order*, pp. 107-108.

Yet, the turn to metaphysics in an attempt to establish transcendental conditions of possibility is meant to offer a metaphysical necessity (the necessary conditions of possibility of any and all experience) as the explanation of our ground.

One cannot have it both ways: the human condition cannot be both characterized by "limits-to" and at the same time grounded in metaphysical necessity. To do so turns anxiety into a mere distortion, i.e., in moments of anxiety we "forget" the necessary conditions of possibility ... Or, if anxiety is an experience pointing to the radical no-thingness of all experience, there can be no necessary ground of that experience.

Tracy hints at another option in a footnote in *Blessed Rage for Order* in which he points out that there are two kinds of necessity, i.e., "metaphysical" or absolute necessity and "contingent" necessity. Metaphysical or absolute necessity is concerned with what must be *regardless* of particularities or "facts" where "contingent necessity" is concerned with what must necessarily be, *given* a certain state of affairs or "facts".[16] It appears that Tracy is viewing what is in fact a form of contingent necessity as if it were an absolute, metaphysical necessity. This is surely the implication of the other kind of limit in human experience, the notion of "limit-to," which is concerned with the role of human contingency, i.e., human beings do not absolutely necessarily exist.[17] The metaphysical consequences to be drawn from any conclusions regarding necessity based on the contingency of human experience, then, is that those necessities, i.e., the necessary conditions of possibility for that human experience, are themselves contingent necessities not absolute necessities. If Tracy's metaphysics is really concerned with contingent necessity (the contingent, necessary conditions of possibility for us to experience as we in fact do experience), then there is nothing absolute about this metaphysics and its grounding is truly a "belief" which in moments of anxiety can be seen to be rooted in no-thingness.

If we may only speak of contingent necessity (as the present project maintains), then Tracy's metaphysics is aesthetic (as Whitehead understood his Process metaphysics to be) and an example of Nygren's "conceptual poetry"[18] of the order of Ferré's "metaphysical model," that is, it is at best coherent and adequate to all our experience[19] but not metaphysically or absolutely necessary. In fact, Tracy's metaphysics then becomes an instance of

---

[16] See Tracy, *Blessed Rage for Order*, p. 224, n. 11.
[17] See Tracy, *Blessed Rage for Order*, p. 93.
[18] See Tracy, *Blessed Rage for Order*, p. 159.
[19] See Tracy, *Blessed Rage for Order*, p. 152.

Ian Ramsey's "cosmic mapping" "with reference to which we may both plot our 'cosmic position' and integrate both our scientifically observable and non-observable languages (e.g., "I" [the "I" here is taken to be the non-observable integrator of all experience])."[20] Whitehead's dipolar deity satisfies precisely Ramsey's criteria by offering a description of reality (both super-human and sub-human) on the basis of an analogy built on the abstract and concrete moments of the human individual which are contingent not absolute moments.

On the Role of Concealment in What is Manifest

What Tracy is calling metaphysical or absolute necessity is in fact contingent necessity, for it is grounded in an analogate (the self) that is contingent. But there is a second moment in Tracy's analysis that requires a shift of attention away from metaphysics to aporetics. Having overlooked the aporetic character of human experience, the imperceptible depths of the human as well as the "irrational" (or inability of rationality to ground itself) character of human experience have been concealed. This allows Tracy to focus on the pragmatic dimension of experience. The alternative, however, is not to call for unfettering fantasy from the moorings of rationality. Surely, critical reflection must reign in unwarranted speculation let loose once one has moved beyond understanding religious language to consist of literal or objective claims. But that critical reflection remains poetic not metaphysical, paradoxical not transparent, open-ended not absolute. Although to speak of the poetic, paradoxical, and open-ended nature of the human condition might at first sound like opening the floodgates of irrationality, this project maintains that there are critical moments insisting upon our remaining accountable to constitutive components of human experience that not only insist upon rigorous reflection but establish criteria for ethical action.

Tracy's call for a second naiveté and return to the "character building" or transforming power of figurative language,[21] following critical reflection about experience, indicates the limits to defining theology in terms of cognitive theistic claims (based on metaphysics) which "... depart from properly metaphorical, proverbial, common-sense, and symbolic language and ... develop an explicitly conceptual language."[22] The very next sentence in

---

[20] Tracy, *Blessed Rage for Order*, p. 150.
[21] See Tracy, *Blessed Rage for Order*, pp. 190-192 and Chapter 9: "The Representative Limit-Language of Christology."
[22] Tracy, *Blessed Rage for Order*, p. 148.

Tracy's text clearly affirms the limits of cognitive theistic claims: "This latter language [explicitly conceptual language] does not claim to capture the full existential meaningfulness of the originating language."[23] Tracy distinguishes between what is "meaningful," those experiences which resonate positively with one's immediate experience (and is concerned with feeling, mood, tone, and bodily awareness)[24], and "meaning," those experiences confirmed as valid as a consequence of critical reflection and internal coherence.

> In short, many kinds of experience and language (e.g., aesthetic, ethical, political, economic, and religious) may be "meaningful" in the sense of genuinely disclosive of our authentic lived experience. But any meaningful experience and language bears the note of a *religious meaning*, we shall argue, only when its logical limit-character is also disclosed by explicit philosophical analysis.[25]

He insists that theology, following the critical reflection which establishes its meaning, must return to the originating figurative language of the New Testament tradition in order to retrieve the full existential meaningfulness of the theological situation.

David Tracy has thought through more thoroughly than others the implications of the theological situation resting upon the two moments of inherited tradition and contemporary experience. These two moments constitute a framework of correlation that serves as the parameters for doing theology.[26] He identifies these as the two sources of theology, that is,

---

[23] Tracy, *Blessed Rage for Order*, p. 148.
[24] See Tracy, *Blessed Rage for Order*, p. 66.
[25] Tracy, *Blessed Rage for Order*, pp. 69-70.
[26] Paul Tillich, of course, is responsible for developing the notion of theology as a method of correlation. See *Systematic Theology*, vol. I, pp. 59f. His method of correlation is based on philosophy's question (see, *ibid.*, pp. 18-22) and theology's answer (see, *ibid.*, pp. 22-28). Tracy rejects this method of correlation by observing in *Blessed Rage for Order*, p. 46: "... Tillich's method of correlation is crucially inadequate. Tillich's implicit commitment to two sources and his explicit insistence upon a theological ideal [answer] which transcends both naturalism and supernaturalism could be successfully executed only by a method which develops critical criteria for correlating the questions and the answers found in both the 'situation' and the 'message' ... Tillich's method does not actually correlate; it juxtaposes questions from the 'situation' with answers from the 'message.'"

Schubert Ogden employs a notion of correlation in theology similar to Tillich's. See thesis two of Ogden's "What is Theology?," p. 23: "... theology presupposes as a condition of its possibility the correlation of the Christian witness of faith and human existence, both poles of which alike have a variable as well as a constant aspect." This, too, is a juxtaposition rather than a correlation.

"Christian texts and common human experience and language."[27] These two sources require a "critical correlation" making theology a "second order reflection" about Christian texts and common human experience and language. Such a correlation radically affirms pluralism in theological formulations, for all theological claims are analogous to statements made about the self. That is, the self is an inexpressible constant throughout the individual's experience, but no single statement (or set of statements) about the self exhausts who the self is.

Tracy distinguishes Christian theology from Philosophy of Religion by insisting on the correlation of these two sources for Christian theology. Christian theology is not concerned with theological claims in general, but with theological claims arising out of a particular tradition. Fundamental theology's first task is the responsibility of "clarifying the Christian fact."[28]

Though the initial net for catching the Christian fact is cast very broadly by Tracy to include "... the significant texts, actions, gestures, and symbols of the entire Christian tradition,"[29] the parameters are subsequently narrowed to the New Testament[30] and finally to the God question:

> To many contemporary analysts of Christian experience and language, moreover, the central, indeed the constitutive cognitive claim of that [Christian] religion is its articulation of the Christian God as the sole and single objective ground of all reality. With that judgment I am in full agreement.[31]

As much as the responsibility of the theologian consists, according to Tracy, of "clarifying the Christian fact," there is no question that there is a second theological source, serving as the final touchstone for adjudicating any and all theological claims. In addition to the Christian fact, one must employ critical understanding of "our common human experience and language" in the present. Tracy's theses three, four, and five of the "Revision-

---

[27] See thesis one of the "revisionist model" of theology proposed by Tracy in *Blessed Rage for Order*, pp. 43-45.

[28] Tracy, *Blessed Rage for Order*, p. 72. According to Tracy, fundamental theology is concerned with the doctrine of God; systematic theology is concerned with a "paradigmatic focal meaning," seen to be central to the entire Christian tradition (in Tracy's case this paradigmatic focal meaning is the Christ of the apostolic witness); and practical theology is concerned with transforming praxis (see *The Analogical Imagination*, p. 95-6, n. 104).

[29] Tracy, *Blessed Rage for Order*, p. 72.

[30] See Tracy, *Blessed Rage for Order*, p. 72: "[m]ore specifically, the primary although not exclusive expression of the Christian fact may be found in texts, more explicitly the texts of the Christian scriptures."

[31] Tracy, *Blessed Rage for Order*, pp. 146-7.

ist Model" present the tools for the investigation of this context of correlation consisting of our common human experience and the scriptures to be 1) Phenomenology (for the investigation of our common human experience) and 2) historical criticism and hermeneutics (for the investigation of Christian texts). But, finally, the criteria for adjudicating the truth claims of the Christian fact come from the horizon of contemporary reflection, more specifically, Process metaphysics.[32] It is not coincidental that all of these disciplines (Phenomenology, historical criticism, hermeneutics, and Process metaphysics) are progeny of the Enlightenment and, with the exception of historical criticism, products of the 20th century.

Tracy indicates understanding of his contemporary "situation" as a theologian when he writes:

> *Religious language does not present a new, a supernatural world wherein we may escape the only world we know or wish to know.* Rather that language re-presents our always threatened basic confidence and trust in the very meaningfulness of even our most cherished and most noble enterprises, science, morality, and culture. That language discloses the reassurance needed that the final reality of our lives is in fact trustworthy.[33]

Given the alternative as presented, it would, of course, be absurd for one to choose the supernatural at the expense of the natural. But has the supernatural been adequately understood here?

The Enlightenment distinguished between reason confined to empirical experience, governed by a closed nexus of natural law (these natural laws, ironically, are themselves inaccessible to the senses) and a dimension beyond empirical experience called the supernatural, an illusory fantasy which could abrogate natural law. However, such a distinction eliminates our mental life, surely constitutive of experience, and is called by Horace Bushnell precisely the "supernatural."[34] The least noteworthy about the mind ($νοῦς$) is that which can be "explained" empirically. Completely inaccessible to the senses, the mind nevertheless is not some hocus pocus dimension outside of the natural order. More important for the moment, however, is that, to the extent Tracy's project insists on appealing to metaphysics for the determination of

---

[32] See Tracy, *Blessed Rage for Order*, pp. 47-56.
[33] Tracy, *Blessed Rage for Order*, p. 135.
[34] See Sydney E. Ahlstrom's discussion of Horace Bushnell in *A Religious History of the American People* (New Haven: Yale University Press, 1972), p. 612; Parts I and II of *Horace Bushnell: Selected Writings on Language, Religion, and American Culture*, ed. by David L. Smith (Chico, CA: Scholars Press, 1984); and M.H. Abrams, *Natural Supernaturalism* (New York: W.W. Norton and Co., Inc., 1971).

religious truth claims, it remains completely within the horizon of the Enlightenment.

But the paradoxes of the human condition indicate that religion and its second order reflection are concerned with much more than merely "the only world we know or wish to know" understood as the "natural" world of empirical experience.[35] Theology can never forget that the world we know or wish to know involves us in a concealing and suppressing that subverts the hubris of our most noble empirical enterprises, since that concealing is concerned with the invisible depths of any and all experience.

This concealment is nowhere more graphically illustrated in Tracy's work than in his insistence that the God question is the central Christian fact. For it is Tracy's 20th century metaphysical presuppositions (committed to the natural world as understood by secular thought) which encourages him to reduce the central claim of the Christian fact down to the God question.[36] The God question is the crucial problem for a world view that can only admit as true what is perceptible, divisible, measurable, calculable, predictable, and controllable. Twentieth century secular reality insists that the referents of our language be real empirical things in order for our judgments to be meaningful. This has problematized all God language, since there is no perceptible and/or measurable object of experience that corresponds to this term "God." It is the task (the only task?) of critical theology to establish the meaning of this referent allowing a post-critical return to existential meaningfulness.

In response to this empirical conundrum, Tracy observes, 20th century theology has passed through three stages of theological analysis of religious language. The inadequacies of the first two stages of evidentialism ("verification" is represented by the work of A.J. Ayer; "falsification" is represented by the work of Antony Flew[37]) led to the third stage of focussing not on what God language represents (i.e., not on what that language tells us about God) but on how God language is used (i.e., to focus on the pragmatic function of our usage of God language[38]). This stage of the analysis of the

---

[35] Tracy is careful to distinguish between "empirical" and "empiricist methods." See, *The Analogical Imagination*, pp. 195 and 219, n. 8. Tracy is fully aware that religious truth claims cannot be empirically verified through the senses. They are empirical truth claims, however, because, even as concealed from the senses, they are the conditions of possibility for empirical experience.

[36] See Tracy, *Blessed Rage for Order*, pp. 146-147.

[37] See Tracy, *Blessed Rage for Order*, p. 120.

[38] Note here the shift from logical claims to pragmatic claims. This unintentionally points to an aporetic relationship between the logical and the pragmatic. See Chapter 8 below, "The Aporia of Logic and Praxis."

performative function of religious language is represented in Tracy's text by the work of Basil Mitchell, R.M. Hare, R.B. Braithwaite, Ian Ramsey, and Frederick Ferré.[39] Tracy writes of this discussion:

> ... Ramsey is principally concerned to answer two questions about religious language: to what kind of empirical situation does religion appeal; for such situations, what kind of language is appropriate ... To his first question, Ramsey responds that the kind of situation which religious language discloses is a situation which involves both an "odd discernment" and a "total commitment." More exactly, religious language points to the kind of highly personal situation which cannot be described in straightforward indicative language [this is called making a strength out of a weakness] ... In those situations where we find ourselves discerning the meanings of our lives [question two], Ramsey suggests, ... we find religious language useful and thereby meaningful ... Such a combination of an odd personal discernment, a total commitment, and a universal significance is the *empirical* [Tracy's emphasis] "place" for religious and theological statements.[40]

Tracy embraces this third stage of language analysis in theological reflection, because it *empirically* situates religious language within the context of secular language use in general. Religious language is concerned with "those situations where we find ourselves discerning the meanings of our lives" and meaning takes us to the limits of the everyday to such events as odd personal discernment, total commitment, and universal significance. The issue of reference for God language (logic) has been side-stepped by shifting the focus to pragmatic usage.

Pragmatics has replaced logic without any acknowledgment that the pragmatic and logical are aporetically related. Phenomenology's logic and critical reflection require the bracketing of the existence claims to focus on the realm of the pragmatic. This is out of a recognition that phenomenological experience occurs in the intellect (intentional consciousness). The pragmatic dimension is an unprovable "given"[41] whose "existence" must be bracketed, since we don't have logical proof to establish the indubitable existence of anything except the self. Yet intentional consciousness is necessarily dependent upon the pragmatic for the experience of meaning. Here we have a classic aporetic tension between two incommensurable, irreducible, and irreconcilable, dialectical moments that necessarily must be taken into account for the understanding of experience prior to the addressing of the

---

[39] See Tracy, *Blessed Rage for Order*, pp. 120-124.
[40] Tracy, *Blessed Rage for Order*, pp. 121-2.
[41] See Douglas R. McGaughey, "Husserl and Heidegger on Plato's Cave Allegory: A Study of Philosophical Influence," *International Philosophical Quarterly*, XVI/3 (September 1976), 331-348.

question of existential meaning. The third stage of linguistic analysis presupposes and ignores the more fundamental theological issue of the aporetic character of all language use.

By accepting the judgments of the third stage of linguistic analysis, Tracy turns to theological language and the issue of the cognitive status of that language. Process metaphysics allows him to speak logically (with conceptual clarity, to use his terminology) about what is going on in our pragmatic usage of religious language. Although the third stage of linguistic analysis has given up evidentialism, i.e., empirical reference claims, with respect to God, Process metaphysics provides Tracy with a language of reference for telling us something about God. The dipolar theistic model of Process metaphysics is the necessary presupposition for understanding our common human experience and language and the Christian texts. For Process metaphysics analogically describes the necessary conditions of possibility of any and all experience.

The circle is complete: Religious language is understood by the third stage of linguistic analysis to be performative not cognitive (this represents the shift from reference to pragmatic usage). The performative character of religious language indicates the concern with personal limits and meaning which empirically situates religious language among other secular usages of language (this represents the clarification of the pragmatic usage of religious language). Process metaphysics, focussing on the conditions of possibility for all experience even religious, most adequately provides the cognitive clarification of our confidence in the meaning of life as it *explains* the nature of human limits (this represents the return to reference and its logical status).

Tracy writes: "... the central, indeed the constitutive cognitive claim of [Christian experience and language] ... is its articulation of the Christian God as the sole and single objective ground of all reality."[42] Critical clarity and warrants for the referent of our God language serve as the core of the theologian's agenda. Given the difficulties of common-sense reference for God language, however, Tracy employs the dipolar theism of Process metaphysics to adjudicate the adequacy of types of God language.

"Classical theism" is an inadequate God language, because of its monopolarity. Classical theism affirms God as the supremely perfect one, while denying that the concept of perfection includes change. More specifically, classical theism affirms that God is love, while denying any real meaning to that love. God cannot be affected or transformed by the object of its love,

---

[42] Tracy, *Blessed Rage for Order*, pp. 146-147.

according to classical theism, because God is supremely perfect, i.e., unchanging.[43]

The more adequate God language, according to Tracy, is what he calls "neo-classical theism" based upon a dipolarity. God is analogous to the human subject in that the individual is constituted out of both something abstract and permanent (allowing us to identify our individuality) and concrete and transient (accounting for change and growth).[44] God, too, is understood by Tracy to involve these two moments of a "primordial" (abstract and permanent) and a "consequent" (concrete and transient) nature. God is eternal and unchanging in "his" primordial, abstract, nature; God is love and changing in "his" consequent nature.[45]

---

[43] See Tracy, *Blessed Rage for Order*, p. 176.

[44] See Tracy, *Blessed Rage for Order*, p. 179. Such a claim is committed to a notion of individual centeredness denied by post-metaphysical understandings of the self as decentered. See below, chapter 12, "The Aporia of Self and Other."

[45] This dipolar understanding of God corresponds to the two moments of "manifestation" and "proclamation" which Tracy insists are complementary moments grounded in the analogical imagination and informing the Christian tradition in a manner that prohibits a simplistic reduction of the Christian claim to either mere manifestation or proclamation. See "Classical Forms of Religious Expression: Manifestation and Proclamation" in *The Analogical Imagination*, pp. 202-218, "The Trajectories of the Route of Manifestation" in *ibid.*, pp. 376-386, "The Trajectories of the Route of Proclamation" in *ibid*, pp. 386-389, "From Manifestation and Proclamation to History and Praxis: Political and Liberation Theologies" in *ibid.*, pp. 390-398, where Tracy suggests: "... we are primarily neither hearers of the word [proclamation] nor seers of a manifestation. But because we have seen and have heard, we are freed to become doers of the word in history" (*ibid.*, p. 390). If proclamation is dialectical, manifestation is analogical (see *ibid.*, pp. 417-148), they are united, Tracy maintains, by a metaphysical understanding that insists that the third focal meaning of theology is historical action (see *ibid.*, p. 425-426).

Manifestation, Tracy underscores, involves both disclosure and concealment as well as withdrawal (see *ibid.*, p. 219, n. 1). For ". . . we find the paradigmatic [of manifestation], not in the illusions of ordinary time and history, not even in the recovered time of Proust, but in the ahistorical, atemporal time of repetition in the myths, rituals, symbols and images of the true time of the origins of the cosmos" (*ibid.*, 206). But such manifestation is no longer our lot, for it is rarely sensed as erupting from nature itself, as of old (*ibid.*, especially 379 but also 377). History and time are experienced by humanity separated from manifestation as "terrors" that yield no final meaning (*ibid.*, 206), hence, there is a longing for preverbal manifestation of the past where "[t]he whole, a 'limit-of' reality, has manifested itself in the great hirophanies of all the religions (*ibid.*, 206).

However, more than manifestation is proclamation, which negates participation in the preverbal, freeing us to risk entrance into history (*ibid.*, 210). There is only "magic, aesthetics or even mechanics" when proclamation is lost and manifestation alone remains (*ibid.*, 217). Religion needs both manifestation and proclamation, for religion which is "only" manifestation (John, Eliade) or "only" proclamation (Paul, Barth/Bonhoeffer) is an adumbration of religion (*ibid.*, 213, 214, 283). Above all, according to Tracy it is

In *The Analogical Imagination*, Tracy writes:

> Fundamental theology's metaphysical reflections do provide a real, logically necessary and critical warrant for the claims to truth of religion by the development of an abstract universal which is not a false distancing ... Critical fidelity to experience means fidelity to the concrete; fidelity to the concrete means, logically, a fidelity to the sufficient and, in and through that decisive sufficiency, to the necessary and necessarily abstract metaphysical conditions of possibility.[46]

Process metaphysics provides critical clarification of the God question in conformity with the common-sense expectations of 20th century rationality. Religious language is in this manner empirically situated within secular language usage in general. We now know to what our God language refers, i.e., a dipolar deity, who is the "fellow sufferer who endures" and the "lure to the good." Reason's power of representation triumphs, and theology is queen of the rational sciences, for theology alone speaks of the rational metaphysical conditions of possibility for any and all experience.

Yet, because Tracy has engaged in another dialog, i.e., with Ricoeur and hermeneutics, he is suspicious of this rationality. Although he is "convinced that Process thought does provide the most adequate resource for contemporary theism,"[47] he expresses reservations about the success of Process metaphysics.[48] In addition to questions internal to the metaphysics of individual Process thinkers, Tracy insists that we return to a second naiveté with respect to religious language after undertaking critical reflection about the cognitive status of one's God language. Only then, he argues, can one find an adequate account of the "character building" and "praxis dimension" of religious language. "... [C]onceptual analysis alone will not suffice for character-forming action."[49] Adequate praxis requires both "rigorous theory and appropriate symbolization."[50] Contingent fact (symbolic representation) complements metaphysical necessity to empower transforming action in the world.

Nevertheless, the ground enabling the symbolic representation to empower character-forming action remains a metaphysical argument for the adequate referent of God language. This reflects the need of 20th century

---

dipolar theism which unites manifestation (the primordial nature of God) and proclamation (the consequent nature of God) in the most meaningful manner for humanity at the end of the 20th century.

[46] Tracy, *The Analogical Imagination*, p. 198.
[47] See Tracy, *Blessed Rage for Order*, p. 187.
[48] See Tracy, *Blessed Rage for Order*, pp. 187-8.
[49] See Tracy, *Blessed Rage for Order*, p. 209.
[50] See Tracy, *Blessed Rage for Order*, p. 210.

humanity for rational explanation according to its paradigm of empirical understanding. In *The Analogical Imagination* he acknowledges that there are both "hard" and "soft" metaphysical claims, but he insists that his metaphysical position provides us with insight concerning God as the "one necessary existent:"

> ... even those, like myself, who argue the so-called 'hard' (i.e., the metaphysical or transcendental) line on this central issue for fundamental theology, claim no more (and, admittedly, no less) than an ability to partly state - more exactly, to metaphysically state - the abstract, general, universal and necessary features of the reality of God as *the one necessary existent which can account for the reality of a limit-of, ground-to, horizon-to the whole disclosed in earlier phenomenological accounts*. Other fundamental theologians, especially most linguistic analysts and phenomenologists, will advance the "softer" claim that a "limit-of" reality may be displayed, disclosed or shown but cannot in principle be stated.[51] (emphasis added)

This project argues that both "hard" and "soft" metaphysical claims fail to articulate the depths of our religious experience to the extent that they conceal the aporetic moments at the core of every paradigm of understanding (either cataphonic or apophantic). Even Process metaphysics is a wager of faith resting upon presupposed definitions and inexplicable paradoxes. Rather than a discussion of the "conditions of possibility" taking us to a rational foundation for experience, that very discussion takes us to the irrational (the presupposed) and forces acknowledgment of the non-epistemic faith at the core of all we experience, understand, and do.

Tracy's theology of correlation, however helpful it is with respect to critical clarification, remains simply too sanguine about our ability to gain critical clarity about either our tradition or our common human condition and language. What is forgotten here is that these two sources of theological engagement (our inherited tradition and contemporary experience) are constituted by a set of aporetic tensions that defy critical clarity. Aporiai do not empower "reason" in the present to stand sovereign over the past. Reason is paradoxical: on the one hand, it itself does not rest upon the absolute foundations it requires for the certitudes of its judgments; on the other hand, we have no alternative but to employ reason for adjudicating the adequacy of our understanding. The death camps of Europe, the slaughter of indigenous peoples in the Americas and all over the globe, the "disappearances" of Central and South America, along with the rubble of history, where absolutes have justified atrocities unbearable even to describe, these all teach us of the dangers of absolutizing human judgment in the name of reason. The aporiai

---

[51] Tracy, *The Analogical Imagination*, p. 161.

at the core of reason teach us to employ the hermeneutics of suspicion along with the hermeneutics of restoration even more radically, perhaps, than is insisted upon by Tracy.[52] Nevertheless, paradoxically, as we employ reason we must remain suspicious even of reason's claims, for they of necessity conceal in their very clarity.

Tracy is surely correct when he emphasizes reason, for, were we to surrender all appeal to reasonable accountability, coherence, and consistency, we would risk babbling idiocy. Enlightenment rationality, however, has perpetrated a confidence in rationality that is destructive beyond measure. It is time to surrender the agenda of establishing the credibility of theology on the basis of Enlightenment rationality either in terms of evidentialism or on the basis of necessary conditions of possibility. It is time that theology named the non-sense that is at the core of all common-sense to retrieve the aporetic (not least between the logical and the pragmatic) at the core of human experience which makes our condition one of faith seeking understanding as spiritual beings in history. Accepting these paradoxes situates the theologian by definition as a person of faith. A radical reigning in of hubris is perhaps our only hope for truly transforming and liberating character-forming action.

---

[52] See Tracy's discussion of the dangers of systematic distortion in *The Analogical Imagination*, pp. 345, 366, n. 21; 351, 363, requiring a "hermeneutics of suspicion" as one engages in a "hermeneutics of retrieval" (see *ibid.*, 131 (the fourth step in interpretation); 146, n. 80; 190, n. 71; and 320). Ricoeur uses the language "strategy of seduction" for "hermeneutics of retrieval" and "strategy of suspicion" for "hermeneutics of suspicion." See Ricoeur, *Oneself as Another*, p. 159, n. 23.

Chapter 5
On George Lindbeck's Cultural-Linguistic Theological Model

A position such as the one taken in the current project, which insists that theology be grounded in experience, cannot ignore George Lindbeck's *The Nature of Doctrine: Religion and Theology in a Postliberal Age*.[1] In contrast to the liberal "experience-expressivist" theological model, he explicitly develops what he calls a postliberal "cultural-linguistic" theological model which is attractive to many (particularly, among persons influenced by Stanley Fish and Stanley Hauerwas).

Lindbeck distinguishes among four models of theology although for all intents and purposes he discusses only models 1, 2, and 4:

Model 1 - The Cognitive Propositional Model: It "... emphasizes the cognitive aspects of religion and stresses the ways in which church doctrines function as informative propositions or truth claims about objective realities."[2] Lindbeck also calls this model the "simple propositional" model.[3]

Model 2 - The Experiential-Expressive Model: "... [I]t interprets doctrines as noninformative and nondiscursive symbols of inner feelings, attitudes, or existential orientations. The primary representative of the experience-expressivist model, according to Lindbeck, is Schleiermacher.[4]

---

[1] George Lindbeck, *The Nature of Doctrine: Religion and Theology in a Postliberal Age* (Philadelphia: The Westminster Press, 1984).
[2] Lindbeck, *The Nature of Doctrine*, p. 16.
[3] Lindbeck, *The Nature of Doctrine*, p. 17.
[4] See Lindbeck, *The Nature of Doctrine*, p. 16. Brian Gerrish, however, questions this reading of Schleiermacher. See his book review of *The Nature of Doctrine* in *The Journal of Religion*, 68/1 (January 1988), pp. 87-92, especially p. 89: "Christian doctrines, according to Schleiermacher, are not about the prereflective experience underlying all religions but about the distinctively Christian way of believing, in which everything is related to the redemption accomplished by Jesus of Nazareth. The very title of Schleiermacher's dogmatic work makes it clear that his concern is even more specifically with the faith of the evangelical (i.e., Protestant) church, not with some ubiquitous private experience. Few Protestant theologians have ever asserted more strongly than he did the priority of the communal over the individual element in Christianity. In his own words, 'Christian piety never arises independently and of itself in an individual, but only out of the communion and in the communion.'" Gerrish is certainly correct when he observes that "Christian doctrines ... are not about the prereflective experience underlying all religions," because the Infinite, according to Schleiermacher, is never experienced qua Infinite but always in and through particulars. Religious experience is always dif-

Introduction   173

This approach, Lindbeck argues, highlights the resemblances of religions to aesthetic enterprises ...⁵ He calls this model "simple symbolism."⁶ What he wishes to suggest with the notions "noninformative and nondiscursive" is that there is nothing about the linguistic formulation itself that is essential to the religious model. What is essential is prereflective experience.

> ... thinkers of this tradition all locate ultimately significant contact with whatever is finally important to religion in the prereflective experiential depths of the self and regard the public or outer features of religion as expressive and evocative objectifications (i.e., nondiscursive symbols) of internal experience.⁷

Lindbeck lists four primary theses characteristic of experiential-expressivism in general:

---

ferent with respect to particulars, even if it is one with respect to the Infinite. But since the Infinite can never be experienced except through particulars, it is simply incorrect to maintain that Schleiermacher reduces religion down to what is internally experienced. See Friedrich Schleiermacher, *On Religion*, pp. 49-50: "The sum total of religion is to feel that, in its highest unity, all that moves us in feeling is one; to feel that aught single and particular is only possible, by means of this unity; to feel, that is to say, that our being and living is a being and living in and through God." This articulates the fundamental unity, but Schleiermacher proceeds to stress the necessity of particularity. See *ibid.*, pp. 50-51: "Whatever occurs anywhere, whether among many or few as a peculiar and distinct kind of feeling is in itself complete, and by its nature necessary. What you find as religious emotions among Turks or Indians, cannot equally appear among Christians. The essential oneness of religiousness spreads itself out in a great variety of provinces, and again, in each province it contracts itself, and the narrower and smaller the province there is necessarily more excluded as incompatible and more included as characteristic." But contrary to Gerrish, it must be observed that, if Christian piety does not arise independently in the individual, neither does Schleiermacher limit the content of religious experience to the particular formulations of a specific religious tradition. Religious experience can vary from individual to individual precisely because of the particularity unique to that individual. See, *ibid.*, p. 51: "Finally, the piety of each individual, whereby he (sic) is rooted in the greater unity, is a whole by itself. It is a rounded whole, based on his peculiarity, on what you call his character, of which it forms one side. Religion thus fashions itself with endless variety, down even to the single personality." Religion, therefore, has an endless variety because the Infinite can only be experienced as the non-experience of unity in multiplicity. See, *ibid.*, p. 43: "It is this earlier moment I mean, which you always experience yet never experience. The phenomenon of your life is just the result of its constant departure and return."

5   Lindbeck, *The Nature of Doctrine*, p. 16. Though Lindbeck himself argues for the "aesthetic character" appropriate to the "cultural-linguistic" model: "Thus reasonableness in religion and theology, as in other domains, has something of that aesthetic character, that quality of unformalizable skill, which we usually associate with the artist or the linguistically competent." (*bid.*, p. 130)
6   Lindbeck, *The Nature of Doctrine*, p. 17.
7   Lindbeck, *The Nature of Doctrine*, p. 21.

(1) Different religions are diverse expressions or objectifications of a common core experience. It is this experience which identifies them as religions. (2) The experience, while conscious, may be unknown on the level of self-conscious reflection.[8] (3) It is present in all human beings. (4) In most religions, the experience is the source and norm of objectifications: it is by reference to the experience that their adequacy or lack of adequacy is to be judged.[9]

Model 3 - The Hybrid or Two-Dimensional Model: It "... attempts to combine these two emphases [of Models 1 and 2]."[10] This approach, Lindbeck suggests, "... [is] equipped to account more fully than can the first two types for both variable and invariable aspects of religious traditions but have difficulty in coherently combining them."[11] They are simply too complicated to be convincing or easily intelligible, Lindbeck declares.[12]

Model 4 - The Cultural-Linguistic Model: It emphasizes "... those respects in which religions resemble languages together with their correlative forms of life and are thus similar to cultures (insofar as these are understood semiotically as reality and value systems - that is, as idioms for the constructing of reality and the living of life)."[13] Church doctrines, according to this model, are not taken to be expressive symbols of some common human experience, but, rather, they are "communally authoritative rules of dis-

---

[8] The experience may be unknown because it has to do with the necessary conditions of knowledge and experience that are by definition prior to that knowledge and experience. If one does not make the conditions of possibility of experience a focus of one's reflection, then they continue to function preconsciously as constitutive of that experience. Lindbeck's question is whether or not such conditions of possibility are in fact prelinguistic and separable from thematization by linguistic or other conceptual systems (see Lindbeck, *The Nature of Doctrine*, p. 43, n. 18). This is another version of the chicken or the egg dilemma. The more crucial theological question with respect to the issue of necessary conditions of possibility is whether they identify a metaphysical necessity or a contingent necessity. If one concludes that there is nothing metaphysically necessary about our experience in the world, then the conditions of possibility for our contingent experience are equally contingent.

[9] Lindbeck, *The Nature of Doctrine*, p. 31.

[10] Lindbeck, *The Nature of Doctrine*, p. 16.

[11] Lindbeck, *The Nature of Doctrine*, p. 17.

[12] Lindbeck, *The Nature of Doctrine*, p. 17. "Karl Rahner and Bernard Lonergan have developed what are probably the currently most influential versions of this two-dimensional outlook" (*ibid.*, p. 16). Although later in his text they (*ibid.*, pp. 31-32 and 43, n. 18) along with David Tracy (*ibid.*, p. 136, n. 4), Paul Ricoeur (*ibid.*, p. 136, n. 5), Eberhard Ebeling (*ibid.*, p. 119), Hans Küng (*ibid.*, p. 120), Leonard Swidler (*ibid.*, p. 137, n. 13), John Hick (*ibid.*, p. 137, n. 14), and Edward Schillebeeckx (*ibid.*, p. 120) exemplify the Experience-Expressivist model, here Rahner and Lonergan are taken to be representatives of this Hybrid Two-Dimensional Model.

[13] Lindbeck, *The Nature of Doctrine*, p. 18.

course, attitude, and action."[14] Hence, Lindbeck calls this view of church doctrine a "'regulative' or 'rule' theory."[15]

Rather than draw sharp distinctions among these theological models, Lindbeck is careful to acknowledge the ambiguity of the distinctions[16] and to underscore that he has not provided an indubitable proof for the cultural-linguistic model but merely presented it.[17] Nevertheless, he does wish to defend the cultural-linguistic model against both propositional models, i.e., the cognitive-propositional and the experience-expressivist.[18] In so doing he offers some unquestionably valuable insights with which anyone engaged in theological reflection today must come to terms. Nonetheless, although in each instance the insight is valuable, the conclusions he draws from the insight must be seriously questioned.

Reality and Religion as a Social Construct: Truth as Pragmatic Usage

First, he points out that reality is a social construct:

> The sense of what is real or unreal is in large part socially constructed, and what seems credible or incredible to contemporary theologians is likely to be more the product of their milieu and intellectual conditioning than of their science, philosophy, or theological argumentation.[19]

---

[14] Lindbeck, *The Nature of Doctrine*, p. 18.

[15] Lindbeck, *The Nature of Doctrine*, p. 18.

[16] For example, he writes: "The issues involved in this debate are even less susceptible to clear-cut decision than are comparable questions about the best overall theories in the physical sciences; and these, if T.S. Kuhn and others are to be believed, are never finally decidable. Theories are abandoned, not so much because they are refuted (on their own terms, that is), but because they prove unfruitful for new or different questions that come to interest the relevant group of scientists for a wide variety of reasons." Lindbeck, *The Nature of Doctrine*, p. 42.

Here Lindbeck touches on a central weakness of the cultural-linguistic model. There seems to be no accounting for the possibility, much less any suggesting of criteria for avoiding, that what the community takes to be fruitful or of interest may be distorting or even wrong, e.g., racism, sexism, classism, and xenophobias in general.

[17] See Lindbeck, *The Nature of Doctrine*, p. 134.

[18] It is confusing at times just what Lindbeck has in mind when he speaks of propositionalists. He seems to distinguish between dogmatic propositionalists (see, *The Nature of Doctrine*, pp. 16 and 113) and expressivist propositionalists (see, *ibid.*, pp. 104 and 106-107). The latter expressivist propositionalists he calls the "contemporary propositional view" (see, *ibid.*, pp. 104-105) which is then contrasted with the cultural-linguistic model's "regulative propositional view" (see, *ibid.*, p. 104f).

[19] Lindbeck, *The Nature of Doctrine*, p. 63.

He develops the implications of this claim, that reality is a social construct, when he proceeds to distinguish between "intrasystematic" and "ontological" (or "isomorphic") statements of truth. "The first is the truth of coherence; the second, that of correspondence to reality ..."[20] He suggests that "... religion, like a mathematical system, seeks to be a coherent whole within which ... the intrasystematic truth or falsity of particular utterances is of fundamental significance."[21] He proceeds to argue that intrasystematic truth is possible without ontological truth,[22] but, in the end, even his notion of ontological truth is not based on the grounds of "epistemological realism" but on pragmatic performance. He writes: Religious utterances' "... correspondence to reality in the view we are expounding is not an attribute that they have when considered in and of themselves, but is only a function of their role in constituting a form of life, a way of being in the world [i.e., pragmatic usage], which itself corresponds to the Most Important, the Ultimately Real [but, he suggests, this is a correspondence of "adequacy" not "literalness," see p. 65].[23] "... [A] religious utterance ... acquires the propositional truth of ontological correspondence only insofar as it is a performance, an act or deed, which helps create that correspondence."[24] In short, ontological truth is based on individual, but above all communal, reinforcement because it "works."

Lindbeck returns to the theme of pragmatic truth in the final section of his book entitled "Intelligibility as Skill." He first distinguishes the cultural-linguistic model from the experience-expressivist model by accusing the "liberals" of "... commitment to the foundational enterprise of uncovering universal principles or structures - if not metaphysical, then existential, phenomenological, or hermeneutical."[25] On the other hand, "postliberals," according to Lindbeck's definition, are suspicious of all such foundations. But in the absence of universal principles or structures, one can appeal, he argues, to the communal usage of a linguistic system. One becomes "competent" or "acceptable" within the community to the extent that one practices the linguistic game.

> The grammar of religion, like that of language, cannot be explicated or learned by analysis of experience, but only by practice. Religious and linguistic competence may

---

[20] Lindbeck, *The Nature of Doctrine*, p. 64.
[21] Lindbeck, *The Nature of Doctrine*, p. 64.
[22] Lindbeck, *The Nature of Doctrine*, p. 64.
[23] Lindbeck, *The Nature of Doctrine*, p. 65.
[24] Lindbeck, *The Nature of Doctrine*, p. 65.
[25] Lindbeck, *The Nature of Doctrine*, p. 129.

help greatly in dealing with experience, but experience by itself may be more a hindrance than a help to acquiring competence: children, at least in Jesus' parabolic sense, have an advantage over adults. In short, religions, like languages, can be understood only in their own terms, not by transposing them into an alien speech [such as foundationalism or experience].[26]

Hence, if one wants to understand religion, according to Lindbeck, one must understand how religions work as cultural-linguistic systems which function to train the individual in linguistic (religious) competency. Watch what an individual or a community *does* and that will demonstrate what that individual's/community's culture and religion is. "Scholarly non-theologians who want to understand religion are concerned with how religions work for their adherents, not with their credibility."[27] "In short, intelligibility comes from skill, not theory, and credibility comes from good performance, not adherence to independently formulated criteria."[28] Intelligibility and reasonableness are a matter of "art," which Lindbeck calls an "unformalizable skill."[29]

There is something attractive about the cultural-linguistic model. First, it acknowledges that reality is a social construct. Second, it affirms that isomorphic truth is impossible and confirms the place of intrasystematic coherence and pragmatic usage as the route to truth.

But, surely, simply because something works doesn't make it "true." A pragmatic definition of truth (i.e., usage or performance), to be sure, must be acknowledged to be at best a necessary but not a sufficient definition of truth in any ontological sense. It will always only remain "sufficient" or "adequate," not absolute, because of the absence of isomorphic truth. In other words, there is no indubitable isomorphic or ontological truth, so that the closest we can come to such a truth claim is a pragmatic test of sufficiency. In the absence of absolute truth, however, what assures us that the linguistic system or individual/communal usage is true? Intrasystematic coherence can result in blinding the individual and/or the community to what it most needs to understand (e.g., dependence on the automobile is intrasystematically coherent for first world countries, but what are the debilitating long term consequences for our short-term convenience?). Manifest coherence is always and already dependent upon concealment and even sup-

---

[26] Lindbeck, *The Nature of Doctrine*, p. 129. Has not Lindbeck read this in a literal rather than a parabolic sense?
[27] Lindbeck, *The Nature of Doctrine*, p. 130.
[28] Lindbeck, *The Nature of Doctrine*, p. 131.
[29] Lindbeck, *The Nature of Doctrine*, p. 130.

pression. To the extent that possibility is greater than actuality, for example, all actuality conceals unrealized possibility. The greater one focuses on actuality, the more one fails to understand what was lost by the actualization of "what is." Simply to observe what a community does by no means tells one what it *is*, because what it *is* involves both its revealed actuality as well as its concealed possibilities.

Under these circumstances, we must acknowledge the possibility of, and the need to protect a community from, systematic distortion. The issue of systematic distortion constitutes one of the two crucial points of weakness in Lindbeck's cultural-linguistic theological model.

Our Debt to Language: Rules Prior to Paradigms?

Second, Lindbeck argues that we always and already find ourselves, and come to conscious awareness within, a linguistic system. He employs the notion of "paradigm" from Thomas Kuhn to argue that religion "[l]ike a culture or language, ... is a communal phenomenon that shapes the subjectivities of individuals rather than being primarily a manifestation of those subjectivities.[30] While acknowledging in passing that "... the relation of religion and experience ... is not unilateral but dialectical,[31] Lindbeck proceeds to claim in defense of the cultural-linguistic model of theology that "[i]nstead of deriving external features of a religion from inner experience, it is the inner experiences which are viewed as derivative.[32] In short,

> ... unless we acquire language of some kind, we cannot actualize our specifically human capacities for thought, action, and feeling. Similarly ... to become religious involves becoming skilled in the language, the symbol system of a given religion ... A religion is above all an external word, a *verbum externum*, that molds and shapes the self and its world, rather than an expression or thematization of a preexisting self or of preconceptual experience. The *verbum internum* ... is also crucially important, but it would be understood in a theological use of the model as a capacity [given by prevenient grace?] for hearing and accepting the true religion, the true external word, rather than (as experiential-expressivism would have it) as a common experience diversely articulated in different religions.[33]

---

[30] Lindbeck, *The Nature of Doctrine*, p. 33.
[31] Lindbeck, *The Nature of Doctrine*, p. 33.
[32] Lindbeck, *The Nature of Doctrine*, p. 34.
[33] Lindbeck, *The Nature of Doctrine*, p. 34. David Tracy argues just the opposite in *Blessed Rage for Order*, p. 103: "We misunderstand religious language if we claim it *causes* (presents) our general confidence or trust in the meaningfulness of existence. We understand such language correctly only when we recognize that the use of religious language is *an effect* (a *re*-presentation) of an already present basic confidence or trust."

This prereflective shaping function of the *verbum externum* is developed by Lindbeck with the assistance of Noam Chomsky's notion of "depth grammar."[34] He argues that "... it is not the lexicon but rather the grammar of the religion which church doctrines chiefly reflect.[35] This distinction permits him to distinguish the position of the cultural-linguist from the "propositions" of the cognitive-propositional and the "simple symbolism" of the experience-expressivist. The deep grammar of a religion (defended by the cultural-linguist) remains constant. The lexicon and propositional dimensions of a religion at least in principle are constantly changing.

> There is nothing uniquely Christian about this constancy: supernatural explanations are quite unnecessary [though taken to be necessary by the cognitive-propositionalists]. This is simply the kind of stability that languages and religions, and to a lesser extent cultures, observably have. They are the lenses through which human beings see and respond to their changing worlds, or the media in which they formulate their descriptions. The world and its descriptions may vary enormously even while the lenses or media remain the same. Or, to change the simile, just as genetic codes, or computer programs may remain identical even while producing startling

---

(emphasis in the original) The argument here is another classic case of the chicken or the egg. Which comes first, language or experience? That we are always and already immersed in a language, however, does not mean that there is some permanent meaning to language prior to and independent from experience. One can argue, to the contrary, that language is generated out of experience as a consequence of metaphorical tension built on the "foundation" of dead metaphors (i.e., "literal" meaning), and that, therefore, linguistic meaning is always tethered to experience. Nevertheless, linguistic claims foreign to our experience do call us to accountability and constitute part of our debt to the past. Their call, however, is not necessarily a call of truth. It can just as easily be the call of untruth and distortion. What distinguishes aporetic theology from Lindbeck's cultural-linguistic theology is, then, not a denial of our immersion always and already in language, but that an adequate understanding of that immersion requires of us to keep all the language games in play even to the extent of acknowledging the inadequacy of some language games to our experience. In short, all of the tradition must be preserved and protected - "heretic" as well as "orthodox." Precisely those options, which we cannot accept, constantly remind us of the inadequacy of our understanding and of the concealment inherent in every clarity that is embraced. This does not deny commitment. As even Lindbeck observes (*op.cit.*, p. 132), faith precedes language.

34 See Lindbeck, *The Nature of Doctrine*, p. 80. My suspicion is that Lindbeck is misreading Chomsky here. Where Chomsky seems to be trying to establish an argument for individual freedom over against the threat of the determinism or conditioning of behaviorism, Lindbeck is arguing for a usage of regulative propositions to determine whether one has acquired competency in a community. The latter is using "depth grammar" in defense of heteronomy. The former is using "depth grammar" in support of autonomy. I am indebted to my colleague at Willamette University, Kenneth Nolley, for the formulation of this insight with respect to Chomsky.

35 Lindbeck, *The Nature of Doctrine*, p. 81.

different products depending on input and situation, so also with the basic grammars of cultures, languages, and religions. They remain while the products change.[36]

Here we encounter the second of the two major weaknesses of the cultural-linguistic model. The first weakness is the inability of the cultural-linguist to acknowledge, much less address, systematic distortion of the intrasystematic coherence of the linguistic system. The issue at issue now, however, strikes at the heart of Lindbeck's regulative propositional view, and it can be formulated in the form of a question: are rules prior to paradigms or are paradigms prior to rules? Lindbeck's position is that rules precede paradigms:

> Paradigms ... are not simply to be replicated, but are rather to be followed in the making of new formulations ... [I]f the same rules that guided the formation of the original paradigm are operative in the construction of the new formulations, they express one and the same doctrine.[37]

Lindbeck employs the notion of paradigm from Thomas Kuhn throughout his text, but he has overlooked Kuhn's discussion of the relationship of rules to paradigms. The reason Lindbeck has done so is clear. The cultural-linguistic model wants to maintain that language precedes experience, and that the language of the community preserves rules governing the truth claims (both intrasystematic and isomorphic) of that community to which the theologian must conform if s/he wishes to be considered a participant in that community.

If Lindbeck is to employ Kuhn's notion of paradigm for developing his understanding of the cultural-linguistic model of theology, then he cannot ignore Kuhn's insistence that paradigms *precede* rules and not vice versa. Kuhn makes explicitly clear that paradigms are operative even in the absence of rules, for paradigms involve a ". . . strong network of commitments - conceptual, theoretical, instrumental, and methodological ..."[38] which constitute a shared set of assumptions and points of view and provide for the coherence of the normal research tradition *prior to rules*.

> Normal science is a highly determined activity, but it need not be entirely determined by rules. That is why, at the start of this essay, I introduced shared paradigms rather than shared rules, assumptions, and points of view as the source of coherence for normal research traditions. Rules, I suggest, derive from paradigms, but paradigms can guide research even in the absence of rules.[39]

---

[36] Lindbeck, *The Nature of Doctrine*, p. 83.
[37] Lindbeck, *The Nature of Doctrine*, p. 95.
[38] Kuhn, *The Structure of Scientific Revolutions*, p. 42.
[39] Kuhn, *The Structure of Scientific Revolutions*, p. 42.

Kuhn asks: "In the absence of a competent body of rules, what restricts the scientist to a particular normal-scientific tradition?"[40] Here he introduces the notion of "family resemblances" from Wittgenstein to suggest that age old insight from Socrates that absolute definitions of universals are impossible. He then observes that a particular normal-scientific tradition is "... constituted by a network of overlapping and crisscross resemblances. The existence of such a network sufficiently accounts for our success in identifying the corresponding object or activity."[41] He proceeds to say:

> Something of the same sort may very well hold for the various research problems and techniques that arise within a single normal-scientific tradition. What these have in common is not that they satisfy some explicit or even some fully discoverable set of rules and assumptions that gives the tradition its character and its hold upon the scientific mind. Instead, they may relate by resemblance and by modeling to one or another part of the scientific corpus which the community in question already recognizes as among its established achievements. Scientists work from models acquired through education and through subsequent exposure to the literature often without quite knowing or needing to know what characteristics have given these models the status of community paradigms. And because they do so, they need no full set of rules. The coherence displayed by the research tradition in which they participate may not imply even the existence of an underlying body of rules and assumptions that additional historical or philosophical investigation might uncover.[42]

He proceeds to argue that rules become important precisely whenever a paradigm or model is felt to be insecure.[43]

Two concerns surface, once again, with respect to Lindbeck's work. The first is Lindbeck's complete failure to recognize the danger of systematic distortion within a paradigm's tradition. The second indicates precisely why Lindbeck is so enamored with rules. Given the non-defensibility of the cognitive-propositional model in theology, that is, given the indefensibility of biblical literalism, we find ourselves in a situation in which a theological paradigm has collapsed. It is only "natural," one would expect having studied Thomas Kuhn, that one would focus one's attention on rules. Why? Because rules become important with a crisis of the paradigm. In Lindbeck's case, the crisis is a crisis of authority in the community. He is arguing for a

---

[40] Kuhn, *The Structure of Scientific Revolutions*, p. 44.
[41] Kuhn, *The Structure of Scientific Revolutions*, p. 45.
[42] Kuhn, *The Structure of Scientific Revolutions*, pp. 45-46.
[43] See. Kuhn, *The Structure of Scientific Revolutions*, p. 47: "Normal science can proceed without rules only so long as the relevant scientific community accepts without question the particular problem-solutions already achieved. Rules should therefore become important and the characteristic unconcern about them should vanish whenever paradigms or models are felt to be insecure. That is ... exactly what does occur."

heteronomous authority, that is, linguistic competence in conformity with regulative propositions established by a normative community, in opposition to an autonomous authority that demands accountability to the text, tradition, the individual, and communal experience.

It is precisely because paradigms function as both "sociological" and "exemplary past achievements,"[44] functioning prior to the full development of regulative propositions or rules, that the community must be vigilant lest focus on rules prohibits awareness of a distorted understanding of "reality" as a consequence of always and already being committed to a paradigm. The issue is not commitment versus non-commitment. There is no Being-in-the-world that is not always and already committed to an understanding of reality and to exemplary past achievements that serve as models of behavior in the present. The issue, rather, is whether one embraces a paradigm uncritically or builds in some kind of self-correcting criticism based on awareness of the danger of distortion.

Lindbeck is so eager to retrieve a normative discourse as rule governing for the community that he has passed over Kuhn's analysis of the priority of paradigms over rules and substituted Chomsky's notion of "depth grammar" as a way of developing a theory of regulative propositionalism.

> As T.S. Kuhn has argued in reference to science, and Wittgenstein in philosophy, the norms of reasonableness are too rich and subtle to be adequately specified in any general theory of reason or knowledge. These norms, to repeat a point often made in this book, are like the rules of depth grammar, which linguists search for and may at times approximate but never grasp. Thus reasonableness in religion and theology, as in other domains, has something of that aesthetic character, that quality of unformalizable skill, which we usually associate with the artist or the linguistically competent.[45]

Notice here that Lindbeck reduces paradigms to norms and norms to depth grammar. These rules or norms constitute "hidden constraints"[46] governing what may or may not be said and done within a linguistic/cultural system.

Lindbeck has confused the rules for the paradigm. What this ignores, however, is that one embraces a set of rules because one is already committed to the reality (the intrasystematic coherence) that informs and empowers the rules. Taking the rules to be the reality places the cart before the horse. It fails to grasp the wagers that all notions of reality rest upon. In short, it fails to grasp the role of presuppositions, paradox, and concealment

---

[44] See Kuhn, *The Structure of Scientific Revolutions*, p. 175.
[45] Lindbeck, *The Nature of Doctrine*, p. 130.
[46] Lindbeck, *The Nature of Doctrine*, p. 96.

that is necessary for every construct of reality which then results in a system of rules to preserve and protect that reality.

When rules are taken to precede paradigms, then theology becomes an epiphenomenon severed from itself by focussing on what is manifest (said and done) by individuals and communities rather than acknowledging and responding to what is beyond appearance. Hold onto the rules when reality appears to be collapsing around one.

Lindbeck does his best to make this vice a virtue, but his very example undermines his point. He suggests that we are to take doctrines to be "second-order guidelines for Christian discourse rather than first-order affirmations."[47] Second-order guidelines, according to Lindbeck, are regulative rules analogous to the hidden constraints of depth grammar. First-order affirmations, on the other hand, are taken to be isomorphic or ontological claims which require experience for their confirmation. This is, in fact, a confused usage of the distinction between first- and second-order language in theological reflection,[48] but for the moment we may accept Lindbeck's formulation. He proceeds to suggest that Athanasius was concerned to express a rule not an experience with ontological significance as he defended the scripturally unjustified *homoousios* of the Nicean formulation.

> ... the theologian most responsible for the final triumph of Nicaea [Athanasius] thought of it, not as a first-order proposition with ontological reference, but as a second-order rule of speech. For him, to accept the doctrine meant to agree to speak in a certain way [the rule: "... whatever is said of the Father is said of the Son, except that the Son is not the Father."[49]].[50]

---

[47] Lindbeck, *The Nature of Doctrine*, p. 94.
[48] Lindbeck asserts that one distinguishes between "first-order affirmations" and "second-order guidelines." See, Lindbeck, *The Nature of Doctrine*, p. 94. The aim is to distinguish between what Lindbeck sees as the idiosyncrasies of inner experience and the normative claims of communal life. The present project, in contrast, follows Mortinmer Adler's distinction in *How to Read a Book* and distinguishes between first- and second-order experience in terms of distinguishing between pre-reflective and reflective experience. For example, first-order experience consists of the routines and rituals of life which we rarely, if ever, place under the scrutiny of critical reflection. The activity of critical reflection, however, is a reflection about first-order experience. Second-order reflection has its grounding in first-order experience and not vice versa as Lindbeck wishes to argue. Both pre-reflective and reflective experience, however, are fundamentally shaped by what is inaccessible to reflection, e.g., the dependence of all reflection upon presuppositions and upon a dynamic of revealing and concealing that denies the totalizing project of reflective rationality.
[49] Lindbeck, *The Nature of Doctrine*, p. 94.
[50] Lindbeck, *The Nature of Doctrine*, p. 94.

Ignoring the issue of Lindbeck's anachronistic use of the intentional fallacy or one's believing to know the intention of an author to make it the sole criterion for determining the correctness of the interpretation of a text, one cannot help but observe that it is patently absurd to conclude that Athanasius was *only* concerned that there be agreement about the way Christians speak. To the contrary, his paradigm (or reality) was at stake. The rule (creed) was rooted in the reality not the reality in the rule. The divinization of the believer was dependent upon the proper relationship between the Father and the Son. There has to be a unity in Being between God and humanity, according to Athanasius, that could in fact liberate humanity from Becoming. Consubstantiality is essential to salvation.

The quarrel with Arius was not merely about a linguistic formulation. Arius and Athanasius, in fact, shared the same metaphysical framework of the Logos Christology. One can understand their disagreement in terms of a struggle about what constitutes the reality promised to the believer. In short, two models of soteriology are at stake.[51] Is that soteriological reality a promised participation in the Father (i.e., divinization of the believer, as Athanasius believed) or is it participation in the eternal Logos of the Son (i.e., a form of divinization but subordinate to the Father, as Arius believed)?

Arius argues that there was a time when the Logos did not exist. It was the first creature (God's eternal thoughts) which was then employed by God to create the world.[52] Yet, God is more than His thoughts (Logos). This is

---

[51] See Maurice Wiles analysis of the soteriology of the Arian movement in the context of the Lutheran (= Lindbeck) - Catholic (= John Courtney Murray) dialogue in the United States entitled "Eunomius: hair-splitting dialectician or defender of the accessibility of salvation?" in *The Making of Orthodoxy: Essays in Honour of Henry Chadwick*, ed. by Rowan Williams (Cambridge: Cambridge University Press, 1989) 157-172. Wiles' conclusion about that dialogue: "The ecumenical usefulness of their failure to acknowledge a religious or soteriological dimension to the Arian position is only too evident" (*ibid.*, p. 158).

For a detailed analysis of the Arian controversy, see Rowan Williams, *Arius: Heresy and Tradition* (London: Darton, Longman and Todd, 1987) in which he concurs with Wiles that soteriology is the heart of Arianism, e.g., pp. 17 and 21. Williams' thesis, that Arius is the victim of the emerging dominance of the episcopacy over the "school tradition of wisdom" (*ibid.*, p. 85), offers an intriguing partial explanation for the demise of the Alexandrian theology in general, the eclipse of Arianism in particular, and the emerging Latin church emphasis on ritual and physical sotoriology.

[52] See Max Mühl, "Der λόγος ἐνδιάθετος und προφορικός von der älteren Stoa bis zur Synode von Sirmium 351" in *Archiv für Begriffsgeschichte* (1962) 7-56, for a detailed analysis of the Logos tradition. He observes that the notion of a double Logos and a double creation (thought and material) finds its "vollendete Hypostase" (*ibid.*, p. 39) in Philo of Alexandria (see Philo of Alexandria *de opificio mundi* 16, 134 and *de Abrahamo* 83), and from Philo there is a direct influence on Christianity (op. cit., p.

totally consistent with John's prologue. Human beings already have partial access to that Logos[53] to the extent that humans are dependent upon universals in order to experience meaningfully (in the absence of universals there is only chaos). But, for Arius, humans in the flesh are only dimly aware of the fullness of the Logos. The fullness of the Logos can only be experienced completely with the resurrection which liberates humans from the flesh (in conformity with Paul's teaching, e.g., I Corinthians 15:50). Human experience now is a sufficient witness to the fullness yet to come, and that partial experience in the present fuels faith. Hence, the aphorism "there was a time when the Son was not" expressed a faith in the providential role of God in the created order calling humans to acknowledge their participation in the reality of the Son in anticipation of the life to come when that participation would be complete and in conformity with the subordination of the Son and the rest of reality to the Father as expressed by Paul in I Corinthians 15:28. Humans, according to Arius, participate in the reality of the Son not in the full reality of the Father.[54] This is the meaning of the Son's begottenness. It

---

39). See, as well, Birger A. Pearson, "Philo and Gnosticism" in *Aufstieg und Niedergang der Römischen Welt (ANRW)* II/21.1 (1984) 295-342, in which he argues for a Jewish origin for Gnosticism (321) but maintains that Philo is indebted to Middle-Platonism (319, 314, 340) and rejects the notion that Philo's thought "... lies in a trajectory that logically and chronologically issues in Gnosticism" (340). Pearson points out that Philo's use of Logos sees the material world as "an 'image of an image'" (323, n. 106).

For further analysis of the Logos tradition, see Ragnar Holte, "Logos Spermatikos. Christianity and Ancient Philosophy According to St. Justin's Apologies" in *Studia Theologica* 12 (1958) 109-168, and the critique of Holte's work by Jan Hendrik Waszink, "Bemerkungen zu Justins Lehre vom Logos Spermatikos" in *Mullus. Festschrift Theodor Klauser* of the *Jahrbuch für Antike und Christentum*, Ergänzungsband 1 (Münster Westfalen: Aschendorffsche Verlagsbuchhandlung, 1964), 380-390.

[53] Paul, on the other hand, rarely speaks of the Logos. Rather than limit the Christ and our participation in the Christ to the Logos, Paul speaks of our participation in the entire νοῦς, or mind, of Christ, e.g., I Corinthians 13:12

[54] See Maurice Wiles, "In Defence of Arius" in *Journal of Theological Studies* 13 (1962), p. 346: "... even within the terms of an understanding of salvation as deification, the argument remains open to question. The deification which is man's goal [according to Arius] is not to become ὁ θεός [God, the Father, as is the case with Athanasius] but θεοὶ κατὰ χάριν [gods according to grace]. The Son, on the Arian understanding of his person, is the prototype of θεοὶ κατὰ χάριν. It is not clear, therefore, why he should not logically be able to bring men to be what he is." Earlier Wiles reminded his reader that "[i]n his desire to maintain the absolute uniqueness and supremacy of the Father, Origen, as is well known, lays great stress on the secondary, derivative, and subordinate nature of the Son. The saying that 'the Father is greater than I' [John 14:28] is, he declares, true in every conceivable respect. And this statement is no mere declaration of a general principle; it is worked out in very specific and detailed terms. The Father alone is ὁ θεός or ἀληθινὸς θεός; the Son is simply θεός" (*ibid.*, p. 342).

was enough for humanity to participate in the reality of the Son, and such participation in the Christ is precisely what makes one a Christian. Furthermore, it curtailed hybris in that it limited to the level of the Logos human participation in divinity, for everything, including humanity, is to be brought to proper subordination under the Father in the Son.

Athanasius, on the other hand, was confident that salvation meant complete divinization. To participate in the Logos meant to participate in God, and the fullness of the resurrection meant participation in the fullness of God.[55] Hence, there could not have been a time when the Son was not. The Logos is co-eternal with the Father. This is an ontological proposition by Athanasius, and it was understood to be rooted in human experience. To argue, as does Lindbeck, that this is merely a quarrel about "a second-order rule of speech," is only to indicate how far our language game has distanced itself from the language game of the 4th century. Lindbeck has made an anachronistic reading as a consequence of our current epoch's having lost any experiential sense of what was at stake with the Logos tradition. Having done so, Lindbeck can argue that all that was at stake was a set of regulative principles (a monotheistic principle, a principle of historical specificity, and a principle of Christological maximalism[56]). Reality has thereby been sacri-

---

This suggests that Arius is defending a form of what Albert Schweitzer called "Christ mysticism" in contrast to Athanasius who would, then, represent a form of "God mysticism." See Albert Schweitzer, *Die Mystik des Apostels Paulus* (Tübingen, J.C.B. Mohr (Paul Siebeck), 1981).

Peter Hofrichter in "Logoslehre und Gottesbild bei Apologeten, Modalisten und Gnostikern. Johanneische Christologie im Lichte ihrer frühesten Rezeption" in *Monotheismus und Christologie. Zur Gottesfrage im hellenistischen Judentum und im Urchristentum* (Freiburg, Herder, 1992), p. 192, n. 14, points out that Philo of Alexandria already distinguished between the Logos as God (θεός without an article) and "another" (ἑτέρου), "the true and one God" (ὁ μὲν ἀληθείᾳ θεὸς εἷς ἐστιν) in *de somniis I*, 228f. See Mühl, "Der λόγος ἐνδιάθετος und προφορικός," p. 19 and, especially, p. 23, where Mühl calls attention to the significance of Philo's assertion in *De fuga et inventione 101* for later Christian understandings of the Logos.

[55] See Wiles, "In Defence of Arius," p. 346, where he quotes Athanasius' *De synodis*, 51: "'By partaking of him, we partake of the Father, because the Word is the Father's own. If the Word himself were what he is by participation and were not in his own right substantial deity and image of the Father, he would not be able to deify, being himself deified. For it is impossible for one who merely possesses something by participation to pass on what he partakes to others, since what he has is not his own but the giver's, and what he receives is barely grace sufficient for his own needs.'"

It is striking that Athanasius employs both ὁμοουσία and ὁμοίωσις in the same line without, apparently, seeing any tension much less contradiction.

[56] Lindbeck, *The Nature of Doctrine*, p. 94.

ficed for the rules. It has been forgotten that "the sabbath was made for man, not man for the sabbath" (Mark 2:27).

We do owe a debt to language as "the great institution ... that has preceded each and every one of us,[57] but we dare not blindly inherit that institution. We must critically engage it ever anew in the open process of interpretation and reinterpretation. Paul Ricoeur borrows Reinhart Koselleck's categories of the "space of experience" and "horizon of expectation" to develop a notion of the present, which is always relative to an individual (i.e., only individual's have a "present"[58]), as standing in tension between the inherited actions and sufferings of both those who have gone before the individual and the imaginative vision of possibility that serves as the horizon of initiative and engagement for the individual[59] (and Ricoeur adds, for the community). Here the emphasis is on action informed by the imagination, what Ricoeur calls mimesis$_3$, rather than upon a mere decision as a result of catechesis or socialization. This focus on the "individual" here in no way diminishes the importance of the "communal" for Ricoeur. Understanding is a dialectical process radically rooted in the Otherness of things and persons.

Faith Precedes Language: But is Certainty the Pre-Condition of Doubt?

Given the priority of the linguistic system over human experience in Lindbeck's cultural-linguistic model, it is understandable that Lindbeck affirms Aquinas' subordinating of reason to faith.[60] One must commit oneself to a linguistic game before one can become proficient and competent in it. In this sense, then, faith precedes language. Catechesis or socialization becomes the vehicle for leading faith to linguistic fulfillment, i.e., linguistic competency.

Lindbeck goes even further, however, to maintain that certitude is the pre-condition of doubt. Echoing the popular chorus that we must avoid Cartesianism at all costs, he rejects Descartes' claim that universal doubt is prior to certitude.[61] He argues:

---

[57] Paul Ricoeur, *Time and Narrative*, vol. 3, p. 221.
[58] See, Ricoeur, *Time and Narrative*, vol. 3, pp. 108-9.
[59] See, Ricoeur, *Time and Narrative*, vol. 3, pp. 208f.
[60] Lindbeck, *The Nature of Doctrine*, p. 131.
[61] Lindbeck, *The Nature of Doctrine*, p. 102.

> Actually ... certitude always comes first. It is the precondition for doubt. To doubt what is generally accepted is unreal and unreasonable, an emotion or a pathology, unless there are statable reasons for doubting (such as, for example, a conflict in evidence or in authorities).[62]

This is a curious logic. There is, to be sure, a Cartesian sense, i.e., cogito ergo sum, in which certitude precedes doubt. I must first exist in order to doubt that I am existing. But since when does such certitude lead to the acceptance of opinion or teaching as normative simply because that opinion or teaching has been held by a community? Again, racism, sexism, classism, and xenophobias have all been embraced at one point or another by the Christian community. Is it an emotion or a pathology to claim that what was generally accepted with respect to racism, etc., is both unreal and unreasonable? There is a hidden agenda in Lindbeck's cultural-linguistic model. It is a fundamental confidence that there is something equivalent to a hidden hand to history mysteriously at work in the community:

> As is true for individuals, so also a religious community's salvation is not by works, nor is its faith for the sake of practical efficacy, and yet good works of unforeseeable kinds flow from faithfulness. It was thus, rather than by intentional effort, that biblical religion helped produced democracy and science, as well as other values Westerners treasure; and it is in similarly unimaginable and unplanned ways, if at all, that biblical religion will help save the world (for Western civilization is now world civilization) from the demonic corruptions of these same values.[63]

What are these "unimaginable and unplanned ways?" How can we have confidence that they are benevolent? Is it not a presupposition of the cultural-linguist that they are? But, further, we find here an example of true distortion that must be, and can only be, checked by the broader community of dialogue, i.e., the notion that democracy and science are peculiarly Western values and treasures. John Brooke, for example, does a convincing job of demonstrating that science, at least, does not owe its exclusive provenance to Western culture.[64]

We are caught in a vicious circle (rather than a hermeneutical circle) with the cultural-linguistic model that knows already in advance both what its goal is ("Jerusalem"[65]) and that it is on the right road because of its confidence that the linguistic usage of the community is trustworthy as well as normative. Not only is this model dependent upon a statistical profile of the

---

[62] Lindbeck, *The Nature of Doctrine*, p. 102.
[63] Lindbeck, *The Nature of Doctrine*, p. 128.
[64] See John Hedley Brooke, *Science and Religion: Some Historical Perspectives* (New York: Cambridge University Press, 1991).
[65] See, Lindbeck, *The Nature of Doctrine*, pp. 52, 53, 54.

Christian tradition for its determination of what constitutes the normative consensus,[66] but it is ultimately Barthian as is confirmed by Lindbeck's own acknowledgment[67] and by both his supportive[68] and critical readers.[69]

What Lindbeck fails to appreciate is that faith does not privilege a particular community's language game. He would have it that one must surrender to the language of the community, for entrance into the community does not permit critical accountability. Reason can be engaged only after one has become proficient in a language game.

> As Aquinas ... notes, reasoning in support of the faith is not meritorious before faith, but only afterward; or, in the conceptuality employed in this book, the logic of coming to believe, because it is like that of learning a language, has little room for argument, but once one has learned to speak the language of faith, argument becomes possible.[70]

Yet one can accept that faith precedes language and one can acknowledge that reason is grounded by a leap of faith and not vice versa without eliminating critical reflection during the acquisition of linguistic competency. The present project argues that the human condition is shaped by aporetics, but aporiai call for critical vigilance lest they be reduced to facile explanations by one side or the other of the paradoxical tension, e.g., that the human condition is shaped by universals and particulars means that both must be acknowledged without explaining one by means of the other. Faith does go before both language and reason, but precisely in the acquisition of linguistic competency there *must* be "room for argument" over the legitimacy and authority of linguistic conventionality. Otherwise, there is no acknowledgment that every model of faith excludes and conceals as it includes and makes manifest, and there is simply no protection against systematic distortion.

A New Heteronomy

The above observations with respect to reality as a social construct, our debt to the language that has always gone before us, and the role of faith preceding language leads Lindbeck to champion

---

[66] See, for example, Lindbeck, *The Nature of Doctrine*, pp. 99-100.
[67] See, Lindbeck, *The Nature of Doctrine*, pp. 120-121 and 135.
[68] See, for example, George Schner, "Hume's *Dialogues* and the Redefinition of the Philosophy of Religion" in *The Thomist*, 55/1 (1991), p. 98.
[69] See, for example, David Tracy, "Lindbeck's New Program for Theology: A Reflection" in *The Thomist*, 49 (1985), p. 465.
[70] Lindbeck, *The Nature of Doctrine*, p. 132.

> ... the viability of a unified world of the future [which] may well depend on counteracting the acids of modernity. It may depend on communal enclaves that socialize their members into highly particular outlooks supportive of concern for others rather than for individual rights and entitlements, and a sense of responsibility for the wider social rather than for personal fulfillment.[71]

The claim is that the "liberal experience-expressivist" model of theology emphasizes exclusively personal fulfillment without any sense of solidarity for the welfare of others or the good of society. This is simply too simplistic, unacceptable, and a misrepresentation.[72] Lindbeck has attempted to raise a bulwark against the disease of modernity as he understands it:

> Sociologists have been telling us for a hundred years or more[73] that the rationalization, pluralism, and mobility of modern life dissolve the bonds of tradition and community. This produces multitudes of men and women who are impelled, if they have religious yearnings, to embark on their own individual quests for symbols of transcendence. The churches have become purveyors of this commodity rather than communities that socialize their members into coherent and comprehensive religious outlooks and forms of life. Society paradoxically conditions human beings to experience selfhood as somehow prior to social influences ... Selfhood is experienced as a given rather than as either a gift or an achievement, and fulfillment comes from exfoliating or penetrating into the inner depths rather than from communally responsible action in the public world. Thus the cultural climate is on the whole antithetical to postliberalism [i.e., the cultural-linguistic model Lindbeck defends].[74]

Such dichotomies as those between "inner" versus "outer," individual versus society, egocentric versus communal welfare, a "unilateral" relation versus a "dialectical" relation between religion and experience,[75] individual quests versus communal verities,[76] "self-identical content" versus "form,"[77] first-order "affirmations versus" second-order "guidelines,"[78] "ontological propositions" versus "regulative propositions,"[79] "extratextual" versus "intratextual,"[80] liberal focussing on God's being versus postliberal focussing on how

---

[71] Lindbeck, *The Nature of Doctrine*, p. 127.
[72] For example, it totally ignores the revisionist agenda outlined by David Tracy in chapter 10, "History, Theory, and *Praxis*" (emphasis in the original), of *Blessed Rage for Order*.
[73] The discipline of Sociology is not a hundred years old yet.
[74] Lindbeck, *The Nature of Doctrine*, p. 126. See, as well, Lindbeck's discussion *ibid.*, pp. 77-78.
[75] See Lindbeck, *The Nature of Doctrine*, p. 33. See, as well, David Tracy's critique in "Lindbeck's New Program for Theology," pp. 462-463.
[76] See Lindbeck, *The Nature of Doctrine*, pp. 77-8.
[77] See Lindbeck, *The Nature of Doctrine*, p. 93.
[78] See Lindbeck, *The Nature of Doctrine*, p. 94.
[79] See Lindbeck, *The Nature of Doctrine*, pp. 94, 106-7.
[80] See Lindbeck, *The Nature of Doctrine*, p. 114, where Lindbeck assigns the "extratextual" reading to the experiential-expressive and the "intratextual" reading to the cultural-linguistic model.

life is to be lived and reality construed in light of God's character as revealed in Jesus,[81] experience as the key to the future kingdom versus the future kingdom as key to experience,[82] the liberal experienced universal of an underlying unity common to all persons versus postliberal championing of "highly particular outlooks,"[83] intelligibility as a matter of "theory" versus "skill,"[84] "independent criteria" versus "performance,"[85] "translation" versus "socialization,"[86] etc., make for wonderful rhetoric. But they shed little disclosive light on the human condition constituted out of a tension between a life-world shaped by a linguistic heritage and the sufferings and actions of the past that is challenged with responsible actions in a yet to be realized future. This dialectical or aporetic situation requires not merely a hermeneutics of restoration, but a hermeneutics of suspicion. Above all, it places a premium on imaginative variations rather than simple repetition of regulative propositions.

Where in most cases one would want to argue for a "both/and", Lindbeck's project, in fact, represents a new form of heteronomy which requires subservience and servitude with only a semblance of critical accountability and a complete discounting of imaginative construction. Critical accountability (the role of the theoretician[87]) is defined by Lindbeck as the ability to properly choose between each dichotomy, sketched above, on the basis of a prior commitment to the normative faith of the community as a consequence of catechesis or socialization.[88]

If we take Paul Tillich's notion of heteronomy as our guiding definition, then one can perceive the siren call of a pleasure principle functioning in Lindbeck's cultural-linguistic model. Tillich writes that heteronomy means to obey a strange authority and continues by suggesting that defenders of heteronomy

> ... are looking for the security of a foreign authority which deprives us of the courage to use our reason because of the fear of punishment or of falling into insoluble problems. So we come to the surprising result that heteronomy is ultimately

---

[81] See Lindbeck, *The Nature of Doctrine*, p. 121.
[82] See Lindbeck, *The Nature of Doctrine*, pp. 125-6.
[83] See Lindbeck, *The Nature of Doctrine*, p. 127.
[84] See Lindbeck, *The Nature of Doctrine*, pp. 128 and 131.
[85] See Lindbeck, *The Nature of Doctrine*, p. 131.
[86] See Lindbeck, *The Nature of Doctrine*, p. 132.
[87] See Lindbeck, *The Nature of Doctrine*, p. 79.
[88] See Lindbeck, *The Nature of Doctrine*, pp. 132-134.

the attempt to escape fear, not by courage but by subjection to an authority which gives us security. In this sense heteronomy indirectly appeals to the pleasure principle and denies our own rational structure.[89]

This is perhaps nowhere more clearly seen in Lindbeck's project than in his discussion of the "typological" interpretation of the text. This is "to interpret a text in terms of its immanent meanings"[90] In short, "[t]o describe the basic meaning of [classics[91]] ... is an intratextual task, a matter of explicating their contents and the perspectives on extratextual reality that they generate.[92] The heteronomy of the text is complete: "A scriptural world is thus able to absorb the universe. It supplies the interpretive framework within which believers seek to live their lives and understand reality."[93] The subsequent pages of Lindbeck's text are full of more of the same. The believer submits to the reality of the text making its story her/his story.[94]

> More generally stated, it is the religion instantiated in Scripture which defines being, truth, goodness, and beauty, and the nonscriptural exemplifications of these realities need to be transformed into figures (or types or antitypes) of the scriptural ones. Intratextual theology redescribes reality within the scriptural framework rather than translating Scripture into extrascriptural categories. *It is the text ... which absorbs the world, rather than the world the text.*[95] (emphasis added)

There is simply no appreciation here of the danger of reading into the text what one reads out of the text. There is, to the contrary, a naive assumption that the text is transparent and generally accessible. Here one can ignore the influence and shaping power of intervening history on the reading of the text.[96] Here there is no regard paid to the redactional activity of the biblical authors. Here the metaphorical nature of the text is simply denied: "Typology does not make scriptural contents into metaphors for extrascriptural realities, but the other way around."[97] The heteronomous world of the text

---

[89] Paul Tillich, *Perspectives on 19th and 20th Century Protestant Theology*, ed. by Carl E. Braaten (New York: Harper & Row, Pub., 1967), p. 26. See, as well, the discussion of heteronomy in *Systematic Theology*, vol. 1 (Chicago: University of Chicago Press, 1971), pp. 84-5.
[90] Lindbeck, *The Nature of Doctrine*, p. 116.
[91] See Lindbeck, *The Nature of Doctrine*, p. 116. To be sure, Lindbeck distinguishes his notion of "classic" from David Tracy's. See *ibid.*, p. 136, n. 4.
[92] Lindbeck, *The Nature of Doctrine*, p. 117.
[93] Lindbeck, *The Nature of Doctrine*, p. 117.
[94] See Lindbeck, *The Nature of Doctrine*, p. 118.
[95] Lindbeck, *The Nature of Doctrine*, p. 118.
[96] What Hans-Georg Gadamer calls *Wirkungsgeschichte* or Troeltsch called the influence of historicism on understanding.
[97] Lindbeck, *The Nature of Doctrine*, p. 118.

shapes the reader, who has become subservient to the normative reading of the text found in "the community."

Although Lindbeck avows that he shares with Deconstructionism the emphasis on the text and its "constituting the (or a) world within which everything is or can be construed,"[98] and even claims that he shares with Deconstructionism "'the play of figural language,' 'the grammar of tropes,' and 'the rhetoric of textual performance,'"[99] he complains that Deconstructionists have failed to acknowledge a "... privileged idiom, text, or text-constituted world."[100] He calls the Deconstructionists "*inter*textual rather than intratextual"[101] (emphasis in the original), and argues that "[i]n an intratextual religious or theological reading, in contrast, there is ... a privileged interpretive direction from whatever counts as holy writ to everything else."[102] Truly, the text has absorbed the universe.

Finally, Lindbeck's notion of "regulative propositions," discussed above, serves the same heteronomous function. Attributing the idea of a depth grammar to religious doctrine places both language and doctrine above critical accountability. Rules are claimed to determine paradigms rather than paradigms recognized as prior to rules. But this fails to acknowledge the role of commitment prior to one's embracing of a set of rules. Heteronomy is a comforting form of protection from the buffetings of a world of incalculable suffering, oppression, and the confusions of pluralism when one's paradigm appears to be crumbling. The postliberal cultural-linguistic project calls for withdrawal into the reassuring securities of one's uncritically embraced language game. But the costs?.

The price both the theologian and the community must pay for such heteronomy is extremely high. Failure to acknowledge the role of concealment in every linguistic formulation (e.g., the suppression of what might have been said rather than what was said; or the intentional and unintentional eliminating of possibilities that are the prerequisite of all coming to actuality), opens the barn door to the dangers of systematic distortion and all of the hybris of those privileged in the power hierarchy to be able to defend their "orthodoxy" as normative over "heterodoxy." The prescription for the

---

[98] Lindbeck, *The Nature of Doctrine*, p. 136, n. 5.
[99] Lindbeck, *The Nature of Doctrine*, p. 136, n. 5. I believe, one can seriously challenge Lindbeck's allegiance to figurative language. I would argue that he is, however, attracted to the rhetoric of the *grammar* of tropes, because that echoes his emphasis on "regulative propositionalism" analogous to "depth grammar."
[100] Lindbeck, *The Nature of Doctrine*, p. 136, n. 5.
[101] Lindbeck, *The Nature of Doctrine*, p. 136, n. 5.
[102] Lindbeck, *The Nature of Doctrine*, p. 136, n. 5.

loss of appreciation of the tradition is not a return to "communal enclaves" of particularity, but, rather, an appropriate embracing of the hermeneutical situation and the need for imaginative variation. There is more light yet to break forth, there is more time to blossom forth, there are alternative social systems and networkings of solidarity yet to be achieved, but, above all, there is a crying need to rigorously experientially understand both the claims and the distortions of the past. There is a performance test for judging the adequacy if not the truth of a religious proposition, but it is not Lindbeck's statistical test[103] of normative consensus in the religious practices of a community. Rather, it is the performative test of what enhances life, what builds up community and solidarity and tears down walls of destructive prejudice and misunderstanding as a consequence of isolationism, protectionism, and xenophobias. The fear is not a loss of commitment. Each individual and community is committed to her/his/its understanding of reality and how it functions. Rather, the fear is that our commitments will blind us to what our realities conceal from us.

---

[103] See Lindbeck, *The Nature of Doctrine*, pp. 99-100.

Chapter 6
Theology as Inquiry into Paradox: Strangers and Pilgrims

The two moments of the aporetic and spirituality are at the core of this theological project. The title "Strangers and Pilgrims" seeks to express the paradoxical character of our experience of aporiai. We are strangers, for example, because of the unique unrepeatability of the experience and understanding that is the individual. There never was and never again can be a person with the same experience and understanding as you, the individual, have. No one can reach the depths that you are - not even you yourself. Even after years of companionship, we remain strangers to ourselves, in our environment, and to Others. Yet, equally, we are fellow pilgrims rooted in a "present" defined by our natural environment, our tradition, language, country, home out of which a shared historical horizon of experience and understanding is constituted. We have no choice but to come to ourselves both as individuals (as strangers) and within the context of a shared historicality with Others (as fellow pilgrims) in the present.

The greater our lack of attachment to locality, the greater our mobility, the greater our self-conscious participation in the global village, the more our role as pilgrims always on the move is exposed. Nevertheless, no matter how transient our personal lives, there is no escaping the shared historical horizon of experience and understanding that of necessity makes us *fellow* pilgrims in the present. Coming to understand our human condition as deeply and broadly as possible requires our investigating this paradox of our being strangers and pilgrims. We are strangers in the sense that we are ultimately inaccessible to Others and to ourselves. We are fellow pilgrims in the sense that as individuals we are increasingly on the move physically and as communities we are on the move in terms of a corporate historical experience and open-ended understanding that is never exhaustive in its transparency or entirely accessible to consciousness.

Augustine?

The reader might hear an echoing of Augustine of Hippo in this title, "strangers and pilgrims."[1] Augustine speaks of Christians as strangers "hidden among the wicked" and not just among a world of wicked non-Christians but as an invisible church in the midst of the visible church. Christians, he suggests further, are "pilgrims even in their own homes,"[2] because they do not belong in the "earthly city," where one loves "self unto the contempt of God," but rather belong to the "heavenly city of Christ," where one loves "God unto the contempt of self."[3] Augustine writes in *The City of God*:

> Let these and similar answers (if any fuller and fitter answers can be found) be given to their enemies by the redeemed family of the Lord Christ, and by the pilgrim city of King Christ. But let this city bear in mind, that among her enemies lie hid those who are destined to be fellow citizens, that she may not think it a fruitless labour to bear what they inflict as enemies until they become confessors of the faith. So, too, as long as she is a stranger in the world, the city of God has in her communion, and bound to her by the sacraments, some who shall not eternally dwell in the lot of the saints ... In truth, these two cities are entangled together in this world, and intermixed until the last judgment effect their separation.[4]

The theological metaphor "strangers and pilgrims" in this project in no way depends upon, nor is it meant to evoke, this two-city dualism of Augustine. Rather than Hebrews 11:13 appealed to by Augustine (which reads: "These all died in faith, not having received what was promised, but having seen it and greeted it from afar, and having acknowledged that they were strangers and exiles on the earth"), a more ancient and fruitful textual provenance for the purposes of this project are Genesis 23:4, where Abraham says to the Hittites, "I am a stranger and a sojourner among you,"

---

[1] Though the notion is pre-Augustine. See the introduction to *Western Asceticism* in The Library of Christian Classics: Ichthus Edition, ed. by Owen Chadwick (Philadelphia: The Westminster Press, 1958), p. 14, where in reference to second century Christianity's championing of martyrdom it is claimed: "The blood of the martyrs not only propagated the gospel: it ensured that the kind of gospel propagated was that which showed the Christians as strangers and pilgrims upon earth, that their life was in another and a heavenly Zion." For the present project, everything hinges on just what is meant by "another and a heavenly Zion." Is one talking of some kind of afterlife, or is one talking about the imperceptible spiritual dimension beyond the material, sensed world, yet inseparable from this life?

[2] Augustine of Hippo, *The City of God*, trans by Marcos Dods (New York: The Modern Library, 1950), p. 21.

[3] Augustine, *The City of God*, p. 477.

[4] Augustine, *The City of God*, p. 38.

and Psalm 39:12, where the psalmist sings, "Here my prayer, O Lord, and give ear to my cry; hold not thy peace at my tears. For I am thy passing guest, a sojourner, like all my fathers."

Beyond Dualism

The human condition is not one of dualism but of paradox. A strict dualism divides experience (e.g., subject-object; the heavenly city-the earthly city; etc.) and then rejects any ultimate meaning, worth, or status to one half of the dualism (e.g., both solipsism and Augustinian Christianity deny any ultimate meaningful status to the world; materialism denies any ultimate meaningful status to spirituality).

Focussing on the aporiai at the core of life, on the other hand, enables recognition of the *necessary* tension generated by the incommensurability or the contradiction of two elements in tension in each aporia. In the case of the aporetic, we must employ both elements, incommensurable and contradictory as they are, to adequately grasp the condition named by the paradox. The classic example from physics is the necessity of using both particle and wave theories to account for light although these are contradictory theories. Light is paradoxical. So, too, is the human as constituted by a number of paradoxes, the most readily observable being that of intellect and world.[5] Nevertheless, to reduce the human down to one pole or the other, either as a soul not bound to this world or as pure materiality with even our mental life explained exhaustively by materialism, is to miss the fullness, the breadth, and the depth of the human condition.

We are strangers and pilgrims not because we possess (or are) a soul that connects us with an eternal and unchanging realm of Platonic ideas (at the core of Augustine's logic for distinguishing between the earthly and the heavenly cities). We are strangers and pilgrims not because, then, we are the hidden few eagerly awaiting full citizenship in the heavenly city (as well as awaiting retribution on our enemies, the wicked of the world). Rather, we are strangers and pilgrims because our very condition in this world (involving both what is manifest and what is concealed) is one of aporiai.

There are two senses in which the manifested and the concealed are understood in this project. The most obvious is the sense of foreground and

---

[5] One cannot help but observe that the juxtaposition of the paradox of light, according to contemporary physics, and the paradox of intellect and world ironically echoes the central "sun metaphor" (the heliotrope) of all of Western spirituality which is found in the Eastern tradition, as well, e.g., *The Tibetan Book of the Dead*, Evans-Wentz, W. Y., ed. (London: Oxford University Press, 1969).

background. True of all experience but especially in the case of aporiai, the manifest foreground conceals its background. To the extent that the foreground occupies our attention, it is easy to forget the background that is as equally necessary for our experiencing of the foreground as is the foreground itself. This tension between foreground and background is particularly important for understanding that the aporiai sketched in Part II of the present project are not mere dualisms. Each component of the aporia in question is necessary for the other component to be what it is.

The second sense of manifest and concealed informing the discussion here is even more ubiquitous, for it goes beyond the focussing of attention to characterize all that is. The Western tradition has focussed its attention almost exclusively on actualities either of the physical world (objects and actual events) or of the mind (ideas or universals as opposed to fantasies and illusions). But we have not begun to understand anything, most assuredly not either ourselves or our world, if we only focus on actuality. Higher than actuality is possibility. We don't understand anything without engaging its possibilities. Understanding is concerned precisely with grasping the possibilities of some-*thing* or event in a situation. Yet those possibilities are not manifest. They are so concealed that we tend to forget that our own possibilities are inseparable from our situation. In other words, we are no more able to remove ourselves from our situation than a spider can be without its web, which, of course, connects the spider with the entire world. Actuality conceals possibility, and for no species is that concealing more complex than is the case with human beings. We are the being that understands that it is more than its actual situation. We alone of all species have the ability to understand that "more" that is concealed in all manifestation. This understanding has us living always ahead of our present situation as we, always inadequately, sketch out for ourselves in advance the possibilities of our immediate and distant future.

To be sure, the notion of manifestation employed here is not the kind emphasized by Mircea Eliade (and David Tracy) by means of the notions of hierophany or theophany.[6] A hierophany/theophany, according to Eliade, is the manifesting of the invisible in the visible that sets an invisible metaphysical, Platonic, eternal dimension over against a visible, physical, ever impermanent and uncertain, linearly historical world of suffering.[7] Religious hu-

---

[6] See Mircea Eliade, *The Sacred and the Profane: The Nature of Religion* (New York: Harcourt Brace Jovanovich, Publishers, 1959), pp. 26-29, and Tracy, *The Analogical Imagination*, pp. 202-218; 376-386.

[7] See Mircea Eliade, *The Myth of the Eternal Return*, trans. by Willard R. Trask (New York: Bollingen Foundation, 1965), p. 34: "... [I]t could be said that ... 'primitive'

manity, according to Eliade, seeks the succor of wisdom or of a redeemer to achieve liberation from the "terror of history" with its unrepeatability and irreversibility.[8]

In contrast to Eliade, manifestation and concealment root humanity in history in an inextricable manner. It will require the sketching out of the aporiai of the human condition before we can begin to sense the full implication of the historical character of manifestation. Only when manifestation and concealment are properly "seen" as historical can we adequately own our situation as a spiritual odyssey of faith seeking understanding.

Unknowing is not Ignorance

Not surprisingly, Augustine of Hippo knows more than this author. Perhaps out of defensiveness, but certainly out of an insatiable desire to understand the human condition, this project maintains that lack of knowledge, however, is an advantage rather than a weakness. By no means is this a proposal that theology become a form of ignorance, though. Ignorance is the siren call of post-modernism and deconstructionism, where giddiness over the discovery of human, linguistic spirituality,[9] liberated from an eternal Logos and

---

ontology has a Platonic structure; and in that case Plato could be regarded as the outstanding philosopher of 'primitive mentality,' that is, as the thinker who succeeded in giving philosophic currency and validity to the modes of life and behavior of archaic humanity." Of course, Plato did so by substituting universals for the mythic stories. The consequence of this substitution, however, was no different for the philosopher than with Eliade's "religious humanity" which seeks to deny linear time and the terror of history by embracing cyclical time and the "eternal return" of archetypes.

[8] See, Eliade, *The Myth of the Eternal Return*, pp. 34-35, 141-162.: Religion seeks "... the abolition of time through the imitation of archetypes and the repetition of paradigmatic gestures" (*ibid.*, p. 35).

[9] Linguistic (or semantic) spirituality is rooted in the tension between Saussurean *semiotics*, indebted to Ludwig Noire and Wilhelm von Humboldt, and Benveniste/Ricoeurian *semantics*. Semiotics treats language as merely a system of signs completely closed in on itself without any reference to a world external to the sign system. This means that semiotics is in no sense material. Language as a semiotic system is "spiritual." But, rather than constituting merely a solipsistic non-referential spiritual reality, negating the connectedness to world and others, semiotics is understood in this project as post-semantic, i.e., semiotics presupposes what Ricoeur calls discourse or the pragmatic use of language in a world of lived experience. See Paul Ricoeur, *The Rule of Metaphor*, p. 217: "... we must go beyond the simple opposition between the semiotic and the semantic viewpoint, and clearly subordinate the former to the latter. Not only are the two planes of the sign and of discourse distinct, but the first is an abstraction of the second; in the last analysis, the sign owes its very meaning as sign to its usage in discourse."

from reference to a world outside of itself which would give us access to "truth," has led to babbling idiocy rather than meaningful insight into the human condition.[10] We must not only learn from our tradition in all of its historicality (and, to the best extent possible given the limits of our own horizon of understanding, to know other traditions), but we must equally know that our knowledge rests upon an "unknowing." Knowledge rests upon a host of presuppositions, assumptions, and hypotheses that are either indefinable or unprovable as well as resting on a concealing/revealing dynamic process of possibility in actuality that suppresses as it selects what stands forth in our attention and experience.

This does not mean that knowledge and understanding are purely relative and that there is no authoritative "reading" of an event, a text, or a work of art. Recognizing the role of pre-judgments and presuppositions in all understanding does not mean that we must embrace every reading. This is an important issue addressed by Hans-Georg Gadamer in *Truth and Method*. Gadamer engages in what appears on the surface to be a contradiction when he suggests that there is no such thing as "better" only "different" un-

---

[10] Both deconstructionism and those theologies influenced by it delight in neologisms and non-metaphorical metaphors. Derrida argues, for example, that, if there is no primary meaning of a sign, then there can be no metaphor, since metaphor is understood by him to be a play between the "proper" meaning and an improper meaning. The proper meaning would be grounded in some kind of metaphysical univocity. See Jacques Derrida, "White Mythology," *Margins of Philosophy*, p. 229. Yet deconstructionists and postmodernists delight in the figurative usage of language as if in agreement with Aristotle that metaphor is to be taken as the sign of genius. See Aristotle's *Poetics* 1459a5: "But the greatest thing by far is to be a master of metaphor. It is the one thing that cannot be learnt from others; and it is also a sign of genius, since a good metaphor implies an intuitive perception of the similarity in dissimilars."

Ricoeur's theory of metaphor completely disagrees with the notion that metaphor is a form of naming. See Ricoeur, *The Rule of Metaphor*, pp. 9-43, 65-100. Derrida and the deconstructionists/post - modernists all appear to have taken their understanding of metaphor from Heidegger, who argues that metaphor depends upon metaphysics. See Martin Heidegger, *Hölderlins Hymne 'Andenken,'* (Frankfurt a.M.: Klostermann, 1982), pp. 39-40; *Hölderlins Hymne 'Der Ister,'* (Frankfurt a.M.: Klostermann, 1984), pp. 17-23; *Der Satz vom Grund* (Pfullingen: Neske, 1957), pp. 77-90; *Unterwegs zur Sprache* (Pfullingen: Neske, 1959), pp. 199-216, English translation by Peter d. Hertz, *On the Way to Language* (New York: Harper and row, 1971), pp. 93-108; and Joseph J. Kockelmans, "Heidegger on Metaphor and Metaphysics," *Tijdschrift voor Filosofie*, XLVII (1985), 415-450. For an extended discussion of deconstructionism and post-modernism in theology, see Wyschogrod, Edith, ed., "On Deconstructing Theology: A Symposium on ERRING: A Postmodern A/theology" in *Journal of the American Academy of Religion*, LIV/3 (Fall 1986), 523-557. See, in addition, Mark C. Taylor, *Erring, A Postmodern A/theology* (Chicago: The University of Chicago Press, 1984).

derstanding[11] while having just made a case for "authority" as not "blind obedience" but "superior knowledge."[12] But authority does not deny the role of presuppositions and the historicality of understanding. For Gadamer authority rests upon "a wider view of things or is better informed."[13] Gadamer insists that "... the goal of all communication and understanding is agreement concerning the object"[14] or "[u]nderstanding begins ... when something addresses us."[15] The perplexing dynamic, of course, is that we never have direct and immediate access to the "object" or to that which addresses us. In short, "... the essence of authority belongs in the context of a theory of prejudices ..."[16] The greater the horizon of understanding, the greater the authority.

Theology *is* concerned with clarity about the human condition. But theology's clarity no longer can rest upon either a mental Logos or the empirical "things-in-themselves." Theology's clarity can no longer rest upon metaphysical explanations of experience even in the sense of transcendental conditions of possibility. Theology neither needs, nor can it appeal any longer with credibility to the knowledge of Augustine and his modified Platonic metaphysics. Nor can theology appeal to versions of Aristotelian metaphysics[17] rooted in materialism. On the other hand, theology has critical clarity about, and is accountable to, far more than the post-modernists and deconstructionists permit.

Faith Seeking Understanding

In short, theology is "faith seeking understanding" (*fides quarens intellectum*). Once again, as in the case of the title "strangers and pilgrims," one must be warned against following past theologians with respect to what is at issue in this aphorism. Faith is too readily defined as belief in some doctrine

---

[11] See Gadamer, *Truth and Method*, p. 264.
[12] See Gadamer, *Truth and Method*, p. 248.
[13] See Gadamer, *Truth and Method*, p. 248.
[14] Gadamer, *Truth and Method*, p. 260.
[15] Gadamer, *Truth and Method*, p. 266.
[16] Gadamer, *Truth and Method*, p. 249.
[17] For an insightful analysis of Whitehead's Aristotelianism, see Reto Luzius Fetz, "Aristotelian and Whiteheadian Conceptions of Actuality: I" in *Process Studies*, 19/1 (1990), 15-27, and "Aristotelian and Whiteheadian Conceptions of Actuality: II" in *Process Studies*, 19/3 (1990), 145-156. Heidegger's project, too, is an Aristotelian project seeking to overcome metaphysics by redefining Aristotle's material cause as "possibility," i.e., no-thing.

or other. Take, for example, the formulation "unless you believe, you shall not understand" (*Nisi credideritis, non intelligetis*).[18] This aphorism, too, can be read in at least two ways. Either one must already believe in God's salvific act through Christ in order to understand the Scriptures or the Christian tradition (I almost said Christian faith, but that would be too obviously tautological) or all understanding ultimately rests upon presuppositions (what Gadamer means by prejudices), which are indefinable yet necessary. The first way treats a particular presupposition as a "fact," the second way treats presuppositions as presuppositions and recognizes that all understanding (even the most empirically "factual" not to mention the more enigmatic spiritual "universals") rest upon a wager of faith.

It is a commonplace in theology today to champion the role of presuppositions in theology (seen by these theologians to constitute theology's contrast to philosophy which is represented to claim to be presuppositionless)[19]

---

[18] From Schubert Ogden, "The Task of Philosophical Theology," *The Future of Philosophical Theology*, ed. by Robert A. Evans (Philadelphia: The Westminster Press, 1971), p. 56.

[19] The issue at issue with respect to presuppositions is not whether one commences with presuppositions or not. Everyone commences with presuppositions. Nor is the issue whether one embraces the dogmatically correct presupposition keeping one within the horizon of a particular tradition of faith. One cannot escape the horizon of one's tradition of faith. Rather, the issue at issue is what is the disclosive power of a particular presupposition (or set of assumptions). How does this presupposition or set of assumptions assist our gaining clarity about the human condition, our present responsibilities, and our future hopes? It is only once one has addressed the issue of the disclosive power of (a) presupposition(s) that one can begin to adjudicate among options with respect to their legitimacy and adequacy. But theology has a task to perform even prior to addressing the issue of presuppositions. Theology must first clarify the paradoxes at the core of the human condition which makes the exercise of clarifying presuppositions an existential necessity.

While Christian theology is engaged in the dynamic tension between inherited tradition and contemporary understanding of human experience (and far "more" when one turns to paradox), Christian theology (to borrow from Hans-Georg Gadamer) "... is not merely a reproductive, but always a productive attitude as well" (*Truth and Method*, p. 264). There simply is no one dogmatic claim (either resurrection, the Kingdom of God, the Christ, forgiveness, guilt, prevenient or cooperating grace, the Trinity, etc.) that defines Christianity. On the other hand, everything in the tradition remains open to investigation for its disclosive power in the present. Theology must engage in both a hermeneutics of restoration and a hermeneutics of suspicion. The hermeneutics of restoration is engaged in the task of seeking out and employing those claims from the tradition that are disclosive in the present. The hermeneutics of suspicion recognizes that present human understanding may be inadequate, and the claims of the tradition taken to be not disclosive in the present may yet throw new light on human experience.

Eberhard Jüngel and Schubert Ogden seek to contrast theology and philosophy by claiming a starting point for theology distinct from philosophy's "presuppositionless"

in terms of seeking out a specific belief (e.g., in the resurrection,[20] in Jesus as the crucified Christ,[21] in Jesus as the Christ,[22] or Agape[23]) that then defines one not only as a theologian but more specifically as a Christian theologian.

---

starting point. See Jüngel, *Gott als Geheimnis der Welt: Zur Begründung der Theologie des Gekreuzigten im Streit zwischen Theismus und Atheismus* (Tübingen: J.C.B. Mohr (Paul Siebeck), 1978), pp. 205-6; and "Meine Theologie - kurz gefaßt," *Theologisches Jahrbuch* (Leipzig) (1988), 98-114. Schubert Ogden insists that there are two poles constituting the concern of theological reflection: the pole of the inherited tradition and the pole of the present human condition (see Ogden, "What is Theology," pp. 23f). Although the latter (present human experience) provides the understanding of the meaning of faith for Ogden, what makes for specifically *Christian* theology, according to Ogden, is "the affirmation, 'Jesus is the Christ'" which "is the constitutive affirmation of the Christian witness and, therefore, the integral object of theological reflection as well" (*ibid.*, p. 23). Here one has a *specific presupposition*, that remains an uncritically accepted presupposition, at the core of the Christian faith for both Jüngel and Ogden. At this level of their work these two theologians represent the worst form of uncritical fideism. Given that there is no existence, much less understanding and reason, without presuppositions, theology cannot simply arbitrarily and uncritically declare a particular presupposition to be the key to the entire Christian tradition. This turns a presupposition into a metaphysical claim analogous to Platonic universals. In other words, there is an archetype that explains particularity. In the case of the claim for the Christ, the archetype is not just a universal, e.g., chair, accounting for our being able to make sense out of our sense experience of a particular chair, but the archetype of the Christ is offered as the way to make sense out of all of history. Setting aside all of the problems of how universals (archetypes) are related to particulars, archetypes are denials of the particularity of individuals. In the case of the Christ, and we have seen this in theological formulations over and over again in the tradition, the Christ as an archetype really is a denial of history not an affirmation of history. It is only aporetic theology that is, and can be, historical.

20 This option, based on the historical fact of Jesus's resurrection, is defended by Wolfhart Pannenberg. See, for example, Pannenberg, *Jesus - God and Man*, trans. by Lewis L. Wilkins and Duane A. Priebe (Philadelphia: The Westminster Press, 1974) and *Theology and the Kingdom of God* (Philadelphia: The Westminster Press, 1969).

21 "Jesus as the crucified Christ" is the presupposition of preference for Eberhard Jüngel.

22 "Jesus as the Christ" is the presupposition of preference for Schubert Ogden and is the central "paradigmatic" (in the sense of an "exemplary past achievement" rather than a sociological paradigm) to Tracy's project in systematic theology in *The Analogical Imagination*.

23 Anders Nygren distinguishes between the "philosophy of religion," concerned with "a context of meaning," and theology per se, concerned with "a motif context." See Nygren, *Meaning and Method: Prolegomena to a Scientific Philosophy of Religion and a Scientific Theology*, trans. by Philip S. Watson (Philadelphia: Fortress Press, 1972), pp. 348-9. The key to Christian theology, according to Nygren, then, is the leitmotif of "agape." See *ibid.*, pp. 351-378, and Nygren, *Agape and Eros*, trans. by Philip S. Watson (New York: Harper and Row, 1969).

But we are theological beings by our very existence not because we have committed ourselves to a particular presupposition, but because faith is at the core of all experience, understanding, and action. We are Christian theologians (or Jewish, or Moslem, or Hindu, or Buddhist, Taoist, or Shinto, etc.), because of the horizon within which we experience and reflect. The strength of the so-called world religions rests not on their indubitable truths, but on their ability to speak disclosively to a wide range of human experience. One is a Christian theologian, because one is engaged consciously in the task of faith seeking understanding rooted in, and inseparable from, concrete historicality.

Ogden's Reflective Faith

Schubert Ogden claims that theology is critical reflection about the conditions of possibility for our basic confidence in the worthwhileness of life. Faith is defined by Ogden in terms of what George Santayana called "animal faith," or

> an instinctive confidence in its [the animal's] environment as permissive of its struggles to live and to reproduce its kind ... The difference in the human case, which is, of course, enormous, is that the acceptance and adjustment in question are not merely instinctive but are self-conscious acts.[24]

The task of theology, according to Ogden then, is to engage in critical reflection about our instinctive faith which leads to an examination of the "transcendental" or "metaphysical" conditions of possibility enabling our experience. But Ogden reminds us that this animal faith "always precedes reason."[25] This means that theological reflection is understood here as a form of "faith seeking understanding" in the sense of a critical analysis of the conditions of possibility for our experience of meaningfulness and/or worthwhileness in the human condition. As intellectually seductive as this task is, it is inadequate.

Where Eberhard Jüngel misses the role of presuppositions in all reason, Ogden reduces theology to a mere cognitive science. The alternative to Ogden, however, is not to oppose his cognitive science with an affective, polymorphous perversity. In short, it is not as if the heart (in the sense of emotionalism) must be given priority over the head. Rather, theology must retrieve the fullness of faith at the core of human experience. Only then can

---

[24] Ogden, "The Task of Philosophical Theology," p. 56.
[25] Ogden, "The Task of Philosophical Theology," p. 58

it regain an appropriate use of critical reflection as an essential constituent of the theological task.

Second Naiveté and Praxis

David Tracy reminds us that, in addition to critical reflection, theology involves two further moments: 1) The first he calls a "second naiveté," which returns to the fundamentally figurative language expressive of faith both in the tradition and contemporary human experience. In short, this is a retrieval of the aesthetic or imaginative moment of experience for theology.[26] 2) The second he labels *praxis*, which he describes as concrete, transforming and liberating.[27]

Emphasizing the role of figurative language (or the imagination) as an essential component in the expression of faith, suggests that faith is far more radical then mere confidence in the meaningfulness or worthwhileness of our human condition. Not only is faith concerned with what is accessible to us in terms of such psychological judgments as meaning and worth, but faith is concerned with what is by necessity inaccessible and concealed by experience. In short, the human condition is far more than merely that which is *transparent* either pre- or post-critically. It is shaped and enabled above all by what is *opaque* and that which of necessity must remain opaque/concealed/suppressed.[28] Opaqueness is the consequence of the mani-

---

[26] See, Tracy, *Blessed Rage for Order*, pp. 78-80.

[27] Tracy concurs with Ogden with respect to understanding faith to be a basic confidence in the meaningfulness of life. See *Blessed Rage for Order*, pp. 47, 55-56, 69-70, 71, 93, 96, 98, 99, 103, 135, 147, 153-5, 163, 174, 187, 214, 221-2, 245, 247. Tracy also concurs with Ogden that theology is critical reflection about the transcendental conditions of possibility for such "animal faith," but he is not satisfied with defining theology as purely an exercise in critical reflection (see, for example, *ibid.*, pp. 189-191, 209). While cognizant of the danger one risks when failing to engage in critical reflection (see *ibid.*, pp. 180 and 249), he calls for both a second naiveté, or return to pre-critical figurative language, but now informed in a life-transforming manner by critical reflection (*ibid.*, pp. 209-210) and for *praxis* (*ibid.*, pp. 209-210, 214, 221, 243., 247, 249). Tracy writes regarding *praxis*: "... the task of philosophy (here theology) is not to interpret the world but to change it; that task is best fulfilled when critical theory always informs, and is informed by, actual economic, social, and political practice. In short, the aim of all thought is *praxis*" (*ibid.*, p. 243). This statement occurs in the context of Tracy's summarizing the teachings of "Liberation Theology," but Tracy leaves no doubt about the importance of *praxis* for his own theological agenda (see *ibid.*, p. 244) as he leaves no doubt about his rejection of the neo-orthodox model of theology which informs most of these eschatological theologies of *praxis* (see *ibid.*, p. 244).

[28] The "necessary" suppression here is not political, economic, or social repression as if theology by definition supported oppression. Instead, suppression, as it is understood

ing and concealing of possibility in each and every situation of actuality. The human condition, resting on constitutive paradoxical elements necessary to, and enabling all, experience, is faith seeking understanding.

Beyond Reductionism

With this judgment we return to theology as the living in and reflecting upon aporiai. Paradox is the necessary holding in tension of two or more items when those items are by definition or experience irreconcilable, incommensurable, and incompatible. One such paradox, as has just been underscored,

---

here, serves as an aid in the reflectively critical understanding of what is occurring in situations of oppression. It is important to distinguish between the "ontic" and the "ontological" to make the proper distinction here. The ontic has to do with objects of one's measurement, calculation, prediction, manipulation, and control. The ontological is concerned with the contingent, necessary conditions of possibility constitutive of, but necessarily presupposed by, all ontic encountering and engagement with things. In a situation of oppression, then, the power structure is exploiting an ontic concealing, selection, and suppression for the sake of the few. But the reason the oppressors are often insensitive to the oppressed is that they confuse the given, apparently static, ontic constellation (which rests on a concealment, selection, and suppression to which the oppressors are oblivious) of the present for the true dynamic and ontological depths of concealing, selection, and suppression of time. Appropriate hearing (this involves both a passive and an active moment) of concealing, selection, and suppression, however, can open one to the transforming and subversive power tearing away at every status quo grounded in an ontic constellation in the present. Such hearing empowers one to respond to injustice, exploitation, and oppression from the perspective now of the ontological and not merely of the ontic. One can then see how both the ontic and narrative (personal, social, and cultural) by necessity conceal, select, and suppress, but they need not do so in blind and non-critically reflective ways. Theology, as David Tracy reminds us (see *Blessed Rage for Order*, pp. 238-9), is both a hermeneutics of retrieval.

Heidegger speaks of the "danger" of the concealed, but hints that there is something positive to the concealing when he quoted Hölderlin:
"But where danger is, grows
The saving power also."
Heidegger concludes his essay saying: "The closer we come to the danger, the more brightly do the ways into the saving power begin to shine and the more questioning we become. For questioning is the piety of thought." Martin Heidegger, *The Question Concerning Technology*, pp. 34 and 35. Implicit in Heidegger's insistence, that he is making no claim to "complete authenticity" in distinguishing between the "authentic" and "inauthentic" in *Being and Time* (see pp. 168, 312, 345-6, 399, and 422), is our inability to escape concealment. The true danger is in forgetting concealment as constitutive of the human condition. Paul Ricoeur emphasizes the necessity of concealment in both his metaphor and narrative theories where suppression (the "is not" or the "once upon a time") and selection (the "is" or the story line) are two sides of the same coin in the realm of the figurative and narrative kingdom of the as if.

is precisely that the manifest necessarily involves concealing, selection, and suppression. Concealing, selection, and suppression are the necessary conditions of possibility for us to experience what is manifest "before us" in any moment. They, alone, should teach us to be suspicious, and not merely thankful, with respect to what is manifest.

One can agree with Ogden that the task of theology is the understanding of faith at the core of the human condition. But what does one mean by the "human condition?" Do we mean the *animal rationale* - as if the human was definable in its essence exclusively in terms of rationality? Do we mean our emotionality - as if the human was definable in its essence exclusively in terms of our affectivity? Do we mean our physicality - as if the human was definable in its essence exclusively in terms of its derivation from (evolutionary and genetic) the material world, or in terms of gender? Do we mean the "thumb" - as if the human was definable exclusively in terms of our ability to calculate, predict, manipulate, and control the things of the world?

Such answers to the question "what is the human condition?" are obviously reductionistic. They take some aspect, which appears to be a distinguishing characteristic of human beings, and employ that aspect to define what the human is *really* all about. At best, reason, the affective, and the physical are usually placed in some kind of hierarchy by such reductionists - and the primary characteristic chosen (be it reason, the affective, or the physical) is placed at the top of the hierarchy as the ultimate explanation of the whole. At worst, reductionists explain away all other characteristics of the human on the basis of the exclusivity of the one characteristic chosen to define the human. For example, extreme rationalists dismiss the affective and physical as mere copy and shadow of the really real which consists of the archetypal universals. Affectivists see rationality and materialism as repressive, and ultimately destructive, of the true human spirit. Materialists derisively call the rationalists "idealists" and the affectivists "touchy feelies" and cry out for a shift from such adolescent fixations on "idealism" and "emotions" to the acceptance of the cold, harsh physical realities of maturity. The materialists claim that all that is can be explained according to physical laws, and the human is at best a "mistake" in the evolutionary scheme.[29]

The consequence of such reductionisms is ironically the hierarchization of reality analogous to the hierarchization for which Platonism is charged.

---

[29] See Stephen Jay Gould, *Wonderful Life: The Burgess Shale and the Nature of History* (New York: W.W. Norton, 1989).

Just when Enlightenment reason was supposed to be liberating humanity from the consequences of institutional hierarchy based upon a spiritual metaphysics, material metaphysics champions a new hierarchy. It is manifest in terms of racism, sexism, and/or classism. Particularly in a culture of materialism, where humans are defined almost exclusively in terms of physical laws, control over their environment, and the consumption of limited resources, goods, and services, racism, sexism, and classism are rampant evils. With no meaningful alternative for describing and understanding the human condition, materialism reduces humans to objects, knowledge to sound bites, critical thought to such ridiculous observations that "finger licking good" is a PR gimmick to exploit positively the most negative aspect of deep fat fried chicken, and rewards go to those who exercise power in the form of controlling persons and things. Of course, the measure of success is: how much can you get paid for doing as little as possible.

Theology as a Subversive Enterprise

The theological task is as subversive and revolutionary as it is illuminating, because it forces the questioning of all such reductionisms to focus on paradox in the human condition. The terminology "human condition" has been chosen deliberately (rather than speaking of the human exclusively in relationship to the divine), because "human condition" suggests that what is at stake in theology is more than the individual self or the human community to the exclusion of the environment. At stake is what Martin Heidegger and Hans-Georg Gadamer call our "situation."[30] Our human condition or situation is not merely describable in terms of the individual ego, but includes our contexts and texts (that is, the narrative that we are in a community, in an ecosystem, and in a lived or "life-world" to borrow from Husserl). Speaking of the aporiai of the human condition, then, means to attend to the dialectical tensions constituting human experience in all of its contexts and in dialogue with its texts. These paradoxical tensions require us to look deeper into experience than mere political ideologies, market forces, the securities and pleasures of personal consumption, or to some metaphysical explanation of order in the midst of chaos. The human condition is a dynamic personal and social reality, narrated and contextualized by both nature and community, informed and shaped by its history as a trajectory of tradition within

---

[30] See Heidegger's discussion of "Befindlichkeit" or "state-of-mind" in *Being and Time*, pp. 172-179, and Gadamer's discussion of the "hermeneutical situation," "horizon," and "historical horizon" in *Truth and Method*, pp. 269-274.

traditions, which of necessity includes both an active (by means of our creating our individual and corporate narratives) and a passive revealing and concealing. Owning our human condition or situation involves both a hermeneutics of restoration (i.e., sensitive to the potential benefits that the concealed and suppressed enable, and not merely for the few) and a hermeneutics of suspicion (i.e., sensitive to the danger of the concealed and suppressed).

Such a project is illuminating, subversive, and revolutionary, because theology challenges the certitudes, the presuppositions, the prejudices, the axioms, the hypotheses, and the very definitions of social and metaphysical convention to indicate precisely not only how fragile (even when backed by the most deadly and destructive weapons), but how arbitrary, how concealing, how manipulative, and how oppressive even for the oppressor our prevailing understanding of the human condition is.

Theology actively subverts conventionalities, not simply for the sake of subversion, but for the sake of truth. But to speak of truth at this stage in the project can only be to self-consciously suppress what this work means by theological truth. Theological truth is not merely "what is in fact the case," nor is it *adequatio intellectus et re* (the correspondence between judgment and that which is judged about), but theological truth is built upon the tension of manifesting and concealing of possibilities in any and all actuality independent of, and is the very condition of possibility for, the truth of our judgments in reference to "things." In short, theological truth is aporetic.

PART II:
ON THE ROLE OF APORIAI IN THEOLOGY

Chapter 7
The Aporia of Spirit and Matter

Because the aporetic addresses the core of human experience, it facilitates a retrieval (without the metaphysics) of what can be called the heart of the Western tradition. This heart is concerned with the dialectic between spirit and matter (universal and particular; intellect and world; invisible and visible; spirit and flesh; abstract and concrete; possibility and actuality) without turning these pairs into mere binary opposites and subordinating one to the other. Exactly how these two dimensions of experience are related, given their incommensurability and irreducibility, constitutes a, if not the, fundamental aporia of the human condition. Human beings are the place where spirit and matter come to self-consciousness by means of a dynamic of concealing and revealing where spirit and matter are united in creative tension. Here in a nutshell is articulated the *historical* nature of human faith demanding hermeneutics (both of restoration and of suspicion) and ethical praxis.

This project, however, identifies six aporiai that are constitutive of the human condition of faith. Although they are intimately interrelated, and in some cases one is merely a sub-form of another, distinguishing among them is important for gaining clarity about the theological condition and task. Anders Nygren once confronted a similar dilemma and observed: "It is always risky to be careless about distinctions. The old saying, *Qui bene distinguit bene docet* ('He (sic) teaches well who distinguishes well'), is extremely pertinent in the present instance."[1] Not only is it hoped that the following will assist in making careful distinctions between the "this" and the "that," which can never be absolute distinctions for they are indefinable and intimately intertwined, but what must constantly be "set before the eyes" is the process of concealing, suppression, and opaqueness that serves as the necessary condition of possibility for one to be able to distinguish between the "this" and the "that." Here one reaches the radical depths of *fides quarens intellectum* ("faith seeking understanding").

---

[1] Anders Nygren, *Meaning and Method*, p. 23.

The Aporia of Spirit and Matter

The paradox of intellect and world of sense perception constitutes two incommensurable and contradictory dimensions of experience that necessarily are in dialectical tension with one another or there would be no experience as we know it. If dialectic involves a synthesis between a thesis and an antithesis, the synthesis of this dialectic of intellect and world is no common substance, nor is it some form of abstract unity that transcends difference. Rather, one best speaks of the synthesis of this dialectic as the nothingness of possibility that is continuously concealed by actuality.

This aporia, then, does not consist of a mere dualism of "inside" and "outside." Although one must identify the radically different dimensions to our experience of spirit and matter, being human does not mean being merely a spirit either "next to" the world or "in" a body like liquid in a bottle. Such characterizations, although common in the tradition and even encouraged by Cartesianism, focus only upon actuality and completely fail to acknowledge the role of possibility uniting spirit and matter. In other words, experience is not a mere collection or adding together of actual things or actual events. The whole of experience is not simply the sum of its actual parts. The whole is a dynamic process built out of the revealing and concealing tension between actuality (the multiplicity and difference of both materiality and spirituality) and possibility.

The "not yet" of our experience, that which one necessarily must yet become, although one doesn't (and can't) know what it actually will be, constitutes the framework for all experience both spiritual and material. On the one hand, that "not yet" is unsettling if not threatening. For the "not yet" is at once an indefinite if not empty possibility, but equally it involves the denial both of at least part of what already actually is and of certain unrealizable possibilities to which one can never return, causing one to want to hold onto what already actually is. On the other hand, the "not yet" is what makes life an adventure, an odyssey, a task, a future of event(s), an anticipation. Without the "not yet" there can be no thrill of discovery, of the new, or of finding something new in the old. Although not a substance, the negativity of possibility constitutes the enabling of the positivity of life, individually and collectively. Ignoring both the negative/positive dynamic of possibility as well as the spiritual dimension of our actuality as human beings, truncates the human as a desperate material being concerned with mere physical activity(ies). Hence, this aporia is the key to an experiential retrieval both of a classical form of spirituality (and even of the supernatural according to Bushnell[2]) permeating the western tradition and of a classical notion of possibility (found in Aristotle[3]) that is the central key to both despair and hope. Here one has the pivotal aporia for understanding the human condition as necessarily faith seeking understanding in the dynamic process of the revealing and concealing, affirming and denying, of possibility and actuality which must now be seen as a revealing and concealing dynamic between the actuality and possibility both of "visible" materiality and of "invisible" spirituality.

---

[2] See *Horace Bushnell: Selected Writings on Language, Religion, and American Culture*, and Ahlstrom's discussion of Bushnell in *A Religious History of the American People*, p. 610-613. Ahlstrom observes with respect to Bushnell: "Taken together, nature and the supernatural constitute 'the one system of God'" (*ibid.*, p. 613).

[3] Rather than see Aristotle and Plato as contradictory positions, the Stoics recognized the complementarity of the two even if the Stoics tended to reject the theologies of both. See Max Pohlenz, *Die Stoa*, pp. 13-15, 54, 65 Aristotle's emphasis on the priority of actual knowledge (form in matter) is epistemological not ontological. What is first in the order of logic is not necessarily first in the order of Being (Metaphysics, 1077b1-4). Human beings come to know first as form in matter (actually) prior to knowing form without matter (potentially) (see Metaphysics, 1049b5). However, since we cannot know matter directly but only indirectly through form, matter itself is pure potentiality (see Metaphysics, 1036a9, 1042a9-12, 1045a20-25, 1050a15-18, 1060a20). Hence, potentiality is ontologically prior to actuality if actuality is epistemologically prior to potentiality. Nevertheless, if "... knowledge of the actual must be present before there is knowledge of the potential" (1049b16-18), Aristotle agrees with Plato that there is a realm of actual, eternal beings. "... [A]ctuality is prior in an even more fundamental sense; for eternal beings are by their very being prior to those that perish, since nothing eternal is potentiality ... Accordingly, whatever is eternal is actual. Nor is anything potentially which is necessarily [i.e., that is "necessary" which cannot be other than the way it is (see 1072b 8-15)], and necessary beings are primary; for, without them, nothing would be at all" (1050b5-19).
  The insight Heidegger discovered in Aristotle and developed in his piece submitted to Göttingen and Marburg in 1922 as part of his candidacy for a teaching position was that potentiality or movement is the key to understanding human Being-in-the-world (see "Phänomenologische Interpretation zu Aristoteles." The dynamic between potentiality and actuality later becomes the meaning of Being and time. To be sure, a major focus of *Being and Time* is the articulation of the structure of Care (the existentials), e.g., state-of-mind (Befindlichkeit), understanding, discourse, concern and solicitude, which as a structure he later rejects as too metaphysical. Nevertheless, the ontological theme of the project, the key to the meaning of both Being and time as they are redefined here, is possibility. See, for example, above Chapter 3, note 13, and "Phänomenologische Interpretation zu Aristoteles," p. 245: "Die Möglichkeit der Existenz ist immer die der konkreten Faktizität als ein Wie der Zeitigung dieser in ihrer Zeitlichkeit. Was die Existenz zeigt, kann direkt und allgemein überhaupt nicht gefragt werden. Sie wird an ihr selbst nur einsichtig im Vollzug des Fraglichmachens der Faktizität, in der jeweiligen konkreten Destruktion der Faktizität auf ihre Bewegtheitsmotive, Richtungen und willentlichen Verfügbarkeiten."

Although the following presentation of the aporia of spirit and matter must stress the distinctiveness of these two dimensions, it always must be remembered that they constitute a tension between two kinds of actuality ultimately united by the revealing and concealing dynamic of possibility. Nevertheless, in order to grasp what is at stake with this aporia, it is necessary to acknowledge that the human is constituted out of two irreducible and irreconcilable dimensions of the visible and the invisible, for the "material" dimension *is* actually different from the "spiritual" even as they are united in possibility.

Matter in Contrast to Spirit

What is material (here not making any judgment about its substantiality but only observing its distinctiveness) is, first and foremost, at least in principle accessible to the senses: all that which is accessible to us through sight, touch, hearing, smelling, and tasting. This dimension of the human is such a commonplace that A.J. Ayer and the logical positivists could suggest that everything that is not accessible to the senses is a matter of emotion.[4] Such a superficial and merely logical judgment based upon what is "actually" accessible through the senses, of course, reduces to mere emotion all of our mental experience, for our minds are inaccessible to the senses. But, prior to turning to the non-material dimension of experience itself, it is important that the distinctiveness of the world of the senses be observed:

The material world is divisible into parts, that is, it is limited or has limits. It is not difficult to tell where the telephone stops and the desk begins, one can take the engine apart and put it back together, one can say where the tree trunk stops and the ground begins, the bridge and the river, etc.

Furthermore, the material is measurable. One can tell the size of a skyscraper, the length, breadth, height, and depth of a lake, the distance to the moon, the age of the planet.

Yet, a final, readily observable characteristic of the material dimension of life is that it is constantly changing. Heraclites' aphorism, "you can't put your foot in the same river twice," articulates this insight that change is fundamental to what is accessible through the senses even if that change is imperceptible in many, if not most, respects. Even the Rock of Gibraltar will

---

[4] See, Alfred Jules Ayer, *Language, Truth and Logic* (New York: Dover Publications, Inc., 1952), pp. 102-3. See, as well, Ricoeur, *The Rule of Metaphor*, pp. 226-227.

not eternally be what it now is, and at the sub-atomic level, as everyone "knows," there is only constant interaction and change.

Entirely overlooked by most, and by A.J. Ayer and the logical positivists in particular, is that there is another dimension to the human that is totally inaccessible to the senses and constitutes the very content of all experience. This is one's mental life (consciousness). One cannot see, touch, hear, smell, or taste one's consciousness. The non-material dimension of experience is directly in contrast, if not diametrically opposite, to the world accessible to the senses:

In contrast to the material world, the mind is not divisible into parts. The mind is illimitable. One cannot tell where one thought starts and the other stops. One cannot draw a line between one idea and the next much less separate them from one another.

Neither are thoughts measurable. One cannot measure the size of one's idea of a skyscraper, nor can one establish the length, breadth, height, and depth of one's idea of a lake. Is the idea of an elephant larger or smaller than one's idea of a mouse?

Lastly, to the extent that mental life rests upon ideas (sometimes called universals or essences in order to prevent confusing "idea" from "opinion" - for one often erroneously says, "I've changed my 'idea' about something," when one really means, "I've changed my 'opinion' about something."), ideas remain the same yesterday, today, and tomorrow. One's idea of an elephant does not increase or decrease; it does not deteriorate. Once one "has" the idea it remains the same.[5]

Having introduced the notion of universals, however, there is another characteristic distinguishing the material dimension of experience from the mental. The material dimension of experience is always perspectival because it is exclusively concerned with particulars or individuals. This material dimension can always be other than the way it appears, since no one has direct and immediate access to the way it is in itself. The mental dimension of experience, on the other hand, is rooted in universals which, of course, can only be experienced by the individual in a particular context of reflection, but the universal (or essence, idea) one is thinking in any particular context is necessarily that universal and nothing else but it. This is because universals must necessarily be what they are in contrast to objects of sense,

---

[5] At this point it is not necessary to speculate about where these "eternal" ideas come from. The point is that once they are either constituted or discovered they do not change, for they are what must stay the same if we are to make sense of the constant flow of sense and mental data of experience.

which can be other than the way they appear to be. If one is thinking of an elephant, one is necessarily thinking of an elephant and not a unicorn. But, were one to watch the movement of the sun, one must judge from appearance that the sun is moving around the earth. That is an error of judgment, of course, for the earth's movement with respect to the sun is very different from the way it appears to be.

As an aporia, these two dimensions of the material and the immaterial (or spirituality) indicate a necessary and unavoidable dynamic tension between the sense and non-sense dimensions of human experience - between what is perceptible and imperceptible or between what is manifest and concealed to the senses.

That all experience transpires in the intellect (consciousness), which is totally inaccessible to the senses, does not discount our radical dependence upon an empirical world accessible by means of the senses. Yet the same pragmatic argument that justifies our acceptance of an empirical world independent of consciousness equally applies to our dependence upon universals in the intellect. Nevertheless, a pragmatic argument is a wager of faith in uncertainty rather than establishing absolute necessity, because *a pragmatic argument rests only upon contingent necessity not metaphysical or absolute necessity*. That something can be done, or cannot be ignored, or must be presupposed in order for the doing or ignoring of something is only possible so long as something is. But there is nothing that absolutely, or metaphysically, must be. The closest one comes is Descartes' *cogito ergo sum*, but that affirms only that an "I" must be in the moment of doubting, that is, the "I" is merely contingently necessary - were it absolutely necessary that the "I" be, that would be a metaphysically necessary "I." But there is no such metaphysically necessary "I." So long as the "I" exists,[6] but no one claims that the "I" will not one day cease to exist, one can talk about the contingent necessary conditions, proved by pragmatic actions, enabling the "I" to do whatever it does. But those conditions are by no means absolutely necessary, i.e., metaphysically necessary, conditions.

There is no more influential description of this aporia of spirit and matter for the Western tradition than that found in Book VI of Plato's "Republic." In this dialog Plato is arguing that the philosophers should be the

---

[6] The notion of existence involves location in space, i.e., existence applies to the status of some thing in the material world. To exist means materially located. This "locative" meaning of being in contrast to the "quantitative" meaning of being, i.e., the degree to which something participates in being, emerges in the 13th century. See John Nijenhuis, "'Ens' Described as 'Being or Existent.'"

rulers of society, because they alone ask about the Good (under the presumption that leaders should be concerned with making society good). Eventually, Glaucon prods Socrates to tell what he means by the Good by chiding him for avoiding the theme. Socrates says that he is unable to say directly what he means by the Good, for, were he to do so, his conversation partners would only laugh. In place of a direct definition of the Good, Socrates offers to talk about the visible "child" of the Good in order that his conversation partners can learn something about the invisible "parent."

The Problem of Definition

What Glaucon is looking for is a definition of the Good by Socrates. If there is anything that Plato learned from Socrates, however, it is the problem of definition. One cannot define one's ideas much less define the Good.[7] An idea is what a number of "things" have in common that enable us to apply the same idea to all of them while simultaneously distinguishing those "things" from everything else. A definition, then, involves both sameness and difference (identity and difference). Both aspects of definition create difficulties. For example with respect to "identity," defining just what that is, that is held in common between, say, everything that we call "beautiful," is impossible. The same "thing" in one context is called "beautiful" in another context "ugly." Yet everyone "knows" what beauty is.

There is a problem with definition, however, not merely with respect to such "subjective" notions like "beauty" and "goodness." Even the ideas of the most common things of our world, though, escape definition, especially, when the criterion of difference is added on to the task of definition. What is it that all the diverse "things," which are called chairs, have in common (identity) that permit one to apply the idea chair to them all? Not all chairs have legs, arms, or backs. When we turn to the criterion of difference, the problems confronting definition become compounded. Not all things, upon which one sits, are chairs (sometimes one stands on chairs; does that make a chair a floor or a ladder?). When we wish to define, or tell someone, what a chair is, we, usually, just point to a particular chair and say, "this is what a chair is." But the particular is not the idea that is actually thought. What is thought is the universal, and, the first criterion of a definition (identity) establishes that a definition applies to the universal not the particular. The particular is only an example of the idea. As an example, a particular thing is accessible to the senses, but the idea is not accessible to the senses.

---

[7] See Plato, *Republic*, Book VI and Aristotle, *Metaphysics* 1040a5-10.

Keeping this dilemma with respect to definitions in mind helps one to understand why Socrates alienated so many people and could be accused of defaming the Gods and corrupting the youth of Athens. The "Apology" tells how Socrates examined the politicians, artisans, and poets only to discover that they did not know either what they were talking about or what they were purporting to be doing. Why? Because they couldn't give a definition of what they knew and/or did. Socrates went away convinced that he was better off than they, for he knew that he didn't know; he knew that he couldn't define the ideas upon which his knowledge and actions depend. Yet, this is not an un-knowing that can be corrected with experience or effort. This is not the not knowing of an ignorance that with enough time and with the proper instrumentation could be corrected. This unknowing has nothing to do with correctly or incorrectly knowing something. It is an inescapable and necessary unknowing at the core of human experience. One cannot define the universals upon which all understanding depends. They can only be assumed or presupposed, and no amount of time, discipline, or effort is able to overcome this unknowing.

No wonder the youth of Athens were all too eager to ridicule authority and that Socrates could be charged with attempting to make a better case for the worse. The youth delighted in their champion exposing the "ignorance" and arrogance of his opponents.

With respect to the charge that he defamed the Gods, Socrates could say, based on the issue of definitions, that, to the contrary, he believed in the Gods in a "far higher sense" than the everyday citizen.[8] This belief in the Gods is not demonstrated simply because he used an oracle from Delphi in his defense, but because he knew that, like any other idea, one cannot define God. One must necessarily presuppose the idea God just as one must presuppose any other idea. One cannot think the idea God without believing in the

---

[8] Plato, *The Apology*, 35d. Schleiermacher edited and translated the works of Plato, and he wrote detailed introductions to the dialogs. Although educated in Moravian schools, he lost any chance to have a career as a Moravian pastor or teacher in 1787 after a personal religious crisis in which he came to doubt the church's teaching on the divinity of Christ and Christ's suffering substitution. Is it a mere coincidence that, following the publication of his *On Religion* in 1799 in which he questions such central church teachings as the role of miracles, the notion of individual immortality, and the personality of God, he would say in 1802 in a letter to his sister Charlotte, who had herself become a Moravian: "'I can say that, after everything, I have again become a Moravian - only of a higher order.' (*Briefe*, I, 295)" (from Hans-Joachim Birkner, "Friedrich Schleiermacher (1768-1834)" in *Theologen des Protestantismus im 19. und 20. Jahrhundert*, vol. 1 (Stuttgart: Verlag W. Kohlhammer, 1978), p. 10).

idea, if by belief one means assumption, in other words, the indefinability of each and every idea which requires us to employ them without truly knowing them. All ideas, whether of gravity or of a unicorn, are matters of assumption, i.e., belief. Ideas, however, are inaccessible to the senses, so that all everyday belief in the Gods' ability to act in the dimension of the senses transforms the Gods into material, limited, i.e., finite, things in contrast to the immateriality, illimitability, infinity, and incorruptibility of ideas. Such a transformation makes the Gods mere particulars rather than universals. Yet Plato, if not Socrates, pointed to a dimension even "higher" than the actual ideas of thought. This dimension Plato calls the Good or the First Principle which, for example, in the Timaeus is spoken of as God. Hence, the belief in the Gods in a "far higher sense" has at least a double meaning: a) in the sense that what is thought when one thinks of the Gods is an idea that, like every idea, is indefinable and necessarily presupposed, i.e., it is a matter of belief; and b) in the sense that the Good or First Principle of the whole is itself not an idea but higher than any essence. Hence, at the least, there may not be any substitution of what is available through the senses with what the Gods are (or God is), for any activity in the material world understood to be an activity of the Gods would be only the copy and shadow of the illimitable, divine dimension of the imperceptible that is the condition of possibility for anything to be or to act in the material world.

Hence, Plato could write: "the many that are seen are not known; the ideas that are known are not seen."[9] What one "knows" when one encounters some particular and individual thing is not the thing itself but an idea which is inaccessible to the senses. What one sees, then, is not what one knows. Yet "know" here must be placed in quotation marks, because one doesn't truly know the ideas if by knowledge is meant definition, for the ideas cannot be defined. They are, and only can be, presupposed or assumed.

Simile of the Sun

Plato, therefore, begins his discussion of the Good by talking about the "child" of the Good which is accessible to the senses. To this end, he builds an analogy (announcing a dialectical structure) upon the experience of seeing a particular object. He suggests that sight depends upon a "third thing" in addition to the eye and the object perceived. This "third thing" is light. Re-

---

[9] Plato, *The Republic*, 507b.

move light and there is no sight. Yet the light is not the eye nor is it the object. The light is the condition of possibility for the eye to perceive the object. The origin of light in this world is the sun, which, Plato observes, is the source of all generation or life. Hence, the ultimate synthesis enabling the perception of difference (the object is perceived as an object different from other objects) is the light of the sun. From the example of the child, one is led to conclude that the Good is some "third thing" inaccessible to the senses enabling one's experience of all difference (ideas). However, Plato explicitly says that the Good is itself not an idea, as is the "sun," for the Good is above all ideas.

Simile of the Line

Glaucon asks if there is not more to be said about this analogy between the sun and the Good. Plato's response is the account of the simile of the line (paradoxically, a line that one can see is to be used to help us think what cannot be seen). He says to draw a line divided into two unequal lengths. He does not say whether the line is to be drawn horizontally or vertically; nor does he say whether the longer portion of the line is to the left, right, top or bottom. He does talk later about upper and lower portions of the line which suggests that the line is to be drawn vertically. His discussion of the one and the many, i.e., "the many (objects) are seen but not known, where the one (idea) is known but not seen,"[10] suggests that the portions of the line can be proportioned according to quantity. That would mean that one is to draw a vertical line divided into two unequal lengths with the longer portion at the bottom. These two portions represent the visible world at the bottom and the invisible world of the intellect at the top.[11] Plato then says to divide these two segments once more into two unequal lengths with the same proportionalities. That would mean that one is left with a vertical line divided into four segments with the length of each segment getting shorter as one goes up the line.

---

[10] Plato, *The Republic*, 507b.
[11] The following two diagrams represent the image of the line. Note that the first basic division is represented by a cross. For the similarities to the "cosmic cross" of the Christian tradition, see, for example, Gregor von Nyssa, *Die Drei Tage zwischen Tod und Auferstehung unseres Herrn Jesus Christus*, trans. by Hubertus R. Drobner (Leiden: E.J. Brill, 1982), especially pp. 147-155.

The Line Simile

(Imperceptible)
Intellect
(Being)

(Perceptible)
Realm of Sense
Perception
(Becoming)

                                  First Principle of the Whole
                                       (The Good)

(Imperceptible)   Reason/Dialectic
Intellect   Logos/Law
(Being)

                     Understanding

        Images/Imagination

                          Objects
(Perceptible)
Realm of Sense
Perception
(Becoming)

                        Shadows and
                        Reflections

Plato proceeds to describe what each of these segments is meant to represent. The largest segment at the bottom of the line represents the shadows and reflections of objects which are far more in number than the objects that they are reflections of; which in turn are more numerous than universals. Any one object can cast an infinite number of shadows by simply moving the light source, causing the casting of a different shadow. In the same manner, any one object can be reflected in a mirror (or shiny metal object) by an infinite number of images as one moves the mirror ever so slightly. Shadows and reflections are in principle the most numerous type of sensed phenomena.

The next segment in the visible world is smaller, and it represents the objects themselves. There are, obviously, less objects than there are shadows or reflections of those same objects. Plato says of these two segments of the visible world that they constitute the realm of becoming, for they are characterized by change. No matter how stable objects appear to be, they are not eternal. If not in the short run, then in the long run, they will deteriorate. These objects and shadows come into, and go out of, being which means that they are not permanent but becoming. Plato, therefore, speaks of the objects as constituting a realm of opinion or faith, because they are constantly changing, and they can be understood only by employing universals which are indefinable.

Plato uses an analogy to talk about the relationship between the invisible intellect and the visible realm of objects and shadows/reflections. This is an analogy based upon copy and original. The shadows/reflections are copies of the original objects. Similarly, the intellect contains the originals of which the objects and shadows/reflections below the objects are mere copies. These originals are the ideas (or essences/universals).

The third segment from the bottom of the line represents the lower of two segments constituting the invisible intellect. Here Plato says that the mind uses the ideas to make sense of the images in the mind of the objects and shadows/reflections of the visible world. One does not have the objects, etc., of the visible world in one's mind. One only has representations, or images, of them in the mind.[12] Plato specifically refers to angles as an example here. What one thinks in the mind, however, are not the angles one can draw in the sand. What is in the sand one cannot put directly into one's

---

[12] Descartes, of course, spoke of this same phenomena of the mind when he uses the piece of wax at the end of the second Meditation to demonstrate that perception is a series of mental judgments. Perception is not some direct and immediate access to objects and things as they are in themselves. Perception is a matter of mental representation.

mind. One thinks, the idea of a right, obtuse, or acute angle. Yet such angles by definition cannot truly be, for an angle is the result of the intersection of two lines. But neither the point of intersection nor lines truly are by definition, for a point with any extension is a line (by definition points have no extension; only lines have extension) and a line with any width is a plane (by definition lines have no width; only planes have length and width).[13] One must assume that one knows what these angles are, because one cannot truly define them nor can they be by definition. For this reason, i.e., that ideas or universals are incapable of definition but must necessarily be used by the intellect, Plato calls ideas/universals "hypotheses." These hypotheses are not tentative judgments to be corrected by empirical observation as one is taught to use hypothesis in the scientific method. Plato's hypotheses are necessary assumptions which enable one to make sense of one's experience of the visible world. Therefore, Plato's hypotheses (ideas) are presupposed by the hypotheses (tentative judgments) of the scientific method.

Hence, the first activity of the intellect is the use of ideas to make sense of the imagined world accessible to the senses. This activity Plato calls "understanding." Here the assumed ideas are employed for making sense of what is imaged in the mind of the "external" world. What distinguishes this activity from the realm of opinion or faith is that it is rooted in, or employs, that which is unchanging in order to make sense of the changing phantasma of images of the "external" world had in the imagination (not to be confused with fantasy which consists of purely mental constructs that in no way are concerned to image, nor are they confined to, the realm of sensed objects).

Ideas, even if they cannot be defined and, hence, even if they must necessarily be, and unavoidably are, presumed, these ideas are nevertheless the same yesterday, today, and tomorrow. An idea does not increase or decrease in any way.[14] Ideas do not change. Opinions are changed. An

---

[13] In addition, there can be no definition of a plane, either, for, as soon as a plane has any depth, it is no longer a plane but space (by definition planes have no depth; only space has length, width, and depth).

[14] Ideas are dis-covered. Even if one wishes to conclude that they are arrived at through one's experience of the "external" world, i.e., that they are ectypal rather than archetypal, this only begs the question of the permanence of ideas. Not only does the correlation between an ordered universe and ideas lead to astonishment that there can be such a correlation between material objects and a mental idea, but that correlation confirms that there is an order to objects to which they must conform. That is, objects conform to ideas, which somehow must be prior to the particularlity of objects, since all similar objects conform to the same idea. The more important point is that these "prior" ideas are inseparable from a physical world, for both actual ideas and the actual world are rooted in a dynamic of possibility which unites them in the project of life.

opinion is formed by making a judgment about the imaged world of objects. That opinion is rooted in ideas which must be employed of necessity to make sense out of the images of the imagination. The formed opinion presupposes this activity of having already made sense of the images by the application of unchanging ideas. To the extent that the opinion is concerned with transient phenomena, the opinion is itself transient. This mental activity of opinion making tends to completely ignore that it is dependent upon ideas (or assumptions) that are constant. Nevertheless, it is not as if there was no change in the intellect in contrast to the changing world of the senses. The understanding employs what is unchanging, the ideas, to make sense of what itself constitutes a constant flow of changing data - the world as it is represented to the intellect in the imagination.

Finally, Plato speaks of a fourth segment, the smallest on the line, which is concerned exclusively with ideas and has nothing whatsoever to do with the changing images of the "visible" world. This segment he labels "reason," and it is concerned with a dialectic of the ideas that takes one "up" to the First Principle of the whole, that is, the Good, and returns "down" to, and remains exclusively in, the unchanging dimension of ideas.

This is a curious dialectic, however. Unlike the dialectic of perception concerned with the "child" of the Good in the realm of the material world of sense perception, this dialectic in the intellect a) involves no change and b) results in a synthesis that is not another idea among the ideas. Unlike a dialog where a synthesis is accomplished by change either within the thesis or the antithesis, the dialectic of the intellect, spoken of by Plato here, "by definition" cannot involve change of either the thesis or the synthesis, because here they are universals which are unchanging. How can there be a dialectic which does not involve some transformation of the thesis and antithesis on the way to drawing a synthesis? The task is a remarkable one as Socrates' conversation partners observe.

Plato insists that there is such a dialectic, but he offers no explanation of it. Just as at other important points in the presentation of the line simile, the reader/hearer is required to work out for her/himself what Plato is suggesting. As with the other cases, however, there are many hints: a) the Good cannot be spoken of directly but only indirectly; b) the Good is not an idea or thing among other ideas or things, it is "beyond essence;" c) the Good is the First Principle of the whole; d) the parent (the Good) is analogous to the child (the Sun); e) ideas, which serve as the multiplicity or distinctions upon which the dialectic's thesis and antithesis depend, are incapable of changing; f) the dialectic spoken of here is entirely inaccessible to the senses not employing any images as does the understanding; and g) here one is concerned exclusively with Being and not Becoming.

At least three possibilities for understanding this dialectic can be formulated on the basis of this information. The first possibility is that the synthesis spoken of here is a summation of the parts, that is, the synthesis arrived at is the whole that is achieved by adding all the ideas together into the unity of a set. The difficulties with this synthesis are at least two: first, it gives us a synthesis that is itself an idea, i.e., the idea of the sum of parts in contrast to individual parts, etc. Second, this synthesis is in no way analogous to the "child." The sun does not "unite" the eye with its object by adding them together. The sun, rather, is a "third thing."

A second possibility for understanding this dialectic of the reason depends upon the uniqueness of the present participle "Being." There is no other present participle like this one. Present participles function both nominally and verbally. The nominal meaning of Being is expressed by the term "being(s)" or things/multiplicity. It applies to objects (these different things are beings); but it equally applies to ideas (each idea is a being). Plato has suggested that the term Being most appropriately applies to ideas, since these ideas do not change where objects in the physical, perceptible world change or are becoming. However, at the end of the simile of the line there is a suggestion that there is a notion of Being that applies even to the changing dimension of Becoming. Nevertheless, it is not inappropriate to speak of ideas as beings, for there are many ideas, hence, ideas constitute many beings.

In addition to a nominal meaning, however, a present participle has equally a verbal meaning. Here is where the uniqueness of the present participle "Being" is announced. The verbal meaning of Being is the verb "to be." There is no other verb comparable to the verb "to be." Unlike any other verb, it is presupposed by all that was, is, and can be. In addition, this verb is presupposed by all other verbs. The verb "to be," then, is temporal. It unites past, present, and future as a horizon of was, is, and will be. Furthermore, the verb "to be" is not a thing, nor is it an idea, among other things or ideas; the verb "to be" does not express the eternal permanence of some actual thing in contrast to what can "pass away," because as a verb it is not a thing. The verb "to be" is that "beyond ideas" that every idea and thing that "is" must of necessity presuppose. If one could remove the "is" from some idea or thing, then that idea or thing could not "be."

The present participle "Being" enables a manner of speaking about a dialectic of the reason that involves no change, provides a synthesis that is higher than all essence, and is analogous to the sun as the "third thing" that enables not merely perception and generation or life as does the sun but everything that "is." The First Principle of the whole or the Good is both "the light of the mind" and the condition of possibility for the entire line. In other words, the Good as "is-ness" is what enables us to distinguish in the mind between universals that are illimitable. Take away "is" from a universal, and we can't begin to think it. But the Good is, also, the "is" for all that "is" (including what was and will be) encompassing not only the mental but the physical world of sense perception, as well. Yet one cannot see or speak directly of it, for one can only see or speak directly of that which can be distinguished from something else. The Good or First Principle of the whole is thought here as the no-thing of "is-ness." As such, "it" can only be "seen" and addressed indirectly by means of dialectic, analogy, and, foremost, metaphor which are the ways in which what is definite points beyond itself, because "is-ness" is not an "it" that can be "seen" or distinguished from other things.

Nevertheless, a third possibility for speaking of the dialectic of the reason focuses on "possibility" rather than merely the verb "to be" in order to avoid any confusion about the copula as some kind of unifying sub-stance, existence, or the actual in a locative sense.[15] This understanding of reason's dialectic observes that the dialectic is built upon what actually can be distinguished from something else (even if they cannot be separated from one another), i.e., at least two ideas actually thought. Yet the greater synthesis in which the actual ideas are embedded is seen to be the no-thingness of possibility. What unites not only the ideas but the entire line in a synthetic whole, then, is possibility, which is not an idea (for it is no one thing). Possibility is imperceptible, constitutes a unity among all that is actual, and is a "third thing" analogous to the sun. Possibility is a more adequate way of thinking the "is" that is always and already "not yet" enabling all actuality. In short, the advantage of thinking the synthesis of Plato's dialectic in terms of possibility is that it includes an open-ended "not yet." What actually "is" is com-

---

[15] If the Good or First Principle of the Whole is thought in terms of possibility, then the one-ness of the Whole is not some kind of unitary identity or substance in the sense of some "intropathic fusion" before the subject and object (see Ricoeur, *The Rule of Metaphor*, p. 246) that one could somehow in meditation experience directly. It is appropriate to speak of possibility as "one," but not in the sense of universal univocity. This is because possibility is always tied to a particular situation. The actual circumstances of a particular situation reign in the possibilities of that situation even as those possibilities are by no means grasped in some conscious way in their entirety. Hence, while possibility "is" shared by all that is and could be, the possibility of any one thing "is not" the same as the possibility for something else.

plete; what is possible is yet to be actualized. At the same time, the possible unites as "no-thingness" all actuality both of spirit and matter in a dynamic process of revealing and concealing, negativity and positivity, despair and hope.

What must be clearly underscored, however, is that this aporia of spirit and matter prohibits along with all other aporiai the employing of any metaphysical foundationalism either of the empirical or of the Logos to explain away the aporia by reducing the aporia down to one side or the other. This is no dualism. It is a dynamic dialectical tension that cannot be explained either spiritually or materially, for this tension is rooted in Being, temporality or possibility, which can neither be explained nor grasped. Being is possibility, i.e., nothingness, that enables all being(s).

Human experience consists of the interrelationship of two dimensions of experience related to one another as an aporia. These two dimensions are the visible and the invisible. Experience as we know it is impossible without both dimensions, but neither dimension can account for the other. Universals are indefinable and we can only speculate about how particulars "participate" in these universals,[16] i.e., how is it that the particular is related to the universal? On the other hand, any material explanation we might give for consciousness is a mental model, i.e., as an immaterial model, it seeks to be a physical "explanation" for consciousness but constructed *within* the immaterial dimension of experience, i.e., consciousness. Furthermore, both dimensions are rooted in the aporia of actuality and possibility, i.e., that all actuality both of consciousness and of the physical is rooted in the nothingness of possibility with no two circumstances sharing exactly the same possibilities.

Everydayness and the Real

Well aware that every beginning is arbitrary, for we are always and already in the midst of that which we are experiencing and wish to reflect about, it is helpful to start an investigation of the meaning of "reality" with what is meant to be a description of our common everyday experience. Just what is real?

There is little if any doubt in our everyday lives that we take the world of things, experienced by means of the senses, to be the real world. What

---

[16] This is Aristotle's critique of the doctrine of the ideas. See, for example, Aristotle's *Metaphysics* 1078b30-1079b3.

we mean by real is something existing independent of our perception of it. In other words, things are there whether or not we perceive them. In terms of our common sense experience of the real world, it is patently absurd to suggest that the tree falling in the forest makes no sound if there is nobody there to hear it.[17]

Most of our everyday lives is spent in the calculation, prediction, manipulation, and control of things in the world. Reality, for us, consists of those things in the world perceived to be necessary for either sustaining or enriching our lives. For too large a majority of persons, life consists exclusively of a constant struggle for the acquisition of the basics of life consisting of the things necessary for material survival: food, clothing, shelter, health, and physical security. Often such struggle is under repressive social systems based on racism, classism, and sexism or under governments which violate basic human rights. Life is a constant struggle or a constant terror for the powerless, marginalized, and oppressed. Nevertheless, no matter what one's nationality, race, class, sex, or sexual orientation, daily routines are structured by the search for those things and those relationships among things and Others that are essential to preserving and/or enhancing material life.

Only the few on the pinnacle of the world hierarchy can simply presume such necessary things in their lives to concentrate on what school to attend, to plan careers, to face perhaps the "dilemma" of juggling careers and child raising. Our concern at this level of the world's social system is more how to aesthetically arrange things and/or repair them when they are broken, than with the question where will the next meal come from. Things inconvenience us in the form of auto repairs, faulty plumbing, disrupted plane schedules, and incompleted tasks in the face of deadlines. Both the value of the individual and her/his status in the community are measured in terms of access to and control over things. The message is clear: money and the control over things, that money represents, brings not only security but power and prestige. We were trained and are training our next generation to exploit those avenues to high incomes which will bring us and them the status and security symbols our society mirrors to us all. Our double stand ard here is unavoidable: for the upper end of the hierarchy, the standard of success is how much can one be paid for doing the least; for the lower end

---

[17] The more important question with respect to the tree in the forest is not whether it makes a sound, but *how* do human beings experience whatever sound there is? In other words, what are the conditions of possibility for the experience of sound and where does that sound get experienced? Immediately and directly, or mediated and indirectly?

of the hierarchy, doing the least is grounds for social and personal condemnation. In any event, the criterion used to adjudicate success or failure, worth or unworthiness, even happiness or unhappiness, is the extent of sovereignty one has over things in the world of the senses.

Challenging this notion of the real, defined in terms of the things that both enable and threaten our lives, would be tantamount to questioning one's own sanity. We could no longer function, nor would we have a sense of self-definition, without our implicit and explicit commitment to the world of things "out there" existing independently of us. To be sure, this notion of the real is not limited to our dependence upon social and economic orders. This definition of the real is at the core of our self-understanding as individuals.

Ernst Bloch observes that all human drives are rooted in the body of an individual[18] (for example, there is not simply a vague and general sexual drive, but one's sexuality is linked specifically with "my" body). This body we take to be the "thing" that we are. Observing that there are many basic human drives with one or the other (or a complex of several) working often even against each other at any one time,[19] Bloch concludes, however, that the most basic human drive is hunger.[20] The fundamental human drive, upon which all others, including our sexual and nesting drives, are dependent, is the life instinct that is physically and immediately manifest as hunger. Once our need for food is satisfied, then we can be concerned about other fundamental human needs such as our sexuality or our "space," which is a constitutive part of the human as Paul Tillich reminds us.[21]

---

[18] See Ernst Bloch, *Das Prinzip Hoffnung*, vol. 1 (Frankfurt a.M.: Suhrkamp Verlag, 1982), p. 53.
[19] Bloch, *Das Prinzip Hoffnung*, p. 55.
[20] Bloch, *Das Prinzip Hoffnung*, p. 71.
[21] Tillich describes four levels of ontological concepts. The fourth consists of the categories: space, causality, and substance (see Tillich, *Systematic Theology*, vol. I, pp. 165-6). Concerning "space," Tillich writes (*ibid.*, p. 194): "To be means to have space. Every being strives to provide and to preserve space for itself. This means above all a physical location - the body, a piece of soil, a home, a city, a country, the world. It also means a social 'space' - a vocation, a sphere of influence, a group, a historical period, a place in remembrance and anticipation, a place within a structure of values and meanings ... Thus in all realms of life striving for space is an ontological necessity." The body constitutes the most fundamental spatial locating of the self, and it is first and foremost manifest in hunger prior to any other "need" or notion of space.

Tillich's second level concepts consists of three polarities: individuality and universality, dynamics and form, freedom and destiny." Tillich, *Systematic Theology*, vol. I, p. 165. These are reminiscent of Kierkegaard's three polarities of infinitude and finitude, possibility and necessity, eternity and temporality. See Alastair Hannay, *Kierkegaard* (London: Routledge and K. Paul, 1981), p. 142.

There can be no doubt that our abhorrence at the violation of basic human rights, as well as our almost exhaustive understanding of the self, centers on our understanding of reality to consist of things. We treat things, Others, and even ourselves as things to be calculated, predicted, manipulated and controlled. Whether it be expressed by the construction of a world economic system that systematically exploits the resources and persons of the world to the advantage of the few in the First World, or whether it be expressed by our insatiable concern for our personal appearance, or whether it be expressed by our allowing ourselves to be shaped by the shine and glamour of our fascination with "super stardom," there is a confirmation of our fundamental grasp of, and commitment to, what reality means (and what is necessary) in all of this. Reality is "external" and free from the arbitrariness of the subjective and personal. Reality is arrived at precisely by "disinterested" investigation that tries to bracket out everything that might constitute subjective interest as one examines empirical reality. We as an individual subject, then, are free of responsibility for this empirical reality. It constitutes the way things are. Not to accept things as they are is to risk even further alienation from reality as an "idealist," New Ager, mystic, or mad.

The common sense base line of experience is that the world of objects "out there" is what endures. "I" as an individual am merely passing through. To the extent that there is any permanence, it is the world that is permanent. Certainly the mind is the most transient. The individual can hardly come to a judgment without revising it, or at least qualifying it, almost immediately. As a self, the "I" is a swirl of impressions, emotions, shifting values, intuitions, judgments, and actions that is almost frightening in terms of its chaotic nature. Security, defined as continuity and a semblance of permanence, is gained only with disciplined focus, planned compromise, careful cultivation of talents, and luck. But above all, the self is a ceaseless flow of data and impressions which either has order because the data and impressions come from the real, empirical world "out there" or the self has imposed that order on its personal chaos.

Yet the individual life is a series of events over which one has little or no control. One does not choose to come into the world at a particular point in time, within a particular filial relationship, as part of, or with a specific context of, a particular culture. Part of reality for the self is the sheer "givenness" of such tangibles and intangibles whose intricacy boggles the imagination. One's self-understanding, emotional makeup, eating and exercising habits, etc., are all more the consequence of a preconscious assimilation of variables inherited genetically or acquired from one's environment then they are of conscious choice. That is nowhere more obvious than in the case of one's "mother" tongue. This language is the one the individual has taken in since the womb. Its structure and range of expression both enable and limit the self. It is the key ingredient in the making sense out of the flow of data and impressions out of which the self is constituted, but it is not the creation of the self. It is inherited like the color of one's eyes.

Were anyone to question the reality of one's "thrownness" into this world of relationships, things, order, and culture would mean the destruction of any and all foundation to self-understanding and experience. At whatever level we commence our analysis of the "real," whether it be of the individual, society, or the world, whether it be a political, economic, religious, or a scientific analysis, we cannot begin to ignore the priority of "things" and their interrelationships without ultimately denying the self and its experience. Such an observation, however, does not make for an indubitable ontological argument for the existence of a world of things independent of our consciousness of them. It is only to acknowledge the pragmatic fact that ignoring the world would be disastrous for the self and its experience. For example, ignoring the edge of a cliff or ignoring an approaching auto in your lane could be deadly. In short, we must of necessity (pragmatic necessity, to be sure, rather than ontological necessity) acknowledge and learn to calculate, manipulate, predict and control the reality of those things which constitute our material world of experience.

On Universals

Despite the obvious pragmatic necessity, confirming the legitimacy of this description of "reality" in terms of our experience of things and their interrelationships, it does not begin to account for either what or how we experience either the world or ourselves. It completely takes for granted, for example, two most perplexing characteristics of human beings: 1) that everything we experience of the world of objects (i.e., what we call the "real" world) we experience entirely within the horizon of our mental life; and 2) sense perception itself, not to mention any notion of the affective or the intuitive, is dependent upon universals which must remain the same throughout all of our experiences of the flux and flow of experiential data in the world of objects.

Aristotle's *Metaphysics* opens with the famous line "[a]ll men (sic) naturally have an impulse to get knowledge."[22] He proceeds to suggest that the desire for knowledge leads human beings to prize sight above all of the senses, because "of all the senses it can best bring us knowledge and best discerns the many differences among things."[23] Yet sight alone, Aristotle continues on, cannot give us knowledge. Recognition of difference, the key to acquiring knowledge, requires a peculiar capacity that humans possess apparently superior to all other forms of life: memory. Memory gives humans (and all other forms of life as well, but not to the same degree) "the power of unified experience."[24] Without the capacity to recognize similarity in difference (without unity in the flow of multiplicity), humans could not acquire knowledge.

Although the opening lines of the *Metaphysics* can be understood as containing Aristotle's entire epistemology, they conceal more than they reveal. What is not stated in those lines is more than what follows in the *Metaphysics* or even in the entire Aristotelian corpus. What is not said are a whole set of assumptions or presuppositions both concerning *what* constitutes knowledge and *how* knowledge is acquired. For example, the assumption of these lines is that sight of all the five senses is the basis for understanding the acquisition of knowledge. In contrast, for a Platonist the acquisition of knowledge is a process of anamnesis.[25] At best, sense perception forces a recollection of a universal (of an eternal and unchanging form) that our fixity on change has clouded over. Likewise, the tradition of Process thought sees the emphasis on sense perception as discounting the roles of "emotions, valuations, purposes, adversions, aversions, consciousness," etc.,[26] in the acquisition of knowledge. Choosing Aristotle's definition of knowledge and how one acquires it can be done only at the exclusion of these other metaphysical options of Platonism or Process thought.

Just what is it that constitutes our experience? How do we go about experiencing, understanding, and acting in a world of things encountered and simply taken for granted in the world? As much as the self cannot ignore the world of things and their interrelationships without serious pragmatic con-

---

[22] Aristotle, *Metaphysics*, trans. by Richard Hope (Ann Arbor: University of Michigan Press), p. 3.

[23] Aristotle, *Metaphysics*, p. 3.

[24] Aristotle, *Metaphysics*, p. 3.

[25] See Hans-Georg Gadamer, *Die Idee des Guten zwischen Plato und Aristoteles* (Heidelberg: Carl Winter Universitätsverlag, 1978), pp. 35f.

[26] Alfred North Whitehead, *Process and Reality: An Essay in Cosmology* (New York: The Free Press, 1969), p. 28.

sequences (ecologically, economically, and personally), our focus on things as the key to our reality has distracted us from precisely that which constitutes our experience. In fact, our common sense notion of reality forces a radical alienation from our own experience on the self.

We do not experience the world directly and immediately as the world is in and to itself. At best we experience "surfaces" or appearances. We "read" things in terms of how they appear to us. Essential to our understanding (and subsequent acting upon that understanding) of our own experience is for us to observe that the things of our world are "external" to us precisely because we do not experience them as they are to themselves "internally." The only "internal" that we ever will experience is our own "internal."

If things are external to us, if we experience things only as they appear to us and not as they are in themselves, then our experience consists in a constant flow of images or perceptions. But our experience teaches us that this flow of perceptions or appearances is not chaotic at least to the extent that our perceptions are not a mere blur. Where does our experience of continuity and identity (or sense of sameness to the world of things) come from if our experience is *not* of these things as they are in their self-identity but as a mere flow of perceptions?

We do not and cannot experience the continuous identity of things immediately from the object of perception, because we experience only appearances or profiles of that object. Where does this experience of continuous identity of things, then, come from? If perception is merely appearances, one can be extreme and say that perception is simply a constant flow of light and shadows. How do patterns emerge out of this flow of light and shadows? Aristotle reminds us of the role of memory in our experience. It is because we possess memory, he tells us, that we are able to recognize continuity, sameness, and finally identity in the flow of light and shadows that constitutes our experience of things. Of course, even recognition of light and shadow as a flow of light and shadow is accomplished only by means of memory which recognizes that what is experienced in this moment is the same flow of light and shadow experienced a moment ago, an hour ago, a day ago, a month ago, a year ago, etc. In other words, in our experience of the appearances of things we have access through memory to sameness and identity.

The technical term for this sameness or identity is "universal." A "universal" is in contrast to "particulars." Particular experience is the flow of data (light and shadow) that is this moment. Universals are what we are able to remember which allow us to experience sameness or identity in our experience of the particular. They are called universals because they are not bound to any particular phenomena, but they are what is used to make sense out of all particular phenomena. In short, universals remain the same, particulars constantly change. Universals transcend the particular and are somehow constant and accessible to memory in principle at any and all times. We are able to experience identity in the flow of perceptions (light and shadow), constituting our experience, because we have access through memory to universals. Prior to addressing the question of the origin of these universals, we need to acquire a sense of the ramifications of this analysis for human experience, understanding, and acting.

We have by no means exhausted our description of our experience of a world of things (or our experience of reality) simply by observing that experience is constituted out of a flow of perceptions which we make sense of by remembering universals. We have merely crossed the Rubicon into the realm of the intellect from out of the realm of concrete things. We commenced our analysis with a description of the material world of things as constitutive of reality. Then we observed that our experience of things is a combination of a constant flow of appearances that acquire sameness and identity by means of universals. But in doing so we have moved into an entirely different dimension than mere external things in our discussion of experience.

External things are perceptible, material, divisible, and measurable even as they consist of a realm that is constantly changing, i.e., of coming into and going out of (or of arising in and deteriorating in) the world. We can touch, smell, taste, hear, and see things. Ignoring the physicists for the moment, who tell us that matter is an illusion and the computer I am now writing at is more empty space than anything else, things are taken in our everydayness to be material in the sense of occupying a definite space. We can cut these things into pieces (or take them apart) and with luck put them back together again. These pieces we can measure according to their length, depth, width, and height. But is this true of the intellect?

Universals or ideas are not things in the same way objects in the world are things. We cannot touch, smell, taste, hear, or see universals. They are not material objects, and we cannot begin to cut them into pieces (or take them apart) much less put them back together again. We cannot even identify where one universal stops and another begins. Where does the idea of a table stop and the idea of a chair begin? Furthermore, we cannot measure the size, shape, or location of a universal. How big is the idea of a table? a chair? What are their length, depth, width, and height? Here we encounter a real perplexity.

The "real" world of things, which we can ignore only at our own pragmatic peril, is experienced by the intellect which itself is of an entirely different character than that material world of objects. The material world of objects is made sense of by an immaterial intellect that is not accessible to the senses, is indivisible, immeasurable, and by definition (since it rests upon universals which permit our experiencing sameness and identity in the flow of perceptions) unchanging (universals are the same yesterday, today, and tomorrow).

What we call "real" or reality has suddenly taken on an entirely different meaning. As much as we cannot ignore the world of things pragmatically, it is not things "out there" that we really experience. Our experience is made up of a flow of perceptions (appearances) of things which we make sense of by means of universals. We now see that it is these universals which are unchanging in the flux of our experience of things. The world of things is experienced as constantly coming into and going out of experience, i.e., constantly in flux and changing. But did we not conclude above that the mind is the least stable of our experiencing? Did we not conclude "the world of objects 'out there' is what endures. 'I' as an individual am merely passing through. To the extent that there is any permanence, it is the material world that is permanent. Certainly the mind is the most transient. The individual can hardly come to a judgment without revising it, or at least qualifying it, almost immediately. As a self, is not the 'I' a swirl of impressions, emotions, shifting values, intuitions, judgments, and actions that is almost frightening in terms of its chaotic nature"?

In spite of such confusing judgments, carefully observing what constitutes and enables our experience of a world of sense perception suggests that we must entirely reverse our notion of "reality." It appears that that which exists independent of our consciousness of it is not a world of objects "out there" accessible to the senses and arrived at through a process of disinterested investigation. Rather, that which exists independent of our consciousness is a system of universals deeper yet "within" than the flow and flux of perceptions, impressions, emotions, shifting values, intuitions, judgments, and arbitrary actions of a chaotic self. These universals are accessible to our memory and are what permit our recognition of sameness and identity in the chaotic flow of data that is the self's experience. Reality, then, is not "out there." It is deeper within. Reality is the system of universals, which remains the same yesterday, today, and tomorrow, and to which we have access in our conscious lives.[27]

---

[27] This observation, *based on our experience*, is precisely the key to reality as it was understood by most of the Christian tradition both East and West shaped as it was by Christian Platonism exclusively down to the 5th century.

Aristotle, with whom this analysis of universals began, represents a particular stage of a dominating dialectic between particulars and universals in the Western tradition. For Plato, Aristotle's teacher, universals have the priority. They are eternal and unchanging. They are accessible to each individual soul. Particulars are mere transient copies and shadows of these universals. For Aristotle, singulars have the priority. We arrive at universals only in and through our experience of particulars. This project understands itself to be a part of this dialectical tradition. The present project returns to the spirit if not the letter of Aristotle with which this analysis commenced. Rather than take Aristotle to be emphasizing merely "sight" as the key to all knowledge, I want to read this passage from Aristotle's *Metaphysics* to be concerned with *how* we are able to experience and understand anything whatsoever. Aristotle does not write that all knowledge is seeing. He writes that the acquisition of knowledge rests upon our being able to experience similarity in difference.[28] Sight is merely the most obvious case of our ability to experience similarity in difference, but it is not an exclusive case. We are able to experience similarity in difference because of memory which gives us access to universals.

Do these universals exist independent of our consciousness of them? Can we give an indubitable proof (a logical argument) for their existence independent of our consciousness of them?

There is no logical argument proving the ontological existence of a material world of objects "out there" independent of our perceptions of it. That world of objects is experienced exclusively in the intellect. Even when we are testing out our mental judgments with respect to our sense perceptions of objects, we are merely comparing two sets of mental data. We are not comparing a judgment "within" with an object "out there." Yet, this lack of a logical proof for the world of objects accessible through the senses does not deny our pragmatic dependence upon that world of objects. The pragmatic argument for the existence of the world of objects "out there" is simply: try ignoring that world and see what happens. In David Hume's *Dialogues Concerning Natural Religion*, Cleanthes initially categorizes Philo as a "vulgar skeptic," and ridicules his logical argument, denying a material world, by appealing to the pragmatic argument.[29] In short, with respect to the world of sensed objects, we can give a pragmatic argument for its presence independent of our consciousness of it, but we cannot give a logical

---

[28] See Aristotle, *Posterior Analytics*, II,19,104-110, and *Memory and Reminiscence*.
[29] See Hume, *Dialogues Concerning Natural Religion*, p. 5.

argument. Everything that we experience in the world of sensed objects transpires exclusively within the horizon of the intellect. Descartes makes this point at the end of Meditation II.[30] Perception is a series of mental judgments. Logically, there is certainty only with respect to that mental experience. As long as I am, that mental experience must be. It cannot be otherwise than what it is. For that reason, it is spoken of in the Western tradition as "necessary"[31] in contrast to our experience of the world of sensed objects consisting of that which can be other than the way it appears to be. Experience is exclusively spiritual. Only pragmatically can we/must we acknowledge a material dimension to our experience.

At this point, a new set of questions emerges: Just what are the necessary conditions of possibility that we can experience and understand both particulars and universals at all? How can we account for universals in our experience of particulars? What role do assumptions/presuppositions/prejudices play in our experience of universals? What role do models or paradigms play in shaping what we understand to be reality? If reality for us is a representation of the way we take "things" to be, how is this representation related to the "world" it is trying to re-present (in other words, can or do we ever "get outside" our representation to the "real world?")? Given the pervasiveness of representation in both presenting and constituting reality for human beings, what are the roles of metaphor, symbol, and narrative in giving us access to truth? Are they not merely blatant mis-representations? Finally, one can conclude that theological questions are concerned with critical reflection about the necessary conditions of possibility of experience[32] which includes the dynamic of manifesting and concealing, opening up and suppression. How might we adequately express those conditions of possibility in a way that gives us access into the Western religious tradition?

The Aporia of Universals and Particulars

Our investigation into everyday experience places us before a perplexity. Initially, we concluded that reality has to do with that which is independent of our consciousness of it and is unchanging. In other words, reality is some-

---

[30] See Descartes, *Meditations on First Philosophy*, p. 22.
[31] See, for example, Aristotle *Posterior Analytics* 71b8-12, 74b5f; *On the Heavens* 279b22; *Metaphysics* 1015a34; *Nicomachean Ethics*, 1139a1-10; and *On the Soul* 433a30.
[32] See David Tracy, *Blessed Rage for Order*, Chapter 8: "The Meaning, Meaningfulness, and Truth of God-Language," pp. 172-203. Though the kind of necessity spoken of by Tracy is really not metaphysical necessity but, rather, factual (or contingent) necessity.

thing that is not dependent upon the whims of subjective judgment and is repeatable, i.e., we can return ever again to it in confidence that our experience will be the same.

Next, we observed that for popular, everyday consciousness that dimension of experience that satisfies these criteria of reality (independence, unchangeability, and repeatability) are met by the objects in the material world accessible to sense perception (sight, touch, sound, taste, and smell). These objects are definitely taken to be independent of our consciousness of them, they remain at least relatively the same over time, and we can return to them over and over again (e.g., the trees, bushes, flowers, and lawn of my backyard are repeatably demanding of my attention independent of my consciousness or will even when I take deep pleasure in working with them).

Finally, however, we were led to conclude that, contrary to our everyday notions about the nature of our experience, we never experience immediately and directly a world consisting of objects of sense perception. Objects of the world of sense perception are perceptible, material, divisible, measurable, and changing. Since the dimension in which we experience, i.e., the intellect, is imperceptible, immaterial, indivisible, immeasurable, and rests upon unchanging universals, we only experience these "objects" as mediated in consciousness. Our experience of the world of sense perception is a mediated, not an immediate, experience.

This constitutes a fundamental aporia in experience. What we cannot ignore, the material world, we cannot experience directly, and what we experience directly is an open-ended sequence of indirect impressions or images of the material world that we can sort out only because we are able to employ "universals," which we cannot define, to establish the sameness in the flow of difference. The aporia of spirit and matter announces a profound unknowing at the very core of the human condition affecting any and all experience.

Experience is constituted out of the paradoxical interface of the visible and the invisible, but, nevertheless, the invisible (intellect/consciousness) has "priority" (to be sure, this cannot be logically proved to be an ontological priority; it is a priority of ontic experience) over the visible because it is the dimension in which all experience transpires. In order to grasp how significant and pervasive the mediated character of that experience is, it is beneficial to investigate the notion of paradigms in the work of Thomas Kuhn.

Chapter 8
The Aporia of Logic and Praxis

A second paradox calls attention explicitly to the dialectical tension between logic and pragmatics in experience.[1] This aporia is a central component in the work of Hume, Husserl, Kuhn, Ricoeur and Tracy. It is concerned with the impossibility of providing a logical argument (from within the mind) for a world external to consciousness[2] while acknowledging 1) that ignoring the external world can lead to disastrous consequences[3] and 2) that ultimate causality is a speculative construction of the intellect, since we never perceive ultimate causal connections in things. On the basis of effects, we speculate about cause.[4]

This aporia is presented here by analyzing Thomas Kuhn's notion of paradigm in *The Structure of Scientific Revolutions*. One could say that Kuhn's notion of paradigm is a reformulation of the activity of understanding developed by Plato in the simile of the line. Kuhn's analysis of the role of paradigms in human experience, however, is not merely a reformulation

---

[1] This paradox of logic and pragmatics is the key to Paul Ricoeur's distinguishing between "semiotics" and "semantics" (see *The Rule of Metaphor*, pp. 65-76) based upon the distinction between a "nominal" and a "real" definition: "The nominal definition allows us to identify something; the real definition shows how it is brought about" (*ibid.*, p. 65). In other words, the nominal definition names something within a linguistic system (as a construct of the mind, i.e., logic); the real definition is concerned with the pragmatic usage of the term in the context of a world of lived experience or reference. This paradox is at the core of the "dipolar" conception of reality in Process thought, as well. That is, reality is thought of as constituted out of an "abstract" and a "concrete" pole. See, for example, the discussion of dipolarity in Whitehead, *Process and Reality*, pp. 42, 59, 128, 280, 285, 322, and 407. Likewise, David Tracy uses the paradox of "metaphysical necessity" (logical necessity) and "contingent necessity" (pragmatic necessity) in order to move from an exclusivist to an inclusivist Christology. See Tracy, *Blessed Rage for Order*, pp. 205-206 and 224-225, n. 11.
[2] This is what Edmund Husserl's famous "phenomenological epoche" sets to the side, i.e., the entire question of the existence of an exogenous world. See, for example, Husserl, *Ideas: General Introduction to Pure Phenomenology*, trans. by W. R. Boyce Gibson (New York: Collier, 1962), pp. 99-100, and Husserl, *Cartesian Meditations: An Introduction to Phenomenology*, trans. by Dorion Cairns (The Hague: Martinus Nijhoff, 1964), pp. 18-21.
[3] See Hume, *Diologues Concerning Natural Religion*, p. 5.
[4] See Hume, *Treatise on Human Nature*, Book I, Part 3; and *Enquiry Concerning Human Understanding*, Sections 4-7.

of Plato's description of understanding, for it expands the notion of understanding to include how human beings constitute *communal* models of reality. Understanding by the individual, as Plato describes it, is extended by Kuhn to include and encompass a communal dimension of human making sense out of the world. As will be discussed below, however, both Plato and Kuhn have not made explicit the aporetic, temporal dynamic at the core of human understanding and paradigms. Yet it is not the aporia of temporality that surfaces here in the discussion of paradigms. The crucial dilemma announced by paradigms is that even understandings of causality are relative to a communal construct of how "reality" functions, for humans do not perceive ultimate causes. Nevertheless, one cannot act as if reality was merely a mental construct. As soon as one must act, and one cannot not act, one affirms one's confidence in a world of objects, structured by a coherent order of causality, although paradoxically there is no way for us to gain immediate access to that world or its causes.

Two Kinds of Paradigms

Paradigms are models, and Kuhn identifies two kinds: models of "exemplary past achievements" and "sociological models."[5] A ready example of such models of exemplary past achievement are grammatical tables of declension or conjugation.[6] Such grammatical models constitute repetitive patterns of order in nouns (declension) and verbs (conjugation) that enable quick identification of gender, number, and case with nouns (or person, number, tense, mood, and voice in the case of verbs) in order that one can ultimately arrive at the meaning of a sentence. As long as one must consciously employ the grammatical model, one expends great effort and must concentrate as much on the model (the declension and conjugation tables) as on the application in the sentence. But such paradigms with time and repetition become silent, efficient, and effortless partners in one's reading and communicating. As such, they are "forgotten" even as they permeate the process of reading. Such models of "exemplary past achievement" are found everywhere, for they constitute the analogical structure for all learning: moving from that with

---

[5] See Kuhn, *The Structure of Scientific Revolutions*, p. 175.

[6] Kuhn refers to such grammatical paradigms that function by mere repetition when he first introduces the notion of paradigm. See *The Structure of Scientific Revolutions*, p. 23. Models of exemplary past achievement are analogous to "universals" in the sense that they become "permanent forms" which one then employs to accomplish something "particular."

which one is familiar to that which one wants to understand on the presumption that what one wants to understand conforms to a similar order with what one is already familiar. Examples of such models of exemplary past achievement are computer software, which structures the computer environment in order that one can undertake some task with the computer, recipes that one "copies" in cooking, manuals for the repair of automobiles, patterns for sewing clothes, etc. All these are paradigms or ordered systems that are repeated in order to understand some thing or accomplish some particular task.[7]

Yet more central to Kuhn's analysis are "sociological models," for here Kuhn is referring to the way in which reality is a social construct. The

---

[7] Eliade emphasizes the role of repetition in the self-consciousness of religious communities. The exemplary past achievements of the Gods and heroes are repeated in ritual (Eliade even suggests that perhaps there was a point where every human action was understood to be a repetition of a primordial action of the Gods or hero, see *The Sacred and the Profane: The Nature of Religion*, trans. by Willard R. Trask (New York: Harper and Row, Harper Torchbooks/The Cloister Library, 1961), pp. 167-8) in order to preserve the cosmic order upon which all life depends.

The notion of repetition surfaces in Heidegger's discussion of the so-called hermeneutical circle in *Being and Time*. Human experience is rooted in a pre-conscious sea of possibility as a consequence of human thrownness in a world of things and Others (see *ibid.*, pp. 362-3). These possibilities are already understood, even if not explicitly, for life consists in realizing those possibilities that are not yet actual. This actualization of possibilities involves the human in a primordial process of repetition. See *ibid.*, pp. 437-8.

Both Eliade and Heidegger are indebted to Nietzsche's notion of the "ever recurrence of the same" found in *Thus Spoke Zarathustra* for the formulation of their understandings of repetition. See Heidegger's discussion of the eternal return of the same in *Nietzsche*, vol. 1, pp. 296 and, especially, 369. See, as well, Heidegger, *Nietzsche*, vol. 2, p. 388: "Was ist, ist das, was geschieht. Was geschieht, ist schon geschehen. Das meint nicht, es sei vergangen. Was schon geschehen ist, ist allein jenes, was sich ins Wesen des Seins versammelt hat, das Ge-Wesen, aus dem und als welches die Ankunft des Seins selbst ist ... Was geschieht, ist die Geschichte des Seins, ist das Sein als die Geschichte des Ausbleibens ... Das Ausbleiben des Seins kommt dergestalt auf das Wesen des Menschen zu, daß der Mensch in seinem Bezug zum Sein vor diesem, ohne es zu kennen, ausweicht, indem er das Sein nur aus dem Seienden her versteht und jede Frage nach dem 'Sein' so verstanden wissen will."

That there is never a complete "repetition," i.e., that the hermeneutical circle is rather a spiral, is nowhere struggled with existentially with greater despair than in the work of Kierkegaard although Kierkegaard and Eliade understand repetition not in the sense of Heidegger's re-covery of past possibilities. Repetition for Kierkegaard and Eliade consists of attempting to manifest in particular, sense experience what is actually only a universal, non-sensed, eternal form. In short, Kierkegaard and Eliade are concerned with the repetition of invisible actualities. Heidegger is concerned with the repetition of invisible possibilities. At the level of possibility, all that will be already is.

first aporia, discussed above, has already indicated that all experience occurs in the mind. One does not have direct access to the world of objects and Others.[8] One can only represent the world of objects and Others to one's self mediated through the imagination.[9] However, Kuhn emphasizes that this activity of representation is not accomplished in isolation, but is as much, if not more so, communal as it is individual. Sociological paradigms are those communal, cultural constructs that constitute "reality" for a group.

Sociological Paradigms and Understanding

Sociological paradigms are cognitive, coherent, require commitment, and are normative, communal, and the mediator of our understanding of causality.

First, sociological models are *cognitive*. This does not mean that they are entirely conscious, because, for the most part, they function preconsciously. Rather, the sense in which they are cognitive meant here is that they are a mental construction constituting a model of the way a group represents things to be (or represents reality to itself). Paradigms (from now on the term will apply to sociological paradigms) are conceptual models that, foremost, inform their adherents about the basic ontological order of reality. Kuhn expresses this aspect of paradigms as ontological models by observing: "Normal science, the activity in which most scientists inevitably spend almost all their time, is predicated on *the assumption* that the scientific community knows what the world is like."[10] In short, it is a mental model which establishes for the community in advance the way the world must be:

> Effective research [in a scientific discipline] scarcely begins before a scientific community thinks it has acquired firm answers to questions like the following: What are the fundamental entities of which the universe is composed? How do these interact

---

[8] There is no one, who has formulated the ubiquity, pervasiveness, and unavoidability of mediation in consciousness more thoroughly than Paul Ricoeur. This is the point of his three-fold mimetic theory developed in his three volume work *Time and Narrative*. See Ricoeur's "Chapter 3: 'Time and Narrative: Threefold Mimesis'" in *Time and Narrative*, vol. I, pp. 52-87.

[9] Heidegger points out that our everyday representation is limited to what we would call "actuality." Our representation is of things and Others as discrete objects that can be calculated, predicted, manipulated and controlled. Such representation remains totally oblivious to the rootedness of all actuality in possibility, the "nothing" that is the horizon of all actuality. However, the notion of sociological paradigm does not have to ignore the ontological depths of possibility. It can, and of course does pre-consciously if not consciously, include possibility in a dynamic of revealing and concealing.

[10] Kuhn, *The Structure of Scientific Revolutions*, p. 5, (emphasis not in the original).

with each other and with the senses? What questions may legitimately be asked about such entities and what techniques employed in seeking solutions?[11]

Given that we do not have direct access to an exogenous world (e.g., we cannot put this manuscript directly into our minds), the way we experience a manuscript is through the mental images we have of it. The world (both "external" and "internal") consists of a complex mental model by means of which we mediate the world to ourselves.

Second, a paradigm is embraced because it is a *coherent* model. In other words, the elements of the model must not be contradictory. A fundamental presupposition of paradigms is that the "whole" of all the parts is systematically consistent. In short, paradigms are intolerant of contradiction. It is precisely the coherence of the mental model that allows for the perception and/or acknowledgment of the anomalous, the inconsistent, that can lead to changes in the paradigm.[12]

Third, one must, then, already be *committed* to a mental model, which tells us in advance what reality is all about, even before one can begin to act. The unavoidably necessary, cognitive modelling of reality, Kuhn observes, involves "metaphysical commitments." For example, he writes of the corpuscular model of nature:

> [a]s metaphysical, it told scientists what sorts of entities the universe did and did not contain: there was only shaped matter in motion. As methodological, it told them what ultimate laws and fundamental explanations must be like: laws must specify corpuscular motion and interaction, and explanation must reduce any given natural phenomenon to corpuscular action under these laws. More important still, the corpuscular conception of the universe told scientists what many of their research problems should be.[13]

The paradigm provides the framework within which one can apply one's methodology or rules. As a mental mapping of reality, paradigms are prior to any rules governing behavior which can only occur within the reality illuminated by the paradigm's assumptions. As a mental mapping of reality, paradigms are prior to any rules governing behavior which can only occur within the reality illuminated by the paradigm's assumptions.[14] That is, para-

---

[11] Kuhn, *The Structure of Scientific Revolutions*, pp. 4-5.
[12] In Chapter 10, "The Aporiai of Truth," we will see that what we call the truth of the correspondence theory of truth is in fact only a form of systematic coherence.
[13] Kuhn, *The Structure of Scientific Revolutions*, p. 41.
[14] This insight is of great importance for understanding the place of "law" in societies and in religions. It is also crucial with respect to the "formalist fallacy," which assumes that the right method will disclose the proper meaning of a text or event, to which every methodology is potentially subject. See the discussion of the "formalist fallacy" along with the "intentional fallacy" and the "affective fallacy" by W.K. Wimsatt, Jr., and

digms are prior to any methodology. "Rules ... derive from paradigms, but paradigms can guide research even in the absence of rules."[15]

What this means, of course, is that what distinguishes a "scientist" from a "charlatan" is not primarily a "scientific method." What distinguishes them is not that one tests her/his hypotheses out by a careful, duplicatable process of experimentation, involving control groups and care that all secondary causality be eliminated from influencing the data of observation and the conclusions drawn from that observation, and the other does not. What fundamentally distinguishes them is not that one is self-correcting while the other is not. Rather, what distinguishes them is their commitment to different cognitive models of what constitutes the basic and most fundamental characteristics of reality.

Kuhn points out that paradigms necessarily function without their having been completely "rationalized," i.e., without the adherent to the paradigm being fully conscious of how the paradigm is functioning and shaping her/his understanding and actions. Echoing the problem of definition at the core of the Socratic dialectic but appealing specifically to Wittgenstein's *Philosophical Investigations*, Kuhn points to the impossibility of definition which means we are dependent upon "family resemblance" for identifying things rather than indubitable and absolute knowledge of what our concepts and rules are.[16] In the absence of their clear and absolute formulation, concepts and rules are assumed, even in scientific communities, as a matter of common sense. What is overlooked too often, however, is that every judgment of common sense is relative to the paradigm to which one is already committed.

Fourth, perhaps more important than even rules and methods, paradigms provide a "strong network of commitments - conceptual, theoretical, instrumental, and methodological"[17] that serve as the framework of common sense *normalcy* necessary for one to function in any discipline (or any "world"). The normative function of paradigms

---

Monroe C. Beardsley in *The Verbal Icon: Studies in the Meaning of Poetry* (Lexington: The University Press of Kentucky, 1954). In the third essay in this volume Wimsatt argues against the insights and limitations of the "formalist fallacy."

[15] Kuhn, *The Structure of Scientific Revolutions*, p. 42.
[16] See Kuhn, *The Structure of Scientific Revolutions*, pp. 44-45.
[17] Kuhn, *The Structure of Scientific Revolutions*, p. 42. Kuhn wrote earlier, p. 11: "Men (sic) whose research is based on shared paradigms are committed to the same rules and standards for scientific practice. That commitment and the apparent consensus it produces are prerequisites for normal science, i.e., for the genesis and continuation of a particular research tradition."

... show[s] that paradigms provide scientists not only with a map but also with some of the directions essential for map-making. In learning a paradigm the scientist acquires theory, methods, and standards together, usually in an inextricable mixture. Therefore, when paradigms change, there are usually significant shifts in the criteria determining the legitimacy both of problems and of proposed solutions.[18]

Therefore, fifth, paradigms are social constructs, in other words, they are *communal*. This, of course, is the key to the very notion of sociological paradigms which "... stands for the entire constellation of believes, values, techniques, and so on shared by the members of a given community."[19] The communal character of paradigms reinforces the paradigms monitoring of normalcy, because behavior that is inconsistent with, and thereby is abnormal, will be censored by the group. The insistence upon coherence combined with the commitment to normative behavior (of research or of actions in general) within a paradigm indicate, then, the communal character of paradigms. Hence, what is significant about paradigms is not merely the cognitive, coherent, and normative commitments of an individual, but that these characteristics constituting a particular paradigm are shared by a community.[20]

Finally, there is an aspect of paradigms not developed by Kuhn that is crucial for our grasping their silent, but imperial, role in all understanding and acting. Paradigms provide us with *causal explanation of events*. It was Hume observed that we do not perceive ultimate causes.[21] David Hume who pointed out that causality is a matter of "habit" and not of perception, for we only perceive effects and *never* ultimate causes:

> Suppose two objects to be presented to us, of which the one is the cause and the other the effect; 'tis plain, that from the simple consideration of one, or both these objects we never shall *perceive* the tie, by which they are united, or be able to certainly to pronounce, that there is a connexion betwixt them. 'Tis not, therefore, from any one instance, that we arrive at the idea of cause and effect, of a necessary connection of power, of force, of energy, and of efficacy. Did we never see any but particular conjunctions of objects, entirely different from each other, we shou'd never be able to form any such ideas.[22]

We only perceive penultimate causes. For example, we perceive the cause of the damage to the telephone pole to be the car that hit it. But what we don't

---

[18] Kuhn, *The Structure of Scientific Revolutions*, p. 109.
[19] Kuhn, *The Structure of Scientific Revolutions*, p. 175.
[20] See Kuhn, *The Structure of Scientific Revolutions*, pp. viii and 153.
[21] See David Hume, "Of the Understanding," pp. 44-51, 115-143, 146-160.
[22] David Hume, "Of the Understanding," p. 48.

perceive is the ultimate cause, i.e., energy. Energy is a key form of causal explanation in the Western paradigm, and it is entirely inaccessible to the senses. In short, every notion of causality is relative to the socially constructed model of reality informing that community about the way things work. Causality is relative to one's paradigm, for it is dependent upon the coherence shaping all habit, and a fundamental characteristic of paradigms is their insistence upon, and provision for, coherence.

Where do our notions of causality come from then? They are arrived at as a matter of "custom" and habit:

> ... suppose we observe several instances, in which the same objects are always conjoin'd together, we immediately conceive a connexion betwixt them, and begin to draw an inference from one to another. This multiplicity of resembling instances, therefore, constitutes the very essence of power or connection, and is the source, from which the idea of it arises ...
>
> The necessary connection btwixt causes and effects is the foundation of our inference from one to the other. The foundation of our inference is the transition arising from the accustom'd union. These are, therefore, the same.
>
> ... Upon the whole, necessity is something, that exists in the mind, not in objects ... Either we have no idea of necessity, or necessity is nothing but that determination of the thought to pass from causes to effects and from effects to causes, according to their experienced union ...
>
> ... [H]ow often must we repeat to ourselves, *that* the simple view of any two objects or actions, however related, can never give us any idea of power, or of a connexion betwixt them: *that* this idea arises from the repetition of their union: *that* the repetition neither discovers nor causes anything in the objects, but has an influence only on the mind, by that customary transition it produces: *that* this customary transition is, therefore, the same with power and necessity; which are consequently qualities of perceptions, not of objects, and are internally felt by the soul, and not perceiv'd externally in bodies?[23]

Human understanding is impossible without commitment to a sociological paradigm. It is not merely that there is no other way for us to experience the world than through the lenses or filters of our communal mental models, but our very notions of causality are mediated to us through sociological paradigms. We cannot begin to act without confidence in our grasp of cause, hence, our common sense, pragmatic activity is shaped in advance by the sociological paradigm we embrace. Common sense, pragmatic activity, then, is relative to our paradigm.

---

[23] Hume, "Of the Understanding," pp. 48-51.

The Subversion of Coherence as the Consequence of Coherence

Ironically, the very characteristics determinative of sociological paradigms (cognitive, coherent, commitment, normative, communal, and causality) are what lead to change within a paradigm and perhaps, if an onset of incoherence is threatening enough to the order of the paradigm warrants, to the adoption of a new paradigm. The communally conservative character of a paradigm is precisely what permits it, and even forces it, to acknowledge anomalous data.

> ... we can at last begin to see why normal science, a pursuit not directed to novelties and tending at first to suppress them, should nevertheless be so effective in causing them to arise.
>
> In the development of any science, the first received paradigm is usually felt to account quite successfully for most of the observations and experiments easily accessible to that science's practitioners. Further development, therefore, ordinarily calls for the construction of elaborate equipment, the development of an esoteric vocabulary and skills, and a refinement of concepts that increasingly lessens their resemblance to their usual common-sense prototypes. That professionalization leads, on the one hand, to an immense restriction of the scientists's vision and to a considerable resistance to paradigm change. The science has become increasingly rigid. On the other hand, within those areas to which the paradigm directs the attention of the group, normal science leads to a detail of information and to a precision of the observation-theory match that could be achieved in no other way. Furthermore, that detail and precision-of-match have a value that transcends their not always very high intrinsic interest. Without the special apparatus that is constructed mainly for anticipated functions, the results that lead ultimately to novelty could not occur. And even when the apparatus exists, novelty ordinarily emerges only for the man (sic) who, knowing *with precision* what he (sic) should expect, is able to recognize that something has gone wrong. *Anomaly appears only against the background provided by the paradigm.*[24] (in part emphasis added)

The normative paradigm has the additional function of ensuring that anomalous data not easily result in surrendering of the paradigm.

> By ensuring that the paradigm will not be too easily surrendered, resistance guarantees that scientists will not be lightly distracted and that the anomalies that lead to paradigm change will penetrate existing knowledge to the core.[25]

In light of such anomalous data, a paradigm reacts in one of two ways (if the data are simply "new" and not anomalous, it merely proves to be consistent with the theoretical expectations of the existing paradigm and requires no substantive change). The paradigm may have to develop an entirely new and even radical theoretical articulation to account for the anomalous data in

---

[24] Kuhn, *The Structure of Scientific Revolutions*, pp. 64-5.
[25] Kuhn, *The Structure of Scientific Revolutions*, p. 65.

order to respond to a serious challenge to the overall coherence of the paradigm. Such new theoretical articulation can cause major shifts within the field without requiring the surrendering of the dominant paradigm itself. The second consequence of truly anomalous data can be a paradigm revolution. Such a revolution involves the substitution of the dominant paradigm by a new paradigm able to account not only for the anomalous data but for some, if not most, of the unresolved problems of the old paradigm.[26]

The Non-Cumulative Character of Human Knowledge

Thomas Kuhn has convincingly demonstrated that the very notion that the natural sciences are engaged in a process of cumulatively gaining knowledge with respect to stable data is an illusion. So long as a single paradigm dominates in a research tradition, so long as the anomalous data are either unthreatening or eventually able to be integrated into that dominate paradigm, only so long can one speak of cumulative knowledge. But science (and human understanding in general) is ultimately characterized by paradigm revolutions rather than mere paradigm shifts. Hence, cumulative knowledge is a passing illusion. He asks in *The Structure of Scientific Revolutions*:

> ... is sensory experience fixed and neutral? Are theories simply man-made interpretations of given [fixed] data? The epistemological viewpoint that has most often guided Western philosophy for three centuries dictates an immediate and unequivocal, Yes. In the absence of a developed alternative, I find it impossible to relinquish entirely that viewpoint. Yet it no longer functions effectively, and the attempts to make it do so through the introduction of a neutral language of observations now seem to me hopeless.[27]
>
> The operations and measurements that a scientist undertakes in the laboratory are not 'the given' of experience ... They are not what the scientist sees ... Far more clearly than the immediate experience from which they in part derive, *operations and measurements are paradigm-determined.*[28] (emphasis added)

Kuhn reminded his reader earlier in the text that "[w]hat occurs during a scientific revolution is not fully reducible to a reinterpretation of individual and stable data. In the first place, the data are not unequivocally stable."[29] If

---

[26] See Kuhn, *The Structure of Scientific Revolutions*, p. 97.
[27] See Kuhn's similar judgments with respect to epistemology since Descartes, *The Structure of Scientific Revolutions*, pp. 126 and 195.
[28] Kuhn, *The Structure of Scientific Revolutions*, p. 126.
[29] Kuhn, *The Structure of Scientific Revolutions*, p. 121. See, in addition, *ibid.*, pp. 135, 150, 192, 195, and 206.

the data are not unequivocally stable in the natural sciences, then we must relinguish the notion that "knowledge" is a cumulative process.[30] Perception is already pre-shaped by a paradigm or model that is the prerequisite for our observing anything. As we walk into the laboratory, we carry with us not only a model (or set of lenses) shaping the discipline of the particular laboratory entered, but we carry a whole world view that functions so subliminally that we are usually completely unaware of it.

Perception is never neutral, but, rather, it is always dependent upon a filter system or a set of lenses mediating the data of perception. Hence, experience itself involves a contradiction or aporia: perception is based on an illusion of stable data, which in fact are paradigm relative, but at the same time we have no other arena to appeal to for adjudicating the adequacy of our perceptions than the correspondence of our judgments coherently and non-contradictorily with this data. In addition, that which we appeal to in perception for the confirming of our judgments is itself a concealing and suppression of what necessarily cannot be present in any particular perception. Hence, the correspondence theory of truth essential to pragmatic experience rests upon two levels of paradox: 1) our inability to unequivocally test out the truth of our judgments because a) the data do not possess the stability we believe they do and, b) more importantly, we have no immediate (only mediate) access to that data; and 2) the very dynamic of revealing and concealing (actuality and possibility) that is essential to an event prohibits any judgment of certainty with respect to that experience. In short, the correspondence theory of truth, on the one hand, has us only comparing two sets of mental phenomena when supposedly "testing" our judgments, because we cannot get "outside" our mental paradigm to test out our judgments. On the other hand, the correspondence theory of truth has us concerned with, if not with mere actuality then with only a limited range of, those possibilities that we are able to consciously grasp. However, far more is concealed from us than what we are able to consciously grasp.

Two observations made by Kuhn, regarding the non-cumulative character of knowledge and his denial of any one absolute paradigm, are instructive for understanding the aporetic character of human experience. Speaking of the emergence of a new paradigm brought on by a radical crisis in a dominant paradigm, Kuhn observes:

> The transition from a paradigm in crisis to a new one from which a new tradition of normal science can emerge is far from a cumulative process, one achieved by an

---

[30] See Kuhn, *The Structure of Scientific Revolutions*, pp. 84, 92, 96, 108, 123, 128, 150.

articulation or extension of the old paradigm. Rather it is a reconstruction of the field *from new fundamentals*, a reconstruction that changes some of the field's most elementary theoretical generalizations as well as many of its paradigm methods and applications. During the transition period there will be a large but never complete overlap between the problems that can be solved by the old and by the new paradigm. But there will also be a decisive difference in the modes of solution. When the transition is complete, the profession will have changed its view of the field, its methods, and its goals.[31] (emphasis added)

Such a change in view of the field, method, and goals is the result of what Kuhn calls a Gestalt transformation of the discipline and not simply the consequence of the adding on of new information.

Just because it is a transition between incommensurables, the transition between competing paradigms cannot be made a step at a time, forced by logic and neutral experience. Like the gestalt switch, it must occur all at once (though not necessarily in an instant) or not at all.[32]

Furthermore, Kuhn argues that no one paradigm can solve all problems and any one paradigm will, therefore, solve the problems that it takes to be most significant. It is precisely this situation combined with the normative coherence within each competing paradigm, he suggests, that accounts for the difficulties of communicating across paradigm horizons.

To the extent ... that two scientific schools disagree about what is a problem and what a solution, they will inevitably talk through each other when debating the relative merits of their respective paradigms. In the partially circular arguments that regularly result, each paradigm will be shown to satisfy more or less the criteria that it dictates for itself and to fall short of a few of those dictated by its opponent. There are other reasons, too, for the incompleteness of logical contact that consistently characterizes paradigm debates. For example, since no paradigm ever solves all the problems it defines and since no two paradigms leave all the same problems unsolved, paradigm debates always involve the question: Which problems is it more significant to have solved?[33]

Kuhn does not stop with such theoretical incommensurability between paradigms. He argues that paradigms are not mere interpretations of nature. They are "constitutive of nature as well."[34] It is with this issue that the aporia of logic and praxis most radically emerges in Kuhn's analysis.

---

[31] Kuhn, *The Structure of Scientific Revolutions*, pp. 84-5.
[32] Kuhn, *The Structure of Scientific Revolutions*, p. 150.
[33] Kuhn, *The Structure of Scientific Revolutions*, pp. 109-110.
[34] Kuhn, *The Structure of Scientific Revolutions*, p. 110.

Paradigm Revolutions and the Aporia of Logic and Praxis

Thomas Kuhn is confronted with the aporia of logic and praxis in his discussion of the issue whether or not the scientist is in a "new world" after a paradigm revolution. By every measurement of "new" (e.g., different data, different interpretative framework, different research agenda, the need to develop new instrumentation, etc.) the scientist is in a "new world" in such a circumstance. Yet Kuhn struggles to hold on to a notion that the world is, nevertheless, to some extent exogenous. Beginning with Chapter X, "Revolutions as Changes of World View," Kuhn wrestles with the inadequacies of what he calls the epistemological model since Descartes which has maintained that understanding is simply a process of interpretation of a stable, external reality.[35] After a paradigm revolution, Kuhn maintains that, although there is no "geographical transplantation," scientists "are responding to a different world."[36] But he insists that this is not merely a responding to a different interpretation of the world, for

> What occurs during a scientific revolution is not fully reducible to a reinterpretation of individual and stable data. In the first place, the data are not unequivocally stable ... Rather than being an interpreter, the scientist who embraces a new paradigm is like the man wearing inverting lenses. Confronting the same constellation of objects as before and knowing that he (sic) does so, he nevertheless finds them transformed through and through in many of their details.[37]

There is perhaps no claim by Kuhn that has caused more consternation than the issue of stable data. The conundrum is the consequence of our ability to logically distinguish between stimuli and sensations, when, in fact, pragmatically we do not experience "pure" stimuli but only sensations.[38] In

---

[35] See Kuhn, *The Structure of Scientific Revolutions*, pp. 120-1, 126. He repeats his dissatisfaction with the Cartesian model of epistemology in the "Postscript," p. 195: "What I have been opposing in this book is ... the attempt, traditional since Descartes but not before, to analyze perception as an interpretive process, as an unconscious version of what we do after we have perceived."

[36] Kuhn, *The Structure of Scientific Revolutions*, p. 111.

[37] Kuhn, *The Structure of Scientific Revolutions*, pp. 121-2.

[38] Kuhn suggests in *The Structure of Scientific Revolutions*, p. 193: "Notice ... that two groups, the members of which have systematically different sensations on receipt of the same stimuli, do *in some sense* live in different worlds. We posit the existence of stimuli to explain our perceptions of the world, and we posit their immutability to avoid both individual and social solipsism. About neither posit have I the slightest reservation. But our world is populated in the first instance not by stimuli but by the objects of our sensations, and these need not be the same, individual to individual or group to group. To the extent, of course, that individuals belong to the same group and thus share education, language, experience, and culture, we have good reason to suppose that their sensations are the same."

short, *it is not that it can be established unequivocally that the data are stable or that the data are not stable.* Given the mediated character of all perceptions (sensations), it is logically impossible for us to tell whether the data are stable or not. Kuhn speaks of "concrete indices" pointing toward the particulars of perception,[39] but such concrete indices are a form of mediated experience that are influenced by a whole host of assumptions, for example, about the way the world must be and what kinds of causal agency accounts for events in the world, which we have learned so well that we are no longer aware of their presence in perception. On the other hand, pragmatically, there can be no question about the stability of the data, for we cannot not act, and we must act on the basis of our confidence that the world has a certain level of sameness to it.

The aporia of logic and praxis, however, surfaces at the point where we must recognize that the pragmatic does not give us absolute knowledge about anything (even ourselves). Pragmatic knowledge provides us at best with contingent understanding of the world in any circumstance, and, for the most part, such contingent understanding is sufficient for the conducting of our lives. Nonetheless, pragmatic knowledge consists of, and is dependent upon, contingent conditions of possibility not upon absolutes. Pragmatic knowledge indicates what we must understand to act in any particular circumstance. But there is nothing absolute about particular circumstances. You and I don't absolutely have to be reading this text. Hence, any "knowledge" based upon praxis is itself contingent. There is nothing absolute about it. Even the so-called absoluteness of the "cogito ergo sum" is contingent. So long as the cogito "is," it must necessarily be (but only contingently). The cogito does not absolutely necessarily have to be. Any "knowledge" dependent upon such contingency is itself contingent.

Kuhn is grappling here with the recognition that paradigms, which are individual and social constructs of reality, and ultimate causal explanation, which is always tied to a paradigm, stand in tension with the necessity of one's engaging in pragmatic actions in the world which we cannot know - a world to which we do not have immediate and direct access, a world which itself is not stable, and a praxis which can occur only by means of one's al-

---

[39] See Kuhn, *The Structure of Scientific Revolutions*, p. 126: "The operations and measurements that a scientist undertakes ... are not what the scientist sees ... Rather, they are concrete indices to the content of more elementary perceptions, and as such they are selected for the close scrutiny of normal research only because they promise opportunity for the fruitful elaboration of an [already] accepted paradigm."

ready being committed to a paradigm with its causal explanation modeling to us the way we should take the world to be. Furthermore, although no paradigm is or can be absolute and exhaustive of the way things are, we must pragmatically act "as if" our paradigm was absolute and exhaustive.[40]

At the very core of our notion of reality and at the very core of our notions of causality, then, Kuhn is speaking of an essential unknowing that annuls all absolute claims to one's grasp on reality and causality. Nevertheless, as individuals and as a community we cannot not act. The acknowledgment of this radical unknowing does not lead to paralysis. To be in the world is to act, despite our lack of knowledge. Hence, to be in the world involves the human community in an odyssey of faith seeking understanding as a consequence of the aporiai at the core of our reality: that we at best can

---

[40] This "as if" character of experience can be found in theological projects across the theological spectrum. Perhaps the first to explicitly embrace the "as if" character of human experience was Fichte, who is often misrepresented as a solipsist. Yet Fichte's "as if" is Kant's notion of the "moral order" that connects "knowledge" and "practice." We are not merely passive knowers who then act. Rather, we are first actors, grounded in a moral order, who then know. See Fichte, *Die Bestimmung des Menschen*, pp. 264-5, 280, and 284. In addition, see pp. 145-311, particularly the third book entitled "Glaube" or "Faith," pp. 253-309.

Karl Barth's "as if" is the infinite difference between time and eternity that enables the dialectic of history leading back to God. See Barth's discussion of this dialectic in "The Christian's Place in Society" in *The Word of God and the Word of Man*, trans. by Douglas Horton (Gloucester, Mass.: Peter Smith, 1978), pp. 299-327.

The "as if" of George Lindbeck's project is that the cultural-linguistic model of theology doesn't distort, and we can know the "road to Jerusalem." With respect to deference to those possessing "linguistic competency," leaving us no test to protect against systematic distortion, see Lindbeck, *The Nature of Doctrine*, p. 82. With respect to the "road to Jerusalem, see Lindbeck, *The Nature of Doctrine*, pp. 52, 53, 54.

For David Tracy, the "as if" is confidence in the God who, as the "fellow sufferer who endures, ensures our capacity to love and confirms our confidence in the trustworthiness and worthwhile character of our lives." With respect to the theme of God is love, see Tracy, *Blessed Rage for Order*, p. 189. With respect to the reality of God as the guarantor of the trustworthiness and worthwhile character of our lives, see *Blessed Rage for Order*, p. 186.

For much feminist theology the "as if" is the emphasis on the priority of experience and relatedness over unchanging hierarchy. See, for example, Sallie MacFague, *Metaphorical Theology*, pp. 21, 106, 125-127, 129, and Elizabeth Moltmann-Wendel, "Zur Kreuzestheologie heute. Gibt es eine feministische Kreuzestheologie?" in *Evangelische Theologie*, 50/6 (1990), 546-558.

In Paul Ricoeur one can identify two "as ifs." The first is a dependence upon the ahistorical transcendental of the ideal speech act which alone can protect against systematic distortion. See Ricoeur, *Time and Narrative*, vol. 3, pp. 226, 258, and 277. The second is the notion of "time that envelops." See *ibid.*, p. 274.

only represent reality to ourselves as an individual and corporate paradigm, yet we cannot not act. We must as individuals and a community act as if we knew what reality is and how it functions.

Religious Language and the Aporia of Logic and Praxis

The aporia of logic and praxis emerges as central to theological reflection concerning religious claims, as well. David Tracy observes that it is precisely a shift from logic to pragmatics that characterizes what he calls the move to the "third stage" of the analysis of religious language in our century. The first two stages are those of attempts at "verification" and "falsification" of religious language, particularly God language, in the work of A.J. Ayer and Antony Flew.[41]

Both verification and falsification are concerned with establishing the truth claims of judgments. They involve the above mentioned correspondence theory of truth which maintains that a judgment is true when it corresponds to that which it is meant to represent. For example, the judgment, "there is a large, three trunked oak tree in the front yard of our house," is true, if in fact there is such a tree in the front yard. It is neither the judgment itself that is true nor is it the referent itself that is true, but truth consists of the correspondence between the judgment and the referent (which assumes, of course, that we can be confident that the referent is what we take it to be).

The *logical* limitations of such a theory of truth are obvious at this point. Consciousness has no direct access to an exogenous world. The world is accessible to human beings only as it is mediated through a paradigm/language. Further, a crucial distinction between the intellect and the world of sense perception is that the intellect can't be other than the way it is; where the objects of sense can be other than the way they appear to be. A judgment may be verified 999 times only to be contradicted the 1,000 time. For example, one can live one's whole life in the northern hemisphere with the false judgment that "all swans are white." Only if one were to encounter an Australian black swan, would one have to correct the error of one's judgment. Hence, the turn to falsification. Rather than seek to confirm one's judgment, the task in the second stage of the analysis of religious language turned to asking what would count as a contradiction or falsification of a judgment. The promise of falsification was short lived, because any such ex-

---

[41] See Tracy, *Blessed Rage for Order*, p. 120.

ercise can only be a judgment of logic, i.e., a judgment in the mind. As an actual test for the truth of one's judgment, it, too, succumbs to the same limitations as the verification theory of truth, lack of access.

Falsification is rooted in the notion that there is some reality external to consciousness to which our judgments correspond. But human beings have no indubitable access to such a reality. Already in Plato's simile of the line one learns that the world of "objects" is accessible to consciousness only to the extent that those objects are imaged in the understanding. What kind of truth is this, then, that can never be certain that even when its judgments are being contradicted, i.e., falsified, the cause of the falsification is not some secondary cause rather than a failure of our judgment? Surely, this is no form of eternal truth. At best, verification or falsification can arrive at adequacy of judgment not indubitable certainty.

Hence, there can be no logical verification or falsification of any reality independent of our consciousness of it - any reality, either exogenous empirical reality or (the conclusion applies, as well, to any claims for an eternal realm of ideas independent of our consciousness of them) a spiritual dimension independent of human spirit. Humans only have mediated access to such dimensions. It is not merely that such tests of truth fail with respect to the God question. Such tests of truth fail with respect to all experience. At best, such tests give us mediated adequacy not direct and indubitable certainty.

In stage 3 of the analysis of religious language, such language was examined in terms of the acknowledgment that all experience occurs within a linguistic horizon. This is the same as saying that all experience is mediated by a paradigm, since paradigms are representations of the way we take reality to be. These representations are mediated to consciousness by symbol systems, i.e., language. Within the linguistic horizon of human experience, however, religious language has a unique "use and function." This turn to usage and function is a turn to pragmatic application rather than logical proof, for asking about the kind of "job" performed by religious language is to examine religious language as a pragmatic instrument. Stage 3, Tracy suggests, is represented by the work of Basil Mitchell, R.M. Hare, R.B. Braithwaite, Ian Ramsey, and Frederick Ferré.[42]

Religious language functions to disclose what Tracy calls our "limit situation" as human beings[43] in that it is that usage of language that employs

---

[42] See Tracy, *Blessed Rage*, pp. 121-124.
[43] See Tracy, *Blessed Rage*, Chapter 5: "The Religious Dimension of Common Human Experience and Language," particularly p. 93

"... such 'odd' qualifies as 'infinitely'; a qualitatively *odd* discernment; a *total* commitment; a *universal* applicability.[44]"

This is simply to say that religious language is concerned with the "whole" where other language games are concerned with parts or regions of experience. In the language of Kuhn, religious language is talking about the limits to any and all paradigms while simultaneously referring to the conditions of possibility for any and all paradigms. The placing of religious language among the other human language games in this manner is what gives theology its priority over all the other sciences.[45] There is no pragmatic test or argument, however, that can provide an absolute ground for any language game. Once again, pragmatic tests can establish "contingent" necessity at best. In other words, given that a language is employed, what are its conditions of possibility. But no particular language absolutely has to be. Hence, the conditions of possibility for a language are not absolute conditions but only contingent conditions. Pragmatic tests of language only confirm that the human condition is one of radical faith seeking understanding.

Tracy concludes his analysis of the three stages of religious language by saying: "Limit-language seems a correct way to indicate the logically odd character of religious language and *the qualitatively different empirical placing for that language* [= pragmatic placing] in our common experience."[46] (emphasis added)

---

[44] Tracy, *Blessed Rage*, p. 123

[45] See, Tracy, *Blessed Rage for Order*, chapter 5, where he rejects the "two language" approach to clarifying the relationship between religion and science (religious language as "self-involving" and scientific language as "spectatorial" - Austin and Evans; or theology as concerned with revelation - Barth - where science is concerned with "neutral discoveries"). Tracy concurs with Bernard Lonergan's notion of "self-transcendence" for speaking about science: "... scientific questioning impels one past an experienced world of sensitive immediacy to an intelligently mediated and deliberately constituted world of meaning" (*ibid.*, p. 96). The scientist's confidence, that her/his work transpires in a "world of meaning," suggests that there are deeper, religious questions, informing the scientific enterprise: 1) with respect to the basic character of this universe and "the very possibility of fruitful inquiry" (*ibid.*, p. 98); 2) whether "there can be any virtually unconditioned judgments unless there exists also a formally unconditioned judgment" (*ibid.*, p. 98), i.e., necessary metaphysical judgments; and 3) whether the scientist's goals, purposes, and ideals are themselves worthwhile (*ibid.*, p. 93). Tracy concludes: "No inquirer can commit himself (sic) to the task of authentic self-transcendence (i.e., intelligent, rational, and responsible thought and action) and then deny his own need to seek the ultimate intelligent, rational, and responsible grounds for such inquiry and action" (*ibid.*, p. 99). In short, religious inquiry has priority over scientific inquiry, because religious inquiry is concerned with the fundamental, metaphysical conditions of possibility of any and all inquiry.

[46] Tracy, *Blessed Rage for Order*, pp. 123-4.

Conclusion

Pragmatic arguments of praxis do not establish absolute logical or metaphysical necessity. Such pragmatic arguments can at best establish relative likelihood or contingent necessity. The aporia of logic and praxis constitutes a wake-up call with respect to the pragmatic certainties of everydayness: First, the paradox is that the realm of the senses, so important to our confidence in an empirical world independent of our consciousness, itself is exclusively experienced as mediated in the intellect in a dimension of nonmaterial non-sense or the spiritual. Second, there is equal pragmatic ground to embrace the notion of a Logos independent of our consciousness of it as there is to embrace the notion of an empirical reality independent of our consciousness of it if we employ a pragmatic argument to confirm our contingently necessary dependence upon some dimension independent of consciousness: try to ignore universals and see what the consequences are. Not only can one no more ignore universals than one can the train rushing toward one stuck in an automobile on the tracks, for a person couldn't begin to understand that it was a train rushing toward her/him, much less that s/he is stuck in a car on the tracks, without universals, i.e., the ideas "train," "car," "tracks," and "self," which pragmatically prove to be universals accessible to, and shared by, all consciousness. These universals are as necessary to experience as the physical objects themselves. On what grounds does one immediately understand in such a situation? On the grounds of the disclosing/concealing dynamic of actuality and possibility made possible by the human as both spirit ($νοῦς$, $λόγος$, and $νόμος$) and the physical in a world of pragmatic activities. But just how these components of disclosure and concealment, i.e., just how actuality and possibility, spirit and world, are irreducibly related constitutes the fundamental aporia of pragmatic action.

This is the same aporia at the core of Thomas Kuhn's analysis of sociological paradigms. When there is a paradigm revolution, one is in a new world, and the data themselves change along with the instrumentation and causal explanation employed by the paradigm to understand the phenomena. Nevertheless, in some sense the world is the same even if the simplistic structure of fact - interpretation must be surrendered. Why must this simplistic structure of interpretation be given up? Because humans have no direct access to the world. Reality is available to us only to the extent that we re-present reality to ourselves in the intellect. There can be no indubitable surety that the world is the way any particular communal paradigm takes it to be. This means there can be no indubitable surety that one's communal paradigm has the correct causal understanding of events. It is for this reason that critical inquiry is self-transcending, i.e., is suspicious of its present understanding and insists on self-correction when the evidence (of whatever kind) justifies and requires revision. This self-transcendence does not rest upon confidence that there is an ultimate, much less a metaphysical, explanation of reality. It rests upon faith, i.e., our radical unknowing, and our suspicion over against any form of explanation although simultaneously aware that one can be suspicious only because one is, paradoxically, already committed to a paradigm of reality.

Chapter 9
The Aporiai of Language

The medium of the mediation accomplished by a sociological paradigm is always some kind of linguistic system. This is the reason why one must speak of reality not as some exogenous world independent of consciousness but as a social construct and, more importantly, as a socio-linguistic construct. To be sure, the linguistic system need not be a language of cultural range, such as English, Greek, Latin, Chinese, etc., but can be any coherent social "sign system."[1] Just as paradigms are communal, so is language a communal achievement although the community may be a discipline within a language of cultural range or, as is the case with mathematics, it may be a sign system transcending cultural languages. All of the aporetic dilemmas of cultural paradigms resurface when the discussion makes the turn to linguistics, for the relationship between language and that to which it refers is precisely the same problematic as the relationship between a paradigm and the "world" it models.

Nevertheless, it would be a mistake to treat language, just as it would be a mistake to take perception in general, as mediating only what is actual. The aporetic character of language is that it is a mirror that is simultaneously actual and possible which means that language is no mere reflection of a given actual reality external to it than it is an internally closed system of self-reference. Language mediates and transforms, because language represents the world (both "inner" and "outer") as simultaneously actual and possible. Therefore, consciousness is no more in control of the medium than it is of the referent. It is because one takes language and reference to be primarily literal that one gives priority to actuality, the factually given, at the expense of the non-literal and the possible. But as Philip Wheelwright suggests, "If reality is largely fluid and half-paradoxical, steel nets are not the best instruments for taking samples of it."[2]

---

[1] On the individual, social, and temporal character of language as a sign system, see Saussure, *Course in General Linguistics*, especially pp. 77-78.

[2] Philip Wheelwright, *Metaphor and Reality* (Bloomington: Indiana University Press, 1968), p. 128. See, p. 39, as well: "Now while logical language is manifestly of very great importance for situations and types of questions to which it legitimately applies, its powers of reference are limited. To try to deal with all matters by logic-scientific language is as self-defeating as to try to capture water in a net, or a breeze in a bag. Meanings always flit mockingly beyond the reach of men with nets and measuring sticks."

What is at issue in the concern with the aporetics of language, then, is complicated precisely by the uncontrollable dynamic of linguistic mediation involving both actuality and possibility. No referential understanding of language (or truth), that treats language as some kind of mere one-to-one correspondence between a linguistic unit and that which is external to the linguistic unit, can do justice to the function of language in human experience. Such a theory is brutally reductionistic not merely because it ignores all of the epistemological problems associated with such a claim for reference, but because it completely ignores potentiality by treating experience as limited to only what is actual (either mentally or materially actual). To present adequately the aporiai of language, then, requires one's keeping the first two aporiai (of intellect and world and of logic and praxis) in mind as one examines the issue of the dynamic of identity and difference in experience that emerges once one moves beyond thinking in terms of mere actuality to consider the revealing/concealing of possibility in all actuality.

This third paradox is concerned, then, with the dialectical tension between literal and figurative language as essential to the human condition. Humans find themselves always and already within a linguistic horizon (or paradigm) that shapes perception and meaning. Yet that linguistic horizon is not grounded in a literal, factual world of reference. Rather, experience and understanding are shaped by the imagination (we can only understand the world to the extent that we can imagine it) which ultimately will force the acknowledgment of the priority of the figurative over the literal. The literal does not ground the figurative; rather, it's the other way around.[3] The central aporia here is that, to the extent the figurative precedes the literal (i.e., the literal is dead metaphor), universals are ectypal (a posteriori). However, to the extent that we always and already find ourselves within a linguistic horizon (i.e., language is the great institution which precedes us all[4]), universals are archetypal (a priori). This aporia makes no final claim with respect to universals existing independent of our consciousness of them. In short, this paradox does not rest on metaphysical claims. It does, however, acknowledge the ambiguity with respect to the relationship between identity and difference in experience. Which comes first, identity or difference? The answer is, neither. Identity and difference are paradoxically related, incom-

---

[3] This is what Ricoeur calls "our most extreme hypothesis, that the 'metaphoric' that transgresses the categorial order also begets it." *Rule of Metaphor*, p. 24. See, also, *ibid.*, 22-3, 121-122, 197.

[4] See Ricoeur, *Time and Narrative*, vol. 3, p. 221.

mensurable and irreducible one to the other. Out of this aporia emerges an entirely different understanding of truth in distinction from the correspondence theory of truth, for this aporia announces the fundamental tension between an "is" and an "is not" constitutive of any and all experience.

Reality as Vitally Metaphoric

Everyday life is shaped by confidence that one has access by means of the senses to the world as it actually is. For the most part, such confidence is justified, since the conduct of one's affairs demands and confirms such a presupposition. The routines of one's life from getting out of bed in the morning to meals, transportation, work, household chores, etc., all rest upon one's confidence that not only is there order to one's experience, but that one can count upon a certain kind of repetition to experience. Such confidence is necessary to life, but it, nevertheless, remains an assumption beyond logical proof.[5] Such assumptions are determinative of the human condition as an odyssey of faith seeking understanding.

However, the routines and repetitions of everyday life are a way of distracting one from examining the true character of one's experience. The task of examining the true character of one's experience may not be an activity that everyone will want to undertake. Nevertheless, a life that focuses only upon "whats" and not upon "hows" is dangerous both for the individual and the community.[6] There is more to humanity than the calculation, prediction, manipulation and control of things and other persons.

If life consisted only of one's having access to, and control over, only what is actual, life would be static and, therefore, not really life but death.[7] The actual, in fact, only has significance, because it is dripping with possi-

---

[5] A case could be made that this is the origin of all (religious) ritual, i.e., ritual celebrates the repetitive order of reality, and is, therefore, a formalized derivative from experience in general. Rituals not only reassure that there is order to experience, they reinforce the legitimacy of a particular paradigm's understanding of reality. Given that reality is only accessible through a communal paradigm, the repetitive order is self-confirming.

[6] There are two manners of asking "how?" One is the "how" of methodology: knowing what I want to accomplish or acquire, how, or what steps must I follow, to accomplish it? The second way of asking "how?" is concerned with the aporiai that shape and enable all experience. The "how" of methodology is a form of knowing; the "how" of aporiai is a form of unknowing. Everything hinges upon acknowledging the difference.

[7] This applies to a reality that might consist exclusively of universals as it applies to a reality that might consist exclusively of static particularities. Both would not only be governed by absolute necessity, but in neither could there be any change. The latter is proportional to the amount of possibility concealed by the actual.

bilities. Possibilities are the source of all impatience and dissatisfaction, of all suffering and disappointment, of all tragedy and oppression, and of all excitement, adventure, liberation, and hope. To be sure, possibilities are limited by the capabilities of the constellation of actuality that is one's world.[8] To be sure, as well, it is precisely the unique configuration of actuality and possibility established by one's historical context that accounts for one's singularity. Nevertheless, possibilities are in no way accessible through the senses. The world constituting one's life situation is a world of possibilities by no means exhausted by whatever actuality one *perceives*. Nor are possibilities accessible to the mind. What one is thinking at any moment is, precisely, what one is actually thinking - and it cannot be other than what one is actually thinking. That which one is thinking in any moment, however, conceals the potentialities of that thought - though those possibilities are not consciously accessible, entirely, in that moment. It is potentialities which "drive thought onward;" it is potentialities which account for the constant change in the world despite all indications of routine and repetition.

Hence, if one wants to talk about life, one needs a paradigm, a language, a vehicle of mediation, that is more than merely literal. The literal is only expressive of the actual, and it fosters the illusion that reality is universally the same and transparently accessible to all. What is valuable about the discussion of metaphor that follows from I.A. Richards, over Philip Wheelwright and Douglas Berggren, to Paul Ricoeur is that it unequivocally shifts the significance of the figurative from the margin to the center of human experience and understanding.

But this is jumping ahead to the end of this query of metaphor. When one "starts at the beginning" with Aristotle, one finds that, in this case, the initial impetus for reflection is more damaging than helpful. Aristotle's defi-

---

[8] An important essay by Alfonso García Marqués, "Der Begriff von 'Möglichkeit' nach 'Metaphysik' IX,3-4" in *Philosophisches Jahrbuch* 100/2 (1993), pp. 357-365, points out that Aristotle understood "possibility" as always tied to "capacity" (Vermögen). See *ibid.*, p. 358. "Impossibility" has to do with a lack of capacity. See *ibid.*, p. 358. This means that "in reality we don't encounter possibilities and impossibilities, but acts and potencies (capacities)" ["In der Realität stoßen wir nicht auf Mögliches und Unmögliches, sondern auf Akte und Potenzen (Vermögen)"] (*ibid.*, p. 359). This insight has important consequences for understanding the relationship between actuality and possibility. It is not as if one's horizon of possibilities was limitless. Rather, one's possibilities are limited by the capacities of one's actual situation. The limit to possibilities is what ensures that the Other (as object(s) or person(s)) emerges as an Other to which one is accountable. If possibility was not limited by actuality, one would life in a solipsistic fantasy world.

nition of metaphor as well as his championing of metaphor as a sign of genius deflects attention away from the metaphoric process at the heart of reality to reduce metaphor to a mere ornate way of naming things. Right at the beginning of the Western discussion of metaphor, then, there is a diversion that assigns metaphor to the margin either as a form of laziness or as a kind of ornamentation, which makes it the preserve of the exceptional rather than the ordinary.

Aristotle defines metaphor as follows: "Metaphor consists in giving the thing a name that belongs to something else; the transference being either from genus to species, or from species to genus, or from species to species, or on grounds of analogy."[9] Two observations are important here: 1) Metaphor is defined as a form of "substitution." Metaphor is the substitution of an inappropriate name for what, one presumes, would be a more appropriate, literal name. This is what leads to the judgment that metaphor is an indication of laziness, for metaphor is taken to be an inappropriate form of "naming" things that, were one to take the time and energy, one could name more properly with a literal label. 2) This definition, in fact, turns metaphor into an abbreviated form of analogy, for what Aristotle calls the transference "from genus to species, or from species to genus, or from species to species" is not metaphor but synecdoche and/or metonymy. Webster defines "synecdoche" to be "a figure of speech in which a part or individual is used for a whole or class, or the reverse of this. Example: *bread* for *food*, or *the army* for *a soldier*." Hence, "from genus to species or from species to genus" is not metaphor, but synecdoche. Webster defines "metonymy," on the other hand to be "use of the name of one thing for that of another associated with or suggested by it (e.g., 'the White House has decided' for 'the President has decided')." Hence, "from species to species" is not metaphor, but metonymy. Something else is going on with metaphor than mere synecdoche or metonymy.[10] What follows is concerned to indicate not only what

---

[9] Aristotle, *Poetics* 1457b.7-9.

[10] Nietzsche writes in his lecture notes for his "Rhetoric" course of 1874: "There were embittered disputes over the number and subspecies of the tropes; one came to thirty-eight kinds or more. We will speak about metaphor, synecdoche, metonymy, antonomasia, onomatopoeia, catachresis, metalepsis, epitheton, allegory, irony, periphrasis, hyperbaton, anastrophe, parenthesis, and hyperbole." From "Nietzsche's Lecture Notes on Rhetoric: A Translation," trans. by Carole Blair in *Philosophy and Rhetoric* 16/2 (1983), pp. 123-124. However, of these fourteen, Nietzsche's notes address only the three of metaphor (*ibid.*, pp. 124-125), synecdoche (*ibid.*, pp. 125-6), and metonymy (*ibid.*, pp. 126-7). Webster's defines the other tropes as follows: Antonomasia (ἀντονομασία) means "to name instead" and consists of the substitution of an epithet or appellative, or of the name of an office or dignity, for a person's proper name; converse-

this "something else" is all about but to indicate, also, how metaphor "stands on its own" and plays a central role with respect to the aporetic character of reality and of one's understanding of reality completely independent of, and more significantly than, analogy.

I.A. Richards: From Analogy to Tenor and Vehicle

I.A. Richards suggested an alternative definition of metaphor in his Mary Flexner lectures at Bryn Mawr College in 1936.[11] Richards argues for *an interactive theory* of metaphor to replace *the substitution theory* which had understood metaphor to be a trope for what could, and should, otherwise be expressed more adequately by literal language. First of all, the substitution theory is questionable, because there are severe limitations to literal language. Literal language has acquired its dominant status because of the illusion that there are fixed meanings to words:

> Literal language is rare outside the central parts of the sciences. We think it more frequent than it is through the influence of that form of the usage doctrine which as-

---

ly, the use of a proper name to express a general idea, e.g., calling an orator, Cicero. Onomatopoeia (ὀνοματοποιία) means "making of words" and is the formation or making of a name or word by an imitation of the sound associated with the thing or action designated (echoism); in rhetoric: the use of ὀνοματοποιία: naturally suggestive words, sentences, and forms for rhetorical effect. Catachresis (κατάχρησις) means "misuse of a word" or the improper use of a word; application of a term to a thing which it does not properly denote; abuse or perversion of a trope or metaphor. Metalepsis (μετάληψις) comes from μετα-λαμβάνειν which means to substitute, to change the sense of words, hence, metalepsis is a form of metonymy but the substitution of one word for another which is itself figurative. Epitheton (ἐπίθετον) means what is ascribed to a person; an attribute; epithet. Allegory (ἀλληγορία) is "speaking otherwise than one seems to speak," or the description of a subject under the guise of some other subject of aptly suggestive resemblances. Irony (εἰρονεία) is "dissimulation, ignorance purposely affected," and is a figure of speech in which the intended meaning is the opposite of that expressed by the words used. Periphrasis (περίφρασις) is "circumlocution" or paraphrasing. Hyperbaton (ὑπέρβατων) means "overstepping" in which the customary or logical order of words or phrases is inverted. Anastrophe (ἀναστροφή) means "a turning back," and is the inversion, or unusual arrangement, of the words or clauses of a sentence. Parenthesis (παρένθεσις) means "to put in beside," and is the explanatory or qualifying word, clause or sentence inserted into a passage with which it does not have any necessary grammatical connection - usually set off. Hyperbole (ὑπερβολή) means "exaggeration," and is an exaggerated or extravagant statement to express strong feeling or produce a strong impression which is not intended to be understood literally.

[11] See I.A. Richards, *The Philosophy of Rhetoric* (New York: Oxford University Press, 1965).

cribes single fixed meanings to words and that is why I have spent so much time in these lectures inveighing against that doctrine.[12]

Richards, therefore, introduces "... two technical terms to assist ... in distinguishing from one another what Dr. Johnson called the two ideas that any metaphor ... give us."[13] He suggests the terms "tenor" and "vehicle" for distinguishing the two halves of a metaphor while acknowledging that

> [a]t present we have only some clumsy descriptive phrases with which to separate them. 'The original idea' and 'the borrowed one'; 'what is really being said or thought of' and 'what it is compared to'; 'the underlying idea' and 'the imagined nature'; 'the principal subject' and 'what it resembles' or, still more confusing, simply 'the meaning' and 'the metaphor' or 'the idea' and 'its image.'[14]

These "clumsy descriptive phrases" are inadequate, according to Richards, because they fail to grasp the interactive character of the two ideas constitutive of a metaphor.

> We need the word 'metaphor' for the whole double unit, and to use it sometimes for one of the two components in separation from the other is as injudicious as that other trick by which we use 'the meaning' here sometimes for the work that the whole double unit does and sometimes for the other component - the tenor, as I am calling it - the underlying idea or principal subject which the vehicle or figure means.[15]

Hence, the meaning of the metaphor is dependent upon "the co-presence of the vehicle and the tenor:"[16] "... the vehicle is not normally a mere embellishment of a tenor which is otherwise unchanged by it but that *vehicle and tenor in co-operation give a meaning of more varied powers than can be ascribed to either.*"[17] (emphasis added)

Hence, rather than speak of metaphor by means of the logic of analogy, Richards is employing the notions of "tenor" and "vehicle" in order to

---

[12] Richards, *Philosophy of Rhetoric*, p. 120. Not to mention how literal language prioritizes the empirical and creates the further illusion, in addition to the illusion of univocity, that humans have immediate and direct access to the world (or to universals, the self, etc.). The full limitations of literal language can only be appreciated in light of the aporiai sketched out in the present project. In the absence of direct access to, and the lack of definition for, either universals or particulars and, given the mediated character of all experience through a linguistic system that is polyvalent and metaphorical, literal language emerges as a very specialized case in which one (or a community/discipline) is blind to the metaphorical conditions that make it appear plausible.
[13] Richards, *Philosophy of Rhetoric*, p. 96.
[14] Richards, *Philosophy of Rhetoric*, p. 96.
[15] Richards, *Philosophy of Rhetoric*, pp. 96-7.
[16] Richards, *Philosophy of Rhetoric*, p. 100.
[17] Richards, *Philosophy of Rhetoric*, p. 100.

shift the attention in metaphor away from mere naming to thoughts in interaction with contexts.

> The traditional theory ... made metaphor seem to be a verbal matter, shifting and displacement of words, whereas fundamentally it is a borrowing between and intercourse of *thoughts*, a transaction between contexts. *Thought* is metaphoric, and proceeds by comparison, and the metaphors of language derive therefrom.[18]

This is an important observation about metaphor, for it situates metaphor not at the level of logic (or Aristotelian genius[19]) but at the interface between thought and "contexts." Lest there be confusion about what "context" means here, one need only observe Richards' insistence that language and especially metaphor are of significance only to the extent that they contribute to the (pragmatic) conduct of life. Speaking of our need to learn "how to live" and to impart that "'greatest gift of all,' a command of metaphor,"[20] Richards writes:

> ... to profit we must remember, with Hobbes, that "the scope of all speculation is the *performance of some action* or thing to be done" and, with Kant, that - "We can by no means require of the pure practical reason to be subordinated to the speculative, and thus to reverse the order, since every interest is at last practical, and *even that of the speculative reason* is but conditional, and *is complete only in its practical use.*" Our theory, as it has its roots in practice, must also have its fruit in improved skill.[21] (emphasis added)

There is something happening with metaphors that results in transforming of both the tenor and the vehicle to the end of enhancing the meaning of what is said that simply could not be articulated otherwise. Richards employs lines from Denham speaking about the mind (the tenor) by means of the Thames (the vehicle) to illustrate his point:

> O could I flow like thee, and make thy stream
> My great exemplar as it is my theme.
> Though deep, yet clear; though gentle, yet not dull;
> Strong without rage; without o'erflowing, full.[22]

---

[18] Richards, *Philosophy of Rhetoric*, p. 94.

[19] Richards is well aware of Aristotle's association of metaphor with genius. He writes (*Philosophy of Rhetoric*, p. 95): "In asking how language works we ask about how thought and feeling and all the other modes of the mind's activity proceed, about how we are to learn to live and how that 'greatest thing of all,' a command of metaphor - which is great only because it is a command of life - may best, in spite of Aristotle, 'be imparted to another.'"

[20] Richards, *Philosophy of Rhetoric*, p. 95.

[21] Richards, *Philosophy of Rhetoric*, p. 95. Note that Richards does not deny the validity of speculative reason. Speculative reason, however, is reigned in by pragmatic usage - even as he defends a naive ontology in the process.

[22] Richards, *Philosophy of Rhetoric*, p. 121.

Richards observes with respect to the relationship between the tenor and the vehicle:

> The more carefully and attentively we go over the senses and implications of *deep, clear, gentle, strong,* and *full* as they apply to a stream and to a mind, the less shall we find the resemblances between vehicle and tenor counting and the more will the vehicle, the river, come to seem an excuse for saying about the mind something which could not be said about the river.[23]

Hence, "[t]he opposed conception of comparison - as a mere putting together of two things to see what will happen - is a contemporary fashionable aberration, which takes an extreme case as the norm."[24] Philip Wheelwright will call such a juxtaposition "diaphor" in contrast to "epiphor," but the point to be made here is that Richards' theory of metaphor is "interactive" and not one of "substitution."

Metaphor not only enables the emergence of meanings that otherwise could not be expressed, but it constitutes that which makes for one's humanity (hence, it is not the exclusive preserve of the geniuses, but the distinguishing characteristic of everyone).

> So far from verbal language being a "compromise for a language of intuition" [logical] - a thin, but better-than-nothing, substitute for real experience [literal] - language, well used, is a *completion* and does what the intuitions of sensation by themselves cannot do. *Words are the meeting points at which regions of experience which can never combine in sensation or intuition, come together. They are the occasion and the means of that growth which is the mind's endless endeavour to order itself.* That is why we have language. It is no mere signalling system. It is the instrument of all our distinctively human development, of everything in which we go beyond the other animals.[25] (partial emphasis added)

Richards rejects the notion of a mere antithesis between "inner" and "outer" as if language was a system of "Words" over against "Things." Quoting Coleridge he suggests: "'I would endeavour to destroy the old antithesis of Words and Things: elevating, as it were, Words into Things and living things too.'"[26] Language is life, according to Richards, and no one saw the importance of that tautology more clearly than Philip Wheelwright.

---

[23] Richards, *Philosophy of Rhetoric*, p. 122.
[24] Richards, *Philosophy of Rhetoric*, p. 123.
[25] Richards, *Philosophy of Rhetoric*, pp. 130-131.
[26] Richards, *Philosophy of Rhetoric*, p. 131.

Wheelwright: Metaphor and Tensive Reality

What characterizes human life, according to Wheelwright, is that, in contrast to things, which have *contexts*, "only a person has *perspectives*."[27] (emphasis added) This, of course, is to speak of "context" in a different manner than Richards. Richards is concerned to emphasize the pragmatic dimension of language, and for that reason he speaks of the context of thought as inseparable from a world. Wheelwright is concerned to underscore that humans are *not simply situated* among things, *but* that humans by necessity have *a perspective* on those things.[28] Hence, by introducing the notion of "perspective," Wheelwright is able to more adequately emphasize the mediated character of human experience with respect to both universals and particulars.

> The difference is not between the perspectival and the universal; for every universal, at least every humanly intelligible universal, is perspectivally conceived. No, the difference is between perspectives that have become standardized and perspectives that are freshly born and individual.[29]

The means by which perspectives are mediated, according to Wheelwright, is language. Language "... designate[s] any element in human experience which is not merely contemplated for its own sake alone, but is employed to *mean*, to *intend*, to *stand proxy for*, something beyond itself."[30]

---

[27] Wheelwright, *Metaphor and Reality*, p. 16.
[28] See the discussion of the "perspectival character of reality," according to Wheelwright below.
[29] Wheelwright, *Metaphor and Reality*, p. 16.
[30] Wheelwright, *Metaphor and Reality*, p. 29. Just what the status of "the beyond" or the "outside" of language is, remains problematic. Wheelwright seems to confirm the self-referential character of language of Saussurian linguistics and Deconstructionism when he suggests that everything one can "grasp" or everything for which language "can stand proxy for," occurs in a linguistic medium: "if ... [one] makes the language itself the object of ... [one's] attention ... [one's] question will then take the form of asking not what ... [one] means (i.e., is trying to grasp) but what the language means (i.e., stands proxy for) ... On the one hand the person himself (sic) wants to stand in relation to What Is, although he cannot avoid some dependence on language in so doing. On the other hand he must believe and feel that the language which he employs stands proxy for What Is; that the referential relation L-->O [Language-->Object] is a real one, even though when he tries to *say* what L means he finds himself having to deal with a relation of the form L_1 -->L_2." (Wheelwright, *Metaphor and Reality*, p. 31) Wheelwright, as was the case with Richards, is naively presupposing that language somehow "stands proxy for" something outside of language even as he recognizes that all that we know about the "outside" is mediated by language. It will take the pragmatic turn in Ricoeur's analysis of a semantic theory of metaphor in *The Rule of Metaphor* to justify this naive presupposition found in Richards and Wheelwright. It is not insignificant, however, that in his later writing (see, for example, *Time and Narrative*, vol. 3, p. 158), Ricoeur seeks to reformulate how he

Consequently the traditional Cartesian dualism of mind vs. matter, or in its later forms subjective vs. objective, which has tended to give shape and direction to much of the philosophical thought since the seventeenth century, has begun to yield in many quarters to a threefold thought-structure, in which subject, object, and linguistic medium play *irreducible and inter-causative* roles in the formation of what ... we may call reality.[31] (emphasis added)

Wheelwright proceeds to investigate the role of language in mediating reality distinguishing between two classes of linguistic meaning: what he calls "steno" and "tensive" language. Steno language is "block," "literal," "digital"[32] or "closed language,"[33] whose ideal is the "semantic positivism"[34] of "scientific,"[35] "exact,"[36] or "logical"[37] language, in contrast to "tensive" language which he calls "fluid" or "open" language.

> By 'block language' I mean language that ideally consists of *terms defined and employed according to the law of identity*, such terms being combined in such a way as to produce *propositions obeying the law of non-contradiction*. This is not a complete definition of block language, but it will serve in an ordinary way to identify it. Block language can also be designated as 'literal language', or ... 'steno language'.[38] (emphasis added)

In *Metaphor and Reality* Wheelwright spoke of steno-meanings as "... meanings that can be shared in exactly the same way by a very large number of persons"[39] "... or meanings that can be publicly and exactly shared, [that] are not limited to objects and groups of objects in the immediate environment. They include sharable abstractions too."[40] The ideal form of steno lan-

---

speaks of language's indebtedness to something "outside" of itself by no longer talking of "reference" but of "application" which now must be thought in terms of the "threefold mimesis" of narrativity (see *Time and Narrative*, vol. 1, chapter 3, "Time and Narrative: Threefold *Mimesis*," pp. 52-87), i.e., application must be thought in terms of "refiguration" following the two earlier stages of mimesis of "pre-figuration" and "configuration" (see *Time and Narrative*, vol. 1, p. 53). This places the emphasis more explicitly upon pragmatic action and interaction rather than on a mere "internal" - "external" relationship between language and world while recognizing that there is no non-mediated (non-figured) level or dimension of experience.

[31] Wheelwright, *Metaphor and Reality*, p. 26.
[32] Wheelwright, *Metaphor and Reality*, p. 34.
[33] Wheelwright, *Metaphor and Reality*, p. 37.
[34] Wheelwright, *Metaphor and Reality*, p. 38.
[35] Wheelwright, *Metaphor and Reality*, p. 37.
[36] Wheelwright, *Metaphor and Reality*, p. 40.
[37] Wheelwright, *Metaphor and Reality*, p. 38.
[38] Philip Wheelwright, "Semantics and Ontology" in *Metaphor and Symbol*, ed. by L.C. Knights and Basil Cottle (London: Butterwords, 1960), pp. 3-4.
[39] Wheelwright, *Metaphor and Reality*, p. 33.
[40] Wheelwright, *Metaphor and Reality*, p. 35.

guage is scientific language. Yet, while scientific language is limited with respect to the number of those who understand it because of its technical precision, "... the point is that so far as they do understand it they can understand it in exactly the same way."[41] However, Wheelwright, just as in the case of Richards, observes that "... while logical language is manifestly of very great importance for situations and types of question to which it legitimately applies, its powers of reference are limited."[42] This is because, again in Wheelwright's words, "[m]eanings always flit mockingly beyond the reach of men with nets and measuring sticks."[43] In contrast to Richards, however, Wheelwright seems to be implying that common agreement of meaning among those sharing literal language appears to be the strength of literal language rather than it having some privileged access to an exogenous world. Hence, literal language is language that intentionally has limited polyvalence, i.e., multiplicity of meaning, to enhance a shared precision of understanding. Such an implication would see literal language as a special case of metaphor rather than metaphor as a special case of literal language.

The assumptions informing semantic positivism are that truth is only arrived at by means of *exact*, steno language, and that open or tensive language is by its nature *inexact*.[44] Wheelwright's response is that truth is not necessarily exact. Why? Because exactness fails to appreciate the concealing character of nature and reality.[45]

> Where ... humanly important situations are involved - the sufferings of Oedipus, the ambivalent purposefulness of Hamlet, the tragic disorientation of mankind, the ambiguous conflict in a human relationship between love and egoism - the employment of alien forms of exactitude is *a fortiori* meaningless and absurd.[46]

In order to articulate and wrestle with such situations, if not to adequately articulate most of human experience, one needs in Wheelwright's judgment a more fluid and open language that is more appropriate than exact steno language for expressing the dynamism and ambiguity of life. In resonance with the aporetic character of experience, which this present project seeks to emphasize, Wheelwright observes that "[i]n all organic life there is a ceaseless but varying struggle between opposite forces, and without such struggle

---

[41] Wheelwright, *Metaphor and Reality*, p. 37.
[42] Wheelwright, *Metaphor and Reality*, p. 39.
[43] Wheelwright, *Metaphor and Reality*, p. 39.
[44] Wheelwright, *Metaphor and Reality*, p. 40.
[45] Wheelwright, *Metaphor and Reality*, p. 41.
[46] Wheelwright, *Metaphor and Reality*, pp. 42-3.

the organism would go dead."⁴⁷ The same ceaseless struggle is manifest in humanity, as well.

> In man the basic organic strife shows itself in various tensions of which he (sic) may be unconscious or at most only partly conscious - the tension between self and other persons, between self and physical environment, between love and antagonism, between one's impulses and the decisions of rational thought, between the life-urge and the dark fascination of death. As man gropes to express his complex nature and his sense of the complex world, he seeks or creates representational and expressive forms (the two adjectives standing for complementary aspects of a single endeavor) which shall give some hint, always finally insufficient, of the turbulent moods within and the turbulent world of qualities and forces, promises and threats, outside him. His life oscillates between contrary pulls, and out of his Dionysian condition he seeks, and sometimes for lingering moments attains, an Apollonian vision. But if the vision is not to be escapist and a merely stubborn refusal to face things as they are, it will bear traces of the tensions and problematic character of the experience that gave it birth.⁴⁸

Nonetheless, Wheelwright is very aware that the value of tensive and fluid language, which must be employed in order to articulate these organic tensions and ambiguities of life, is equally subject to abuse and imprecision. He is concerned that the emphasis upon the openness of tensive language, exemplified but by no means limited to poetic language, not open the floodgates to any and all meanings. Wheelwright critically refers to the position taken by William Empson, who suggests that "all the particulars denoted by a word are brought into play in a poem."⁴⁹ If all the particular meanings of a word are to be brought into play, then one would be caught up by the affective fallacy, for

> whatever meanings and values a word in a poem might have for any reader's rambling fancy would be a part of the poem's own meaning, and there could not be any question of whether the poem was being interpreted well or ill, suitably or arbitrarily.⁵⁰

Much as Gadamer insists that all reading is accountable to the text, Wheelwright, too, suggests that the text establishes limits to the possible meanings of even its tensive language. He finds "more accurate" than Empson's claim Lascelles Abercrombie's statement

> that poetry, by its devices of juxtaposition, delimits a "sector" of meanings, and thereby enriches the word with "the individual vigor of some individual quality." In-

---

⁴⁷ Wheelwright, *Metaphor and Reality*, p. 45.
⁴⁸ Wheelwright, *Metaphor and Reality*, p. 46.
⁴⁹ Wheelwright, *Metaphor and Reality*, p. 59.
⁵⁰ Wheelwright, *Metaphor and Reality*, p. 60.

terpretation is concerned not with all the meanings a word might have, but with what is revealed or hinted by the immediate passage and the poetic context working in collaboration.[51]

Again, sounding very Gadamerian, Wheelwright asks: "... may it not be, and to what extent can it be, that the legitimate meaning of a poem grows and changes as the typical responses of fitly responsive readers change?"[52]

Wheelwright suggests that, of the proposed candidates for the linguistic unit most adequate for representing the tensive quality of reality, i.e., image, symbol, and metaphor, it is metaphor that is most qualified for articulating the full range of tensiveness. His argument is that, where "image" is too concrete and narrow,[53] "symbol" is derivative from metaphor.[54]

A primary factor in favor of metaphor is that it incorporates both the tensiveness born out of perspectival "individuality" and of "universality." The strength of poetic or metaphorical language with respect to individuality is that

> ... it *partly creates and partly discloses* certain hitherto unknown, unguessed aspects of What Is. Every such aspect represents a perspective that is individual, that cannot be put into a class with other similar perspectives (except in abstract and largely irrelevant ways), and that is capable of eliciting a fresh response and fresh insight on the part of every attentive hearer or reader.[55] (emphasis added)

On the other hand, there are what Wheelwright calls "overtones of universality" in metaphor as a consequence of the metaphor's "vehicle" and "tenor" (terminology which he consciously borrows from I.A. Richards[56]). As with the case of contexts and perspectives, however, Wheelwright is effecting a shift of emphasis from Richards' discussion of tenor and vehicle. Richards' concern is to locate metaphor as a process of thought in interaction with its context rather than as a mere process of naming. This is his way of

---

[51] Wheelwright, *Metaphor and Reality*, p. 61.
[52] Wheelwright, *Metaphor and Reality*, p. 62. Gadamer, of course, would argue that that is precisely the case and that the extent to which the legitimate meaning of a poem or text grows depends upon how aware the reader is of the presuppositions at work in the reading as a result of the fore-structure of understanding, i.e., the legitimate reading is one that is both accountable to the text and the historicality of understanding. See Gadamer's discussion of "*Wirkungsgeschichte*" in *Truth and Method*, pp. 267f.
[53] See Wheelwright, *Metaphor and Reality*, pp. 66-68.
[54] This is the thesis he develops in chapter V ("From Metaphor to Symbol") in *Metaphor and Reality*, pp. 92-110.
[55] Wheelwright, *Metaphor and Reality*, p. 51. Again, note the naive ontology presupposed by the notion "What Is."
[56] Wheelwright, *Metaphor and Reality*, p. 55.

shifting the analysis of metaphor away from the substitution of naming to an interactive theory dependent upon the tensions and congruence between the tenor and vehicle. On the other hand, Wheelwright's concern for the dimension of universality, opened up by the interaction between tenor and vehicle, is a response to those who would charge that metaphor is purely subjective and private. To the contrary, Wheelwright suggests, universality or meaning is a consequence of the tension between the vehicle, employed as the means for eliciting an "ulterior significance," and the tenor as the intended meaning evoked in the responsive imagination of the hearer/reader.

> Poetic language [Wheelwright means metaphor] generally, by reason of its openness, tends toward semantic plenitude rather than toward a cautious semantic economy. The power of speaking by indirection and by *evoking larger, more universal meanings than the same utterance taken in its literal sense would warrant*, is one species of semantic plenitude. But it may also be that the tenor of an image or of a surface statement is not single; the semantic arrow may point in more than one direction. When two such diversely intended meanings are sharply opposed, the result is paradox. But even when the doubleness of meaning is not pushed to the point of contrariety, it may often be the case that more than one meaning is suggested simultaneously by a certain word or phrase or image ... with the result that *the interplay of meanings and half-meanings is far more copious than any literal paraphrase could ever formulate.*[57] (emphasis added)

Wheelwright's use of "universality" here is not concerned with Platonic universals of the intellect in contrast to the singular particulars of sense perception. Rather, he is concerned to suggest that metaphorical language breaks open the horizon of language from the narrowness of the literal to the plenitude and richness of meaning more reflective of life. This is his motivation for rejecting the "substitution" theory of metaphor which suggests that metaphor is a poor substitution for what one could say more directly with steno or literal language were one to have the time and the intellectual ability. Wheelwright argues elsewhere that metaphors, to the contrary, can-

---

[57] Wheelwright, *Metaphor and Reality*, p. 57. Douglas Berggren suggests such "copiousness of meanings" makes it impossible for Wheelwright to distinguish between the ravings of the schizophrenic and the appropriate metaphoric meanings of truly "universal" range. See Berggren, "The Use and Abuse of Metaphor, II," p. 472. Though this charge against Wheelwright of what Berggren calls "mythic absurdity" may be unfair precisely because Wheelwright argued that interpretation is not concerned with *all the meanings of a word*, but with "what is revealed or hinted by the immediate passage and the poetic context working in collaboration" (Wheelwright, *Metaphor and Reality*, p. 61), Berggren's judgment is focussed primarily not on this discussion of the power of metaphor to evoke tensions of particularity and universality, but, rather, on Wheelwright's suggestion that "... metamorphosis, the continual passing of one qualitative state into another, is a primary ontological fact" (Wheelwright, *ibid.*, p. 169).

not be paraphrased nor can they be translated.[58] There is an "irreducible novelty" that emerges in and through metaphor that no form of steno, block, literal, digital, closed, scientific, exact, or logical language, in short, no form of semantic positivism, can begin to capture. This is the "universalism" in contrast to narrowness that is announced by metaphoric language which breaks open the constraints of semantic positivism to articulate not merely the emotional but more so the organic tensions of life which cannot be voiced by a language that insists on the law of identity and non-contradiction. These emotional and organic tensions, Wheelwright insists, are the key to universal significance, and it is the task of the two components of metaphor, the tenor and the vehicle, to vocalize this universality.

A further contribution made by Wheelwright with respect to clarifying the way metaphors function to illuminate and represent the tensiveness of life, is his distinguishing between "epiphor" and "diaphor:" "... the one standing for the outreach and extension of meaning through comparison and the other for the creation of new meaning by juxtaposition and synthesis."[59] Epiphor depends upon a level of familiarity whose meaning is then extended in a coherent way to speak of the unfamiliar. This is the kind of metaphorical activity that is closest to analogy, i.e., Aristotle's definition of metaphor. Epiphor consists in extending or broadening the horizon of meaning from the accustomed to the unaccustomed:

> Since the essential mark of epiphor - which is to say, metaphor in the conventional Aristotelian sense - is to express a similarity between something relatively well known or concretely known (the semantic vehicle) and something which, although of greater worth or importance, is less known or more obscurely known (the semantic tenor), and since it must make its point by means of words, it follows that an epiphor presupposes a vehicular image or notion that can readily be understood when indicated by a suitable word or phrase. In short, *there must be a literal base of operations to start from.*[60]

---

[58] See Wheelwright, "Semantics and Ontology," p. 6.

[59] Wheelwright, *Metaphor and Reality*, p. 72.

[60] Wheelwright, *Metaphor and Reality*, p. 73. Wheelwright repeats this claim that epiphor presupposes the literal meaning, while extending and transforming it, to be sure, when he writes: "'A sign is metaphorical if it is used in reference to an object which it does not denote literally, but which has certain properties that its literal denotandum has.' This is Aristotle's definition couched in current academic terminology [by Paul Henle]; the revealing thing about it is that there is taken for granted to be, at the outset of any metaphorical activity, *a literal meaning, a standard usage*, from which comparisons are drawn. And so there is - *to the extent that* the metaphor functions epiphorically." (partial emphasis added) (Wheelwright, *Metaphor and Reality*, p. 74)

This presupposition of the literal meaning as the foundation for epiphor will be challenged by Ricoeur as it already has been called into question by Nietzsche and the Deconstructionists. See the discussion of Ricoeur's theory of metaphorical truth below.

Although epiphor is rooted in the familiar, this does not mean that there can be no surprise with epiphor. Rather, epiphor is precisely that metaphorical activity able to identify similarity in difference which can result in shock, i.e., the shock of recognition.[61]

In the case of diaphor, however, one is concerned with mere juxtaposition of dissimilarities. With diaphor, "[a]ny similarity that a reader may find or think he (sic) finds between the terms is not so much antecedent as ... induced."[62] "The essential possibility of diaphor lies in the broad ontological fact that new qualities and new meanings can emerge, simply come into being, out of some hitherto ungrouped combination of elements."[63]

Wheelwright's contributions to the understanding of metaphorical reality are: a) the insistence that reality (itself tensive rather than static and unambiguous) is adequately articulated only by means of the tensive openness of metaphorical language in contrast to steno or literal language; b) the employment of Richards' notion of "tenor" or the intended idea and "vehicle" in order to emphasize the universal meaning opened by metaphor for articulating life's emotional and organic tensions, rather than take metaphor to be concerned with mere private or subjective experience; c) and the distinction between "epiphor" and "diaphor" for describing the two extremes of metaphorical activity that foster the recognition of similarities in dissimilarities. He concludes his discussion of metaphor by saying:

> The take-it-or-leave-it attitude that is implicit in all good metaphor is in itself, so far as it goes, diaphoric; the sense of an invisible finger ambiguously pointing is epiphoric. The role of epiphor is to hint significance, the role of diaphor is to create presence. Serious metaphor demands both.[64]

As has already been observed, Wheelwright's analysis of metaphor is not an end in and of itself. He shares the same goal as Richards, that is, to find that linguistic medium that can adequately evoke the dynamic character of human life beyond language. Having argued that no literal language, that no language conforming to the laws of identity and non-contradiction, is

---

[61] See Wheelwright, *Metaphor and Reality*, p. 74.
[62] Wheelwright, *Metaphor and Reality*, p. 80. Wheelwright offers the following as an example of diaphor (*ibid.*, p. 78):
   My country 'tis of thee
   Sweet land of liberty
   Higgledy-piggledy my black hen.
[63] Wheelwright, *Metaphor and Reality*, p. 85.
[64] Wheelwright, *Metaphor and Reality*, p. 91.

adequate for articulating the organic nature of life, Wheelwright turns in the final chapter of *Metaphor and Reality* to describe what he labels "three characteristics of reality" which emerge from an analysis of the tensive language of metaphor: reality as "presential;" reality as "coalescent;" and reality as "perspectival."[65]

Fundamentally, these three characteristics are inseparable and interrelated.[66] Yet, for the sake of description, it is possible to distinguish among

---

[65] See Wheelwright, *Metaphor and Reality*, p. 154.

[66] This should caution the Derridians from too easily concluding, for example, that Wheelwright's notion of "presential" is simply a form of "presence" in contrast to its binary opposite "absence" which both presuppose differance or an infinite process of supplementation by the trace.

Presence, according to Derrida, is not to be confused with "the present." "While *presence* is the general form of what is, the *present*, for its part, is always different." (Derrida, "Plato's Pharmacy," in *Dissemination*, p. 114) In "'... That Dangerous Supplement...'" in *Of Grammatology*, p. 143, Derrida wrote: "Differance makes presence and absence possible: ... differance makes the opposition of presence and absence possible. Without the possibility of differance, the desire of presence as such would not find its breathing-space. That means by the same token that this desire carries in itself the destiny of its non-satisfaction. Differance produces what it forbids, makes possible the very thing that it makes impossible."

Presence, according to Derrida, is equivalent to metaphysics, for it forgets its dependence on "absence." "Since the sense of being is never produced as history outside of its determination as presence, has it not always already been caught within the history of metaphysics as the epoche of presence? This is perhaps what Nietzsche wanted to write and what resists the Heideggerian reading of Nietzsche; *differance* in its *active* moment - *what* is comprehended in the concept of *differance* without exhausting it - is what not only precedes metaphysics but also extends beyond the thought of being. The latter speaks *nothing other than* metaphysics, even if it exceeds it and thinks it as what it is within its closure." (Derrida, "'...That Dangerous Supplement'," p. 143.

While it is true that "presence" is dependent upon "absence," and that the "what is" of presence is taken in the inadequate sense of "things," the binary of presence and absence need not lead to absolute skepticism. The dynamic of concealment in what is manifest can be seen to be a virtue rather than a vice, for this dynamic is the key to all tensiveness. The alternative to absolute understanding is not absolute skepticism. The alternative to absolute understanding is openness to the world as an odyssey of understanding in community that allows the otherness of the text and the Other to demand one's accountability precisely because its integrity is manifest in repeatability. We can return to the text. We can return to the Other. We cannot return in precisely the same way as either the first or the most recent time, but, nevertheless, there is an integrity demanding one's accountability in the midst of the difference/differance.

However, Wheelwright is not speaking of the mere "presence" of things in a manner that ignores the inseparability of "absence" when he introduces this notion of the "presential." Rather, the presential character of reality is concerned with a mystery and awe that is inseparable from the three forms of coalescence, developed below by Wheelwright, and the perspectival character of reality that gives each one a voice rather than turns each voice into a babbling cacophony.

them in a way that justifies separate discussions. What is at stake in Wheelwright's analysis is the concern to indicate how radically inadequate steno language is for providing insight into reality. Literal language is not only reductionistic in that it can only grasp the "surface" of things, literal language presupposes a profound dichotomy between subject and object and, by implication at least, is seen by Wheelwright to be the result of prior metaphoric activity that has been either forgotten or ignored. Wheelwright's entire project is an attempt to indicate the interconnecting and interactive linking of subject and object by language that evokes the "interpenetrative and coalescent" characteristic of reality to demonstrate mere dichotomies to be superficial abstractions that only have logical legitimacy, if any at all, but cannot begin to account for the pragmatic wholeness of experience.

That humans cannot not act is an insight already at the heart of the Kantian move from the "pure" to the "practical" reason. Furthermore, that humans cannot not act is what protects Fichte's project from solipsism, for he insists that one does not understand in order to act; rather, one acts therefore one can (and must seek to) understand.[67] Coherent and in agreement with this Kantian insight, Wheelwright's discussion of the role of language in mediating reality for humanity is both practical and logical. His presentation of the three characteristics of reality explicitly rejects any suggestion that there is some unbridgeable gap between the "inner" and the "outer." There is a difference, to be sure, between "inner" and "outer," but they are inseparable because of the linguistic constitution of experience. Above all, it is tensive language that most adequately mediates reality as "presential," "coalescent," and "perspectival."

Wheelwright introduces the notion of "presential" reality by suggesting a fundamental difference between early humanity and contemporary humanity. As much as Wheelwright's description of the two types of consciousness might be accurate, there is no little anachronistic utopianism in his maintaining

> that early man unlike ourselves, did not dichotomize his (sic) world into a law-abiding physical universe on the one hand and a confused overflow of subjective ideas on the other. Nature and self, reality and fancy, for him were radically interpenetrative and coalescent.[68]

---

[67] See Fichte, *Die Bestimmung des Menschen*, pp. 264-5, 280, and 284. In addition, see pp. 145-311, particularly the third book entitled "Glaube" or "Faith," pp. 253-309.

[68] Wheelwright, *Metaphor and Reality*, p. 134.

In addition, Wheelwright's description of "presential reality" sounds all too much like a form of perfectionism from which humanity in the meantime has fallen. One would no more be able to accept the generalization made about humanity today than one would be able to accept the generalization made about the past. Nevertheless, there is something valuable about the distinction even though one would more appropriately say that the literary evidence suggests that *many* human beings today dichotomize their world into an objective law-governed natural order in contrast to a subjective emotional order, and there is literary evidence which suggests that *some* in the past experienced "nature and self, reality and fancy" as "interpenetrative and coalescent." Wheelwright's more significant point, however, is that an awareness of presential reality is imperative if one is to understand consciousness.

> His (sic) [early humanity's] world, we may say, was *presential*. By this word I mean something fairly close to what Rudolph Otto has called "the numinous." The word "presential" has the advantage, however, of avoiding specifically religious connotations, although by no means excluding them; it will therefore be better suited to describe that quality of the world which the primitive myth-maker, the man of religious sensitivity, and the developed poetic consciousness all have in common.[69]

What they all have in common is an understanding of the human place in the order of things similar to that articulated by Martin Buber's language of "I" and "Thou"[70] which suggests an open responsiveness is involved in understanding reality as "presential." Central to Wheelwright's notion of presential reality is a sense of wonder, awe, and mystery about the human condition.[71] This is no call to simple primitivism but a check on the all too frequent contemporary model which approaches reality as a disinterested individual only concerned with the calculation, prediction, manipulation, and control of things. Wheelwright suggests that what is missing in that world of objectification is imaginative responsiveness:

> In describing the sense of presence as an independent dimension of reality I intend the descriptive word in a precise sense. A dimension, properly speaking, is an independent variable; *the sense of presence can vary quite independently of empirical circumstances*. The most common objects and everyday situations, as well as the most unpromising human individuals, may reveal sudden and astounding *possibilities of presence* when they are ignited by a suitably responsive-imaginative act. The hyphen is used intentionally; for *a genuine responsiveness is imaginative, and a genuine imaginativeness is responsive.*[72] (emphasis added)

---

[69] Wheelwright, *Metaphor and Reality*, p. 135.
[70] See Wheelwright, *Metaphor and Reality*, p. 155.
[71] See Wheelwright, *Metaphor and Reality*, p. 158.
[72] Wheelwright, *Metaphor and Reality*, p. 156.

Unfortunately, there is a certain vagueness about Wheelwright's discussion of presential reality. What remains a set of assertions requires more clarification if one wishes to avoid collapsing "presential reality" into mere enthusiastic rapture even as Wheelwright wishes to avoid cold, calculating objectivity as some exclusive criterion for reality. It is only by turning to all the aporiai permeating "reality" that one can begin to gain adequate clarity about the truly presential character of experience that Wheelwright wishes to bring to the fore.

There is no point in Wheelwright's description of the three characteristics of reality where the aporetic tensions emerge any more clearly, however, than in his discussion of reality as coalescent. What Wheelwright means by "coalescence" is complementarity. In short, reality is not adequately thought as dichotomized but as aporetic. He is suggesting that the notion that "reality" is something objective to which individual's have subjective, emotional reactions or that the notion that "reality" is to be dichotomized into "primary" (objective and measurable) and "secondary" (subjective and relative) qualities simply does not adequately account for what humans experience. Rather, objective and subjective must be seen as intimately and inseparably interrelated.

> The *I* who am aware and the *that* of which I am aware are but two aspects of a single sure actuality, *as inseparable as the convex and concave aspects of a single geometrical curve*. They can be distinguished intellectually ... but both subject and object are present as complementary aspects of every possible situation, however much the emphasis and the proportion might shift. Reality, as distinguished from the intellectual artifacts that often usurp the name, is neither object nor subject, neither matter nor mind, nor can it be limited to any other philosophical category ...[73] (partial emphasis added)

Wheelwright identifies three kinds of coalescence (or aporiai) shaping of reality: that between self and not-self; the coalescence of particular and universal; and the coalescence of entities and change, what he calls the "time dimension."[74] The first form of coalescence implies the second.

> Abstract universals are a product of logical analysis;[75] in Greece an understanding of them was of slow growth, resulting from the successive contributions of (in the

---

[73] Wheelwright, *Metaphor and Reality*, pp. 166-167.

[74] This present project has combined these first two forms of coalescence in its discussion of the aporia of intellect and world, and it treats temporality as a separate aporia.

[75] This claim will not be outright rejected by the present author, but it will be qualified by saying that universals are experienced by the individual as ectypal or a posteriori, to the extent that they are arrived at only in and through experience; they are archetypal or a priori, however, to the extent that they are inseparably embedded in the language one inherits.

main) Parmenides, Socrates, Plato, and Aristotle. Concrete universals, on the other hand - in which the particular actuality is one with all other things of the species - are the natural and usual terms of thought in a pre-sophisticated civilization[76] ...

Hence, the present project agrees with the Husserlian formulation of the Nominalist explanation of essence as the constitution of intentional consciousness to the extent that constituting consciousness accounts for how we come to experience universals and leaves unanswered the ontological status of universals. Universals are experienced as abstractions arrived at in consciousness after one has experienced (universals are ectypal). What remains a perplexity in Husserl's Phenomenology and in Nominalism is the issue: how is it that the "given" of the world conforms to imperceptible abstractions when matter cannot produce form; it can only employ form? In other words, the material order appears to presuppose the non-material ontologically; where anthropologically the non-material order clearly presupposes the material.

This contemporary ambiguity is anticipated in the fundamental conflict between the Stoics and the Epicureans. On the one hand, both the Stoics and the Epicureans agreed with Aristotle (*De Anima* 414a18-22) that there is no "soul" without a body. (See Pohlenz, *Die Stoa*, pp. 64 and 295 and Epicurus' teaching on the inseparability of soul and body in his "Letter to Herodotus" in *The Essential Epicurus*, trans. by Eugene O'Connor (Buffalo, N.Y.: Prometheus Books, 1993), p. 33.) For example, the Stoics, according to their founder, Zeno, taught that effects can occur only through the physical, the non-physical is incapable of doing or of suffering anything. True being can only be said of the body.

On the other hand, where the Stoics differed from the Epicureans, when both technically are "materialists," was precisely over the issue raised here: does the spiritual serve as the foundation and origin of everything, as the Stoics maintained with their teaching of the Logos (granted, it is still "substance," according to the Stoics), or does the spiritual arise out of the material as Epicurus taught? See Pohlenz, *Die Stoa*, p. 216. The materialists, empiricist, and "hedonists" agree with Epicurus.

This project, on the other hand, maintains that anthropologically both Epicurians and the Stoics are correct: the Epicurians because the activity of abstraction, the "spiritual," is experienced only a posteriori or ectypally; yet the Stoics are equally correct that universals exist prior to the individual. Though now the Stoic insight must be modified in that universals are experienced as prior to the extent that they are inherited in language as a priori or archetypal, and their doctrine of creation must be taken speculatively. Nevertheless, it is not contrary to experience (though it is surely speculative) to assume with the Stoics that the spiritual ($\nu o \hat{v} \varsigma$) is presupposed by the material which would account for the emergence of the finite spiritual out of the material as is the case of the occurrence of consciousness with animals and most richly with humans. This Stoic position has been most recently defended as "metarealism" by Guitton, Bogdanov and Bogdanov in *Gott und die Wissenschaft*, pp. 106, 116.

Nevertheless, this ontological aporia has not begun to be understood so long as it is viewed exclusively in terms of actuality and ignores the concealed dynamic of possibility in all actuality. These aporiai all confirm the priority of faith over both logic and pragmatics.

[76] This notion of "concrete universals" is equivalent to Aristotle's notion of "actual knowledge," i.e., the pros hen (reference to one) nature of Being of actual things where one universal serves as the dominant referent governing the combination of other universals in matter to account for the particularity of that actual thing. The actual thing, of course,

> [According to Plato] a particular exists ... by participation (*methexis*) in the universal reality that gives it its main significance, and conversely the universal reality permeates all particular things to different degrees, much as the pure light of the sun illuminates the different objects of a landscape to different degrees, each according to its capacity for receiving. Particular things bulge with significance, to whatever extent they participate in, coalesce with, a something more that is consubstantial with themselves.[77]

Once again, there is a valuable insight here that requires more precision to adequately describe experience: particulars participate in universals as "a something more"[78] that imparts them significance and a meaning. Just "how" that occurs can only be adequately understood out of the coalescence of all the linguistic aporiai informing the human condition. Nevertheless, the linguistic turn which Wheelwright makes in order to claim the priority of the figurative over the literal, i.e., to retrieve the radically metaphorical character of reality, is one important step in illuminating how the coalescence of aporiai function. It will require an investigation of Douglas Berggren's analysis of metaphor and "metaphysics" by means of the notion of "stereoscopic vision," borrowed from W. Bedell Stanford,[79] and Ricoeur's tension theory of metaphor in order to obtain greater clarification of just how metaphorical "reality" truly is without slipping into metaphysical presuppositions about "What Is."

Equally incompletely developed, as it is crucial, is Wheelwright's third aspect of coalescence which he calls the "phenomenon of radical change." Here the juxtaposition is between things and their lack of permanence. "Taking experience as it comes, instead of as it can be rationalized, what we obviously discover is that while some things change rapidly and others with laborious slowness, nothing whatever escapes metamorphosis."[80] Wheelwright is denying any dimension to experience that is not subject to change. "... [I]t follows that metamorphosis, the continual passing of one qualitative state into another, is a primary ontological fact."[81] This is, of course, a cor-

---

is the consequence of the interaction of the four primary causes: form, matter, efficient, and teleological. See Joseph Owens' discussion of pros hen equivocity in *The Doctrine of Being in the Aristotelian 'Metaphysics'*.

[77] Wheelwright, *Metaphor and Reality*, p. 168.
[78] It must be seen how one would want to equally say that universals participate in particulars before one has grasped the full import of the coalescence of reality.
[79] See Berggren, "The Use and Abuse of Metaphor, I," p. 243.
[80] Wheelwright, *Metaphor and Reality*, p. 169.
[81] Wheelwright, *Metaphor and Reality*, p. 169.

nerstone to Wheelwright's claim that reality is metaphoric, because only tensive language can adequately represent a world of constant change.

As was mentioned above, this claim for ontological change by Wheelwright serves as the basis for Douglas Berggren's critique of Wheelwright's discussion of metaphor. Berggren maintains that such an ontological claim of permanent metamorphosis leaves no grounds for distinguishing between the ravings of the schizophrenic or the fragmentations of the aphasic's world. Here it is important to observe the descriptive appropriateness of Wheelwright's threefold notion of coalescence even as each component is in need of greater precision. For one has not adequately understood what "reality" is all about until one recognizes that reality is not dichotomized into the self and not-self, that particulars presuppose universals and vice versa, and that constitutive of reality is, at least in part, constant metamorphosis.

The third characteristic of reality suggested by Wheelwright is that reality is "perspectival." Once again, at stake here is the tensive character of reality. If reality were not radically shaped by perspective, then literal language would be the most appropriate language for grasping the one, true reality.

> The communication of presential and coalescent reality is not possible by relying on words with inflexible meanings; if it is to be achieved at all (and the achievement is always imperfect at best) the common words must be chosen and contextualized with discriminating suitability ... The fresh context may be regarded as an angle of vision, a perspective, through which reality can be beheld in a certain way, a unique way, not entirely commensurate with any other way. *A genuine perspective must partly create, justify and interpret the language by which it finds expression; therefore no such perspective can be reduced to another.*[82] (emphasis added)

Wheelwright is fully aware that, given the perspectival character of reality, the "real" is inseparable from wagers of faith. "For the problem of reality is man's ultimate problem; his (sic) judgment, 'Such-or-such is more real, or more deeply real, than something else,' is a major expression of his intellectual faith."[83] Reality "is intrinsically and ultimately hidden from any finite exploration."[84] Rather than such a judgment leading Wheelwright to vulgar skepticism and contempt for the human condition as is the case with Nietzsche and Derrida, he, along with Spranger, Heidegger, Gadamer, and Ricoeur, sees this "fact," that reality is ultimately hidden, not as a vice but

---

[82] Wheelwright, *Metaphor and Reality*, p. 170.
[83] Wheelwright, *Metaphor and Reality*, pp. 171-2.
[84] Wheelwright, *Metaphor and Reality*, p. 172.

as a virtue luring the human to ever richer experience through understanding.

> Reality is ultimately problematical, not contingently so; for to grasp and formulate it, even as a set of questions, is to fragmentize it. *There is always, in any inquiry, something more than meets the eye, even the inner eye*; the permanent possibility of extending one's imaginative awareness has no limits. *A person of intellectual sensitivity is plagued by the sense of a perpetual Something More* beyond anything that is actually known or conceived. A wise beginning for any large inquiry is to entertain the postulate that reality ... is latent, subtle, and shy.
>
> If reality is intrinsically latent and unwilling to give up its innermost secrets even to the most enterprising explorer, then the best we can hope to do is catch partisan glimpses, reasonably diversified, all of them imperfect, but some more suited to one occasion and need, others to another. *If we cannot hope ever to be perfectly right, we can perhaps find both enlightenment and refreshment by changing, from time to time, our ways of being wrong.*[85] (emphasis added)

Wheelwright anticipates Ricoeur's discussion of the metaphorical nature of truth when he suggests that "[p]erhaps truth, like certain precious metals, is presented best in alloys."[86] If truth is inseparable from reality, and reality is presential, coalescent, and perspectival, then truth is not concerned with some system of unequivocal literal assertions either about the world of sense perception or about the "Something More" of "What Is." Truth is radically ambiguous and inseparable from the concealment of both actualities and possibilities included in, and presupposed by, all that is manifest. But then, that would mean that truth and faith are inseparable.

Wheelwright's analysis of the metaphorical nature of reality is without doubt extremely suggestive, but its implications need to be more explicitly developed in order to avoid mere emotional rapture or blind metaphysical commitments. In addition to those hesitations observed above with respect to the imprecision of Wheelwright's discussion of the "presential" and "coalescent" characteristics of reality, there remains a contradiction in Wheelwright's analysis that points to the fundamental linguistic aporia but remains equally imprecise as it is presented here. Wheelwright maintains that there

---

[85] Wheelwright, *Metaphor and Reality*, pp. 172-3. Once again, the Socratic ethical ideal emerges. Not knowing, and knowing that one does not know, prevents one from engaging in destructive behavior based upon one's conviction that one absolutely knows. Descartes defines "evil" in the fourth Meditation, as the applying of the will prior to one's having acquired proper understanding. Much evil could be avoided in the world were one to question the indubitable character of one's knowledge.

Again, though, one must point out the naive ontology of the "Something More" presupposed here.

[86] Wheelwright, *Metaphor and Reality*, p. 173.

must be a "literal base"[87] from which the metaphoric extension of meaning commences. Nevertheless, he later unequivocally maintains that all language is ultimately figurative: "When a straightforward thinker sets out to free himself (sic) from symbolic and metaphorical thinking, what he actually means to do is limit himself to those symbols and rigidified metaphors which have become habitual stereotypes in everyday life."[88] The "literal base" depended upon for present metaphoric activity is the consequence of prior metaphoric activity. That would mean that literal language is merely dead or faded metaphor which, in turn, would greatly strengthen Wheelwright's claim that truth is ultimately metaphoric. However, this implication doesn't acquire its full significance until one turns to Ricoeur's theory of metaphor.

Prior to turning to Ricoeur's theory of metaphor and metaphorical truth, however, insight into the aporetic character of language and reality is benefited by a detour through the work of Douglas Berggren. Berggren's discussion of metaphor assists in acquiring greater precision with respect to some of those aspects of Wheelwright's work that are vague and potentially misleading. As with the case of Wheelwright, however, there are important observations made by Berggren with respect to both metaphor and reality which require the greater precision of Ricoeur's reflections. Nevertheless, Ricoeur is more easily understood when one engages the discussion that Ricoeur himself presupposes, for he has said of Berggren's work: "No other author to my knowledge has gone as far in the direction of the concept of metaphorical truth.[89]

Metaphorical Tension at the Heart of Language

If I.A. Richards provided the terminology of tenor and vehicle enabling a new approach to the understanding of metaphor over against the Aristotelian substitution theory of metaphor dominating the entire Western tradition, and if Philip Wheelwright provided the insight that reality itself is metaphorical because of its metamorphosis, there remain imprecisions both with respect to "how" the tenor and vehicle are related in the metaphorical process and with respect to the nature of reality illuminated by metaphor. Douglas Berggren offers greater clarity with respect to the way in which tenor and vehicle are related even as he remains inadequately suggestive of the nature of reality illuminated by metaphor. It is not until one turns to Paul Ricoeur's discussion

---

[87] Wheelwright, *Metaphor and Reality*, p. 73. See, also, p. 74.
[88] Wheelwright, *Metaphor and Reality*, p. 128.
[89] Ricoeur, *The Rule of Metaphor*, p. 254.

of metaphor, after having worked through the issues raised and addressed by these predecessors, that one arrives at a more appropriate understanding of the tensions driving metaphor and about the nature of reality that requires one to say it is radically metaphorical.

There is a tendency in Richards and Wheelwright to view the interactive relationship between tenor and vehicle in light of the polyvalence of the vehicle alone. The "more" than the sum of the parts of metaphoric interaction is taken to be the consequence of the tensions within the vehicle, e.g., the Thames, which enable one to say something about the tenor, the mind, that cannot be said of the Thames. While not incorrect, this interactive theory is not sufficient for catching all of the dynamics of metaphor. Greater precision with respect to the abundance of meaning unleashed by the metaphorical is achieved in the work of Berggren. Berggren seeks to walk the line between too much objectivity (e.g., what he calls literal, mathematical, and mythical language) and too much subjectivity (e.g., what he calls the ravings of the schizophrenic or the fragmentations of the aphasic), by insisting that, while there is an integrity, which is neither to be ignored nor violated, to both the objective and the subjective dimensions of experience, there is nothing inviolately absolute about either. True insight into metaphor and experience/reality, he maintains, requires an understanding that acknowledges in the encounter between the objective and the subjective that both not only have an integrity but they are simultaneously transformed, as well. Berggren employs W. Bedell Stanford's notion of "stereoscopic vision" in order to describe this metaphorical interaction that simultaneously affirms integrity while acknowledging transformation.

Berggren maintains that metaphorical tension (what Wheelwright calls "tensiveness") is what unites the arts, the sciences, and philosophy when they are properly understood.[90] The corollary to this claim is that all three tend to "abuse metaphor" by overlooking this very tension and transforming themselves into what Berggren calls "myth" or literal language.[91]

Berggren wishes to make five points with respect to the tension theory of metaphor. First, building upon the minimum of two components to metaphor, he suggests that *every metaphor has at least two referents*.[92]

Second, "... the difference between the referents of any metaphor must be such that a literal or univocal interpretation of their conjunction would produce absurdity."[93] One cannot take the metaphors "the Good is the light

---

[90] See Douglas Berggren, "The Use and Abuse of Metaphor, I," p. 238.
[91] See Berggren, "The Use and Abuse of Metaphor, I," pp. 238 and 245.
[92] See Berggren, "The Use and Abuse of Metaphor, I," p. 238.
[93] Berggren, "The Use and Abuse of Metaphor, I," p. 239.

of the mind" or "Achilles is a lion" to be literal statements without collapsing into absurdity. On the other hand, the metaphors engage two referents, e.g., Good/light and Achilles/lion. It is not that the metaphor depends only upon the univocity of one referent (the vehicle, e.g., light, lion) to say something about the polyvalence of something less well known (the tenor, e.g., Good, Achilles). Rather, metaphor exploits the polyvalence of both referents.

Third, not every logically or empirically absurd statement is a metaphor. "... metaphorical 'sort-crossing' differs from absurd 'sort-trespassing' by virtue of the *as if* character of the metaphor's apparent assertion."[94] In short, according to Berggren, all metaphor must involve some kind of epiphor:

> ... however clear the pretense, or however willing we may be to read the sentence counterfactually, it is extremely difficult to turn the absurdity of "Triangularity drinks coffee" into a metaphor.[95] To achieve what Beardsley calls the "significant self-contradiction" of metaphorical attribution ..., some principle of assimilation which can meaningfully link the two referents must be found.[96]

Yet, that all metaphor involves epiphor does not deny diaphor. Berggren's fourth point with respect to metaphorical tension is that, "[a]s Wheelwright argues, many metaphors are not only epiphoric, but involve a 'diaphoric' dimension as well: 'the creation of new meaning by juxtaposition and synthesis' ..."[97] This creation of new meaning is the consequence of what Berggren calls "construing." "Diaphoric metaphor does not merely compare antecedently given similarities between principle and subsidiary subjects [epiphor], but introduces new meaning by construing the one in terms of the other."[98] Further, diaphoric metaphor "brings the connotations" of the principle and subsidiary subjects "to life:" "... the metaphor of truly novel creation seems far more appropriate than the notion of simply actualizing a meaning which was already implicitly present."[99] "... [W]hile metaphorical

---

[94] Berggren, "The Use and Abuse of Metaphor, I," p. 240.
[95] Berggren adds in a footnote here: "To be sure, this is not to say that it would be impossible. It is never wise to attempt to prejudge the possible ingenuity of the human imagination. The point is, however, that until some context is introduced which can provide an intelligible connection between the two referents of the sign focus, absurdity will not yield to metaphor, even if a counterfactual interpretation is attempted" (Berggren, "The Use and Abuse of Metaphor, I," p. 240, n. 1.)
[96] Berggren, "The Use and Abuse of Metaphor, I," p. 240.
[97] Berggren, "The Use and Abuse of Metaphor, I," pp. 241-242.
[98] Berggren, "The Use and Abuse of Metaphor, I," p. 242.
[99] Berggren, "The Use and Abuse of Metaphor, I," p. 243.

construing may act as a midwife, it may also function as a parent. In any case, the difference is for the most part one largely of degree."[100] This leads Berggren to the central element of his tension theory of metaphor: "... as a result of the process of metaphorical construing, *both the principle and subsidiary subjects are transformed and yet preserved.*"[101] (emphasis added) He applies W. Bedell Stanford's terminology of "stereoscopic vision" to speak of the metaphor's "... ability to entertain two different points of view at the same time."[102]

> That is to say, the perspectives prior to and subsequent to the transformation of the metaphor's principle and subsidiary subjects must both be conjointly maintained. It is precisely this transformation of both referents, moreover, interacting with their normal meanings, which makes it ultimately impossible to reduce completely the cognitive import of any vital metaphor to any set of univocal, literal, or non-tensional statements. For *a special meaning and in some cases even a new sort of reality, is achieved which cannot survive except at the intersection of the two perspectives which produced it.*[103] (emphasis added)

These four ingredients of tension allow Berggren to offer the following definition of metaphor:

> ... any vital metaphor should be defined as a plurisignificative sign focus whose referents can be univocally conjoined or fused only at the expense of absurdity, but which implicitly involves a process of assimilative construing whose cognitive import cannot be entirely resolved into literal or non-tensional assertions. In other words, the tension of the tension theory has two related dimensions. On the one hand, a logical or empirical absurdity stands in apparent conflict with a possible truth. On the other hand, this possible truth may itself depend upon a creative interaction between diverse perspectives which cannot be literalized or disentangled without destroying the kind of insight, truth, or reality which the metaphor provides.[104]

The corollary to this definition of metaphor is that overlooking or suppressing the tensiveness by taking the principle and subsidiary subjects univocally, results in the "abusing of metaphor" and turning the metaphorical insight into "myth"[105] which constitutes Berggren's fifth point with respect to metaphorical tension.

This is an unfortunate use of the term "myth," however. Berggren takes this meaning of "myth" from Turbayne, who "... defines a myth as an

---

[100] Berggren, "The Use and Abuse of Metaphor, I," p. 243.
[101] Berggren, "The Use and Abuse of Metaphor, I," p. 243.
[102] Berggren, "The Use and Abuse of Metaphor, I," p. 243.
[103] Berggren, "The Use and Abuse of Metaphor, I," pp. 243-244.
[104] Berggren, "The Use and Abuse of Metaphor, I," p. 244.
[105] See Berggren, "The Use and Abuse of Metaphor, I," p. 244.

extended metaphor whose apparent or face-value assertions are interpreted univocally. Myth, in other words, is a believed absurdity, believed because the absurdity goes unrecognized."[106] Berggren's purpose in employing the term "myth" in this fashion is to enable a distinction later in his two part essay between "myth" and "metaphysics." It will be clearer below that, despite Berggren's commitment to metaphorical truth, his employment of stereoscopic vision to define metaphorical truth remains embedded in an ontological preference for the dimension of the senses and sense perception as the ultimate touchstone of verisimilitude. What he finds attractive in the notion of stereoscopic vision is the affirmation of "integrity" to the constitutive components which are transformed but remain the same. It will take the move to praxis in Ricoeur's analysis to justify this notion of "integrity," however, for there is no ontological absoluteness to the referents which are metaphorically construed. Any "integrity" of sameness, which, in fact, would justify a literal meaning for articulating the integrity, is itself the product of mediation in consciousness, and that mediation is the consequence itself of metaphorical tensiveness. Whatever "integrity" there is, it is not an integrity of absoluteness, but one that demands provisional, even if reasonable, acknowledgment because to ignore it would lead to misunderstanding, at least, and disaster, at worst.

Rather than speak of "myth" in order to articulate the "believed absurdity" resulting from confusing metaphorical construal for something literal, it would be more helpful to employ Wheelwright's notion of steno language. The absurdity arising from treating metaphorical meanings literally is the result of treating tensive language as steno language. The advantage of the terminology of steno and tensive language is that it allows a more positive valence to myth. Given the socio-linguistic character of sociological paradigms, given that reality, including judgments of causality, is a social construct, one may no longer talk as if one paradigm possessed the truth where other paradigms succumb to mythic absurdities. Rather, all paradigms are myths. The so-called absurd claims of the myths of former epochs are not the result of collapsing the metaphorical into the literal. The "erroneous" claims of former myths are perceived, in retrospect, because our socio-linguistic model for reality today is based on an alternative coherence and causal explanation. The myth of the moment is valid not because it is "true" in the sense of corresponding to the way things are "in fact," but because it "works." To work better than previous myths means: a myth is able to give

---

[106] Berggren, "The Use and Abuse of Metaphor, I," p. 244.

a coherent account of more, and in a more palatable manner, than the former myth(s) were able. But that "more" could only arise as the anomalous against the backdrop of the coherence of the former myth or paradigm. It is simply anachronistic to insist that a prior myth/paradigm should be able to explain what it had not yet "seen."[107]

It may just be that at least some of the adherents to the mythological world views of the past in fact were fully aware that their paradigm was radically metaphorical and that it was understood that the figurative is more important and illuminating than the literal. This would be an explicit contradiction of Berggren's definition of "myth," for rather than making literal claims, such myths would be self-consciously making figurative suggestions. Retrospectively reading them exclusively literally would be to violate them.

If prior "myths" were self-consciously figurative (and such a judgment, if it could be verified, would surely only apply for some and not all), then the present epoch's "scientific" paradigm (equally embraced by some and not all), committed to the empirical as immediately accessible through the senses, is not only an impoverishment in contrast to such mythological world views of the past, according to Berggren's own theory of metaphorical tension, but, by treating the paradigm of the past as making merely literal claims, it is perpetrating an injustice by forcing the past paradigm to conform to the presuppositions of the present. Forcing the other to conform to one's presuppositions, Gadamer points out, means not only not to take the Other seriously but it means not permitting the Other to truly emerge as Other.[108] Berggren's unfortunate vocabulary is contributing to the contemporary epoch's inability to hear what former paradigms might be able to teach it. At the least, it would be a valuable heuristic exercise to examine

---

[107] Formulated in a Gadamarian manner: the horizon of a prior myth/paradigm is shaped by the fore-structure of the understanding which limits the possibilities that can be projected (in short, limits understanding) to those which "fit" or "pass to" that horizon.

A concrete example of the uni-directionality involved here is Emerson's famous observation that one can go from being a materialist to an idealist but there's no return to being a materialist once one has grasped idealism. See Ralph Waldo Emerson, "The Transcendentalist" in *The Complete Essays and Other Writings of Ralph Waldo Emerson*, ed. by Brooks Atkinson (New York: the Modern Library, 1940), p. 87: "Every materialist will be an idealist; but an idealist can never go backward to be a materialist." Given the materialist predisposition of the reigning paradigm in the "developed" world today, there might be much to learn from a mythic world view that is idealist rather than empiricist without succumbing to the metaphysics of idealism. But that would require fundamental transformations of the contemporary paradigm ...

[108] See Gadamer, *Truth and Method*, p. 236.

former myths in terms of their saying more about the figurative character of reality than the literal.

Nevertheless, having developed the four points characterizing his tensive theory (focus with two referents, avoidance of literal absurdity, the as if character of metaphor, and stereoscopic vision), Berggren proceeds to investigate the adequacy of the theory in the arts, the sciences, and philosophy. He distinguishes the arts and the sciences not on the basis that the arts employ tensive language and the sciences employ literal language, but, rather, that, while the sciences seek to avoid what he calls "poetic textures," i.e., emotional metaphors,[109] they do employ "poetic schemata." Poetic schemata are rooted in a "visualizable phenomenon" even as they may serve as "... a vehicle for expressing something about the inner life of man, or non-spatial reality in general ..."[110] With a central modification, Berggren employs Max Black's discussion of the three main types of models used in science (physical, schematic, and formal[111]) in order to indicate the essential role of tensive language permeating the sciences. In other words, Berggren is suggesting that science is engaged in the modeling of reality, i.e., it can

---

[109] See Berggren, "The Use and Abuse of Metaphor, I," p. 241.

[110] Berggren, "The Use and Abuse of Metaphor, I," p. 248.

[111] See Berggren, "The Use and Abuse of Metaphor, II," p. 451. A physical model employs "... some directly observable macroscopic phenomenon [which] is used either to illustrate or explore something other than itself" (*ibid.*, p. 451). There are basically two kinds of physical models: "scale models" such as airplane models or architectural models; and "analogue models" such as hydraulic models of economic systems. See *ibid.*, p. 451. A schematic model is "... no longer anything actually physical or observable, [but] like the poetic schemata ..., is an intuitive creation of the imagination itself" (*ibid.*, p. 452). An example of such schematic models is "Maxwell's use of an imaginary incompressible fluid to represent an electrical field" (*ibid.*, p. 452). Black defined "formal model" as "'a systematic repertoire of ideas by means of which a given thinker describes, by analogical extension, some domain to which those ideas do not immediately and literally apply'" (*ibid.*, p. 453). Berggren is not satisfied with this definition, because it is in the end indistinguishable from physical and schematic models. "Nor is it enough to add Black's further characterization of a scientific archetype as 'an implicit or submerged model operating in a writer's thought' ..." (*ibid.*, p. 453). Rather, "[i]f submerged archetypes of a truly trans-cultural and perennial nature are to be found in science, parallel to such poetic archetypes as up and down, light and darkness, they must be general and basic enough to generate countless transformations or diverse applications while still retaining their fundamental structure. The two that spring to mind, of course, are the basic schemata of machine and organism, with their opposing emphasis on external and internal relations. And, just as the opposing textures of light and darkness, or up and down, are both required to generate the life of poetry, so apparently the atomism of the machine and the matrix of the organism are likewise both necessary to the advance of science" (*ibid.*, p. 453).

only engage in constructing a mediated representation of the way it takes reality to function. But Berggren also identifies what he calls two "abuses" of the models of science: the reduction of science to mathematics[112] and the equating of scientific models with scientific theories.[113]

> ... the positivistic attempt to treat scientific theories or theoretical laws as elliptic formulations, translatable into observation statements, has clearly proved unsuccessful, whether such observation statements are taken to belong to a sense datum language, or to a physicalistic thing language. Not only is such a descriptive theory incapable of doing justice to the central explanatory function of science, it has never succeeded in showing how the theoretical notions of science can be eliminated, or reduced to observation statements, in the first place.[114]

In short, "... reductionist and purist theories are ... no more adequate in science than they are in poetry."[115] Hence, the "explanations" of science involve metaphorical construing built upon "a tensional interaction between the two perspectives of the 'is' and the 'must.'"[116]

Having discussed the role of metaphor in the arts and the sciences, Berggren then turns to philosophy to develop what he calls a "metaphysics" based upon metaphorical tension. His first concern is to reject both metaphysical monisms and metaphysical dualisms.[117] Rather, just as one finds in the arts and the sciences, metaphysics is a kind of construal: "... in neither case is truth supposedly determined by a sovereign decree either from the side of *a priori* ideals or *a posteriori* facts.[118]"

> ... simple ontological monisms are ultimately just as unsatisfactory as simple ontological dualisms. If Parmenides had trouble in accounting for the appearance of motion, the analysts have no less difficulty in doing justice to mental entities, or non-spatial reality in general. Specifically, if it is wrong to dissolve things into sensa, then so it would appear to be equally wrong to transform mental entities either into quasi-spatial things, or into potential bodily manoevers. Or to phrase the argument meta-linguistically, if the physicalistic think language cannot be reduced even to hypothetical, phenomenalistic assertions, then neither can the logic of mental or non-spatial discourse be reduced to even hypothetical, physicalistic assertions.[119]

Berggren's alternative is to suggest a metaphysics based upon stereoscopic vision. The two referents of stereoscopic vision in this case are the

---

[112] See Berggren, "The Use and Abuse of Metaphor, II," p. 454.
[113] See Berggren, "The Use and Abuse of Metaphor, II," p. 455.
[114] Berggren, "The Use and Abuse of Metaphor, II," p. 457.
[115] Berggren, "The Use and Abuse of Metaphor, II," p. 458.
[116] Berggren, "The Use and Abuse of Metaphor, II," p. 459.
[117] See Berggren, "The Use and Abuse of Metaphor, II," p. 465.
[118] Berggren, "The Use and Abuse of Metaphor, II," p. 468.
[119] Berggren, "The Use and Abuse of Metaphor, II," p. 469.

things in the world and consciousness. It is only vital metaphors that enable their interconnection or correlation.[120]

> The only possible solution to the dilemma of monism versus dualism ... is man's intellectual ability to play two diverse language games stereoscopically. *While construing one mode of reality in terms of the other, the autonomy of each must be preserved even while they are being simultaneously assimilated or integrated.*[121] (emphasis added)

Berggren concludes:

> ... metaphysics must be vitally metaphorical for three related reasons. First, the truth of its archetypal schemata is tensionally dependent on the truth of its dialectical arguments. Secondly, such systematic arguments must themselves seek to preserve the independent integrity of the phenomena they integrate. They must attempt to satisfy the demand of external adequacy as well as of internal consistency ... And finally, metaphysics must rely on metaphor in order to deal at all successfully with that particular form of tensional identity-in-difference which obtains between spatial and non-spatial reality.[122]

Only such a metaphysics, Berggren maintains, can protect one from the "... aphasic's world of isolated simples, the timeless and ultimately ineffable One of Parmenides, the process reality of schizophrenia, or the self-contradictions of literally transgressed dichotomies."[123]

Just as the present project has difficulties with Berggren's notion of "myth," so, too, reservations must be expressed with respect to his notion of "metaphysics." While one would applaud the rejection of monisms, dualisms, exclusive metamorphosis, and dichotomies, the interaction between the world and the mind cannot be explained by appealing to the autonomous integrity of both in interaction with one another as if they were merely "next to" each other as *actual* non-spatial and spatial realities. Berggren is surely on the right track when he observes "... there would still seem to be considerable force behind Sartre's argument that 'two types of existence, as thing in the world and as consciousness, is an ontological law.'"[124] Berggren recognizes that this is a dualism:

> Having proposed an irrevocable dualism between the spatial and the non-spatial, both Sartre and Yolton immediately proceed to cross their own avowed barriers. As Sartre

---

[120] See Berggren, "The Use and Abuse of Metaphor, II," p. 470.
[121] Berggren, "The Use and Abuse of Metaphor, II," p. 471.
[122] Berggren, "The Use and Abuse of Metaphor, II," p. 471.
[123] Berggren, "The Use and Abuse of Metaphor, II," p. 472.
[124] Berggren, "The Use and Abuse of Metaphor, II," p. 470.

concludes, "an image is a consciousness of[125] some thing," ... - where the simple word "of" tends absurdly to conjoin supposedly unconjoinable realms.[126]

Berggren's suggestion is that the absurdity, arising from a literal connection between these "supposedly unconjoinable realms," can only be avoided by employing his tensive theory of metaphor:

> While it is possible to develop a literal or univocal language for spatial reality, and while an equally univocal language for non-spatial reality is also at least theoretically conceivable, their philosophically necessary interconnections or correlations can be formulated only in terms of vital metaphors.[127]

Nevertheless, there are three key problems with Berggren's formulation. First, there is a presumption of the possibility of a univocal language with respect to spatial reality, even though such a univocal language for non-spatial reality is only "theoretically conceivable," which betrays an ontological prejudice towards sense experience and a lack of appreciation of how radically metaphorical *all* language is (even so-called literal language) given the mediated character of all experience.[128] Second, this same prejudice is announced with respect to Berggren's claim that "the truth of ... archetypal schemata is tensionally dependent on the truth of ... dialectical arguments. Third, and crucially, Berggren's theory of metaphorical tension ignores the horizon of possibility that enables all metaphorical tensions.

The first problem hints at a privileged "materialism" despite Berggren's insistence on the "integrity" of the non-material. Clearly, Berggren's statements about the possibility of developing a literal language for spatial reality indicate a privileged status for the sensuous in his theory. This privileged moment is suggested, in addition, by his statement concerning truth. Were he to be able to reverse the statement, then his theory would be truly stereoscopic. He would then be able to say not only that the truth of archetypal schemata is tensionally dependent on the truth of dialectical arguments, but that the truth of dialectical arguments is tensionally dependent on the truth of archetypal schemata.

---

[125] It is Husserl who defines intentionality in terms of consciousness being always consciousness-of something. See Edmund Husserl, *Ideas*, p. 214: "... the experiencing Ego is still nothing that might be taken *for itself* and made into an object of inquiry on its *own* account. Apart from its 'ways of being related' or 'ways of behaving,' it is completely empty of essential components, it has no content that could be unraveled ..."

[126] Berggren, "The Use and Abuse of Metaphor, II," p. 470.

[127] Berggren, "The Use and Abuse of Metaphor, II," p. 470.

[128] The radically metaphorical character of experience is what drives Nietzsche's argument in "Truth and Lies in a Nonmoral Sense."

Until one can reverse the sentence, one has not fully appreciated the issue of universals and intellect at the core of the aporiai of language. Until one can reverse the sentence, one is still fundamentally committed to the priority of sense perception over the intellect, and one is subordinating the intellect to what is material, divisible, measurable, and changing. Yet, to do so is to discount one's own experience, for experience itself is non-material, indivisible, immeasurable, and rooted in the unchanging. Further, the inability to reverse the statement does not acknowledge the ambiguous status of either the world or universals. True, Berggren has rejected the claim that one has direct access to the world in order to make literal claims about the way the world "is," leaving one with an acknowledged tension between the way one believes the world "must" be and the way it "is." Nevertheless, the full implication of ambiguity with respect to the "as if" character of reality is not clearly articulated leaving one with an underlying confidence that there "is" a world independent of one's consciousness of it - without appreciating one's inability to "get to it." In fact, Berggren's confidence with respect to developing a literal language for spatial reality and his hesitation about one's ability to do the same for non-spatial reality strongly imply that he is still shaped by a two substance theory of reality - as much as he is trying to move beyond such dualisms. What this ultimately means is that the status of universals with respect to their being a posteriori or a priori remains completely unresolved. It is not until one turns to Ricoeur's analysis of metaphorical tensiveness that the pragmatic ambiguity (rather than logical certainty) of reference and the ambiguous status of universals unequivocally emerge.

The third problematic factor with Berggren's presupposed "metaphysics" is concerned with his having ignored that which is *concealed* by whatever is manifest in the tensions between the "inner" and the "outer." What is at stake in this concealment is not merely that process of elimination and suppression that necessarily, though not determinatively, occurs with the focus of one's attention on some things rather than others. Certainly, the focus of attention involves a selectivity and concealment by pushing to the background what is unrelated to or tangential to what one is focussed on in the foreground of the moment. However, that does not exhaust the dynamic of concealment in experience. Such concealment as a consequence of shifting attention has exclusively to do with what is actual, for one can focus attention only upon entities either mental or physical. What one cannot make transparent are possibilities. Possibilities remain radically opaque to one's attention, perception, and thought. One simply cannot have all of the possibilities in the foreground as one is engaged in understanding one's world. And even those possibilities which are "perceived" conceal other possibilities that are equally, if not more, likely to become actualized. It is only at this level of reflection that the ambiguous and aporetic character of experience can fully emerge in a way that undermines all naive metaphysical assumptions. Rather than speak of metaphysics, one must speak of aporiai. Only then can the dimension of faith in human understanding fully emerge.

Nevertheless, a wrestling with Berggren is valuable, for it assists in clarifying just what the issues are in terms of metaphorical truth. His development of the understanding of metaphor by pointing to the tensions involved with *both* referents of the metaphor best articulated in terms of stereoscopic vision; his warning against the abuse of metaphor which ignores its tensions by reducing the metaphorical to literal or steno claims; his concurrence with Wheelwright that "... neither scientific nor poetic metaphors can reveal except by creating, precisely because they partially create what they in fact reveal;"[129] in short, his warning against too much objectivity as well as too much subjectivity and his implicit support of the notion that reality itself is tensive, establish a framework for following Ricoeur's development of a tensive theory of metaphor.

Metaphorical Tension at the Heart of Reality

What strikes one when reading Ricoeur's *The Rule of Metaphor* is that the atmosphere of the entire discussion with respect to language and metaphor has dramatically shifted. This shift is a confirmation of Gadamer's insight that one's understanding is inseparable from one's historical context. In Ricoeur's case, his context involves both the Continental and the Anglo-American traditions.

A dramatic new tact was taken by some in French philosophy after the political crisis of 1968. In these years two currents came together in French Structuralism (shaped by Ferdinand de Saussure and Levi Strauß) and in a turn to Nietzsche influenced by Heidegger's decades' long wrestling with Nietzsche to produce Deconstructionism. However, Heidegger's dominance in French philosophy did not commence with the appearance of his two volume opus on Nietzsche.[130] He has long been a determining factor in

---

[129] Berggren, "The Use and Abuse of Metaphor, II," p. 462.
[130] Heidegger's *Nietzsche*, 2 vols., consist of Heidegger's lectures on Nietzsche at Freiburg, i.Br., between 1936 and 1940. They were first translated into French in 1971. In addition, Heidegger's *What is Called Thinking?* written in 1951-1952 (published in 1954) is primarily a reading of Nietzsche.

French philosophy[131] ever since Sartre's version of *Being and Time* appeared as *Being and Nothingness*.[132] It was this long tradition of Heidegger scholarship which prepared the way for the attention given to Nietzsche in the early 1970s in France.

How is this atmosphere of Structuralism and Nietzsche scholarship manifest in Ricoeur's work? Foremost, it is expressed in the central theme of "reference" in Ricoeur's analysis. If there is a naive assumption of linguistic reference in Richards, Wheelwright, and Berggren, in other words, if there is a presupposition of empirical realism ultimately shaping their reflections on metaphor, what strikes one in reading *The Rule of Metaphor* is that this presupposition is precisely what has been called into question. Surely, this is the consequence of the emerging French school of Deconstructionism and particularly of Ricoeur's student Derrida upon Ricoeur's work.[133]

It is with the pragmatic moment that Ricoeur, certainly influenced by his sojourn among the Anglo-Americans, engages the discussion. The task is to reject the claims of literal language, as having some privileged ontological status by means of an indubitable correspondence between words and things, without succumbing to solipsism and yet to maintain a notion of reference without succumbing to metaphysics. It will be seen that metaphor provides the linguistic bridge between consciousness and world in a manner that requires understanding of *both* particulars and universals to be open ended rather than metaphysically absolute. Once again, νοῦς emerges, this time as

---

[131] See the history of the role of German philosophy in general and Heidegger in particular in shaping 20th century French philosophy by Luc Ferry and Alain Renaut, *Antihumanistisches Denken. Gegen die französischen Meisterphilosophen*, trans. by Ulrike Bokelmann (München: Carl Hanser Verlag, 1987). The determining influence of Heidegger on French circles contributed to the shock waves unleashed in France by the publication of Victor Farias, *Heidegger and Nazism* (Philadelphia: Temple University Press, 1989) originally published in French in 1987.

[132] See Jean-Paul Sartre. *Being and Nothingness: An Essay on Phenomenological Ontology*., trans by Hazel E. Barnes (New York: Philosophical Library, 1956). Hugo Ott reports that it was because of the esteem with which Sartre and the French held Heidegger that he was able to keep his library after 1947 when the French occupation forces wanted to use Heidegger's library as part of the library for the refounding of the university in Mainz. See Ott, *Martin Heidegger. Unterwegs zur seiner Biographie*, pp. 324-325. Conversation notes taken by the Rector of the university in Freiburg report that Heidegger had an invitation to visit Sartre in Baden-Baden in 1945, but that was prevented by the decision of the occupation forces. See *ibid*., pp. 308-9. This same time period saw invitations to Heidegger to publish something in French in the *Revue Fontaine*. See *ibid*., p. 309.

[133] Derrida's "White Mythology" is central to Study 8, "Metaphor and Philosophical Discourse," in *The Rule of Metaphor*, though his influence is noted already on page 34.

the locus of the aporetic interface between universals and particulars but now shaped by all of the aporiai of language as the medium of the interaction between self and other/Other,[134] even as νοῦς is merely presupposed by Ricoeur. Nevertheless, the analysis of the aporiai of language is not complete until the dynamic of revealing/concealing of possibilities in actualities is perceived. This is the second moment in Ricoeur's analysis of metaphor, the moment of metaphorical truth, that is essential for grasping the extent to which aporiai inform the human odyssey of faith/understanding.

An indication of the role of praxis as opposed to mere logic in Ricoeur's analysis is that he seeks what he calls a "real" definition of metaphor in contrast to a mere "nominal" definition. The "nominal" definition of metaphor sees metaphor in the classic Aristotelian sense of "substitution," i.e., metaphor is a form of naming in which a trope is substituted for more direct literal language. By searching for the "real" definition, Ricoeur is shifting the focus away from transpositions within, i.e., internal to, language to place metaphor at the heart of all linguistic activity as precisely an "event." His theory, then, builds upon a distinction between semiotics and semantics from Emile Benveniste, which shifts attention away from the "word," which can take the linguistic "event" to be a mere shifting or substituting of signs within a sign system, to the "sentence," which sees the linguistic "event" as an act of speech, i.e., discourse. Ricoeur commences Study 3 of *The Rule of Metaphor*, entitled "Metaphor and the semantics of discourse" with the claim:

> In our first two Studies, the change of meaning constituting the trope and continually referred to as metaphor in ancient and classical rhetoric found its locus in the *word*. This allowed us to adopt, as an initial approximation, a definition of metaphor that identifies it with giving an unaccustomed name to some other thing, which thereby is not being given its proper name. But the investigation of the interrelationships of meaning that give rise to this transposition of the name also relentlessly forces open the frame of reference determined by the word ... and imposes the *statement* as the sole contextual milieu within which the transposition of meaning takes place. The present Study is devoted to a direct examination of the role of the statement, as the carrier of 'complete and finished meaning' ..., in the production of metaphorical meaning. Hence, we will speak from now on of the *metaphorical statement*.
>
> Does this mean that the definition of metaphor as transposition of the name is wrong? I prefer to say that it is nominal only and not real, using these terms as Leibniz does. *The nominal definition allows us to identify something; the real definition shows how it is brought about.*[135] (partial emphasis added)

---

[134] This project uses the term "other" to refer to things and "Other" to refer to persons. The terms "other" and" Other" do *not* refer to "persons" and "God," respectively.
[135] Ricoeur, *The Rule of Metaphor*, p. 65.

This turn toward the "real" definition, however, does not eliminate the meaning of the "nominal" definition: "... the real definition of metaphor in terms of statement cannot obliterate its nominal definition in terms of word or name, because the word remains the locus of the effect of metaphorical meaning."[136] It will be seen, however, that the meaning of the word is not taken by Ricoeur to arise solely inner-linguistically, nor does it have an independent ontological status by means of literal reference, but itself emerges out of a metaphorical process that involves ambiguous reference - what he calls "split reference." In short, where the word is central to the event of metaphor, since all metaphor depends upon a "common linguistic usage" (not to be confused with the literal meaning), nevertheless, the event of metaphor involves the entire metaphorical statement and occurs, or functions, only when it is taken up in an event of discourse. In other words, discourse involves and engages the world "external" to language either as a speech act or as an act of reading. In either event, the linguistic moment is not complete until the event of "utterance" in the broadest sense, i.e., above all, until it includes a hearer/reader.

Ricoeur finds support for his theory of discourse in what he calls six "traits" of discourse that constitute six pairs of characteristics about language that indicate how the linguistic event is inseparable from a world of discourse greater than the linguistic sign system itself. Ricoeur, in fact, is accomplishing with his theory of discourse what Heidegger accomplished with his analysis of the Being-question in *Being and Time* in terms of the existential-structure of "Care," i.e., indicating how the human is inseparable from, and clearly mutually defined by, its worldly context.

These six pairs or traits of discourse are described as follows:

1) The first pair is that of "event" and "meaning," i.e., language is diachronic and synchronic: "... discourse always occurs as an event, but is to be understood as meaning."[137] In other words, Saussure had focussed on the synchronic at the expense of the diachronic bracketing the question of the speaker's "intention," taken in the broadest sense as having something to say to someone at a particular point in time. Saussure's concern was with the ability of language to preserve the same meaning of a sign over time,[138] which drew attention to the structural and self-referential moment of the synchronic. But language is simultaneously both "permanent" *and* "fleeting." To the extent that it is "permanent" language can be analyzed as a closed

---

[136] Ricoeur, *The Rule of Metaphor*, p. 66.
[137] Ricoeur, *The Rule of Metaphor*, p. 70.
[138] Ricoeur, *The Rule of Metaphor*, p. 70.

self-referential system of signs, i.e., language is synchronic and semiotic. To the extent that it is "fleeting" language must be analyzed as inseparable from a world of event, i.e., language is diachronic and includes a world of reference external to language. In other words, language is semantic.

2) The second pair consists of what P.F. Strawson calls "the fundamental polarity of language,"[139] i.e., its "identifying function" and its "predicative function." The identifying function of language is its ability to name singular individuals by means of proper nouns, demonstratives, pronouns, and "definite description."[140] The predicative function of language is concerned with universals, i.e., qualities, classes, relations, and actions.[141] This time Ricoeur is underscoring how language as discourse is not only tied to a particular speaker in a particular context even as it is employing the universal sign system available to all who share it. In addition, there is a tension within language itself, independent of a particular speaker, which allows language to unite singular individuals with universals. The universal moment is concerned with semiotics (again, the self-referential closed system of signs) where the particular or individual moment is the concern of semantics.[142] "... [O]nly within discourse does a generic term take on a singularizing function ... [T]he predicate, which in itself has a universalizing function, only has this circumstantial character to the extent that it determines a proper logical subject."[143]

3) The third pair of traits Ricoeur takes from J.L. Austin, and they consist of the distinction between "locution" and "illocution." Locution has to do with the act of saying, i.e., what one does when one brings the identifying function and the predicative function together to actually say something.[144] Illocution, on the other hand, has to do with the "force" of the saying, e.g., a mere statement, a command, a wish, regret, or a promise, etc.[145] This pair of traits characterizing discourse anchors language in a speaking agent, i.e., locution and illocution involve more than the mere manipulation of signs; they engage a world.

4) The fourth pair consists of the distinction between "Sinn" and "Bedeutung" which Ricoeur finds in Gottlob Frege.[146] Sinn (sense) is con-

---

[139] Ricoeur, *The Rule of Metaphor*, p. 71.
[140] Ricoeur, *The Rule of Metaphor*, p. 71.
[141] See Ricoeur, *The Rule of Metaphor*, p. 71.
[142] Ricoeur, *The Rule of Metaphor*, p. 72.
[143] Ricoeur, *The Rule of Metaphor*, p. 72.
[144] See Ricoeur, *The Rule of Metaphor*, p. 73.
[145] See Ricoeur, *The Rule of Metaphor*, p. 73.
[146] See Ricoeur, *The Rule of Metaphor*, p. 73.

cerned with the internal and is semiotic; where Bedeutung (reference) is concerned with the external and is semantic.[147] In his essay "Paul Ricoeur on Biblical Hermeneutics," Ricoeur writes:

> *Sinn* is the ideal objective content of a proposition [internal]; *Bedeutung* is its claim to truth [reference]. My hypothesis is that this distinction is of interest not only to the logician, but concerns the functioning of discourse in its whole scope.[148] Meaning is *what* a statement says, reference is *that about which* it says it. What a statement says is immanent within it - it is its internal arrangement. That with which it deals is extra-linguistic. It is the real insofar as it is conveyed in language; it is what is said about the world.[149]

As long as one is concerned with language as a semiotic system of signs, then there is no problem of reference in language. It is only when language is treated semantically, at the level of sentences of communication, i.e., at the pragmatic level of actually speaking, writing, and hearing/reading, that language necessarily involves a world. Taken merely logically, i.e., semiotically, language leads to vulgar skepticism about a world of reference. Taken pragmatically, i.e., semantically, language is inseparable from a world of reference. This does not mean that one can or need embrace a naive ontology of literal reference even at the level of pragmatic usage. Ricoeur's analysis of metaphor as "discourse *par excellence*"[150] thoroughly rejects naive literal reference to language. Nevertheless, the peculiarly human event of language is not solipsistic. Everything hinges on just how language refers, i.e., metaphorically, to enable shared meaning.

5) The fifth pair is concerned to distinguish two kinds of reference in discourse: "reference to reality" and "reference to the speaker."[151] Language refers to "the world" external to language both with respect to Sinn and Bedeutung, i.e., meaning and reference to things, events, and language refers to its speaker in a particular speech act. Here Ricoeur points to the function of pronouns (particularly, the first person singular, "I"), tenses of verbs (particularly, the role of the present), adverbs, and demonstratives to

---

[147] See Ricoeur, *The Rule of Metaphor*, p. 74.
[148] In *The Rule of Metaphor* Ricoeur suggests that "[t]his trait, more than others perhaps, marks the fundamental difference between semantics and semiotics. Semiotics is aware only of intra-linguistic relationships, whereas semantics takes up the relationship between the sign and the things denoted - that is, ultimately, the relationship between language and world" (*ibid.*, p. 74).
[149] Paul Ricoeur, "Biblical Hermeneutics" in John Dominic Crossan, *Semeia 4: Paul Ricoeur on Biblical Hermeneutics* (Missoula: Scholars Press, 1975), p. 81.
[150] See Ricoeur, *The Rule of Metaphor*, p. 97.
[151] See Ricoeur, *The Rule of Metaphor*, p. 75.

indicate how discourse is "auto-referential" and establishes an "absolute this-here-now."[152] Though it will be clear below that this is not a naive reference to an exogenous this-here-now.

6) The final pair of traits Ricoeur borrows from Roman Jakobson and consists of the role of the "paradigmatic" and the "syntagmatic" in discourse.[153] If the paradigmatic is best represented by the formal grammatical model (what Thomas Kuhn calls paradigms of "exemplary past achievements" in contrast to sociological paradigms), then the syntagmatic is the joining together of the constitutive paradigmatic moments and components to produce the sentence. In principle, then, the paradigmatic can be substituted or is interchangeable; the syntagmatic is unique and unrepeatable since it is always tied to a specific and particular context. The paradigmatic is concerned with language as semiotic; the syntagmatic with language as semantic.

This pair of traits is important for the further development of Ricoeur's theory of metaphor, because traditionally, as has been noted, metaphor has been taken to be a kind of "substitution," i.e., the substitution of the figurative for a more precise literal naming. Hence, the traditional theory of metaphor sees metaphor as paradigmatic. On the contrary, Ricoeur seeks to build upon the interactive theory of metaphor that emerges with I.A. Richards, and this understanding sees metaphor as syntagmatic, i.e., the result of the unique "setting together" of words to "take on qualities they did not possess in themselves."[154] What will become clear below is that the paradigmatic is itself seen to be generated by the metaphorical dynamic of the syntagmatic. This takes one to the heart of the aporetic character of language.

Having established a rootedness in the world that is extra-linguistic (both with respect to things/Others and with respect to universals), Ricoeur seeks to understand that rootedness in a non-literal, i.e., in a non-empiricist, sense. This is the motivation for turning to metaphor, for Ricoeur maintains, quoting Shelley, that "language is 'vitally metaphorical.'"[155] In fact, the nominal definition becomes the conventional meaning not the proper meaning, which results in redefining what "literal" itself means *on the basis of metaphor*:

---

[152] Ricoeur, *The Rule of Metaphor*, p. 75.
[153] See Ricoeur, *The Rule of Metaphor*, p. 75.
[154] Quoting Benveniste in Ricoeur, *The Rule of Metaphor*, p. 76.
[155] Ricoeur, *The Rule of Metaphor*, p. 80.

> The sole criterion of metaphor ... is that the word presents two ideas at once, that it comprises at once both tenor and vehicle in interaction. By contrast, this criterion can serve to define literal meaning: a word in which tenor and vehicle cannot be distinguished can be taken provisionally to be literal. So this distinction is not wholly lost; however, it does not arise from a characteristic indigenous to words, but from the manner in which interaction functions, on the basis of the contextual meaning theorem. But then literal meaning has no connection any longer with proper meaning. Moreover, literal language becomes quite rare outside of the technical language of the sciences.[156]

Literal language is no longer to be seen in contrast to, and given a privileged status over, metaphor. Literal language is a special case of the metaphorical where the "two ideas" of tenor and vehicle are indistinguishable. Translating this into experience: All consciousness involves mediation, linguistic mediation. In the absence of immediacy, language serves as the medium of the mediation. Language, however, is distinct from that to which it refers, i.e., there is always a radical "twoness" to words; a twoness of "is"/"is not" at the very least given the mediated character of experience. The best that language can do is play off of that irreducible twoness in order to share meaning in a speech act or an event of reading a text (text can be taken here in the broadest sense). But even the "referred to" of the linguistic reference is accessed by consciousness in and through language. Hence, this "twoness" is always, even with the most literal usage of language, a twoness of linguistic mediation. Literal language results where all difference between the "twoness" has collapsed, but, then, that is a case where the twoness is forgotten. Consciousness is, rather, radically metaphorical: it is incessantly engaged in exploiting difference in order to find similarity leading to a judgment of identity. Why? Because difference is precisely what is announced by mediation. Just as with Gadamer one can hear the other/Other only once one can acknowledge that one's understanding is shaped by one's pre-understanding (presuppositions), so with one's experience of the world: one can listen to the referent (the world or the universal) only once one can acknowledge that all experience is mediated in and through language. This is the lesson of Gadamer and now Ricoeur.: Gadamer with respect to prejudices and understanding; Ricoeur with respect to mediation and linguistic reference.[157]

---

[156] Ricoeur, *The Rule of Metaphor*, p. 81.
[157] Ricoeur wrote in "Erzählung, Metapher und Interpretationstheorie," *Zeitschrift für Theologie und Kirche* 84, no. 2 (1987), p. 248: "Ich fasse diese erkenntnistheoretische Konsequenz in der folgenden Formulierung zusammen: Es gibt kein Verständnis von sich, das nicht durch Zeichen, Symbole und Texte *vermittelt* wird; das Verständnis von sich fällt in letzter Instanz mit der Interpretation zusammen, die auf diese vermittelnden Begriffe angewandt wird. Indem die Hermeneutik von dem einen zum anderen übergeht, befreit sie sich zunehmend vom Idealismus, mit dem Husserl die Phänome-

Metaphor surfaces for Ricoeur as the model for language and understanding in the place of the "proper meaning" of the literal. Yet Ricoeur adds to the analysis of metaphor over Richards, Wheelwright, Berggren, Black, and Beardsley the emphasis on the event character of metaphor as an event of discourse. In short, the weight for Ricoeur is placed on the event of speaking/writing and, implicit to that event, the event of hearing/reading. In fact, turning from the siren call of the intentional fallacy altogether, Ricoeur emphasizes the role of the reader in the production of meaning.[158]

> The important point to be underlined in the subsequent discussion concerns what I will call the production of meaning ... It is the reader, in effect, who works out the connotations of the modifier that are likely to be meaningful ... No speaker ever completely exhausts the connotative possibilities of his (sic) words.[159] [They require a hearer/reader in order for their range to be worked out.]

However, this does not open the door to the affective fallacy, either. Ricoeur immediately adds that the event of the production of meaning commenced by the author yet only completed by the reader is reigned in by the principle of "fittingness" and a principle of "plenitude." Fittingness "... has to do with 'deciding which of the modifier's connotations can *fit* the subject',"[160] i.e., not all the meanings but only the universals (the predicates) that fit the particular (the individual) are acceptable. Nevertheless, "[t]he second principle counterbalances the first, being a principle of *plenitude*. All the connotations that can 'go with' the rest of the context must be attributed

---

nologie gleichsetzen wollte." "Die wichtigste Konsequenz ist, daß dem cartesischen, fichteschen und zum Teil auch husserlschen Ideal einer Transparenz des Subjektes für sich selbst ein Ende bereitet wird ... Keine der beiden Subjektivitäten, weder die des Autors noch die des Lesers, ist also primär im Sinn einer ursprünglichen Gegenwärtigkeit seiner selbst für sich selbst" (*ibid.*, p. 250). "Die Aufgabe der Hermeneutik ... ist eine doppelte: die Rekonstruktion der inneren Dynamik des Textes und die Wiederherstellung des Vermögens des Werkes, über sich selbst hinauszuweisen, in der Vorstellung einer Welt, die ich bewohnen könnte" (*ibid.*, p. 251).

[158] This is central to Ricoeur's narrative theory of threefold mimesis developed in *Time and Narrative*, 3 vols. Mimesis$_3$ is concerned with the re-figuring process, ultimately a process of application, accomplished by the reader/hearer without which the meaning of the narrative is incomplete. See *Time and Narrative*, vol. 1, pp. 53, especially 70-71; *Time and Narrative*, vol. 2, pp. 10, 20, 164, n. 20, 27. See, as well, Paul Ricoeur, "Narrated Time," trans. by Robert Sweeney in *Philosophy Today* 29 (Winter 1985), pp. 268a-268b.

[159] Ricoeur, *The Rule of Metaphor*, p. 95.

[160] Ricoeur, *The Rule of Metaphor*, p. 96.

to the poem, which 'means all it *can* mean'."[161] Taken together these two principles are "sufficient to exorcise the demon of relativism."[162]

Yet the production of meaning that emerges out of the connotations of the context transformed by the change in context for each reader presents a problem for Ricoeur. Changed contexts would appear to be just another version of substitution, but now at a more sophisticated level. In short, one would be substituting a "new context" for an "original context" to account for the novelty of meaning generated by the metaphor.[163] Instead of a figurative meaning being substituted for a literal meaning, metaphor would be concerned with substituting novel linguistic contexts for lost linguistic contexts.

This dilemma arises because of the distinction made by Beardsley between "denotation" and "connotation." If denotation is concerned with "explicit meaning," connotation is concerned with "implicit meaning."[164] Ricoeur observes:

> In certain contexts, the other words eliminate the undesirable connotations of a given word; such is the case with respect to technical and scientific language, where everything is explicit. But 'in other contexts, [the] connotations are liberated; these are most notably the contexts in which language becomes figurative, and especially metaphorical' [quoting Beardsley]. Such discourse can be said to involve a primary level and a secondary level of meaning at the same time.[165]

If the classic substitution theory is an "Object-comparison Theory," then Beardsley is suggesting a substitution theory which is a "Verbal-opposition Theory" of metaphor.[166] Ricoeur's concern here is that the dimension of "reference" be lost that he has struggled to achieve with his six traits of discourse as opposed to language as a closed system of self-

---

[161] Ricoeur, *The Rule of Metaphor*, p. 96.

[162] "If it is kept in mind that the principle of plenitude complements the principle of congruence and that complexity counterbalances coherence, it becomes clear that the principle of economy that rules over this logic does not just eliminate impossibilities. It also tends towards 'maximizing' the meaning, that is, towards getting as much meaning out of the poem as possible. The only thing this logic must do is maintain a division between getting meaning out of the poem and reading (i.e. forcing) meaning into the poem." Ricoeur, *The Rule of Metaphor*, p. 96. If one can never be absolutely sure that one is not reading out of the text what one reads into it, one can at least assure that one is trying to listen to the text by engaging in active clarification and illumination of those prejudices/presuppositions one has brought to the text.

[163] See Ricoeur, *The Rule of Metaphor*, p. 98.

[164] See Ricoeur, *The Rule of Metaphor*, p. 91.

[165] Ricoeur, *The Rule of Metaphor*, p. 91.

[166] See Ricoeur, *The Rule of Metaphor*, p. 97.

referential signs. This is because Beardsley's "contexts" are verbal contexts, i.e., linguistic, and are not either I.A. Richards' "contexts," concerned with a naive empirical realism, or Wheelwright's "contexts," limited to things, where persons have "perspectives." In order to avoid the linguistic pitfalls of Beardsley's Verbal-opposition theory, Ricoeur re-opens the question of the nature of reference by examining what kind of reference is essential to metaphor as an event of discourse. Metaphor serves for Ricoeur as the 'instance of discourse' *par excellence.* "The dictionary contains no metaphors; they exist only in discourse."[167] This means that metaphor must have a larger horizon of reference than merely its linguistic context limiting its connotations. How do these "primary" and "secondary" levels of meaning come about in language? Beardsley naively presupposes them. Ricoeur's theory of metaphorical reference and metaphorical truth seeks to give an account of metaphorical meaning that is decidedly real and not merely nominal.

In Study 7 of *The Rule of Metaphor* Ricoeur takes up the issues of metaphorical reference and metaphorical truth. Here he suggests that there are two levels of reference: semantic and hermeneutic reference. Semantic reference is concerned "only with entities belonging to the order of the sentence" where hermeneutic reference "addresses entities that are larger than the sentence."[168] Semantic reference is concerned with the reference implicit to discourse and the pragmatic usage of language. The six traits of discourse, described above, are constitutive of what is in play with semantic reference. Now Ricoeur turns to those complex units of discourse that are not reducible to the sentence, i.e., the text as a "work."[169] With a "work" three new pragmatic categories enter the stage: "disposition" (*dispositio* in ancient rhetoric), that which makes the work a "totality;" "genre," or the formal rules that "regulate the practice of a work;" and "style," which "makes the work a singular, individual thing."[170] At this level of discourse and with these new pragmatic categories, the issue of reference is transformed from concerns of semantic reference to the "world of the work" that is "larger than" the mere "structure of the work."

> ... instead of saying that we are not satisfied with the sense and so presuppose reference besides, we would say that we are not satisfied with the structure of the work and presuppose a world of the work. The structure of the work is in fact its

---

[167] Ricoeur, *The Rule of Metaphor*, p. 97.
[168] Ricoeur, *The Rule of Metaphor*, p. 216.
[169] See Ricoeur, *The Rule of Metaphor*, p. 219.
[170] See Ricoeur, *The Rule of Metaphor*, p. 219.

sense, and the world of the work its reference [echoing the analysis of Frege]. This simple substitution of terms is sufficient as a first approximation. Hermeneutics then is simply the theory that regulates the transition from structure of the work to world of the work. *To interpret a work is to display the world to which it refers by virtue of its 'arrangement,' its 'genre,' and its 'style'* ... I contrast this postulate with the romantic and psychologizing conception of hermeneutics originating with Schleiermacher and Dilthey, for whom the supreme law of interpretation is the search for a harmony between the spirit of the author and that of the reader. *To this always difficult and often impossible quest for an intention hidden behind the work, I oppose a quest that addresses the world displayed before the work.*[171] (emphasis added)

Just how is a world displayed before the work? It is clear that there is a difference between the way that scientific discourse displays the world and the way that literature displays the world. Yet the difference is not that scientific discourse literally links sense and reference and literature is merely the pleasurable play of senses without reference. "My whole aim [Ricoeur maintains] is to do away with this restriction of reference to scientific statements."[172] Literary works refer, as well, but in a different way that enhances humanity by exploiting human capacities shared with no other beings.

> ... the literary work through the structure proper to it displays a world only under the condition that the reference of descriptive discourse is suspended. Or to put it another way, discourse in the literary work sets out its denotation as a second-level denotation, by means of the suspension of the first-level denotation of discourse.[173]

Rather than speak of an interplay between denotation and connotation, as did Beardsley, Ricoeur is concerned to see the literary work as a form of denotation. Yet here the interplay is between a "first-level" and a "second-level" denotation which brings the discussion back to metaphor:

> It may be, indeed, that the metaphorical statement is precisely the one that points out most clearly this relationship between suspended reference and displayed reference. Just as the metaphorical statement captures its sense as metaphorical midst the ruins of the literal sense, it also achieves its reference upon the ruins of what might be called ... its literal reference. If it is true that literal sense and metaphorical sense are distinguished and articulated within an interpretation, so too it is within an interpretation that a second-level reference, which is properly the metaphorical reference, is set free by means of the suspension of the first-level reference.[174]

This interplay between levels of reference serves as the basis for developing a theory of "split reference" with respect to metaphor: "... what hap-

---

[171] Ricoeur, *The Rule of Metaphor*, p. 220.
[172] Ricoeur, *The Rule of Metaphor*, p. 221.
[173] Ricoeur, *The Rule of Metaphor*, p. 221.
[174] Ricoeur, *The Rule of Metaphor*, p. 221.

pens in poetry is not the suppression of the referential function but its profound alteration by the workings of ambiguity."[175]

> The double-sensed message finds correspondence in a split addresser, in a split addressee, and what is more in a split reference, as is cogently exposed in the preambles to fairy tales of various peoples, for instance, in the usual exordium of the Majorca storytellers: "Aixo era y no era" (It was and it was not).
> Let us keep this notion of *split reference* in mind, as well as the wonderful 'It was and it was not,' which contains *in nuce* all that can be said about metaphorical truth.[176]

Here with the idea of split reference the metaphorical statement and the world of the work find themselves inseparable from the activity of hermeneutics, i.e., interpretation. Metaphorical truth, and the truth of not merely literature but all linguistic mediation (= experience), is dependent upon a tension between a negative condition of impertinence which enables the appearance of a more adequate positive innovative meaning of pertinence.[177] All that has been anticipated but only implicitly by Richards' discussion of tenor and vehicle, by Wheelwright's addition of epiphor, diaphor, and the presential, coalescent, and perspectival character of reality, and by Berggren's stereoscopic vision, i.e., the naive ontology of a world external to language, all that finds its justification and full articulation finally through the notion of split reference. This tension between the negative and the positive is no less than the tension between possibilities and actuality. "Is it not the function of poetry to establish another world - another world that corresponds to other possibilities of existence, to possibilities that would be most deeply our own?"[178] Metaphor is concerned with the projection of possibilities that serve as "imaginative variations"[179] for the living of one's life (always in community with Others[180]).

It is precisely at this point that Heidegger re-emerges in Ricoeur's text, i.e., at the point where projection of possibilities comes to the foreground. Here the connection is now made between metaphor and what Heidegger

---

[175] Ricoeur, *The Rule of Metaphor*, p. 224.
[176] Ricoeur, *The Rule of Metaphor*, p. 224.
[177] See Ricoeur, *The Rule of Metaphor*, pp. 229-230.
[178] Ricoeur, *The Rule of Metaphor*, p. 229.
[179] The notion of "imaginative variations" appears in Ricoeur, *Time and Narrative*, vol. 3, pp. 127-128, 139, and 142f. Ricoeur stresses, especially, the tension between one's "debt to the past" and imaginative variations as what links fiction and history. See *ibid.*, pp. 145 and 397, n. 13. In addition, the theme of imaginative variations is important to Ricoeur's *Oneself as Another*, pp. 148, 159, and 288.
[180] See below the discussion of the aporia of Self and Other.

calls "state of mind" (*Befindlichkeit*) which in his analysis is equally primordial to understanding's projection of possibilities.[181] The world of the work, particularly the literary work but equally all works (including the scientific), constitutes a unity of "mood." Yet Ricoeur is quick to point out that this is not merely psychological.

> Under the name of mood, an extra-linguistic factor is introduced, which is the index of a manner of being (on condition that it is not treated psychologically). *A mood or 'state of soul' ... is a way of finding or sensing oneself in the midst of reality.* It is, in the language of Heidegger, a way of finding oneself among things (*Befindlichkeit*). Here again, the *epoché* of natural reality is the condition that allows poetry to develop a world on the basis of the mood that the poet articulates. *It will be the task of interpretation to elaborate the design of a world liberated, by suspension, from descriptive reference.* The creation of a concrete object - the poem itself - cuts language off from the didactic function of the sign, but at the same time opens up access to reality in the mode of fiction and feeling.[182] (partial emphasis added)

Here Ricoeur introduces the notion of feeling, to be sure, but not as a mere psychological emotionalism. Feeling, state-of-mind or *Befindlichkeit*, is the most primordial manner in which one is in the world. It is the most primordial way by which one's situation is announced, and it confirms that one is never without a situation. The word *Befindlichkeit* involves the meaning "finding" one's self. This finding is not a mere establishment of the facts of one's physical location. It is a disclosure that one's situation establishes the parameters of one's possibilities. *Befindlichkeit* ("feeling") announces the valence of ambiguity accompanying all understanding of one's situation, since it consists of one's response (positive or negative) to the non-grasped and, perhaps, non-graspable possibilities of that situation. "Feeling," then, is equiprimordial with one's possibilities just as those very possibilities are equally concealed by the world of the senses and of abstract thought.[183] Nei-

---

[181] See section 29 ("Being there as State-of-Mind"), of Heidegger's *Being and Time*, pp. 172-179, and, especially, the opening lines of section 31 ("Being-there as Understanding"), p. 182: "State-of-mind [*Befindlichkeit*] is *one* of the existential structures in which the Being of the 'there' maintains itself. Equiprimordial with it in constituting this Being is *understanding*."

[182] Ricoeur, *The Rule of Metaphor*, p. 229.

[183] I am in thorough agreement with Ricoeur that the notion of an external physical world as an "outside" to an "inside" of thought is not adequate for reflecting experience (see Ricoeur, *Time and Narrative*, vol. 3, p. 147), for both the world and thought are too narrowly mediated by such a dichotomy (see Ricoeur's call for an expansion of the notion of "thought" in *ibid.*, p. 145). Nevertheless, Ricoeur has not sufficiently appreciated either the importance or the extent of νοῦς in experience. He "expands" thought to include "the whole field of intentions and motivations" (*ibid.*, p. 145), to be sure, but that barely hints at the illimitable, imperceptible, immaterial, immeasurable whole rooted in the unchangeable that is involved in the notion of νοῦς.

ther the senses nor abstraction can grasp or contain either possibilities or one's state-of-mind, because both are at least partially suppressed by what is dominant in one's attention. Ricoeur writes of feeling: "The paradox of the poetic can be summed up entirely in this, that the elevation of feeling to fiction is the condition of its mimetic use. Only a feeling transformed into myth can open and discover the world."[184] What Ricoeur means by "myth" here is not mere anthropomorphic stories about the Greek gods, but, rather, myth is another way of talking about the mediated character of experience shaped by presuppositions and models/paradigms.[185] Mimêsis (imitation, mediation, representation) is to consciousness what water is to a fish. When Ricoeur writes, then, that "only a feeling transformed into myth can open and discover the world," this is no world-denying escapism or submersion into polymorphous perversity. There is no "feeling" without a world. Feeling is not merely a subjective condition separable and distinct from the world. State-of-mind is fundamental to how the world is announced to one as a world of possibilities and not mere factual actuality. In other words, "feeling" and "myth" are complementary moments of mediation by means of which reality is disclosed and simultaneously concealed. It is only because "representation" in the sense of some direct and immediate one-to-oneness of literal language has come to dominate the way one takes "reality" (read "actuality") to be; it is only because of the dominance of sense perception as the vehicle for access to "reality" (read "actuality"); it is only because materialism (read "physical actuality") has overpowered spirituality (read "mind") even turning the spirit into a material force; it is only because concealment has turned into pathological denial, that "feeling" and "myth" have lost their power to illuminate reality and to remind us that imagination and possibilities are higher than all actuality.

> If this heuristic function of mood is so difficult to recognize, it is doubtless because 'representation' has become the sole route to knowledge and the model of every relationship between subject and object. Yet *feeling* has an ontological status different from relationship at a distance; it *makes for participation in things*.[186]
> (emphasis added)

Reality is always had at a price. Just as one's life is the result of the actualization of some possibilities at the expense of others that can never be

---

[184] Ricoeur, *The Rule of Metaphor*, p. 245.
[185] Ricoeur engages in a discussion of models and metaphor in the work of Max Black in conjunction with Aristotle's connection of *mimêsis* and *muthos*. See Ricoeur, *The Rule of Metaphor*, pp. 239-245.
[186] Ricoeur, *The Rule of Metaphor*, pp. 245-246.

actualized as a consequence, so metaphor and linguistic mediation in general is concerned with the opening up of novel, i.e., possible, reference at the expense of the commonplace. Precisely because of this dynamic of negativity and positivity, an inhabitable world is made possible.

> ... the meaning of a metaphorical statement rises up from the blockage of any literal interpretation of the statement ...
>
> But this is only the first phase, or rather the negative counterpart, of a positive strategy. Within the perspective of semantic impertinence, the self-destruction of meaning is merely the other side of an innovation in meaning at the level of the entire statement, an innovation obtained through the 'twist' of the literal meaning of the words. It is this innovation in meaning that constitutes living metaphor. But are we not in the same motion given the key to metaphorical reference? Can one not say that, by drawing a new semantic pertinence out of the ruins of the literal meaning, the metaphoric interpretation *also* sustains a new referential design, through those same means of abolition of the reference corresponding to the literal interpretation of the statement? A proportional argument, therefore: the other reference, the object of our search, would be to the new semantic pertinence what the abolished reference is to the literal meaning destroyed by the semantic impertinence.[187]

Hence, metaphor would be engaging in a "category mistake that clears the way to a new vision."[188] But Ricoeur is clear that this "new vision" is not merely the product of subjective fantasy playing with linguistic signs. This becomes manifest when one, once again, turns to the *usage* of metaphor. Some metaphors work and others don't. Why? If all that was involved in metaphor was a substituting of signs, what would constitute a mistake or even prohibit usage, since metaphor by definition means a violation of the sign system, i.e., it depends upon a category mistake within the system? Ricoeur's answer:

---

[187] Ricoeur, *The Rule of Metaphor*, p. 230. The new semantic pertinence Ricoeur spoke of earlier in Study 6, p. 197, as well, in terms of its presupposing an obliteration of the logical and established meanings of everyday language: "Can one not say that the strategy of language at work in metaphor consists in obliterating the logical and established frontiers of language, in order to bring to light new resemblances the previous classification kept us from seeing? In other words, *the power of metaphor would be to break an old categorization, in order to establish new logical frontiers on the ruins of their forerunners.*" (emphasis added) See, as well, *ibid.*, p. 214, where Ricoeur stresses the role of the imagination which stretches beyond the conundrum, resulting from the clash within the logical meaning, to generate the new metaphorical meaning: "Metaphorical meaning ... is not the enigma itself, the semantic clash pure and simple, but the solution of the enigma, the inauguration of the new semantic pertinence. In this connection, the interaction designates only the *diaphora*; the *epiphora* properly speaking is something else. It cannot take place without fusion, without intuitive passage." See, as well, pp. 190, 194, 196, 197

[188] Ricoeur, *The Rule of Metaphor*, p. 230.

> The 'appropriateness' of metaphorical as well as literal application of a predicate is not fully justified within a purely nominalist conception of language. Although such a conception has no trouble explaining the choreography of labels, since there is no essence to block re-labelling, it has greater difficulty accounting for the air of *rightness* that certain more fortunate instances of language and art seem to exude. To my mind, this is the place to part ways with ... nominalism. Does not the fittingness, the appropriateness of certain verbal and non-verbal predicates, indicate that language *not only has organized reality in a different way, but also made manifest a way of being of things, which is brought to language thanks to semantic innovation?*[189] (partial emphasis added)

Figurative language illuminates the world. Is this illumination merely of the actual or, at the other extreme, merely speculative, or does it indicate a new kind of reference that shows one the way "things are" by breaking things open to their new possibilities? In order to grasp just how radical the illumination process truly is, one must come to terms with the meaning and significance of the "split reference" of metaphor.

Just how is reference "split" with respect to metaphor (and, therefore, with respect to reality)? The metaphor functions because of a tension between impertinence and pertinence; between first-level denotation and second-level denotation; between the eclipsing of the literal and the innovation of meaning; between the category mistake and the new emerging category; between the "is not" and the "is." In short, "[i]n the metaphorical discourse ... referential power is linked to the eclipse of ordinary reference; the creation of heuristic fiction is the road to redescription; and reality brought to language unites manifestation and creation."[190] If there is anything misleading in this cryptic summary of the illumination of the world (reality) by split reference, it is the lack of explicit observation that manifestation presupposes concealment. This oversight is remedied when Ricoeur turns to describe the kind of truth that split reference makes possible. A full discussion of metaphorical truth, however, will be reserved for the analysis of the aporia of truth in the next chapter.

A valuable insight into the central aporia of language with respect to the emergence of the categorical out of the non-categorical or of archetypes out of the ectypal is to be gleaned from what Ricoeur calls the "three applications" of tension involved in metaphorical truth :

> a) tension within the statement: between tenor and vehicle [Richards, Wheelwright], between focus and frame [Black], between principal subject and secondary subject [Berggren];

---

[189] Ricoeur, *The Rule of Metaphor*, p. 239.
[190] Ricoeur, *The Rule of Metaphor*, p. 239.

b) tension between two interpretations: between a literal interpretation that perishes as the hands of semantic impertinence and a metaphorical interpretation whose sense emerges through non-sense [split reference];

c) tension in the relational function of the copula: between identity and difference in the interplay of resemblance.[191]

It is this third moment of tension that demands consideration with respect to the linguistic aporia, for the two prior moments presuppose the third which ultimately accounts for the other two. In other words, this tension at the level of the copula (the ontological moment) is merely a more radical formulation of the tension between the literal and the non-sensical, which is the condition of possibility for the first tension between the signs of the semantic metaphorical event (the ontic moment), but it goes to the jugular vein of ontology. For deeper than the tension between impertinence and pertinence is the recognition of "identity" in the midst of "difference" presupposed by a judgment of impertinence. Something must be seen as "the same," i.e., as identical, before it can be eclipsed by an emergent new meaning. Here Ricoeur is pushing split reference, i.e., metaphorical truth, even further back than the mere interplay of the literal and the figurative of a particular metaphorical statement. Where does this judgment of "identity" or "sameness" come from that permits acknowledgment of a conventional meaning (the literal) which can then be "twisted" by the metaphorical statement? "... is there not a metaphorical sense of the verb *to be* itself, in which the same tension would be preserved that we found first between words ..., then between two interpretations ..., and finally between identity and difference?"[192]

> In order to elucidate this tension deep within the logical force of the verb *to be*, we must expose an 'is not,' itself implied in the impossibility of the literal interpretation, yet present as a filigree in the metaphorical 'is.' Thus, the tension would prevail between an 'is' and an 'is not.' This tension would not be marked grammatically ... [E]ven if not marked, the 'is' of equivalence is distinct from the 'is' of determination.[193]

The central aporiai of language, concerned with the emergence of the categorical out of the non-categorical, i.e., identity out of difference, universals out of metaphoric activity, is announced here in the tension of the copula as is the "is"/"is not" of possibility as the ever concealed horizon of actuality. For the tension within the copula (the "is"), concealed by the

---

[191] Ricoeur, *The Rule of Metaphor*, p. 247.
[192] Ricoeur, *The Rule of Metaphor*, p. 248.
[193] Ricoeur, *The Rule of Metaphor*, p. 248.

grammatical conjugation of "to be," arises out of "... two senses of the verb *to be*, the relational and the existential."[194] The relational function of the verb "to be" enables the establishment of equivalence between two elements: "'nature is a temple where living columns ...'" But the copula ("is") here not only establishes a relation between nature and temple; the copula is being used here to redescribe in a manner that says something about what is real, what exists. These two functions of equivalence/relation and determination/existential can arise only because of a radical tension within the verb "to be" that is presupposed and never unambiguous and self-evident. At the heart of the copula is a tension between "is" and "is not" between actuality and possibility. "'Nature *is* a temple where living columns ...'," and it patently *is not*. Such a splitting of reference rests upon the ontological implication of Being that enables any and all experience of the world. Beyond all actuality is an interplay of actuality and possibility in and by means of which all things are in one sense the "same", i.e., they all participate in the universal character of possibility (identity) concealed by the actual, but, precisely because possibility is inseparable from the concealing of actuality, no two things have the identical possibilities, i.e., the possibilities of each are distinct (difference).

However, one does not need to turn to poetic metaphors to observe this tension of the copula. If experience is mediated through the vehicle of language, then language and reality are radically metaphoric, for language, one's experienced reality, can only mediately never immediately grasp "what is." Hence, every usage of the copula involves an "is"/"is not." What appears as an obviously literal statement, "the tree is in the yard," is not as unequivocal as it appears. Which tree? There can easily be several requiring other indicators not contained in the statement to single out which is under discussion. In any event, the tree is a mediated "image" and "suggestion" in one's mind. Which yard? In order for the tree to be in "this" yard, other yards must be excluded from attention, and, again, the yard is experienced mediately not immediately. If truth is concerned with what "really is," then "the tree is in the yard" tells one very little, for, in order for trees to be in yards there must be a world that is both actual and possible, and for one to make such a "truth claim" there must be an actual and possible world mediated in consciousness. "The tree is in the yard" tells one, at best, something about what is actual, but it completely conceals the possibilities, e.g., the cycle of the seasons affecting the tree, the kinds of flowers such a tree

---

[194] Ricoeur, *The Rule of Metaphor*, p. 248.

allows for and prohibits, whether the tree shades the house keeping it cool in the heat of the summer, whether branches can/will fall potentially injuring someone, is it a coniferous or a deciduous - the latter requiring the raking of leaves and by whom? What is at issue here is not that one cannot "progress" from the "simple" statement "the tree is in the yard" to talking about aesthetics and environmental issues related to air conditioning, or concern about the welfare of children or whose turn it is to rake the leaves. What is at issue in the "simple" statement is that such a "straight forward" "literal" judgment is metaphorical, i.e., it is projecting, usually pre-consciously to be sure, a world of possibilities, a world that one may truly inhabit, but it is a world that both "is" and "is not."

Hence, Ricoeur asks: "... [D]oes not the tension that affects the copula in its relational function also affect the copula in its existential function? This question contains the key to the notion of *metaphorical truth.*"[195] The tension of the copula is most clear with an explicit metaphor: "'nature is a temple where living columns ...'" Nature is a temple, yet nature is not a temple. However, whether nature is a temple or not suggests something about the reality one inhabits. Yet the same can be said of the tree in the yard: the tree is/is not in the yard; the tree is/is not part of a horizon of possibility. One's inhabitable world is enriched or impoverished by the truth or non-truth of the metaphor which is not merely evoking possibilities (the existential function) but is tied to the actualities (the relational function), as well..

What is crucial with respect to the tension of the copula is that the existential function not be taken as a naive and uncritical "ontological vehemence."[196] In other words, simply saying something "is" does not make it factually the case. Because the "is" is hermeneutical, there are limits established by the context to which the "is" must be accountable just as in the reading of a text. Not all possible meanings are truly possible. Every "is" contains the echoed, if not the voiced, "is not." Yet without this ontological vehemence the suggestiveness of the metaphor would lose its power. The metaphor would merely float in the air and not open up a real world that one might possibly inhabit.

> ... [T]he metaphorical utterance functions in two referential fields at once ... The first meaning relates to a known field of reference ... The second meaning ... relates to a referential field for which there is no direct characterization ...
>
> Two energies converge here: the gravitational pull exerted by the second referential field on meaning, giving it the force to leave its place of origin; and the

---

[195] Ricoeur, *The Rule of Metaphor*, p. 248.
[196] See Ricoeur, *The Rule of Metaphor*, p. 249.

> dynamism of meaning itself as the inductive principle of sense. The semantic aim that animates the metaphorical utterance places these two energies in relation, in order *to inscribe a semantic potential* ... within the sphere of influence of the second referential field to which it relates.
>
> ... At the origin of this process, therefore, there is what I shall call the ontological vehemence of a semantic aim, hinting at an unknown field that sets it in motion. This ontological vehemence cuts meaning from its initial anchor, frees it as the form of movement and transposes it to a new field to which the meaning can give form by means of its own figurative property. But *in order to declare itself this ontological vehemence makes use of mere hints of meaning, which are in no way determinations of meaning*.[197] (emphasis added)

These hints of meaning can be had only at the price of negating the naive, literal meaning of the "is." The hints of meaning can only surface out of the ashes of a "no." Hence, metaphorical ontological vehemence requires that language go beyond itself as it evokes potential reality within the horizon of actual reality.

> ... *actuality has meaning only in the discourse on being*. This signifies ... that the semantic aim of metaphorical utterance does intersect most decisively with the aim of ontological discourse, not at the point where metaphor by analogy and categorial analogy [Aristotle] meet, but *at the point where the reference of metaphorical utterance brings being as actuality and as potentiality into play*.[198] (emphasis added)

But potentiality has its price: one cannot stay statically attached to steno actuality:

> There is no better testimony to this affirmative vehemence than the poetic experience. Along one of its dimensions, at least, this experience expresses the *ecstatic* moment of language - language going beyond itself. It seems, accordingly, to attest that discourse prefers to obliterate itself, to die, at the confines of the being-said.[199]

It is clear, however, that not all dying leads to resurrection. Only some disclosive meanings emerge out of the negativity at the heart of the copula. Hence, to point to the abuse of metaphor (i.e., in the sense of the tendency for metaphor to lose its negativity by being reduced to an actual meaning) indicating how metaphor too easily collapses into literal, steno language or to point out how metaphor violates the conventions of meaning (as do Berggren[200] and Colin Turbayne,[201] respectively) does not mean one can ignore, much less reject, metaphor. That would lead to the crippling of human un-

---

[197] Ricoeur, *The Rule of Metaphor*, p. 299-300.
[198] Ricoeur, *The Rule of Metaphor*, p. 307.
[199] Ricoeur, *The Rule of Metaphor*, p. 249.
[200] See the discussion of Berggren above.
[201] See Ricoeur, *The Rule of Metaphor*, pp. 251-53.

derstanding by limiting understanding to the actual at the expense of the possible. One can enter into the circle of understanding in the "right way" only by means of conscious awareness of the tensiveness of metaphor, the very heart of language in general. Hence, negativity in metaphor functions analogously to Gadamer's observation with respect to the understanding of a "text," that there is no understanding free of prejudices/presuppositions. This does not lead to the elimination of all understanding any more than the negativity of metaphor eliminates disclosive meaning. To the contrary, critical awareness of the dynamics of negativity and disclosure in metaphor allows the text to challenge one's assumed grasp of its meaning (analogous to the way critical awareness of one's presuppositions allows the text to challenge the understanding one brings to the text). It allows one to engage the text in a manner that illuminates how one might yet be in the world. Quoting Turbayne, Ricoeur observes:

> 'We cannot say what reality is, only what it seems like to us' ... If there can be a non-mythic state,[202] there can be no non-metaphorical state of language. So there is no other issue than to 'replace the masks,' but to do so consciously ... In brief, critical consciousness of the distinction between use and abuse leads not to disuse but to re-use of metaphors, in the endless search for other metaphors, namely a metaphor that would be the best one possible.[203]

Hence, truth is equivocal and paradoxical in a productive rather than merely destructive fashion in contrast to the radical skepticism of Nietzsche and Derrida. Truth depends upon concealment, selection, and negativity which serves as the necessary condition of possibility for disclosure, attention, and meaning opening up a world within which one can live. Hence, there are no absolutes; there are only wagers. For there is an

> ... inescapably paradoxical [this project would say aporetic] character surrounding a metaphorical concept of truth. The paradox consists in the fact [that] ... there is no other way to do justice to the notion of metaphorical truth than to include the critical incision of the (literal) 'is not' within the ontological vehemence of the (metaphorical) 'is.'[204]

How does this notion of metaphorical truth lead to the central aporetic moment of language as an interplay between identity and difference? The

---

[202] As with the case of Berggren, I would challenge this notion that there can be a "non-mythic state." Such a state would be equivalent to there being a non-paradigm state, i.e., to one's being in the world without a sociological paradigm. It is simply not possible.
[203] Ricoeur, *The Rule of Metaphor*, p. 253.
[204] Ricoeur, *The Rule of Metaphor*, p. 255.

aporia at issue here is that which emerges as a consequence of the metaphorical circularity at the heart of language where language becomes living discourse:

> The circle can be described in the following manner. Initial polysemy equals 'language,' the living metaphor equals 'speech,' metaphor in common use represents the return of speech towards language, and subsequent polysemy equals 'language.'[205]

What this circle is describing is the process within discourse (and not merely within language) that both depends upon and generates sameness in otherness, identity in difference:

> ... [M]etaphor reveals the logical structure of 'the similar' because, in the metaphorical statement, 'the similar' is perceived *despite* difference, *in spite of* contradiction ... In other words, metaphor displays the work of resemblance because the literal contradiction preserves difference within the metaphorical statement; 'same' and 'different' are not just mixed together, they also remain opposed. Through this specific trait, enigma lives on in the heart of metaphor. In metaphor, 'the same' operates *in spite of* 'the different.'[206]

And it is this power of metaphor to discover "same" in the "different" without losing their tension, i.e., without collapsing into naive sameness, that elevates metaphor to its unchallenged place in language for illuminating reality. "Metaphor, a figure of speech [discourse], presents in an *open* fashion, by means of a conflict *between* identity and difference, the process that, in a *covert* manner, generates semantic grids by fusion of differences *into* identity."[207] What is the reality illuminated here? It is a reality of identity and difference at the level of ontic things dependent upon the ability of consciousness to grasp the universal in the particular, and it is a reality of identity and difference at the ontological level of possibility and actuality upon which the ontic tension of identity (there is no ontic thing without concealed possibilities) and difference (the actual circumstances of each ontic thing circumscribes its unique possibilities) depends.[208]

This then accounts for the circularity at the heart of language mentioned above. Metaphor at the ontic level generates the common meaning,

---

[205] Ricoeur, *The Rule of Metaphor*, p. 121.
[206] Ricoeur, *The Rule of Metaphor*, p. 196.
[207] Ricoeur, *The Rule of Metaphor*, p. 198.
[208] The theological implication of this metaphorical moment of ontology is the questioning of any notion of mystical union or desire to become one with a univocal "is" by escaping any and all "is not." Just as the tension of metaphorical truth requires the suspension of a literal referent at the ontic level of things, challenging the positivism of empiricism, so the tension of metaphorical truth calls humanity to resist the siren call of mystical oneness drawing one out of history.

i.e., the literal meaning, that it depends upon to dis-cover new meaning, i.e., sameness and identity, which in turn serves as the common meaning in the dis-covery of new meaning. The dictionary is full of dead metaphors, or as Ricoeur formulates it: "The dictionary contains no metaphors; they exist only in discourse."[209]

---

[209] Ricoeur, *The Rule of Metaphor*, p. 97. This is precisely how Ernst Cassirer spoke of metaphor, also. See "Sprache und Mythos: Ein Beitrag zum Problem der Götternamen" in *Wesen und Wirkung des Symbolbegriffs*, pp. 148 and 154. Cassirer credits Friedrich Max Müller for the notion. Müller speaks of "radical metaphor" as distinguished from the "poetic metaphor" in terms of this paradoxical metaphorical creation of the "literal" upon which the metaphorical then depends. See, *Vorlesungen über die Wissenschaft der Sprache* (Leipzig: Verlag von Gustav Mayer, 1866), pp. 334, 367-368, 392, and 407. Not to be overlooked in this respect is Ludwig Noire's *Die Welt als Entwicklung des Geistes*, pp. 294-295. Yet Nietzsche reports that such an account for the emergence of literal language is already found in Jean Paul's *Vorschule der Aesthetik* in *Sämmtliche Werke*, Vols. 41-42 (Berlin: S. Reimer, 1827) originally published in 1804. Nietzsche writes (from Carole Blair, "Nietzsche's Lecture Notes on Rhetoric: A Translation," p. 123): "On the other hand, and correctly, Jean Paul, *Vorschule der Aesthetik*, says: 'Just as in writing, the writing with hieroglyphics was older than writing with the letters of the alphabet, so it was that in speaking, the metaphor, insofar as it denotes relationships and not objects, was the *earlier* word, which had only to fade into the *proper expression*. The besouling and the embodiment still constituted a unity, because I and world were still fused. Thus, with respect to spiritual relationships, *each language is a dictionary of faded metaphors*.'" (emphasis added)

I am indebted to Paul Ricoeur's *Oneself as Another*, p. 12, n. 17, for the reference to this passage from Jean Paul and to the invaluable service of Ted Peters, who arranged for my gaining access to Jean Paul's text held in storage in Richmond, CA. Nevertheless, Paul Ricoeur's statement that "Jean-Paul's (sic) *Vorschule der Aesthetik* ... concludes with the following statement ..." (*ibid.*, p. 12, n. 17) is incorrect. Carol Blaire's citation in the English translation "Nietzsche's Lecture Notes on Rhetoric" (p. 128, n. 38) as "*Sämmtliche Werke*, Abt. II, vol. 9 (Berlin, 1861), no. 50, p. 179. - Trans." is equally incorrect. Nietzsche himself, of course, only quotes the text, he doesn't provide a citation. Far from being found at the conclusion of either the first or the second volume of Jean Paul's *Vorschule der Aesthetik*, this passage is found on pp. 24-25 of the second volume which is a total of 228 pages long.

There is much in Jean Paul's *Vorschule der Aesthetik* (1804) that is amazingly anticipatory of themes that have become commonplace only in the 20th century. For example, one might think Wheelwright was speaking about the priority of metaphor over literal language when one reads in Paul: "... wie das organische Reich das mechanische aufgreift, umgestaltet und behrrschet und knüpft, so übt die poetische Welt dieselbe Kraft an der wirklichen und das Geisterreich am Körperreich" (*Vorschule der Aesthetik*, vol. 1 (vol. 41 of the *Sämmtliche Werke*), p. 44). Anticipatory of Gadamer: "Weder der Stoff der Natur, noch weniger deren Form ist dem Dichter roh brauchbar. Die Nachahmung des erstern setzt ein höheres Prinzip voraus; denn jedem Menschen erscheint eine andere Natur; und es kommt nur darauf an, welchem die schönste erscheint. *Die Natur ist für den Menschen in ewiger Menschwerdung begriffen* ..." (*ibid.*, pp. 42-43). (emphasis added)

Berggren had argued that there must be some level of "integrity" in the midst of transformation in order for there to be an experience of ontic change. It is not until one turns to Ricoeur, however, that one learns how the "integrity" of the categorical (the sameness or identity of the universal) is itself the consequence of the activity of metaphor. This is what takes one to the key aporia of language, for the same emerges out of the difference of ontic particulars which then serves as the basis for an ongoing process of discovery of similarity in difference to sometimes lead to a judgment of identity and the emergence of a new universal which can then serve as the basis for an ongoing process of discovery ... In other words, *universals are a posteriori abstractions that distillate into permanent categories which are preserved in one's inherited language where they function a priori.* At the same time this ontic "integrity" in the midst of transformation is illuminated by Ricoeur's metaphor theory ontologically as the *universality* of possibility that is always and already a range of *particular* possibilities.

Ricoeur's "... most extreme hypothesis, [is] that the 'metaphoric' that transgresses the categorial order also begets it:"[210]

> If metaphor belongs to an heuristic of thought, could we not imagine that the process that disturbs and displaces a certain logical order, a certain conceptual hierarchy, a certain classification scheme, is the same as that from which all classification proceeds? Certainly, the only functioning of language we are aware of operates within an already constituted order; metaphor does not produce a new order except by creating rifts in an old order. Nevertheless, could we not imagine that the order itself is born in the same way that it changes? Is there not, in Gadamer's terms, a 'metaphoric' at work at the origin of logical thought, at the root of all classification?[211]

Language is radically aporetic, for it is the product of the very metaphorical process that it is. Language is either living or dead metaphor. To the extent that language is steno, it is dead metaphor; to the extent that language is tensive, it is living metaphor; yet all living metaphor presupposes dead metaphor, and all dead metaphor presupposes living metaphor. There can be no stronger aporia, and it is at the heart of the human condition.

It is the task of theology to identify such aporiai in order to adequately illuminate how faith is not ultimately concerned with dogma and belief in "things" either unknown or unseen (the ontic). Rather, reality is a matter of faith, for things do not begin to exhaust reality (the ontological). Reality is

---

[210] Ricoeur, *The Rule of Metaphor*, p. 24.
[211] Ricoeur, *The Rule of Metaphor*, p. 22.

potential, it emerges only at the expense of the concealed, life presupposes death, the "is" can only be experienced in tension with the "is not." But, above all, that unseen order of "things," i.e., universals or the Logos, that helped the early church formulate its doctrine; that unseen order of the Logos is now seen (metaphorically) to be itself the consequence of metaphoric activity: universals are experienced by humans ectypally. Yet universals are archetypal, i.e., universals are the Logos, to the extent that there is no human experience that is not shaped by an inherited language system of dead metaphors, "... for language is the great institution, the institution of institutions, that has preceded each and every one of us."[212] Yet "higher" than the Logos (ontic "things") is the metaphorical playing out of the tensions between possibility and actuality that prohibit any claims to absolute univocity either to universals or particulars.

Even as the circularity determining both language and understanding is acknowledged, one naturally desires to question beyond the limits of the circle to ask how it came to be. However, once one moves beyond the metaphorical process that generates the universal to ask, where does the order in the material world come from, since it is not capable of generating that non-material order out of itself (given that opposites cannot generate one another); where does this order in the material world come from that permits its non-material or spiritual experience in consciousness?, to answer, there must be a non-material horizon of information that serves as the ordering principle of the material which can then be non-materially thought by humans,[213] once one offers such answers, one must acknowledge that one is speculating beyond the limits of human capacity. This does not mean that the speculation is incorrect.[214] As Plato maintained with respect to the notion of the trans-

---

212 Ricoeur, *Time and Narrative*, vol. 3, p. 221.
213 This is the conclusion of "metarealism" claimed by Guitton, Bogdanov, and Bogdanov in *Gott und die Wissenschaft*, pp. 106, 116.
214 Whether or not the non-material precedes the material or vice versa is one way of formulating the disagreement between the two friends Alois Emanuel Biedermann and Otto Pfleiderer, for the issue at issue between them was the question whether or not one stops one's reflections within the limits of human experience (so Biedermann) or does one leave open speculative possibilities beyond those limits (so Pfleiderer). Emanuel Hirsch sees the primary difference between Biedermann and Pfleiderer (and he sides with Pfleiderer) to be over the question of individual eternal life. Biedermann argues that the concept is completely indefensible (see Emanuel Hirsch, *Geschichte der neuern evangelischen Theologie*, p. 560; see Biedermann's analysis in his *Christliche Dogmatik*, 1869, p. 748 and his implicit critique of Pfleiderer's position, p. 749). Rather than deny the notion of an objective eternal existence in the afterlife, Pfleiderer maintains that scholarship can neither establish nor disprove the point. Hirsch concludes: "Hinsichtlich der Unsterblichkeit des Einzelnen aber gilt, daß eine ihrer Gren-

migration of souls (that such an opinion is not incompatible with "reason,"[215] given his understanding of the soul as what connects the material and the intelligible orders, but it can only be a speculative claim[216]), so here

---

zen bewußte wissenschaftliche Metaphysik sie weder behaupten noch verwerfen kann. Solange das Verhältnis des absoluten Geistes zum endlichen Bloß Gegenstand einer allgemeinen Prinzipienlehre ist, ergibt sich keine Möglichkeit der Entscheidung. Eben damit aber ist wissenschaftlich freier Raum für die christliche Gewißheit der Unsterblichkeit, wie sie sich gründet in dem Bewußtsein der Kinder Gottes, in der lebendigen Gemeinschaft mit dem ewigen Gotte des ewigen Lebens teilhaft zu sein. Diesem christlichen Postulate widersprechen [as is the case with Biedermann], heißt, das persönliche religiöse Verhältnis der Gotteskindschaft für eine leere subjektive Einbildung erklären ..." (Hirsch, *Geschichte der neuern evangelischen Theologie*, p. 565)

Biedermann, of course, understands one's status as a child of God to consist not in subjective immortality but in the elevation into the Spirit, i.e., in recognizing that one experiences the eternal spiritual order now and not in some future life. See Biedermann, *Christliche Dogmatik*, 1869, p. 30: "Der allgemeine, wesentliche Inhalt des religiösen Proceses im menschlichen Geistesleben ist die Erhebung des Menschen, als endlichen Geistes, aus der eigenen endlichen Naturbedingtheit zur Freiheit über sie in einer unendlichen Abhängigkeit." Yet this elevation into Spirit is not a human work alone: "Das menschliche Ich als endlicher Geist erfährt und bethätigt selbst seine Freiheit überhaupt nur, indem der absolute Geist sich in ihm offenbart: nicht mehr bloss als Grund für sein Dasein; nicht mehr bloss als Norm gegenüber seiner formal freien Selbstbethätigung; sondern nun auch als die wirksame Kraft in seinen realen Freiheitsacten als Geist" (*ibid.*, p. 282).

[215] Reason, according to Plato, is not instrumental reason, i.e., the rationality of calculation, prediction, manipulation, and control. Reason, rather, is contemplative as that unique activity of consciousness that is an engaging in a dialectic exclusively within νοῦς commencing with the universals (which he calls hypotheses, since they are incapable of being defined) leading "upward" to the First Principle of the whole (or what he calls the Good analogous in the mind to the sun in the realm of sense perception, but the Good is no universal among universals - it is beyond all essence). See Book VI of Plato's *Republic*.

[216] See Ernst Benz, *Indische Einflüsse auf die frühchristliche Theologie* in *Akademie der Wissenschaften und der Literatur. Abhandlungen der Geistes- und Sozialwissenschaftlichen Klasse*, vol. 3 (Wiesbaden: Franz Steiner Verlag Gmbh, 1951), p., 192: "... all diese Anspielungen auf die Seelenwanderung, die sich bei Plato finden, sind von ihm niemals als eine philosophische Lehre, als ein Dogma entwickelt worden. Bedeutungsvoll ist, daß all diese Beschreibungen von Reinkarnationen in den platonischen Dialogen entweder Bestandteile eines *Mythos* sind oder wenigstens eine mythische Färbung haben, aber nicht als ein Logos, als eine philosophische zu erweisende Lehre vorgetragen werden. Für all diese Mythen aber gilt die Warnung, die der platonische Sokrates im Phaedo ausspricht: 'Niemand wird behaupten, daß diese Dinge sich genau so abgespielt haben, wie ich sie beschrieben habe. Aber die Annahme, daß entweder dies oder etwas Ähnliches die Wahrheit ist im Hinblick auf unsere Seelen und ihre Wohnungen, scheint mir kein unvernünftiges Wagnis zu sein, nachdem die Unsterblichkeit der Seele nachgewiesen wurde.'"

with respect to the interrelationship between universals and particulars. It is not a violation of experience to suppose that universals are the ultimate source of all particularity, but such a judgment must necessarily remain speculative. Contributing to the legitimacy of the judgment is, surely, the fact that experience itself is non-material, i.e., it occurs exclusively in, and by means of, linguistic mediation or consciousness impossible without universals. Nevertheless, the most we can say from within experience is that universals and particulars are *experienced* as aporetically inseparable yet irreducible one to the other.[217] Universals are themselves aporetic, since they are produced in individual consciousness a posteriori as a product of the metaphorical, yet they function a priori through one's inherited language.

Conclusion

The aporiai of language are all in one way or another related to the circularity of human experience arising out of the dynamic interaction between actuality and possibility (stasis and dynamis, negativity and positivity, rest and motion, "is"/ "is not," etc.). *Whether* one turns from language as synchronic to the diachronic event of discourse, which is a move from treating language as a self-referential internal system of signs to language as an event of communication between persons and with the self to wrestle with the ambiguity of reality, which can only be experienced within a linguistic horizon yet is more than a mere language event and is most adequately "grasped" with metaphor; or *whether* one engages the split reference of language itself which announces one's dependence upon an "is not" in order to say what "is;" or *whether* one is concerned with the priority of the figurative over the literal since the categorical (or Logos) can emerge only at the expense of the violation of its own order enabling the discovering of identity in difference to account for the experience of universals as a posteriori, arising out of experience ectypally, yet, to the extent that universals are preserved in the lin-

---

For a further discussion of the notion of reincarnation in early Christianity, see Norbert Brox, "Die frühchristliche Debatte um die Seelenwanderung" in *Concilium* 29/5 (October 1993), pp. 427-430.

[217] Hugh of St. Victor recognized humanity's middle role, but, rather than speak of humanity in the Augustinian sense of hanging in the middle between salvation and damnation, Hugo of St. Victor spoke of the human as in the middle between angels and animals with a providential responsibility for the natural world (he employs metaphors of agricultural cultivation in contrast to metaphors of domination). See Eckard Wolz-Gottwald, "Oculus Triplex."

guistic system one has inherited and shapes one's sociological paradigm, they are experienced as archetypal; in the end, all three of these linguistic aporiai are fundamentally related to the concealing and revealing of the organic interaction between possibility and actuality. The split reference of all linguistic events call one to reject the hegemony and heteronomy of literal language without succumbing to mere emotionalism, metaphysics, or blind speculation. But this means acknowledging a radical unknowing permeating all experience. That unknowing is announced not only with respect to the impossibility of defining the very universals upon which all "knowledge" is based. But in addition, now one can see that that unknowing is the consequence of the aporetic concealing of possibility and actuality as all understanding is perspectival and historical and an open-ended odyssey that is ever richer, even as it can be dangerous and traumatic to the point of unbearability.

The trajectory of analysis in this chapter is a not so silent scream against the literal in order to retrieve the figurative as mediator of the dynamic process of possibility and actuality enabling and constituting life. At the core of all experience is an ambiguous dynamic of *both* "is" and "is not," of both positivity and negativity, that is essential to life. Emphasis needs to be placed on the ambiguity of this dynamic, for not all possibilities are mutually compossible - not all possibilities can be actualized. This means that there is a fundamental negativity at the core of experience no matter what one does.[218] Yet without this negativity there would be absolute determinism. The cost of human freedom is the negativity that inseparably accompanies all positivity - the denial of possibilities that necessarily, but not determinatively, accompanies the actualization of some alternative possibilities.

Once again, a non-epistemic faith finds expression from the very center of human experience and understanding. With the aporiai of language, faith is seen as the very condition of possibility of the linguistic character of all experience.

It is obvious that the aporiai of linguisticality have tremendous implications for theological reflection. Particularly for those Protestant Christian traditions, who believe that they are returning to some pristine form of Christianity empowered by the shibboleth of *sola scriptura*, the aporiai of language are unavoidably crucial as they are devastating. At the

---

[218] This is what Heidegger speaks of as the fundamental "nullity" (Nichtigkeit) that characterizes human guilt, but the opposite of guilt is not innocence. The opposite of guilt is determinism. See Heidegger, *Being and Time*, pp. 329, 330, 331.

least, these aporiai require surrendering any form of mere biblical literalism as the *foundation* for faith. It is not simply that biblical literalism has ignored the open-ended character of understanding - that is, the recognition that the historical character of human experience makes any exact repetition impossible because of the ever new context of each reading, which means there can be no absolutely fixed meaning (no *actually* correct meaning) for any text - not even the biblical text (see the discussion of "historicality" in the next chapter). But in addition, biblical literalism rests upon the assumption that one has access to an exogenous, objective reality through the senses. The biblical literalist and the empirical scientist share the same ontology - they disagree only about what constitutes valid evidence, i.e., the bible or nature.

The very strength of a living religious tradition depends upon its ability to speak meaningfully to the wide spectrum of human contexts and understandings, but it is able to do so only because of the historicality of all understanding, i.e., only because of the open-endedness of understanding. Hence, a (religious) tradition's ability to illuminate the particular context of any reading does not rest upon some absolute essence, or trans-historical universal (or Word), that is copied or repeated in that changing historical context, either. Such a belief in repetition based upon participation of the particular in the universal depends upon a metaphysical judgment that is at best speculative and at worst distracting from grasping the full dimension of faith shaping the historical, human condition. This is not to deny all forms of repetition in human experience; nor is it to deny that human experience is dependent upon universals - any more than one may deny that human experience is dependent upon a world of particularity. Rather, what must be questioned is whether repetition is exact duplication and whether universals have some indubitable metaphysical status independent of consciousness or the material order.

Furthermore, biblical literalism is a form of positivism that completely ignores the fact that humans have only mediated access to whatever exogenous world is "out there." What this means is that the epistemological problems of verification and falsification make it impossible for there to be any assurance, much less salvific assurance, that the mediation of any particular point in time or of any particular text is actually the "correct" one. Reality is only mediate not immediate; reality is potential not merely actual. What is experienced in the most concrete moment of sense perception is in fact an event of understanding in the mind mediated through the images of the imagination and informed by universals, which are of questionable status, with the entire event floating upon the manifest concealment of one's historical horizon of possibilities. It is this doubtful status of universals at the core of all linguistic mediation which is ever in tension with the world within a horizon of both actuality and possibility that is at issue in the aporiai of language. In moments of weakness, one may wish to, or think one does, possess the "correct" salvific mediation, i.e., one may wish to possess the Logos. In moments of inward focus, one may wish to, or think one does, experience a univocal oneness behind, in, and through all things. But a more careful examination of the human situation teaches that such a possession would be not only a contradiction of that situation (for it would be entirely actual and a denial of any new possibilities) but a violation of the very components that make humanity what it is: an odyssey of faith seeking understanding responsible to the Other and to the self. Higher than λόγος or νόμος is νοῦς as δύναμις.

Chapter 10
The Aporiai of Truth

All six of the aporiai described in this project confirm that a dynamic of manifestation and covering over is the fundamental condition of possibility for human experience. Hence, any understanding of truth must be sensitive to the aporia of the ever present concealment in disclosure that enables human experience of that which cannot be other than what it is (one's experience of simple universals and of one's mental life in any particular moment) which is experienced always and already in the context of that which can be other than the way it appears to be (the physical world of the senses).

The aporia of truth, then, points to the radically historical character of the human condition, for the dynamic of revealing/concealing addressed by this aporia is the key to temporality (to be discussed as an aporia for itself in the next chapter). One has not established historical truth, however, simply by claiming to have established what "actually" happened in an event. On the other hand, this does not mean that the truth of history must be concerned with some "eternal truths" as opposed to "historical accidents." History is as much its possibilities as it is what actually happened. At best there may be a record or a set of traces of what actually occurred, along with some of the perceived alternatives by some of the participants of what might have happened, but such records and traces can't begin to exhaust the concealed possibilities in play that contributed to, and/or were suppressed by, what actually happened. Not only, then, does this dynamic influence the meaning of truth, but it is this dynamic between the revealing and concealing of possibility in actuality that prohibits the reversal of linear time.

This project seeks to underscore that the unchanging and the changing (the One and the Many) are aporetically inseparable, and, thereby, qualify each other by preventing a simple reduction of one to the other. The aporia of truth is concerned with human understanding which can distinguish between that which is the same yesterday, today, and tomorrow (i.e., the universals of the mind that enable one's grasping identity in difference) and that which is constantly changing (the phenomena of sense experience), but neither is grasped in and of themselves in an absolute sense which could then in turn serve as a criterion for truth for making "correct judgments" with respect to itself and/or to the other.¹ For one experiences the Logos² only within the historical context of perception.³ Truth is a veil that hints, and it never enables possession of what is veiled.

Human beings are inseparable from their world. That world is not something that the individual is just next to over a stretch of time as a mere collection of objects and persons (others and Others) standing over against the self. The world constitutes the horizon of reality both actual and possible for the self, and the self, in turn, is simultaneously and aporetically mental and physical (spiritual and material). Hence, one has not begun to grasp what "reality" is all about if one takes truth to be defined as the correspondence of the individual's mental judgments to an "external" or "independent" collection of universals, things, and persons merely "over against" and/or "outside" of the judgment/self. Such a correspondence formulation of truth and reality (either physical or mental) tends to take the individual's world as shaped and defined only by what is actual and ignores the role of potentiality in experience.⁴ The aporia of truth is rooted in the dynamic of revealing and concealing involved in the covering over of potentiality by every actual context of understanding and action.

As the next chapter will suggest, the temporality of experience (involving action and understanding) is concerned with this dynamic of concealing and revealing in play with the potentiality of every form of actuality. Time is far more than a linear sequence of measurable, "actual" moments that tick off on a clock, for time must somehow include the simultaneity of possibility within the "linearity" of actuality, making time a unified whole in a more primordial sense than even mere human memory. Time, history, and truth are inextricably interrelated.

---

[1] The central conclusion of the aporiai of language, above, is that universals are a posteriori, ectypal, to the extent that they are generated from experience by the metaphorical process of establishing identity in difference; nonetheless, universals are experienced as a priori, archetypal, at least to the extent that they are deposited in language and inherited ever anew by each generation and individual.

[2] Λόγος constitutes the unchanging order of universals enabling it to mean not even primarily "Word", but "story," "speech," "calculation," "argumentation."

[3] The word for perception in Greek is αἴσθησις (aesthesis) indicating that perception has to do with the aesthetic, which is transient, in contrast to λόγος, which is the enduring.

[4] Potentiality is consciously acknowledged, if at all, as fate or, if one is a theist, as providence, but both provide excuses for ignoring possibility. This project follows Gadamer's insight, who takes it from Heidegger, who takes it from Aristotle, that rather than ignoring possibility, possibility is central to our experience of the self and other/Other. In fact, consciously engaging one's own possibilities/prejudices is, aporetically, the only route to enabling the other/Other to obtain an acknowledged independent status over against the self.

In order to describe the aporia of truth, then, it becomes necessary to draw on, and to anticipate all of, the aporiai with which the present project is concerned, for by definition the aporetic is concerned with the irreducible tension between two inseparable components which involve some kind of mutual exclusion, i.e., concealing, of the other. Hence, any focus on one of the components of an aporia leads to the concealment of the other. The aporia of truth is concerned precisely with this complex and pervasive dynamic in all of experience.

There is a second aporia with respect to truth as a consequence of the linguistic mediation of truth: this aporia has to do precisely with the fact that understanding is always dependent upon an event, that is, with *a linguistic mediation of some prior event*. On the one hand, understanding is always playing "catch up" ball. Something must happen for there to be understanding. On the other hand, it is only because of possibilities of meaning, which one already possesses, that one can begin to understand what happened. When one sees beyond the actual to the possible of the event character of experience, one can glimpse the aporetic circularity of understanding that is never separate from one's pre-understanding (one's ceaseless projecting of possibilities as an open process of attempting to "make sense" of one's experience), yet, it is precisely critical awareness of one's pre-understanding (i.e., critical awareness of one's presuppositions/prejudices) that can allow a text (or the Other) to emerge with integrity as an "over against" to which one is accountable.[5] Therefore, the aporia of truth, i.e., the aporia of the necessarily historical or temporal nature of human understanding, anticipates, as well, the final aporia of the present project, i.e., the aporetic relationship between "self" and "Other."

Keeping the comprehensiveness of the aporetic character of truth in mind, i.e., that it is involved in all of the other five aporiai presented in the project, the discussion here will focus on contrasting what has come to be called the "correspondence theory" of truth with the "disclosure theory" of truth, and it will suggest that the latter is more appropriate to understanding human experience. Once truth is liberated from mere "internal" and "external" reference between a linguistic form and that to which it refers, the dynamic, i.e., historical, character of truth can come into its own. Truth as disclosure is inseparable from the event character of all that is.

The aporia of truth confirms that all understanding, precisely, true and proper understanding, presupposes that something be concealed (the horizon

---

[5] See Gadamer, *Truth and Method*, p. 238.

of possibilities as well as other actualities not the focus of one's attention in any moment) in order for some-thing to be "correctly" understood. In short, there is a radical unknowing at the heart of all truth, that is an unknowing both "internal" (intellect/νοῦς/Geist) and "external" (material reality). The etymology of the Greek word for truth, ἀλήθεια (aletheia), offers an opportunity to situate the truth of correspondence as derivative of metaphorical truth, but, more so, to re-focus on the fundamental revealing and concealing that is νοῦς/Geist/consciousness inseparable from its material world. Ἀλήθεια is a metaphor providing a vehicle for expressing the tenor of human spirituality in the world that is informed by the most radical understanding of the dynamic of truth. This, in turn, will permit a re-engagement of the notion of the symbolic as essential to human experience. Nevertheless, neither ἀλήθεια nor the symbolic will be taken as providing one with indubitable access to a "correct" truth about the nature of reality either ultimate or finite. Truth and understanding are a process not a conclusion.

Truth as Correspondence: Verification and Falsification

It has become a commonplace to think of truth in terms of "correctness.[6]" What follows will not deny the role of making correct judgments in everyday life. As with the case of metaphor above, however, it is important that one seek not merely what Leibniz called a "nominal" but a "real" definition of truth.[7] In other words, when truth is limited to the correct correspondence between a word (or words) and that to which the word (or words) refer(s), one is engaging in a "nominal" definition of truth. A "real" definition of truth would be concerned, then, with "how" the nominal definition can come

---

[6] See Aristotle, *Metaphysics* 1027b25-27: "For the false and the true are not in things ... but they are in the judgment." See, as well, *ibid.*, Book IX, chapter 10; and Kant, "Inaugural Dissertation" in *Kant's Inaugural Dissertation and Early Writings on Space*, trans. by John Handyside (Westport, Conn.: Hyperion Press, Inc., 1979), p. 51: "... to take judgments about what is known by sense, the truth of a judgment consists in the agreement of its predicate with the given subject. But the concept of the subject, so far as it is a phenomenon, can be given only by its relation to the sensitive faculty of knowledge; and it is by the same faculty that sensitively observable predicates are also given." Where Kant is here suggesting that the truth of judgments consists in a comparison of the judgment with other mental experience, the "sensitive faculty of knowledge," Aristotle acknowledges that there are truths of the intellect, not given by sense, and these consist of those actualities which cannot be other than what they are. See, for example, Aristotle, *Metaphysics*, 1015a34, 1052a29-33; *Posterior Analytics*, 71b8-16, 74b5f; *On the Heavens*, 279b22; and *Nicomachean Ethics* 1139a7-10.

[7] See Ricoeur, *The Rule of Metaphor*, p. 65.

about. Once again, though, this "how" is not the "how" of methodology which would presume a goal and be concerned with only what steps must be taken to arrive at that goal. The methodological "how" of truth presumes that there already is something called correct judgments, and it is concerned with only the steps one must take in order to arrive at a correct judgment. But the "how" shaping the following analysis is a different "how." It addresses what such a methodological "how" presupposes in order for it to be even *possible* to make correct judgments.

Nevertheless, it is instructive to commence the analysis with commonplace experience in order to demonstrate the limits to the everyday notion of truth as "correctness." Contrary to Descartes, who concluded that humans would be perfect if they would simply withhold the application of the will (i.e., if they would withhold consent) until they had correct understanding,[8] such a claim fails to understand the dynamic of revealing *and* concealing that is truth. Correct judgments are un-true simply because they only take one part, and, often, an extremely isolated part, of experience into account. In fact, this inability of correct judging to take the whole into account constitutes the limits to truth as "verification," and recognition of the limits of verification motivated the turn to falsification as the criterion for a truth claim of correctness. Falsification, however, is only a species of truth as correspondence, and, therefore, it suffers from all of the limitations of the correspondence theory of truth insofar as it fails to take concealment into consideration as fundamental to its own possibility.

But all this is merely an assertion of conclusions. Before one can grasp limitations and look for an alternative one must understand what the correspondence theory of truth is all about. The classic definition of truth as correspondence is offered by Edgar Brightman:[9] "... we ordinarily mean to assert that a true judgment is one that describes or refers to a state of affairs that is as described. In other words, a true judgment is one that corresponds to reality."[10] Truth is concerned with *adequatio intellectus et re*, i.e., the

---

[8] See Descartes, Meditation 4 of *Meditations on First Philosophy*.

[9] Brightman's work is far earlier than A.J. Ayer's *Language, Truth and Logic* published in 1946.

[10] Edgar S. Brightman, *An Introduction to Philosophy* (New York: Henry Holt and Company, 1935), pp. 34-35. Brightman is well aware of the limitations of this definition, for he already observed: "What, then, is truth? This question, as we ask it, does not mean, What is the whole truth about things? Nor does it mean to imply the skepticism of a scornful Pilate. It means simply, How shall we define the word *true*? Sometimes, evidently, we denote by it the moral quality of loyalty, or of honesty, or of veracity. Logic is interested in the term, not as applied to the character of persons, but as applied to judgments" (*ibid.*, p. 34).

correspondence between intellect and "what is." The correspondence theory of truth leads to the issue of verification at that point when one raises the question: How do I know that my judgment (intellect) in fact does correspond to reality (what is)? How do I verify the truth of my judgments?

Brightman proceeds to investigate ten criteria for verifying the true correspondence of a judgment to that to which it refers: instinct, custom, tradition, *consensus gentium*, feeling, sense experience, intuition, correspondence, pragmatism, and coherence. The first seven of these criteria, however appealing and no matter how often employed, simply do not offer assurance of the truth of one's judgments, because they are inconsistent, self-contradictory, too limited,[11] or, as with the case of intuitions, they offer no way of distinguishing among them which are true from which are false.

The crucial dilemma that surfaces with the correspondence theory of truth, however, is the very issue of correspondence. What is corresponding to what? One might think that a mental judgment, for example, is corresponding to some physical state of affairs. But, as has become clear already with the notion of sociological paradigms, there is no immediate access to anything external to the mind. In the case of the correspondence of a judgment to a physical object, what is being compared is one kind of mental data with another kind: a judgment with a product of the imagination, for the physical object can only be imaged in the mind.

> If the reality of things were accessible to me, in the same sense as are ideas, and knowledge of reality were thus immediately certain, in the same sense as are ideas, we should then already be in possession of a true knowledge of reality, and we could easily adjust our ideas to it. But if all that we have is our experience, *it is impossible for us to compare ideas, which are part of experience, with any reality other than our experience. We cannot compare ideas with things. We can only compare ideas with other ideas or experiences.*[12]

Since mental experience (one should say simply experience) is what it is and cannot be other than what it is in any particular moment; since not everything that one experiences is true, e.g., not all of one's fantasies *correspond* to things or events that actually are or potentially could be; and, finally, since everything but one's mental experience can be other than the way it appears to be, there is nothing about correspondence in and of itself that certifies the truth of a judgment.

---

[11] For example, sense experience is unable to provide one with the truths of consciousness, for experience itself cannot be perceived by the senses. See Brightman, *Introduction to Philosophy*, pp. 43-46.
[12] Brightman, *Introduction to Philosophy*, p. 50.

Not even pragmatism offers a certification of truth. Even if one were to distinguish between humanistic,[13] experimental,[14] nominalistic,[15] and biological/instrumental[16] pragmatism:

> [w]hat is true from the humanistic standpoint (e.g., immortality) may be false from the nominalistic; for at no particular time in this world or in the world to come could one's idea of endless life lead one up to the particulars which it denotes. What is experimentally true might be biologically useless for adjustment ...
>
> It is also evident that untrue ideas may lead to results which, in the long run, appear to be practical. Christian Science and Roman Catholicism, for example, are both systems of belief that have led to practical results; yet both cannot be true at the same time unless the universe is a madhouse ...
>
> It is equally evident that some true ideas are not pragmatically verifiable in the nominalistic or the biological sense. If there be such a fact as self-consciousness, my idea about your self-consciousness can never lead to the concrete fact that is your self-consciousness.[17]

In short, "Pragmatism may include the untrue or exclude the true."[18]

> A philosophical criterion of truth must not be narrow in its range or limited to one class of truth only. It must be inclusive of all types of experience, all objects of knowledge and belief. To pick out one of the special sciences [e.g., biology as a form of pragmatic instrumentalism] as the source of the criterion of all truth is arbitrary procedure. If at one time biology is the fashionable science, at another it is physics,[19] or mathematics, or psychology; but philosophy [and theology] ought to be

---

[13] Humanistic pragmatism maintains that "what satisfies human nature as a whole is true" (Brightman, *Introduction to Philosophy*, p. 51). "Whatever fulfills my purposes, satisfies my desires, develops my life, is true" (Brightman, *ibid.*, p. 52).

[14] Experimental pragmatism maintains that "whatever can be experimentally verified is true; or, more simply still, What works is true." Brightman, *Introduction to Philosophy*, p. 52)

[15] Nominalistic pragmatism is a "sub-form of the experimental type." A nominalistic pragmatist says that "any idea is simply a prediction of certain expected, possible results. I say 'red-apple-in-orchard,' and mean that if I go to the orchard I shall see the red apple that I meant. These results are said by the nominalistic pragmatist always to be concrete particulars; nothing general, universal or abstract ... [U]niversals are mere names for the particulars to which they may lead ... This kind of pragmatism is closely affiliated with sense experience as a criterion [for the truth of one's judgments], for the particulars that we meet are mostly sense data" (Brightman, *Introduction to Philosophy*, pp. 52-53).

[16] For the biological/instrumental pragmatist "the pragmatic test is found in the function of thought in adapting the human organism to its environment" (Brightman, *Introduction to Philosophy*, p. 53). "Because it regards thought as an instrument of adjustment, this view is often called instrumentalism" (Brightman, *ibid.*, p. 54).

[17] Brightman, *Introduction to Philosophy*, pp. 55-56.

[18] Brightman, *Introduction to Philosophy*, p. 56.

[19] This is, of course, exactly what has happened. Evolution and adaptation have given way to Heisenberg's uncertainty principles and wave and particle theories as the favorite of critical theologians for seeking credibility for theological positions.

superior to the whims of fashion, and should allow no special science to usurp her rightful seat. Biology, as a special science, leaves many important facts out of account. It makes no attempt to prove or disprove the law of falling bodies, or the Pythagorean theorem, or the principles of democracy.[20]

Brightman concludes with respect to pragmatism by referring to Vaihinger, who "... points out the biological significance of our fundamental ideas, but is bold enough to assert that their biological utility is no proof of their truth; we must act and think, he holds, 'as if' these ideas were true, knowing all the while that they are only 'fictions.'"[21]

Brightman maintains that the sole criterion for a correspondence theory of truth is "coherence." Coherence, as was suggested in the discussion of Kuhn's notion of sociological paradigm, means "systematic consistency."[22] Hence, any judgment that one makes must conform to the "law of contradiction"[23] and the "law of identity."[24] "Whatever conforms to the laws of contradiction and identity, then, is said to be self-consistent, capable, as the Latin means, of standing together."[25] But not all self-consistent propositions are true.[26] Such a criterion might only give one "a welter of confusion, a chaos without rime or reason"[27] with the only virtue that the individual elements don't contradict one another.[28] Therefore, one must add to the criterion of coherence, in addition to the laws of contradiction and identity, the compatibility of one's judgment with all else that one knows to be true:

> Any judgment is true, if it is both self-consistent and coherently connected with our *system of judgments as a whole*. Thus the working test of truth is our maximum

---

[20] Brightman, *Introduction to Philosophy*, p. 57.
[21] Brightman, *Introduction to Philosophy*, p. 58.
[22] See Brightman, *Introduction to Philosophy*, p. 59.
[23] The law of contradiction states: "a thing cannot both be and not be at the same time." See Brightman, *Introduction to Philosophy*, p. 59. Notice the presupposition of "time" by this "law." The next chapter will indicate the aporetic character of time.
[24] The law of identity states: "whatever you are talking about, you must mean that and not something else." Brightman, *Introduction to Philosophy*, p. 59. The law of identity is also dependent on the presupposition of time which is aporetic.
[25] Brightman, *Introduction to Philosophy*, p. 59.
[26] This is an insight already observed by Plotinus. See Plotinus, "Beauty" in *The Essential Plotinus*, p. 35: "There may be accord [coherence], even complete agreement, where there is nothing particularly estimable: the idea that 'temperance is folly' fits in with the idea that 'justice is naïve generosity"; the accord is perfect."
[27] Brightman, *Introduction to Philosophy*, p. 60.
[28] Habermas warns of the danger of "systematic distortion" where coherence conceals rather than illuminates. See Jürgen Habermas, "On Systematically Distorted Communication," pp. 205-218. See, as well, Ricoeur, *Time and Narrative*, vol. 3, pp. 225-227, and Tracy, *The Analogical Imagination*, pp. 345 and 366, n. 21.

coherent system of judgments; by "maximum" is meant including in the most coherent way the whole range of our judgments about experience. Yet this "working test" is not static, for the system needs revisions in the interests of improved coherence ...[29] (emphasis added)

Hence, the correspondence theory of truth must include the notion of "self-correction" given the limitations of even comprehensive systems with respect to coherence. Coherence alone, systematic consistency, does not guarantee truth. This means that even with the best of scenarios there is a circularity to truth as correspondence, for what one takes to be true must be coherent with what one already holds to be true. But wasn't the task to find a criterion or set of criteria to establish what is true in the first place? What this circularity means is that one holds a coherent set of *convictions* that serve as the litmus test for the embracing of new *convictions*. At its best, then, the correspondence theory of truth is a circular wager of faith.

A very pragmatic consequence of the limitation to the correspondence theory of truth is that one may experience consistent verification of a falsehood. One can live one's whole life convinced of the truth that "all swans are white" so long as one never encounters a black swan. How is one to know that one's most cherished truths are not equally capable of an instance of contradiction? Simply because a judgment is "verified" (remembering, of course, that, even then, the verification is always the comparison of two kinds of mental data) 999,999 times does not make it true when it is contradicted on the 1,000,000th time. But one cannot begin to subject all one's convictions to such an endless process of verification. One returns to some version of pragmatic confirmation, but now with the understanding that there are dramatic limitations to such pragmatic confirmation challenging one's confidence in the absolute certainty of the truth of one's judgments.

The correspondence theory of truth in its version of verification confronts a dual limitation: 1) it is, at best, circular; and 2) it can only give one tentative confidence with respect to the truth of one's judgments. It is because of the second limitation that attempts were made to shore up the correspondence theory of truth by turning to falsification rather than verification.

---

[29] Brightman, *Introduction to Philosophy*, pp. 61-62. It sounds like Brightman is anticipating Thomas Kuhn's notion of paradigm revolution when he suggests: "We are right in accepting any judgment as the best truth, i.e., the best account of reality as it is, that we can get, if it is not contradicted by any judgment in the system we accept as true, and we are able to find connections between it and the rest of truth: - the more connections, the better. It often happens, however, that an entire system of old truth has to be revised in the interests of new fact ..." (Brightman, *Introduction to Philosophy*, p. 62).

Here the goal was to establish what would count as a falsification of one's judgment rather than merely seek what verifies the judgment.[30]

Two important naive presuppositions were made in the process: 1) it was assumed that judgments correspond to empirical states of affairs; and 2)

---

[30] For a discussion of falsification in general and the issues it has raised for theology, see the conversation among Antony Flew, R.M. Hare, and Basil Mitchell with comments by I.M. Crombie in "Theology and Falsification" in Antony Flew and Alasdair MacIntyre, *New Essays in Philosophical Theology* (New York: The Macmillan Company, 1964), pp. 96-130; Basil Mitchell, ed., *The Philosophy of Religion* (Oxford: Oxford University Press, 1971), which commences with a reprint of the Flew, Hare, Mitchell discussion; and Alastair McKinnon, *Falsification and Belief* (The Hague: Mouton, 1970), and David Tracy's discussion in *Blessed Rage for Order*, pp. 120-124.

Tracy's strategy for responding to the inadequacies of verification and falsification is to turn to Ian Ramsey's *Religious Language: An Empirical Placing of Theological Phrases* (New York: Macmillan, 1963) to establish the "empirical place" of religious language as those situations that involve "odd personal discernment," "total commitment," and "universal significance." See Tracy, *Blessed Rage for Order*, pp. 121-123. The logic of religious language is meant not to describe the world but to express attitudes and behaviors in that world. See, *ibid.*, p. 121. This represents a shift from logical verification to pragmatic action: what is the use and function of religious language, what kinds of commitments and actions does it involve? Tracy, of course, is not satisfied with just any kind of odd discernment, total commitment, or claim for universal significance, for such could lead to illusions if not delusions. He turns to Frederick Ferré's work to suggest that "[i]f such language is not merely logically odd but also internally incoherent, it should be revised" (*ibid.*, p. 123). For Tracy, the key here is that proper religious language "... does not present a new, a supernatural world wherein we may escape the only world we know or wish to know. Rather that language re-presents our always threatened basic confidence and trust in the very meaningfulness of even our most cherished and most noble enterprises, science, morality and culture. *That language discloses the reassurance needed that the final reality of our lives is in fact trustworthy* (*ibid.*, p. 135). (emphasis added) The turn to the pragmatic performative character of religious language offers Tracy an empirical location for talking about that language as distinct from other language games.

The present project would not question the phenomenological legitimacy of such a linguistic turn to performative language. What it would question is its sufficiency. Without speaking, in addition, of the aporiai of intellect and world, of the sociolinguistic paradigms providing communities with a socially constructed reality (including judgments of causality), of the aporiai of language, particularly its *circularity* of understanding and the centrality of the figurative over the literal, the turn to performance can be misleading. Tracy's own turn to Process metaphysics as a way of legitimizing performative religious language is particularly suspect, because it fails to acknowledge the limits of analogy to human experience for "explaining" the universe and merely assumes that, having described the necessary conditions of possibility for transient human experience, one has given an account of an eternal order guaranteeing the trustworthiness and meaning of life.

An understanding of truth as disclosure and of the metaphorical nature of truth requires a retrieval of the aporetics of spirituality and the existential dynamic of faith as a process of *seeking*, not guaranteeing, understanding.

that a judgment that could not, at least in principle, be falsified was vacuous. Yet both presuppositions are questionable, for at its best correspondence involves the comparing of two different kinds of mental data, and simply because one cannot begin to either verify or falsify the mental experience of another does not make the other's experience meaningless. In short, the presupposition of falsification is not only that empirical confirmation for mental judgments is possible but that empirical criteria alone provide one with truth. In both cases, one's mental experience, i.e., experience whatsoever, is excluded from the realm of truth.

Truth as Disclosure: Metaphorical Truth

The three regions of aporiai already investigated in this project (intellect and world; logic and praxis; and language) have already indicated the paradoxical character of human experience. Truth is equally aporetic. At the heart of this aporia are the conclusions that emerge with an investigation into the inadequacies of the correspondence theory of truth. 1) Empirical verification and falsification are an illusion: a) they fail to acknowledge the role of consciousness in experience which by definition cannot be empirically verified or falsified and b) they fail to acknowledge that perception itself is not the comparing of a mental judgment with something physically real outside of the mind, for perception is merely the comparing of two different kinds of mental data: judgments and images. 2) Empirical verification and falsification are ultimately circular, for they depend upon the coherence of that which one already "knows" as a test of the truth of what one is discovering. There is nothing indubitable about the coherence of what one already "knows."

Coherence can be a matter of what is comfortable, and, surely, merely because something has not yet been contradicted is no absolute test that it cannot be contradicted at some future point. The correspondence theory of truth forgets that one does not really know what one thinks one "knows" - and this applies not only to sense perception but to the very universals upon which all judgments depend for their very formulation. The investigation of language indicated that universals themselves are simultaneously experienced as ectypal and archetypal, i.e., to the extent that they emerge out of one's experience a posteriori through the metaphorical activity of consciousness, they are ectypal; only to the extent that they are preserved and passed on in language, they are archetypal or a priori as far as we can establish from our experience although this minimal presence a priori does not exclude the possibility that they in fact are all a prior and archetypal.[31]

The questionable character of coherence, in addition, becomes particularly problematic, for example, when one learns from the aporia of logic and praxis that causality itself is relative to the coherence of one's sociological paradigm and not a matter of perception. It is not simply that one does not know what one thinks one knows, one, also, can't be absolutely confident of the causal explanation one offers for any particular experience.[32]

---

[31] Once one moves beyond this aporetic insight to question where the order in the "material" world comes from that is able to correspond to a "non-material" order in the mind, one has taken the step beyond experience to engage in speculation. It is not that such speculation is unjustified, but it is simply incapable of verification and is often accompanied by the employment of analogies based on experience as if the primary analogates out of experience were themselves somehow indubitable and absolute. In short, such speculation seeks an epistemic faith consisting of knowledge of things unseen when faith is more appropriately non-epistemic, i.e., an acknowledgment of the radicality of one's lack of knowledge.

[32] This insight has obvious consequences for any theological discussion of miracles. The critical theological response to miracles has usually taken some form of the following: given that God created the laws governing natural events, for Him (sic) to violate those laws would constitute God's violating His own order. Human beings might violate the laws they create, but God's violation of His laws would involve a capriciousness incompatible with God's nature. Since miracles by definition maintain that the laws of nature can be ignored by God, miracles are impossible.

Such critical theology presupposes, however, far more than it clarifies. Given that ultimate causal explanation is relative to a sociological paradigm, what is at stake in a discussion of miracles is nothing that one can know about God. Rather, it has everything to do with the adequacy of one's paradigm which one can never indubitably prove. One can, at best, argue for greater coherence, but, as this present discussion indicates, that is ultimately a circular argument. Once one acknowledges that ultimate causality is a human judgment, that all human judgments are relative to the paradigm they presuppose, and that no paradigm gives one immediate and indubitable access to the "correct" way, that things are, then it becomes clear that not merely miracles but all of experience is a wager of faith.

The legitimacy of one's embracing miracles would then need to turn to experience and not merely logic for its verification. All verification presupposes concealment. Hence, it could be argued that it is more legitimate to accept the surprise of possibility concealed by the actual acknowledging that, although not everything is possible, one cannot begin to know all that is actually possible in any given circumstance. But that would involve surrendering one's claim to know that there is a conscious intentionality behind the events of the world ...; which proves, of course, to be a very dubious claim when one allows oneself to see all of the suffering, exploitation, and injustice in the world.

Such a re-examination of miracle might lead one to agree with Schleiermacher, that there is only one miracle: life itself. See, Schleiermacher, *On Religion: Speeches to*

Calling the correspondence theory into question is not undertaken here in order to embrace vulgar skepticism in a Humean, Nietzschean, or Derridian sense. One's lack of access to absolute knowledge does not mean that one's experience is capricious and/or worthless. After all, there is a certain absoluteness to the knowledge that one does not know, which in turn, all too often, fuels the arrogance of vulgar skeptics. But absolutes and arrogance are not only foolish, they are dangerous. For they are blind to the consequences of taking their "truths" as absolutes, when they are in fact not absolute but ambiguous, suggestive, and creative, with the result that they insist on their own way and fail to acknowledge that there are other perspectives/voices than their own. If all one may hold onto are absolutes, then one can only hold onto negation and death. It is not naive optimism to observe that there is more to life than negation and death. Perhaps by paying attention to one's lack of knowledge and the dynamic metaphorical process by which one does dis-cover insights into experience, one can reign in arrogance if not avoid the follies and even dangers to which such arrogance leads one. But, then, the arrogant are blind to their own follies and rarely perceive the dangers until its too late ...

The more adequate understanding of truth is that of truth as disclosure rather than truth as correspondence. Disclosure includes concealment as inseparable from its very possibility. Since experience is radically dependent upon concealment in order for there to be an experience of something manifest, any theory of truth that only focuses on what is manifest will be truncated if not, as has been said, dangerously misleading.

There are two senses in which concealment is central to one's experience. The first is the obvious sense that, in order for one to focus one's attention on some thing, other things must be pushed into the background. Every foreground necessarily involves the concealment of its background. The truth of the foreground is inseparable, then, from that which is concealed in the background - something not always acknowledged by the correspondence theory of truth.[33]

Its Cultured Despisers, p. 88: "Miracle is simply the religious name for event. Every event, even the most natural and usual, becomes a miracle, as soon as the religious view of it can be the dominant." But, then, how can the rule be an exception ... If miracle means exception, then there is no miracle if every event is a miracle, unless one sees the aporetic character of event as a revealing and concealing of actuality and possibility which makes every particular event an exception - because of its uniqueness.

[33] See Paula Gunn Allen's discussion of the differences between Indian and white perceptions in "Kochinnenako in Academe: Three Approaches to Interpreting a Keres Indian Tale" in *The Sacred Hoop: Recovering the Feminine in American Indian Traditions* (Boston: Beacon Press, 1986), pp. 222-244. She suggests that for native Americans

But there is a second kind of concealment that is essential to experience. That is the concealment of the horizon of possibility in-forming all experience. To narrow truth down to correct judgments about what is actually manifest in experience is to ignore the conscious and pre-conscious possibilities in play in every experience. Truth, then, must address the negativity (though not an absolute negation) that is essential to every actual experience. In order for one to experience the actual world with its particular configuration of things and Others, there must be simultaneously a suppression of a range of possibilities, equally compatible with the limitations of one's actual situation, that are denied actualization, i.e., they are suppressed and concealed by what does/did happen. It would be an illusion, however, to assume that those suppressed and concealed possibilities simply ceased to be. They continue to be present in the subterranean regions of one's reality, and they can become manifest, if in a transformed way, at some later point. For everything has its possibilities, and the continued organic interaction by the self with the things and Others (persons) is possible only because the real possibilities of all the components in the situation are constantly brought into play.

The inadequacies of the correspondence theory of truth, then, are not limited to the fact that correspondence is always the correspondence between one kind of mental data and another; rather, correspondence is seeking to mix apples and pears in that it is assuming a direct correlation between that which cannot be other than what it is, one's mental life, and that which can be other than the way it appears to be, the realm of sense perception; but, in addition, all correspondence is radically dependent upon concealment.

Consciousness is nothing if not the process of seeking sameness and identity in difference. Meaning or the making sense of experience,[34] including texts, things, and Others, is concerned with what endures in the midst of the transiency of phenomena. Meaning is possible because of re-identification. Hence, all meaning is dependent upon a prior event, or process of events, that enables the emergence of identity out of multiplicity. Again, merely limiting truth to the correspondence of a judgment with that to which

---

(all?) neither the foreground nor the background is ever privileged as is the case with European culture's emphasis on individuals, competition, and power. Rather, for native Americans perception is an inclusive or unified field.

[34] The term "meaning" here is being used in a logical sense. Not all meaning involves a judgment of positive value. In this discussion, meaning is taken as "making sense of" some-thing/Other/self, and is not to be immediately equated with affirming or denying the "meaning," i.e., the value, of life.

it refers presupposes the prior process of establishing identity in difference. For one cannot begin to say that "the sunset is gorgeous" without some identity (re-identification, repetition) to "sunset" and "gorgeous." But, surely, truth cannot be restricted to something derivative. Truth must include that which makes it possible, i.e., the entire dynamic of concealing and revealing that enables the experience of identity in difference. Once again, the limits of the correspondence theory of truth are announced.

The issue of identity in difference confronts one with the radically metaphorical character of reality, for identity emerges in consciousness out of metaphorical tension. There is no other activity of consciousness that is comparable. As was suggested in the discussion of the aporiai of language, metaphor is tensional and can function only on the basis of the tension between an "is" and an "is not." Lack of identity, difference, becomes the occasion for dis-covering sameness and, perhaps in time, i.e., with repetition, a wager of identity. This is Paul Ricoeur's most venturesome hypothesis: that the categorial is generated by the very process that violates it.

The pertinent meaning can emerge only by exploiting and ultimately suppressing the impertinent. Hence, truth establishes the conditions for its own subversion, for concealment can always be exploited to create deception and one can exploit and suppress for selfish and destructive ends. *The defense against untruth is aporetically accomplished by being diligent about one's unknowing* not by being confident that one's possession of absolute truth.

Here is where the aporia of truth extends into praxis, for the aporia of truth consists in simultaneously knowing that one cannot not act and that all action involves concealment, exploitation, and suppression as it consists of manifestation, cultivation, and enrichment. Once again, one is confronted with a choice, but not a choice between correctness and incorrectness. Rather, the choice is between what Hume called vulgar and refined skepticism. Vulgar skepticism sees one condemned to untruth no matter what one does. Refined skepticism acknowledges, and seeks conscious awareness of, the unknowing, concealment, exploitation, and suppression constitutive of truth while wagering one's commitments in a manner that seeks to enhance the possibilities of oneself and others/Others by living in the awareness of one's debt to the actions and sufferings of those who have gone before, and by seeking to establish more just institutions for all.[35]

---

[35] This ethical agenda emerging out of the aporia of truth is indebted for its formulation to Paul Ricoeur's *Oneself as Another*. Here Ricoeur distinguishes between morality, concerned with norms, and ethics, concerned with aims (see *ibid.*, p. 170), and proceeds to structure the remainder of his comments as a response to his definition of "ethical inten-

When seeking criteria for one's actions, it is not inappropriate to recall here the criteria Ricoeur employs to ensure an appropriate reading of a text while acknowledging that there is no "correct" reading of a text: a poor reading is narrow and far fetched, while a good reading is congruent and a plenitude. These criteria can be seen as applying to all of one's experience, since experience is a mediated process of linguistic interpretation. What must be kept in mind with respect to the aporia of truth and praxis, however, is that success is never achieved on the basis merely of what is manifest and actual. Success only happens on the basis of what is concealed and possible.[36] Actuality (the text) establishes the parameters of possibility, which means that not all possibilities are realistically possible, but actuality only hints at the truth of experience. We are not able to make entirely conscious the possibilities which the actual limits.

Furthermore, as long as the focus of attention is merely upon correctness and even as long as the focus is merely upon understanding, the tendency is to conceal and to suppress the imperceptible, immaterial, the illimitable, and the immeasurable to the enhancement of what is perceptible, material, limited, and measurable. In short, as long as the focus is on correctness and understanding as an open-ended process of making sense out of things and others/Others, νοῦς or the intellect is presupposed and forgotten. Metaphorical truth draws one's attention to the process enabling the emergence of universals, but metaphorieal truth in turn presupposes the aporia of intellect (νοῦς) and world that is its condition of possibility. Hence, the aporia of truth as revealing and concealing extends beyond the tension between foreground and background and the tension between possibility and actuality to include the aporetic concealment of spirit in the mate-

---

tion:" "Let us define 'ethical intention' as *aiming at the 'good life' with and for others, in just institutions*" (*ibid.*, p. 172, emphasis in the original). Though he is clear that the "ethical intention" is indebted to the actions and sufferings of those who have gone before: "The ultimate equivocalness with respect to the status of the Other in the phenomenon of conscience is perhaps what needs to be preserved in the final analysis ... Although set on the plane of science, psychoanalysis concurs here with innumerable popular beliefs that the voices of our ancestors continue to make themselves heard among the living and in this way ensure, not only the transmission of wisdom, but its intimate personal reception at every stage. This dimension, which could be called *generational*, is an undeniable component of the phenomenon of injunction and, all the more so, of that of indebtedness" (*ibid.*, p. 353).

[36] Hence, one must temper Nietzsche's "Übermensch" with an awareness of one's radical "unknowing," i.e., faith. Great deeds involve more than determined resolution. They require informed acknowledgment of ambiguity.

rial world that is the condition of possibility for all experience. Ultimately, then, truth is spiritual, but not in the sense of some hocus-pocus revelation from some other dimension than that of experience in the world. Spiritual truth is radically rooted in the world and is concerned with the aporia of concealing and revealing that is experience.

The truth of disclosure or metaphorical truth is "higher" than *adequatio intellectus et re* or the correspondence theory of truth, not because metaphorical truth teaches absolute certainties, but because metaphorical truth illuminates more of reality than the correspondence theory of truth. For the correspondence theory of truth emphasizes the actual, the referent that is somehow accessible and "obvious," as it tends to elevate sense perception to serve as the model and primary analogate for truth claims. Yet the correspondence theory of truth, even if one adds the further criteria of coherence and non-contradiction, is riddled with presuppositions and is dependent upon a radical mis-*take*. For the correspondence theory of truth can only *take* what is actual into account.

How much reality is there to which one has not and cannot direct her/his attention? How much reality is there to which one, even in principle, has not and cannot direct her/his attention? For example, the possibilities that were inseparable from a past event (not to mention a present or a future event) are not, even in principle, entirely accessible to conscious attention. To be sure, a few are accessible, those which some chronicler happened to mention in addition to her/his description of what did, in fact, *actually* happen; or those few that one can raise to consciousness in the deliberation and calculations of a present moment in anticipation of the future. But those few are only a tantalizing remnant of all the possibilities that escape conscious attention. More often than not it is precisely those possibilities that remain concealed that had everything to do with whatever actually occurred in a past event or that will in fact come to pass in the future. Does not reality include these *concealed possibilities*? What kind of a world would it be were there no possibilities? Possibilities cannot only surprise; they can radically transform,[37] for they are surely higher than actuality.[38]

---

[37] In short, possibilities are the key to all redemption (which experience teaches can only be redemption in the/a world of both actuality and possibility).

[38] This is the key to Heidegger's ironic critique of Husserl's Phenomenology which was dependent upon describing noematic presence. Heidegger wrote at the end of section 7 of *Being and Time*, pp. 62-63: "Our comments on the preliminary conception of phenomenology have shown that what is essential in it does not lie in its *actuality* as a philosophical 'movement' ["Richtung"]. Higher than actuality stands *possibility*. We can understand phenomenology only by seizing upon it as a possibility."

Is there anything about the linguistic mediation of reality that would break open this truncated notion of truth while acknowledging the limited adequacy of this correspondence notion of truth? Is there anything about the linguistic mediation of reality that exposes the illusion of immediacy and the correspondence of one's judgments to it? Ricoeur's unequivocal response is: Yes, metaphor! Reality and, therefore, truth are metaphorical. Reality depends upon the re-description of metaphor in order to illuminate its possibilities. Aporetically, metaphor functions by exploiting the conventional (what is taken to be the literal) by saying "no" in order to illuminate a "yes." By calling into check direct description, metaphor discovers by setting free. One is thereby liberated from the tyranny of the literal in order to hear the higher truth of life that is a dynamic process of disclosure at the expense of concealment. This is not an understanding of truth that intentionally desires to conceal (and leave concealed). Nor is this a defense of a truth as unbridled speculation, for not all metaphors "fit."

Metaphor presupposes the prior mediation of language. It depends upon the "conventional meaning" in order for it to "twist" out the new meaning. Still further, metaphor is semantic, and, therefore, one has an accountability to its semantic event as a whole as well as to the "disposition," "genre," and "style" of the work in which the metaphor is embedded (and the "work" can be a life). Above all, metaphor is an event of discourse that seeks to illuminate the world. That world is not merely a solipsistic world, but a shared world. Metaphor, then, forces one not only to consider the aporia of truth, but takes one to the heart of the aporia of self and Other.

Ricoeur's metaphorical truth is tensional not steno. Perhaps this is the most distressing conclusion of a study of metaphor. For by defining truth as tensive rather than steno, one seems to be introducing a qualification to the universal character of truth. Steno language[39] by definition is universal. Everyone who uses the notion "π" in mathematics understands "exactly" the same thing.[40] Suggesting that reality is metaphorical and truth is tensive seems to be reintroducing a notion of Aristotelian aristocratic genius as the key to truth rather than the democratic universalism of the correspondence theory of truth. Does that mean that only a few have insight into the truth - if reality is non-steno?

The tensive theory of truth is no more aristocratic than the correspondence theory of truth. The illusion of democracy in the correspondence

---

[39] See Wheelwright, *Metaphor and Reality*, pp. 34-40.
[40] Though, truthfully, no two people ever understand in precisely the same way, because understanding concerns both possibility and actuality and each person's possibilities are unique to her/his actual context and experiences.

theory of truth is that it maintains in principle that all persons would form the same judgment with respect to a particular referent. In fact, however, not all persons have access to the referent. This is as true for political access as it is for educational and information access. Some persons will live their entire lives with no understanding of "π." A case can be easily made that it is the correspondence theory of truth, which is dependent upon privilege, where the tensive theory of truth requires the acknowledgment of concealment and, therefore, the acknowledgment of the worth of every person's experience. There is a universalism to tensive truth that is just as legitimate, if not more so, than the privileged universalism of the truth of correspondence.

Metaphorical truth as a truth of disclosure is a more adequate take on the notion of truth than the correspondence theory, because truth as disclosure takes into account the conditions of possibility for truth as correspondence. In addition, truth as disclosure accounts for the process of human understanding as the dynamic of projecting possibilities both mental and physical in a world that enables a judgment to correspond with a state of affairs in the first place. Hence, metaphorical truth or truth as disclosure does not deny all legitimacy to truth as correspondence. It contextualizes correspondence in a manner that both accounts for its appeal and its possibility in a way that enables one to accept the limitations of truth as correspondence as a virtue rather than a vice. For, again, higher than actuality is possibility. Yet both metaphorical truth and the truth of correspondence presuppose the spiritual truth of experience. Without the revealing and concealing that is central to the aporia of world and intellect there can be neither metaphorical truth nor the truth of correspondence.

On the Open-endedness of Understanding

There is no point at which the issue of truth claims become more problematic, complex, and crucial than when it comes to the reading/hearing of texts. Are texts true? Above all, how does one know whether one has made a truthful reading of a text? Are any and all readings legitimate? Yet, these issues are all the more significant when it is acknowledged, as with the aporia of logic and praxis and the aporiai of language above, that there is no experience that is not mediated by language in one form or another. Life is a text, and all understanding is a process of encountering the text.

Hermeneutic phenomenology has taken the encounter with a text to be the most illuminative means for indicating the activity of understanding and of the truth claims that emerge in that understanding. The encounter with a text becomes paradigmatic for illustrating the complex process of understanding in general. A text is in one sense an object in the world analogous to any object, be it a chair, the sun, or a lover. Yet a text is once removed from the objects and persons it is talking about. Hence, in reading the text, the reader is processing a linguistic object that is "about" objects and persons that cannot be literally present in the text.[41] S/he must rely on the "trustworthiness" of the author's account of the objects and persons about which the text is concerned, so that the reading of a text is itself a wager of faith even when the text is non-fiction. But when the text is fictional, then the trust is that the author seeks to illuminate some meaning that justifies the reader's time rather than that the author is giving a trustworthy account of how the things and persons in the story factually are.[42] In the encounter with a text, then, there are at least two levels of duplication involved (there are more levels of duplication if the text itself contains texts, i.e., quotes, stories, etc., from others): the author's representation of an actual (nonfictional) or a possibly actual (fictional) world; and the reader's representation of the text. Hence, reading involves a representation of a representation. Obviously, the question of truth emerges wherever there is a representation. Is the representation by the author a true account of the circumstances described? Just what constitutes a "true" account, for there is a truth to fiction just as there is a truth to factual claims. How can truth function in these two contexts so differently? But then, have I, as reader, understood correctly the author's representation? Or in the case of fiction, have I, as reader, understood properly the meaning the text was formulated to convey?

Truth is usually taken to be concerned with the "true account," the "correct reading," the "proper reading." Yet even a so-called "objective"

---

[41] This, however, is precisely what all experience is.

[42] Ricoeur speaks in this regard of "the pact of reading" or the "note of trust that counterbalances the violence concealed in the strategy of persuasion." Ricoeur, *Time and Narrative*, vol. 3, p. 162. He adds, "[t]he degree to which the narrator is reliable is one of the clauses of this reading pact. As for the reader's responsibility, it is another clause of the same pact.." (Ricoeur, *ibid.*, p. 163). The dilemma of the author is that s/he will ask "too much" of the reader. "At quite the other extreme from readers on the edge of boredom from following a work that is too didactic, whose instructions leave no room for creative activity, modern readers risk buckling under the load of an impossible task when they are asked to make up for this lack of readability fabricated by the author" (Ricoeur, *ibid.*, p. 169).

description is problematic concerning its truth claim(s), because there is no way to "get out" to that "object" to test whether the mental judgments concerning it are "correct."

If truth is concerned with the "correctness" or the "properness" of judgments about objects/persons, then there is no indubitable truth. This is clearly what the encounter with texts (even the most objectively descriptive texts) illustrates. The difficulties become exponentially more difficult when the text is talking about motivations and/or causality. For neither motivations nor ultimate causes are accessible to the senses. Every judgment of motivation and causality involves speculation.

Hermeneutic phenomenology not only helps with the specific task of attempting to understand a particular text but indicates the historical and linguistic character of that very understanding. The reading of a text is analogous to a dialogue. Contrary to the living dialogue, however, in the case of reading the "speaker" is no longer present in the dialogue. Her or his vocal pitch, gestures, and other non-verbal elements of communication are absent. In addition, the speaker's "world of immediate reference" (to be sure, a world of both actual things and potentialities) is also no longer part of the dialogue. Finally, the text or discourse is "fixed." Contrary to a living dialogue, the author (or speaker) cannot respond to the perplexities and ponderings of the reader or hearer. The rigidity of the text, then, is both a blessing and a curse. Since the text is "fixed discourse," there remains, on the one hand no ambiguity about precisely *what actually* was said. On the other hand, because the text is fixed, it can no longer adapt its discourse to the needs of the reader no longer immersed in the world of immediate reference of the original world of the utterance. What the possibilities of understanding were for the original audience of the utterance are lost to the actuality of the text. Rather, the horizon of possibilities for understanding the text have dramatically expanded to include the world (again, both actual and possible) of a reader/hearer far removed from that original world. This becomes particularly problematic, obviously, when a text consciously employs figurative language (though, as was shown above, since all reality is mediated, all language is figurative). In any event, the very structure of the situation of reading keeps the interpreter always on "this side of" the text,[43] that is, unable to probe the linguistic horizon of the author as would be the case in a living dialogue.

Since reading a text is analogous to discourse, however, the reader can appropriately assume that the text "makes sense" (*Sinn*). The reader must

---

[43] See Paul Ricoeur, "Biblical Hermeneutics," p. 82.

gather the meaning(s) (*Bedeutung(en)*) for which the text serves as a repository opening up a referent world of discourse. The world of the text at the time of writing, however, is no longer the world of reference at the time of reading. The world of the text now *includes*, in addition, the world (both actual and possible) of reference and application of the reader as well as the influences of the temporal gap between the text's original "now" and its "now" of being read. In the words of Paul Ricoeur:

> ... interpretation does not stop at a structuralist analysis of works, that is, at their immanent meaning [in contrast to de Saussure's internal linguistics] but ... aims at unfolding the sort of world that a work projects ... [The] hermeneutical implication of the distinction between meaning [the fixed sense of the text - *Sinn*] and reference [the meaning(s) dis-covered by the reader - *Bedeutung(en)*] becomes completely striking if we contrast it with the romantic conception of hermeneutics in which interpretation aimed at recovering the intention of an author *behind* the text. The Fregian distinction [between *Sinn* and *Bedeutung*] invites us rather to follow the movement which conveys meaning, that is, the movement of the internal structure of the work towards its reference, toward the sort of world which the work opens up *in front of* the text.[44]

Ricoeur adds in *The Rule of Metaphor*:

> The important point ... concerns what I ... call the production of meaning [le travail du sens]. It is the reader, in effect, who works out the connotations of the modifier that are likely to be meaningful ... No speaker ever completely exhausts *the connotative possibilities* of his (sic) words.[45] (emphasis added)

Later in *Time and Narrative* Ricoeur develops a threefold theory of mimesis in an attempt to describe the process of the production of meaning across the arch of the author's formulation (*con-figuration* of the already *pre-figured* mediations of language inherited by the author) and the reader's formulation (*re-figuration* of that which was initially *con-figured* by the author) consisting of the reader's application of the possibly inhabitable world of the work to her/his world of actualities and possibilities. Note, however, how the three mimetic moments are always and already linguistic, that is, they are concerned with mediated ("figured") experience and understanding. The author is no more in control of the meaning of her/his text than is the reader, for there is no primary, un-mediated or non-figured experience or language to which either can appeal. The author encounters an already "pre-figured"[46] world, which s/he then has "con-figured" by the writing of the

---

[44] Ricoeur, "Biblical Hermeneutics," p. 82.
[45] Ricoeur, *The Rule of Metaphor*, p. 95.
[46] See Ricoeur, *Time and Narrative*, vol. 1, pp. 53, 182.

work,[47] which is completed only when a reader "re-figures" the text through application to her/his world.[48]

Hans-Georg Gadamer describes the hermeneutical situation as not merely a reproductive event, but as a productive event in which new readings are different not superior or better:

> Not occasionally only, but always, the meaning of a text goes beyond its author. That is why *understanding is not merely a reproductive, but always a productive attitude as well*. Perhaps it is not correct to refer to this productive element in understanding as "superior understanding" ... Understanding is not, in fact, superior understanding, neither in the sense of superior knowledge of the subject because of clearer ideas, nor in the sense of fundamental superiority that the conscious has over the unconscious nature of creation. *It is enough to say that we understand in a different way, if we understand at all* [Es genügt zu sagen, daß man *anders* versteht, wenn man überhaupt versteht].[49] (emphasis added)

E.D. Hirsch suggests that any reading of a text which takes one beyond the search for the intention of the author either violates the "fundamental ethical maxim" for interpretation[50] or opens the floodgates of carelessness in reading and the worst form of relativity (subjective whim). However, Ricoeur warns equally against both the "affective fallacy" and the "intentional fallacy."[51] Rather than let a million flowers bloom, hermeneutic

---

[47] See Ricoeur, *Time and Narrative*, vol. 1, pp. 53, 182; *Time and Narrative*, vol. 2, pp. 10, 20, 27, and 164, n. 20.

[48] See Ricoeur, *Time and Narrative*, vol. 1, pp. 53 and *Time and Narrative*, vol. 2, pp. 10, 20, 27, and 164, n. 20.

[49] Gadamer, *Truth and Method*, p. 264.

[50] Hirsch reduces the hermeneutical options down to "original and anachronistic meaning" making the search for the author's intention a "fundamental ethical maxim for interpretation." See E.D. Hirsch, Jr., *The Aims of Interpretation* (Chicago: The University of Chicago Press, 1976), pp. 89f.

[51] See Paul Ricoeur, "Erzählung, Metapher und Interpretationstheorie," p. 250: "Die Intention des Autors wird nicht mehr unmittelbar weitergegeben, wie es die des Sprechers in einer aufrichtigen und direkten Rede sein will. Sie muß in einem mit der Bedeutung des Textes selber rekonstruiert werden ... Die Intention des Autors ist aufgrund ihrer Entfernung von seinem Text selber eine hermeneutische Frage geworden. Was die andere Subjektivität, die des Lesers betrifft, so ist sie insoweit das Werk der Lektüre und die Gabe des Textes, als sie der Träger der Erwartungen ist, mit denen dieser Leser den Text aufnimmt und rezipiert. Es ist also nicht mehr die Frage, die Hermeneutik durch den Primat der lesenden Subjektivität über den Text zu definieren, d.h. durch eine Rezeptionsästhetik. Es würde zu nichts dienen, eine 'intentional fallacy' durch eine 'affective fallacy' zu ersetzen. Sich verstehen bedeutet, sich *vor dem Text* zu verstehen und von ihm die Bedingungen eines Selbst zu erhalten, das ein anderes ist als das Ich, das sich an die Lektüre macht. Keine der beiden Subjektivitäten, weder die des Autors noch die des Lesers, ist also primär im Sinn einer ursprünglichen Gegenwärtigkeit seiner selbst für sich selbst."

phenomenology calls every reading to an accountability to the text. Gadamer reminds his reader "... that the goal of all communication and understanding is agreement concerning the object. Hence the task of hermeneutics has always been to establish agreement where it had failed to come about or been disturbed in some way."[52] He had observed earlier that

> [a]ll correct interpretation must be on guard against arbitrary fancies and the limitations imposed by imperceptible habits of thought and direct its gaze 'on the things themselves' (which, in the case of the literary critic, are meaningful texts, which themselves are again concerned with objects). It is clear that to let the object take over in this way is not a matter for the interpreter of a single decision, but is 'the first, last and constant task'. For it is necessary to keep one's gaze fixed on the thing throughout all the distractions that the interpreter will constantly experience in the process and which originate in himself.[53]

Ricoeur speaks of a "hermeneutical arc" demanding the reader's most strenuous attention.[54] Pursuing the analogy of dialogue, he suggests that the reader must concomitantly seek to understand the entire arc leading from the author's world to the reader's. Hence, one must seek to understand the author to the extent possible (though recognizing that the author's intention is beyond the reach of the reader as are most of the motivations and possibilities of the author, since all of them were not even clear to her/him at the time of writing). In addition, however one must seek to understand the

---

For further reference to the notion of the "affective fallacy," see Ricoeur, *Time and Narrative*, p. 171, n. 38, and David Tracy, *The Analogical Imagination*, pp. 118 and 143, n. 60.

See the discussion of the "intentional fallacy" and the "affective fallacy" by W.K. Wimsatt, Jr., and Monroe C. Beardsley in *The Verbal Icon*, pp. 3-39. I am indebted to David Tracy for this reference to Wimsatt and Beardsley in *The Analogical Imagination*, p. 143, n. 60. In the third essay in this volume Wimsatt argues against the "formalist fallacy," as well. Gadamer's version of the formalist fallacy, which he too rejects, is the central concern of *Truth and Method*, for Gadamer's title should more accurately read "Truth or Method." To the extent that one concentrates on "method" (or the technical criticisms of the "formalist fallacy" in Wimsatt's terms), one loses truth, for the formalist fallacy can only treat the text as actual and not possible resulting in the denial of the historical dynamic of understanding dependent upon revealing and concealing.

52 Gadamer, *Truth and Method*, p. 260.
53 Gadamer, *Truth and Method*, p. 236.
54 The "hermeneutical arc" was a central theme of a course entitled "Hermeneutical Problems in Contemporary Theology and Philosophy" offered by Professor Ricoeur in the Spring of 1970 at the Divinity School of the University of Chicago. For an analysis of this concept's significance in Ricoeur's work, see Sanford Schwartz, "Hermeneutics and the Productive Imagination: Paul Ricoeur in the 1970s" in *The Journal of Religion*, 63/3 (July, 1983), pp. 290-300.

original world of the text as well as those linguistic and structural meanings immanent to the text. Equally, one must be sensitive to what has happened to the text in the interval between writing and reading which requires that the reader engage in a quest for awareness of her/his presuppositions or prejudices inherited as a consequence of the temporal gap between the author and the text's original world/audience and the reader's. Finally, the reader must rigorously examine the influence of, and possibilities in, the new world of reference and application that the text now has in its new "present," the present now of reading.[55] The recognition of the presence and demands of the elements of this "hermeneutical arc" (developed more exhaustively in terms of the threefold theory of mimesis in *Time and Narrative*), functioning whenever one is reading a text (or hearing an address, looking at a work of art, attempting to makes sense of an event) increases one's awareness of both the complexity of the event of meaning (much less of truth claims) as well as the responsibilities challenging the reader rather than simplifying the task of interpretation by merely affirming that just any reading is adequate. One must avoid both the "intentional fallacy" and the "affective fallacy." A proper reading of the text, then, is one that is accountable to the text, i.e., congruent, but generative of "imaginative variations," i.e., evocative of a plenitude, informing the reader's possibilities for living in a space made possible by the acting and suffering of Others and one's self.

On the Historicality of Understanding

Although the 20th century did not discover the role of history, in, and the influence of historical contexts upon, human understanding,[56] the his-

---

[55] Gadamer speaks of this process of understanding across the "hermeneutical arc" as a process of "fusion of horizons." See Gadamer, *Truth and Method*, p. 258, 271-274. This is an unfortunate metaphor, however, for contrary to Gadamer's explicit formulations to the contrary, it implies that there can be a bridging of the gap between the author's/text's horizon of meaning and application and the reader's horizon of meaning and application.

[56] One might want to argue that at least implicit in Descartes' judgment, that perception is a series of mental judgments, one can find the shaping role of history and historical context on any and all understanding. Surely with Kant's distinction between "appearance" and "thing-in-itself" there can be no separation of historical context from the content of one's understanding. In theology Schleiermacher wrote already in the "Second Speech" in 1799: "History is not of value for religion, because it hastens or controls in any way the progress of humanity in its development, but because it is the greatest and most general revelation of the deepest and holiest. In this sense ... religion begins and ends with history" (Schleiermacher, *On Religion*, p. 80). Earlier he had written that true religion is not to be narrowly defined, but it has to do as much with the particular experiences of not only organizations but individuals as much as it does with inward unity: "... the

toricality of experience and understanding has become a central concern in this century as linguisticality and hermeneutics have emerged as pivotal for describing the human situation.

Martin Heidegger introduced the concept of historicality (*Geschichtlichkeit*) into the 20th century discussion in *Being and Time*.[57] Historicality is not concerned simply with the fact that humans have a past and can re-

---

whole circumference of religion is infinite, and is not to be comprehended under one form, but only under the sum total of all forms. It is infinite, not merely because any single religious organization has a limited horizon, and, not being able to embrace all, cannot believe that there is nothing beyond; but more particularly, because *everyone is a person by himself, and is only to be moved in his own way, so that for everyone the elements of religion have most characteristic differences*. Religion is infinite, not only because something new is ever being produced in time, by the endless relations both active and passive between different minds and the same limited matter; not only because the capacity for religion is never perfected, but is ever being developed anew, is ever being more beautifully produced, is ever entering deeper into the nature of man; but religion is infinite on all sides ... It is the very feeling of religion, and must therefore accompany everyone that (sic) really has religion. He (sic) must be conscious that *his religion is only part of the whole; that about the same circumstances there may be views and sentiments quite different from his, yet just as pious; and that there may be perceptions and feelings belonging to other modifications of religion, for which the sense may entirely fail him*" (*ibid.*, p. 54, emphasis added). It is the combination of historical multiplicity and inward unity that constitutes the true religious life according to Schleiermacher: "The whole religious life consists of two elements, that man (sic) surrender himself to the Universe and allow himself to be influenced by the side of it that is turned towards him is one part, and that he transplant this contact which is one definite feeling, within, and take it up into the inner unity of his life and being, is the other" (*ibid.*, p. 58). Hence, any debate about which has priority "the universal-objective" or "the particular-subjective" (or what Schleiermacher calls the "grammatical interpretation" and the "psychological interpretation"), which fails to take into account the radically historical character of religion, truncates Schleiermacher's entire project. Religion beings and ends with history. See James Duke, "Schleiermacher: On Hermeneutics" in Schleiermacher, *Hermeneutics: The Handwritten Manuscripts*, trans. by James Duke and Jack Forstman (Missoula: Scholars Press, 1977), pp. 1-14.

One would not want to ignore Hegel's work on the role of history in consciousness. See, for example, Georg Wilhelm Friedrich Hegel, *Phenomenology of Spirit*, trans. by A. V. Miller, (Oxford: Oxford University Press, 1977) and *Lectures On The Philosophy Of World History*.

Wilhelm Dilthey perhaps more than anyone distinguished between the natural sciences and the humanities on the basis of the role of history in understanding for the latter.

Finally, Nietzsche observed: "... 'das *Perspektivische* [ist] die Grundbedingung alles Lebens' (VII,4)" (Heidegger, *Nietzsche*, vol. 1, p. 244).

[57] See Heidegger, "Temporality and Historicality ("Zeitlichkeit und Geschichtlichkeit") in *Being and Time*, pp. 424-455.

member that past. Rather, historicality has far more to do with the inseparability of the human from its particular, temporal world of experience. Humanity is not some alien spiritual entity in a material container. Whatever alienation might mean, it cannot mean that the human belongs somewhere else than in the world. Of course, everything hinges, then, upon what is meant by "world." One has not begun to grasp the meaning of "world" if one thinks of the world as a the sum of actual things.

To represent the human as a mere thing among things not only conceals the non-material dimension of all of human experience (a crucial oversight in Heidegger's analysis even with his emphasis on concealed possibility). In addition, such a representation can (though Heidegger, to be sure, avoids this mistake) take humans to be a particular kind of thing somehow next to other things. A more adequate representation of the world is to "observe" that, far more than a mere collection of actual things, the world constitutes a horizon of possibility. Those possibilities are often, in fact, concealed by what is taken to be actuality. However, the individual human being is inseparable from the possibilities of her/his environment. S/he cannot even begin to be consciously aware of all of those possibilities much less actualize them all. Hence, human beings are involved in a truly dynamic if not volatile process of actualizing, and thereby simultaneously suppressing, possibilities both perceived and unperceived, both conscious and unconscious. What connects the individual to her/his world of things and Others, then, is the individual's horizon of possibilities - not mere actualities.

Focussing attention on the dynamic of possibility in every actual context illuminates the non-substantial and non-material "unity" that connects not only the individual to its present context but the non-substantial unity (temporality) that, in addition, connects the perceptible actual events of the future and the past with the present as a seamless horizon of possibility (emphasized by Heidegger) as well as with the non-perceptible, illimitable unity of consciousness/intellect ($νοῦς$) with its actual and potential contents (precisely what is overlooked by Heidegger's work). Yet, this "unity" is not univocal. All actuality is embedded in possibility (the "same"), but no two actual situations duplicate the same possibilities ("difference"). Historicality, then, has to do with this non-substantial unity of possibility to any and all experience that is the condition of possibility for there to be clocks which measure the passing of moments of "time." Focussing on what is quantifiable, including the measurement of moments, however, sells the human birthright of possibility by reducing all of perception down to the actual.

To be sure, the notion of historicality does not deny actuality, nor does it seek to ignore it. Rather, historicality is concerned to emphasize the paradoxical dynamic of actuality and possibility while elevating possibility to its rightful role in experience.

The term historicality insists that there is a historical character to consciousness. Historicality, however, does not mean history as a linear sequence or objective time-line. Such a linearity implies that there could/should be an ever greater objective description of events and even of consciousness itself as our knowledge improved. Coming to terms with our historicality as mere linearity would mean filling in the ignorance gaps on the time line of history both corporate and personal. The more proper notion of historicality, however, challenges the adequacy of understanding time as a mere linear sequence of actual events, and, therefore, denies the capability of such progressive knowledge. There can be no exhaustive grasp of possibility which is intimately related to, and inseparable from, actuality.

Furthermore, consciousness cannot rise objectively above historical events as a dis-interested observer. The human is rooted in the dynamic of actuality and possibility, embedded in history, and unable to escape its contextual placedness in time. This lived placedness in time influences all understanding and interpretation. An objective, totally transparent, absolute knowledge of any kind is an illusion either in fact or as a goal as Gadamer observes.

> Does the fact that one is set within various traditions mean really and primarily that one is subject to prejudices and limited in one's freedom? Is not, rather, all human existence, even the freest, limited and qualified in various ways? If this is true, then the idea of an absolute reason is impossible for historical humanity. Reason exists for us only in concrete, historical terms, i.e., it is not its own master, but remains constantly dependent on the given circumstances in which it operates.[58]

When reading a text, one is intimately connected with the text as its range of possible meanings emerges. The temporal distance is easily overlooked as those meanings emerge. Therefore, that temporal distance requires a hermeneutics of suspicion as much as a hermeneutics of restoration in the process of reading. But that temporal distance is not an ugly ditch in Lessing's sense. It is only such if one approaches the text in terms of its mere thingness and not as a repository of possible meaning for a reader. The reader is limited by the constraints of the encounter, but it is precisely those constraints that enable the encounter. As the horizon of possible meaning for the text shifts with the ever new contexts of its reading, so, too, does the text enable possible illuminations of meaning unactualizable in the original con-

---

[58] Gadamer, *Truth and Method*, p. 245.

text. The text can say more, but there is no guarantee that it will. It can be so bound to the particularities, the limiting actuality, of its original horizon that in time it says less. Nevertheless, it can speak at all only to the extent that it is "connected" to the present of the reader by a common horizon of possibility shared between the text and the reader.

Here one encounters the "double-edged quality of language"[59] which as the *pharmakon* of written language both poisons and heals. Plato wrote in the *Phaedrus*:

> ... when it came to writing Theuth said, 'Here, O king, is a branch of learning that will make the people of Egypt wiser and improve their memories; my discovery provides a recipe [*pharmakon*] for memory and wisdom.' But the king answered and said, 'O man full of arts, to one it is given to create the things of art, and to another to judge what measure of harm and of profit they have for those that shall employ them. And so it is that you, by reason of your tender regard for the writing that is your offspring, have declared the very opposite of its true effect. If men learn this, it will implant forgetfulness in their souls; they will cease to exercise memory because they rely on that which is written, calling things to remembrance no longer from within themselves, but by means of external marks. What you have discovered is a recipe [*pharmakon*] not for memory, but for reminder. And it is no true wisdom that you offer your disciples, but only its semblance, for by telling them of many things without teaching them you will make them seem to know much, while for the most part they know nothing, and as men filled, not with wisdom, but with the conceit of wisdom, they will be a burden to their fellows.'[60]

Jacques Derrida observes from his analysis of this passage:

> The disappearance of truth as presence, the withdrawal of the present origin of presence, is the condition of all (manifestation of) truth. Nontruth is the truth. Nonpresence is presence. Differance, the disappearance of any originary presence, is *at once* the condition of possibility *and* the condition of impossibility of truth.[61]

I prefer to say that nontruth is the condition of possibility of truth, nonpresence is the condition of possibility of presence, in order to avoid sug-

---

[59] Patricia Cox Miller, "In Praise of Nonsense" in A.H. Armstrong, ed., *Classical Mediterranean Spirituality: Egyptian, Greek, Roman* (New York: Crossroad Press, 1986), p. 492.

[60] Plato, *Phaedrus*, 274e - 275b.

[61] Jacques Derrida, "Plato's Pharmacy" in *Dissemination*, p. 168. I would take exception with Derrida here, however. It is not that nontruth is the truth, but that nontruth is the condition of possibility for truth while truth is the condition of possibility for nontruth. This insight is perhaps even preserved in the oxymoron of *demma daqqa* in I Kings 19:12 (and found only in Psalm 107:29 and Job 4:15 but in reference to the Elijah story). This unique theophany account in the Elijah cycle can mean both "a voice of gentle stillness" (silence) or a "roaring thunderous sound" (sound). See J. Lust, "A Gentle Breeze or a Roaring Thunderous Sound?. Elijah at Horeb. 1 Kings xix 12" in *Vetus Testamentum*, 25 (1975), 110-115.

gesting that the manifest be taken as subordinate to the non-manifest. Nevertheless, this paradox of language, above all, points to our radical dependence upon what is concealed as much as, if not more than, what is revealed. The value of Derrida's formulation is that it shocks one out of one's everydayness which prioritizes the unconcealed over the concealed. But this does not lead to a grounding in either a metaphysically concealed, i.e., the Logos, or a metaphysically revealed, i.e., empiricism. Hence, a text is never absolutely transparent and clear. It is transparent, if at all, only to the extent that it is read exclusively as actual, hence, only by a reading that is oblivious to its rootedness in a world of possibility. Knowing the text is no guarantee that the text has been understood. Understanding the text involves the projecting of the possibilities of the text on a world yet to be.

Language as the Mediator of Possibility

If Thomas Kuhn's analysis of paradigms does indicate how reality is a mediated, social construct and if that analysis does indicate the importance of the anomalous for initiating internal adjustments (if not a revolution) of any given paradigm, it does not adequately account for either the linguistic character of paradigm mediation or the continuous dynamic of internal transformation of a paradigm as a consequence of its temporality. In short, while Kuhn suggests that the anomalous is the cause of change in a paradigm, paradigms are more stable for him than dynamic.[62] On the other hand, turning to the role of language as the medium enabling paradigm development and to the centrality of historicality enabling human understanding permits observation of the intricate and incessant dynamism of paradigms even in the absence of the "threateningly" anomalous.

Hans-Georg Gadamer is concerned with raising to conscious attention this incessant dynamism of human understanding. Gadamer indicates that his notion of hermeneutical experience is dependent upon Heidegger's analysis of the "fore-structure of understanding" in *Being and Time*, though Gadamer observes that his own interest in pre-understanding is not limited to Heidegger's ontological concern for overcoming "scientific objectivity" as it is to underscore the role of historicality in understanding generally.[63]

---

[62] See, for example, Kuhn, *The Structure of Scientific Revolutions*, p. 64.
[63] See Gadamer, *Truth and Method*, p. 235. Much of what Heidegger and Gadamer have to say about the "fore-structure of understanding" (*ibid.*, p. 389) the "historicality" of understanding (*ibid.*, pp. 386, 388), as well as Gadamer's notions of "horizon" ("Lebenszusammenhang") (*ibid.*, p. 395), the "open-ended character of all understanding" (*ibid.*, pp. 38, 388, 389), and "application" (with its emphasis on the reader as the completer of

The Aporiai of Truth

Heidegger defines "understanding" as the process by which Dasein projects its possibilities before itself.[64] This is the key to the "fore-structure" of understanding, for, in order to project (a) possibility(ies), one must somehow already be in possession of them - even when, for the most part, one certainly does not have conscious possession of all of one's possibilities. This is why the question of an "authentic" projection of one's ownmost possibilities is *always* ambiguous, for even conscious possession of one's possibilities is no assurance that they constitute one's ownmost possibilities. They can just as well come from the "public They-world's" expectations and silent shapings of the individual as from the individual her/himself. Therefore,

---

the text) (*ibid.*, p. 363) and Heidegger's notion of "the giving" ("Schickung") (*ibid.*, p. 389), has already been anticipated by Eduard Spranger in "Zur Theorie des Verstehens und zur geisteswissenschaftlichen Psychologie," pp. 357-403.

Interestingly, Gadamer's initial footnote to Heidegger's analysis of the "fore-structure of understanding" is not to section 32 of *Being and Time* (i.e., pp. 188-195, especially p. 191 where Heidegger describes Dasein's "fore-having," "fore-sight," and "fore-conception" of understanding) but to page 359 (H312), which presupposes section 32, but where Heidegger clearly indicates the ontological focus of his concern with the "fore-structure of understanding:" "Dasein's *kind of Being* thus *demands* that any ontological Interpretation which sets itself the goal of exhibiting the phenomena in their primordiality, *should capture the Being of this entity, in spite of this entity's own tendency to cover things up*. Existential analysis, therefore, constantly has the character of *doing violence* [*Gewaltsamkeit*], whether to the claims of the everyday interpretation, or to its complacency and its tranquilized obviousness. While indeed this characteristic is specially distinctive of the ontology of Dasein, it belongs properly to any Interpretation, because *the understanding which develops in Interpretation has the structure of a projection* ... Where are ontological projects to get the evidence that their 'finds' are phenomenally appropriate? *Ontological Interpretation projects the entity presented to it upon the Being which is that entity's own, so as to conceptualize it with regard to its structure*" (Heidegger, *Being and Time*, p. 359). (partial emphasis added) Gadamer does eventually footnote to section 32, though not to the description of the "fore-structure of understanding" on page 191 of *Being and Time*, but to Heidegger's discussion of the hermeneutical circle on pages 194-195 of *ibid.*: "... *if we see this circle as a vicious one and look out for ways of avoiding it, even if we just 'sense' it as an inevitable imperfection*, then the act of understanding has been misunderstood from the ground up ... If the basic conditions which make interpretation possible are to be fulfilled, this must rather be done by not failing to recognize beforehand the essential conditions under which it can be performed. *What is decisive is not to get out of the circle but to come into it in the right way* ... In the circle is hidden a positive possibility of the most primordial kind of knowing. To be sure, we genuinely take hold of this possibility only when, in our interpretation, we have understood that our first, last, and constant task is never to allow our fore-having, fore-sight, and fore-conception to be presented to us by fancies and popular conceptions, but rather to make the scientific theme secure by working out these fore-structures in terms of the things themselves." (partial emphasis added)

[64] See *Being and Time*, pp. 188-189.

If the Being of Dasein is essentially potentiality-for-Being [i.e., possibility], if it is Being-free for its ownmost possibilities, and if, in every case, it exists only in freedom for these possibilities or in lack of freedom for them, can ontological Interpretation do anything else than base itself on *ontical possibilities* - ways of potentiality-for-Being - and project these possibilities upon *their ontological possibilities*? And if, for the most part, Dasein interprets itself in terms of its lostness in concerning itself with the 'world', does not the appropriate way of disclosure for such an entity lie in determining the ontico-existentiell possibilities ... and then providing an existential analysis grounded upon these possibilities? *In that case, will not the violence of this projection amount to freeing Dasein's undisguised phenomenal content?*[65]

This passage from Heidegger indicates both *the content* of Heidegger's concern for understanding as the "projection of possibilities,"[66] and *the focus* by Heidegger on the ontological Being-question (i.e., possibilities) in general. It is this content and focus which leads Heidegger to underscore the circular structure of all understanding precisely because *the activity of projecting of one's possibilities requires that one somehow already be in "possession" of them before one can project them.* This "possession" is hardly a conscious possession because of the complexities of one's horizon of possibilities which can only be concealed by one's actual circumstances.[67] (Oh, that we knew all of the possibilities in any single moment. Or would we really like to know all of them all of the time?) Despite this limitation of one's awareness of those possibilities which one always and already "is," ontological authenticity is dependent upon the individual's wrestling with the ambiguity of the projection of one's possibilities with respect to taking ownership of them as one's own.

Gadamer's concern with the circular structure of the projection of possibilities, on the other hand, is more specifically concerned with the under-

---

[65] Heidegger, *Being and Time*, p. 360.
[66] See Heidegger, *Being and Time*, pp. 188-189.
[67] An important essay by Alfonso García Marqués, "Der Begriff von 'Möglichkeit' nach 'Metaphysik' IX,3-4" in *Philosophisches Jahrbuch* 100/2 (1993), pp. 357-365, points out that Aristotle understood "possibility" as always tied to "capacity" (Vermögen). See *ibid.*, p. 358. "Impossibility" has to do with a lack of capacity. See *ibid.*, p. 358. This means that "in reality we don't encounter possibilities and impossibilities, but acts and potencies (capacities)" ["In der Realität stoßen wir nicht auf Mögliches und Unmögliches, sondern auf Akte und Potenzen (Vermögen)"] (*ibid.*, p. 359). This insight has important consequences for understanding the relationship between actuality and possibility. It is not as if one's horizon of possibilities was limitless. Rather, one's possibilities are limited by the capacities of one's actual situation. The limit to possibilities is what ensures that the Other (as object(s) or person(s)) emerges as an Other to which one is accountable. If possibility was not limited by actuality, one would life in a solipsistic fantasy world.

standing of "texts" in the human sciences.[68] The aporetic moment here, however, is precisely the circularity. Thomas Kuhn indicates how the notion of an independent exogenous world accessible to all as an enduring sameness but interpreted differently, depending upon one's paradigm, is problematic, at best. The individual and community are always and already shaped by pre-understandings or a filtering process because of her/his and their paradigms which is as intimate as one's own and the community's possibilities.

Concretely, with respect to the activity of reading a text, one begins to understand a text at that point where the text connects up with the conscious understanding that one already possesses. What is this conscious understanding if not the projecting of possible meanings which one throws onto the text as one struggles to uncover the text's meaning (i.e., the text's possibilities). This projecting of possible meaning is continued so long as the text conforms to that meaning or until the text contradicts it. Hence, reading is a constant process of tentative wagering and revision because of the dynamic interplay between projected understanding and textual confirmation and/or resistance.

> A person who is trying to understand a text is always performing an act of projecting. He (sic) projects before himself a meaning for the text as a whole as soon as some initial meaning emerges in the text. Again, the latter emerges only because he is reading the text with particular expectations in regard to a certain meaning. The working out of this fore-project, which is constantly revised in terms of what emerges as he penetrates into the meaning, is understanding what is there.[69]

Hence, the emerging meaning of the text is inseparable from the task of clarifying one's presuppositions, one's horizon of meaning, brought to the text. And this clarification is accomplished by a dialectic of questioning and listening that is inseparable from the possibilities shaped by the actual text and those possibilities brought by the reader from her/his situation which shape her/his projection of meaning onto, in, and out of the text. If understanding is truly such a dynamic interchange, rather than a mere "reading off" of the "objective meaning" of the text, then understanding is as much an "unknowing" as it is a "knowing."

Gadamer speaks of "the famous Socratic docta ignorantia"[70] as "a radical negativity: the knowledge of not knowing."[71] Yet the unknowing informing Gadamer's notion of historicality in the human sciences is not simply a

---

[68] Gadamer, *Truth and Method*, p. 235.
[69] Gadamer, *Truth and Method*, p. 236.
[70] Gadamer, *Truth and Method*, p. 326.
[71] Gadamer, *Truth and Method*, p. 325.

Socratic unknowing. Socratic unknowing is concerned with the inability to establish definitions of universals that apply in every particular instance in which the universal properly occurs. It is his examination of those who thought they knew what they were talking about, or doing, (the politicians, artisans, and poets) that led him into trouble with his fellow citizens and eventually to his being charged with defaming the Gods and corrupting the youths of Athens. His defense at the trial consisted in his reporting how he tried to prove the Delphic Oracle incorrect when the oracle maintained that there was no one wiser than Socrates. What Socrates reported at the trial was that his inquiring of those who were either taken to be, or thought themselves, wise resulted in his establishing that they didn't know what they were talking about, because they could not define the universals upon which their wisdom consisted. This led Socrates to conclude that he was at least wiser in the sense, not that he knew more than they did, but that he knew that he didn't know what he thought he knew.[72]

However, the unknowing informing Gadamer's project is equally pervasive if no less crucial. It is not simply that all knowledge is dependent upon universals that are indefinable. In other words, it is not simply that all knowledge rests upon presuppositions that one cannot logically prove or define. What concerns Gadamer, in addition to Socratic unknowing, is that the task of interpretation, i.e., of understanding, is an open-ended project because the human condition is radically historical. *Unknowing is a consequence, then, not only of "internal" limitations but of "external" limitations, as well.* To be sure, acknowledgment of the limits of the external is not something new with Gadamer. One could say such limits are recognized already by Heraclitus with his famous aphorism about not being able to put one's foot in the same river twice. Though, it was Plato who reduced the "external" world to the dimension of "opinion."[73] Nevertheless, the novel emphasis of Heidegger and Gadamer with respect to the limits of the external is not that such skepticism turns one's attention "away from, and out of, the external world" to the "internal,"[74] but, rather, their appropriating those limits in a positive project on the basis of the inseparability of human experience from the world. Unknowing becomes the condition of possibility for an open-ended odyssey of understanding as a projecting of possibilities

---

[72] See Plato's *Apology*.
[73] See the line simile in Book VI of the *Republic*.
[74] This is, of course, the high ethical ideal of Platonism inherited from the Pythagorean ascetics and eventually manifesting itself in Christian martyriology, asceticism, and monasticism.

that acknowledges the integrity of self and Other while accepting that both the self and Other are transformed by the encounter.

There is no absolute knowledge with respect to a text (or an event, a work of art, a piece of music) much less with respect to another person. There is no return to some ideal "true" meaning of a text either as the intended meaning of its author or the "first" meaning of its original audience/readership. The circularity of human understanding reveals that understanding is inseparable from the possibilities of the individuals and communities involved. Those possibilities are never absolutely transparent or graspable by the individual or community. Hence, it is not merely that language is polyvalent, i.e., that there are no absolute or literal meanings to words. In other words, it is not merely that language is suggestive as it is descriptive. More importantly, there is no absolute knowledge because neither the author, nor the original audience/reader(s), nor the audience (reader) at a temporal distance can grasp or control the possibilities of the linguistic mediation. Language itself is no static medium. Language's dynamism is itself a reflection of the potentiality of words (the semiotic) and sentences (the semantic).[75] Implicit in Heidegger's analysis of Dasein in *Being and Time*, where Dasein is understood as inseparable from Being-in-the-world,[76] but now explicit in Gadamer's analysis of the role of historical situatedness in shaping any and all understanding, is the aporetic insight that the human is not in control of either "internal" meaning or "external" understanding.

> From this viewpoint the concept of the belongingness between subject and object is no longer seen as the teleological relation of the mind to the ontological structure of what exists, as this relation is conceived in metaphysics. Quite a different state of affairs follows from the fact that the hermeneutical experience is linguistic in nature, that there is converse between tradition and its interpreter. The fundamental thing here is that something is happening. Neither is the mind of the interpreter in control of what words of tradition reach him (sic), nor can one suitably describe what

---

[75] Ricoeur points out that the distinction between semiotics (signs) and semantics (sentence) was first made by Émile Benveniste, who "... introduces the distinction between the fundamental units of language and of discourse: the signs and the sentence respectively." Ricoeur, *The Rule of Metaphor*, p. 67.

[76] See Heidegger, *Being and Time*, pp. 78-86, particularly the discussion of Dasein's "facticity," p. 82: "Whenever Dasein is, it is a Fact; and the factuality of such a Fact is what we shall call Dasein's *"facticity"*. This is a definite way of Being [Seinsbestimmtheit], and it has a complicated structure which cannot even be grasped *as a problem* until Dasein's basic existential states have been worked out. The concept of "facticity" implies that an entity 'within-the-world' has Being-in-the-world in such a way that it can understand itself as bound up in its 'destiny' with the Being of those entities which it encounters within its own world."

happens here as the progressive knowledge of what exists, so that an infinite intellect would contain everything that could ever speak out of the whole of tradition. Seen from the point of view of the interpreter, 'event' means that he does not, as a knower, seek his object, 'discovering' by methodological means what was meant and what the situation actually was, if slightly hindered and affected by his own prejudices ...

For on the other side, that of the 'object', this event means the coming into play, the working itself out, of the context of tradition in its constantly new possibilities of significance and resonance, newly extended by the other person receiving it. In as much as the tradition is newly expressed in language, something comes into being that had not existed before and that exists from now on ... Whether what is handed down is a poetic work of art or tells us of a great event, in each case what is transmitted emerges newly into existence just as it presents itself. It is not being-in-itself that is increasingly revealed when Homer's *Iliad* or Alexander's *Indian Campaign* speaks to us in the new appropriation of tradition but, as in genuine conversation, *something emerges that is contained in neither of the partners by himself.*[77] (emphasis added)

It is this "something" contained in neither of the partners by him/herself, which nevertheless emerges in the event of understanding, that suggests the aporetic dimension of understanding mediated by linguistic systems. Neither the author nor the interpreter is in control of the meaning of the text. The problematic issue that emerges here is that of the limits to human freedom as a result of presuppositions, prejudices and meanings shaping one's understanding and over which one has no control:

In fact history does not belong to us, but we belong to it. Long before we understand ourselves through the process of self-examination, we understand ourselves in a self-evident way in the family, society and state in which we live. The focus of subjectivity is a distorting mirror. The self-awareness of the individual is only a flickering in the closed circuits of historical life. That is why the prejudices of the individual, far more than his judgments, constitute the historical reality of his being.[78]

Gadamer takes this situation to be a virtue not a vice. Why is this a virtue? Would we not be better off were we to have absolute knowledge of an exogenous world to which we simply had to "open our eyes" to see the truth? How can it be a virtue to live in the dark? Again, the stories of Socrates or of Jesus of Nazareth provide a possible answer. Clearly, in the case of Socrates, Plato explicitly states in the *Apology* that the consequence for Socrates of his unknowing was a call for the pursuit of virtue. The four cardinal virtues of the classic Greek world are: insight ($\phi\rho\acute{o}\nu\eta\sigma\iota\varsigma$), self-control ($\sigma\omega\phi\rho\sigma\sigma\acute{\nu}\nu\eta$), justice ($\delta\iota\kappa\alpha\iota\sigma\sigma\acute{\nu}\nu\eta$) and courage ($\grave{\alpha}\nu\delta\rho\varepsilon\acute{\iota}\alpha$).[79] The aporia, of

---

[77] Gadamer, *Truth and Method*, p. 419.
[78] Gadamer, *Truth and Method*, p. 245.
[79] See Pohlenz, *Die Stoa*, p. 126. "Der Phronesis ordnet er [Chrysipp (d. 208/204 BCE)] die Wohlberatenheit, Wohlüberlegenheit, Geistesgegenwart, praktische Klugheit,

course, is: how can one "pursue" something that one cannot know? The Socratic response is to present the alternative: what happens when one is certain that one does know? The voting citizens of Athens were certain that they knew that Socrates had defamed the gods and corrupted the youth of Athens - equivalent to a charge of high treason. On the basis of their certainty, they voted to execute Socrates. The alternative is clear: lack of knowledge leaves one in an open-ended search for understanding informed by the virtues; possession of knowledge leads one convinced of one's certain individual and communal wisdom and to destruction of the Other (either persons or the environment). There is a similar message in the crucifixion of Jesus of Nazareth. Jesus' story indicates that one lives and acts on faith not absolutes.[80] Those who possess absolutes are not only intolerant but destructive.

Gadamer articulates the virtue of the aporetic of understanding in terms of the prejudices/presuppositions functioning to make possible whatever understanding one can have, because *awareness that one's understanding is shaped by prejudices/presuppositions allows one to pay closer attention to the Other* in her/his/its otherness. Humanity is a questioning animal which is a testimony that there is an other/Other beyond the limitations of one's self:

> The hermeneutical task becomes automatically a questioning of things and is always in part determined by this. This places hermeneutical work on a firm basis. If a person is trying to understand something, he (sic) will not be able to rely from the start on his own chance previous ideas, missing as logically and stubbornly as possible the actual meaning of the text until the latter becomes so persistently audible that it breaks through the imagined understanding of it. Rather, a person trying to under-

---

Zielstrebigkeit und Gewandtheit im Auffinden der Mittel unter, der Sophrosyne Ordnungssinn, Anstand und die sittliche Scheu vor Tadel, der Tapferkeit Enthaltsmakeit, Festhalten an dem als recht Erkannten, Zuversichtlichkeit, Hochsinn, Mut und Tatkraft, der Gerechtigkeit endlich Frömmigkeit, Wohltätigkeit, Gemeinsinn und Verträglichkeit."

[80] This is, to be sure, not the only message found in the crucifixion. What the crucifixion, in addition, might mean depends entirely upon one's anthropology: whether one sees humanity as radically separated from God (Barth and the Neo-Orthodox) or intimately if not organically always and already united with God/Christ (Paul, John, Patristic theology, Eastern Orthodoxy, Christian monasticism, German Idealism, New England Puritanism and Transcendentalism, etc.). The former seeks in the crucifixion a sacrifice to remove sin; the latter seeks in the crucifixion a model of liberation from, if with a temporary reorientation within, the realm of the senses. What one must learn, however, is that one's anthropology is itself a matter of faith given the aporetic character of experience and understanding. Hence, the crucifixion offers no absolute conclusions. It can only raise questions. The human is an odyssey of faith ...

stand a text is prepared for it to tell him something. That is why a hermeneutically trained mind must be, from the start, sensitive to the text's quality of newness. But this kind of sensitivity involves neither 'neutrality' in the matter of the object nor the extinction of one's self, but the conscious assimilation of one's own fore-meanings and prejudices. *The important thing is to be aware of one's own bias, so that the text may present itself in all its newness and thus be able to assert its own truth against one's own fore-meanings.*[81] (emphasis added)

Ironically, awareness of one's prejudices/presuppositions permits the "newness" of the text (the Other) to be announced. Awareness of one's lack of knowledge enables one to listen.

This is why Gadamer can insist that it is the "object" or the "text" itself that governs the interpreting process. Such a claim seems to contradict common sense once one concludes that reality is a social construct mediated by a linguistic system. How can the "object" itself govern the interpreting process when everything that is experienced of it occurs in one's consciousness which itself is shaped by prejudices/presuppositions? This is the dilemma that confronted Thomas Kuhn with respect to the epistemological model since Descartes that claims we have access to an independent, exogenous world. Kuhn rejects such an understanding of interpretation, but has no alternative for it, as yet.

> ... is sensory experience fixed and neutral? Are theories simply man-made interpretations of given data? The epistemological viewpoint that has most often guided Western philosophy for three centuries dictates an immediate and unequivocal, Yes. In the absence of a developed alternative, I find it impossible to relinquish entirely that viewpoint. Yet it no longer functions effectively, and the attempts to make it do so through the introduction of a neutral language of observations now seem to me hopeless.[82]

One may not and cannot surrender the confidence in the integrity of something "external" to one's mental paradigm without succumbing to solipsism - although one has no direct access to that exogenous world. Gadamer points out that it is precisely awareness, that one's understanding is radically circular, that one's pre-understanding shapes what one is able to understand, which enables one to hear the Other as an Other, because it requires acknowledgment that one not blindly insist that one's understanding of the Other is absolutely correct. Precisely at that moment, the Other acquires her/his/its autonomous confirmation. The assumption of correctness can only result in one's missing the Other, perhaps entirely, because it refuses to allow the Other to be Other.

---

[81] Gadamer, *Truth and Method*, p. 238.
[82] Kuhn, *The Structure of Scientific Revolutions*, p. 126.

> If we examine the situation more closely ..., we find that meanings cannot be understood in an arbitrary way. Just as we cannot continually misunderstand the use of a word without its affecting the meaning of the whole, so we cannot hold blindly to our own fore-meaning of the thing if we would understand the meaning of another. Of course this does not mean that when we listen to someone or read a book we must forget all our fore-meanings concerning the content, and all our own ideas. All that is asked is that we remain open to the meaning of the other person or of the text. But this openness always includes our placing the other meaning in a relation with the whole of our own meanings or ourselves in a relation to it. Now it is the case that meanings represent a fluid variety of possibilities ..., but it is still not the case that ... everything is possible ... The hermeneutical task becomes automatically a questioning of things and is always in part determined by this.[83]

Hence, Gadamer can insist that "... the goal of all communication and understanding is agreement concerning the object,"[84] although now this agreement is enabled and informed by the aporia of the circularity of understanding.

What was once taken to be a straightforward activity, the reading of a text as a conversation in which one speaker is absent but whose words have been preserved, and what was once taken to be a process by which the intention of the absent speaker was presumed to govern the meaning of the preserved words, has now to be seen for what it truly is: an open-ended odyssey of enriching understanding, for understanding is radically historical.

> Not occasionally only, but always, the meaning of a text goes beyond its author. That is why understanding is not merely a reproductive, but always a productive attitude as well. Perhaps it is not correct to refer to this productive element in understanding as 'superior understanding'. For this phrase is ... the application of a principle of criticism from the age of the enlightenment on the basis of the aesthetics of genius. Understanding is not, in fact, superior understanding, neither in the sense of superior knowledge of the subject because of clearer ideas, nor in the sense of funda-

---

[83] Gadamer, *Truth and Method*, p. 238.
[84] Gadamer, *Truth and Method*, p. 260. Gadamer had written p. 236: "The point of Heidegger's hermeneutical thinking is not so much to prove that there is a circle as to show that this circle possesses an ontologically positive significance. The description as such will be obvious to every interpreter who knows what he (sic) is about. All correct interpretation must be on guard against arbitrary fancies and the limitations imposed by imperceptible habits of thought and direct its gaze 'on the things themselves' (which, in the case of the literary critic, are meaningful texts, which themselves are again concerned with objects). It is clear that to let the object take over in this way is not a matter for the interpreter of a single decision, but is 'the first, last and constant task'. For it is necessary to keep one's gaze fixed on the thing throughout all the distractions that the interpreter will constantly experience in the process and which originate in himself." See Ricoeur, *Time and Narrative*, III, p. 328, n. 41.

mental superiority that the conscious has over the unconscious nature of creation. It is enough to say that we understand in a different way, if we understand at all.[85]

Gadamer suggests that the temporal distance opened up by the writing of a text "is not something that must be overcome."[86] "In fact the important thing is to recognize the distance in time as a positive and productive possibility of understanding. It is not a yawning abyss, but is filled with the continuity of custom and tradition, in the light of what all that is handed down presents itself to us."[87]

Just as the circularity of understanding is appropriated as valuable and productive for allowing the Other to emerge out of a careful reading/listening suspicious of the pre-shaping of the text's possible meaning by the reader's pre-conscious prejudices/presuppositions, so, now, temporal distance between the text and its reader is seen to have a positive significance. This is not because temporal distance has brought a closure to the world of the text and its meaning, liberating it from the subjective influences of its original audience. Rather, temporal distance expands the horizon of the text to include the horizons of new readers/hearers informed by the events, readings, and transitions that have occurred over that temporal distance.

> True historical thinking must take account of its own historicality. Only then will it not chase the phantom of an historical object which is the object of progressive research, but learn to see in the object the counterpart of itself and hence understand both. The true historical object is not an object at all, but the unity of the one and the other, a relationship in which exist both the reality of history and the reality of historical understanding. A proper hermeneutics would have to demonstrate the effectivity of history within understanding itself. I shall refer to this as 'effective-history' [*Wirkungsgeschichte*]. Understanding is, essentially, an effective-historical relation.[88]

The static relationship between a reader and an absent or dead conversation partner has been transformed into a dynamic event. The horizon of meaning of the text is seen to be shifting just as the horizon of understanding of the hearer/reader is shifting.

> Just as the individual is never simply an individual, because he (sic) is always involved with others, so too the closed horizon that is supposed to enclose a culture is an abstraction. The historical movement of human life consists in the fact that it is never utterly bound to any one standpoint, and hence can never have a truly closed horizon. The horizon is, rather, something into which we move and that moves with

---

[85] Gadamer, *Truth and Method*, p. 264.
[86] Gadamer, *Truth and Method*, p. 264.
[87] Gadamer, *Truth and Method*, pp. 264-265.
[88] Gadamer, *Truth and Method*, p. 267.

> us. Horizons change for a person who is moving. Thus *the horizon of the past*, out of which all human life lives and which exists in the form of tradition, *is always in motion. It is not historical consciousness that first sets the surrounding horizon in motion. But in it this motion becomes aware of itself.*[89] (emphasis added)

Gadamer talks about "the one great horizon" that unites the present with the historical depths of the past. This "one great horizon" is nothing else but the horizon of possibilities out of which all actuality emerges. Recalling that Gadamer understands "prejudice" to be the projected possibilities of pre-understanding, he writes

> [w]hatever is being distinguished must be distinguished from something which, in turn, must be distinguished from it. Thus all distinguishing also makes visible that from which something is distinguished. We have described this above as the operation of prejudices. We started by saying that a hermeneutical situation is determined by the prejudices [the projected possibilities of one's pre-understanding] that we bring with us. They constitute, then, the horizon of a particular present, for they represent that beyond which it is impossible to see.[90]

One cannot see beyond one's possibilities of seeing, just as one cannot see all of those possibilities which make up one's present. It is precisely this horizon of possibilities which constitutes the "present" of a reader/hearer, and this horizon of possibilities is necessarily different from the horizon of possibilities out of which a text emerged (or the horizon of possibilities of any Other). Nevertheless, the separation that constitutes these distinct horizons of possibilities is itself possible because all understanding arises out of the process of projecting possibilities informing and illuminating one's world. The "one great horizon" of possibility enables the "fusion of horizons" between a text of the past and the present.

> Every encounter with tradition ... involves the experience of the tension between the text and the present. The hermeneutic task consists not in covering up this tension by attempting a naive assimilation but consciously bringing it out. This is why it is part of the hermeneutic approach to project an historical horizon that is different from the horizon of the present. Historical consciousness is aware of its own otherness and hence distinguishes the horizon of tradition from its own. On the other hand, it is itself ... only something laid over a continuing tradition, and hence it immediately recombines what it has distinguished in order, in the unity of the historical horizon that it thus acquires, to become again one with itself.[91]

It should be clear that Gadamer is no proponent of a naive "reader response criticism." Despite the fact that the author does not have control over

---

[89] Gadamer, *Truth and Method*, p. 271.
[90] Gadamer, *Truth and Method*, p. 272.
[91] Gadamer, *Truth and Method*, p. 273.

her/his words, despite the fact that the reader is not in control over her/his prejudices/presuppositions, despite the fact that understanding is an openended process as a result of the historical character of all understanding, Gadamer is not suggesting that just any and every reading of the text is appropriate. If one must avoid the "intentional fallacy," which maintains that the intention of the author governs the correct reading of the text, so must one avoid the "affective fallacy," which maintains that whatever the reader finds, or reads into, the text is valid. For example, Gadamer writes

> There is a polarity of familiarity and strangeness on which hermeneutic work is based: only that this polarity is not to be seen, psychologically, with Schleiermacher,[92] as the tension that conceals the mystery of individuality, but truly hermeneutically, ie (sic) in regard to what has been said: the language in which the text addresses us, the story that it tells us. Here too there is a tension. The place between strangeness and familiarity that a transmitted text has for us is that intermediate place between being an historically intended separate object and being part of a tradition. The true home of hermeneutics is in this intermediate area.[93]

Gadamer has insisted throughout his analysis that the "strangeness" of the text holds the interpreter accountable to it. "All that is asked is that we remain open to the meaning of the other person or of the text ... Now it is possible that meanings represent a fluid variety of possibilities ..., but it is still not the case that ... everything is possible ..."[94] Ricoeur takes a similar position by developing a parallelism to Beardsley's criteria for deciding if

---

[92] This refers to Schleiermacher's hermeneutics based on the goal of reconstruction of the mental experience of the text's author in an attempt to understand an author better than the author has understood her/himself. See Richard E. Palmer, *Hermeneutics: Interpretation Theory in Schleiermacher, Dilthey, Heidegger, and Gadamer* (Evanston: Northwestern University Press, 1969), p. 89. Does Schleiermacher owe this hermeneutical goal to Kant? See Kant's *Critique of Pure Reason*, B370: "I need only remark that it is by no means unusual, upon comparing the thoughts which an author has expressed in regard to his subject, whether in ordinary conversation or in writing, to find that we understand him better than he (sic) has understood himself. As he has not sufficiently determined his concept, he has sometimes spoken, or even thought, in opposition to his own intention." Kant's comment comes precisely in the context of his discussion of Plato. Since Schleiermacher produced an authoritative edition with thorough introductory commentaries of Plato's works, it would not come as a surprise where he to have been familiar with this statement from Kant concerning Plato.

[93] Gadamer, *Truth and Method*, pp. 262-263.

[94] Gadamer, *Truth and Method*, p. 238. See, as well, p. 236: "All correct interpretation must be on guard against arbitrary fancies and the limitations imposed by imperceptible habits of thought and direct its gaze 'on the things themselves' (which, in the case of the literary critic, are meaningful texts, which themselves are again concerned with objects)." See, in addition, p. 260: "... the goal of all communication and understanding is agreement concerning the object."

one has made a "good" reading of a text. A good reading, according to Beardsley, involves "congruence and plenitude," i.e., coherent accountability to the text and insightful suggestiveness. Ricoeur adds that a "poor" reading of a text as one that is "narrow and far fetched."

> We may summarize ... the analogy between the explication of a metaphoric statement and a literary work as a whole.
>
> In both cases the construction relies on the 'clues' contained in the text itself: a clue is a kind of index for a specific construction, both a set of permissions and a set of prohibitions; it excludes some unfitting constructions and allows some others which make more sense of the same words.
>
> Secondly, in both cases a construction may be said more probable than another, but not true. The most probable is that which (1) accounts for the greatest number of facts provided by the text, including potential connotations, and (2) offers a better qualitative convergence between the traits which it takes into account. A poor explication may be said to be narrow or farfetched.
>
> I agree here with Beardsley that a good explication satisfies two principles: that of congruence and that of plenitude ... The principle of plenitude ... reads: 'all the connotations that can fit are to be attached; the poem means all it can mean.'[95]

Such principles ensure that one listens to the text, but now this listening is seen to be in-formed by the aporetic ambiguities of the reading situation. There is nothing direct and immediate about the reading of a text. Yet the open-ended process of mediation is not an open invitation to unrestrained flights of speculative fancy. Even in light of the paradox of the hermeneutical circle, the reader has an accountability to listen to, and hear, the text which can only happen by acknowledging and attempting to clarify the presuppositions/prejudices that one brings to the text. Only then can the text emerge as an other/Other.

Here a second aporia emerges in the process of understanding. It is not merely that the hermeneutical circle paradoxically allows the other/Other to emerge for itself. In addition, texts and hearers/readers are properly understood not as static entities, encountered somehow ahistorically, but, as horizons of dynamic possibility in themselves united by a concealed horizon of possibility. *Unknowing is a consequence not only of "internal" limitations* (the inability to define universals) *but of "external" limitations* (the inability to arrive at absolute knowledge of the text/other). Aporetically, then, Gadamer observes

> ... the discovery of the true meaning of a text or a work of art is never finished; it is in fact an infinite process. Not only are fresh sources of error constantly excluded, so

---

[95] Paul Ricoeur, "Metaphor and the Main Problem of Hermeneutics" in *New Literary History* VI/1 (1974), p. 104.

that the true meaning has filtered out of it all kinds of things that obscure it, but there emerge continually new sources of understanding, which reveal unsuspected elements of meaning. The temporal distance which performs the filtering process is not a closed dimension, but is itself undergoing constant movement and extension. And with the negative side of the filtering process brought about by temporal distance there is also the positive side, namely the value it has for understanding. It not only lets those prejudices that are of a particular and limited nature die away, but causes those that bring about genuine understanding to emerge clearly as such.[96]

The virtue of presuppositions arises precisely as they enable one to permit the text to be its own horizon of possibilities while, aporetically, the text assists in clarifying and articulating those presuppositions of the reader/hearer which make for appropriate understanding of the text with the consequence that "... *something emerges that is contained in neither of the partners by himself* (sic)."[97] (emphasis added) Understanding, that which emerges as not contained in either of the partners by him/herself, is driven and sustained by a radical unknowing and unknowability. There can be no stronger formulation of an aporia. All understanding rests upon an unknowing that is simultaneously an internal and an external concealing-understanding enabling human possibilities in the world.

Hermeneutics and hermeneutic phenomenology, then, are not simply concerned with the narrow interpretation of texts. Hermeneutics is concerned with understanding: whether it be of a sunrise, rebuilding an engine, baking bread, building a life with a significant other, cleaning the toilet, jogging, reading, everything and anything. Understanding is rooted in the world. That world is a shared world, to be sure, but it is always the world of a specific individual. Possibilities are inseparable from the configuration of particular actualities, which both limit and enable possibilities by their capacities. The particular, however, is always the singular. This is why life is radically lonely. Yet, it is precisely because reality is more than the particulars of actuality, it is precisely because reality is a dynamic of actuality and possibility, the manifest and the concealed, that life is both individual and communal - not only because the mediation of the manifest and the concealed is accomplished only by means of a communal paradigm, but because possibilities are never merely particular although they are inseparable from a particular context. The individual's possibilities are inseparable from the possibilities of her/his historical context. Hence, the aporiai of language and, therefore, of hermeneutic understanding, are central to life. The circularity

---

[96] Gadamer, *Truth and Method*, p. 265-266.
[97] Gadamer, *Truth and Method*, p. 419.

of understanding which paradoxically not only permits, but requires, the emergence of the Other; the paradox that all understanding rests upon an internal and external unknowing that is dependent upon concealing and making manifest; the paradox that linguistic paradigms, mediating all experience, are neither static nor simply waiting for the anomalous to emerge, but are both stable and radically dynamic and constantly shifting - these insights of hermeneutics are not merely methodologically valuable. They are existentially essential, because the possibilities for an inhabitable world are at stake.

Aletheia and Symbolic Reality

The shift from the correspondence theory of truth, grounded in judgments, to the disclosure theory of truth, enabled by metaphor yet grounded in the aporia of νοῦς and world, coupled with the notion of human understanding as radically historical in the sense of an open-ended process of projecting of possibilities within the horizon of one's context of actuality, permits a rethinking of the meaning of truth encouraged by the etymology of the Greek word for truth: ἀλήθεια (aletheia) derived from the privative "α" plus λανθάνω (to conceal from someone). Etymologically, then, truth is an unconcealing or dis-closure, or metaphorically a bringing into the light of day.

On the basis of this etymology, Heidegger suggests that truth primordially has to do with the projecting of one's ownmost possibilities as authentic understanding.[98] For only such a self-conscious understanding of one's own possibilities can constitute real disclosure of one's context. Such disclosure of one's ownmost possibilities, such truth, is contrasted by Heidegger with "untruth," which in this case does not mean "lie," but one's "fallenness" into the everyday expectations and definitions of the self from the public "they-world," i.e., one's fallenness into inauthenticity.[99] Hence, the disclosedness of truth for Heidegger is not merely that things are manifest, but, rather, that the possibilities of those things are critically evaluated and owned by the individual. Therefore, Heidegger can write: "Truth (uncoveredness) is something that must always first be wrested from entities."[100]

> The goddess of Truth who guides Parmenides, puts two pathways before him, one of uncovering, one of hiding; but this signifies nothing else than that Dasein is already both in the truth and in untruth. The way of uncovering is achieved only in

---

[98] See Heidegger's discussion in *Being and Time*, p. 264f.
[99] See Heidegger, *Being and Time*, p. 264.
[100] Heidegger, *Being and Time*, p. 265.

κρίνειν λόγῳ - in distinguishing between these understandingly, and making one's decision for the one rather than the other.[101]

But one can now maintain that Heidegger's notions of truth and untruth are too narrowly confined to the individual's struggle with authenticity in the midst of inauthenticity, and that a turn to Ricoeur's notion of the metaphorical tension centered on the copula, i.e., the tension of the "is"/"is not," enables a more comprehensive understanding of ἀλήθεια.

It cannot be an accident, though surely long forgotten, that the etymology of the Greek term depends upon the tension between manifesting and concealing. Here there is an acknowledgment that concealment is equally constitutive of what is manifest in truth. This would be entirely compatible with all that has been said by Ricoeur about metaphorical truth. To be sure, such a dynamic at the heart of truth includes both the concealing of the background by every focussing of one's attention as well as the necessary dynamic of concealing and revealing that is the interplay between actuality and possibility. For what is manifest at any moment (and not merely what is apparent as the consequence of one's focussed attention) is the consequence of the negating and concealing of possibilities that cannot be manifest. The truth is always had at a price, and coming into truth in the broadest sense of the term means coming into the awareness of that price. This understanding of truth, then, is far more inclusive than the struggle by an individual to wrest her/his ownmost possibilities out of the givenness of one's world, for the individual's struggle presupposes this truth of concealing manifestation. Truth as ἀλήθεια is most adequately understood as metaphorical truth which conceals as it discloses, because it involves a "no" as it simultaneously is a "yes."

A further advantage of Ricoeur's metaphor theory is that it enables a re-engagement of the central role of the symbolic in human experience. In

---

[101] Heidegger, *Being and Time*, p. 265. Gadamer seems not to have grasped this point that truth is not merely the disclosure of some-*thing* but has to do with the wresting of its possibilities which alone uncovers what a thing truly is. For Gadamer seems to be satisfied merely with the "appearance itself" as primordial truth. See Gadamer, *Truth and Method*, pp. 439 and 443. Gadamer places his discussion of truth in the setting of the priority of the object which calls the interpreter to accountability (see *ibid.*, p. 441) which may account for his having forgotten the central concern of Heidegger that truth has to do with the possibilities of the object as much as with the fact of the object. Surely, however, the Heideggerian account of truth is entirely compatible with Gadamer's notion of *Wirkungsgeschichte* (effective history).

other contexts,[102] I have attempted to develop an alternative understanding of symbol independent of metaphysics. The classical notion of symbol is indebted to Platonic metaphysics, for it understands symbol to be a pointing from what is visible to what is invisible with the invisible providing the ultimate explanation of the visible.[103] A more recent attempt to resuscitate a notion of symbol was that of Paul Tillich's who claimed that, in contrast to signs, symbols participate in the reality of that to which they refer.[104] What was meant to provide a privileged status to symbols as the means for mediating Being on Tillich's part turns out to be incapable of distinguishing symbol from any other sign, for all of reality participates in Being. Tillich's attempt to distinguish between signs and symbols was surely indebted to Immanuel Kant who defines signs as in no way belonging to that which they represent in contrast to symbols which form an analogy connecting the visible and the invisible.[105]

Rather than distinguish signs from symbols on the basis of their separateness or connectedness to that which they point to, Gadamer offers a more helpful contrast:

> There is an obvious distinction between a symbol and a sign, in that the former is more like a picture. The representational function of a symbol is not merely to point to something that is not present [as does a sign]. Instead, a symbol manifests as present something that is really present.[106]

---

[102] See my doctoral dissertation "On the Soteriological Significance of the Symbol of the Kingdom of God in the Language of the Historical Jesus," pp. 72-186, and Douglas McGaughey, "Ricoeur's Metaphor and Narrative Theories as a Foundation for a Theory of Symbol" in *Religious Studies* 24 (1988), pp. 415-437.

[103] This is the meaning of symbol for Eliade. See Mircea Eliade, *The Myth of the Eternal Return* and *The Sacred and the Profane*.

[104] See Paul Tillich, *Systematic Theology*, vol. 1, p. 239.

[105] See Immanuel Kant, §59 "Von der Schönheit als Symbol der Sittlichkeit" in *Kritik der Urteilskraft* (Hamburg: Verlag von Felix Meiner, 1974), pp. 211-212. Gadamer pronounces Kant's insight that "symbolic representation does not present a concept directly ... but only indirectly" to be "one of the most brilliant results of Kantian thought," because "[h]e thus does justice to the theological truth that had found its scholastic form in the analogia entis and keeps human concepts separate from God." Gadamer, *Truth and Method*, p. 67. Kant had written: "... so ist alle unsere Erkenntnis von Gott bloß symbolisch [i.e., indirect and mediated representation], und der, welcher sie ... für schematisch [i.e., as direct and unmediated representation] nimmt, gerät in den Anthropomorphism ..." (Kant, *ibid*.., p. 213).

Gadamer had added (*op cit*, p. 67), parenthetically, that Kant had connected symbol and metaphor presumably on the assumption of the Aristotelian definition of metaphor as analogy, for nowhere in §59 does Kant explicitly refer to metaphor.

[106] Gadamer, *Truth and Method*, pp. 135-136.

To be sure, everything hinges upon what is meant by presenting "something that is really present."

Gadamer's discussion of signs and symbols occurs at that point in *Truth and Method* where he is attempting to retrieve a positive notion of allegory from its negative association with mythology and dogmatics.[107] His manner of argumentation is that "... there is a metaphysical background to the concept of symbol which is entirely lacking in the rhetorical use of allegory."[108] The metaphysical background of symbols enabled the 19th century to appeal to symbols as part of a theory of aesthetic genius, for symbols depend upon an idea which must be "recognized in some way or another"[109] in contrast to an allegory which was determined in advance by an exact meaning."[110] The "genius" recognizes the idea "as what can be interpreted inexhaustibly, because it is indefinite;"[111] where the rest of us merely memorize the meaning meant to be conveyed by the allegory, because allegory stands "in a more exact relation to meaning."[112] Gadamer's argument is that allegory and symbol must now be seen as relativized, because a symbol, "admitting various interpretations," "can no longer be characterized by its privative relation to the concept"[113] possessed by the genius. The genial vision of aesthetic consciousness can no longer be sharply distinguished from the dogmatics of the mythical.[114]

As important as Gadamer's pointing to the relativizing of symbol and allegory is, because of the crumbling distinction between aesthetic consciousness and mythology (for, this project would say, the consciousness of critical genius can no longer be seen as "superior to" mythology for both are forms of sociological paradigms), his analysis is most challenging and suggestive at that point where he equates symbol with metaphysics. By connecting symbol with the invisible metaphysical order of ideas, which was presumed to lead to a hierarchy of intellectual capacity leading from the ordinary individual to the genius, a wedge was driven between intellectuals and commoners, Gadamer maintains. But now "ideas" or universals must be seen to be relative to experience not to intellectual capacity. All consciousness is a metaphorical activity uniting of difference by means of the

---

[107] See Gadamer, *Truth and Method*, pp. 67 and 71.
[108] Gadamer, *Truth and Method*, p. 66.
[109] Gadamer, *Truth and Method*, p. 66.
[110] See Gadamer, *Truth and Method*, p. 67.
[111] Gadamer, *Truth and Method*, p. 67.
[112] Gadamer, *Truth and Method*, p. 67.
[113] Gadamer, *Truth and Method*, p. 72.
[114] See Gadamer, *Truth and Method*, p. 72.

identity enabled by metaphorical construal. The invisible realm of the intellect is no more the special preserve of the "genius" than the mythological world view is the consequence of an inferior stage of consciousness tied to particulars and unable to draw abstractions.

A new appreciation of signs and symbols as central to all conscious activity can now emerge. Signs are dead metaphors even as they point to that which is not present, e.g., the stop sign on the curve leading to an intersection, "π" for a mathematical number. What characterizes a sign can now be seen not in the sense that it doesn't participate in the reality of that to which it points, for reality is a mediated whole where none of the parts are separate from the others, rather *signs point to what is not present*. On the other hand, *symbols point to what is invisibly present*, i.e., the entire dimension of sense perception can be seen as symbolic. For everything experienced in the senses points beyond itself to the mediation of the intellect which is invisible. What is invisibly present in all sense experience is the spiritual or non-material dimension of consciousness. All material reality symbolically evokes the spiritual depths of experience. One does not have to be an intellectual genius to acknowledge the difference between the material and the non-material; one does not have to be an intellectual to recognize the spiritual depths and richness of one's own experience.

In addition, however, acknowledging the metaphorical character of signs and symbols liberates both signs and symbols from metaphysics, either of materialism or of idealism. The empirical or physical is exclusively experienced as mediated just as universals are exclusively experienced as mediated (both ectypally and archetypally). Signs and symbols are events of language and metaphorical tension with neither having a privileged status because of their rootedness in some indubitable ground. Signs and symbols evoke the profound truth of experience, because they are both rooted in, though evoke differently, the concealed of what is manifest.

Conclusion

The aporia of truth requires distinguishing between truth as correspondence and truth as disclosure. Truth as correspondence presupposes the truth of disclosure which is the condition of possibility for the former and not an alternative kind of truth. The privative of the term dis-closure indicates the aporetic moment of truth: un-covering is dependent upon a covering, the manifest is inseparable from the concealed. This is not simply a truism about experience, i.e., that every foreground conceals a background, but rather truth as disclosure draws unequivocal attention to the aporetic priority of possibility over actuality in experience. The truth of disclosure is foremost concerned with the role of possibilities in human experience and understanding. There is no experience without the manifesting of actuality as the actualization of some possibilities at the expense of others whose actualization then serves as the context limiting and enabling the emergence of new possibilities in an endless spiral of understanding projecting possibilities. This hermeneutical circle of possibilities and actuality is what experience is all about. Life is aporetically a limiting and negating that opens up possibilities and the positive. Life is truth.

This is nowhere more tantalizingly suggested than in the Greek word for truth: ἀλήθεια. Its composition out of the alpha privative and "concealing" suggests that truth is a simultaneous revealing and concealing. Far more adequately than Heidegger's limiting of truth and untruth to the struggle of the individual for authenticity in the midst of inauthenticity, the metaphorical truth of disclosure indicates how the aporetic dynamic of revealing and concealing is central to any and all experience. There is no emergence of actuality out of possibility without the simultaneous exclusion and suppression of other possibilities; just as their can be no focus of attention without the exclusion of the background. This is the truth of experience in general, and it serves as the presupposition for any wrestling with personal authenticity in particular.

Furthermore, the aporia of metaphorical truth permits a distinguishing between sign and symbol that acknowledges the figurative character of both. Signs are dead metaphors, for they are conventions that have sedimented out of earlier metaphorical insights. Equally metaphorical are symbols, which can be understood as metaphors functioning at the level of narrative if narrative is taken in the broadest sense of mimetic mediation. This would lead to an understanding of reality as radically symbolic, for all that is experienced with the senses is a pointing to something that is present yet absent from the senses themselves, i.e., consciousness, νοῦς.

Hence, the aporia of truth ultimately leads to a spiritual truth that is the condition of possibility for metaphorical truth which, in turn, is the condition of possibility for truth as correspondence. As dependent upon, and as inseparable from, the material as our experience surely is, focus upon both the emergence of universals and the process of understanding of others/Others tends to conceal the immaterial, imperceptible, illimited, and immeasurable character of experience itself. In other words, concern merely for universals either as ideas or as laws governing the material order conceals νοῦς which is where experience exclusively transpires. For this reason, the scientific mathematization of reality and concern for natural law has resulted in the loss of the spirit. It is νοῦς which must be re-covered, for it is the spiritual truth of νοῦς which provides an invaluable key for understanding the origin of religious experience and reflection as it informs Christian theology throughout the ages.

The aporia of the figurative character of language, i.e., metaphorical truth, leaves radically undecided whether or not universals are ectypal or archetypal upon which all truths of correspondence depend. Yet the theological significance of metaphorical truth is announced by the spiritual character of experience. Whether universals are ectypal or archetypal, whether one is using steno signs, or whether one is aware of the symbolic character of reality, universals, signs, and symbols, all indicate that experience is radically non-material, i.e., spiritual. What is important for theology to recover is not merely Law or Logos, but νοῦς. This is surely not overlooked by Paul, whose theological position is shaped neither by the Law nor by the Logos but by having the "mind" (νοῦς) of Christ (I Corinthians 2:16).

In addition, the dynamic of the concealed and revealed raises the speculative moment in theology: Whence the dynamic process of revealing and concealing in the first place? Whence the non-material order to which the material order appears to conform? The legitimacy of theology's speculative claims, however, is dependent upon how adequately the six aporiai are understood and taken into account with respect to their establishing the horizon of faith. This inquiry requires the engaging of reason both to insist on clarifying and maintaining the dialectical tensions of the aporiai constitutive of the human condition and to reign in unbridled speculation while it simultaneously acknowledges the necessity of faith as the non-ground of all reason and truth.

Chapter 11
The Aporiai of Temporality

A fifth aporia is concerned with temporality. Time is aporetic in at least three respects. The first is that time is both a linear sequence and a simultaneous whole.[1] Although time is experienced as a sequence of events with a "before" and an "after," there is always a simultaneity, an illimitable whole, to time uniting future, past, and present that is more than the whole of any one moment. The second aporia with respect to time is that of cosmological and phenomenological time.[2] In terms of the cosmological perspective, time is a mere sequence of "instants" in which the individual human being is cosmically insignificant. In terms of the phenomenological perspective, time has a "present" precisely because significance occurs with the individual human being. Yet a third aporia with respect to time is that all events in time depend upon the "pause" or "gap" of the "present."[3] Aporetically, the present is a not-Being which enables beings to be in time. It will be claimed, however, that the aporia of temporality is not to be confused with a tension between Eternity and time. Such a tension misrepresents temporality as a metaphysical phenomenon of actuality and fails to grasp the role of possibility in defining the temporal.

Clock Time and Eternity

Everyday understanding of time is concerned with measurement. Everyday time is a quantity of duration that one measures, for example, by means of a clock. What one is measuring is endurance, a stretch of time. Yet it is not time itself that endures. Rather, what endures is some-*thing in* time. What is being measured by the clock is not time itself but the motion of the internal components (some *things*) of the clock in terms of conventional intervals.

---

[1] This way of speaking of the aporia of time is central to the analysis of time by both Martin Heidegger and Paul Ricoeur. See Heidegger's distinction between our "ordinary conception of time," i.e., linearity, and the "ecstatico-horizon" or "stretched along" temporality of experience in *Being and Time*, pp. 416, 456-480. See, as well, Ricoeur's discussion of time as a "three-fold present" in *Time and Narrative*, vol. 1, pp. 9, 11, 59-63.
[2] See Ricoeur, *Time and Narrative*, vol. 3., p. 90, 93, and 96.
[3] See Aristotle, *Physics* 220a5-13; 222a10-19.

Those motions are a certain quantity, e.g., a "second," "minutes," or "hours," which in turn are taken to be a measurement of time. But, again, that quantity is not time; *any quantifiable duration presupposes the time it is quantifying*. What is called a "day" or a "year" is not time, but an interval of cultural convention super-imposed upon time. It is quite possible to substitute some other conventional interval for "day" or "year" as indicated by the switch from daylight saving to standard time or is obvious in the difference in the length of a year between lunar and solar calendars.[4] Time, then, is not quantity. Everyday understanding of time, concerned with quantities of time, does not tell one what time itself is, but shifts attention from time to conventional intervals which have been commonly agreed upon as representing some duration of time - and they are highly arbitrary intervals. Quantity presupposes time.

If "stretches" of time present a dilemma for one's seeking to understand what time is, since any quantifiable stretch of time presupposes the time it is measuring, so does any attempt at grasping time as some simultaneous, concomitent, or accumulative collection of stretches of time. Surely, it takes a certain duration of time for plants to grow, to be harvested, for the produce to be transported to warehouses and distributed to stores, for one to get to the grocery store, to prepare a meal, and to clean up after the meal. Yet time is itself indivisible. The duration of time needed for plants to grow can occur simultaneously with the duration of time needed to build a skyscraper. These are not divisible chunks of time, as if a duration of time could be exclusively devoted to one purpose and some other duration of time devoted to another purpose. Even when it comes to the individual's experience, the same duration of time can be "used" for watching the evening news as one simultaneously prepares supper. Everyday experience teaches, then, that events occur sequentially, simultaneously, and overlap. Surely, this is cause for no little curiosity. Time cannot be the mere duration of events (the duration in which something happens), for that would mean that time could be broken up into chunks and divided out into singular events, but, rather, events occur in time. Although time involves duration, then, time itself is indivisible, an illimitable whole.[5]

---

[4] Witnessed in the differences between the Julian/Gregorian calendar and the Moslem calendar.

[5] Kant observes: "... the possibility of all changes and successions - the principle of which, so far as it is sensitively known [through the senses], resides in the concept of time - presupposes the persistence of a subject whose opposite states succeed one another. But that whose states change does not persist unless maintained by another; and thus the concept of time as single, infinite, and immutable ... is the *aeternitas phaenomenon*

The notion of "whole" suggests a difference between time and eternity. It is common to define "eternity" as the "whole" of time, i.e., as the sum of the duration of all events. In other words, the illimitable whole of time is understood to be an "eternity" which is taken to consist of an endless duration.[6] But such an eternity would not be an open-ended sequence but an endless moment without sequence. Eternity cannot simultaneously be the sum of the parts of time and an endless duration of sequence without being an impossible contradiction. Something cannot simultaneously be one, single moment and the sum of all moments, for this would mean that all actuality (future and past as well as present actuality) would be contained in the present moment as actuality and not as mere potentiality. Such a state of actuality is patently impossible. One does not have the whole of the parts if the parts are only potentially present. If the parts were only potentially present, then there would be an outstanding actuality not present, and that outstanding actuality either past or future, would have to be added onto the sum of the parts. Hence, if eternity is the sum of the parts, then eternity would be a moment in which all actuality and potentiality occurred simultaneously. But that would mean the elimination of potentiality, for, if all actuality was realized in a singular moment, there could be nothing potential to be actualized. Eternity would then be a momentary endless, actual state of affairs without potentiality. Such an eternity is a logical and pragmatic absurdity.

Such a definition of eternity as the sum of all events which could occur in time is more appropriately called "infinity" in contrast to "eternity." Eter-

---

of the general cause." ("Inaugural Dissertation," p. 71) Further: "The moments of time do not present themselves as successive to one another; for, in that case another time would have to be presupposed for the succession of the moments; but in sensitive intuition [of the senses] actual things seem to descend, as it were, through a continuous series of moments" (*ibid.*, p. 71, n. 1).

[6] This notion of eternity as an endless state informs both amateur and professional theology. The "afterlife" is taken to be an endless duration of time. The thought alone is enough to inspire fear, but not because such an eternity might be a state of endless pain. Rather, it is terrifying, because it means a loss of freedom. An endless, perfect state of affairs is necessarily unchanging. Any eternal state, including heaven, independent of change would surely be hell, for by definition what is necessarily unchanging is determined in advance (in this case eternally) and un-free. Even as a pleasurable state (surely, the most extreme form of hedonism), such an unending, necessarily unchanging state of affairs would be intolerable.

The everyday notion of the afterlife as an endless duration of time is the consequence of absolutizing one aspect of experience: actuality. Eternity in this case is the absence of possibility. It is motivated out of a desire to escape the uncertainties, temptations, and tragedies of transience. But the escape is had at an extremely high price.

nity, on the other hand, might not be the sum of all actuality but only of those actualities which are the necessary presupposition for experience and cannot be other than the way they appear to be. Both qualifications are essential. It is not sufficient to define eternity merely in terms of "those things which cannot be other than the way they appear to be," for that would require including not only "universals" but the products of the imagination in one's notion of eternity, as well. For what one is experiencing in the imagination *is* what one is experiencing and cannot be other than what one is experiencing. Although at some later point in time, that which one was experiencing might be judged to be "incorrect," nevertheless what one experienced *is* what one experienced. But, obviously, what transpires in the imagination, i.e., the representations of the "external" world as well as the sequence of "internal" mental thoughts, is dependent upon time, for they involve change, i.e., are dependent upon sequence. Eternity cannot change; there is no duration or stretch of time to eternity. Hence, to the criterion of those things which cannot be other than the way they appear to be must be added: those things "which serve as the necessary (though not determinative) condition of possibility for experience, that is, those things that are the same yesterday, today, and tomorrow. Such "things" are the universals and their conditions of possibility. Experience alone is not sufficient to define the "eternal;" one must add the criterion "necessary condition of possibility," i.e., the transcendental conditions of possibility. But we don't have access to any transcendental conditions of possibility that are metaphysically necessary, because what we experience is at most only contingently necessary. The notion of eternity remains always at best a speculative moment.

The Western tradition has thought "eternity," in this respect, as the dimension of the universals including what caused and enabled them to be (e.g., the Platonic Good or First Principle of the whole, Aristotle's Unmoved Mover, Philo's and Plotinus' The One and The Intelligence). In contrast to all other things, universals are simple and singular (not composite and individual) and, therefore, they cannot be other than what they are and endure without change. However, the investigations above have called the status of universals into question as at best aporetic, i.e., incapable of definition and as much the a posteriori product of, as they are preserved a priori in, language. Hence, the eternal status of universals is itself relative to human experience, and their reality for humans, as necessary as they are for one's making sense out of experience, is a matter of unknowing faith (nonepistemic faith). Furthermore, since ultimate causality of every kind is relative to one's socio-linguistic paradigm and imperceptible in itself (one only experiences effects) and since consciousness requires two-ness (the ability to distinguish one thing from another) in order to be conscious, the cause of universals (e.g., as the Good, the Unmoved Mover, The One) is equally a matter of non-epistemic faith.

Hence, "eternity" as an "Eternal Now," including all that is what it is and cannot be other than what it appears to be, which serves as the necessary condition of possibility for everything else, is at best a "contingent" eternal, for it is relative to contingent human experience and understanding. It requires a speculative leap (even if one acknowledges that it is not an "unreasonable" leap) beyond the limits of experience for one to maintain that it is an "absolute" eternal.

Yet more importantly, one should not confuse an actual "infinite" for an "eternal" unchanging cause: one should not confuse actuality for possibility, or infinity for the eternal. Infinity defined as the accumulation of all actuality ignores possibility. The "Eternal" composed of universals and "that" which causes them, despite all protests by their defenders as beyond essence and incapable of definition or determination, is consistently thought in the Western tradition as something "actual," e.g., God, because of the presupposition from Xenophanes and Anaxagoras that "nothing can come from nothing."[7] According to this presupposition, actuality must precede potentiality. Yet, there is a hint throughout the Western tradition (preserved most emphatically in theological circles) that ultimate reality escapes the limits of actuality and constitutes an indefinable potentiality.[8]

---

[7] This presupposition reigns throughout the Western tradition from the pre-Socratics to Descartes and beyond along with the presupposition from Epedocles that only like can recognize like. When these presuppositions are combined with the presupposition of the law of excluded middle (entirely dependent upon "time," for at different times A can be not-A), one has not only the cosmological argument for God, but one has "grounds" for affirming the radical similarity between the human spirit and God (imageo dei) as well as assurance of coherence, if not providence, in experience. Yet there are radical aporiai connected with these presuppositions which force acknowledgment of their speculative nature as well as acknowledgment that they are embraced out of a leap of faith.

[8] This project distinguishes between two kinds of "possibility," i.e., "formal possibility" in the Kantian sense, as that which can be experienced given the formal conditions of consciousness, and "ontological possibility" in the Heideggerian sense, as that which all actuality as well as understanding presupposes. See Bernard Charles Flynn, "From Finitude to the Absolute: Kant's Doctrine of Subjectivity" in *Philosophy Today* XXIX/4/4 (1985), pp. 284-301; Martin Heidegger's *Kants These über das Sein* (Frankfurt a.M.: Vittorio Klostermann, 1963) also available in English translation as "Kant's Thesis About Being," trans. by Ted Klein and William Pohl in *Southwestern Journal of Philosophy*, 4/3 (1973), pp. 7-33. Heidegger connects this late meditation on Kant with *Being and Time*, where Being is thought as possibility. He writes, pp. 35-36: "Im unscheinbaren 'ist' verbirgt sich alles Denkwürdige des Seins. Das Denkwürdigste darin bleibt jedoch, daß wir bedenken, ob 'Sein', ob das 'ist' selbst sein kann, oder ob

The investigations of time in the tradition, having enduring significance, are those from Plato's *Timaeus* 37-38, Aristotle's Book IV, chapters 10-14, of the *Physics*; Plotinus's *Enneads* III 7; Augustine's Book 11 of the *Confessions*; Kant's discussion of the intuition (time and space) in his inaugural dissertation of 1770[9] and in *The Critique of Pure Reason*;[10] Husserl's *Phenomenology of Internal Time Consciousness*, edited by Heidegger; and Heidegger's various analyses of time commencing with *Being and Time*.[11] Ricoeur's three volume project *Time and Narrative*, particularly chapter 1 of volume 1 and chapters 1 through 5 of volume 3, offers a detailed analysis of these classic discussions in the context of the fundamental narrativity of experience. This long tradition of investigation demonstrates that the meaning of time is entirely dependent upon the metaphysical presuppositions brought to the analysis.

Cosmological Time

Plato

The classical discussions of time, i.e., Plato, Aristotle, Plotinus, and Augustine are shaped by a metaphysical understanding that clearly distinguishes

---

Sein niemals 'ist' und daß gleichwohl wahr bleibt: Es gibt Sein.
   Doch woher kommt, an wen geht die Gabe im 'Es gibt',
      und in welcher Weise des Gebens?
   Sein kann nicht *sein*. Würde es sein, bliebe es nicht mehr Sein,
      sondern wäre ein Seiendes.
   ... Steht es so, dann muß die Frage nach dem Sein
      unter den Leittitel gelangen: 'Sein und Zeit'."
Being cannot be actual, for if it is actual it is a thing among things. If Being is not actuality, then actuality conceals Being as potentiality, and, hence, Being and time are one and the same.

9   See, particularly, §14 in Immanuel Kant, "Dissertation on the Form and Principles of the Sensible and Intelligible World [1770]" in his "Inaugural Dissertation."

10 See Immanuel Kant, *Critique of Pure Reason*, B46-73.

11 This is not to simply dismiss the work of Aquinas, e.g., in *De Veritate* 2,12 ad 9, *IV Physica*, and *ST* I, 10; 14, see Brian Leftow, "Aquinas on Time and Eternity" in *New Scholasticism* 62/2-4 (1990), 387-429; Bergson, e.g., *Time and Free Will* (New York: Harper & Row, 1960); or Merleau-Ponty, e.g., *Phenomenology of Perception*, trans. by Colin Smith (New York: Humanities Press, 1970), pp. 410-433, *The Visible and the Invisible*, trans. by Alphonso Lingis (Evanston: Northwestern University Press, 1968), pp. 190-191, 194-195. No list on such a topic would be able to, much less want to, exhaust all the discussions of time in the tradition. It is precisely such issues that drive a living tradition onward in the quest of understanding. Nevertheless, there are seminal moments in the investigation of time, to which the discussions time and again (the entire aporia is intentionally echoed) turn, and those are to be discussed here.

time and eternity. Plato speaks metaphorically of time as "a moving image of eternity" (*Timaeus* 37d). Time is sequential and moves "according to number," i.e., measurement. Eternity, in contrast, is a unity:

> ... the past and future are created species of time, which we unconsciously but wrongly transfer to eternal being, for we say that it 'was,' or 'is,' or 'will be,' but the truth is that 'is' alone is properly attributed to it, and that 'was' and 'will be' are only to be spoken of becoming in time, for they are motions, but that which is immovably the same forever cannot become older or younger by time, nor can it be said that it came into being in the past, or has come into being now, or will come into being in the future, nor is it subject at all to any of those states which affect moving and sensible things and of which generation is the cause. These are the forms of time, which imitates eternity and revolves according to a law of number. Moreover, when we say that what has become *is* become and what becomes *is* becoming, and that what will become *is* about to become and that the nonexistent *is* nonexistent - all these are inaccurate modes of expression.[12]

These are inaccurate modes of expression, because "is" cannot "become." It is this characteristic of Being that makes today always today and prohibits tomorrow from ever coming. Only eternity, according to Plato, "is," and this eternity is an eternal "now."[13] Time, on the other hand, involves the change of becoming, and, according to this classical discussion of time: time is an image or an imitation of the eternal. Here is where the metaphysical presuppositions surface. The eternal does not move "according to number," but "itself rests in unity." It is the image of this unity that is called time, according to Plato.

Plato presents a "mythological" account[14] of the origin of time by saying:

> Time ... and the heaven came into being at the same instant in order that, having been created together, if ever there was to be a dissolution of them, they might be dissolved together. *It was framed after the pattern of the eternal nature - that it might resemble this as far as was possible, for the pattern exists from eternity, and the created heaven has been and is and will be in all time.* Such was the mind and thought of God in the creation of time.[15] (emphasis added)

---

[12] Plato, *Timaeus* 37e-38b.

[13] This insight must be seen as an aporia and not as an explanation. It forces acknowledgment of human limits and dependence, but equally forces the reigning in of blind speculation about the content and intent of such an eternity. Why? Because humans only experience it as an effect, and its content is indefinable. It will be argued that it is, in fact, an "is" of "not-Being" and not to be confused with the "is" of some *thing*.

[14] I employ the term "mythological" here in the sense of Ernst Benz in *Indische Einflüsse auf die frühchristliche Theologie*, p. 192, i.e., as a consciously speculative, narrative account not incompatible with reason but nevertheless not a defensible logical argument precisely because it must remain speculative.

[15] Plato, *Timaeus* 38b-c.

The metaphysical presupposition of this discussion of time and eternity by Plato is that the world of sensation is a copy of the eternal, or the dimension of change is an image of the unchanging. Hence, eternity is understood here neither as the totality of time nor as the summation of all material actuality (in the sense of all that was materially actual in the past, materially actual in the present, and what would be materially actual in the future) to the elimination of potentiality. Rather, eternity is that "unity" which always "is" and remains the same yesterday, today, and tomorrow that cannot be other than the way it appears to be and is the condition of possibility for everything in time. Becoming, then, is an *image* of Being both resembling and *participating in Being* "as far as possible."

Plato is employing an analogy based on human "creativity" for talking about the creation of time and all that is in time. Just as an individual has an "idea" that s/he then sets about to actualize in the world, that is, just as the individual begins with an "original" and makes a "copy" (an always imperfect copy, since the copy can never exactly duplicate the original), so has God created time and all that is in time as a copy of an original.

Plotinus draws the logical metaphysical conclusion from these presuppositions that the copy, or created order is *deficient*, i.e., it needs sequence, it needs time. The eternal is not temporal, because it is an indivisible unity, lacking in nothing, "complete without sequence."[16]

> ... [A] close enough definition of Eternity[17] would be that it is a life limitless in the full sense of being all the life there is and a life which, knowing nothing of past or future to shatter its completeness, possesses itself intact for ever. To the notion of a life (a Living-Principle) all-comprehensive add that it never spends itself, and we have the statement of a Life instantaneously infinite.[18]

The unity of the Life-principle spoken of here is the unity of νοῦς,[19] "intellect" or more appropriately, Spirit, that contains the illimitable whole of uni-

---

[16] Plotinus, *Third Ennead* VII. 7 in *The Six Enneads* in *Great Books of the Western World*, ed. by Mortimer J. Adler (Chicago: Encyclopedia Britannica, Inc., 1952), p. 122.

[17] Plotinus can at best give a "close enough" definition, because precise definitions (as Socrates taught) are impossible.

[18] Plotinus, *Third Ennead* VII.7, pp. 121-122.

[19] William Ralph Inge speaks of the difficulties of translating νοῦς in Plotinus in *The Philosophy of Plotinus. The Gifford Lectures at St. Andrews, 1917-1918*, vol. II (New York: Longmans, Green and Co., 1923), p. 37-38: "For λόγος there is no single English word. It is quite different from the Logos of Christian theology, whom the Christian Platonists invested with the attributes of the Plotinian Νοῦς ... Even more serious is the difficulty of finding a satisfactory equivalent for Νοῦς. Modern writers on Neoplatonism have chosen 'intellect,' 'intelligence,' 'thought,' 'reason,' 'mind,' '*das Denken.*' All these are misleading. Plotinus was neither an intellectualist (in the sense in which Hegel has been called an intellectualist or 'panlogist'), nor, in the modern sense,

versals which remain the same yesterday, today, and tomorrow.[20] Plotinus wrote in *The Enneads* V,9 "[t]he Intelligence [νοῦς] in its totality is made up of the Ideas ..."[21] Where νοῦς is complete, time, in contrast, is deficient: "Things and Beings in the Time order ... are ... bound to sequence; they are deficient to the extent of that thing, Time, which they need."[22]

Aristotle

Hence, time and eternity are two different "things." Everyday conceptions of time confuse infinite time with limitless eternity. But infinite time has to do with what is quantifiable; eternity, since it is limitless, is non-quantifiable, i.e., it has no length, width, depth, or height, and, since it cannot be divided, it cannot be numbered. In contrast to eternity, time is concerned with what is divisible and numerable.

This is precisely Aristotle's definition of time: "time is the number of movement."[23] Time, therefore, according to Aristotle, is not movement itself.[24] Yet, it is not independent of movement: "It is evident ... that time is

---

an idealist. He does not exalt the discursive reason (διάνοια or λογισμός) to the highest place. These are the activities proper to Soul, not to the principle higher than Soul. The discursive reason has its function in separating, distributing, and recombining the data of experience ... But Νοῦς beholds all things in their true relations without the need of this process ...

By far the best equivalent is *Spirit*. It need not cause confusion with πνεῦμα, for this word is very little used by Plotinus, and does not stand for anything important in his system. It has the right associations. We think of spirit as something supremely real, but incorporeal, invisible, and timeless. Our familiarity with the Pauline and patristic psychology makes us ready to accept Spirit, Soul, and Body as three parts of our nature, and to put Spirit in the highest place. St. Paul also teaches us to regard Spirit as super-individual, not so much a part of ourselves as a Divine life which we may share. In all these ways, νοῦς and Spirit correspond closely.

[20] See Plato's mythological description of creation in the *Timaeus* 38-42, and 49-50, where Plato adds to the "intelligible" and its "imitation" (the created order) the notion of the "receptacle" or "that which is to receive all forms," which has no form, as necessary to give an account of the created order. This receptacle ... is an invisible and formless being which receives all things and in some mysterious way partakes of the intelligible, and is most incomprehensible." (Plato, *Timaeus* 51a-b) Aristotle, to the contrary, calls this "receptacle" the material cause. See Aristotle, *Metaphysics*, Book I, chapters 1-3; Book VII, chapter 3; and, particularly, Book VII, chapter 10: "... matter is unknowable in itself."

[21] Plotinus, *The Essential Plotinus*, p. 53.

[22] Plotinus, *Third Ennead* VII.7 in *The Six Enneads*, p. 122.

[23] Aristotle, *Physics* 223a18-20.

[24] See Aristotle, *Physics* 218b19: "Clearly then it [time] is not movement."

neither movement nor independent of movement."²⁵ For all movement is *in* time, hence, movement presupposes time; but time "... is just this - number of motion in respect of 'before' and 'after'"²⁶ - though time is not itself the number; rather, the number is a measure of time.²⁷

There can be no "before" and "after," however, without the boundary of the "now." Aristotle calls the "now" the "link of time:"

> The 'now' is the link of time ... (for it connects past and future time), and it is a limit²⁸ of time (for it is the beginning of the one and the end of the other). But this is not obvious as it is with the point [of a line], which is fixed. *It divides potentially, and in so far as it is dividing the'now' is always different, but in so far as it connects it is always the same* ...
>
> So the 'now' ... is in one way *a potential dividing of time*, in another the termination of both parts, and their unity. And the dividing and the uniting are the same thing and in the same reference, but in essence they are not the same.²⁹ (emphasis added)

Aristotle is pointing to a true curiosity about the "now" or the moment that is the present. His discussion employs an analogy between time and points on a line. Time, he suggests, is as paradoxical as the notion of "point," for a "point" is not "one" but "two."

> Time ... is both made continuous by the 'now' and divided at it ... Here, too, there is a correspondence with the point; for the point also both connects and terminates the length - it is the beginning of one and the end of another. But when you take it in this way, using the one point as two, *a pause is necessary*, if the same point is to be the beginning and the end. The 'now' on the other hand, since the body carried is moving, is always different.³⁰ (emphasis added)

Since the now both connects and terminates the length, it is "two," which is "[t]he smallest number, in the strict sense of the word 'number' ..."³¹ Two is the smallest number not only with respect to the "now" as the end of the "before" and the beginning of the "after," but it is also the smallest number

---

25 Aristotle, *Physics* 219a1.
26 Aristotle, *Physics* 219b2.
27 See Aristotle, *Physics* 219b5-9: "Time then is a kind of number. (Number, we must note, is used in two senses - both of what is counted or the countable and also of that with which we count. *Time obviously is what is counted, not that with which we count*: these are different kinds of thing.)" (emphasis added)
28 See Aristotle's definition of "limit" at *Metaphysics* 1022a17-1022b.
29 Aristotle, *Physics* 222a10-19. See 223a5-7, as well: "... we say 'before' and 'after' with reference to the distance from the 'now', and the 'now' is the boundary of the past and the future ..."
30 Aristotle, *Physics* 220a5-13.
31 Aristotle, *Physics* 220a26.

with respect to epistemology: in order for something to be experienced there must be at least "two," for identification requires distinguishing something from something else.

These observations with respect to points are not mere sophistry. Just as a point cannot exist by definition, since any point with extension is a line, except as an imaginary beginning or end, so the "now" cannot exist except as a "pause" or "gap" that is constantly "different," i.e., continuous and moving.[32] This "gap," which is the "now," is always only potential as a dividing of time just as it is the termination of the past and the future as well as their point of unification. And this "now" only emerges as a consequence of movement; although, as was said above, it is not itself the movement.

When Aristotle initially raised the question about time, he asked: "First, does it belong to the class of things that exist or to that of things that do not exist? Then, secondly, what is its nature?"[33] There is reason to believe that time is not-Being:

> ... the following considerations would make one suspect that *it either does not exist at all or barely, and in an obscure way*. One part of it has been and is not, while the other is going to be and is not yet. Yet time - both infinite time and any time you like to take - is made up of these. One would naturally suppose that what is made up of things which do not exist could have no share in reality [μετέχειν οὐσίας = to participate in Being].[34] (emphasis added)

To the extent that time does not participate in Being it is not-Being. To the extent that time is the link between a "before" and an "after" it does not exist. That is what leads Aristotle to focus on the "now," though not as a part (οὐ μέρος) of time but as a "limit" (πέρας, an end, termination).

Time as the measure of movement is not a number any more than the "now" is movement. Time eludes all attempts to grasp it, since it is the "gap" that makes movement possible. The "now," as the link or boundary connecting "before" and "after" (past and future), is an elusive gap which is potential and never actual.[35]

---

[32] Aristotle distinguishes the "now" from a "point" on a line in that a point on a line is fixed where the "now" is continuously changing. Hence, he is careful to insist that the "now" as a "pause" in the sense of some fixed point between a "before" and "after" is no more time than is number or movement, but an "attribute" of time. See Aristotle, *Physics* 220a21-25. The present analysis suggests that the "pause" or "gap" suggested here is not time itself but an indication of, a pointing to, the "not-Being" that "is" time.

[33] Aristotle, *Physics* 217b31-32.

[34] Aristotle, *Physics* 217b33-218a3.

[35] See Aristotle's definition of "potency" at *Metaphysics* 1019a15-1020a6.

Aristotle's discussion of time treats time as sequential,[36] since time fundamentally is concerned with movement or motion. This represents Aristotle's metaphysical presupposition. He defined motion earlier in the *Physics* as "the fulfillment of what exists potentially,"[37] which is the key to all human experience and knowledge as Aristotle indicated in the *Posterior Analytics*, for it is only by this fulfillment (motion) that something becomes actual and can be an object of sense:

> ... out of sense-perception comes to be what we call memory, and out of frequently repeated memories of the same thing develops experience; for a number of memories constitute a single experience. From experience again - i.e. from the universal now stabilized in its entirety within the soul, the one beside the many which is a single identity within them all - originate the skill of the craftsman and the knowledge of the man of science, skill in the sphere of coming to be and science in the sphere of being.[38]

The metaphysical presupposition of motion is Aristotle's way of protecting himself from what he takes to be a teaching by Plato that ideas are self-subsistent and independent of everything else.[39] Although Aristotle himself insists that "forms" are actual (*Metaphysics* 1072a20-23) and that actuality precedes potentiality (*De Anima* 430a20-22), even as "in the individual, potential knowledge is in time prior to actual knowledge,"[40] Aristotle's ontological commitment is to knowledge which arises in the senses, i.e., as a consequence of motion. The *Metaphysics* begins:

> All men by nature desire to know. An indication of this is the delight we take in our senses; for even apart from their usefulness they are loved for themselves; and above all others the sense of sight. For not only with a view to action, but even when we are not going to do anything, we prefer seeing (one might say) to everything else. The reason is that this, most of all the senses, makes us know and brings to light many differences between things.[41]

---

[36] Although, Aristotle understands time to be circular rather than linear. See Aristotle, *Physics* 223b24-35.

[37] See Aristotle, *Physics* 201a10 and 208a30.

[38] Aristotle, *Posterior Analytics* 100a4-8; notice how universals are treated ectypally here.

[39] See Aristotle, *Metaphysics* 1031a29-1031b18; and 1079b 23-26: "... other things do not come 'from' the ideas in any of the usual senses of 'from.' But to say that the ideas are patterns and that other things participate in them is to use empty words and poetical metaphors." Though there are several passages in Plato that would challenge the correctness of Aristotle's reading of Plato. See, for example, *Sophist* 249d; *Timeaus* 59d; and *Philebus* 22a-b, 60c-d.

[40] Aristotle, *De Anima* (430a20-21).

[41] Aristotle, *Metaphysics* 980a23-28.

Plotinus

Plotinus' discussion of time in the *Third Ennead* can be seen as a dialog with Aristotle, for Plotinus is particularly concerned to argue that time is not only not movement, but time is not the measure of movement either. Time cannot be movement, as Aristotle agreed, since movement, "whether a definite act of moving is meant or a united total made up of all such acts[,] ... in either sense, takes place in time."[42] Yet, in addition, although the Celestial Circuit [universe] in principle can be measured both in terms of its space (extent) and in terms of its

> continuity, of its tendency not to stop but to proceed indefinitely; ... this is merely amplitude of Movement; search it, tell its vastness, and, still, Time has no more appeared, no more enters into the matter, than when one certifies a high pitch of heat; all we have discovered is Motion in ceaseless succession, like water flowing ceaselessly, motion and extent of motion.[43]

Furthermore, time cannot be the measure of movement, for all measurement not only presupposes that which it is measuring, but every measure "... must have a quantity, like a foot-rule; it must have magnitude."[44] But movement presupposes time not vice versa, and time itself has no quantity; it has no magnitude. "Time means something very different from any definite period: before all question as to quantity is the question as to the thing of which a certain quantity is present."[45] Explicitly using Aristotle's example of horses, Plotinus observes:

> Time, we are told, is the number outside Movement and measuring it, like the tens applied to the reckoning of the horses and cows but not inherent in them: we are not told what this Number is; yet, applied or not, it must, like that decade, have some nature of its own.[46]

But any quantity (or number) must presuppose the time it is meant to measure:

> ... once a thing - whether by point or standard or any other means - measures succession, it must measure according to time: this number appraising movement degree by degree must, therefore, if it is to serve as a measure at all, be something dependent upon time and in contact with it: for, either, degree is spatial, merely - the beginning and end of the Stadium, for example - or in the only alternative, it is a pure matter of Time: the succession of early and late is stage of Time, Time ending upon a certain Now or Time beginning from a Now.

---

[42] Plotinus, *Third Ennead* VII.8 in *The Six Enneads*, 123.
[43] Plotinus, *Third Ennead* VII.8, p. 124.
[44] Plotinus, *Third Ennead* VII.9, p. 124.
[45] Plotinus, *Third Ennead* VII.9, p. 125.
[46] Plotinus, *Third Ennead* VII.9, p. 125.

> Time, therefore, is something other than the mere number measuring Movement, whether Movement in general or any particular tract of Movement.[47]

Having dismissed Aristotle's definition to his satisfaction, Plotinus returns to Plato's definition of time, i.e., that time is an "image of Eternity."[48] In fairness to Aristotle, though by no means to suggest that Aristotle is any closer to defining what time is than Plato or Plotinus, Aristotle did not equate time either with movement or with number. Time is a "gap" that is the "twoness" of the "now;" the gap that is the link and boundary between the end of the past and the beginning of the future. That gap is potential not actual, hence, it is neither movement nor the measure of movement. Aristotle's point with respect to the relationship between movement and time is that time emerges only with motion and number, but time itself is neither.

However, Aristotle limits his discussion of time to sequence, where Plotinus sets sequence over against simultaneity in an attempt to describe the full perplexity of time. In so doing, he describes the aporia of time:

> ... Eternity, we have said, is Life in repose, unchanging, self-identical, always endlessly complete; and there is to be an image of Eternity - Time - such an image as this lower All presents of the Higher Sphere. Therefore over against that higher life there must be another life, known by the same name as the more veritable life of the Soul; over against that movement of the Intellectual Soul there must be the movement of some partial phase; over against that identity, unchangeableness and stability there must be that which is not constant in the one hold but puts forth multitudinous acts; over against that oneness without extent or interval there must be an image of oneness, a unity of link and succession; over against the immediately infinite and all-comprehending, that which tends, yes, to infinity but by tending to a perpetual futurity; over against the Whole in concentration, there *must* be that which is to be a Whole by stages never final.[49] (emphasis added)

But this only describes what time "must" be, not what time "is." The closest Plotinus comes to saying what time "is" is to say that time is "... primarily a Kind to itself"[50] echoing Plato's discussion of the five primary Kinds (existence, motion, rest, sameness, and not-Being) in the *Sophist* 253b-260b. When one combines Aristotle's notion of time as a linking or boundary "gap" with the description of time as an image of Eternity from Plotinus, one is led to conclude that time is not a primary Kind to itself, but time is the key to Plato's primary Kind of "not-Being."

---

[47] Plotinus, *Third Ennead* VII.9, p. 125.
[48] See Plotinus, *Third Ennead* VII.11, p. 126.
[49] Plotinus, *Third Ennead* VII.11, p. 126.
[50] Plotinus, *Third Ennead* VII.12, p. 127. Plotinus repeats this observation in 13, p. 127: Time "... must be primary, a thing 'within itself.'"

Time and Not-Being

Plato carefully distinguished not-Being from that which is contrary to reality as existent. Not-Being is "only what is different from that existent."[51] Not-Being is the "different" from things that exist.

> May we now be bold to say that 'that which is not' unquestionably *is* a thing that has a nature of its own - just as the tall was tall and the beautiful was beautiful, so too with the not-tall and the not-beautiful - and in that sense 'that which is not' also, on the same principle, both was and *is* 'what is not,' a single form to be reckoned among the many realities? ... [W]e have brought to light the real character of 'not-being.' We have shown that the nature of the different has existence and is parceled out over the whole field of existent things with reference to one another, and of every part of it that is set in contrast to 'that which is' we have dared to say that precisely that *is really* 'that which is not.'[52]

May this primary Kind of "not-Being" be thought of as time? It will take the discussion of time as Being, i.e., possibility (no-thingness), in Heidegger to draw out the full implication of these hints about time emerging with Plato, Aristotle, and Plotinus.

This analysis of time in Plato, Aristotle, and Plotinus is meant to describe time cosmologically - as it applies to all that is and/or to all events and not with respect to the individual person's having a privileged status for the emergence of time. The analysis of these discussions indicates that time is a radical enigma. It is not itself a "thing," but is at best a "link," "boundary," or "gap" between "before" and "after" that emerges only where there is motion. Yet time itself is neither motion nor the number used to measure motion. At the same time, time is sequential and an indivisible whole both as some kind of "unity" of "before" and "after" in Aristotle's sense and/or the indivisible unity of the illimitable and immeasurable, i.e., Eternity, in Plato's and Plotinus' sense.

Anthropological Time

Augustine

Although Aristotle acknowledges in passing that time is relative to the soul,[53] it is Augustine who makes the relationship to the self central to his reflections about time.[54] The first thirteen chapters of Book XI of his *Con-*

---

[51] Plato, *Sophist*, 258b.
[52] Plato, *Sophist* 258c-e.
[53] See Aristotle, *Physics* 223a25-27.
[54] I am indebted to Friedrich-Wilhelm von Hermann's article "Augustinus und die phänomenologische Frage nach der Zeit" in *Philosophisches Jahrbuch* 100, no. 1 (1993), pp. 96-113, for most of the analysis of Augustine which follows.

fessions constitute a meditation on the opening verses of Genesis and the notion of eternity to draw the conclusion that eternity is to be understood as the Platonists taught, i.e., eternity is a "permanent present." Chapters fourteen to twenty are concerned with the three ways in which time is manifest, rather than in asking about the essence of time. After initially concluding that time doesn't exist, because both past and future are not and the present moment is fleeting (chapters 14 and 15), with chapter 16 a new direction is taken with respect to the question of time. It is no longer the cosmological character of time, but, rather, the human or anthropological perception of time that is the focus of investigation.

Chapter twenty formulates the conclusions of this investigation: the three modalities of time (past, present, future) are in fact three kinds of "present" or a "three-fold present:" the past-present, present-present, and future-present, because the past and the future can only be perceived/experienced by the individual in terms of the present. This locates time squarely in the individual, for the present is always the present for a particular individual, although this means that time is aporetic in that it is both accessible in its everydayness and concealed.[55] As Augustine observed: "What, then, is time? If no one ask of me, I know; if I wish to explain to him who asks, I know not."[56]

However, not all of the past is explicitly present nor is all of the future explicitly present. It is not until chapter 26 that the relation of time to the individual finds its full formulation. Here Augustine introduces the notion of "*distentio animi*" or the "extension of the soul" (or the extension of temporal consciousness) as a three-fold present. Chapter 27 indicates that it is because of memory that there is an internal understanding of time by the individual. Memory preserves the continuum of the past with the present. The continuum of the past, preserved in memory, combines with the attention of the present to permit an anticipation of the future. *Memoria*, *attentio*, and *expectatio* enable the experience of time as a "stretch" of time: *distentio animi*.

Clearly, Augustine represents a dramatic shift in the analysis of time in the Western tradition. The earlier discussion classically formulated by Plato,

---

[55] See F.-W. von Hermann, "Augustinus und die phänomenologische Frage nach der Zeit," p. 109: "Die aporetische Situation ist die zwischen dem scire des natürlichen Zeitumgangs und dem non scire des philosophischen Begreifens."

[56] Augustine, *The Confessions* in *Basic Writings of Saint Augustine*, ed. by Whitney J. Oates (New York: Random House, 1948), Chapter XIV, p. 191. See Chapter XXV, p. 198, as well, where Augustine contrasts the knowledge of ordinary experience of time and one's epistemological ignorance of time.

Aristotle, and Plotinus was concerned with time in its cosmological sense. What is the "essence" of time that enables it to accompany all events and to be measured? That discussion led to the conclusion that time escapes observation, motion, and measurement although it is impossible without them. Time is a kind of "not-Being" without which there can be no becoming. This discussion ultimately has no privileged place for the individual. Cosmologically, time as the flow of "nows" privileges no moment above any other moment.

With Augustine, however, the analysis of time turns explicitly to the individual by providing an anthropological (or phenomenological) description of time in terms of *distentio animi* (*memoria, attentio, expectatio*). Anthropological time focuses on the individual for the meaning, or making sense of, time. Time acquires its present from the individual, and it is the individual who, paradoxically, gives even cosmological time whatever meaning it has although the individual moment is meaningless for cosmological time.[57] Ricoeur calls this "... the main difficulty that the aporetics of temporality will reveal, namely, the irreducibility of one to the other ... of a purely phenomenological perspective of time and an opposed perspective that ... I will call the cosmological one."[58] Ricoeur articulates this aporia of time succinctly as follows: "The length of time of a human life, compared to the range of cosmic time-spans, appears insignificant, whereas it is the very place from which every question of significance arises."[59]

Kant

The Enlightenment returned to the question of time in an anthropological sense, once again, with Immanuel Kant. Kant located time with space not in the dimension of the sensed things[60] themselves but in the intuition which is only and always concerned with phenomena of sense.

> ... [A]ll our intuition is bound to a certain formal principle under which alone anything can be apprehended by the mind immediately, that is, as *singular*, and not as merely conceived discursively through general concepts. But this formal principle of our intuition (space and time) is the condition under which anything can be an object of our senses; and being thus the condition of sensitive knowledge ...[61]

---

[57] See Ricoeur, *Time and Narrative*, vol. 3., p. 90, 93, and 96.
[58] Ricoeur, *Time and Narrative*, vol. 3, p. 4.
[59] Ricoeur, *Time and Narrative*, vol. 3, p. 90. Ricoeur said earlier: "... a psychological theory [phenomenological time] and a cosmological theory [cosmological time] mutually occlude each other to the very extent they imply each other" (*ibid.*, p. 14).
[60] "*The idea of time does not originate in the senses, but is presupposed by them.*" Kant, "Inaugural Dissertation," p. 53 (emphasis in the original).
[61] Kant, "Inaugural Dissertation," p. 50.

He distinguished among phenomena (sense experience), intuition (space and time), and the intellectual (logical concepts).

> All things which, as objects, are referred to our senses, are phenomena; whatever does not affect the senses but contains merely the special form of sensibility, belongs to pure intuition (i.e., to intuition empty of sensations, but not for that reason intellectual). The phenomena of outer sense are reviewed and expounded in physics, those of inner sense in empirical psychology. But pure intuition (in man) is not a universal or logical concept *under* which, but a singular concept *in* which, all sensibles are apprehended.[62]

In other words, time is something that the individual brings to the experience of singular things of the senses. However, just as in the case of Augustine, Kant has not explained what time is; he has merely presupposed it as inseparable from human experience in the world.

> *Time is not something objective and real.* It is neither substance nor accident nor relation, but is a subjective condition, necessary owing to the nature of the human mind, of the co-ordinating of all sensibles according to a fixed law; and it is a *pure intuition*. For we co-ordinate alike substances and accidents, whether according to simultaneity or according to succession, only through the concept of time; and thus the notion of time, as a formal principle, is prior to the concepts of simultaneity and succession.[63]

Though what Kant means by "simultaneity" here is the simultaneity of all that is actual at any particular point in time and not that sequence requires that all of time (past, future, and present) somehow be present in any moment.

> ... though time possesses only one dimension, yet the ubiquity of time ..., owing to which all things conceivable by sense are *at some time, adds to the quantum of actuals* a second dimension, *so far as they hang*, as it were, *from the same point of time*. For if you represent time by a straight line produced to infinity, and simultaneous things at any point of time by lines drawn perpendicular to it, the plane thus generated will represent the phenomenal world, both as to its substance and as to its accidents.[64] (partial emphasis added)

Time, according to Kant, is a necessary, internal condition of possibility (along with space) not only for the individual's experience of outer sensations, but time is essential for reason itself for which the law of the excluded middle is essential, i.e., "... A and not-A are not incompatible unless they are judged of the same thing *together* (i.e., in the same time); but when they

---

[62] Kant, "Inaugural Dissertation," p. 51.
[63] Kant, "Inaugural Dissertation," p. 56.
[64] Kant, "Inaugural Dissertation," p. 57, n. 1.

are judged of a thing successively (i.e., at different times), they may both belong to it."65 The very principle of contradiction, then, presupposes time, and without this principle reason would be impossible.

> ... *only if infinite space and time be given*, can any definite space or time be marked out by limitation of it; neither a point nor a moment can be thought by itself; they are conceived only as limits in any already given space or time. Thus all primary properties of these concepts are beyond the jurisdiction of reason, and so cannot in any way be intellectually explained. But *none the less they are the pre-suppositions upon which the intellect rests* ...66 (emphasis added)

Of these necessary intuitions presupposed by experience, time has a priority over space, according to Kant, because space is applied as an "image" to time where time "approaches more nearly to a universal:"

> Of these concepts, the one [i.e., space] properly concerns the intuition of an *object* , the other [i.e., time] a *state*, namely, that of representation. Thus space is applied as an image to the concept of time itself, representing it by a line, and its limits (moments) by points. But time approaches more nearly to a universal, rational concept, in that it embraces absolutely everything within its survey, namely, space itself, and in addition the accidents which are not comprehended in space-relations, such as the thoughts of the soul.67

Space and time (along with the categories of the understanding[68]) are "transcendental deductions," i.e., what must necessarily be *given* in order for there to be any human experience whatsoever. Hence, space and time are not demonstrated or explained; they are presupposed *as a consequence of individual experience*.

Husserl

Husserl maintains the tradition of analyzing time anthropologically/phenomenologically in the tradition of Augustine, yet his work, also, constitutes no greater explanation of time, but, rather, in Husserl's case one finds merely a re-articulation of Augustine's notion of *distentio animi* in terms of "retention," "intention"/Urbewußtsein, and "protention."[69] Just as with Augustine, the present moment of an individual's consciousness is the focal point for understanding time - though that present moment is not to be confused with the instant. The "now" of conscious experience is itself a "stretch of time"

---

[65] Kant, "Inaugural Dissertation," p. 58.
[66] Kant, "Inaugural Dissertation," p. 64.
[67] Kant, "Inaugural Dissertation," pp. 64-65.
[68] See Kant, *Critique of Pure Reason* B106.
[69] See Edmund Husserl, *Vorlesungen zur Phänomenologie des inneren Zeitbewußtseins*, 2. Auflage, ed. by Martin Heidegger (Tübingen: Max Niemeyer Verlag, 1980), p. 398.

which evaporates only when it is sought among what is given to experience, i.e., the givenness of temporal objects:

> If we ... relate what has been said about perception to the *differences of the givenness* with which temporal Objects make their appearance, then the *antithesis of perception* is *primary remembrance*, which appears here, and *primary expectation* (retention and protention), whereby *perception and non-perception continually* pass over into one another. In the consciousness of the direct, intuitive comprehension of a temporal Object, e.g., a melody, the passage, tone, or part now heard is perceived, and not perceived is what is momentarily intuited as past. Apprehensions here pass continually over into one another and terminate in an apprehension constituting the now; this apprehension, however, is only an ideal limit. We are concerned here with a *continuum of gradations in the direction of an ideal limit*, like the convergence of various shades of red toward an ideally pure red. However, in this case, we do not have individual apprehensions corresponding to the individual shades of red, which, indeed, *can be given for themselves*. Rather, we always have and, according to the nature of the matter, can only have continuities of apprehensions, or better, *a single continuum which is constantly modified*. If somehow we divide this continuum into two adjoining parts, that part which includes the now, or is capable of constituting it, designates and constitutes the "gross" now, which, as soon as we divide it further, immediately breaks down again into a finer now and a past, etc.
>
> ... In an ideal sense, then, perception (impression) would be the phase of consciousness which constitutes the pure now, and memory every other phase of the continuity. But this is just an ideal limit, something abstract which can be nothing for itself. Moreover, it is also true that even this ideal now is not something *toto caelo* different from the not-now but continually accommodates itself thereto. The continual transition from perception to primary remembrance conforms to this accommodation.[70]

Time, according to Husserl, is a constant flow of "nows" that has its identity because of its content:

> The consciousness of unity, spreading out in the pre-empirical flow of time, posits unity in the temporal flow of the exhibitive images, in that it turns every image into precisely an exhibitive one, posits givenness in it and with every new image, givenness "of the same." What is given in every phase, however, is given and posited as a now with such and such a content. In the transition to the next phase it is held fast in its now. Thus the new phase (and very new phase) is given with its now held fast; therefore, in the continuous transition, the phases are so posited in unity that every phase in the Objectivation keeps its now, and the series of now-points (as Objective temporal points) is filled with a continuously uniform and identical content. When phase *a* is actual, it has the character of the actual now. But in the temporal flux, phase joins to phase, and as soon as we have the new actual phase those which have just "now" been have altered their character as actual. In this flux of alterations, temporal Objectivation takes place so far as, in the flux of phenomenological alteration which *a* undergoes in sinking back, a continuous positing of the

---

[70] Husserl, *The Phenomenology of Internal Time-Consciousness*, trans. by James S. Churchill (Bloomington: Indiana University Press, 1969), pp. 62-63.

identical *a* with the determinate temporal point results. In Objectifying consciousness, the flux of images running off appears as a flux of alterations of sensible contents. If every image with its now were so Objectified as it is in itself, the unity of this multiplicity would be the unity "lying in it," and to be inferred from it.[71]

If there is something new added with Husserl's analysis of time over against Augustine, therefore, it is the concern to ensure that time is not exclusively subjective, but belongs to objects, as well. This conclusion he justifies on the basis of the principle of intentionality:

> The foreground is nothing without the background; the appearing side is nothing without the non-appearing. It is the same with regard to the unity of time-consciousness - the duration reproduced is the foreground; the classifying intentions make us aware of a background, a temporal background. And in certain ways, this is continued in the constitution of the temporality of the enduring thing itself with its now, before, and after. We have the following analogies: for the spatial thing, the ordering into the surrounding space and the spatial world on the one side, and on the other, the spatial thing itself with its foreground and background. For the temporal thing, we have the ordering into the temporal form and the temporal world on the one side, and on the other the temporal thing itself and its changing orientation with regard to the living now.[72]

The emphasis is placed by Husserl not in terms of transcendental deductions, as with Kant, but in terms of the "Urimpression," the originating, primal impression dependent upon a given objective content, which is the absolute starting point of the constitution of the continuum of temporality.

> This is the characteristic of continuous generation. Modifications continuously beget ever new modifications. The primal impression is the absolute beginning of this generation - the primal source, that from which all others are continuously generated. In itself, however, it is not generated; it does not come into existence as that which is generated but through spontaneous generation. It does not grow up (it has no seed): it is primal creation. Does this mean that a fresh now is continuously added on to the now which is modified into a not-now? Or does the now generate, spring up all of a sudden, a source? These are the images. One can only say that consciousness is nothing without an impression.[73]

Consciousness is nothing but the content of its impressions. These impressions are a "given," and the condition of the possibility of that "giv-

---

[71] Husserl, *The Phenomenology of Internal Time Consciousness*, p. 167.
[72] Husserl, *Phenomenology of Internal Time-Consciousness*, pp. 78-79. See, as well, *ibid.*, p. 165: "It appears, indeed, that something temporal, temporality itself, belongs essentially to the appearing object and, in our case, temporality in the form of the duration of the unaltered, static thing."
[73] Husserl, *Phenomenology of Internal Time-Consciousness*, p. 131.

enness," in the way that those impressions are in fact given, is temporality. Temporality is both the condition of possibility for the impressions and it is inseparable from the acts of constituting consciousness that makes sense of those impressions.

> I have a primordial schema, a flux with its content, but in addition a primordial multiplicity of "I can": I can go back to any place in the flux and produce it "once more." As with the constitution of Objective spatiality, we also have an optimum here. The image of the duration in a simple retrospective glance [*Rückblick*] is unclear. In clear re-production [*Wiedererzeugungen*] I have it "itself," and more clearly, the more nearly complete.[74]

However, one can and must ask whether it is in fact possible to "go back to any place in the flux." This is, rather, an illusion created by the assumption that time is concerned with what is actual. Once one observes the role of possibility in all actuality, then the illusion that one can "go back to any place in the flux" is manifest, for, at best, one could "go back" to what actually happened. But what actually happened occurs always at the expense of what possibilities were denied. Those possibilities in their comprehensive range are incapable of reconstruction, since they are concealed by actuality.

Ricoeur points out[75] that the price Kant pays for situating time in the intuition as the condition of possibility for the experience of the sensed world is the loss of the identity of the self (*Critique of Pure Reason* B152-153) and of the other/Other. This is because the self is analogous to any other object of experience, i.e., one has access only to the appearance of the object not its reality. Time is the necessary condition of possibility for the emergence of any content in experience, but, as such, the object recedes behind its appearances and time (as well as space) remains *an inexplicable given* in the intellect. On the other hand, Husserl retains the dependence of time upon an enduring identity of the objects of experience, for ultimately it is that enduring (temporal) identity that accounts for one's experience of both other/Other and self. Consciousness is always conscious-of something. Hence, for Husserl *the inexplicable given* is the enduring, temporal identity of the object (the noema) to which one can return.

Ricoeur concludes his analysis of temporality in Husserl and Kant by observing a paradoxical relationship between them:

> Neither the phenomenological approach [Husserl] nor the transcendental one [Kant] is sufficient unto itself. Each refers back to the other. But this referral presents the paradoxical character of a mutual borrowing, on the condition of a mutual exclusion

---

[74] Husserl, *Phenomenology of Internal Time-Consciousness*, p. 145.
[75] See Ricoeur, *Time and Narrative*, vol. 3, pp. 48, 49, 50, 54.

[clearly an aporia]. On the one hand, we can enter the Husserlian problematic only by bracketing the Kantian problematic [which treats time as mere intuition distinct from objects]; a phenomenology of time can be articulated only by borrowing from objective time, which, in its principal determinations, remains a Kantian time [contrary to Husserl's claim]. On the other hand, we can enter the Kantian problematic only on the condition of abstaining from all recourse to any inner sense that would reintroduce an ontology of the soul [since the identity of the self eludes one], which the distinction between phenomenon and thing in itself has bracketed. Yet the determinations by which time is distinguished from a mere magnitude must themselves be based on an implicit phenomenology [on the presupposition of an enduring self over against the enduring identity of temporal objects in the world], whose empty place is evident in every step of the transcendental argument. In this way, phenomenology and critical thought borrow from each other only on the condition of mutually excluding each other. *We cannot look at both sides of a single coin at the same time.*[76] (emphasis added)

Ricoeur's project intends to bridge the two inexplicable givens of the intuition (time and space) in the intellect and of noematic temporal identity of the object by means of the mediating process of narrativity - specifically, the pervasive role of mimesis in all experience. There are only degrees of mediation in experience and not differences in kind for accessing reality independent of mediation.

As much as the present project applauds that agenda embracing mediation, it cannot be allowed to merely conceal the aporetic complexities upon which narrative experience depends. It is only when consciousness encounters its limits openly that it can become accountable for its individual and communal actions out of the humility of faith. Ricoeur is well aware that narrativity alone does not protect one from systematic distortion.[77] It is only by combining a hermeneutics of restoration with a hermeneutics of suspicion that the religious depths of the human condition can begin to be, even if remotely, understood.

Ontological Time

If the classic discussion of time found in Plato, Aristotle, and Plotinus is cosmological, and if the anthropological/phenomenological turn is taken

---

[76] Ricoeur, *Time and Narrative*, vol. 3, p. 57.
[77] The danger's of meta-narrativity, even the "cunning of reason" of the Hegelian project so attractive to the intellectual, are clearly acknowledged by Ricoeur. See Ricoeur, *Time and Narrative*, vol. 3, p. 274: "... our eulogy to narrative unthinkingly has given life again to the claims of the constituting subject to master all meaning. On the contrary, it is fitting that every mode of thought should verify the validity of its employment in the domain assigned to it, by taking an exact measure of the limits to its employment."

with respect to time already with Augustine only to be developed in terms of its paradoxical character in the mutually excluding yet complementary projects of Kant and Husserl by whom the triad of self, world, and temporal presupposition emerge as *a tension between an illusive self*, by, and within whom, time is the necessary condition of possibility for one to experience a world, *and the illusive unity and constancy of the world*, permitting one's returning to it and retaining of it in consciousness in order for time to be experienced, then an examination of the meaning of time in Heidegger will enable a direct encounter with the dynamic of self and world as inseparable from the horizon of temporality. Yet, what is new in the Heideggerian analysis is that the self, world, and temporality are analyzed not in terms of actuality, but in terms of possibility.

If Aristotle is the first to ask how time is real, he can ask the question as he does only because for him what is real is what is "actual." Hence, only the "present" of time is real, because only the present is actual. This allows him to understand non-material "forms" to be both actual and eternally present as the cause of form in matter, for, if "forms" are actual (and they must be, according to Aristotle, *Metaphysics* 1071b20-23), then "they must ever be actual." Since knowledge for Aristotle consists in causal explanation (*Metaphysics* 981b27-30; 983a25-26), knowledge is concerned foremost, if not exclusively, with what can and must actually be, i.e., form, matter, efficient causality, and the final cause. Time, according to Aristotle, is the enigmatic moment of the moving point, i.e., the pause that is the "two" of end and beginning, which is the condition of possibility not only for one's knowing any-*thing* but for all experience (for, if there is motion, there must always be motion, *Metaphysics* 1071b7-14) of actuality. But there is no further investigation into this "gap" by Aristotle. The "gap" resurfaces in Plotinus in his equally aporetic description of time combining Plato's notion of time as the "image of Eternity" with time as "a unity of link and succession," which is neither movement nor number but "a Kind to itself." It has been suggested that the Kind of time is the Kind of "not-Being," taking Plato's five Kinds as the framework for Plotinus' notion of Kind. "Not-Being" can be most fully understood as the key to temporality only once one moves beyond restricting time to the confines of actuality to include the open dynamic of possibility into the discussion. This is the achievement of Heidegger in *Being and Time*, for even the anthropological/phenomenological discussion of time by Augustine, Kant, and Husserl rests upon the narrow metaphysical presupposition of actuality. Augustine's case for *distentio animi* or the "three-fold present" presupposes, just as Aristotle does, that only the present is actual. Both Kant and Husserl are interested in time as the presupposed condition for human experience of actual things.

Heidegger

No other category (or "Kind") discloses the metaphysical presuppositions of the Western tradition more graphically than time. If actuality is the key to the discussion of time prior to the Enlightenment, nevertheless, that actuality included the actuality of a non-material dimension (e.g., Plato's νοῦς and the Good; Aristotle's forms and Unmoved Mover). With the Enlightenment, however, a shift commences with respect to what constitutes actuality to the point that *by the beginning of the 20th century actuality is exclusively material*. Hence, Heidegger's retrieval of the Aristotelian notion of potency as the key to human experience and understanding in the world marks a certain kind of revolution in the tradition of metaphysics, for, not only does Heidegger attack the metaphysics of actuality, he elevates possibility above actuality while simultaneously concerned to limit the discussion of Dasein (or the human) to its concern with the things of the world. *A human being "is" its world, because Dasein is inseparable from the possibilities of its world.* Experience is analyzed in terms of understanding consisting of an open-ended process of projection of possibilities based upon the circumstances of the individual's world. Humans are unthinkable without the world as an horizon of possibility.[78]

It will be seen in the next chapter that Heidegger's discussion of the Self in terms of its authentic possibilities, i.e., those possibilities that are its own rather than merely defined by the public "they-world," is central to his rethinking the problematic of the Self raised by Kant while concomitantly linking the Self to the temporal dynamic of the world. Hence, it is time, or the no-thingness of possibility, that ensures that the Self is inseparable from its world and the other/Other in that world.

What must be done here is a careful analysis of what temporality means for Heidegger. It will become clear that the title of Heidegger's opus should not be *Being and Time* but *Being is Time*, i.e., Being as the Being-of beings is possibility.

When one asks about the "meaning" of something, according to Heidegger, one is asking about its Being and that can only occur within a temporal horizon or totality.

---

[78] Again, one must acknowledge a difference between "formal" and "ontological" possibility as discussed above in footnote 8.

> "Meaning" signifies the "upon-which" [*das Woraufhin*] of a primary projection in terms of which something can be conceived in its possibility as that which it is. Projecting discloses possibilities - that is to say, it discloses the sort of thing that makes possible.[79]

But this is not some blind projecting of possibilities. The projecting of possibilities is impossible without, and inseparable from, the world of entities in which the individual (Dasein) finds itself.

> All ontical experience of entities - both circumspective calculation of the ready-to-hand, and positive scientific cognition of the present-at-hand[80] - is based upon projections of the Being of the corresponding entities - projections which in every case are more or less transparent. But in these projections there lies hidden the "upon-which" of the projection; and on this, as it were, the understanding of Being nourishes itself.[81]

What is this "upon-which" that is "hidden" and "nourishes" understanding? This hidden source is time as possibility. The individual (Dasein) makes sense of its experience in and through the actualization of possibilities. In order to do so, Dasein must acknowledge that it already finds itself in a world, and the possibilities that it will actualize are inherited out of the pastness of that specific world of the individual. But Dasein can project possibilities, it can seek to make sense of its experience, only because it lives toward the future. Projection of one's possibilities is always a projection from where one now "is" towards what one "is" yet to be. Hence, the horizon of possibilities is the "upon-which" that is "hidden" and "nourishes" understanding. That horizon of possibilities is radically temporal: Dasein is inseparable from historicality.

> In temporality ... the constitutive totality of care has a possible *basis* for its unity. Accordingly it is within the horizon of Dasein's temporal constitution that we must approach the ontological clarification of the 'connectedness of life' - that is to say, the stretching-along, the movement, and the persistence which are specific for Dasein. The movement [*Bewegtheit*] of existence is not the motion [Bewegung] of something present-at-hand. It is definable in terms of the way Dasein stretches along. The specific movement[82] in which Dasein *is stretched along and stretches itself along*, we call its "*historizing*". The question of Dasein's 'connectedness' is the

---

[79] Heidegger, *Being and Time*, p. 371.
[80] For the distinction between the "present-at-hand" and the "ready-to-hand," see Heidegger, *Being and Time*, pp. 79, 97-98, 200.
[81] Heidegger, *Being and Time*, p. 371.
[82] Notice the connection here between temporality and movement echoing the Aristotelian discussion. Heidegger's point is very Aristotelian: time is not movement; time is the condition of possibility of "stretching along" that is movement. Time is the concealed horizon of possibility ...

ontological problem of Dasein's historizing. To lay bare the *structure of historizing*, and the existential-temporal conditions of its possibility, signifies that one has achieved an *ontological* understanding of *historicality*.[83]

To be sure, this "historicality" is *not* world history. World history is a mere re-construction of the actual and is, therefore, derivative from Dasein's historicality, i.e., from Dasein's existence as projecting of possibilities.

> We contend that what is *primarily* historical is Dasein. That which is *secondarily* historical, however, is what we encounter within-the-world - not only equipment ready-to-hand in the widest sense, but also the environing *Nature* as 'the very soil of history.' Entities other than Dasein which are historical by reason of belonging to the world, are what we call 'world-historical'. It can be shown that the ordinary conception of 'world-history' arises precisely from our orientation to what is thus secondarily historical. World-historical entities do not first get their historical character, let us say, by reason of an historiological Objectification; they get it rather *as those entities* which they are in themselves when they are encountered with-the-world.[84]

Heidegger summarizes this derivative character of world-history as follows:

> the 'birth' of historiology from authentic historicality ... signifies that in taking as our primary theme the historiological object we are projecting the Dasein which has-been-there upon its ownmost possibility of existence. Is historiology thus to have the *possible* for its theme? Does not its whole 'meaning' point solely to the 'facts' - to how something has factually been?
>
> But what does it signify to say that Dasein is 'factual'? If Dasein is 'really' actual only in existence, then its 'factuality' is constituted precisely by its resolute projection of itself upon a chosen potentiality-for-Being. But if so, that which authentically has-been-there 'factually' is the existentiell possibility in which fate, destiny, and world-history have been factically determined. Because in each case existence is only as factically thrown, *historiology will disclose the quiet force of the possible with greater penetration the more simply and the more concretely having-been-in-the-world is understood in terms of its possibility, and 'only' presented as such.*[85] (partial emphasis added)

Clock time is itself a derivative from the primordial temporality of Dasein with its possibilities.[86] It is only because Dasein is a stretching along

---

[83] Heidegger, *Being and Time*, p. 427.
[84] Heidegger, *Being and Time*, p. 433.
[85] Heidegger, *Being and Time*, p. 446.
[86] See Heidegger, *Being and Time*, pp. 476-477. Ricoeur identifies the most valuable contribution of Heidegger with respect to the analysis of temporality to be his advancing of the "idea of a plurality of temporal levels" (*Time and Narrative*, vol. 1, p. 84). In *Time and Narrative*, vol. 3, p. 71 he adds: "There is no way I can measure my debt as regards the ultimate contribution of Heidegger's hermeneutic phenomenology to the theory of time. The most valuable discoveries in it give rise to the most disconcerting perplexities. The distinction between temporality, historicality, and within-time-ness ... can be added to its two other remarkable discoveries - the recourse to Care as that which makes tem-

of possibilities: inherited, projected, and actualized thereby suppressing other possibilities which are part of the new background of inherited possibilities of realized actuality that are, in turn, projected and actualized ...; it is only because Dasein is a stretching along of possibilities that there can be movement that is measurable.[87] *"The 'there'* [Dasein literally means "there-Being"] *is disclosed in a way which is grounded in Dasein's own temporality as ecstatically*[88] *stretched along, and with this disclosure a 'time' is allotted to Dasein; only because of this can Dasein, as factically thrown, 'take' its time and lose it."*[89]

Hence, time is not the quantifiable sequence of moments, for such a quantifiable movement presupposes time. Neither is time to be confused with a linear sequence of actuality, for in such a linear sequence time presents itself merely as a "pause" or "gap" of "not-Being" as the between at the end of the past and the beginning of the future. Rather, time is more ade-

---

porality possible and the plural unity of the three ecstasies of temporality." What Ricoeur sees as perplexing in Heidegger's analysis is what Ricoeur takes to be his exclusive concern with "Being-towards-death" or mortal time for an understanding of temporality at the exclusion of the "public time of narrative." See Ricoeur *Time and Narrative*, vol. 1, p. 86. This leads Heidegger in Ricoeur's judgment to ignore the significance of the "trace" (a narrative trace) as the key to historicality. See Ricoeur, *Time and Narrative*, vol. 3, pp. 78, 120, 122-123. In "Narrated Time," p. 265, Ricoeur wrote: "... how does *Dasein* interpret its having-been-there if not by relying on the autonomy of marks left by the passage of former humans? Heidegger's failure to understand the phenomenon of the trace reflects the failure of *Sein und Zeit* to give an account of the time of the world, which has no care for our care." While this critique of Heidegger is well taken with respect to Heidegger's not attempting to give an account of cosmological time over against phenomenological time, Ricoeur's focus on the trace can be taken to be an emphasis on the "actual" at the expense of the horizon of possibilities that makes for historical Dasein as a "having-been-there." Perhaps Ricoeur's misunderstanding of Heidegger's analysis of time as possibility is most clearly disclosed when he writes: "I cannot see how the repetition of possibilities inherited by each of us as a result of being thrown into the world can measure up to the scope of the historical past. Extending the notion of historizing to co-historizing ... provides, of course, a wider basis for having-been. But the gap between having-been and the past remains, insofar as what, in fact, opens the way for an inquiry into the past are visible remains" (Ricoeur, *Time and Narrative*, vol. 3, p. 79). Heidegger's analysis demonstrates that "history" or the "historical past" is derivative from time and historicality. See Heidegger, *Being and Time*, pp. 444f. Hence, Heidegger has not forgotten the role of the "trace," but, to the contrary, he is concerned to point to the *concealed* horizon of possibility that constitutes the temporal horizon of human experience and understanding. What greater force can the past have?

[87] See Heidegger, *Being and Time*, p. 457f.
[88] See Heidegger, *Being and Time*, p. 380: "Temporality is essentially ecstatical."
[89] Heidegger, *Being and Time*, p. 463.

quately "ontologically" understood as that limitless sea of possibility uniting actuality in a whole of past, present and future within which human beings find themselves. Since possibility is inseparable from actuality, however, actuality places constraints on the limits of possibility. However, those constraints, are usually not the ones the individual thinks they are, either because the individual tends to focus exclusively on actualities rather than possibilities or, when the individual does tender possibilities, s/he cannot ever be conscious of the entire range of possibilities enabling any actual context and, thereby, tends to exclude possibilities that consequently are actualized. In addition, though, the individual can actualize a particular possibility only at the exclusion of other possibilities to which the individual can never return to in exactly the same constellation. This accounts for the aporetic moment associated with time as a mere linear sequence.

For, although in principle it would be possible to "reverse" time, were time merely a linear sequence of actual events, in fact time is the not-Being of possibility presupposed by all actuality. As such, it is impossible to reconstruct the horizon of possibilities accompanying any particular point of actuality. Therefore, time cannot be "reversed." Yet, having forgotten the role of possibility in experience, the linearity of actuality, in turn, encourages the individual to focus on time as a measurable quantity rather than as the limitless horizon of possibility uniting future, past, and present. Aporetically, then, the very horizon of possibility which determines that time is irreversible encourages the focus on time as linear which contributes to the "forgetting" or "concealing" of the role of possibilities/time in experience.

Being as Time Unites the Unchanging and the Temporal
Frequently in the tradition, Being has been contrasted with Becoming and Eternity with Time. This is because Being was understood as "reality" and the really real was the eternal and unchanging order of universals. Reality applied to what endured, hence, what truly is, i.e., Being and Eternity, as opposed to what was transient, i.e., Becoming and Time. The realm of Becoming was explained as consisting of a mirror image or copy of the realm of Being; Time, then, was understood to be a mirror image of Eternity.

It is now clear that such a metaphysical explanation of Being or Becoming is no longer defensible. Universals are aporetic in that they are the contingent condition of possibility for one to make sense of one's experience but they are, on the one hand, indefinable and are constituted through experience ectypally. On the other hand, they are archetypal and a priori in experience to the extent that they are encountered as inherited in language, that "great institution that has gone before us all" in the words of Paul Ricoeur.

They constitute the unchanging order necessary for one's making sense of the flow of phenomena in consciousness. In other words, in the absence of universals it would be impossible for one to understand anything of the incessant flow of mediated phenomena from the world in the mind. Universals constitute the enduring actualities of mental life, yet, just as with the actualities of the physical world, universals are involved in the dynamic of revealing and concealing of possibilities by actuality. Hence, both the unchanging and the changing are involved in the same dynamic of manifestation and concealment.

Similarly with the physical world, the dimension of Becoming is experienced as an aporia, for it is experienced only by means of the mediations of one's socio-linguistic paradigm through which everything is filtered. Again with reference to Ricoeur, there is no escaping mimesis$_1$. Furthermore, the dimension of Becoming is secondary in experience to the illimitable and immeasurable dimension of the mind. First, because all experience of the realm of Becoming occurs exclusively in the mind. Second, mind can combine the ingredients of the physical world in ways that the physical world cannot by itself. For example, the components of a computer, when spread out on a table, can never combine themselves to create a computer. It is only with the addition of the "eminent" (as opposed to "formal") causality[90] of the mind that the components can be turned into a functioning computer. Such observations cannot be employed to logically justify a retrieval of the teleological argument or argument from design for God, however, because of the aporetic limits to both universals and the socio-linguistic structuring of reality.[91] Once again, the physical world of Becoming is ambiguously characterized by the dynamic of manifestation and concealment played out by actuality and possibility in historical experience similar to the same dynamic of actuality and possibility in the intellect.

Taking Being as time to be possibility, then, thoroughly transforms the frequent contrast between Being and Becoming; Eternity and Time. The aporetic tension of experience is not appropriately articulated by these contrasts. Rather, the aporetic tensions of experience consist of the inseparable and yet irreducible dynamic of interaction between the intellect and world, paradigms and speculative causality, the aporia of language, truth, and temporality already discussed, and it includes the aporia of self and other/Other

---

[90] See Descartes Meditation III.
[91] It will be suggested at the conclusion of this project that the teleological argument is not necessarily incompatible with the logical judgments arrived at in the present project, but it constitutes a speculative leap beyond those logical judgments.

presented in the next chapter. Ontologically, it is the no-thingness of Being as time that unites these aporetic tensions in the interplay of actuality and possibility. Hence, Being as time unites the intellect and the world of sense perception. As no-thingness, however, Being as time offers no metaphysical explanation or foundation to experience. In fact, Being as time is itself aporetically concealed by the actuality of experience. Being as time unites the unchanging and the temporal in the aporetic dynamic of revealing and concealing, in other words, in the aporetic dynamic of actuality and possibility.

Conclusion

One can identify three aporetic moments with respect to temporality. Everyday experience of time indicates that time is not merely a sequence of moments, but, as *distentio animi*, time includes the simultaneity of the past and the future in the present. This is not a mere simultaneous whole of all that is transpiring as event in any particular moment, but, rather, the simultaneity of the past and future for enabling the present. Aporetically, then, time is a contradiction of sequence and simultaneity.

Second, time is aporetic with respect to cosmological and phenomenological or anthropological time. In terms of the cosmic moment, the "present" of the individual is insignificant, not even a mere blip on the cosmic screen. On the other hand, there is only significance because of the "present" of an individual's experience. Cosmological time itself is meaningless without phenomenological time. Here the aporia consists in the whole negating the part upon which the whole is dependent.

The third aporia of time surfaces out of the Aristotelian and Plotinian attempt to reconcile time with movement and measurement. Aporetically, the "present" is not "one" but "two." It is the end of the past and the beginning of the future. As such, the "present" is not any-*thing*. It is a "pause" or "gap" of not-Being which Plotinus speaks of as a "Kind" in the Platonic sense from the *Sophist* of the "great Kinds." This allows a connecting of Heidegger's analysis of time as the "no-thingness" of possibility with the "not-Being" of this classical discussion. Time, then, can be thought as the no-thingness of possibility presupposed and concealed by all actuality. As such, possibility is what negates the reversibility of time while simultaneously encouraging focus on time as a linear sequence of actuality thereby concealing the role of possibility. For this reason, although everyone knows what time is, i.e., sequence, movement, and measurement, when confronted with the task of defining time, it escapes delineation. For time is possibility inseparable from, enabling, and limited by actuality.

This ontological notion of time as possibility permits a rethinking of the tension between time and Eternity suggested by Plato and fully developed by Plotinus. According to Plato and Plotinus, time is the image of Eternity as a copy is the image of its original. Such a definition of time presupposes a metaphysics of Eternal universals existing independent of time. Yet the analysis of the aporiai of language has shown that universals are experienced both as a posteriori and a priori, i.e., as generated by metaphorical language and preserved or inherited with language. In short, universals are aporetically inseparable from the world of sense in human experience. A metaphysics of Eternal universals, while perhaps not an unreasonable leap, remains a speculative leap that too easily covers over the aporetic status of universals.

Hence, the classic tension between Being and Becoming, Eternity and Time, must be reformulated. Being is time as the concealed horizon of possibility for all actuality both invisible and visible, internal and external, mental and physical. This post-metaphysical position radically challenges the presupposition that actuality precedes potentiality, the presupposition of the Western tradition since at least Xenophanes in the 6th century BCE and Anaxagoras in the 5th who maintained that "nothing can come from nothing." Possibility is no-thing, and all actuality is embedded in a sea of possibility even as that constellation of the actual limits, but by no means determines, what possibilities will be actualized. Being and time are not two dimensions of reality in dualistic contrast to one another, i.e., Being in contrast to Becoming; Eternity in contrast to Time; hence Being and Eternity in contrast to Becoming and Time. Rather, Being is time as the horizon of possibility concealed by all spiritual and material actuality. The human condition, then, is an aporetic dynamic process of revealing and concealing/actuality and possibility which accounts for, but doesn't metaphysically explain, the ever changing context of experience.

The aporetics of temporality have consequences at the heart of human reason. It is not merely that universals must remain presuppositions (i.e., ideas are indefinable); it is not merely that reality is a socio-linguistic construct; it is not merely that the fundamental presuppositions of Western thought of "nothing can come from nothing" and "like perceives like" either depend upon a metaphysics of actuality or a metaphysics of Mind, i.e., aporetically conceal the role of possibility; but even the coherence of one's socio-linguistic construct of reality presupposes time which now must be seen as aporetic. For both the law of the excluded middle and the law of identity, upon which all coherence is dependent, presuppose time. Eluding all conceptual clarification and definition, time is the not-Being presupposed by all events/actuality; yet, to the extent that it is distinguishable as cosmological and phenomenological it is aporetic. Similarly, the Eternal escapes definition, for the unchanging aporetically takes one back to the self, but now to retrieve the spiritual depths and richness of the human intellect (the door opened by one's awareness of universals/λόγος and νοῦς which are the key to the Eternal in the Western tradition) as a complement to the analysis of the human as Being-in-the-world by Heidegger.

Heidegger's analysis stressed the role of possibility in establishing the inseparability of the human from its world, i.e., the world of sense perception. It can now be seen that possibility establishes the inseparability of the "inner" and the "outer" in human experience in a way that opens up the unique, if aporetically unreachable, depths of the self. The self is rooted in the sea of possibility common to all things, but the individual's own possibilities are unique to the circumstances in which s/he finds her/him-self. But, even further, the self is contradictorily (aporetically) dependent upon, and accountable to, the other/Other for its self-understanding and worth.

Chapter 12
The Aporia of Self and Other

The discussion of the aporia of self and Other (person) has been left to the last by no means because it is of least significance, but because experiential spirituality commences with the individual even as the individual is inseparably interconnected with the world and Others (persons). Even though the prior five chapters on aporiai in experience have spoken frequently in the third person singular, the attentive reader will have long since observed that the entire project is in reality concerned not only with the first person plural "we" but with the world of action, including objects and persons, as well. However, it is only after taking the long route over the issues at issue with νοῦς (Spirit/Intellect/Consciousness) and world, with sociological paradigms and causality, with language, truth, and time that the themes related to the aporiai of the self and the Other can come into adequate focus.

Defining the Self?

Who is the self? If anything has been established by the preceding discussions, the self is not a mere "what" or "thing." While it is true in the First World that the self is defined by its appearance, power, and social status, no such criteria for defining the self can begin to apply to the imperceptible, illimitable, immeasurable depths of the self. It could easily be maintained that all criteria for defining the self in terms of appearances in fact are misguided distortions of the self, for they seek to reduce the self to some form of external manifestation.

On the other hand, it has become popular today to define the self psychologically in terms of invisible, suppressed emotions that have come to blindly determine the self. To regain one's self one must somehow return to the initial emotionally charged events to rework and complete an emotional process that has been blocked off by repression. The accuracy of this description of the self consists of the acknowledgment that there is no experience unaccompanied by "mood" or an emotional valence. For this reason, it is always possible to focus on emotion. But it would be a distortion of the self if it was to be defined only by its mood. If mood is essential for the illumination of one's situation, equally significant are the possibilities of that situation which alone can transform the situation including the mood. Moods on their own can change nothing; they can only perpetuate themselves. Only possibilities can change moods and situations.

A more reflective understanding of the self is that definition of the self as the "essence" of the individual. This notion of the self depends upon the logical distinction between form and accidents. The self, according to this definition, is that permanent substrate (form or substance) that enables one to be identified as the self-same throughout all of the changes (accidents) that make for a life. In short, the self is that which unites the baby I once was with the adult that I now am although not even the cells are the same between these two manifestations of the self. Here one encounters several characteristics of selfhood that are best more precisely distinguished.

The idea of a permanent substrate includes two notions: permanent suggests always present; substrate suggests substance. Hence, the self, according to this definition, is a permanent substantial presence uniting all of the accidents that make up the historical contingencies of the self. Yet there is more to this notion of the self as a substance of presence. The self as an abiding substantial presence includes the claim that the self, as imperceptible, illimitable, and an indivisible unity, is something permanently "inside" from which one "goes out" into the world and to which one "returns." The "going out" and the "coming in" are transient events constituting the accidents of the permanent substance of the self as presence.

All of these constitutive components associated with a definition of the self as an individual essence, however, are limited to defining the self in terms of actuality. To speak of the self as an essence, as a substance of enduring presence from which one goes out into the world and to which one returns, is only to acknowledge as the self what the self "actually is." It leaves out of account all that of the self that is possible. But of course, that is because one's possibilities are not real until they are actualized, and the self is not a self until it is actualized. Nonetheless, as true as it is, that we cannot say "who" this self is until something of that self is actualized, to define the self merely in terms of its actuality would be to sever the self from its very taproot: the ambiguous nothingness, yet limited, hence somehow definite, range, of its possibilities.

No more greater violation of selfhood has been perpetuated than that which has sought to define the self exclusively in terms of its actuality. More has been lost by the human species insistence on refusing to acknowledge potentialities than has ever been destroyed by wars, racism, sexism, nationalism, capitalism, technology, etc. All of these define the self and its world in terms of actual things to be calculated, predicted, manipulated, and controlled to enhance the interests of the few. Yet, they all rest upon a "knowledge" of actuality that is either ignorant of, or wishes to avoid, the radical unknowing faith at the core of all experience.

Merely emphasizing the dimension of possibility in seeking the "who" of the self, however, is not sufficient. Heidegger has sought to define the self exclusively in terms of its "authentic ownmost possibilities."[1] Such a definition of the self not only risks failing to acknowledge the radical ambiguity of identifying one's "authentic ownmost possibilities," but Heidegger's analysis has emphasized only those possibilities with respect to one's thrown Being-in-the-world of things both present- and ready-to-hand[2] of our concern and the possibilities of Dasein-with of Others in solicitude.[3] In other words, Heidegger's analysis of the self correctly, but narrowly, insists that the individual is inseparable from its world of things and Others, because they constitute part of the horizon of possibility that is essential for each individual to be the individual that s/he is. But Heidegger ignores the role of possibilities in the intellect, i.e., the spiritual depths of the human.

Appropriately, Heidegger focuses on the role of the projecting of one's possibilities in light of the context of things and Others in which the self finds itself. This allows him to distinguish authentic and inauthentic possibilities in terms of those truly appropriate to the individual and those defined for the individual by its socio-historical context. The "true Self" for Heidegger remains the resolute individual in possession of her/his ownmost possibilities without the distortions and illusions of the public they-world:

> If Dasein discovers the world in its own way [eigens] and brings it close, if it discloses to itself its own authentic Being, then this discovery of the 'world' and this disclosure of Dasein are always accomplished as a clearing-away of concealments and obscurities, as a breaking up of the disguises with which Dasein bars its own way.[4]

However, according to Heidegger, inauthenticity serves as the framework within which any and all authenticity may occur. Hence, if the self means authentic self-constancy, then the structure serving as the condition of possibility for our experience is not grounded in the self, i.e., in the authentic self, but in non-Self, i.e., the inauthentic "they" world: "'Resoluteness' sig-

---

[1] See Heidegger, *Being and Time*, pp. 368-369.
[2] Things "present-at-hand" are all objects in the world. See Heidegger, *Being and Time*, pp. 79 and 200. Things "ready-to-hand" are those employed by Dasein in some manner. See Heidegger, *Being and Time*, pp. 97-98.
[3] For the distinction between "concern" and "solicitude," see Heidegger, *Being and Time*, pp. 157, 237, and 344. Concern has to do with one's involvement with "things." Solicitude, on the other hand, has to do with one's relationships to Other Dasein's, i.e., persons.
[4] Heidegger, *Being and Time*, p. 167.

nifies letting oneself be summoned out of one's lostness in the 'they'. The irresoluteness of the 'they' remains dominant notwithstanding, but it cannot impugn resolute existence."[5] It is only in this context that Heidegger can claim that

> *Care does not need to be founded in a Self. But existentiality, as constitutive for care, provides the ontological constitution of Dasein's Self-constancy, to which there belongs, in accordance with the full structural content of care, its Being-fallen factically into non-Self-constancy.*[6]

This comes as a shocking statement, for the analysis of the Being of Dasein (the individual) is the analysis of "Care" as the existential structure enabling any and all experience. Hence, to suggest that Care does not need to be founded in a Self seems to suggest that Care can be independent of Dasein. The confusion is resolved once it is seen that the meaning of "Self" is limited to the "authentic self," the self owning its unique individualization and seeking to own its possibilities responsibly, in contrast to the "inauthentic self" lost in the public they-world. Care is manifest by both authentic and inauthentic Dasein. One can live one's whole life, in Heidegger's judgment, inauthentically, for that is far "easier" than struggling to live authentically. Such an inauthentic life is very much a life of Care. Hence, "Care does not need to be founded in a[n authentic] Self." Rather, one can live one's whole life inauthentically, and it still would be a life of Care. On the other hand, if Care does not need to be founded in an authentic self, the authentic Self is founded in the inauthentic self.

The analysis of the authentic self by Heidegger seems at times to be shaped by a naive optimism about authenticity that ignores the implications of his own analysis with respect to the ambiguity of this relationship between authentic and inauthentic possibilities.[7] This becomes manifest when he insists that only as authentic possibilities is the self truly the Self.[8] Heidegger

---

[5] Heidegger, *Being and Time*, p. 345:
[6] Heidegger, *Being and Time*, p. 370.
[7] This naive optimism is shared by Robert Funk who reformulates the notions of inauthenticity and authenticity in terms of the conflict between "literal" (= inauthentic language) and "poetic" (= authentic language) without awareness of the ambiguities involved. See Robert W. Funk, "Myth and the Literal Non-Literal" in *Parables and Presence* (Philadelphia: Fortress Press, 1982), pp. 134-135; especially, p. 130: "Absolute metaphor represents a suitable purgatory for the literalistic mind; parable offers kenotic redemption for those willing to venture beyond the precincts of the comfortable but illusory solidity of the received world."
[8] Heidegger wrote in *Being and Time*, p. 369: "Selfhood is to be discerned existentially only in one's authentic potentiality-for-Being-one's-Self - that is to say, in the authenticity of Dasein's Being *as care.*"

states on more than one occasion that inauthenticity is the *existentiale*, i.e., it is primordial, where authenticity is an *existentiell*, i.e., it is episodic and impermanent.[9] Nevertheless, according to Heidegger, this rootedness of the authentic Self in inauthenticity is neither determinative nor ambiguous for the authentic Self. The "they" cannot "impugn resolute existence." It is for this reason that Heidegger embraces Nietzsche's notion of "monumental history."[10] Monumental history, according to Heidegger, is the consequence of authentic resolution into the future which arises out of "resolute repetition" of the great possibilities of the past.[11]

However, such an authentic Self and, hence, monumental history, as Heidegger and Nietzsche would have it, are truly ambiguous, for one can never be sure that one is actualizing one's ownmost possibilities any more than one can have certain knowledge of any-*thing*. Heidegger seems to be aware of this ambiguity when he writes: "In the moment of vision [the authentic insight], indeed and often just 'for that moment', existence can even gain the mastery over the 'everyday' [inauthenticity]; but it can never extinguish it."[12] The most authentic possibilities are tied to the "world" of the individual and, thereby, subject to the influence of the public "they." The notion of a sovereign authentic self is an illusion.

Furthermore, as indicated above, Heidegger's analysis of Dasein only in terms of the possibilities with respect to things (the objects of "concern") and Others (the persons engaged in "solicitude") of its world[13] has completely turned attention away from the dimension of the intellect/consciousness or νοῦς (Spirit) with its own "internal" dynamic of actuality and possibilities *as inseparable as that "internal" dynamic is from the things of one's "concern"*

---

[9] See Heidegger, *Being and Time*, pp. 167-168, especially, p. 168: "*Authentic Being-one's-Self* does not rest upon an exceptional condition of the subject, a condition that has been detached from the "they"; *it is rather an existentiell modification of the "they" - of the "they" as an essential existentiale.*" Later, however, Heidegger wrote, p. 365: "It has been shown that proximally and for the most part Dasein is *not* itself but is lost in the they-self, which is an existentiell modification of the authentic Self." See, however, *ibid.*, p. 312: "Authentic Being-one's-Self takes the definite form of an existentiell modification of the 'they' ..."

[10] See Heidegger, *Being and Time*, p. 448.

[11] See Heidegger, *Being and Time*, pp. 443-444.

[12] Heidegger, *Being and Time*, p. 422. The notion "moment of vision" echoes the theme of the "Moment" from Kierkegaard. See Chapter 1, n. 28.

[13] This is what Heidegger calls Dasein's "*facticity*." See *Being and Time*, p. 82: "the concept of 'facticity' implies that an entity 'within-the-world' has Being-in-the-world in such a way that it can understand itself as bound up in its 'destiny' with the Being of those entities which it encounters within its own world."

and the persons of one's "solicitude." Heidegger's neglect of νοῦς leads him to define λόγος (Logos) exclusively in terms of διαίρεσις (diaeresis) and σύνθεσις (synthesis) rather than including theoria in the discussion of λόγος. His desire to avoid an "ontology of ideas" that can serve as the foundation for knowledge as well as his abhorrence of all "idealism" prohibits his retaining any valuable notion of θεωρία in his reflections. Understanding (διαίρεσις or discursive reason[14]) has eliminated reason (θεωρία).[15]

The present investigation of the aporia of the self and other/Other (things/persons) seeks to correct the onesidedness of Heidegger's analysis by retrieving the spiritual depths of possibility equally constitutive of the self as much as the self, surely, is inseparable from the horizon of possibilities of others/Others in the world as Heidegger maintained. Despite its limitations, however, the value of Heidegger's analysis of the self is his calling into question traditional notions of the self: "In the prevalent way of saying 'I', it is constantly suggested that what we have in advance is a Self-Thing, persistently present-at-hand; the ontological question of the Being of the Self must turn away from any such suggestion."[16]

The Self: Beyond Actuality to the Dynamic Tension of Possibilities Between Intellect and World

The Self that emerges in the present project is neither a thing, nor a bundle of uncensored and censored emotions, nor a substance, nor a mere presence, nor merely a set of authentic possibilities. The self is, in addition, neither a thing nor a place from which we go out into the world and to which we return. The self is no more a mere "inside" than it is a mere "outside." Above all, the self is nothing merely actual. The self is inseparable from its Being, and its Being is an open-ended process of projecting of possibilities both material and mental, i.e., inseparable from its communal paradigm, the linguistic mediation of all experience, the dynamic of revealing and concealing of possibilities in actuality, and the horizon of time.

Although the self is nothing other than an understanding projecting of its possibilities, those possibilities are, to be sure, limited by the actual context of the individual self even as such limitation always leaves room for the

---

[14] See Plotinus, "The Good or the One" in Enneads VI, 9 [9] found in *The Essential Plotinus*, pp. 78-79.

[15] For clarification of the distinction between "understanding" and "reason" employed here, see the simile of the line in Book VI of Plato's Republic.

[16] Heidegger, *Being and Time*, p. 370.

unexpected. In any event, the self is not in complete conscious control of its possibilities, for the dynamic of actuality and possibility is a dynamic of manifestation and concealment that involves both the actualization and the nullification of possibilities in any moment (although nullified possibilities can, on occasion, be in part resuscitated if never in exactly the same constellation[17]). Hence, there is a circularity to understanding that is as preconscious, if not more so, than it is conscious. *One can only actualize one's possibilities that one somehow already "possesses" even as one is not necessarily conscious of those possibilities.*

Yet, the self is not just any and every dynamic of possibility and actuality. The situation of the self is always unique if not at the level of actuality then assuredly at the level of possibilities. It may be that two individuals share the same living accommodations, travel the same route to work, even work in the same office, but their experience is individually unique. That uniqueness is the consequence of each individual's historicality. In other words, it is not merely that each individual has a unique perspective.[18] Rather, each individual inherits a certain range of presuppositions (Gadamer's "prejudices" or what one can call filters or lenses) as well as acquires her/his own presuppositions out of the unique experience as a result of the interface between one's presuppositions and the actual events of one's personal life. A perspective is the consequence of this process of constant interaction between the understanding (the projection of those possibilities open to the individual) the individual brings to the event *and* the constellation of possibilities enabled by the constitutive things/Others of the event. That interface of possibilities and actuality is, and must be, unique for each individual. It is precisely this uniqueness that is the key to the individual's claim to dignity and integrity.

Aporetically, each individual is a unique world just as the world is the same world for everyone. No greater lesson can be learned than this paradox. In an age in which the differences among races, ethnic groups, nationalities, genders, and classes have come to dominate individual and social perceptions and policies, nothing could be more valuable than to grasp the meaning of individual uniqueness, dignity, and worth born out of the necessarily unrepeatable character of each individual's acquisition of a world. But that insight is inseparable from the recovery of the role of possibility in all

---

[17] This is the real potential informing Monumental History. See Heidegger, *Being and Time*, pp. 396-397.

[18] Argued by Nietzsche in *Thus Spoke Zarathustra* and Wheelwright in *Metaphor and Reality*.

actuality in experience. So long as individuals, genders, races, social groups, societies, and nations only focus on, or are only defined in terms of, actualities, so long will individuals, groups, and societies be tempted to cultivate only mis-understanding, distrust, and fear which are the source of oppression, exploitation, and attempts at eradication of the Other.

Yet here the aporia of the world as both unique and shared plays into the mis-understanding. For one can only project those possibilities which are one's own, i.e., one can only understand the world from out of the interface of possibilities and actualities that are a unique configuration for each individual. Hence, the encounter with the Other is compromised from the start, because one cannot project (one can only imagine[19]) the possibilities of the Other.

When one adds the dynamic of socio-linguistic paradigms for the constitution of the individual's reality to the set of filters shaping the uniqueness of the individual's world, then the vastness and pervasiveness of the built-in tendency to mis-understand (i.e., a distorted imaging of the Other in one's own imagination) in the encounter between the individual and the Other clearly emerges. This is precisely what Gadamer teaches with respect to the necessity of acknowledging one's own presuppositions/prejudices/filters in order for the Other to be acknowledged as Other.

However, Gadamer's notion of presuppositions applies not only to the "text" but also to νοῦς (spirit/intellect/consciousness), for the possibilities of the self include *simultaneously* the "inside" and the "outside;" the "invisible" and the "visible." As much as the self is inseparable from its world of things and Others, as Heidegger taught, the experiencing self is inaccessible to the senses just as it is inaccessible to itself - as was taught by Kant and underscored by Ricoeur.[20] However, what has been overlooked by Kant, Heideg-

---

[19] The imagination does not refer to fantasy and imagining is not fantasizing. Rather, the imagination is that capacity of consciousness that "images," represents, or mediates the contents(s) of conscious experience to the self. It is directed "outward" from consciousness in contrast to understanding which is an "inner" activity of establishing coherence by means of establishing identity in the flow of differences of the imagination. The activity of understanding employs universals and the imagination in the projecting of possibilities in order to "make sense" of experience.

[20] See Kant, *Critique of Pure Reason*, B152-153. Ricoeur observes in *Time and Narrative*, vol. 3, p. 55: "... we know ourselves as an object - and not as we are ..." Quoting Kant he adds, *ibid.*, p. 55: "'... the determinations of inner sense have therefore to be arranged as appearances in time in precisely the same manner in which we arrange those of outer sense in space' ... Of course, what is important to Kant in this argument is that self-affection is strictly parallel to affection from outside: 'so far as inner intuition is concerned, we know our own subject only as appearance, not as it is by itself' ..."

ger, and Ricoeur is the role of νοῦς as central for the understanding of the self. Νοῦς is the imperceptible, illimitable, indivisible whole of consciousness (the "invisible unity" of experience) that is inseparable from the aporia of universals as ectypal and archetypal as well as the aporiai of paradigms and praxis, truth, and temporality. Without the aporia of universals there would be no experience of similarity much less identity in individual and corporate experience. The "content" of one's spirit (νοῦς) is not merely the flow of images by means of which the "external" world is represented to the self in the imagination, but, as Husserl taught, the "content" of one's spirit simultaneously includes the essences or universals that one employs to make sense of those images[21] and, as Kuhn points out, that content does not consist of the mere matching up of a single universal with its appropriate images of the imagination as if isolated in a vacuum. Rather, understanding involves the coherent (i.e., non-contradictory) inter-relationship of all experienced universals and images, i.e., it involves the totality of a paradigm with its quasi-metaphysical commitments, rules, instrumentation, communal agreement, and causal habitualities.[22] In other words, experience is a dynamic, interface between language and the imagination as an illimitable, coherent unity. However, now it must be observed that this dynamic interface is incompletely understood so long as it is taken to be merely an interface of actuality.

This can be seen as the central oversight of Descartes, who separates the paradoxical interfacing of intellect and world into two substances.[23] Language, the imagination, and the illimitable coherence of a paradigm, however, are events of possibility more than they are of actuality (or more than they are any form of substantiality[24]). Descartes, however, ignores possibili-

---

[21] See Husserl's discussion in "Philosophy and the Crisis of the European Man" in *Phenomenology and the Crisis of Philosophy*, trans. by Quentin Lauer (New York: Harper Torchbooks, 1965), pp. 188f.

[22] See Kuhn, *The Structure of Scientific Revolutions*, pp. 41-42.

[23] See Descartes, *Meditations*, particularly Meditation VI.

[24] A case could be made that Aristotle makes the same error as a consequence of uncritically accepting the aphorism of Xenophanes and Anaxagoras that "nothing can come from nothing." Hence, actuality must precede potentiality according to Aristotle. This is precisely where his position embraces the metaphysics of Plato. Forms must exist actually prior to their being manifest as form in matter although epistemologically we experience form first as form in matter. It is in this sense that Aristotle suggests that "not everything logically prior is also prior in being [substantiality]." (Metaphysics 1077b) For a discussion of the unity of Aristotle's metaphysics in terms of the inseparability of the law of excluded middle, the principle of non-contradiction, and the concept of substance, where οὐσια is taken to mean εἶδος, see Fernando Inciarte, "Die Einheit der Aristotelischen Metaphysik" in *Philosophisches Jahrbuch* 101/1 (1994), pp. 6-7.

ty. Yet it is precisely possibility that accounts for the ambiguity of experience far more than one's ability to doubt the actuality of the "external" world. For possibilities are not only concealed by all actuality, but, in addition, their presence and concealedness are not restricted to the "external" world. The possibilities that "I" am include simultaneously and inseparably those emerging out of the unique and unrepeatable experience of the self as νοῦς in dynamic interaction with a life-world of things and Others.

As was discussed with respect to the aporiai of language, universals are indefinable, i.e., they remain indefinite presuppositions of possibility. This judgment is independent of the issue whether or not universals are a posteriori or a priori - as aporetic as that issue is in itself. Hence, the very dimension of experience that enables the perception of identity in difference is as much if not more a phenomenon of possibility than it is actual. Once again, the inadequacy of any and all literal language surfaces in the analysis, for literal language is no more adequate for grasping universals than it is for grasping particulars. Just as Wheelwright argued that steel nets are not the best means for taking samples of reality that is "largely fluid and half-paradoxical,"[25] so, too, do universals escape the rigid formulations of the literal language of actuality.

Not only is the realm of sense perception not the content of experience (for we don't think the angle drawn on the blackboard; we think the idea "angle" imperceptible to the senses), but all particularity is made sense of by means of universals that escape the precision of literal actuality. Hence, if the reality of particularity is most adequately understood as a dynamic of actuality and possibility, so, too, is the reality of universals and that unity of illimitable, coherent wholeness that is νοῦς/spirit.

In any event, this discussion of νοῦς in no way is meant to reintroduce a twoness in experience as if there was an "I" that was some passive observer of its contents both mental and physical. Such an understanding of the "I" that separated it from its contents was maintained by Natrop and vigorously rejected by Husserl. Natrop maintained that

> "[t]he I as the subjective center of relatedness to all contents of my consciousness stands over against those contents as decidedly different from them. It does not have the same relationship to them as they do to it ... It cannot be a content for itself and is entirely different from anything that can be a content for it. It is incapable of

---

This issue is a chicken or egg issue. It is not simply that something must be actual before it can be possible. For prior to all actuality must be possibility. Otherwise, the actual could not become manifest if it was not previously possible.

[25] See Wheelwright, *Metaphor and Reality*, p. 128.

closer description; for everything we might employ in order to describe the I or our relationship to it could be taken only out of the content of consciousness and, thereby, the I itself or the relationship to the I is missed."[26]

Husserl responds:

> Now I must confess, that I am simply not able to find this primitive I of the subjective center of relatedness. All that I notice, or that is possible for me to perceive, is the empirical I and its empirical relation to its own experiences or external objects available to it in any given moment as precisely those objects of particular attention ...[27]

According to Husserl, consciousness is nothing other than its contents. This is what he means by "intentionality."

> In perception something is perceived, in the imagining of images some image is imagined, in love something is loved, in hate something hated, in desiring something desired, etc. The mystery indicated by these examples was what Brentano had in mind when he said: "Every psychical phenomenon is characterized by that which the Scholastics in the Middle Ages called the intentional (to be sure, entirely mental) non-existence of an object, and what we would call, although not without ambiguity, the relationship to a content, the directedness toward an object (whereby one does not understand a reality) or immanent objectivity. This immanent objectivity contains something in it as an object, although not always in the same manner."[28]

This permits Husserl to observe:

> It is not ... two psychical things present, it is not the experienced object and next to it the intentional act directed toward the object; it is also not two things in the sense of part and encompassing whole, but only one thing is present, the intentional experience, whose essential descriptive character is precisely the mentioned intention ... Is this experience in its psychical, concrete fullness present, so is *eo ipso* the intentional "relationship to an object" accomplished, *eo ipso* an object is "intentionally present"; for both say exactly the same thing.[29]

Consciousness is always and already consciousness-of something,[30] and this consciousness-of constitutes an indivisible unity which can be described in terms of "parts," but, nevertheless, remains a whole.[31] Therefore, it is the unitary whole of νοῦς, that is nothing but its contents, which is of central

---

[26] Edmund Husserl, *V. Logische Untersuchung. Über intentionale Erlebnisse und ihre "Inhalte"* (Hamburg: Felix Meiner Verlag, 1975), p. 20. All translations from this text are those of this author unless indicated otherwise.
[27] Husserl, *V. Logische Untersuchung*, p. 21.
[28] Husserl, *V. Logische Untersuchung*, p. 26.
[29] Husserl, *V. Logische Untersuchung.*, pp. 31-32.
[30] See Husserl, *Ideas*, p. 108: "It belongs as a general feature to the essence of every actual *cogito* to be a consciousness *of* something."
[31] See Husserl, *V. Logische Untersuchung*, pp. 35-6, 37.

significance for the present project. There is no going above or behind consciousness to any actuality (when one does engage in speculation one is sketching possibilities not actualities), any self, that somehow contains the experience of the individual, guides that experience, or from which one "goes out" and to which one "returns." Consciousness is a unitary whole imperceptible, immaterial, indivisible, immeasurable, and "rooted" in the unchanging as it is struggling to understand the changing.

Above all, however, consciousness and, hence, the self, are inadequately understood from the ground up when it is treated exclusively in terms of actuality. This is the key critique made by Heidegger of Husserl's Phenomenology.[32] Higher than actuality is possibility, Heidegger silently screams at the end of §7 in *Being and Time*. It is precisely the horizon of possibility unique to each individual that holds the "visible" and the "invisible;" the "inside" and the "outside" in an inseparable dynamic tension as a whole. Once again, Heidegger's analysis of Dasein in terms of Care has indicated the inseparability of the individual from her/his world of things and Others, for Dasein is nothing but its possibilities and its understanding consists precisely in the constant projecting of possibilities. On the other hand, Husserl's analysis of consciousness indicates the inseparability of consciousness, what this project prefers to call νοῦς, from its contents. Yet the illimitable unity of νοῦς/spirit is only adequately understood when it, too, is seen in terms of its rootedness in possibilities, i.e., not merely of the imagination (not to speak of the fantasy), i.e., in terms of the self's inseparability from the horizon of possibilities of the world of things and Others as analyzed by Heidegger, but, in addition, of universals, as well.

Beyond Heidegger's Logos to Nous

Heidegger's analysis of "interpretation" in §32 and §33 of *Being and Time* remains incomplete without an appreciation of the role of universals in the taking of something "as something." The "as-structure" of interpretation is incomprehensible without the notion of universals and their aporetic status. This failure on Heidegger's part may be accounted for by his tendency to treat λόγος exclusively in terms of "discourse."[33]

---

[32] See McGaughey, "Husserl and Heidegger on Plato's Cave Allegory."
[33] See section B of §7 entitled "The Concept of the Logos" in Heidegger, *Being and Time*. Later, Heidegger suggests that discourse is equiprimordial with state-of-mind (Befindlichkeit) and understanding. See *ibid.*, p. 203. See, as well, his discussion of λόγος in "Letter on Humanism."

Heidegger's analysis centers on the role of the λόγος in "letting something be seen" in the sense of "to make manifest what one is 'talking about' in one's discourse."³⁴ "And only *because* the function of the λόγος as ἀπόφανσις lies in letting something be seen by pointing it out, can the λόγος have the structural form of σύνθεσις."³⁵ This reading allows Heidegger to understand λόγος exclusively in terms of entities:

> When considered philosophically, the λόγος itself is an entity, and, according to the orientation of ancient ontology, it is something present-at-hand ... In this first search for the structure of the λόγος as thus present-at-hand, what was found was the *Being-present-at-hand-together* of several words. What establishes the unity of this "together"? As Plato knew, this unity lies in the fact that the λόγος is always λόγος τινός. In the λόγος an entity is manifest, and with a view to this entity, the words are put together in *one* verbal whole. Aristotle saw this more radically: every λόγος is both σύνθεσις and διαίρεσις, not just the one (call it 'affirmative judgment') or the other (call it 'negative judgment'). Rather, every assertion, whether it affirms or denies, whether it is true or false, is σύνθεσις *and* διαίρεσις equiprimordially. To exhibit anything is to take it together and take it apart. It is true, of course, that Aristotle did not pursue the analytical question as far as the problem of which phenomenon within the structure of the λόγος is the one that permits and indeed obliges us to characterize every statement as synthesis and diaeresis.³⁶

Here it is clear that Heidegger, true to the entire project of *Being and Time*, understands λόγος with respect to the letting be manifest of entities in the world. Λόγος is understood exclusively in terms of διαίρεσις and σύνθεσις and not in terms of θεωρία, or, in the vocabulary of Plato in the simile of the line in Book VI of the *Republic*, λόγος is discussed by Heidegger only in terms of "understanding" (what later in the tradition was called discursive reason) rather than in terms of "reason."

Because Heidegger seeks to limit λόγος to the "letting something be seen" in the sense of "to make manifest what one is 'talking about' in one's discourse," he employs the notion of ἴδια (meaning "one's own, belonging to one, personal" and not ἰδέα the notion of form or universal) to speak of the more primordial moment of the simplest and determinate ways of Being.

> Αἴσθησις, the sheer sensory perception of something, is 'true' in the Greek sense, and indeed more primordially than the λόγος which we have been discussing. Just as seeing aims at colours, any αἴσθησις aims at its ἴδια (those entities which are genuinely accessible only *through* it and *for* it); and to that extent this perception is al-

---

³⁴ Heidegger, *Being and Time*, p. 56.
³⁵ Heidegger, *Being and Time*, p. 56.
³⁶ Heidegger, *Being and Time*, pp. 201-202.

ways true.[37] This means that seeing always discovers colours, and hearing always discovers sounds. *Pure νοεῖν is the perception of the simplest determinate ways of Being which entities as such may possess, and it perceives them just by looking at them.* This *νοεῖν* is what is 'true' in the purest and most primordial sense; that is to say, it merely discovers, and it does so in such a way that it can never cover up. This *νοεῖν* can never cover up; it can never be false; it can at worst remain a *non-perceiving*, ἀγνοεῖν, not sufficing for straightforward and appropriate access.[38] (partial emphasis added)

Here ἴδια refers to "the simplest determinate ways of Being which entities as such may possess" without any accounting for the "how" of that determinateness. But that "how" not only involves a dynamic of revealing and concealing of possibility (the event of Being in Heidegger's sense), in addition, it includes the aporetic event of universals which alone allow consciousness to perceive something as a determinate "this" rather than "that."

It is clear that Heidegger wishes to avoid any "'doctrine of ideas' [which alone are to] ... be understood as philosophical *knowledge*,"[39] but when ideas are understood as aporetic and indefinable then they, too, are open to the very dynamic of possibility and actuality that Heidegger wishes to emphasize for the "world" of the individual. Then the "truth" as ἀλήθεια as revealing/concealing of actuality and possibilities emerges for ideas/universals (the most simplest determinate ways of Being) as much as for entities of one's "concern" as for the Others of one's "solicitude" in the world.

Only in this way can one retrieve the spiritual depths and breadth of the self as νοῦς which distinguishes humanity from all other species while enhancing humanity's accountability to, and for, all species. As the "house of Being"[40] language provides the "clearing" for the possibilities of one's world, but at the same time one cannot overlook the aporiai that characterize language and illuminate the spiritual character of any and all experience. The very loss of the spiritual character of experience has been a major factor contributing to the eclipse of theology as an existentially relevant discipline in the contemporary world.

---

[37] This is clearly a reference to the notion that consciousness is what it is and cannot be anything but what it is in contrast to the things and Others in the world accessible through the senses that can be other than the way they appear to be.
[38] Heidegger, *Being and Time*, p. 57.
[39] Heidegger, *Being and Time*, p. 58.
[40] See, for example, Martin Heidegger, "Letter on Humanism," p. 205.

On the Unique and Unrepeatable Character of Individual Consciousness

No one has wrestled with the issue of the unique and unrepeatable character of individual consciousness with respect to the problem of solipsism more than Edmund Husserl. While seeking to maintain an "objectivity" within conscious experience, Husserl commenced with the singular and originating character of consciousness which allows for speaking of the Other as persons only analogically (or by apperception) rather than directly and immediately. But Husserl did not stop with the problem of our having only indirect access to the Other. The limitations of our experience of the Other as the Otherness of someone else, accessible only through analogy/apperception, applies to the world (otherness) in general.[41]

Husserl commences his analysis with the everyday experience of consciousness which is convinced that it has access to the empirical world directly and immediately. This attitude he calls the "natural standpoint." Nevertheless, such a standpoint generates questions like the following:

> How can experience as consciousness give or contact an object? How can experiences be mutually legitimated or corrected by means of each other, and not merely replace each other or confirm each other subjectively? How can the play of a consciousness whose logic is empirical make objectively valid statements, valid for things that are in and for themselves? Why are the playing rules, so to speak, of consciousness not irrelevant for things? How is natural science to be comprehensible in absolutely every case, to the extent that it pretends at every step to posit and to know a nature that is in itself - in itself in opposition to the subjective flow of consciousness?[42]

Husserl's answer to these questions is that they point to the fundamental enigma of consciousness in the sense that consciousness does not have direct and immediate access to an exogenous world external to it. Yet Husserl insists that this does not lead to mere subjective relativism or solipsism. Bracketing out a directly accessible world as *existing independently* of one's consciousness (or what Husserl calls engaging in the phenomenological epoché) does not eliminate the "objective" world of experience.

While it is accurate to say that consciousness is always experienced as "my" consciousness, there is a universal "structure" to consciousness shared by all consciousness.[43] Borrowing from Brentano, Husserl calls this structure

---

[41] See Edmund Husserl, *Cartesian Meditations*, p. 147

[42] Edmund Husserl, "Philosophy as Rigorous Science" in *Phenomenology and the Crisis of Philosophy* (New York: Harper Torchbooks, 1965), pp. 87-88.

[43] Husserl writes in the *Cartesian Meditations*, p. 28-9: "The bare identity of the 'I am' is not the only thing given as indubitable in transcendental self-experience. Rather there extends through all the particular data of actual and possible self-experience - even though

"intentionality." Consciousness is always and already "consciousness-of" something regardless of the status of that something, e.g., actual, fantasy, illusion.

> All that bears the title "consciousness-of" and that "has" a "meaning," "intends" something "objective," which latter - whether from one standpoint or other it is to be called "fiction" or "reality" - permits being described as something "immanently objective," "intended as such," and intended in one or another mode of intending.[44]

Husserl argues, in addition, that, although we cannot establish the indubitable *existence* of anything independent of consciousness, nevertheless there is a dependable order to the intentional structure of consciousness that allows us to establish whether something is actual or not. His point in short is that, although we can never have *direct*, unmediated access to any world "outside" of consciousness, the content of consciousness (and there is always a content) indicates that there are not only "regions" of experience, e.g., fantasy, dreaming, reflection, acting, but each region is distinguishable by its structural constituent elements. The degree to which one can pragmatically "return to" or "repeat" the intentional experience establishes the status of each region. For our purposes here, however, what is crucial is Husserl's insight that the apodictic "ego" is not merely a Cartesian transcendental point of certainty. It always and already involves a structure even though that structure is experienced only from within consciousness.[45]

The fact that experience is "only from within" my own consciousness in no way denies that there is a foreign component (Husserl speaks of the "other" as "Fremd" and of what is *peculiarly my own* as "Nicht-Fremd"[46]) not of my origin as part of the structural moment of experience which is "given."[47] Nevertheless, consciousness remains "*a unitarily coherent stratum*" or what Husserl calls "the *founding* stratum"

> that is to say: I obviously cannot have the "alien" or "other" as experience, and therefore cannot have the sense "Objective world" as an experiential sense, without having this stratum in actual experience; whereas the reverse is not the case.[48]

---

they are not absolutely indubitable in respect of single details - a *universal apodictically experienceable structure* of the Ego (for example, the immanent temporal form belonging to the stream of subjective processes)."

[44] Husserl, "Philosophy as Rigorous Science," p. 109.
[45] See Husserl, *Cartesian Meditations*, p. 103.
[46] See Husserl, *Cartesian Meditations*, p. 95.
[47] See Husserl, *Cartesian Meditations*, p. 111.
[48] Husserl, *Cartesian Meditations*, p. 96.

It is this "founding stratum" (and not some universal, simple point or Natrop's "primitive " of the subjective center of relatedness") that constitutes the singular and unique experience of the individual in the sense that no other individual can have the same "founding stratum."

> But here something remarkable strikes us: a sequence of evidences that yet, *in* their sequence, seem paradoxical. The psychic life of my Ego (this "psychophysical" Ego), including my whole world-experiencing life and therefore including my actual and possible experience *of* what is other, is wholly unaffected by screening off what is other. Consequently there belongs within my psychic being the whole constitution of the world existing for me and, in further consequence, the differentiation of that constitution into the systems that constitute what is included in my peculiar ownness and the systems that constitute what is other. I, the reduced "human Ego" ("psychophysical" Ego), am constituted, accordingly, as a member of the "world" with a multiplicity of "objects outside me". But I myself constitute all this in my "psyche" and bear it intentionally within me.[49]

Husserl's aim is to indicate how all "otherness" is not something that is merely questionably arguable after one has established the existence of an indubitable Cartesian ego.[50] Rather, the ego is nothing other than its content which means that simultaneously with the self is a not-self - even if that not-self can only and exclusively be experienced "in my peculiar ownness."[51]

> Manifestly (and this is of particular importance) the own-essentiality belonging to me as ego comprises more than merely the actualities and potentialities of the stream of subjective processes. Just as it comprises the constitutive systems, *it comprises the constituted unities* - but with a certain *restriction*. That is to way: Where, and *so far as, the constituted unity is inseparable from the original constitution itself*, with the inseparableness that characterizes an immediate *concrete* oneness, *not only the constitutive perceiving but also the perceived existent belongs to my concrete very-ownness*.[52] (partial emphasis added)

There is a paradoxical character to the individual's experience of the world. All experience of any actual or possible "outside" occurs exclusively in the individual's "inside." This points to the radical solitude of the individual.

---

[49] Husserl, *Cartesian Meditations*, pp. 98-99. Husserl adds, p. 99: "In consequence of this parenthesizing [this transcendental reduction], I have become aware of myself as the transcendental ego, who constitutes in his constitutive life everything that is ever Objective for me - the ego of all constitutions, who exists in his actual and potential life-process and Ego-habitualities and who constitutes in them not only everything Objective but also himself as identical ego."

[50] See Husserl, "§18. Descartes's misinterpretation of himself. The psychologistic falsification of the pure ego attained through the epoché" in *The Crisis*, pp. 78-81. See pp. 90, 155, and 171 (*ego-cogitatio-cogitata*), as well.

[51] See Husserl, *Cartesian Meditations*, pp. 102-103.

[52] Husserl, *Cartesian Meditations*, pp. 103-104.

... as soon as ... one sets to work, attempting in a systematic self-investigation and as the pure ego to uncover this ego's whole field of consciousness, one recognizes that *all that exists for the pure ego becomes constituted in him himself* (sic); furthermore, that every kind of being - including every kind characterized as, in any sense, "transcendent" - has its own particular constitution. *Transcendency in every form is an immanent existential characteristic, constituted within the ego*. Every imaginable sense, every imaginable being, whether the latter is called immanent or transcendent, falls within the domain of transcendental subjectivity, as the subjectivity that constitutes sense and being. *The attempt to conceive the universe of true being as something lying outside the universe of possible consciousness, possible knowledge, possible evidence ... is nonsensical. They belong together essentially*; and, as belonging together essentially, they are also concretely one, one in the only absolute concretion: transcendental subjectivity. *If transcendental subjectivity is the universe of possible sense, then an outside is precisely - nonsense.*[53] (emphasis added)

The individual, according to Husserl, is a unique and unrepeatable stream of events whose depths and richness are immeasurable, because each person is

---

[53] Husserl, *Cartesian Meditations*, pp. 83-84. See, in addition, Husserl, *The Crisis*, p. 69: "Transcendentalism ... says: the ontic meaning [*Seinssinn*] of the pregiven life-world is a *subjective structure* [*Gebilde*], it is the achievement of experiencing, prescientific life. In this life the meaning of the ontic validity [*Seinsgeltung*] of the world are built up - of that particular world, that is, which is actually valid for the individual experiencer. As for the 'objectively true' world, the world of science, it is a structure at a higher level, built on prescientific experiencing and thinking [e.g., Kuhn's quasi-metaphysical commitments], or rather on its accomplishments of validity [*Geltungsleistungen*]. Only a radical inquiry back into subjectivity - and specifically the subjectivity which *ultimately* brings about all world-validity, with its content and in all its prescientific and scientific modes, and into the 'what' and the 'how' of the rational accomplishments - can make objective truth comprehensible and arrive at the ultimate ontic meaning of the world. Thus it is not the being of the world as unquestioned, taken for granted, which is primary in itself; and one has not merely to ask what belongs to it objectively; rather, *what is primary in itself is subjectivity, understood as that which naïvely pregives the being of the world and then rationalizes or (what is the same thing) objectifies it.*" (partial emphasis added) See further, *ibid.*, pp. 184-185: "The epoché creates a unique sort of philosophical solitude which is the fundamental methodical requirement for a truly radical philosophy. In this solitude I am not a single individual who has somehow willfully cut himself off from the society of mankind, perhaps even for theoretical reasons, or who is cut off by accident, as in a shipwreck, but who nevertheless knows that he still belongs to that society. I am not *an* ego, who still has his *you*, his *we*, his total community of cosubjects in natural validity. All of mankind, and the whole distinction and ordering of the personal pronouns, has become a phenomenon within my epoché; and so has the privilege of I-the-man among other men ... [T]he always singular 'I,' in the original constituting life proceeding within it, constitutes a first sphere of objects, the 'primordial' sphere; how it then, starting from this, in a motivated fashion, performs a constitutive accomplishment through which an intentional modification of itself and its primordiality achieves ontic validity under the title of 'alien-perception' perception of others, of another 'I' who is for himself an 'I' as I am. This becomes understandable by analogy ..."

a singular historical process. No two individuals could ever be the "same" even were they to live inseparably together. Each perspective is informed by its exclusive horizon of experience which is the consequence of the unfathomable dynamic of what has gone before and what is now transpiring in that individual's experience. There is a radical existential solitude constitutive of the human condition.

Nevertheless, Husserl's description includes more than the mere solitary experience of the individual. As inaccessible as an "outside" is to consciousness, since everything that is and can be experienced occurs within consciousness, as inaccessible as the "outside" is, there is no "inside" without the structural moment of the other as world and the Other as person.

> Genuine theory of knowledge is accordingly possible [*sinnvoll*] only as a transcendental-phenomenological theory, which instead of operating with inconsistent inferences leading from a supposed immanency to a supposed transcendency (that of no matter what "thing in itself", which is alleged to be essentially unknowable), has to do exclusively with *systematic clarification of the knowledge performance, a clarification in which this must become thoroughly understandable as an intentional performance* ... Stated more precisely: First, a self-explication in the pregnant sense, showing systematically how the ego constitutes himself (sic), in respect of his own proper essence, as existent in himself and for himself; then, secondly, a self-explication in the broadened sense, which goes on from there to show how, by virtue of this proper essence, the ego likewise constitutes in himself something "other", something "Objective", and thus constitutes everything without exception that ever has for him, in the Ego, existential status as non-Ego.[54]

This "intentional performance" in individual solitude is paradoxically determined by the structurally necessary moment of the "given" which is not the free or arbitrary invention of the individual.

> Apperception is not inference, not a thinking act. *Every* apperception in which we apprehend at a glance, and noticingly grasp, objects *given beforehand* (emphasis added) - for example, *the already-given everyday world* (emphasis added) - every apperception in which we understand their sense and its horizons forthwith, points back to a *"primal instituting"*, in which an object with a similar sense became constituted for the first time. Even the physical things of this world that are unknown to us are, to speak generally, known in respect of their type ... Thus *each everyday experience* involves an *analogizing transfer* of an originally instituted objective sense to a new case, with its anticipative apprehension of the object as having a similar sense. *To the extent that there is givenness beforehand, there is such a transfer* (partial emphasis added).[55]

What is true of the "everyday world," i.e., that it is the always and already given horizon of all intentional acts of individual consciousness, is

---

[54] Husserl, *Cartesian Meditations*, p. 85.
[55] Husserl, *Cartesian Meditations*, p. 111.

equally true of whatever one means by "nature" and, particularly, of the Other as another individual. Nature and the Other are experienced within individual consciousness by means of an "analogizing transfer" from an "originally instituted objective sense to a new case, with its anticipative apprehension of the object as having a similar sense."

> Openly endless Nature itself then becomes a Nature that includes an open plurality of men (sic) (conceived more generally: animalia), distributed one knows not how in infinite space, as subjects of possible intercommunion. To this community there naturally corresponds, in transcendental concreteness, a similarly open *community of monads*, which we designate as *transcendental intersubjectivity*. We need hardly say that, as existing for me, it is constituted purely within me, the meditating ego, purely by virtue of sources belonging to my intentionality; nevertheless it is constituted thus *as* a community constituted also in every other monad (who, in turn, is constituted with the modification: "other") as the same community - only with a different subjective mode of appearance - and as necessarily bearing within itself the same Objective world.[56]

Husserl is articulating the fundamental aporia of the self that its experience is radically individual and unrepeatable with all of its content subject to the mediation of conscious representation while, nevertheless, all representation presupposes the *givenness* of that which is represented. Representation depends upon a prior presentation that is given and discovered by consciousness. Hence, although experience itself involves a radical solitude, it equally is dependent upon an "objectivity" or the givenness of the life world of the individual that is a shared life world with Others.

> ... [I]s it ... *conceivable* that two or more *separate pluralities of monads*, i.e., pluralities *not in communion*, co-exist, each of which accordingly constitutes *a world of its own*, so that together they constitute *two* worlds that are separate ad infinitum, *two* infinite *spaces and space-times*? Manifestly, instead of being a conceivability, that is a pure absurdity. A priori, as the *unity* of an intersubjectivity ... each of two such groups of monads has, to be sure, its possibly quite different looking "world".

---

[56] Husserl, *Cartesian Meditations*, p. 130. The limits that this "Objective world" places upon transcendental subjectivity are indicated by our ability to distinguish between fantasy and what is "discovered" in that world. "... [I]n a free variation, I can fantasy *first of all myself*, this apodictic de facto ego, as otherwise and can thus acquire the *system of possible variants of myself*, each of which, however, is annulled by each of the others and by the ego who I actually am. It is *a system of a priori incompossibility*. Furthermore the fact, "I am", prescribes *whether* other monads are others for me and *what* they are for me. *I can only find them; I cannot create others that shall exist for me* (emphasis added) ... *[E]ach monad having the status of a concrete possibility predelineates a compossible universe*, a closed "world of monads", and that two worlds of monads are incompossible, just as two possible variants of my ego (or of any presupposedly fantasied ego whatever) are incompossible" (*ibid.*, p. 141).

> But the two worlds are then necessarily *mere "surrounding worlds"*, belonging to these two intersubjectivities respectively, and mere aspects of a single Objective world, which is *common* to them. For indeed the two intersubjectivities are not absolutely isolated. As imagined by me, each of them is in necessary communion with me (or with me in respect of a possible variant of myself) as the constitutive primal monad relative to them. Accordingly they belong in truth to a single universal community, which includes me and comprises unitarily all the monads and groups of monads that can be conceived as co-existent ... Hence there can exist *only one Objective world*, only one Objective time, only one Objective space, only one Objective Nature.[57]

In a recent article, Eckard Wolz-Gottwald draws attention to the interesting parallel between Husserl's transcendental phenomenology and the "three-fold eye of knowing" in the work of Hugh of St. Victor and Bonaventura.[58] The lowest form of perception is that of the "eye of sense perception" (*oculus carnis*) concerned with the existing objects of the physical world external to consciousness. Wolz-Gottwald suggests that this is what Husserl means by the "natural standpoint."[59] The "second eye" is rational knowledge (*oculus rationis*) or what Wolz-Gottwald calls the "eye of understanding."[60] Although he does not himself refer to it, Wolz-Gottwald's analysis here echoes what Plato calls the lowest activity of the intellect, i.e., understanding as distinct from reason: understanding as the making sense of the images in the mind of the external world by matching them up with their appropriate, indefinable universals in contrast to reason, according to Plato, which engages in a dialectic without the aid of external images but employs the indefinable universals to rise up to the First Principle of the whole (i.e., what Hugh of St. Victor calls the "third eye" of contemplation). Wolz-Gottwald sees in this notion of the second eye Husserl's "transcendental sphere of consciousness."

> Every phenomenological analysis must begin with sense experience in order then to shut out the sensed data by means of the epoché to get to the "sense explanation of the way of being of the real world" ... Consciousness includes simultaneously material nature, but it goes beyond it.
>
> Transcendental consciousness is concerned precisely with this region that "goes beyond." It is concerned with the form of rational perception which is no longer concerned with the analysis of particular objects or things in the world. It is concerned, rather, with that dimension of consciousness which makes possible such an analysis, i.e., that of performing and constituting transcendental subjectivity ...[61]

---

[57] Husserl, *Cartesian Meditations*, p. 140.
[58] See Eckard Wolz-Gottwald, "Die transzendentale Phänomenologie und die philosophische Mystik," pp. 98-115.
[59] Wolz-Gottwald, "Die transzendentale Phänomenologie," p. 105.
[60] Wolz-Gottwald, "Die transzendentale Phänomenologie," p. 103.
[61] Wolz-Gottwald, "Die transzendentale Phänomenologie," pp. 105-106.

Wolz-Gottwald is careful to observe that Husserl does not pursue the implications of the three-fold eye to the "highest" third eye of contemplation (*oculus contemplationis* or what the tradition has called theoria),[62] but his analysis of Husserl's notion of transcendental consciousness in light of the three-fold eye provides not only an enlightening perspective on the meaning of the transcendental epoché and the overcoming of the "natural standpoint" to indicate how Husserl can both speak of bracketing out "existence" yet, nevertheless, retain the notion of the "objective world." In addition, it indicates how Husserl is in continuity with perhaps the most ancient epistemological discussion of the Western tradition, for the "three-fold eye" is a reformulation of the three kinds of perception (or faculties of the soul) described by Plato in the simile of the line in Book VI of the *Republic*: sense perception ($\alpha\ddot{\iota}\sigma\theta\eta\sigma\iota\varsigma$), understanding ($\delta\iota\alpha\acute{\iota}\rho\varepsilon\sigma\iota\varsigma$), and reason ($\theta\varepsilon\acute{\omega}\rho\iota\alpha$). Just as in the case of Thomas Kuhn, Husserl's project is concerned with what Plato calls the "understanding," i.e., that level of consciousness concerned with making sense of the images in the mind of the sensed world by matching up universals with the appropriate images. Husserl is as aware as Plato that those universals are of a questionable status. Plato calls them hypotheses or assumptions, since he learned from Socrates that they are incapable of definition. In Husserl's case, the position is taken that the world is given; universals or essences are "constituted" by the individual.[63] In other words, universals are abstractions or ectypal developed by each individual as a consequence of her/his encounter with the "objective" world.

Husserl has appropriately described the experience of the individual both with respect to the status of the "objective" world and the emergence of awareness of universals in individual consciousness. This description insists that we acknowledge both the unique and unrepeatable character of individual experience as well as a "shared," objective world with others. But, as the discussion of the aporiai of language above indicated, the nominalist explanation of the origin of universals in the sense of their being abstractions has only pushed the conundrum of universals one step backward. One must ask, further, where does the "objective order" of the external world come from that enables the mental abstraction (or the constituting of universals to use Husserl's language)? That the material world, which cannot bring about

---

[62] See Wolz-Gottwald, "Die transzendentale Phänomenologie," pp. 106 and 114.
[63] See Robert Sokolowski, *The Formation of Husserl's Concept of Constitution* (The Hague: Martinus Nijhoff, 1964).

order on its own, conforms to a non-material order of universals is a fundamental aporia of the human condition.

Lévinas and Ricoeur on the Self

Emmanuel Lévinas[64] critiques both Heidegger and Husserl for having made the focus of their reflections the self as an individual to the neglect of the Other. He argues that their attention to the experiencing self has neglected the significance of the Other for any understanding of the self. He suggests that Husserl's notion of "intentionality," while not incompatible with a philosophy centered on the Other, nonetheless tends toward the illusion of "interiority."[65] Speaking of Heidegger, Lévinas writes:

> ... according to Heidegger's formula, "in his (sic) existence there is the question of that existence itself"; a subject who defines himself precisely by this concern for himself - and a subject who in happiness accomplishes his "for himself." To this subject we oppose the Desire of the Other which proceeds from a being already full and independent, a desire which does not want for itself. The need of a person who does not have needs - this is recognized in the need for an Other who is Other ...[66]

Although the present project agrees, that the tendency has been to read Heidegger and Husserl as all too limited to Dasein[67] and the constituting ego respectively without due consideration of the Other, Lévinas' critique is inappropriate when one examines carefully what Heidegger and Husserl have to say about the relationship between the self and its "world." For example, as was pointed out above, Heidegger not only refuses to think of the human as anything but rooted in its world, but he distinguishes within the primary existentiale of Care between "concern" for things and "solicitude" for Others.[68] Furthermore, the discussion of Husserl, above, equally indicates the

---

[64] See Walter Strolz, "Vom Sein zum Anderen. Extremer Humanismus im Denken von Emmanuel Lévinas" in *Neue Zeitschrift für Systematische Theologie und Religionsphilosophie* 35/2 (1993), pp. 176-197; Thomas Freyer, "Die Öffnung der Transzendenz. Thesen zum Logos der Theologie anhand der Philosophie" in *Die Zeitschrift für Katholische Theologie* 114/2 (1992), 140-152. For Lévinas' reflections on Heidegger and Nazism, see Emmanuel Lévinas, "As if Consenting to Horror" in *Critical Inquiry* 15/2 (1989), pp. 485-488.

[65] See Emmanuel Lévinas, "On the Trail of the Other" in *Philosophy Today* 10/1 (1966), p. 35b.

[66] Emmanuel Lévinas, "On the Trail of the Other," p. 39a.

[67] Husserl's critique of Heidegger's *Being and Time* was that it was a return to anthropology.

[68] For the distinction between "concern" and "solicitude," see Heidegger, *Being and Time*, pp. 157, 237, and 344.

inappropriateness of censoring Husserl for neglecting the Other. Transcendental intersubjectivity is a central concern of the later Husserl, and his analyses have much to contribute to understanding the self in terms of the Other. Ricoeur summarizes Lévinas' thesis: "... Lévinas dares to reverse the statement 'no other-than-self without a self,' by substituting for it the inverse statement no self without another who summons it to responsibility ..."[69] Concerning the self's responsibility to the "face" of the Other, Ricoeur states:

> I do not think I am unduly limiting the scope of the admirable analyses of Lévinas's *Totality and Infinity*, to say nothing here of his *Otherwise than Being*, by saying that this face is that of a master of justice, of a master who *instructs* and who does so only in the ethical mode: this face forbids murder and commands justice ... What strikes one immediately is the contrast between the reciprocity of friendship and the dissymmetry of the injunction. To be sure, the self is "summoned to responsibility" by the other. But as the initiative of the injunction comes from the other, it is in the *accusative* mode alone that the self is enjoined. And the summons to responsibility has opposite it simply the passivity of an "I" who has been called upon.[70] The question is then whether, to be heard and received, the injunction must not call for a response that compensates for the dissymmetry of the face-to-face encounter. Taken literally, a dissymmetry left uncompensated would break off the exchange of giving and receiving and would exclude any instruction by the face within the field of solicitude. But how could this sort of instruction be inscribed within the dialectic of giving and receiving, if a capacity for giving in return were not freed by the other's very initiative? Now what resources might these be if not the resources of *goodness* which could spring forth only from a being who does not detest itself to the point of being unable to hear the injunction coming from the other?[71]

Ricoeur is not compromising the ethical aim driving Lévinas' project. Although he acknowledges the mediated character of both history and fiction, Ricoeur maintains that

> ... the recourse to documents does indicate a dividing line between history and fiction. Unlike novels, historians' constructions do aim at being *re*constructions of the past. Through documents and their critical examination of documents, historians are subject to what once was. They owe a debt to the past, a debt of recognition to the dead, that makes them insolvent debtors.[72]

Yet he is far more aware than Lévinas of the dynamics in play in the historian's attempt to fulfill the debt. The driving component of his analysis is the movement of all understanding from practical experience (which is al-

---

[69] Ricoeur, *Oneself as Another*, p. 187.
[70] This judgment is confirmed by Thomas Freyer in "Die Öffnung der Transzendenz." See, particularly, the section "Subjektivität als reine Pasivität," pp. 148-149.
[71] Ricoeur, *Oneself as Another*, p. 189.
[72] Ricoeur, *Time and Narrative*, vol. 3, pp. 142-143.

ways and already mediated) through narration/emplotment back to practical experience.[73] The debt owed to the past and to all otherness (of inherited things and order as well as the Others of one's past and present) is not transparent by means of, or through, direct and immediate encounter with the other/Otherness, for it can be understood only through mediation. Ricoeur employs the analysis of R.G. Collingwood on the role of the imagination of the historian in the event of historical "reenactment:"

> Only a historical event lends itself to the dissociation of the "inside" fact of the event, which has to be called "thought," and the "outside" face, which stems from natural changes. To make this radical starting point plausible, Collingwood adds two clarifications. First, the outside face is far from being inessential. Action, in fact, is the unity of the outside and the inside of an event. Furthermore, the term "thought" has to be taken as having a broader extension than just rational thought. It covers the whole field of intentions and motivations.
>
> ... Faced with the authority of written sources, "the historian is his (sic) own authority" ... His autonomy combines the selective aspect of the work of thinking, the audacity of "historical construction," and the suspicious tenacity of someone who, following Bacon's adage, "puts Nature to the question" ... Collingwood does not even hesitate to speak of an "*a priori* imagination" ... to indicate that the historian is the judge of his sources and not the reverse; *the criterion for his judgment is the coherence of his construction.*
>
> Every intuitionist interpretation that would situate the concept of reenactment on a methodological plane is excluded. The place supposedly assigned to intuition is occupied instead by the imagination.[74] (emphasis added)

The dilemma for Ricoeur is that he cannot accept the distinction even between an "internal" and an "external" face as if the face in any way alone offered direct and immediate access to some ontological truth.

> Admitting that no consciousness is transparent to itself, can we conceive of reenactment as going so far as to include the opacity that is as much a portion of the original act in the past as it is of the present reflective act? ... How can we call an act that abolishes its own difference in relation to some original act of creation, re-creation? In a multitude of ways, the "re" in the term reenactment resists the operation that seeks to wipe out temporal distance.
>
> If we continue our path backwards even further, we have also to call into question the very decomposition of an action into an outside, which would be just physical movement, and an inside, which would be just thought ... The very mediations that make historical time a mixed form of time are lost: the survival of the past

---

[73] See Ricoeur, *Time and Narrative*, vol. 1, p. 53.
[74] Ricoeur, *Time and Narrative*, vol. 3, pp. 144-145. In his footnote here, Ricoeur refers to Rex Martin's *Historical Explanation: Reenactment and Practical Inference* (Ithaca: Cornell University Press, 1977) to conclude: "Imagination, practical inference, and reenactment have to be thought together" (Ricoeur, *Time and Narrative*, vol. 3, p. 307, n. 14).

that makes the trace possible, the tradition that we inherit, the preservation that makes a new possession possible. These mediations cannot be placed under the "leading kind" of the Same.[75]

It is precisely because the "reenactment" by the historian is not a mere repetition that Ricoeur's notion of debt, and the idea of our debt to the ations and sufferings of the past,[76] takes on daunting significance.

> If history is a construction, historians, by instinct, would like this construction to be a reconstruction. Indeed, it seems as though this plan to reconstruct something in constructing it is a necessary part of the balance sheet of good historians. Whether they put their work under the sign of friendship or that of curiosity, they are all moved by the desire to do justice to the past. And their relationship to the past is first of all that of someone with an unpaid debt, in which they represent each of us who are the readers of their work. This idea of a debt, which may appear strange at first sight, seems to me to stand out against the background of an expression common both to painters and historians: They all seek to "render" something, a landscape or a course of events. In this term "to render," I see the desire to "render its due" to what is and to what once was.[77]

Therefore, Ricoeur speaks of the task of the historian as a twofold task of debt and "imaginative variations."[78] This means that the encounter with the other/Other is not merely passive nor is it complete as with Lévinas in the accusative injunction. The ethical obligation of our debt to the acting and suffering of others in the past is, to be sure, an obligation of inestimable debt, but it is paid only by means of responsible imaginative variation given our lack of immediate access to the other/Other, i.e., given the mediated character of all experience. Everything hinges, then, not on what is obvious (nothing is obvious), but on how rigorously one fulfills one's responsibility in light of the necessary role of imaginative variation (projection of possibilities) in the encounter with the other/Other.

---

[75] Ricoeur, *Time and Narrative*, vol. 3, p. 147. Ricoeur had just observed: "... historians do not know the past at all but only their own thought about the past. But history is not possible unless historians know that they reenact an act that is not their own" (*ibid.*, p. 146).

Ricoeur "transposes" (see *ibid.*, pp. 143, 154, 207, 228) Plato's "leading kinds" from the Sophist 254b-259d as "the Same, the Other, the Analogous" although he admits that Plato does not discuss the "analogous" (see *ibid.*, p. 152).

[76] Ricoeur emphasizes: "For my part, I never forget to speak of humans as acting and suffering" (Ricoeur, *Oneself as Another*, pp. 144-145).

[77] Ricoeur, *Time and Narrative*, vol. 3, p. 152.

[78] See Ricoeur, *Time and Narrative*, vol. 3, pp. 142, 177-178, 228, and 257.

The Self as Ambiguous Dialectic: The "Structure of Selfhood"

But "who" is this self that owes a debt and engages in imaginative variations? Is this self an autonomous "ego" simply "next to" and merely observing the world, events, and Others? Surely not. Nor is the self passively shaped by the world, events, and Others. An adequate understanding of the self must involve an illumination of the aporia of self and other/Other(s). This self is no more transparent to itself than the world is transparent to it. The self is inseparable from its mediations both of itself to itself and of the world and Others to it. Ricoeur's critique of Husserl, then, is that with him everything is derived from the self. With Lévinas, on the other hand, everything is derived from the Other.[79] Ricoeur calls for acknowledgment of a "structure of selfhood" constituted out of an ambiguous dialectic of interaction between the self and the Other.[80]

> To the reduction of being-in-debt to the strange(r)ness tied to the facticity of being-in-the-world, characteristic of the philosophy of Martin Heidegger, Emmanuel Lévinas opposes a symmetrical reduction of the otherness of conscience to the externality of the other manifested in his face. In this sense, there is no other modality of otherness for Lévinas than *this* externality. The model of all otherness is the other person. To these alternatives - either Heidegger's strange(r)ness or Lévinas's externality - I ... stubbornly oppose the original and originary character of what appears to me to constitute the third modality of otherness, namely *being enjoined as the structure of selfhood*.[81]

What is this "structure" of selfhood? Ricoeur distinguishes between, what he labels, "*idem*-identity" and "*ipse*-identity" as the key to understand-

---

[79] See Ricoeur, *Oneself as Another*, p. 331: "... it is impossible to construct this dialectic [between active "agent" and passive "patient"] in a unilateral manner, whether one attempts, with Husserl, to derive the alter ego from the ego, or whether, with Lévinas, one reserves for the Other the exclusive initiative for asigning responsibility to the self."

Although one might want to agree with Ricoeur that Husserl seeks to "derive the alter ego from the ego" for rhetorical purposes, this "derivation" is not one of creation but of discovery.

[80] See Ricoeur, *Oneself as Another*, p. 339.

[81] Ricoeur, *Oneself as Another*, p. 354. See, further, *ibid.*, p. 317: "It was stated at the beginning of this study that the dialectical tie between selfhood and otherness was more fundamental than the articulation between reflection and analysis ... and even more fundamental than the contrast between selfhood and sameness, the ontological dimension which is marked by the notion of being as act and as potentiality.

The fact that otherness is not added on to selfhood from outside, as though to prevent its solipsistic drift, but that it belongs instead to the tenor of meaning and to the ontological constitution of selfhood is a feature that strongly distinguishes this ... dialectic from that of selfhood and sameness, which maintains a preeminently disjunctive character."

ing the self. *Idem*-identity is that notion of the self that is self-identical, universal, and articulated by the "I" in the sense of "permanence in time."[82] *Ipse*-identity is not concerned with an "unchanging core of the personality," but with "the dialectic of *self* and the *other than self*."[83] He understands "character" to be the consequence of the overlapping of *ipse* and *idem*:

> However, this overlapping of *ipse* and *idem* is not such that it makes us give up all attempts to distinguish between them. The dialectic of innovation [*ipse*] and sedimentation [*idem*], underlying the acquisition of a habit, and the equally rich dialectic of otherness [*ipse*] and internalization [*idem*], underlying the process of identification, are there to remind us that character has a history which it has contracted, one might say, in the twofold sense of the word "contraction": abbreviation and affection.[84]

Although Ricoeur develops the notion of character in light of the role of narrative in contrast to the notion of the self's permanence in time reflected in promise, the present project is concerned to point out the paradox with respect to the self: it is precisely the other as things and institutions and the Other as individuals and communities that establishes the uniqueness, the distinctiveness, the particularity of the self. In short, *idem*-identity, we shall see in Ricoeur's analysis, is interchangeable with Others. It is universal, i.e., that permanency that allows anyone to say "I." But it is *ipse*-identity that provides the self with a history hammered out on the anvil of particular context and changing in time which establishes the uniqueness of the self and distinguishes this self from every other self. "... [T]he life history of each of us is caught up in the histories of others ... What we said ... about practices and about the relations of apprenticeship, cooperation, and competition that they include confirms this entanglement of the history of each person in the histories of numerous others."[85]

To be sure, our particular context is not adequately understood if it is limited merely to its actuality. Context is the consequence of the dynamic of actuality and possibility. Yet context is only possible if it includes the other/Other and its/her/his possibilities. Paradoxically, then, the uniqueness of the self is not determined by the self inaccessible to the senses (and not known even by the self[86]), but the uniqueness of the self is established by its

---

[82] Ricoeur, *Oneself as Another*, p. 2. See *ibid*., pp. 85, 116, 118-119, 121, 124, 137, and 149-150.
[83] Ricoeur, *Oneself as Another*, p. 3.
[84] Ricoeur, *Oneself as Another*, p. 122.
[85] Ricoeur, *Oneself as Another*, p. 161.
[86] See, once again, Kant, *Critique of Pure Reason*, B152-153; and Ricoeur, *Time and Narrative*, vol. 3, p. 55: "... we know our own subject only as appearance, not as it is by itself' ..."

relatedness. It is not that you don't have access to my consciousness nor I to yours that establishes our unique identities. Our uniqueness is born out of the distinctive character of each individual's context and temporal odyssey. The is precisely the point made by Husserl with respect to intentionality: consciousness is always and already consciousness-of something and, hence, consciousness is nothing other than its contents/context.

The notion of the "other" is taken very broadly by Ricoeur to include everything in one's context not created by the self: not only the other of things and persons, but the otherness of the self as "flesh"[87] and the Other as institutions.[88] Nonetheless, the primary focus of Ricoeur's "little ethics"[89] is the Other as person. He employs Heidegger's notion of "solicitude" to speak of the self's relatedness to the Other. He is concerned to stress that solicitude is inseparable from "self-esteem" which is concerned not with one's accomplishments but with one's capacities.[90] "... [S]olicitude is not something added on to self-esteem from outside but ... unfolds the dialogic dimension of self-esteem ... such that self-esteem and solicitude cannot be experienced or reflected upon one without the other.[91] Just as with Heidegger,[92] solicitude involves the "*mediating* role of others between capacities and realization."[93]

> Never, at any stage, will the self ... [be] separated from its other. It remains, however, that this dialectic, the richest of all, as the title of the work recalls, will take on its fullest development only in the studies in the areas of ethics and morality. The *autonomy* of the self will appear then to be tightly bound up with *solicitude* for one's neighbor and with *justice* for each individual.[94]

---

[87] See Ricoeur, *Oneself as Another*, p. 324: "The flesh is the place of all the passive syntheses on which the active syntheses [echoing Husserl's *Cartesian Meditations*] are constructed, the latter alone deserving to be called works (*Leistungen*): the flesh is the matter (*hule*) in resonance with all that can be said to be *hule* in every object perceived, apprehended ... [I]t results that selfhood implies its own 'proper' otherness, so to speak, for which the flesh is the support. In this sense, even if the otherness of the stranger can - by some impossibility - be derived from the sphere of ownness, the otherness of the flesh would still precede it."

[88] See Ricoeur, *Oneself as Another*, pp. 194f.

[89] Ricoeur, *Oneself as Another*, p. 290.

[90] See Ricoeur, *Oneself as Another*, p. 181.

[91] Ricoeur, *Oneself as Another*, p. 180.

[92] See Heidegger, *Being and Time*, pp. 157, 237, and 344.

[93] Ricoeur, *Oneself as Another*, p. 181. Heidegger spoke of solicitude in terms of "leaping ahead" in contrast to "leaping in" for someone.

[94] Ricoeur, *Oneself as Another*, p. 18.

The goal of ethics (concerned with the "*aim* of an accomplished life"), which has priority over morality (concerned with "the articulation of this aim in *norms* characterized at once by the claim to universality and by an effect of constraint),[95] is articulated in light of the dialectic of solicitude for the other and self-esteem. "The very definition of ethics that we have proposed - living well with and for others in just institutions - cannot be conceived without the project of living well being affected by solicitude,"[96] hence, "... to recognize oneself as being enjoined to *live well with and for others in just institutions and to esteem oneself as the bearer of this wish.*"[97]

What higher goal can human life have? One can not, live for oneself alone; one does not establish one's self-esteem by one's accomplishments; one's identity is not some psychic pole hidden from the world and known only to the self; but, rather, one's life is a life inseparable from otherness; one's self-esteem is located in one's capacities not one's accomplishments; and one's identity is the consequence of an aporetic dialectic between the self's unknown and concealed depths and the unknown and concealed depths of otherness of all kinds.

> ... [S]haring Lévinas's conviction that the other is the necessary path of injunction, allows me to stress, more than he would want to, the need to maintain a certain equivocalness of the status of the Other on the strictly philosophical plane ... To be sure, Lévinas does not fail to say that the face is the trace of the Other. The category of the trace seems in this way to correct as well as to complete that of epiphany. Perhaps the philosopher as philosopher has to admit that one does not know and cannot say whether this Other, the source of the injunction, is another person whom I can look in the face or who can stare at me, or my ancestors for whom there is no representation, to so great an extent does my debt to them constitute my very self, or God - living god, absent God - or an empty place. With this aporia of the Other, philosophical discourse comes to an end.[98]

Conclusion

The classical Greek world spoke of that which enables the self to focus its attention either on the external or the internal world as the "soul."[99] But what is this "soul" that focuses? It is no more a thing than is that which

---

[95] See Ricoeur, *Oneself as Another*, p. 170.
[96] Ricoeur, *Oneself as Another*, p. 330.
[97] Ricoeur, *Oneself as Another*, p. 352.
[98] Ricoeur, *Oneself as Another*, p. 355.
[99] See, for example, the simile of the line in Book VI of Plato's "Republic" where the soul can focus its attention both down and up the line and Plotinus' discussion in the Enneads.

enables us to experience ourselves as an identical individual through time. One can only say that it is always a "whole" that has no parts, hence, no limits, but is inseparable from its content which itself is a dynamic of actuality and possibility. The self is far more possibility than it is actual, but these possibilities are concealed and can only be partially conscious in any moment of decision.

The aporia of self and other/Other returns, then, to the radical unknowing that has characterized this entire project. This aporia discloses experience as not the mere interface of the internal and the external, the known self and the known context, but, more profoundly, it discloses experience as an unknown and unknowing paradox in which our very "identity" as unique individuals becomes defined not by our inwardness but by our interaction with the world. The pronoun "I" is empty without its particular content born out of its interaction with the world unduplicated by any other "I." Once again, we encounter the aporia of the universal and the particular. The indefinable, universal "I" obtains its meaning only by its particular experience of otherness, which, again, is characterized by inaccessibility to either one's self or to the other/Other.

How often have we defined "individualism" only as autonomy? How often have we defined the meaning and worth of the Other by her/his appearance? How often have we defined "personal worth" in terms of one's accomplishments? How often have we defined "genius" in terms of the mind as an instrument of calculation, prediction, manipulation, and control? How often have we written the Other off as not our responsibility, because "we live in the land of equal opportunity?" How often have we called for the cutting of taxes on the grounds that I've worked for what I have without acknowledging that the "I" cannot have anything without its context/world making her/his earnings possible? How often have we criticized the freeloaders as we've pursued the goal of how much can I earn with the least amount of work?

So long as the self is defined only in terms of actuality and in terms of what one can know of the self through the senses, so long will the dignity and worth of individuals be denied and so long will our search for the good life be at the expense of others in institutions that are unjust and where self-esteem is trampled. But the key to the self is precisely what is inaccessible to the senses: the spiritual character of experience and the concealed possibilities of its/our "world." This means, however, that the key to the self is faith as an individual and communal odyssey in search of understanding. We are strangers yet fellow pilgrims ...

Conclusion
Faith in a Post-Metaphsycal Context

It is not merely theology that is confronted with a crisis today. This is because our epoch's crisis is not concerned with any specific content of knowledge or specific region of action, but with the very notions of knowledge and praxis in general. We neither know what we think we know nor does pragmatic action establish any indubitable truth. Even acknowledging that a certain kind of assurance of an exogenous world is provided by the pragmatic test (try ignoring it and see what the consequences are), this test does not apply exclusively to what has now become a questionable external world but to the structures of invisible consciousness, as well. Were we to ignore those structures of consciousness *and* the external world, we would not only get ourselves into serious trouble, but we wouldn't be able to experience anything. Yet our contemporary "post-metaphysical" context underscores not only the limits to logical arguments for any dimension independent of consciousness. In addition, it challenges all pragmatic truth claims, for they are at best contingent and not absolute. Pragmatic "proofs" suffice, perhaps, when the focus of concern is the everyday and one's agenda is defined by routines. Theology, however, is concerned with "reality" and not with mere common opinion or what is minimally sufficient for the conduct of life. The individual, who cannot not act, does not absolutely have to be. Every individual is contingent. Hence, the pragmatic truths confirmed by that contingent self are, at best, contingent and not absolute truths.

This crisis situation, however, is not something that has emerged over night. It is the consequence of a 500 year epistemological trajectory. The paradigm revolution commencing in the 14th century consisting of the shift from Christian Platonism to Christian Nominalism, resulted in a dramatic transformation with respect to what it means to know. Where Christian Platonism spoke of reality in terms of imperceptible intellect and the enduring structures of consciousness[1] ($\nu o \hat{u} \varsigma$) entirely independent of the transient

---

[1] To avoid distorting associations with Cartesianism, Kantianism, and Neo-Kantianism, the following is employing the term "consciousness" for the Greek notion of $\nu o \hat{u} \varsigma$. It understands $\nu o \hat{u} \varsigma$ to apply to the two divisions of the upper portion of Plato's simile of the line in Book VI of the *Republic*, but that upper portion ($\nu o \hat{u} \varsigma$) is not separable from the lower portion with its own two divisions of objects and shadows/reflections. Reality for Plato is not restricted to ideas/hypotheses, nor is it reducible to either $\delta \iota \alpha \iota \rho \varepsilon \sigma \iota \varsigma$ or $\theta \varepsilon \omega \rho \iota \alpha$, nor is it self-contained mind or mere abstract reason "outside" of a world of

world of materiality, Christian Nominalism came to embrace a form of Aristotelian rationality which speaks of actual reality as the material order and of reason as providing causal explanation to events.

The subsequent splitting of the sources for knowledge about God into natural and revealed theology provided a refuge for theology by maintaining a parallelism between material rationality and spiritual ultimacy. Nature can teach one about God, for by investigating the causal laws of nature one is following in the eternal footsteps of the divine. Nature, however, cannot teach one about the goal, purpose, and/or meaning of life. Nature can only tell one the "facts" of life. Hence, revealed theology, the scriptures, complemented natural theology by providing an empirical source of information about the ultimate purpose of life, i.e., salvation.[2] Although it disturbed

---

engagement, πρᾶξις. Plato's simile does not divide reality into two unrelated substances. 'Αγαθός or the first principle of the whole enables the entire line not just mind. Furthermore, the first of the four classical virtues (wisdom, justice, courage, and self-control) of Greek thought, φρόνησις, means not mere abstract insight, but practical wisdom (see Max Pohlenz, *Die Stoa*, p. 126).

Paul Ricoeur speaks of νοῦς in his discussion of Aristotle's notion of friendship and the Other as "what is best in one." See Paul Ricoeur, *Oneself as Another*, pp. 184-185. Ricoeur, as does the present project, wishes to avoid any suggestion that he is concerned with Spirit in the sense of a Hegelian meta-narrative. See *ibid.*, p. 249 and 255, and chapter 9, "Should We Renounce Hegel?," in *Time and Narrative*, vol. 3. Nevertheless, the present project seeks to rethink "spirit" precisely in the sense of νοῦς, and, hence, wishes to rethink spirit in a non-Hegelian sense. Therefore, it disagrees with Ricoeur's judgment that Geist (spirit) "... seems to be superfluous in an investigation centered on selfhood" (*Oneself as Another*, p. 240).

[2] In the first half of the nineteenth century the conflict between the "Catastrophists," those arguing that the geological record can only be accounted for by acknowledging supranatural causal agency given that the earth is only some 6,000 years old (exactly 6,000 on October 23, 1997, according to the calculation of Archbishop Usher made in 1650) on the basis of scriptural calculations, and the "Uniformitarians," those proponents of the newly developing science of geology who maintained that the geological record can be explained by uniform causality throughout an unimaginably extensive length of time, was summed up: to surrender the notion of catastrophic cause means the loss of God; where, on the other hand, to surrender the notion of the uniformity of cause means the loss of science. See Charles Coulston Gillispie, *Genesis and Geology*, p. 121.

Both alternatives are too simplistic, for assuming uniform causality throughout all time to account for natural, material phenomena does not deny (or confirm) "nomothetic" creation, i.e., the Christian Aristotelian notion that God established the eternal laws and material conditions for nature to continue creating on its own. On the other hand, if by science one means "knowledge" as is implied by the root "scientia," science is easily seen to be no threat to "theology." If one isn't convinced that the relationship between religion and science is a simple contrast, then one may defend a form of parallelism (to use Ian Barbour's descriptive categories). See chapter 5 of Ian Barbour, *Issues in Science and Religion* (New York: Harper Torchbooks, 1971). The assumption is that one can hold religion and science in parallel, i.e., religion is concerned

some that the transition to empirical rationality pulled humanity "down" exclusively into the world of natural causality, no one seemed disturbed that this paradigm revolution limited the sources for all truth to the senses: truth is learned either from nature or from the scriptures, i.e., there are and must be empirical warrants and backings for all truth claims.

Hence, the stage for the conflict between natural and revealed theology of the so-called Copernican revolution in the 17th century (although Copernicus died in 1543, it is not until Kepler and Galileo in the 17th century that one may speak of the emergence of a consensus with respect to the heliocentric universe) was set already in the 14th century with the emergence of Nominalism following the West's gaining access to the Aristotelian corpus in

---

with the meaning of experience; science with the facts. Hence, theologians have embraced the materialist epistemology of the natural sciences while still carving out a niche for themselves by defending nomothetic beginnings and the insight that nature can only say what life is; not what the meaning, purpose, and goal of life is. The former is the preserve of the natural sciences; the latter that of theology.

Barbour also speaks of a derivative relationship between religion and science in which religious judgments are "confirmed" by scientific insights, e.g., the Heisenberg uncertainty principles confirm the notion of freedom, the Big Bang theory of the universe suggests history has a beginning and an end, or the paradoxical character of the theory of light, requiring contradictory models of wave and particle theories, confirms the paradoxical character of all experience. The derivation model is a sophisticated version of the God of the gaps which is committed to a materialist ontology and seeks to gain confirmation for non-verifiable components of experience on the basis of that materialist ontology.

Parallelism between religion and science is as old as the natural/revealed theology distinction, and even Galileo argued, quoting the Vatican's cardinal librarian, that "'the Bible teaches how to go to heaven, not how the heavens go.'" See Owen Gingerich, "Hypothesis, Proof, and Censorship or How Galileo Changed the Rules of Science," p. 59. Gingerich, Professor of Astronomy/History of Science at the Harvard-Smithsonian Center for Astro Physics, reports this aphorism emerges in the debate over the church's acceptance of Galileo's defense of the Copernican system. He demonstrates that several popular conceptions about the Copernican revolution and the Church are erroneous, e.g., "[n]owhere in the decrees was it actually stated that the Copernican doctrine was heretical" (*ibid.*, p. 61); Galileo was never excommunicated but censored for disobeying the Holy See (*ibid.*, p. 64); and that the distress over the heliocentric model clearly appears to be an Italian ecclesiastical political affair (*ibid.*, p. 61), i.e., outside of Italy there is little evidence that the writings of Copernicus were "corrected," for even in orthodox Spain his works were recommended (*ibid.*, p. 61). There appears to have been a far greater awareness by the ecclesiastical authorities that reality is a limited human model. Gingerich suggests that Galileo changed the rules of science by shifting to coherence rather than empirical evidence as the fundamental criterion for scientific truth (*ibid.*, p. 65). If that is the case, science is just beginning (?) to catch up with him.

the 13th century.³ A process began here which not only championed a new standard of rationality, but it resulted in a shift in understanding Being from having a "quantitative" meaning (i.e., things having Being to the extent of the quantity of their participation in what is unchanging in the imperceptible dimension of intellect) to having a "locative meaning," (i.e., things "are" or exist to the extent that they occupy a particular place in the material world).⁴

Nominalism rests upon the conviction that the material dimension of experience contains the explanation (= causal explanation) not only of empirical events but of mental abstraction and life, as well. According to nominalism, ideas do not exist independent of consciousness. They are mere names for abstractions accomplished by the mind's synthesizing perceptions of the external world.⁵ The physical is what is enduring. The mental is transient. Platonic realism, on the other hand, rests upon exactly the opposi-

---

3   John Nijenhuis in "'Ens' Described as 'Being or Existent,'" p. 3, has pointed to the fascinating fact that "[w]hile St. Thomas uses the VERB *esse* close to half a million times, the verb *existere* is found a mere 4,000 or so times. Equally revealing, of these 4,000 verb forms, more than 3,000 are participles which, as a rule, function as the participles for *esse*." Nijenhuis observes: "The present writer belongs to the small chorus of language-sensitive medievalists who feel pressed to sing *extra chorum* because they have conclusive evidence that the translation of the Latin *esse* (as also of the Greek *einai*) by the usual existence-terminology leads to a flawed interpretation of the 'onto-logical' thought world where use is made of the 'being'-term *ens* (and its Greek equivalent)" (*ibid.*, p. 1). A revolution is contained in Nijenhuis' paragraph (*ibid.*, p. 5): "The *Oxford English Dictionary* notes that the very word 'exist' is not yet found in Cooper's Dictionary of 1565, and seems at a loss to explain this when it states that '[T]he late appearance of the word [read: verb] is remarkable.' Shakespeare uses the verb only three times, and in one of these three cases it is clearly in the etymologically suggested sense, 'The orbs FROM whom we do exist.' Descartes, also writing in the 16th century, seems to be aware, that something was astir in the world of language because his *Cogito ergo SUM* sometimes contains the addition, both in the Latin text and the French translation made under his supervision, '*vel EXISTO*.' Kant, on the other hand, writing as late as the second half of the 18th century, was blandly unaware that 'something had happened' in the world of being and existence or, to use the two German verbal infinitives, *sein* and *existiren*. For he freely interchanges the two verbs, along with the German '*es ist*': this thing '*existirt, ist*' and, God '*ist, oder es ist ein Gott.*'"

4   I am indebted to John Nijenhuis for this distinction between "quantitative" and "locative" meanings for Being. See, Nijenhuis, "'Ens' Described as 'Being or Existent'," pp. 7-8.

5   Fernando Inciarte argues that Aristotle has been mis-represented by the representational theory of forms, i.e., the ectypal theory of universals that argues that universals are a posteriori abstractions. See Inciarte, "Der Begriff der Seele in der Philosophie des Aristoteles," trans. by F. Dirlmeier, in *Seele. Ihre Wirklichkeit, ihr Verhältnis zum Leib und zur menschlichen Person*, ed. by Klaus Kremer (Leiden: E.J. Brill, 1984), pp. 61 and 62.

te metaphysical conviction. The empirical world is derived from mental reality, since the material world is an inadequate copy (it can be other than the way it appears to be) of perfect ideas (which can't be other than what they are). Analogous to the way an individual creates an artifact, i.e., making a copy of a mental model, Platonic realism spoke of the world as a copy of a mental system of eternal ideas.[6] The mental is what is enduring. The physical is transient.

Platonic metaphysics lost credibility in this 14th century revolution, because it could neither give a satisfactory account, much less proof, of its universals (i.e., its inability to define universals[7]) nor could it give an adequate account of the origin of the physical world out of the mental (i.e., the problem of "participation"/$\mu\acute{\varepsilon}\theta\varepsilon\xi\iota\varsigma$ in Being).[8] The pragmatic success of commerce, energized by the Crusades and the Hanseatic League, equally challenged the model of reality associated with Platonic metaphysics.

The presumption of the mathematization of reality[9] as a consequence of the Nominalist and Copernican revolutions and shaping the epistemology of contemporary physics is that all experience can be explained on the basis of material reality and causal calculating rationality. The mathematization of "reality" resulted from Galileo's distinguishing between "primary" and "secondary" qualities. The primary qualities of mass and motion are quantifiable in the "new" sense of "objective," mathematically measurable and spatially located things unlike such secondary non-quantifiable qualities of "subjec-

---

[6] This understanding of creation is from the Timaeus, but its clear entrance into Christian theology is over Philo's *De opificio mundi* 16-36, 29, 134-135 where Philo speaks of a "double creation," i.e., "... first of the ideal exemplar, then of the sense-perceptible version ..." David Runia, *Philo in Early Christian Literature: A Survey* (Minneapolis: Fortress Press, 1993), p. 188. See *ibid.*, pp. 187, 254, 286-287, and 326, as well.

[7] It is not possible to state both what a number of particulars have in common (similarity) that simultaneously distinguishes those particulars from everything else (difference). This is the insight of Socrates. See Plato's *Euthyphro* and *Apology* as well as *Grundprobleme der großen Philosophen. Philosophie des Altertums und des Mittelalters*, ed. by Josef Speck (Göttingen: Vandenhoeck & Ruprecht, 1978), p. 23.

[8] Both of these challenges to Platonic metaphysics are found in Aristotle. See, for example, *Metaphysics* 1078b30-1079b3: "... if the ideas and the things participating in them have the same idea, it will be something they have in common ... But if they do not have the same idea in common, then they have only the same name." Hume pointed out through his character "Philo" in *Dialogues Concerning Natural Religion*, p. 47 and Part VIII, pp.52-53, that all experience teaches that mind is dependent upon vegetation, hence, if God is the first cause, then God must be a vegetable.

[9] For the significance of Galileo and the mathematization of reality see Edmund Husserl, "Galileo's mathematization of nature" in *The Crisis*.

tive" taste, color, etc.[10] The triumph of objective, locative calculability labelled all that was not mathematically quantifiable as subjective capriciousness (mere "emotion" in the positivist sense) to the loss of any value for consciousness except as a more or less capable (yet accidental in the sense of non-essential) witness to material, measurable reality.

The theological crisis engaging us today in particular, but the epistemological crisis in general, has emerged as the confidence in both these metaphysical alternatives has crumbled. For some five centuries Western humanity has been fascinated, if not blinded by, calculating, causal rationality, but now recognition of our lack of immediate access to the physical world indicates the limits of the materialist paradigm, so extensively embraced and cultivated in the Western world since the 14th century, just as that paradigm revolution indicated the limits of the idealist paradigm.

The benefits from the materialist paradigm, of course, have been incalculable, and no one would claim that there should be a return to the pre-Nominalist world. But the costs have been high, as well. Technology is both a blessing and a curse depending upon the kind of understanding driving it. Having let the genie of epistemological materialism out of the bottle, however, there is no putting it back. Nevertheless, the turn toward materialism epistemologically as well as experientially has, above all, resulted in spiritual poverty as the human species has pursued the calculation, prediction, manipulation, and control of what is accessible to the senses at the expense not of some hocus-pocus or fanciful spiritual force created by wishful thinking, but of experience itself which is entirely inaccessible to the senses and immaterial.

This project suggests that a turn to pre-Nominalist spirituality, but not a re-turn, is necessary if theology is to respond constructively to this present crisis of materialism. Emphasizing our material context as a crisis is not meant to justify opening the floodgates of blind spiritual speculation (what one finds too often in popular religion). Although one could exploit the crisis to attack empirical materialism in defense of a "spiritual" order trying to communicate with us "from the other side" analogous to the material order trying to communicate with us from the material side of experience, such a strategy leads to literal ghosts and goblins if not to channeling and

---

[10] Alexander Koyré points out that this shift to the mathematization of reality was not a simple transition from Platonism to Aristotelianism. Rather, a hybrid emerged, consisting of Aristotelian metaphysics (materialism) and Platonic physics (mathematics) as a consequence of the limitation of Aristotelian physics. See Alexander Koyré, "Galileo and Plato."

claims for the after life remarkably "material." However, the epistemological limits to materialism are not to be employed as a call to reject the understanding acquired by the investigation of the material order. There can be no call back into the caves or sticking our heads in the sand. On the other hand, the project is equally on guard against the tendency to treat the spiritual as material, i.e., as some kind of "sense phenomena" in the mind stimulated by "the other side."[11] Such a tendency is a category mistake of the first order, i.e., substituting one order of experience for another when they are irreducible one to the other. Nonetheless, these orders of experience are distinguishable, but they are not separable. This project has sought to retrieve a classic notion of spirituality that is rational but not in the sense of calculating reason as applied to the material order. Nevertheless, both θεωρία (contemplative reason) and διάνοια/διαίρεσις (calculating reason) require acknowledgment of the human condition as faith seeking understanding.[12]

Perhaps the greatest barrier to what can be seen as a necessary course correction is that, what was once understood in the Western tradition by uneducated and educated alike (Cynics and Stoics, Christians and Pagans) to be the very framework and content of experience, i.e., intangible consciousness (νοῦς), has lost all worth except as an instrument or tool.[13] One is either blessed or not blessed with a good mental instrument. The consequence is that the retrieval of human spirituality requires acquiring "knowledge" of what once entirely and exclusively defined one's reality. With life defined

---

[11] It is not surprising that this danger is the centerpiece of Chauncy's critique of the "Great Awakening." See Charles Chauncy, "Enthusiasm Described and Caution'd Against." What is perhaps surprising is that the same danger was warned against by Jonathan Edwards. See Jonathan Edwards, *Religious Affections*, particularly the "First Sign."

[12] This vocabulary of θεωρία (contemplative reason) and διαίρεσις (calculating reason) is at least as old as Plato. In the simile of the line Plato distinguishes between νόησις (reason) and διάνοια (understanding) (*Republic* 511d-e). The activities of both reason and understanding presuppose universals or, in other words, the mental ability to distinguish between a "this" and a "that." Hence, both νόησις and διάνοια depend upon διαίρεσις, i.e., the dividing or separating among universals and/or things/shadows/reflections.

However, θεωρία (contemplation) is the goal of reason's dialectic (*Republic* 511b), i.e., the contemplation of the First Principle of the Whole or the Good. By maintaining a distinction in what follows between θεωρία and διαίρεσις as contemplative reason and calculating reason, the terminology is meant to focus on the ultimate goal of each kind of mental activity. θεωρία contemplates the illimitable and indivisible presupposition of all that is. Διαίρεσις calculates and manipulates on the basis of distinguishing something from something else. Both θεωρία and διαίρεσις depend upon presuppositions, however, that cannot be either defined or proved.

[13] In the vocabulary of Plato's simile of the line, understanding is now called reason and Platonic reason has been forgotten.

narrowly in terms of the senses, one has to "learn" that one cannot touch, smell, taste, hear, or see one's own experience (consciousness/νοῦς) - that very dimension "above nature" which makes one a member of a human community and defines the meaning of culture. One surely does not have to be an intellectual to recognize the non-material nature of experience, but the exotic character of such awareness, given its deviation from everything that is counted as worthwhile in the world today, *makes it appear* like it is the preserve of intellectuals, hence, unfathomable and irrelevant to the average person in the pew much less on the street.

The Crisis of Reason: Two Kinds of Rationality

The first step, then, on the path of spiritual and theological renewal in an age of post-metaphysical materialism is the recognition of the epistemological limits of materialism. This is what Thomas Kuhn was wrestling with in *The Structure of Scientific Revolutions* as he came to realize that reality as an exogenous world external to and/or independent from consciousness eludes any and all attempts to reach it.[14] Reality is a communal,

---

[14] Paul Ricoeur's theory of "threefold mimesis" describes the mediated character of all understanding as an arc from practical experience over emplotment in language/narrative back to practical experience. See Paul Ricoeur, *Time and Narrative*, vol. 1, p. 53. Practical experience, however, is not direct and immediate experience. Practical experience both prior and subsequent to emplotment "... is always already articulated by signs, rules, and norms. It is always already symbolically mediated" (*ibid.*, p. 57). For his discussion of threefold mimesis, see chapter 3, "Time and Narrative: Threefold *Mimesis*" in *ibid.*, pp. 52-87. Ricoeur's point is that all understood mediation influences acting. "It is the task of hermeneutics ... to reconstruct the set of operations by which a work lifts itself above the opaque depths of living, acting, and suffering, to be given by an author to readers who receive it and *thereby change their acting* (emphasis added)" (*ibid.*, p. 53). Speaking of the process of emplotment itself, Ricoeur writes: "Remaining in a Kantian vein, we ought not to hesitate in comparing the production of the configurational act to the work of the productive imagination ... *The productive imagination is not only rule-governed, it constitutes the generative matrix of rules* (emphasis added) ... [T]he productive imagination fundamentally has a synthetic function. It connects understanding and intuition by engendering syntheses that are intellectual and intuitive at the same time [precisely the function of the understanding in Plato's simile of the line.]" (*ibid.*, p. 68). Ricoeur employs the term "paradigm" to speak of the "sedimented" syntheses or the "typologies" of emplotment and adds: "the labor of imagination is not born from nothing. It is bound in one way or another to the tradition's paradigms ... deployed between the two poles of servile application [requiring a hermeneutics of suspicion] and calculated deviation [dependent upon a hermeneutics of retrieval], passing through every degree of 'rule-governed deformation'" (*ibid.*, p. 69). But the mimetic process does not stop at the level of synthesis in emplotment. "[N]arrative has its full meaning when it is restored to the time of action and of suffering in mimesis$_3$" (*ibid.*, p. 70). In agreement

mental model (a sociological paradigm containing *universal* "paradigms of exemplary past achievement"[15] and the *particular* experience of individuals). What Kuhn has not acknowledged in his epic making work is that even causal explanation is relative to one's sociological paradigm. As David Hume observed in the 18th century, we do not perceive ultimate cause; we perceive only effects.[16] For example, the key causal ingredient of our materialist paradigm is energy, but we don't perceive energy directly. We can only perceive (and measure) the effects of energy. Energy is a hypothesis of the paradigm that has become a "fact." The notion of sociological paradigms and imperceptibility of cause raises serious questions about our access to the world "as it truly is." Kuhn almost reluctantly acknowledges that there is no perception independent of the lenses of a paradigm. As a historian of science, it is not surprising that he is obviously uncomfortable with the idea that perception is not simply the interpretation of a world that is the same for every observer.[17]

Thomas Kuhn points out, however, that even in the natural sciences one is concerned with a mental (read, spiritual) modeling of physical reality without there being any means for gaining direct access, independent of the spiritual model, to the physical world of "facts" to confirm or deny the "truth" of the model. At best, one has a confidence of statistical probability that confirms the legitimacy of one's model, but there is no means or method to acquire absolute certainty - the holy grail of the physical sciences. If empirical data accessible through the senses are the warrant for truth claims, then science cannot give us truth, for there is no direct access (Kuhn, at best, speaks of "concrete indices"[18]) to the world through the senses - there is only mediated access filtered through the paradigm lenses of the observer and her/his community.

The Western tradition has reached the point of syzygy with respect to rationality. The materialism of the new Aristotelianism of the 14th century

---

with Gadamer in *Truth and Method* (see "The Hermeneutic Problem of Application" in Hans-Georg Gadamer, *Truth and Method*, pp. 274-278), Ricoeur insists that all reading/understanding is "application." See *ibid.*, p. 70.

[15] See Kuhn's distinction between sociological paradigms and paradigms of exemplary past achievement in his "Postscript" to *The Structure of Scientific Revolutions*, p. 175.

[16] See David Hume, "The Treatise of Human Nature. Book I. On the Understanding" in *Hume: Selections*, pp. 46-51, 115-143, and 146-160.

[17] See, for example, Thomas Kuhn, *The Structure of Scientific Revolutions*, pp. 120-121, 192-193.

[18] See Kuhn, *The Structure of Scientific Revolutions*, p. 126 and the section "Tacit Knowledge and Intuition" in the "Postscript," pp. 191-198.

led to the investigation of nature for its own sake in an attempt to discover the laws of efficient causality governing physical events. This resulted in the championing of an entirely different understanding of rationality over against the notion of reason governing Christian Platonism. Calculating reason, emerging as a consequence of Christian Nominalism, is dependent upon our ability to distinguish one event, or constituent of an event, from another/others. This capacity is called διαίρεσις, the "dividing of a class into its constituent parts." It is the necessary presupposition of any system of causal explanation, for determining what caused something to happen requires one's being able to distinguish a prior state of affairs from a subsequent state. Were we unable to distinguish among "things," we would not be able to develop any model of causal explanation of events. Calculating reason (διαίρεσις) presupposes λόγος (discursive reason's ability to distinguish) and νομός (law) in order to predict, manipulate, and control the "things" of its world. It is precisely our confidence in calculating reason that is challenged by Kuhn's analysis of paradigms and the recognition that causality is speculative not empirical.

Calculating reason is exactly opposite to the "contemplative" reason of Christian Platonism. Christian Platonism understood reason to be an activity entirely unconcerned with the calculation, prediction, manipulation and control of the material world. Rather, reason is dialectic which leads one to a "First Principle of the Whole," i.e., the Good. Hence, dialectical reason is not to be confused with discursive reason. While dialectical reason, too, is dependent upon λόγος, i.e., that system of ideas or universals enabling all distinctions, it employs the λόγος in an entirely opposite activity. Plato only hints at that activity in the simile of the line in Book VI of the *Republic*. A careful reading of the simile, however, indicates a three-fold structure governing both the empirical world of becoming and the mental world of being. That three-fold structure is represented in the empirical world by the "sun" (the "child of the parent," the Good, enabling us to learn something about the Good without having direct access to the Good/parent) which enables the "eye" to see an "object." Eye and object are placed in relation by the sun although the sun is neither the eye nor the object. Likewise, in the intellect the Good, which is not an idea among ideas,[19] places one idea in relation to another without our being able to determine where one idea stops and the next starts and without the Good causing any change in the ideas themselves. Contemplative reason, then, is concerned exclusively with the invisible,

---

[19] See Plato's *Republic* 509b.

spiritual dimension of experience and the ultimate source of any and all experience rather than with the calculating, predicting and controlling of the material dimension of experience. It is these two kinds of rationality which have come to stand in syzygy with one another.

The work of Kuhn and recognition of the mediated character of all experience teaches us that the calculating reason (διαίρεσις) of Aristotelian rationality, seeking causal explanation, is no route to indubitability. It and the contemplative reason (θεωρία) of Platonic rationality, focussing on the eternal imperceptible, immaterial, and illimitable order of reality, are necessary but at best merely adequate in our epoch. Both depend upon metaphysical claims (either material or intellectual) that are indefensible given our understanding of the mediated character of all experience and understanding.

Beyond Critical Realism and Heidegger

It has become popular to take the attitude of "critical realism" to acknowledge the tentativeness of scientific modeling while maintaining one's confidence that there is no better alternative for acquiring a true understanding of the world.[20] Critical realism, however, neither adequately understands its content nor its conditions of possibility. It is, to be sure, a modified realism (since it acknowledges no direct access to an exogenous world), but it remains committed to the agenda of Enlightenment rationality which seeks to

---

[20] Critical realism has its defenders among scientists, theologians, and biblical scholars. See, for example, Ian Barbour, *Issues in Science and Religion*, pp. 172-174; Arthur R. Peacocke, *Creation and the World of Science* (Oxford: Clarendon Press, 1979), pp. 20-21, especially 40-41: "The viewpoint adopted in these lectures is that in both the scientific and theological enterprises the basic stance, the working assumption, is that of a sceptical and qualified realism - the belief that they are processes of finding out the 'way things are'. This belief is justified, in the case of science, by its success in prediction and control. In the case of theology, it is justified by providing resources which give moral purpose, meaning and intelligibility to the individual plotting his (sic) path through life and also, so it has been well argued, by contributing to the survival of society;" and the use of the term in Lonergan circles found in Ben F. Meyer, *Critical Realism and the New Testament* (Allison Park, PA: Pickwick, 1989), particularly the "seven traits of critical realism" discussed by Meyer, pp. x-xiii summarized, p. xiii: "These seven traits - the authority of fact, the correlativity of 'true' and 'real,' the primacy of insight into the text as individual, the 'intended sense' as constitutive of discourse, the indispensability of judgment, the circle of things and words, and the requisite that the interpreter measure up to the text - set critical-realist hermeneutics apart as sane, rigorous, and productive." A conference entitled "Critical Realism in Science and Religion" was held at the Center for Theology and the Natural Sciences at the Graduate Theological Union in Berkeley, CA, March 7-9, 1986.

acquire knowledge of the world in terms of causal explanations enabling calculated predicting of future events. Its error is not that it is incorrect, but that it is too narrow.

Critical realism buys into the materialist paradigm for "common sense" and "pragmatic" reasons, but, by focussing attention exclusively in the direction of materiality, it, like Martin Heidegger, has drawn the human so far down/out into the world that any and all understanding of the human spirit and of faith is covered over in the confidence of a relatively successful understanding of physical events.[21]

For his part, Heidegger insightfully refuses to equate the human "spirit" with the cleverness of calculating reason or a tool, but, he does reduce human spirituality down to "resolve:" "Spirit is neither empty cleverness nor the irresponsible play of the wit, nor the boundless work of dismemberment carried on by the practical intelligence; much less is it world-reason; no, spirit is a fundamental, knowing resolve toward the essence of being. (Rektoratsrede, p. 13)."[22] According to Heidegger, "knowing" resolve consists of Dasein's (human being's) deciding to actualize her/his ownmost possibilities as those possibilities are enabled and limited by the "world" of things present- and ready-to-hand. Heidegger's constructive contribution is twofold: α) He overcomes Descartes' two substance notion of spirit and world by focussing on possibility rather than actuality. In other words, rather than taking human experience to consist of two actual substances (mind and body) creating a gap (Lessing's ugly ditch as a consequence of the difference between necessary and accidental truths) that one must jump over, Heidegger focuses attention upon possibility which indicates Dasein's inseparability (i.e., eliminating any "gap") from its world of engagement: "higher than actuality stands *possibility*."[23] Why? Because the process of understanding is a project of "projecting of possibilities" which one has only in a context of "world."[24] β) Heidegger challenges any founda-

---

[21] Of course, the character of what counts as "successful understanding" is radically different between Heidegger and critical realists. For Heidegger, successful understanding is concerned with resolute projection of one's ownmost possibilities undeterred by the public they world's expectations of the self. For critical realism, successful understanding is concerned with adequate calculation, predication, manipulation, and control over events having neutralized the self as a disinterested observer.

[22] Martin Heidegger, *An Introduction to Metaphysics*, p. 41.

[23] Martin Heidegger, *Being and Time*, p. 63.

[24] See Martin Heidegger, Section 32: Understanding and Interpretation in *Being and Time*, pp. 188-192. Paul Ricoeur employs the language of "imaginative variations" and "thought experiments" to articulate this notion of understanding as projecting of possibilities inseparable from one's context/world. See Paul Ricoeur, *Oneself as Another*, pp.

tionalist or metaphysical grounding of experience precisely because of the role of possibility in all experience: possibility is no-thing, i.e., it is not an actual ground from which one can calculate, predict, manipulate, or control, i.e., it defies explanation. In the process of focussing on drawing our understanding of Dasein out into a world of possibilities and with the goal of overcoming metaphysical explanations, Heidegger turned away from the "spirit" of German Idealism which is a spirit of meta-narrativity explaining all "that is" as a process of non-material Oneness spilling itself out into material, historical multiplicity returning to itself only after a long process by means of which consciousness emerges out of materiality to once again experience Oneness in the unity of non-materiality. Rather than meta-narrativity, spirit, for Heidegger, means resolve in the face of one's accountability to oneself for one's own possibilities. Hence, he truncates the spiritual in the laudable attempt to retrieve the priority of possibility over actuality.[25]

Critical realism similarly truncates the content of experience, for it ignores the imperceptible, immaterial, indivisible, immeasurable, and un-

---

148, 159, and 288. The present project prefers the more encompassing "projecting of possibilities" to imaginative variations and/or thought experiments, because projecting of possibilities includes possibilities of which one is not consciously aware, i.e., which are concealed in the very process of projecting but which nevertheless play a crucial, sometimes determinative, role in understanding. Imaginative variations and thought experiments, while not incorrect, suggest far too much conscious control over the project of understanding.

[25] Heidegger's project is very Aristotelian. He has rejected Platonic realism, but, despite his embracing of Aristotle, he has redefined Aristotle's material cause in terms of possibility (Being) rather than static actual substance (Which is more appropriately Aristotelian than to translate ὀυσία as locative substance, i.e., existence. See footnote 4 above.). He rejects, therefore, Aristotle's claim that actuality precedes possibility (e.g., *Metaphysics* 1049b11-29), at least with respect to understanding the human condition in the world, by insisting on the priority of possibility over actuality. For an analysis of Aristotle's notion of potency and the priority of act over potency, see Gerard Verbeke, "The Meaning of Potency in Aristotle" in *Graceful Reason. Essays in Ancient and Medieval Philosophy Presented to Joseph Owens, CSSR*, ed. by Lloyd P. Gerson (Toronto: Pontifical Institute of Mediaeval Studies, 1983), pp. 55-73.

It should be remembered that *Being and Time* originated out of a project on Aristotle. See Martin Heidegger, "Phänomenologische Interpretation zu Aristoteles." This is Heidegger's description of his writing project as part of his application in 1922 for positions in Marburg and Göttingen (*Being and Time* was published in 1927).

Despite, perhaps precisely because of, his rethinking of metaphysics and ontology, Heidegger continued to insist that the God of Christianity must be *a* being rather than to wrestle with the theological implications of Being as the possibility of beings (das Sein des Seienden). See Martin Heidegger, "Phänomenologie und Theologie."

changing character of human spirituality, i.e., it ignores experiencing (consciousness/νοῦς), to focus attention exclusively on the experienced, the perceptible, material, divisible, measurable, and ever changing physical world. It substitutes what is inaccessible for what alone is accessible. In short, it ignores the content of experience to concern itself with the mere appearances of experience.[26]

As a method, in addition, critical realism has ignored the key insight from Kuhn that rules presuppose paradigms rather than rules defining paradigms.[27] In other words, critical realism has forgotten its own conditions of possibility, i.e., one's always and already being committed to a notion of reality prior to all methodology or any investigation or explanation of events. Again, analogous to Heidegger: if language is the house of Being,[28] one must not forget that there needs to be a lot (in the fullest sense) before one can build a house.[29] If critical realism indicates how one best gains ac-

---

[26] Nietzsche observed the dissimilitude of empiricism when he wrote in "On Truth and Lies in a Nonmoral Sense," pp. 81-2: "... [W]hat about these linguistic conventions themselves? Are they perhaps products of knowledge, that is, of the sense of truth? Are designations congruent with things? Is language the adequate expression of all realities?

It is only by means of forgetfulness that man can ever reach the point of fancying himself (sic) to possess a "truth" of the grade just indicated. If he will not be satisfied with truth in the form of tautology, that is to say, if he will not be content with empty husks, then he will always exchange truths for illusions. What is a word? It is the copy in sound of a nerve stimulus. But the further inference from the nerve stimulus to a cause outside of us is already the result of a false and unjustifiable application of the principle of sufficient reason ... [W]ith words it is never a question of truth, never a question of adequate expression; otherwise, there would not be so many languages. The "thing in itself" ... is likewise something quite incomprehensible to the creator of language and something not in the least worth striving for. This creator only designates the relations of things to men, and for expressing these relations he lays hold of the boldest metaphors. To begin with, a nerve stimulus is transferred into an image: first metaphor. The image, in turn, is imitated in a sound: second metaphor."

[27] See Kuhn, *The Structure of Scientific Revolutions*, pp. 42-43 and Ricoeur's discussion of the relationship between the "productive imagination" and rules in note 14 above.

[28] See, for example, Martin Heidegger, "Letter on Humanism," p. 205: "Man, however, is not only a living being, who besides other faculties possesses language. Language is rather the house of Being, wherein living, man ex-sists, while he, guarding it, belongs to the truth of Being."

[29] Ricoeur observes: "... language does not constitute a world for itself. It is not even a world. Because we are in the world and are affected by situations, we try to orient ourselves in them by means of understanding; we also have something to say, an experience to bring to language and to share.

... Language is for itself the order of the Same. The world is its Other. The attestation of this otherness arises from language's reflexivity with regard to itself, whereby it knows itself as being *in* being in order to bear *on* being" (Ricoeur, *Time and Narrative*, vol. 1, p. 78).

cess to true judgments, it has forgotten that it has already committed itself to an understanding of reality before it goes looking for it. This is the fundamental role of paradigms, i.e., they consist of what Kuhn calls "quasi-metaphysical" commitments concerning the way reality "must" be. He calls them "quasi-metaphysical," because he recognizes that they are indefinable much less provable.[30]

Kuhn, clearly, is not aware of the problem of definition from the Socratic tradition which observes our inability to identify what is both common to a set of perceptions and at the same time distinguishes that set from all other sets (i.e., the problem of identity and difference is at the core of Socrates' aphorism that wisdom consists in one's knowing that one doesn't know what one thinks one knows). Rather, Kuhn has encountered the issue of definition in terms of our inability to identify and differentiate sets not by Socrates but in Wittgenstein,[31] who spoke of "family resemblances" in the absence of indubitable universals as the most satisfactory form of definition available to consciousness. The problem of definition is sufficient in and of itself to prohibit the critique of critical realism from leading to the call to return to traditional Platonic realism - although it is all too readily forgotten that Plato spoke of universals as "hypotheses"[32] and of the necessity of having *both* dimensions of the One and the Many, the intellect and the world of becoming, for an adequate understanding of human experience.[33]

Neither universals nor particulars offer a metaphysical explanation of experience. Humanity is caught in the middle, however, requiring both universals and particulars, organized into a coherent model, in order to experience as it does. If now one must acknowledge that there are no *logical* argu-

---

[30] See Kuhn, *The Structure of Scientific Revolutions*, p. 41: "Less local and temporary, though still not unchanging characteristics of science, are the higher level, quasi-metaphysical commitments that historical study so regularly displays ... That nest of commitments proved to be both metaphysical and methodological. As metaphysical, it told scientists what sorts of entities the universe did and did not contain: there was only shaped matter in motion. As methodological, it told them what ultimate laws and fundamental explanations must be like ..."

[31] See Thomas Kuhn, *The Structure of Scientific Revolutions*, p. 45: We must ... grasp some set of attributes that all games and that only games have in common. Wittgenstein, however, concluded that, given the way we use language and the sort of world to which we apply it, there need be no such set of characteristics. Though a discussion of *some* of the attributes shared by a *number* of games or chairs or leaves often helps us learn how to employ the corresponding term, there is no set of characteristics that is simultaneously applicable to all members of the class and to them alone."

[32] See the simile of the line in Book VI of *The Republic*.

[33] See *The Sophist* 249c-d and Philebus 22a-e; 60c-d; and 61b.

ments that can prove the independent status of either universals or particulars over against consciousness, one does counter such "vulgar skepticism" with the *pragmatic* argument: perhaps you cannot logically prove the existence of the world, but neither can you not act and, as soon as you act, you cannot ignore the exogenous world.[34] What has been too easily overlooked, given our materialistic prejudices, is that the same pragmatic argument justifying one's confidence in the world of sense perception, i.e., try ignoring the world of sense perception and see what happens, that same pragmatic argument applies to universals, i.e., try ignoring ideas that are the same yesterday, today, and tomorrow and see what happens. Nonetheless, we remain always "on this side" of the physical world and universals, we cannot define the very universals nor logically prove the indubitable existence of the physical world so necessary for experience. If Kuhn's notion of sociological paradigms, rooted in exemplary past achievement paradigms (ectypal universals), is an expansion from the individual to include a community over against Plato's notion of the manner of individual understanding in the simile of the line (to be sure, Kuhn ignores what Plato calls "reason," i.e., dialectic), Plato's discussion of dialectic in the simile of the line may itself be taken to be an expansion of Socrates' wisdom aphorism, because it acknowledges precisely the problem of definition even as it attempts to suggest an unknowable "First Principle of the Whole" beyond universals. Plato's dialectic indicates the *tentativeness* of a thought process that commences with hypotheses (i.e., indefinable universals for which one cannot tell where one stops and the next one starts although one can clearly distinguish one idea from another) to arrive at a synthesis uniting all universals, which itself is not a universal[35] and, as an absolute unity, is unable to be experienced directly by consciousness, because consciousness requires twoness to experience (experience consists precisely in our ability to distinguish one thing from something else,[36] e.g., one object from another object or one idea from another idea). This is, indeed, a profound unknowing that is rooted in necessary ingredients (to be sure, contingently necessary ingredients) of experience, which are themselves indefinable, to point to a unity that is not able to be

---

[34] The label "vulgar skepticism" and critique of it comes from Hume's, *Dialogues Concerning Natural Religion*, p. 5. See the discussion of vulgar and refined skepticism below.

[35] *Republic* 509b.

[36] This is why our understanding of experience tends to focus on actuality at the expense of concealed possibility, because experience consists in distinguishing. Schleiermacher was well aware of this when he described consciousness as "sundered" in the Second Speech in *On Religion*, p. 41.

experienced directly. Here one encounters a fundamental aporia of human experience: pragmatically, we can neither ignore the world nor ignore universals; yet, we are unable to give logical proofs for either. Pragmatic wisdom is a matter of faith seeking understanding.

The Christian tradition has too easily overlooked that its metaphysical traditions are radically grounded in unknowing. The critique of critical realism and of Heidegger for failing to acknowledge the full implications of unknowing with respect to the spiritual dimension of all experience, nonetheless, cannot be accompanied by a call back to a "higher" form of knowing, i.e., either anagogical knowledge or a meta-narrative.

Non-epistemic Faith and the Priority of Spirit

The crisis in theology and epistemology in general in a post-metaphysical context means not merely the bracketing of God-talk either with respect to claims about, or for, God - as constitutive as this bracketing is for post-metaphysical theology.[37] Our present crisis requires the same bracketing of

---

[37] This bracketing does not mean a denial of the possibility of God-talk. There is nothing about human spirituality that would deny (or logically prove) God as the ultimate source of all that is, any more than there is anything about human experience that would deny (or logically prove) the existence of an exogenous world independent of consciousness. Yet theology has foremost the task of acknowledging its limits and to indicate where speculation begins. Both calculating and contemplating reason are limited in that their content is always and already mediated. Those limits indicate that faith must reign in unbridled speculation either about material or spiritual causality. As David Hume suggested in *Dialogues Concerning Natural Religion*, p. 89: "to be a philosophical skeptic is, in a man (sic) of letters, the first and most essential step towards being a sound, believing *Christian* ..." Demea, Cleanthes, and Philo in Hume's *Dialogues* agree that the "existence" of God (or (a) first cause(s)) is not in question. What is in question in the *Dialogues* is what can be known about the "nature" of God/first cause(s) on the basis of experience. Philo is the refined skeptic who affirms "existence" but denies the knowability of the nature or characteristics of the first cause(s). This is exactly the position taken by his namesake, Philo of Alexandria, who in "Quod deus sit immutabilis" 62 maintains that outside of the existence we can know nothing of the characteristics of God. Runia reports that one of the three areas of enduring influence of Philo of Alexandria on the tradition is "... the doctrine of God, with the strong emphasis on unchangeability and essential unknowability ..." (Runia, *Philo in Early Christian Literature*, p. 338). However, Runia acknowledges that there is no universal agreement over whether or not Philo "... was the first to enunciate the principle of the unknowability of God" (see, *ibid*., p. 152, n. 88).

Post-metaphysical theology would have to speak of God as possibility, i.e., nothing, out of which every-thing emerges. This is a creatio ex nihilo that is continuous and commences with possibility rather than Aristotelian actuality, i.e., rather than Aristotle's Unmoved Mover which is actual (see Aristotle's *Metaphysics* 1072a20-

indubitable claims about the physical world. Hence, post-metaphysical theology is not a call to return to negative or apophatic theology, but rather commences with the radical unknowing at the core of the human condition: it commences with that non-epistemic faith enabling and structuring all experience (material or spiritual).

Rather than speak of epistemic faith, which provides one with knowledge about ultimate things inaccessible to reason, theology in a post-metaphysical sense is concerned with non-epistemic faith or the radical unknowing and limitation to all rationality either the calculating rationality of Aristotelianism or the contemplative rationality of Platonism (either διαίρεσις or θεωρία). Hence, more than a quest for empowerment of the marginalized and/or oppressed, justice, compassion, and peace (as unquestioningly important as these are), theology is that discipline concerned: α) with the non-epistemic faith, or radical unknowing, at the heart of all experience and β) with that which has been, and is, ignored, forgotten, and concealed by our contemporary understanding of the human condition - both in the sense of human spirituality as the imperceptible, illimited, and indefinable whole of consciousness and in the sense of the open-ended dynamic of the revealed (actuality) and the concealed (possibility) that roots human spirituality in a communal, historical world. These two constitutive elements of theology are precisely what enable theology to call for empowerment of the marginalized and/or oppressed, justice, compassion, and peace. Marginalization, oppression, injustice, and conflict all result from the absolutizing of actuality and the covering over and suppression of possibility. A post-metaphysical theology of liberation is a figurative theology breaking open the hegemony of actuality (the literal) both visible and invisible.

In short, post-metaphysical theology is a call to awareness of the symbolic character of all experience as everything is seen to point somewhere else (things to consciousness; consciousness to things; the actual to concealed possibility; concealed possibility to the actual, etc.) and to awareness of the figurative character of language which is not rooted in a literal meaning but which discovers meaning through a dynamic process of dis-covering

---

1073a15) or Process thought's primordial nature (in contrast to the consequent nature) of God. On the other hand, speaking of God as possibility would require surrendering the notion that God's oneness is some kind of univocity enabling of all multiplicity. Where possibility is the same concealed dimension for all actuality, no two situations share the same possibilities. In short, there is a profound identity and difference ("is"/"is not") to possibility that would then apply to God were one to speak of God as possibility.

similarity and identity in difference (i.e., consciousness/spirituality is metaphoric not literal). Post-metaphysical theology recognizes that no one dimension of experience is in the position to serve as an absolute ground or explanation of the whole, but, rather, both the invisible and the visible are necessary constituents of experience. Neither the empirical offers direct verification of truth claims nor does one have access to an absolute mystical univocity, for constitutive of all experience and truth claims is a tensiveness of "is"/"is not" of possibility in any and all actuality that applies to the concealed in all actuality. Nevertheless, even in light of such tensions there is a priority given by post-metaphysical theology to the spiritual and to concealed possibility - and not simply because they have been ignored and forgotten. Rather, it is because the spiritual is the very dimension of experience (consciousness/νοῦς) and concealed possibility is the key to both experience and understanding. This is no new metaphysics, for νοῦς is non-sense and possibility is no-thing.

Beyond Self and Actuality to Concealed Possibility

All experience (consciousness/νοῦς) transpires in that dimension of the human that is inaccessible to the senses. But, furthermore, we have not begun to understand experience if we only focus on actuality. Understanding is concerned far more with possibility than it is with mere actuality. Yet all experience, understanding, and "knowledge" conceals possibility as it selectively actualizes certain possibilities.[38]

Crucial to post-metaphysical theology is that spirituality is inseparable from possibility. Hence, the errors of Cartesianism are twofold: α) that the self is treated as an isolated ego next to, if not outside of, the world to which it goes out into and from which it returns or retreats; and the corollary β)

---

[38] This is what Heidegger refers to in *Being and Time* as the fundamental "nullity" (Nichtigkeit) of experience. See, for example, *Being and Time*, p. 331. All understanding involves the selective projecting of possibilities that requires the suppression and negation of other possibilities. This is at the heart of Kierkgaard's dilemma/despair over repetition. See Søren Kierkegaard, *Repetition*.

Heidegger, however, rethinks repetition in a new non-Kierkegaardian fashion. For Kierkgaard repetition was of the "actual" (either of the particular circumstances or of the universal). For Heidegger, repetition is the re-covery of the possibilities of the past. This is the key, as well, to Heidegger's notions of the "moment of vision," which he, also, redefines in terms of (authentic) possibility rather than in terms of Kierkegaard's focus on actuality, and "monumental history," redefined in terms of possibility rather than in terms of Nietzsche's focus on actuality.

that mind and body are taken to be two distinct, and separated, substances. Human spirituality is never isolated but is inseparable from the horizon of possibility established by the actuality that is its world. There can be no consciousness that is enclosed exclusively upon itself.[39] Language denies such isolation and affirms the cultural and historical rootedness of all spirituality.[40] One cannot experience, much less think, without language which Ricoeur spoke of as "the great institution, the institution of institutions, that has preceded each and every one of us."[41] To be sure, human experience is always unique and unrepeatable, but that by no means leads to encapsulated isolation. A central aporia of the human condition is that one cannot begin to make sense of one's unique and unrepeatable experience without language and the cultural accumulations of the human community in, and by means of, which one gains consciousness.[42]

---

[39] Already Aristotle, i.e., the teaching does not commence with the Stoics, maintained that "die Seele immer Seele eines Körpers ist." From Fernando Inciarte, "Der Begriff der Seele in der Philosophie des Aristoteles," p. 46, in reference to Aristotle's *De Anima* 414a18-22 and 413a6f. Ricoeur speaks in a similar, though more expansive fashion: "the being of the self presupposes the totality of a world that is the horizon of its thinking, acting, feeling - in short of its *care*.

... the being of the world is the necessary correlate to the being of the self. There is no world without a self who finds itself in it and acts in it; there is no self without a world that is practicable in some fashion" (Ricoeur, *Oneself as Another*, pp. 310-311).

[40] The historical, hence communal, character of all consciousness is identified by Schleiermacher as the key to the "identity" of a religious community rather than its identity being determined by a particular dogmatic content or an individual's inward experience. See Brian Gerrish's review, "The Nature of Doctrine," of George Lindbeck's *The Nature of Doctrine*, particularly his critique of Lindbeck's reading of Schleiermacher as an "experiential-expressivist," pp. 88-90.

Claude Welch calls this "grammatico-historical" interpretation, and locates it in Herder's *Spirit of Hebrew Poetry*. See, Claude Welch, *Protestant Thought in the Nineteenth Century, 1799-1870*, vol. 1 (New Haven: Yale University Press, 1972), p. 41. Troeltsch also stresses the historical and cultural character of the human spirit. See Ernst Troeltsch, *Der Historismus und seine Überwindung* (Aalen: Scientia Verlag, 1979), pp. 77, 101-102.

[41] Ricoeur, *Time and Narrative*, vol. 3, p. 221.

[42] This is precisely why Heidegger's notion of authenticity (Eigentlichkeit) is too narrow for defining the "spirit" of Dasein in terms of "personal resolve." Heidegger's own presentation of this issue is ambiguous, but his conclusion is beyond doubt. See *Being and Time*, p. 168, but pp. 312, 345-346, and 422, as well. The call to authentic resolve for the actualization of one's ownmost possibilities cannot ignore the inseparability of the self from the spiritual and physical environment (as a spiritual and a concrete situation of possibility) within which every individual finds her/himself. What one might choose as one's "ownmost possibility" may be in fact, more likely than not actually is, the consequence of influences from one's situation (but now to be seen as both spiritual and material) of which one has only limitedly, and never entirely, been conscious.

What Cartesianism has neglected, as well as most of the Western tradition including Deconstructionism, is the role of possibility in experience. Attention has focussed on actuality and what "actually is." Of course, one attends to what is actual in order not to be distracted, or led astray, by fantasy and illusion, but there is a huge difference between fantasy and possibility. Furthermore, it is "easier" to focus one's attention on the actual, either actual objects/occasions or actual thoughts, than it is to focus on possibility, precisely because we have access to the actual; where the possible is always concealed. Nevertheless, we have not understood anything, if we have not understood it in terms of its possibilities. For example, a chair is not merely understood as a mere actual thing, it is always and already understood in terms of the possible activities that it enables: sitting at a desk, at a dining table, for reaching to the top shelf for a book, for working at a computer, etc. Hence, simultaneously as one is grasping the possibilities of the actual chair, one's rootedness in a world is announced.

The same applies to the intellect, and this, too, has been overlooked in the Western tradition.[43] One has not grasped the meaning of an idea/universal without having grasped it as a possibility for understanding something particular. All abstraction is rooted in the possibility of both the illimitable wholeness of consciousness inseparable from the possibilities of the world of engagement of the individual consciousness. There are not two substances of mind and body, there is one horizon of concealed possibility that includes both consciousness and matter.

But concealed possibility is no veil for some absolute univocity "behind" all ontic reality. There is a tensiveness to possibility that includes an "is"/"is not" even within possibility. Possibilities are always circumscribed by an actual situation as a consequence of the basic historical character of experience. No two situations have the same possibilities although all situations are rooted in possibility.

The Correspondence Theory of Truth and ἀλήθεια

All of the limitations of the two substance theory are indicated by the inadequacies of the theories of truth that have dominated the Western tradition since the 14th century: first, verification and, more recently, falsification. Both verification and falsification are versions of the correspondence theory

---

[43] Though it was not overlooked by Plato. See the *Sophist* 249c-d and *Philebus* 22a-e; 60c-d; and 61b.

of truth. This theory maintains that truth consists in the correspondence of one's judgment to the "facts" or state of affairs to which one's judgment refers. This notion of truth, however, is limited to actuality at the neglect of possibility.

The correspondence theory of truth does not claim that the judgment itself is true or false; nor does it claim that the "facts" or state of affairs are/is true or false. Rather, it claims that the judgment correctly (truly) *refers to* the facts/state of affairs it seeks to represent. Hence, the same judgment can be both true and false (true when it refers correctly to a fact that it represents; false when it refers incorrectly). No matter what elaborate strategies one develops to ensure the *correctness*, hence, the "truth," of one's judgments, whether those strategies be appeals to warrants and backings of verification (confirming data) or of falsification (seeking those conditions that would count as a denial of the judgment's accuracy), there can be no indubitable confirmation, for all experience is mediated in consciousness: there is no getting outside of consciousness (or outside of one's cultural paradigm) to gain access to the facts/state of affairs as they truly are in themselves. Verification and/or falsification is/are merely the comparing of one kind of mental phenomena with another: a judgment with mental images of sense; or a judgment within a coherent mental model. The consequence is that the search for truth in the Western tradition has been limited to an illusory quest of actuality, and, thereby, its very optimism with respect to its success has denied its limitations and concealed the role of possibility inseparable from all actuality.

The Greek tradition, on the other hand, preserves an altogether different notion of truth: that of dis-closure rather than correctness. The Greek word for truth, ἀλήθεια, is derived from λανθάνω which means "to escape or elude notice, to be unseen, unnoticed" and the alpha privative. The alpha privative negates the noun, hence, truth as ἀλήθεια means "to be noticed" but in the sense of arising out of that which eludes notice and is unnoticed. This is precisely the nature of all experience, which one can acknowledge once one moves beyond limiting one's understanding to actuality to include possibility. In short, what is noticed is the actual; it emerges out of, and simultaneously conceals, what is unnoticed, the possible. Paying attention to "what is" cannot be limited to what is merely actual. "What is" includes the possible. The truth of what is, then, involves a dynamic tension between what is actually "visible" or manifest *and* potentially invisible or concealed. Truth is simultaneously an un-covering, a partial manifesting *and* concealing.

The notion of possibility functioning here, however, should not be confused with Kant's "formal possibility" or what are called the conditions of possibility for any and all experience. Nor should the notion of possibility suggested here be confused with probability. While it is true that all experience requires a presupposed structure or order that makes the experience possible, such formal possibility functions as a kind of actuality.[44] One is observing here that there is an actual structure or order that must be in place before any experience is possible. Possibility, however, is not limited to any particular set of conditions. Just as all conditions of possibility constitute a form of contingent necessity.

The great shift in Western thought initiated by Cartesian skepticism but reaching its zenith in Hume and Kant, that is, the shift from focussing on *what* one can know to the *conditions of possibility* for experience (the *how* of knowledge), that the certitude of the self simultaneously confirms,[45] has led to such projects as Process theology's claims for God in terms of these very

---

[44] See Bernard Charles Flynn, "From Finitude to the Absolute: Kant's Doctrine of Subjectivity;" and Martin Heidegger's *Kants These über das Sein*. Heidegger connects this late meditation on Kant with *Being and Time*, where Being is thought as possibility. He writes, pp. 35-36: "Im unscheinbaren 'ist' verbirgt sich alles Denkwürdige des Seins. Das Denkwürdigste darin bleibt jedoch, daß wir bedenken, ob 'Sein', ob das 'ist' selbst sein kann, oder ob Sein niemals 'ist' und daß gleichwohl wahr bleibt: Es gibt Sein."

Being cannot be actual, for if it is actual it is a thing among things. If Being is not actuality, then actuality conceals Being as potentiality, and, hence, Being and time are one and the same.

[45] Descartes' *cogito ergo sum* establishes the individual's thinking consciousness as a logical absolute: I cannot deny I am conscious without confirming I am conscious. Descartes believed he had logical arguments, commencing with this Archimedian point of indubitable consciousness, to prove both the existence of God and of the external world. His logical arguments depend, however, upon the assumption that something cannot come from nothing. This assumption is the key to Descartes' notion of eminent causality (that the cause can have more reality than its effect) in contrast to formal causality (the cause must have at least as much reality as its effect) which he employs to "prove" that the idea God is not a human construct just as the physical world must exist independent of either God or human consciousness. But there is no logical proof for this key assumption. One can even maintain that possibility (no-thing) precedes actuality (some-thing). Even without this latter claim, however, Hume and Kant challenged the adequacy of Descartes' arguments for God and the external world. Kant, then, made the brilliant move to focus attention not on the *content* of knowledge (what we can know), but, rather, to focus on the conditions of possibility for the Cartesian ego to experience as it does. Hence, the *how* of consciousness becomes the source of certain knowledge. Given that we do in fact experience as we do, then the structures of consciousness that enable that experience must necessarily exist. Yet, the contingent character of consciousness means that, at best, its conditions of possibility are contingent not absolute. Kant's synthetic a priori knowledge is contingent not absolute.

conditions of possibility. This is the logic of dipolar theism which maintains that God is both the primordial conditions of possibility for any and all experience and the consequence of that experience. As important as Process theology's quarrel with classical theism's insistence on an unchanging deity is, there can be no illusion that such an appeal to conditions of possibility does not provide one with absolute knowledge about God. Rather, since experience itself is contingent, the conditions of possibility of experience can at best themselves be judged to be contingent. This requires one distinguishing, then, between contingent and absolute necessity. Formal possibility, i.e., the actual conditions of possibility, is neither possibility itself nor is it absolute.

Such focussing on formal conditions of possibility, however, ignores the spiritual, non-material, nature of experience to emphasize the material nature of the conditions of possibility for experience. One can argue that Whitehead's theory of concressing actual occasions is precisely the redefining of Aristotle's material cause in terms of the insights of contemporary physics[46] analogous to Heidegger's project of rethinking Aristotle's material cause as possibility. In both cases, the tendency is to emphasize "world" at the expense of "spirit." What must be done now is to rethink spirit in light of the world[47] in order to regain an appreciation of human spirituality and faith as constitutive of any and all experience.

Possibility is not probability. Prizing actuality over possibility, the notion of probability is an attempt to quantify possibility to make it quasi-actual, i.e., it is an attempt to deny possibility in a quest to predict actuality. It is the task of diairesis and calculating reason to seek to eliminate possibility and to predict what will actually be the case. Focussing on actuality, conditions of possibility, and/or probability, diairesis and calculating reason are oblivious to truth as ἀλήθεια.

---

[46] See Reto Luzius Fetz, "Aristotelian and Whiteheadian Conceptions of Actuality: I and II."

[47] This is not a new project by any means. Beierwaltes indicates that the issue of thinking spirit *and* world rather than withdrawal from the world into spirit was crucial to Neoplatonism, too often mis-understood by its detractors. See Werner Beierwaltes, *Denken des Einen. Studien zur Neuplatonischen Philosophie und ihrer Wirkungsgeschichte* (Frankfurt a.M.: Vittorio Klostermann, 1985), pp. 24-28. Lest the judgment be too quickly drawn that the relationship between Neoplatonism and Christianity was a one way street with Christianity only borrowing from Neoplatonism, one should not ignore the significance of Iamblichus' addition of a "fifth" virtue of love to the traditional four virtues of wisdom, courage, justice, and self-control in his *The Pythagorian Life*. See Iamblichus, *On the Pythagorean Life*, trans. by Gillian Clark (Liverpool: Liverpool University Press, 1989), pp. 70-100, and Gillian Clark's introduction, pp. x-xiii.

Sola scriptura and Protestant Theology

The need for a retrieval of human spirituality and faith helps to illuminate the limitations of the spectrum of Protestant theological options today. That spectrum can be described as a conservative - liberal spectrum shaped by the notion of *sola scriptura* as a consequence of the Protestant Reformation's belief that one can jump over the history of interpretation in the tradition to encounter God's revelation immediately in the text, i.e., the scriptures. It, of course, completely ignores, if not explicitly denies, the role of presuppositions in play in any reading of the text.[48]

Protestantism is a child of the via moderna[49] or Aristotelian Nominalism. This has crucial consequences for Protestant theology and its interface with its cultural context given the emergence of the natural sciences. For example, the irony of the subsequent struggle between conservative Protestants, who are threatened by the natural sciences, and liberal Protestants, who embrace the natural sciences, is that they *all* share the same epistemology: truth claims have validity only to the extent that they are empirically verifiable, i.e., sense data provide the criteria for truth. Both conservative and liberal Protestants have been cowered by the claim that only quantifiable, primary qualities have validity - all else is subjective whim, fantasy, and emotion. What distinguishes them is not their epistemology, but what counts as evidence. Liberal Protestants and the natural sciences appeal to empirical evidence *in nature*. Conservative Protestants appeal to empirical evidence *in the scriptures*. The impasse in conversation between these groups can be productively overcome by cutting the Gordian knot: observing that the epistemological model is what is misleading not the particular evidence.

Conservative Protestantism is committed to biblical literalism out of confidence in the senses as the source for truth. It maintains that the meaning of the text is available to anyone who opens her/his eyes and reads it.

---

[48] The Enlightenment sought to eliminate all presuppositions in the quest for "disinterested" knowledge. See Hans-Georg Gadamer, *Truth and Method*, pp. 239-240: "... there is one prejudice of the enlightenment that is essential to it: the fundamental prejudice of the enlightenment is the prejudice against prejudice itself, which deprives tradition of its power."

What today is taken to be an immediate encounter with the scriptures, turns out in fact to consist of a reading filtered by the presuppositions of a materialistic paradigm.

[49] Although Zwingli was trained in the via antiqua which perhaps helps to explain the character of Swiss "freisinnige Theologie" which developed in the 19th century independent of German Protestantism. See Nigg, *Geschichte des religiösen Liberalismus*, pp. 223-244.

God does not communicate ambiguously when it comes to the eternal goal of life, and one only has to *look* to learn. If there are subsequent problems with biblical literalism, those are not problems with the text itself. They are problems with the reader. The text is absolute. The reader is finite and distorted by sin. The text builds community, and the community establishes the consensus with respect to the true faith based on open access to the text. Conservative Protestantism is deceptively democratic as it establishes assurance and security in the faith of the ages. The encountering of discrepancies and inconsistencies in the text is resolved by appealing to those "better trained in the faith," i.e., the theologians, who practice gospel harmonization, intertextual explanation regardless of differences of context, and emphasize the miraculous (the exception not the rule) as physical confirmation of God's sovereignty and power over this world. The faith is announced, confirmed, enhanced, and preserved, however, by sense data informed by "common sense." The touchstone is that the faith is perspicuous for anyone who will use her/his senses. God is trying to reach us through the senses: exclusively by means of the only vehicle for gaining knowledge that our epoch acknowledges as valid - sense perception.

Liberal Protestantism is not appealing to an alternative epistemological model, however, which surely fuels the raging fire of contempt between the two groups. Liberal Protestantism is equally committed to sense perception as the key to acquiring truth. Unlike conservative Protestants, however, sense perception is acknowledged to be ambiguous. Hermeneutics has taught liberals that one all too easily reads into the text (eisegesis) what one wants to read out of it (exegesis). Hence, one must develop strategies to neutralize subjective wishes and filters in order to engage the "real" text. Above all, liberal Protestantism must attack anagogical readings of the text which intentionally take one beyond sense experience in a "mystical" reading of the text.

The point here is epistemological: what gives Christian theology legitimacy in a materialist culture (and not merely in the academy) is that it embraces the dominant epistemological model of sensuous materialism informed by the correspondence theory of truth. The difference between conservatives and liberals is not epistemological. It has to do with acknowledgment of ambiguity in sense perception.

Liberal Protestant biblical scholars are basically divided into two camps: the historical/sociological and the principled. The former seeks to establish the correct reading of the text by means of the empirical, historical and/or social evidence of the scriptural community out of which the text emerges. It is a form of literalism, but now no longer in terms of the dotted "i"s and "t"s of the text itself. Rather, secondary textual evidence (including botanical, agricultural, archaeological, architectural, artistic artifacts, etc.) serves as the invaluable source for grasping the meaning of the primary text, the scriptures. For example, one has not understood the communities generating the New Testament documents if one has not taken into consideration the social world that generated those texts. Particularly, what counts as acceptable and what is tabu is relative to a social world. In order to "hear" the shock of the message of Jesus, one must know the values of his original audience. The historical/sociological liberal is epistemologically a materialist, i.e., the warrant for one's truth claims come through the senses. The faith is definable as a "what."

The "principled" reading of the text, on the other hand, is aware that "how" one approaches the text is as important as what one finds in the text. According to this form of liberalism, the principles guiding one's reading are crucial for, if not determinative of, the "proper" reading of the text. Such principles (e.g., acknowledgment of the open-endedness of metaphorical meaning or the search for a hermeneutical key behind the text) are "formal possibilities," i.e., analogous to metaphysical conditions of possibility, for which it is claimed that without them one cannot begin to understand any particular text. Where the historical/sociological approach to the scriptures can be seen as a kind of gnosticism (the key to Christian faith is knowledge about historical events and/or sociological traditions), the strategy of principled liberals can be seen as a kind of legalism, because principles for reading the text constitute a set of rules/laws governing "proper" reading. For example, in the case of a principled reading on the basis of metaphor: one must have a "proper" understanding of metaphor (most often metaphor is understood by liberals to be abbreviated analogy as in the case of Aristotle[50] which privileges the theory of metaphor as substitution or naming over the theory of metaphor that seeks identity in difference while acknowledging concealment and lack of definition[51]). In short, it is deemed sufficient to deny literalism and allegory simply because one emphasizes the metaphorical character of the teaching material of Jesus.

A classic example of a principled reading of the text in search of the hermeneutical key behind the text which one must *know* and bring to the text (in contrast to a *theory* of metaphor that one must bring to the text) can be seen in Robert Hamerton-Kelly's *The Gospel and the Sacred: The Poetics of*

---

[50] See Aristotle, *Poetics* 1457b.
[51] This latter theory of metaphor is indebted to Paul Ricoeur's *The Rule of Metaphor*.

Violence in Mark.[52] Hamerton-Kelly suggests that Mark is a protest against the violence of scapegoating in second temple Judaism. His work is a magisterial attempt to protect Christianity from its own violence of scapegoating in the substitution theory of the sacrificial lamb of God. This is a classic principled reading of the text, for one maintains that one's thesis accounts for the form of the text as it now stands either by indicating that, positively, this hidden principle explains the present form of the text or, negatively, this hidden principle explains the present form of the text since the text sought to suppress or exclude the principle.

Precisely because of its legalism, what is concealed by the "principled" reading of the text is exactly what is concealed by formal possibilities in metaphysics: α) that experiential possibility is always contingent not necessary and, above all, β) that spirit is an illimited, unitary horizon of the imperceptible always and already functioning before one has either chosen principles[53] or engaged in particular readings. One's ontological commitment, establishing what counts as reality and how reality does/should function, precedes one's embracing any set of rules for acting in, and investigating that, reality.[54] Simply focussing on "conditions of possibility" does not ensure one has the proper key for opening up the meaning of the text. In fact, focussing on "conditions of possibility" assumes that one has understood reality properly and can talk about the conditions of possibility of that which one has understood - there is little, if any, acknowledgment of concealment, and ambiguity is simply a matter of incomplete knowledge that one will eventually acquire with time and effort. The principled reading of the text is a classic form of arguing from effects to causes which is speculative at best (since we don't perceive cause) and, more often than not, must argue from silence, since the effects (the text) rarely identify their causal presuppositions.

Principled liberalism surely provides no one with sufficient confidence to justify beating conservative or reactionary Protestants/Christians over the

---

[52] See Hamerton-Kelly, *The Gospel and the Sacred: The Poetics of Violence in Mark* (Minneapolis: Fortress Press, 1994). This work is based upon the work of René Girard, *Violence and the Sacred*, trans. by Patrick Gregory (Baltimore: Johns Hopkins University Press, 1977).

[53] Paradigms precede rules. One has to have a sense of what reality is before one can establish what the structure enabling reality is. That structure equally establishes/confirms one's notion of causality which is always inseparable from the coherence of one's paradigm. Reality for both conservative and liberal Protestants is defined by the senses. Again, it is only a matter of acknowledged levels of ambiguity about sense experience that distinguishes them.

[54] Again, Thomas Kuhn provides insight here. See footnote 30 above.

head for mis-reading the text and causing the fragmentation of Christentum. For, although the principle of plurivocity is a challenge to narrow biblical literalism, it is equally an affirmation of alternative readings of the text. In other words, plurivocity is a strength for living faith surely not because it provides one with an eternal identity (even in principle) uniting Christians, but because it enables a tradition to speak meaningfully to any and all contexts of experience as well as to a broad spectrum of understanding.[55] Hence, there is no room in the faith for bashing either by the fundamentalist or liberal, or by the homophob, sexist or racist, or by the defenders of class or creed. The price paid for such truth as the "correct" faith is the price of exclusion, division, separation, and, above all, narrowness of understanding. We have not begun to understand the richness of the tradition if we limit ourselves to a materialist paradigm of sense perception and/or the conditions of possibility for material experience of actuality (be it an experience of a text or an event) as the sole source of true experience.

Beyond Plurivocity to Spirit and Faith

Nevertheless, plurivocity cannot be *an end* in itself. It is *a means* for breaking down the walls of suspicion over against Others and against fear in life just as it enables opening oneself to the abundance of the life of faith. For above all, it enables the breaking open of each and every paradigm's hegemony over understanding, and it leads one to ever new vistas as one moves from the material to the spiritual depths of experience.

To be sure, the spiritual, for its part, is no source for absolutes. We must avoid metaphysical reductionisms of all kinds no matter what enthusiasm might encourage us to embrace. The spiritual as well as the material dimensions of experience require us to speak of an odyssey of faith seeking understanding, because we do not have direct and immediate access to the material, and the spiritual, at the very least, is rooted in indefinables. But spirit *is* informed by a higher horizon of pragmatic faith. Where the materialist argues that one cannot ignore the physical world without devastating consequences, the person of spirit argues that one cannot ignore the spiritual dimension of life without devastating consequences.

---

[55] This is the conclusion of my doctoral dissertation entitled "On the Soteriological Significance of the Symbol of the Kingdom of God in the Language of the Historical Jesus." The task of that project was to champion pluralism and tolerance in the faith. The present project focuses on unity in the kingdom, but not in terms of an enduring and exclusive identity. What unites Christians is far higher than anything actual or definable.

Human life is spirit in the world, and the Christian models of faith are incomplete so long as one has not encountered the faith that calls for elevation into spirit to re-orient one's involvements in the material world.[56] In

---

[56] The Greeks distinguished among νοῦς (consciousness or Reason in the sense of Plato's simile of the line), λόγος (the structuring system of universals), and νόμος (law), and they understood νοῦς to be "higher" than either λόγος or νόμος, because these notions were understood in terms of an analogy to the human mind. The individual's mind (νοῦς) is more than the content of her thoughts (λόγος) or the principles/laws (νόμος) governing her actions. This is a key to distinguishing between the letters of Paul and John's gospel, the most "spiritual" texts of the New Testament. Paul speaks 164 times of the Christian being "in Christ." See Bernard McGinn, *The Foundations of Mysticism*, p. 73. 1 Cor. 6:16-17 speaks of the Christian's being united in Spirit with Christ (ὁ δὲ κολλώμενος τῷ κυρίῳ ἓν πνεῦμα ἐστιν) and 1 Cor. 2:16 says that the Christian has the mind (νοῦς) of Christ (ἡμεῖς δὲ νοῦν Χριστοῦ ἔχομεν), where John, on the other hand, speaks of the Christ as the "Word" (λόγος). If one follows the Greek meaning of νοῦς when reading Paul, one can "see" that Paul is not speaking of the Christian's sharing the "opinion" or "perspective" of Christ, but, rather, that the Christian participates in the internal mind of Christ, i.e., the illimitable unity of spirit that is life, and thereby the Christian becomes a member of the external body of Christ (1 Cor. 12). In the case of John, on the other hand, the focus is on the indefinable structure of universals (the Logos) that provides the order to any and all experience, i.e., equally the spiritual order that is the key to life.

Yet Paul prefers νοῦς to λόγος, because λόγος is too easily reducible to law. Higher than the law is life: higher than λόγος is νοῦς. This is precisely the interpretive strategy of Origen who speaks of ἡγεμονικός more frequently than νοῦς, because he seeks to draw attention to that aspect of mind that enables one to focus one's concentration and energies. See Endre von Ivánka, "Der 'Apex mentis'" in Werner Beierwaltes, ed., *Platonismus in der Philosophie des Mittelalters* (Darmstadt: Wissenschaftliche Buchgesellschaft, 1969), p. 131: "Erst wo das stoische psychologische Schema sich mit der platonischen Grundidee verband, daß die Grundtendenz des Geistes auf die *Erkenntnis* des Absolutums gerichtet ist, eine Erkenntnis, die aber zugleich ein Hinstreben und ein Hingerichtetsein bedeutet - erst da konnte das stoische ἡγεμονικόν zu einem 'Seelengrunde' im Sinn der mittelalterlichen Mystiker werden. Diese Verbindung des stoischen Schemas mit der platonischen Grundhaltung - zugleich mit der Verchristlichung beider Motive - hat erst Origenes vollzogen." The Christianization of these themes began long before Origen, for they can be found already in Paul.

Kantian deontology seeks to retrieve νόμος and the inner moral disposition as the key to religion within the limits of reason alone. Kant is followed in this regard by Fichte, who, observing that humans cannot *not* act and all action is judged by the actor to be proper or improper, concluded that there must be a prior system of moral law governing all action. See Fichte, J.G., *Versuch einer Critik Aller Offenbarung*, p. 82. However, attention to νόμος conceals one's already being committed to an understanding of reality (one's communal paradigm). Exclusive appeal to νόμος as the key to religion can offer no guarantee that "reality" has been properly understood. It can only insist that its guidelines for action in a presupposed understanding of reality are normative. Νόμος alone cannot protect against systematic distortion of reality any more than it can absolutely ground an understanding of reality.

this respect post-metaphysical theology is picking up a theme of spirit as elevation beyond the limits of the material world, while inseparable from

---

Just how Christianity and Greek philosophy were related is debated among scholars. Heinrich Dörrie takes the extreme position that Christianity borrowed nothing from Greek philosophy, where most other scholars, including Dörrie's mentor Langerbeck, maintain not only some influence but determinative influence. I know of no better descriptions of the positive relationship between Greek philosophy and Christianity than Cornelia de Vogel's "Platonism and Christianity," Antonie Wlosok's, *Laktanz und die Philosphische Gnosis*, and Egon Brandenburger's, *Fleisch und Geist. Paulus und die dualistische Weisheit*.

David Runia distinguishes between four "historians of philosophy" (Wolfson, de Vogel, Popma, and Reale) and four "theologians" (Harnack, Daniélou, Chadwick, and Osborn) and concludes: "The theologians are most interested in the origin and development of distinctive Christian doctrines and attitudes ... The historians of philosophy focus on the underlying continuities of thought, especially as related to the major Greek philosophical positions" (Runia, *Philo in Early Christian Literature*, p. 57). But Runia proceeds to say: "A rigid distinction between philosophy and theology for Philo and early Christian thinkers up to Augustine soon runs into trouble ... Theological problems very often involve philosophical issues, while philosophical problems no less often have a theological focus" (*ibid.*, pp. 57-58). The following additional references are representative of the discussion: C. Andresen, "The Integration of Platonism Into Early Christian Theology," ed. by Elizabeth A. Livingstone in *Studia Patristica* (Berlin: Akademie-Verlag, 1984), pp. 399-413; Cornelia J. de Vogel, "The Problem of Philosophy and Christian Faith in Boethius' Consolatio." in *Romanitas et Christianitas*, ed. by P. G. van der Nat, C. M. J. Sicking, W. den Boer, and J.C.M. van Winden (Amsterdam: North-Holland Publishing Company, 1973), pp. 357-70; Heinrich Dörrie, "Die platonische Theologie des Kelsos in ihrer Auseinandersetzung mit der christlichen Theologie auf Grund von Origenes c. Celsum 6,42ff" in *Nachrichten der Akademie der Wissenschaften in Göttingen. Philologisch-Historische Klasse*. (Göttingen: Vandenhoeck & Ruprecht, 1967); "Was ist 'spätantiker Platonismus'?" in *Theologische Rundschau* 36, no. 4 (1971), pp. 285-302; Hermann Langerbeck, "Paulus und das Griechentum. Zum Problem des Verhältnisses der christlichen Botschaft zum antiken Erkenntnisideal" in *Aufsätze zur Gnosis*, aus dem Nachlaß herausgegeben von Herman Dörries (Göttingen: Vandenhoeck & Ruprecht, 1967), pp. 83-145; E.P. Meijering, "The Doctrine of the Will and of the Trinity in the Orations of Gregory of Nazianzus" in *Nederlands Theologisch Tijdschrift* 27 (1973), pp. 224-34; "Irenaeus' Relation to Philosophy in the Light of His Concept of Free Will" in *Romanitas et Christianitas* (Amsterdam, North-Holland Publishing Co., 1973), pp. 221-232; "Orthodoxy and Platonism in Athanasius" in *Orthodoxy and Platonism in Athanasius: Synthesis or Antithesis?* (Leiden: E.J. Brill, 1974), pp. 114-99; and "Wie platonisierten Christen? Zur Grenzziehung zwischen Platonismus, kirchlichem Credo und patristischer Theologie" in *Vigiliae Christianae* 28 (1974), pp. 15-28; Eric Osborn, "Arguments for Faith in Clement of Alexandria" in *Vigiliae Christianae* 48, no. 1 (1994), pp. 1-25; Karl Praechter, "Christlich-neuplatonische Beziehungen" in *Byzantinische Zeitschrift* 21 (1921), pp. 1-27; R.M. Price, "'Hellenization' and Logos Doctrine in Justin Martyr" in *Vigilae Christianae* 42 (1988), pp. 19-23.

that world, initially formulated by the 19th century Swiss "freisinnige" theologian, Alois Emanuel Biedermann.[57] One can trace the theme over Otto Pfleiderer to Ernst Troeltsch and Ernst Cassirer although the shift in professional context from theology to philosophy indicates how "speculative" theology (an unfortunate label perhaps to English speaking ears but it refers to θεωρητικώτατος, speculative or contemplative thought, rather than unbridled fantasy), as it was called in the 19th century,[58] has been marginalized, even suppressed, in German theological power centers. It is time to take a new look at this theological trajectory in light of our post-metaphysical context.

On the other hand, spirit cannot a priori deny, much less condemn, any model of faith, for spirit informs any and all faith. What one can do *a priori* is warn against any and all reductionism or coherent system that seeks to limit spirit by, or to, a metaphysical and/or metanarrative explanation of experience, or a specific formula, a definition, or a hermeneutic strategy. *A posteriori* one can censure those models of faith that are insensitive to the ambiguities of the conditions of possibility of life. Preservation of the conditions of possibility of life alone as a litmus test is too narrow,[59] however, for it treats all actualities and possibilities as equal. Possibilities and actualities are impossible without both simultaneously. Not all possibilities are mutually

---

[57] According to Biedermann religion is "Erhebung des Menschen, als endlichen Geistes, aus der eigenen endlichen Naturbedingtheit zur Freiheit über sie in einer unendlichen Abhängigkeit." Alois Emanuel Biedermann, *Christliche Dogmatik*, 1869, p. 30. See, also, Biedermann, *Christliche Dogmatik*, 2nd. ed., 1884-5, vol. 1, p. 241: "Die Religion, als subjective Erhebung des menschlichen Ich aus einer negativ empfundenen Weltschranke seines natürlichen Lebens zu einer incommensurabel über derselben erhabenen Macht um von ihr Befreiung zu erlangen, hat zu ihrem subjectiven Motiv alles, worin der Widerspruch zwischen dem Lebensanspruch des Menschen und seiner erfahrenen Schranke hervortreten kann. Zum Inhalte der Religion gehört alles, worin jene Erhebung sich vollzieht. Die psychische Form des Glaubens ist der einheitliche Act persönlicher Erhebung ...: ein Gefühl von Weltschranke und Abhängigkeit als Ausgang und von Freiheit von derselben als Ziel; ein Vorstellen von einer unendlichen Macht über derselben, und ein Wollen, als Act der Selbsterhebung zu ihr mit dem Verlangen nach Freiheit von jener Lebensschranke. Alle diese Acte ... bilden jedoch nicht isolirt selbständige Theile, sondern nur in ihrer innern Wechselwirkung auf einander Momente der Religion; d.h. sie sind nicht isolirt für sich, sei's um ihres Inhaltes sei's um ihrer Form willen, religiöse Gefühle, religiöse Vorstellungen, religiöse Handlungen."

[58] For a discussion of the notion of "Speculation" (Spekulation) in 19th century theology, see Walter Nigg, *Geschichte des religiösen Liberalismus*, pp. 123-125.

[59] This is the position I took in "The Paradox of a Theologian - Weltanschauungen and Conviction: The Problem of Evil." *Explorations: Journal for Adventurous Thought* 4/2 (1986): 39-58, and would now modify. Conditions of possibility alone are not sufficient for grounding a moral system, since they always and already presuppose a commitment to how reality is and functions.

compossible, nor may one ignore the limits of actuality in the pursuit of possibility. One should neither naively discount actuality for the sake of possibility nor naively discount possibilities for the sake of actuality. Any context involves both, and life's decisions remain ambiguous precisely because each context is a dynamic of revealed actuality and concealed possibilities. Any model of faith that ignores that ambiguity and the basic nullity of life (i.e., that any and all future possibilities involve the negation of possibilities in the present) is placing a straight jacket on experience exemplified by dogmatic legalism.[60] Spirit is not a principle or a mere formal condition of possibility. It contains all principles, for spirit is experiential possibility higher than, but inseparable from, all actuality. Spirit is life in the real world.

If liberal Christians may easily accuse conservative Christians of narrow literalism and failing to appreciate the figurative character of all experience, conservative Christians may easily accuse liberals of gnosticism, legalism, and intellectual elitism making the faith inaccessible to the "common" person. Liberal Protestantism requires either knowledge of tools of textual, historical, and sociological criticism, and/or one must grasp the role of presupposed principles silently guiding one's reading - principles which, if not consciously evaluated it is argued, can lead one to a distorted reading. The one hermeneutic strategy calls for "knowledge," the other for the proper interpretive "law(s)." Furthermore, from the perspective of the conservative Protestant, liberal Protestantism has distorted Christianity's scandal and folly to make the faith adaptable to any and whatever context with its hermeneutical open-endedness. The faith is made amenable because it is adaptable. In the eyes of the conservative Christian, the liberal's "two sources" of inherited scripture and contemporary experience[61] have resulted in con-

---

[60] This is what is easily forgotten in the abortion issue. Preservation of the conditions of possibility alone might be employed as a criterion for denying abortion. But such a criterion fails to take the ambiguities of the world of the persons involved into consideration. No one can understand those ambiguities for another. This does not mean that one applauds abortion. It merely underscores the moral necessity of acknowledging that such a choice cannot be made for someone. A spiritual community would create an environment of understanding and support not condemnation and violence.

On the other hand, what is too easily overlooked in a technological age is that our ability to actually do something is taken to justify doing it without awareness of the concealed possibilities of that actuality. By focussing on manifest actuality at the expense of concealed possibility one can cause incalculable damage.

[61] For example, see David Tracy's "revisionist" model of the Christian faith in *Blessed Rage for Order*, although Tracy later warns against the "affective fallacy" (see Tracy, *The Analogical Imagination*, pp. 118 and 143, n. 60) and the dangers of "systematic distortion" (see *ibid.*, pp. 366, n. 21; 351, 363) requiring a "hermeneutics of suspicion" in the dynamic interface of these two sources of theology constituting a "hermeneutics of

temporary experience becoming the dominant driving force of religious truth selecting and rejecting those elements in scripture that it finds acceptable and/or offensive.[62] Christianity has become chameleon, and, precisely because it is chameleon, it has lost its identity and its truth.

Surely, the appropriate response to any and all demands for Christian identity either creedal, historical/sociological, or principled is to point out that all readings and systems of the faith conceal as they reveal, and that one must affirm one's limits in understanding to allow oneself to be challenged by precisely those elements in the tradition that one finds most offensive. It just might be that precisely what one finds offensive today one will discover: α) that it is disclosive and informative in the context of a life experience that one has not yet had or β) that one discovers a new understanding of the offensive claim/teaching when it is placed in a new context of coherence (e.g., a spiritual rather than a material context). Perhaps here is the scandal[63] of faith that drives one onward to increasing spiritual richness. The anomalous, the offensive, the most disturbing is not a diabolical threat, but the strategy of possibility to break down all hegemony, all systems of coherence, in order to open us up to life in the spirit rather than limiting life to the material.

Two Models of the Faith

Surveying the Christian tradition from the perspective of its spiritual and material metaphysical options, we can identity two fundamental models of the faith: unification and separation.[64] There is great variation within these

---

restoration" (see *ibid.*, 131 (the fourth step in interpretation); 146, n. 80; 190, n. 71; and 320). Ricoeur uses the language "strategy of seduction" for "hermeneutics of retrieval" and "strategy of suspicion" for "hermeneutics of suspicion." See Ricoeur, *Oneself as Another*, p. 159, n. 23.

[62] See Chapter 1, n. 117 for G. Leibholz' comment in his "Memoir" to Bonhoeffer's *The Cost of Discipleship*, p. 30, and, as a contrast, Walter Nigg's portrayal in *Geschichte der religiösen Liberalismus*, pp. 203-223, of the German Protestant Society (der deutsche Protestantenverein) founded in the last third of the 19th century.

[63] One meaning of σκάνδαλον is "trap," i.e., metaphorically, what one cannot not affirm. Such a σκάνδαλον is consciousness/νοῦς as the spiritual character of experience equated with the Christ by Paul. If the Christ means νοῦς, then one cannot not affirm the Christ even if one denies one is a Christian.

[64] One cannot speak of models of the Christian faith without reference to David Tracy's five models (Orthodox, Liberal, Neo-Orthodox, Radical, and Revisionist) presented in chapters two and three of *Blessed Rage for Order*. Nonetheless, these five models are either variations on only one of two overarching models shaping the Christian tradition or, as is the case of the Revisionist model, shaped by Aristotelian thought, for Process meta-

two models ranging from apocalyptic, to red and white martyrology, to apophatic/negative theology, to various understandings of the afterlife, to claims for the kingdom of God as partially and/or completely to be realized in this life, etc. Nonetheless, the metaphysical context of these various understandings of the Christian faith allow one to identify these two fundamental options of unification and separation informing Christian understanding. A case can be made, but lack of space prohibits making it here, that there is

---

physics is a reformulation of Aristotelian categories of causality, particularly the material cause, in light of contemporary physics. All five models ignore the unification model of the Christian faith rooted in Christian Platonism.

In *The Analogical Imagination* Tracy talks of God's mystery as an incomprehensibility only on the other side of a theological comprehensibility (*ibid.*, p. 412) echoing his discussion of mystics (*ibid.*, p. 174) that "[s]ilence may indeed be the final and most adequate mode of speech for religion. And yet silence is possible as silence only to a speaker," i.e., silence is possible only on the other side of having spoken (see also *ibid.*, pp. 177 and 202). Here he speaks of this comprehensible-incomprehensible in terms of dialectical theology with its "stark otherness" (see *ibid.*, pp. 177-178), but he distinguishes between two dialectical theological positions (*ibid.*, p. 203): one of participation (the "mystical-priestly-metaphysical-aesthetic"), which he names "manifestation," and one lacking participation (the "prophetic-ethical-historical"), which he names "proclamation." He suggests (p. 204) that "... a study of Western religion shows that a nondialectical understanding of Western religions proves shortsighted. To Western religious eyes, the great Eastern religions as well as the archaic and 'primitive' religions can sometimes seem so mystically and metaphysically oriented that the Western interpreter wonders and ... actually suggests that the classic Eastern traditions fail at ethical, political-historical and thereby *religious* responsibility."

It is precisely the "nondialectical" "metaphysical" tradition of classical Christianity that emphasizes "unification" with ultimate reality rather than "separation" from ultimate reality that constitutes one of the two overarching models of the Christian faith. In other words, Tracy's "manifestation" and "participation" models are variations on the "separation" model of Christian theology.

In a more recent work, "Literary Theory and Return of the Forms for Naming and Thinking God in Theology" in *The Journal of Religion* 74 (1994), Tracy suggests (*ibid.*, p. 312) that "[a]ll Christian theologies ... are grounded in one or the other of ... two classic namings of God: the Hidden-Revealed One or the Comprehensible-Incomprehensible One." He suggests that dialectic language applies to the former and is Pauline (classically Protestant in Barth, p. 312); where analogical language applies to the later and is Johannine (classically Roman Catholic in von Balthasar, p. 312). Though Tracy suggested in *The Analogical Imagination* that even Barth along with the other theologians identified by Tracy as representing "theologies of negative dialectics," e.g., Bultmann, Tillich, Moltmann, Metz, and Schillebeeckx, "... moved forward into the fuller range of the Christian symbol system ... into new ... analogical languages." (*The Analogical Imagination* , p. 417; see, also, pp. 420-421) It should be observed that "all Christian theologies" discussed by Tracy in this article are variations of the Western separation model described here.

a historical sequence to these two models, as well. The church of the New Testament reflects the tensions in the model of unification among λόγος, νοῦς, and νόμος theologies, and, with the decline of Palestinian Christianity, the λόγος and νοῦς theologies of unification come to dominate the Apostolic and Patristic periods down to Augustine. With Augustine we encounter the classic formulation of the theological model of separation that shaped Latin Christianity including the Protestant traditions with some extremely important exceptions (e.g., Pseudo-Dionysius; monastic theology informed by Evagrius of Pontus and Cassian; Eriugina; Bernard of Clairvaux; the Victors; Nicholas of Cusa; Wycliffe; Huss; Zwingli; the Cambridge Platonists; Wesley; Edwards; New England Transcendentalists, Unitarianism; Bushnell, etc.).

What are these two models? The model of separation is most familiar to Western post-Protestant Christianity. It maintains that humanity is separated from God because of original[65] and personal sin.[66] The claim is that there is only one route to overcome this separation, i.e., faith in the sacrificial death and resurrection of Jesus of Nazareth, who as the Christ is the exclusive means for re-unification with God. This model is essentially materialistic. The sin of humanity is obvious when one only opens one's eyes. Humanity is driven by lust, greed, avarice, personal aggrandizement, in short, hubris, and one witnesses humanity's fallenness not only by observing others, but by observing one's own actions and inmost motivations fueled by desires in and for the material world. It's logic is informed by distinguishing humanity from divinity with an entire spectrum of theological reflection

---

[65] Some baptismal rituals maintain that "we were conceived and born in sin" reflecting the evil of concupiscence that has tormented Christianity since Augustine.

[66] Original sin is a doctrine which first emerged as a result of Augustine's mis-reading of Romans 5:12. Karl Barth's "dialectical theology" is a theology of separation. He explicitly rejects any common "being" between God and humanity. See Barth, *Die Kirchliche Dogmatik* (München: Kaiser, 1935-), I/1, pp. viiif., 252; I/2, pp. 158, 41, 48. Though, in an attempt to acknowledge that there must be some form of relationship between God and humanity in order for there to be a restoration of the "image of God" in humanity, Barth speaks of an "analogy of faith." See *ibid.*, I/2, pp. 41, 48f.; I/1, pp. 11, 251. I am indebted to John M. McDermott, S.J., "Dialectical Analogy: The Oscillating Center of Rahner's Thought" in *Gregorianum* 75/4 (1994), p. 675, for this set of citations.

Otherwise, McDermott's paper is disappointing not only for its clinging to metaphysics (e.g., *ibid.*, pp. 691, 695), but because he maintains that "'God' is both 'a part of the world and simultaneously its whole as conscious ... its empowering ground'" (*ibid.*, p. 691) which can only mean that God is finite as an idea among other ideas (i.e., part and whole).

seeking to describe, and account for, whatever role, if any, humanity can play in its restoration to God. The great fracturing of the Western Christian world occurred over this very issue when the Protestant Augustinians, Luther and Calvin, emphasized grace over any and all works in the grand plan of restoration. Here spirit ($\pi\nu\varepsilon\tilde{\upsilon}\mu\alpha$) is understood as a power or force that can overwhelm one from an "outside" source, i.e., spirit is merely a part (rather than the whole) of experience.

This model of separation stands in stark contrast to the model of unification that shaped Hellenistic Christianity. Here the emphasis is upon the always and already accomplished, if only partial, union of the individual Christian with God in spirit, i.e., in immaterial consciousness, that can never be lost. Hence, this model is essentially spiritual. Whether it be formulated in its $\lambda\acute{o}\gamma o\varsigma/\nu o\mu\acute{o}\varsigma$ or $\nu o\tilde{\upsilon}\varsigma$ form, the insight driving the faith here is that we already have access to God's eternal order through the eternal structure of God's thoughts ($\lambda\acute{o}\gamma o\varsigma/\nu o\mu\acute{o}\varsigma$) and spirit ($\nu o\tilde{\upsilon}\varsigma$) whose power is above transience and every desire for the material world of particularity.

Here the locus of conflict is not that separation of the human from God but in a division of focus within the individual: spirit or world; spirit or flesh. Spiritual rebirth is accompanied by a complete transformation of one's frame of reference and motivation in the world. The material world is relativized and one seeks elevation in freedom in the spirit, for the natural goal of life is to participate in reality not any mere transient appearances. If one enters the world and matures initially materially, in the course of one's development one encounters the spiritual dimension of life in the religious community of faith, i.e., that very spiritual dimension that distinguishes humanity from nature and other animals, and one "naturally" seeks growth no longer materially but spiritually. Christ as $\lambda\acute{o}\gamma o\varsigma$ or $\nu o\tilde{\upsilon}\varsigma$ is a constant presence not as some finite, physical being whispering in one's ear warning against eternal damnation, but as cosmic Lord, Savior, and friend providing the very structure to any and all reality.[67]

---

[67] There is perhaps no one more representative of this theology of unification over against Augustinian separation in the Western tradition than Hugh of St. Victor who as a classic Christian Platonist employs the structure of Plato's simile of the line to speak of humanity having three eyes: a physical eye ($\alpha\ddot{\iota}\sigma\theta\eta\sigma\iota\varsigma$), an eye of understanding ($\delta\iota\alpha\acute{\iota}\rho\varepsilon\sigma\iota\varsigma$) and an eye of contemplation ($\theta\varepsilon\omega\rho\acute{\iota}\alpha$). Rather than speak of humanity in the Augustinian sense of hanging in the middle between salvation and damnation, Hugh of St. Victor speaks of the human as in the middle between angels and animals with a providential responsibility for the natural world (he employs metaphors of agricultural cultivation in contrast to metaphors of domination). See Eckard Wolz-Gottwald, "Oculus Triplex". Hugh of St. Victor is a 12th century ecologist.

Faith in a Post-metaphysical Context

The epistemological crisis of our contemporary post-metaphysical context manifests itself in theology by forcing the recognition that both of the fundamental models of the Christian faith (unification and separation) depend upon metaphysical presuppositions that are logically unprovable. The classical attempts in Christianity at foundational explanations on the basis of spirituality or materiality represent reductionist options attempting to explain the material dimension of experience on the basis of the immaterial dimension or vice versa. Such forms of reductionism depend upon metaphysical assertions that are logically indefensible.

This project has sketched out six aporiai central to the human condition that underscore the unknowing character of the human condition.[68] In addition to the spirit/matter aporia (chapter 7), we have examined the mediated character of all experience by means of paradigms (or models) denying immediate access to any foundational structure and indicating that causal explanation itself is relative to one's paradigm, for we can perceive only effects not ultimate causes (chapter 8). In short, these two aporiai deny actual knowledge of facts and indubitable causal explanation.

An examination of language (chapter 9) has indicated how literal meaning dissolves in the acidity of mediated experience, and language must be seen as radically figurative (the dictionary is full of dead metaphors not

---

[68] Rather than an exercise seeking to elevate Christianity above all other religions and rather than employing reason to call for the elimination of religion as an inferior stage of consciousness, that we need to leave behind, this project argues for the universal character of religion across culture, creed, race, gender, or class given the limits to reason and the role of faith in any and all experience. But this form of universalism is not arguing for a specific content that all religions have in common. Eliade suggests that religious humanity is aware that the human condition is constituted out of the interface of the visible and the invisible with hierophanies establishing a cosmos in the midst of chaos for a people. The hierophany is represented by an axis mundi (classically depicted by the human spinal chord or Plato's simile of the line). See *The Sacred and the Profane*.

Eliade's form of universalism, however, is metaphysical. He sees the "terror of history" (see *The Myth of the Eternal Return*) as the motivation for the religious quest in search of the permanent, spiritual order behind, grounding, and informing all historical experience.

Rather than seek a universal metaphysical (ahistorical) explanation of experience, this project underscores the historical and communal character of any and all consciousness as an odyssey of spirit in the sense of faith seeking understanding in the world, i.e., always and always shaped by the actual historical conditions of experience as those both limit and enable, though always conceal, possibilities.

literal truth[69]). It is not that figurative language is a kind of ornamentation to literal language, but, rather, literal language is trivialized and anesthetized figurative language born out of the incessant drive of the human spirit to seek similarity, which often leads to a judgment of identity, in difference which then is subsequently confused for an ontological identity. Furthermore, language may be the house of Being, but language is impossible without spirit and world. In other words, the aporia of language negates any reductionism to language as the exclusive component of experience either as a ceaseless folding over on itself or an endless erasing of the trace.[70]

The project then turned to analyze the Western tradition's notions of truth (chapter 10) commencing with the correspondence theory of truth with its variants of verification and falsification to indicate its indefensibility, because it depends upon direct access to dimensions of experience inaccessible

---

[69] An insight already formulated in 1804 by Jean Paul in *Vorschule der Aesthetik*, p.25: "... *each language is a dictionary of faded metaphors*." (emphasis added).

[70] In "The Double Session" Derrida concludes: "Since everything becomes metaphorical, there is no longer any literal meaning and, hence, no longer any metaphor either ... If there is no such thing as a total or proper meaning, it is because the blank *folds over*" (Jacques Derrida, "The Double Session" in *Dissemination*, p. 258).

Derrida has his notion of the effaced coin and the trace from Nietzsche. Nietzsche had written: "Truths are illusions which we have forgotten are illusions; they are metaphors that have become worn out and have been drained of sensuous force, coins which have lost their embossing and are now considered as metal and no longer as coins." (Nietzsche, "On Truth and Lies in a Nonmoral Sense," p. 84) This is where Derrida picks up Nietzsche's analysis. See Jacques Derrida, "White Mythology: Metaphor in the Text of Philosophy," p. 217, n. 14, 262, n. 74. Derrida's discussion of "coinage" (see *ibid*., p. 210, 216), then, can be traced directly to Nietzsche. Derrida thinks of metaphor, in agreement with Nietzsche, as a form of un-truth. "Metaphor is less in the philosophical text (and the rhetorical text coordinated with it) than the philosophical text is within metaphor. And the latter can no longer receive its name from metaphysics, except by a catachresis, if you will, that would retrace metaphor through its philosophical phantom: as 'nontrue metaphor.'" (Derrida, "White Mythology," p. 258) Already in *Of Grammatology*, Derrida had written, "*There is nothing outside of the text* ..." (Jacques Derrida, "'... That Dangerous Supplement ...,'" in *Of Grammatology* p. 158). If this was not an explicit enough articulation of his thorough skepticism (i.e., "vulgar" skepticism in the sense of Hume), Derrida immediately adds: "... there has never been anything but writing; there have never been anything but supplements, substitutive significations which could only come forth in a chain of differential references, the 'real' supervening, and being added only while taking on meaning from a trace and from an invocation of the supplement, etc. And thus to infinity, for we have read, *in the text*, that the absolute present, Nature, that which words like 'real mother' name, have always already escaped, have never existed; that what opens meaning and language is writing as the disappearance of natural presence" (Derrida, "'... That Dangerous Supplement...',", p. 159).

to us. A case has been made that the Greek notion of truth as ἀλήθεια (disclosing) is more appropriate for speaking of human experience if it is understood in terms of the aporia of actuality and possibility. Where the Western tradition has tended to focus on actuality, it has consistently contributed to the overlooking, forgetting, and suppression of possibility. The truth of human experience is that it consists of a dynamic of the actual concealing the possible where the possible is constantly being projected by the human spirit into the future in acts of understanding.

This aporia of actuality and possibility (the aporia of truth), then, points to a fundamental productive negativity at the core of all life, but this is not Tillich's notion of non-Being threatening, yet subservient to, Being.[71] Rather, Being is both Being and non-Being, for it is the no-thingness of possibility, denying any and all metaphysical ground or foundation, just as it is inseparable from a particular context of historical actuality. Truth is an aporia of revealing and concealing, of actuality and possibility uniting both spirit and matter in one horizon of possibility.

Descartes' two substances and Lessing's ugly ditch are the consequence of limiting one's understanding to actuality while ignoring possibility. The epistemological crisis of post-metaphysical experience has shown that there is no unmediated access to actuality or possibility. Having surrendered the "what" of knowledge by acknowledging that one cannot actually know, the tradition turned to describing the "how" or conditions of possibility of experience in a quest for indubitable knowledge. Yet the "how" in terms of the conditions of possibility gets us no closer to indubitable truth than the "what" of judgment, because every "how" is contingent and not absolutely necessary. Now it is seen that both the "what" and the "how" of knowledge elude claims of indubitability, and our post-metaphysical context confronts us with a radical unknowing in experience born out of the revealing and concealing dynamic of possibility and actuality.[72]

The fifth aporia analyzed in this project has been time (chapter 11). The cosmological understanding of time by Plato/Plotinus (as the image of

---

[71] See Paul Tillich, *The Courage to Be* (New Haven: Yale University Press, 1969), pp. 40, 176-177. Tillich's argument that non-Being is dependent upon Being, since it can only be a negation of Being, is a classic example of an argument for a contingent, rather than an absolute, necessity. So long as one "is," Being has priority over non-Being, but one does not absolutely necessarily have to be. Such logic applies to all arguments for the necessity of "conditions of possibility," e.g., Process thought, as well. They can at best establish contingent but not absolute necessity.

[72] This enables one's speaking of the Christian virtue of hope in light of non-epistemic faith as one lives in, and out of, the illimitable unity of spirit, i.e., love.

eternity) and by Aristotle (as the paradoxical "gap" of the present presupposed by all motion) has been investigated in contrast to the anthropological understandings of time by Augustine, Kant, and Husserl. Perhaps no other component of human experience announces our radical unknowing than does time. Ricoeur speaks of the fundamental paradox of cosmological and phenomenological time in terms of cosmological time consisting of a ceaseless flow of moments in which the individual is *meaningless*; where it is precisely in the phenomenological time of human experience that makes sense of cosmological time (i.e., phenomenological time gives cosmological time its *meaning*). However, this project finds Heidegger's ontological analysis of time as the dynamic horizon of possibility to be precisely what unites the limited cosmological, anthropological, and phenomenological descriptions of time, since it speaks of time as the dimension of no-thingness (possibility) upon which all experience depends and by means of which all experience thrives.

The final aporia investigated by this project has been the paradox of self and Other (chapter 12). Rejecting the Cartesian notion of the self as some kind of permanent substrate (substance) from which we go out into the world and to which we return, this project has focussed on the unique and unrepeatable character of individual experience inaccessible in its depths even to the self while simultaneously the self is inseparable from its context of world and Others which are equally inaccessible to the self. Drawing on the work of Kant, Husserl, Heidegger (particularly his distinction between care and solicitude), Lévinas (on our accountability to the face of the Other), and Ricoeur's analysis of the self as an *ipse*-identity in *Oneself as Another*, the self emerges as an aporia of an unknowing project that is successful only when it acknowledges its inseparability from its equally unknown world and the unknown Others in its world. We are fellow strangers and yet fellow pilgrims on an odyssey of faith seeking understanding.

From Vulgar to Refined Skepticism: Faith Seeking Understanding

Such pervasive unknowing might lead one to conclude that this project is merely a version of what Cleanthes calls "vulgar skepticism" in David Hume's *Dialogues Concerning Natural Religion*. Long before Richard Rorty, Hume challenged vulgar skepticism with the pragmatic argument. But a pragmatic argument is neither a logical proof nor may we limit it to the material dimension of experience as does Cleanthes (i.e., the physical world provides the litmus test of pragmatic truth not the intellect although it is precisely Cleanthes in these dialogues who defends the teleological argument for God as mind). We can no more ignore the role of universals in experience than we can ignore the speeding train. Yet we only have mediated access to both dimensions of experience, i.e., we can only re-present them we can't know them. This, indeed, requires acknowledgment of the role of faith in any and all experience and understanding. This project concludes with Philo:

> ... in proportion to my veneration for true religion is my abhorrence of vulgar superstitions; and I indulge a peculiar pleasure, I confess, in pushing such principles sometimes into absurdity, sometimes into impiety. And you are sensible that all bigots, notwithstanding their great aversion to the latter above the former, are commonly equally guilty of both.[73]

Bigots are guilty of both absurdity and impiety, because their claims are grounded in contradiction(s) and their human "knowledge" is elevated to the status of divine knowledge. Therefore, all that protects humanity from vulgar superstition (of a material or a spiritual order), which exploits the limits of reason to unbridle speculation about ultimate cause(s) with respect to either the material or the spiritual dimensions of experience, all that protects us from blind speculation is our embracing of the non-epistemic faith determinative of spiritual experience. Refined skepticism is the appropriate alternative to vulgar skepticism: "[i]f we distrust human reason we have now no other principle to lead us into religion,"[74] for it is precisely reason that instructs that we live by non-epistemic faith as spiritual beings in the world. Yet, although reason (both calculating $\delta\iota\alpha\iota\rho\varepsilon\sigma\iota\varsigma$ and contemplative $\theta\varepsilon\omega\rho\iota\alpha$) instructs in the necessity of faith, because reason itself is limited, reason equally provides the only means for adjudicating the adequacy of our communal model of reality, i.e., coherence continually examined by the hermeneutics of suspicion[75] given the role of concealed possibility in all experience and understanding. Hence, reason enables self-correction of our understanding, when the data warrant it, and demands self-transcendence as possibility

---

[73] Hume, *Dialogues Concerning Natural Religion*, p. 82.
[74] Hume, *Dialogues Concerning Natural Religion*, p. 12.
[75] Ricoeur offers the formula: an inadequate reading (or any understanding of experience in general, since all experience is a mediated, interpretive process after an event) is narrow and far-fetched; an adequate reading is congruent and a plenitude. See "Metaphor and the Main Problem of Hermeneutics," p. 104.

Ricoeur warns against both the "intentional fallacy" (that the intention of the author is the sole criterion of a proper reading) and the "affective fallacy" (that whatever meaning the reader gets out of, or reads into, the text is valid). See "Erzählung, Metapher und Interpretationstheorie," p. 250. See, as well, *Time and Narrative*, vol. 3, p. 317, n. 38.

pushes us beyond actuality. Even more, reason is higher than this discursive reason of διαίρεσις, which calls for critical, open-ended correction of judgments about an "exogenous" world, for it announces the very illimitable character of consciousness in which all experience occurs. Reason is not knowledge and cannot be replaced by law (νόμος) or universals (λόγος). Reason announces that higher than νόμος and λόγος is spirit (νοῦς) and the θεώρια of contemplation rooted in unknown possibility. Nevertheless, reason is able only to bring one to the threshold of faith. It cannot define the content of that faith. To be sure, there are pragmatic arguments of discursive reason (διαίρεσις) which justify confidence in both matter and spirit. Spirit, however, has truly a pragmatic priority, reason teaches, because spirit (νοῦς) is that dimension in which *all* experience transpires. Yet, on the other hand, spirit is inseparable from a world, grounded as both are in the no-thingness of possibility. We are spirit in the world as an odyssey of faith seeking understanding.

Hugo Staudinger distinguishes among four world views shaping the Western tradition: the magical, mythical, scientific, and historical.[76] He suggests that there is a continuity between the magical and the scientific with the former leading to the latter; and that there is a continuity between the mythical and the historical with the former leading to the latter.[77]

Staudinger describes the magical world view as a closed system in which all events and appearances constitute an inner relatedness. Here the concern is with causality and the exercising of control over occurrences through ceremonies and formulas meant to influence the gods and demons governing events. These magical deities are not free to act as they will. Rather, they are themselves embedded in the great mechanism of the world.[78]

The scientific world view, Staudinger suggests, shares with the magical world view the belief that the natural order consists of a closed system in which all events and appearances constitute an inner relatedness. In addition, the scientific world view is concerned with causality and the exercising of control over occurrences, but here, of course, is where they differ.[79] The inner relatedness of all things is controlled not by gods and demons but by natural laws.

In contrast, the mythical world view, Staudinger continues, is concerned with unique events and occurrences which are not subject to the ne-

---

[76] See Hugo Staudinger "Mythos und Geschichte. Überlegungen zur historisch-kritischen Exegese" in *Forum Katholische Theologie*, 7/3 (1991), 161-174, especially, p. 162..
[77] See Staudinger, *ibid.*, p. 162.
[78] See Staudinger, *ibid.*, p. 162.
[79] See Staudinger, *ibid.*, p. 171.

cessity of any laws but rather spring from spontaneous activities or unique decisions of the gods or super individuals. Here the gods do not react automatically according to formulas and ceremonies, but by human appeal to which they may or may not respond.[80] Characteristic of this world view is that things have not always been the way they are, and the emphasis is on the unique and unrepeatable.[81]

Similar to the analogous relationship between the scientific and the magical world views, the historical world view shares with the mythical world view the concern with unique events and occurrences. Although, unlike the mythical world view, the historical world view engages its task critically with the historian taking personal responsibility for the accuracy of what s/he reports.[82]

Staudinger's thesis is that the mythical-historical world view has proven to be the more accurate over the magical-scientific[83] given the demise of the mechanical model of the universe and the demonstration by physics of the probability character of natural law.[84] He argues that, although much can be said about the material conditions of experience, no one can explain the seam between spirit and matter ("die Nahtstelle zwischen Geist und Materie"[85]) which constitutes human experience.

While Staudinger's description of the Western tradition in terms of these four world views is illuminating, his conclusion, that the triumph of the mythical-historical world view makes it appropriate to conclude that God influences the material order,[86] is an example of a hasty speculative leap from effects to cause that theology must avoid. We are always on this side of effects (of the event or text). If we are to properly understand and recover who we are in the order of things as spirit in the world on an individual and corporate odyssey of faith, we need both the "scientific" and the "historical" world views as described by Staudinger. Rather than emphasize the ultimate priority of the unique and unrepeatable over the internally related, closed system to conclude that there is room for divine agency in the world, we need to acknowledge such judgments about divine agency to be valid at the

---

[80] See Staudinger, *ibid.*, p. 164.
[81] See Staudinger, *ibid.*, p. 165.
[82] See Staudinger, *ibid.*, p. 167.
[83] See Staudinger, *ibid.*, p. 173.
[84] See Staudinger, *ibid.*, p. 172.
[85] See Staudinger, *ibid.*, p. 174.
[86] See Staudinger, *ibid.*, p. 174. He is careful enough to say that we cannot explain it, but he argues we do and can observe that divine intervention (*ibid.*, p. 174).

very most only as speculative but, more importantly we must hold on to both the unique and the internally, coherently related moments of experience as of equal importance if we are to adequately understand who we are. For, in the end, both are aporetically experienced exclusively in the spiritual dimension of our lives. Only by holding on to both moments can the universal character of non-epistemic faith be made clear and the spirit regain a proper balance on its fulcrum with the material.

Furthermore, the model of non-epistemic faith proposed here is a call to freedom, but not a freedom that is oblivious to its damaging consequences as a mere exercise of the will in arbitrary choice. Yet another truncating legacy from Descartes is the defining of the freedom of the will as unrestricted from or by anything external.[87] Such an understanding of freedom is limited to a choice among actualities. It has forgotten that the human condition is inseparable from its horizon of possibilities. In short, it has forgotten the radically historical character of human freedom. Spiritual faith as a call to freedom is higher than law/νόμος. This freedom is an acknowledgment that the human at its best rises above material necessity to νοῦς. It is not what the human chooses that constitutes freedom, but, rather, what the human is in addition to its material conditions that liberates. Hence, spiritual freedom is no stoic resignation before material fate. Spiritual freedom is an actualizing, enabling, and enhancing of possibilities for the self and Other in a historical community that cannot but remember the actions and suffering of those who have gone before if it truly wishes to understand who it is now. Spiritual freedom is what makes for culture, but culture is no unambiguous good. If humanity is to reign in its destructiveness, it must acquire an understanding of the human beyond the confines of its mere material and logical conditions (doubtful as they are) to embrace the illimitable unity of spirit and the role of possibility in an odyssey of faith.

In short, refined skepticism acknowledges the non-epistemic faith essential to all experience and understanding as it seeks to enhance the present and future possibilities of oneself, nature, and Others by accepting its dependence upon that which it did not create itself and its debt to the actions and sufferings of those who have gone before. The refined skepticism of non-epistemic faith focuses on the illimitable spiritual depths of humanity to

---

[87] See Descartes discussion of the will in Meditation IV, 57: "... the will consists solely in the fact that when something is proposed to us by our intellect either to affirm or deny, to pursue or to shun, we are moved by it in such a way that we sense that no external force could have imposed it on us" (*Meditations on First Philosophy*, trans. by Donald A. Cress, p. 37).

enhance those present and future possibilities leading to just institutions and self-esteem, because they preserve the contingent conditions of possibility for the odyssey of faith. It is precisely the spiritual depths of the individual and Other that are the key to self-esteem which is not measured by accomplishments but by capacities. As a spiritual odyssey of faith seeking understanding, refined skepticism acknowledges the contingencies of what is necessary while calling for appreciation of the illimitable spiritual character of humanity.

When we turn to the model of unification (as distinct from the model of separation sketched above) in the Christian tradition, we can hear an echoing throughout Christian history of a call for the "elevation" of the human into the spirit and out of a life of enslavement to mere materialism speaking to our post-metaphysical situation. Christians according to this model are in but not merely of the world (John 17:15-16). Their lives are characterized by the classic Christian virtues (I Corinthians 13:13) of faith (non-epistemic), hope (rooted in possibility higher than any and all actuality) and love (informed by the illimitable spiritual whole of experience), which empower theological renewal by calling for elevation into the spirit in faith precisely because (not in spite) of the skepticism of our post-metaphysical context.[88] Responding to this call from the Christian tradition does not re-

---

[88] Precisely these classic Pauline Christian virtues indicate how faith is a spiritual odyssey seeking understanding inseparable from its historical, communal context. See the following literature of the on-going debate about the source of these virtues in the Pauline literature generated by Richard Reitzenstein's work and Adolf von Harnack's response to it:

Richard Reitzenstein, "Die Entstehung der Formel 'Glaube, Liebe, Hoffnung'" in *Historische Zeitschrift* 116 (1916), pp. 189-208; "Die Formel 'Glaube, Liebe, Hoffnung' bei Paulus" in *Nachrichten von der Königlichen Gesellschaft der Wissenschaften zu Göttingen. Philologisch-historische Klasse* (1916), pp. 367-416; "Die Formel Glaube, Liebe, Hoffnung bei Paulus. Ein Nachwort" in *Nachrichten von der Königlichen Gesellschaft der Wissenschaften zu Göttingen. Philologisch-historische Klasse* (1917), pp. 130-51; *Die hellenistischen Mysterienreligionen. Nach ihren Grundgedanken und Wirkungen*, Vortrag ursprünglich gehalten in dem Wissenschaftlichen Predigerverein für Elsass-Lothringen den 11. November 1909. (Leipzig: Verlag von B.G. Teubner, 1920); *Historia Monachorum und Historia Lausiaca. Eine Studie zur Geschichte des Mönchtums und der frühchristlichen Begriffe Gnostiker und Pneumatiker* (Göttingen: Vandenhoeck und Ruprecht, 1916); and "Iranischer Erlösungsglaube" in *Zeitschrift für die Neutestamentliche Wissenschaft und die Kunde der älteren Kirche* 20 (1921), pp. 1-23; Carsten Colpe, *Die Religionsgeschichtliche Schule. Forschung zur Religion und Literatur des alten und neuen Testaments* (Göttingen: Vandenhoeck & Ruprecht, 1961); Peter Corssen, "Paulus und Porphyrios" in *Sokrates. Zeitschrift für das Gymnasialwesen* 73 (1919), pp. 18-30; Martin Dibelius, "Reitzenstein, R., Historia Monachorum und Historia Lausiaca" in *Wochenschrift für klassische Philologie* 33 (1916), pp. 1037-42; Johannes Geffcken, *Der Ausgang des griechisch-römischen Heidentums* (Heidelberg: Carl Winters Universitätsbuchhandlung, 1920); Adolf von

quire embracing the metaphysics which initially informed the call. It only requires acknowledging the speculative character of any and all metaphysics in faith which allows hearing the call for "elevation" into the spirit as a call into history. The Spirit is manifest, as far as we can know, exclusively in the historical odyssey of individuals in community.

This understanding of the Christian faith will surely not be appealing to all Christians. For some it offers too little, for others it is too vague, for others there is no agenda or succinct formula for arriving at the "true" content of Christianity or for bringing the world to Christ. For its part, it makes no pretense of seeking to bring the world to Christ, but claims that the spiritual depths of Christ are always and already inseparable from what human consciousness (νοῦς) is all about. It openly acknowledges that it is one path or model of the faith among many. Given the mediated character of experience and our inability to adjudicate an absolute paradigm, since we cannot get outside of the paradigm we are committed to in order to test its correctness, it seeks the retrieval of an ancient spirituality informing the Christian tradition since its beginnings that has been too long ignored and forgotten. It appeals to that peace where the lamb has already laid down with the lion in order to spiritually transform individuals, communities, and the world. It is a call to freedom that empowers and enhances. It understands that responsibility requires both a remembrance of, and accountability to, those who have gone before and a sensitivity to those things and possibilities that are unseen. Above all, it affirms the dignity and worth of each individual in the communal odyssey of faith seeking understanding.

Harnack, "Über den Ursprung der Formel 'Glaube, Liebe, Hoffnung'" in *Preußische Jahrbücher* (April bis Juni 1916), pp. 1-14; Hermann Langerbeck, "Paulus und das Griechentum;" R. Schütz, "Der Streit zwischen A. V. Harnack u. R. Reitzenstein über die Formel 'Glaube, Liebe, Hoffnung' 1. Kor. 13,13" in *Theologische Literaturzeitung* 42 (1917), pp. 454-57; Wolfgang Weiss, "Glaube - Liebe - Hoffnung. Zu der Trias bei Paulus" in *Zeitschrift für die Neutestamentliche Wissenschaft* 84, no. 3/4 (1993), pp. 196-217; Geo Widengren, "Die Religionsgeschichtliche Schule und der Iranische Erlösungsglaube" *Orientalistische Literaturzeitung* 58;11/12 (1963), pp. 533-48.

Appendix
Division of the Task of Theology

In his article "What is Theology?" Schubert Ogden follows the example of Friedrich Schleiermacher[1] by dividing theology into a three-fold structure of "historical theology,"[2] "systematic theology,"[3] and "practical theology."[4] Ogden, however, adds the fourth task of "fundamental theology"[5] concerned with establishing the "first principles" of the other three moments "thereby reestablishing communication between (sic) them."[6]

Theology, according to Ogden, is concerned with "the fully reflective understanding of the Christian witness of faith as decisive for human existence."[7] Included in this reflective understanding, and what distinguishes theology from "the special sciences," is "reflection on its [theology's] own conditions of possibility as a form of understanding."[8] The "object" of theology, according to Ogden then, is "not this human activity or that, but the all-inclusive activity of witness, and thus human existence as such."[9] More specifically, "... 'the Christian witness of faith' can mean nothing other than the believing re-presentation of the witness of faith of Jesus of Nazareth ..."[10] Therefore, "... theology as here defined is, in effect, the fully reflective understanding of Jesus as the Christ."[11] "... [T]he task of theology as such is not simply to make this affirmation but also to understand it; and this

---

[1] See Friedrich Schleiermacher, *Brief Outline on the Study of Theology*, trans. by Terrence N. Tice (Richmond, Va.: John Knox Press, 1970).
[2] Ogden, "What is Theology?," Theses 5 and 6, pp. 27-30.
[3] Ogden, "What is Theology?," Thesis 7, pp. 30-32.
[4] Ogden, "What is Theology?," Thesis 8, pp. 32-34.
[5] Ogden, "What is Theology?," Thesis 9, pp. 34-35.
[6] Ogden, "What is Theology?," p. 35.
[7] Ogden, "What is Theology?," p. 22.
[8] Ogden, "What is Theology?," p. 22.
[9] Ogden, "What is Theology?," p. 23. It sounds as if Ogden is defining theology as all-inclusive of experience in a similar way as does the present theological project based on the aporiai at the core of all experience. But Ogden does not really mean all-inclusive paradoxical experience. He means the "all-inclusive activity of witness" to the fundamental worthwhileness of experience. Such a witness presupposes and conceals the aporetic character of faith.
[10] Ogden, "What is Theology?," p. 23.
[11] Ogden, "What is Theology?," p. 23.

consideration is important for a properly theological definition of theology itself."[12]

Ogden follows Tillich's "method of correlation"[13] by maintaining that not simply theology in general but Christian theology in particular exhibits "... the witness of faith as expressive of *the* answer to the one fundamental question expressed or implied by all of man's life and history."[14] The "primary understanding" of the witness of faith contained in the symbolism of its original witness serves as the ultimate criterion for the *appropriateness* of a theological claim.[15] This suggests that we have access to the understanding of that original witness unclouded by intervening history. Yet Ogden is aware that the formulation of "the Christian witness" is contextually dependent:

> ... we now realize only too well that Scripture and dogma themselves, as well as any supposed understanding of them, are so thoroughly historical as to render any such test [e.g., agreement with the received understanding of an allegedly infallible Scripture or dogma] insufficient. Likewise, ... we now recognize that what one epoch or culture accepts as criteria of meaning and truth by no means needs to be accepted by another. As a matter of fact, ... we know that even the most fundamental conditions of understandability may be subject to change.[16]

How does the theologian adjudicate, then, between an appropriate and an inappropriate formulation of "the Christian witness?" Ogden suggests, first, "through intensive discussion with [the] best secular knowledge;"[17] second,

---

[12] Ogden, "What is Theology?," p. 23.

[13] The structure of correlation is expressed by Ogden's Thesis 2: "As such, a theology presupposes as a condition of its possibility the correlation of the Christian witness of faith and human existence, both poles of which alike have a variable as well as a constant aspect." (Ogden, "What is Theology?,", p. 23) For a more extended discussion of the "method of correlation" in theology, see Chapter 4, "David Tracy: Theology as Correlation."

[14] Ogden, "What is Theology?," p. 25.

[15] Ogden, "What is Theology?," p. 25. See, in addition, the discussion of Thesis 4, p. 27: "... the first requirement of the theology of any religion is that its statements give appropriate expression to *the same understanding of faith as is expressed in the witness or 'dogma' it presupposes as its object.*" (emphasis added) Or again, p. 30: "... with all the difficulties of applying it, agreement with the witness of Scripture is still the primary test of the appropriateness of theological statements, practical as well as systematic." Given the nature of contextualization and historicality determining all understanding, this "first requirement" and "primary test" of theology are impossible of fulfillment. This in no way means, however, that we are to give up trying to understand the witness of faith of an earlier epoch or trying to understand Scripture. It merely acknowledges the impossibility of the total fusion of horizon that "agreement" requires.

[16] Ogden, "What is Theology?," p. 26

[17] Ogden, "What is Theology?," p. 27.

through the criterion of universal applicability, and, finally, the free choice of the theologian.[18]

These are weak criteria, to be sure. Secular knowledge is granted the task of establishing the criteria of rationality. Universal applicability either so restricts the domain of theological concern to what is universal that it α) diminishes the significance of the particulars of life, or β) theology becomes ultimately indistinguishable from any and all experience,[19] or γ) it rests upon

---

[18] See Ogden, "What is Theology?," p. 27.

[19] So long as theology is defined as some kind of positive science concerned with a specific content, it fails in its role even when that positive science is concerned with the universal "conditions of possibility of any and all experience." Such a universal "truth" must address the paradox of concealment and suppression in the conditions of possibility for it to be theological. It is precisely this aporetic dynamic of the paradoxical that distinguishes theological experience from all other experience while simultaneously (paradoxically) no different from all other experience.

Ogden follows a classic "essence" and "accident" structure for theological claims which eliminates any sensitivity to the aporetic and permits no distinguishing between theological and other kinds of experience. See, Ogden, "What is Theology?," pp. 28-9: "... it belongs to the very nature of faith that there is no human activity, and hence no form of culture, that does not in some way bear witness to it. [This is analogous to Hegel's notion of the "cunning of reason." See G.W.F. Hegel, *Lectures on the Philosophy of World History*, trans. by H.B. Nisbet (Cambridge: Cambridge University Press, 1975, p. 89.] In general, however, one may distinguish between the *explicit* witness of faith, which is borne by religion as one form of culture among others, and the *implicit* witness of faith, which is borne somehow by all the remaining cultural forms. To say, then, that the question of historical theology is what the Christian witness of faith has already been is to say that it is concerned with the reflective understanding of the history of the Christian religion, its beliefs, rites, social organization, and theology, together with the rest of human activity and culture so far as historically shaped thereby." This "essence"/"accident" structure is confirmed later when Ogden writes, p. 30: "... the real difference between the two disciplines [historical and systematic theology] is logical: the difference between expressing what has already been said or meant by others [= accident] and expressing what is properly said or meant by all [= essence], whether or not anyone up to now has ever actually said it." Further, p. 31: "... the task of systematic theology remains in principle the same [= its essence]: to achieve an understanding of the Christian witness that, however different it may be from all previous witnesses and their theological interpretations, appropriately grasps *their essential meaning* ..." (emphasis added) The same logical structure to theology is expressed in the definition of "fundamental theology," p. 35: "... 'fundamental theology:' reflection undertaken within each of the specialities and disciplines [historical, systematic, and practical theology] directed toward formulating their respective *first principles* and thereby reestablishing communication between (sic) them." (emphasis added)

Ultimately, the essence of Christianity, according to Ogden is articulated by that description of the conditions of possibility for any and all experience found in Process metaphysics. See "Toward a New Theism' in *The Reality of God and Other Essays*, pp. 44-70. Paradox is lost in this descriptive account of the causal conditions of experience. Aristotelianism still reigns in theology as it has since Aquinas.

an opinion poll criterion for truth that runs the risk of systematic distortion. The free choice of criteria by the individual theologian, while no doubt the case, must always be qualified by critical public discussion and clarification if it is to avoid the worst form of relativism.

Building upon Ogden's own analogy to the battlefield as the arena for discussion between the theologian and "secular colleagues,"[20] the theologian has already surrendered the field, because the criteria for what counts as knowledge has been left to the definition of the secular colleagues. Ogden represents the dilemma of the 20th century theologian desperately seeking to define the theological task in a manner acceptable to secular knowledge and understanding. Yet, fully aware of the contextualization of all knowledge, and thereby no longer in a position to give revelation a privileged status for truth claims, the critically reflective 20th century theologian is equally aware that it is secular knowledge and understanding that has now brought us to recognize that all knowledge is relative to a paradigm (i.e., contextualized). Hence, no longer in possession of any criteria of knowledge or understanding outside of secular knowledge and understanding, the critically reflective 20th century theologian has no alternative but to employ the criteria of knowledge and understanding of her/his secular colleagues "more radically" than they do. The theologian, we are told, must turn to either transcendentalism or metaphysics to talk about "the universal conditions of possibility" of all experience and understanding.

Yet, either unwilling or unable to confront the pre-rationality of such universal conditions of possibility, that is, unwilling or unable to acknowledge the role of aporiai and presuppositions that serve as the condition of possibility for transcendental and metaphysical claims, the theologian maintains the illusion of rationality in order not to lose face in the conversation with her/his secular colleagues. In so doing, the theologian has given up her/his proper role in the conversation and surrendered to the secular colleague the task of defining what counts as a rational conversation. After all, no theologian committed to critical reflection wishes to risk being laughed off the podium. Yet so long as the theologian surrenders the definition of rationality to her/his secular colleagues, s/he must either define some kind of metaphysics or transcendentalism, taken to be the more radical grounding of secular rationality, or remain silent. In either case, the task of theology as *fides quaerens intellectum* has not only been compromised, it has been either intentionally or unintentionally concealed.

---

[20] See Ogden, "What is Theology," p. 27.

The fear, if not terror, generated by the retrieval of the theological task as a pre-rational task, is that we sink into a swamp of superstition, magic, and/or tricksterism. The situation is analogous to coming to terms with our ancestry in the ape family. To demonstrate the origin of rationality, defined as the commitment of the human intellect to universals (transcending material particularity[21]), is in superstition, magic, and tricksterism no more diminishes the importance of our capacity to employ universals in reflection than demonstrating the origin of the human species in the ape family diminishes the importance of our species. Failure, however, to self-consciously come to terms with the aporiai of our rationality, continuing to suppress the aporetic in the belief that our rationality gives us access to absolutes (in terms of "natural laws" or more radically in terms of the transcendental, metaphysical claims of "conditions of possibility" which those natural laws depend upon), projects upon secular knowledge the same heteronomous power that was once projected onto the Church with respect to the authority of revelation.

Our age of technology is currently experiencing the consequences of the abuse of such heteronomous, secular power. It is time for theology to call secular knowledge to account, not by returning to heteronomous claims based on revelation, but by pointing out the equivocal foundation of all experience, understanding, and knowing that makes the human condition an odyssey of faith.

---

[21] If rationality commences with the division of life into the spheres of ideas and the factual world (or universals and particulars), then Kurt Hübner argues in *Die Wahrheit des Mythos* (München: Verlag C.H.Beck, 1985) that we owe such rationality to Plato, who was the first demythologizer. It was Plato who substituted the arché (or universal) for the experiential model or activity performed by the Gods that was then eternally repeated by humans. The Idea-world (universals) was substituted for the mythological (the actions of the Gods). See *Die Wahrheit des Mythos*, pp. 137, 428, n. 139 and n. 140, and 138. See, as well, Mircea Eliade, *The Myth of the Eternal Return*, p. 34: "... [I]t could be said that ... 'primitive' ontology has a Platonic structure; and in that case Plato could be regarded as the outstanding philosopher of 'primitive mentality,' that is, as the thinker who succeeded in giving philosophic currency and validity to the modes of life and behavior of archaic humanity." Of course, Plato did so by substituting universals for the mythic stories. The consequence was the same: "... the abolition of time through the imitation of archetypes and the repetition of paradigmatic gestures." Eliade, *Myth of the Eternal Return*, p. 35.

Theology's Threefold Division

In contrast to the threefold division of theology offered by Schleiermacher and Ogden, this project proposes that theology as an academic discipline consists of Philosophical Theology, Systematic Theology, and Practical Theology.[22] These tasks are completely interdependent and each is necessary for the discipline of theology.

---

[22] David Tracy also divides the task of theology into a threefold: "fundamental theology" (the focus of *Blessed Rage for Order*, BRO), "systematic theology" (the focus of *The Analogical Imagination*, AI) and "practical theology" (the third part of the trilogy yet to be written, AI, 95-6, n. 104). As was the case in BRO, Tracy remains heavily influenced by Ogden in his division of the theological task.

The focal issue of fundamental theology is the doctrine of God, claimed in BRO and confirmed in AI (439, n. 7) as most articulated by the Process metaphysical tradition (see BRO 68, 160, 175-187).

AI, on the other hand, is concerned with the task of systematic theology, i.e., establishing systematic theology as a hermeneutics of retrieval and suspicion (AI, 104, 131) constituted out of mutually critical correlations (e.g., AI, 447) that acknowledge the necessity of pluralism as a consequence of the tension between the tradition and the situation of the individual theologian, i.e., the structure of critical correlation. While engaged in, with, and by the three publics of society, academy, and church (AI, 55f), the systematic theologian is lead to make a personal choice (AI, 422-423) of a "paradigmatic focal meaning" (AI, 428) as a consequence of his/her concrete context of correlation between life-world situation and inherited tradition. This "paradigmatic focal meaning," however, is correctively challenged in Christianity by the three further focal meanings of manifestation, proclamation, and historical action (AI, 371, 425).

Tracy's own Christian systematic theology is structured by the paradigmatic focal meaning found in the Christ event (AI, 423). Here in AI he develops, if not corrects, the Christological formulation of BRO by stressing 1) the importance of negation (e.g., AI, n. 58); 2) an emphasis on radical mystery (e.g., AI, 439, n. 7); 3) that the always-already Christology of BRO must be complemented by the "dangerous memory" of Jesus which includes the not-yet, eschatological future (AI, 431, 443, n. 31; though the not-yet is grounded in the always-already, 435, reminiscent of BRO); and 4) the importance of apostolic witness (AI, 337-8, n. 34) expressing the experienced event of the Christ, and dismisses the historical Jesus as "theologically inappropriate" (e.g., among many other instances, AI, 295, n. 68).

In addition to his continued insistence on the role of Process metaphysics in "fundamental theology" (AI, 439, n. 7), there are two central themes in *The Analogical Imagination* that contradict Tracy's embracing of "pluralism" in theology. The first is his insistence that "... any theological discourse which loses its anchorage in the doctrine of God is no longer theological." (AI, 52) The second is his insistence that Christian theology is not concerned with the historical Jesus, but rather the Christ proclaimed by the apostolic witness (e.g., AI, 236, 238, 239).

First, in contrast, this project maintains that theology must commence not with God but with human spiritual experience. Second, rather than claim that "Christianity does not live by an idea, a principle, an axiom but by an event and a person ...," (AI, 427) the present project wishes to stress that Christianity be understood as *a historical*

All three disciplines presuppose a distinction between religion and theology. Religion is the practice (ritual, worship, doctrines, etc.) of a particular religious community. Following Mortimer Adler, it can be called "first order" experience. A religion represents a particular cultic and/or institutional manifestation of religious experience performed by individuals in community. Theology, on the other hand, is a "second order" experience. It is second order not in the sense of having less worth, but in the sense of its being the activity of reflective description and analysis of the factual and faith claims made by a religious community. Since the human condition is always and already experienced from within a tradition, and since theological reflection is always and already engaged within the context of a religious tradition, all three disciplines of theology presuppose first order religious experience.

On the other hand, this division between "first" order experience and "second" order reflection is misleading. First, theology is not to be contrasted with religion as if religion experienced and theology thought. Such a division would be to force a dualism into the human condition, as if thought was not experience and experience was not thought. In addition, such a division ignores the contextual, historical, and hermeneutical character of all experience. The theologian is experiencing religion as s/he describes and analyses it, and is perhaps more immersed in religion than the non-theologian who attends to the institutional and ritual processes of a church regularly if not daily. The theologian "hears echoes" throughout the tradition, and, in short, can have a more rich religious experience than the religiously active non-theologian, because the theologian reflectively engages the tradition and contemporary experience.[23] This is not a statement of arro-

---

trajectory of human faith seeking understanding as the open-ended project of trying to understand who we are in the world. Hence, Christianity is here claimed to be neither a timeless truth, nor a principle, nor a cause, *nor an event or a person, but a historical movement of human spiritual understanding* rooted in faith. Finally, Christianity so understood as an odyssey of historical faith could then appropriate the symbol of the kingdom of God in the teaching material of *the historical Jesus* with all of its multi-faceted and suggestive meanings, precisely as a consequence of the "mutually critical correlations" between inherited story and the new experience of the hearer's situation. I attempted to develop this approach to understanding the central symbol of the kingdom of God in my unpublished dissertation at the University of Chicago: "On the Soteriological Significance of the Symbol of the Kingdom of God in the Language of the Historical Jesus."

[23] One is reminded of Clement of Alexandria's judgment in the *Stromata*: "'Faith,' this is simple, traditional Christianity, is enough for salvation, but the man who adds to his (sic) faith 'knowledge,' has a higher possession." In Williston Walker, *A History of the Christian Church*, 3rd ed., p. 73.

gance, but rather emphasizes the theologian's responsibility to the non-theologian to enable her/his hearing of the rich and vibrant overtones of her/his tradition and to enable the non-theologian's ownership of the individual's odyssey of faith in community.

Second, theology is concerned ultimately with the aporiai which are constitutive of human experience. Hence, theology as reflective does not mean that theology is rational. Rationality rests upon aporiai, and it is the task of theology to acknowledge the irrational foundation of all rationality. The Hegelian "cunning of reason" is the illusory dream of systematic thought, but not of theology. History is not a movement of reason through all unconscious and conscious events leading to the flight of the Owl of Minerva in the twilight. History is an odyssey of faith seeking understanding. Helping to illuminate that historical faith is the task of theology in all three of its moments.

Philosophical Theology: The Aporetic

Philosophical theology is not second order critical reflection about religious experience or the tradition in order to establish the truth claims of either. Unable to critically master its own conditions of possibility, philosophical theology seeks to understand the open-ended, experiential horizon of faith, rooted in the dialectical tensions of aporiai, that demands the vigilance of the head to ensure that the commitments of the heart are not mere illusions or dangerous.

Hence, Philosophical Theology engages in the task of illuminating the most basic constituent moments and historical character of human experience which enable and serve as the horizon of all traditions. If the human condition is more than the repetition of historically transcendent archetypes, in other words, if the human condition is not a denial of linear time,[24] and if the human condition is more than a senseless flow of insignificant instants in a vast cosmic emptiness, in other words, if the human condition is not simply an event of meaningless cosmological time, then it is historical. Historical experience is a process of meaning and significance in spite of the envelopment of the human in the apparent meaninglessness of cosmological time.[25]

---

[24] It is the thesis of Mircea Eliade that religious humanity seeks to deny linear time and the terror of history by embracing cyclical time and the "eternal return" of archetypes. See Eliade, *The Myth of the Eternal Return*, pp. 34-35, 141-162.

[25] This theme of the aporia of cosmological time and phenomenological time is taken from Ricoeur, *Time and Narrative*, vol. 3, p. 90.

The key ingredient of cosmological time is the indifferent instant. The key ingredient of historical time is the meaning-rich present which is always and already relative to an historical individual in community. To be sure, this focus on the "present" here by no means makes for a theology of "presence." The aporetic character of experience prohibits such facile reductionisms.

There are two essential ingredients necessary for historical experience: First, the relationship between possibility and actuality which accounts for the irreversibility or linearity of time (it is absolutely impossible to return to the situation of possibility prior to any present actuality). In short, this ingredient is the dynamic of revealing and concealing essential to any and all experience. Second, the relationship between (at the least, ectypal) universals and particulars in individual human beings which are constitutive for the experience of meaning in events. In short, this ingredient is the dynamic of the one and the many essential to any and all experience.

The key contribution of Philosophical Theology to the theological task is that it addresses the aporetic components that are constitutive of historical experience to ensure that each is given its appropriate attention. This task has been continually neglected. Time and again in the Western tradition the aporetic character of experience has been understood as a dualism that was ultimately reducible to, or explained by, one side of the twofoldness. For example, what counts as reality today is our experience of the world of the senses. Rationality in this reality is the calculation, prediction, manipulation, and control of the objects of sense experience. But, ironically, this definition of reality denies any credibility to our actual experience. For experience is inaccessible to the senses. Experience is the individual's life of the mind which is radically different from, and paradoxically opposite to, the world of the senses. If the world of the senses is perceptible, material, divisible, measurable, and changing, our mental life is imperceptible, immaterial, indivisible, immeasurable, and dependent upon unchanging "universals." The tradition has defined the rationality appropriate to our mental life to be the contemplation of these universals without which there could be no experience but only chaos. If our materialism today denies the true significance of the individual's life of the intellect, the spirituality of the tradition denies any true significance to the unrepeatability and uniqueness of the individual's personal and communal historical life.

The Western tradition can be understood as a giant pendulum swinging between these two forms of rationality. The success of technology in our age has resulted in the preponderance of the rationality of calculation, prediction, manipulation, and control of the world of the senses. No one can argue with success (though one has grounds for seriously doubting the success). The consequence has been the complete loss of appreciation for the spiritual life of the mind. Yet prior to the 13th century reason was exclusively defined in terms of the contemplation of universals with the world of sense experience being reduced to a mere transient copy and shadow of those eternal universals.

The task of Philosophical Theology is not to retrieve the absolute reality of the sacred over against the profane that this dualistic contrast with respect to rationality encourages. It is not as if our materialistic age needs to, or even can, simply retrieve and repeat the traditional spirituality classically shaping Christian theology.

Precisely because the life of the intellect has not been given any recognition by the predominant system of technological rationality, however, the "discovery" of one's spiritual life of the intellect leads all too often to a simplistic contrast and outright rejection of technological rationality as a perversion and a threat to spirituality. But Philosophical Theology has the responsibility to indicate and preserve the aporetic tensions that constitute historical experience. As a result, the fundamental goal of Philosophical Theology is the identification of the role of faith that is at the core of all human experience. This is not a faith that commences from knowledge of God or of any absolute spiritual reality. This is the faith that is demanded by our experience of inexplicable, irreducible, and incommensurable aporiai in life. At the same time, this is not a faith that surrenders critical reflection to embrace mystery. Philosophical Theology has the task of acknowledging, investigating, and critically evaluating the dialectical moments of the aporiai shaping human experience upon which that experience is radically dependent.

Only after having performed this task can Philosophical Theology venture into speculative judgments about the ultimate nature of our radical dependence. Even then, Philosophical Theology acknowledges that it always does so inadequately because of the historical parameters within which it necessarily functions. The speculative moment in Philosophical Theology, above all, insists upon a hermeneutics of suspicion sensitive to the danger of manipulative human interests, systematic distortion, and the *Unübersichtlichkeit* of human experience.[26]

---

[26] See Jürgen Habermas, "On Systematically Distorted Communication;" "Towards a Theory of Communicative Competence;" *Knowledge and Human Interests*, trans. by Jeremy J. Shapiro, Jr. (Boston: Beacon Press, 1972); *Theorie des kommunikativen Handelns* (Frankfurt a. M., Suhrkamp, 1981), translated by Thomas McCarthy as *Theory of*

Only after one has engaged the task of Philosophical Theology can one adequately fulfill the obligations of Systematic Theology. The diachronic and synchronic moments of Systematic Theology are historical concretizations of the aporiai identified by Philosophical Theology. Once one has performed the task of Philosophical Theology, however, one can appreciate the tremendous richness of historical faith arising out of the tensions between inherited tradition (the individual and collective memory of past suffering and acting) and new individual and corporate experience. This correlation between tradition and experience, however, is not a mere external or objective comparison between a mythologically compromised or other erroneous metaphysical truth claim of the past and a critically transparent truth claim about experience today. Nor is this correlation between tradition and experience a simple repetition of eternal archetypes as Eliade and Kurt Hübner[27] would have it, as comforting as that might be.[28] Not only are such understandings

---

Communicative Praxis (Boston: Beacon Press, 1984); and *Die neue Unübersichtlichkeit. Kleine politische Schriften* (Frankfurt a. M., Suhrkamp, 1985).

[27] See Kurt Hübner, *Die Wahrheit des Mythos* (Munich: Verlag C.H.Beck, 1985) and "Der Mythos, der Logos und das spezifisch Religiöse. Drei Elemente des Christlichen Glaubens" in *Mythos und Rationalität*, hrsg. von Hans Heinrich Schmid (Gütersloh: Gütersloher Verlagshaus Gerd Mohn, 1988), 27-43.

[28] David Tracy seems to be enamored with this notion of repetition in Eliade, but one wonders if Tracy's "reinterpretation" is the same as Eliade's hierophany: "In the extraordinary, indeed classic hermeneutics of religion by Mircea Eliade one may see this understanding of religious expression as manifestation at its clearest, and in many ways its most radical. Indeed, the radicality of Eliade's understanding of religion is the result of the neglected (by Western interpreters) power of religion as manifestation. Eliade has articulated that power in his remarkable *oeuvre* uniting scholarship, philosophy, art and religious passion. In fact, Eliade's classic achievement - still too little appreciated by most Western theologians - paradoxically serves a prophetic religious role to challenge the dominant prophetic, ethical, historical trajectory of Western religion in favor of its grounds in the power of manifestation" (*The Analogical Imagination*, p. 205). Further, "[b]y entering the ritual, by retelling the myth, even by creatively reinterpreting the symbol, we escape from the 'nightmare' of history and even the 'terror' of ordinary time" (*ibid.*, 205). Tracy seems to lament that "[e]arlier forms of manifestation as the sheer eruption of the powers of the cosmos - all those forms of originary, archaic religions analyzed by Mircea Eliade - seem, in our day, relatively muted" (*ibid.*, pp. 376-7). Speaking of the "power of manifestation" he adds: "That power is rarely sensed as erupting from nature itself, as of old. Rather the power is now disclosed through the critical mediations of reason reflecting upon the original experience of wonder in existence only to yield through philosophical reflection to a mediated sense of a fundamental trust in the ultimate reality of God as well as an attendant trust in all reality as graced" (*ibid.*, p. 379).

One could make a case that Eliade's notion of hierophany establishing the axis mundi (or a cosmos in the midst of chaos) for religious humanity, is no longer a live option for contemporary (profane) humanity precisely because the imperceptible spiritual

of the correlation between tradition and experience an ultimate denial of history for the sake of "truth" or "eternity," but they constitute a denial of the aporetic tensions essential to historical experience. In short, the tradition is not one of failed mythology or false metaphysics. Nor is the present in possession of the true mythology or true metaphysics. Both tradition and present experience are constituted by a dynamic process of aporetic, dialectical tensions that insist that our tenure in this world is one of faith seeking understanding.

Finally, the task of Philosophical Theology recognizes the necessity of, and enables an appreciation for, radical pluralism both within and among religious traditions. Human understanding is a construct of the intellect (a paradigm) of the way the world is taken to be. Even our judgments of what constitutes a causal explanation always relative to a paradigm. Hence, given the opaqueness constitutive of every paradigm, because of the aporiai essential to them, and given the historicality of human experience, varieties of religious understanding are both essential and necessary. They are essential, because they call all absolute claims to accountability and illuminate the delusions of such absolute claims. They are necessary, because the varieties of religious understanding constitute the communities and contexts for presenting the broad spectrum of human experience and understanding.

In short, the varieties of religious understanding are a virtue rather than a vice. They reflect to us the range of human experience within the horizon of the aporiai constitutive of that experience. It is the very horizon of those aporiai, however, which establish the limits to the varieties of religious paradigms. In other words, it is not as if religious relativism opens some floodgate of chaos permitting a million flowers to bloom. Rather, the con-

---

dimension of human experience is almost totally unappreciated, even by Tracy. See Eliade's *The Sacred and the Profane: The Nature of Religion* and *The Myth of the Eternal Return*. Eliade represents a form of Platonism that champions the invisible arché, the eternal, over the visible particularities of history, the transient terror of history. Hence, the "manifestation" of the hierophany is not an "objective" event "erupting from nature itself," but, rather, the re-cognition that nature mirrors an eternal order from the midst of nature's chaos to which humanity and the individual always and already have access. In short, nature is merely the shadow of the spiritual which one can "grasp" once one has acquired the "appropriate," spiritual understanding. The "truth" of nature is, in fact, a spiritual, "subjective truth."

Tracy attempts to wed the critical reflections of a Process metaphysics with the "primordial manifestations" of Eliade's Platonism to affirm a basic confidence and worth in human experience. The marriage fails, however, not because of a lack of insight, but because of the turn by both Eliade and Tracy to metaphysics.

stitutive paradoxes of life establish clearly the range of options that Philosophical Theology can then adjudicate with respect to their relative adequacy in the contemporary world.

The threat of chaos with respect to religious or experiential meaning in the face of relativism proves to be an illusion. Historical human experience is always and already within the horizon of a paradigm of understanding that ensures coherence, consistency, and meaning to our judgments and actions. If not, experience would be radically solipsistic, and the reader could not even begin to grasp the meaning of these words. It is impossible to experience outside of a paradigm. The crumbling of the notion of an absolute paradigm does not mean the end of either understanding or meaning. It means their commencement. Were the conditions of human experience not paradoxical, we would not, and could not, be the historical odyssey which we are. At the same time, the crumbling of the notion of an absolute paradigm and the recognition that our experience and understanding is always and already within the horizon of a paradigm (we can perceive even the anomalous only against the background of a paradigm, Thomas Kuhn reminds us[29]), leads us again to the engaging of a hermeneutics of suspicion. How much is our paradigm serving unrecognized interests, how much is it distorting rather than making accessible, how much is it concealing as it makes clear?

On the other hand, the necessity of a horizon of understanding provided by our inherited paradigm requires that we engage in a hermeneutics of restoration. The hermeneutics of restoration is a two-way process: First, it consists of retrieving out of our inheritance those texts and events that are disclosive for our experience in the present (though Gadamer reminds us that we are not in control even over this process[30]); yet, second, it consists of allowing ourselves to be placed into question by that inheritance. How adequately have we understood our experience in all of its contextuality and historicality? How adequately have we understood the claims of our inheritance? Can we ever be sure that what we reject today from that inheritance will not be experientially disclosive in the future?

These are the questions addressed by Philosophical Theology of every religious tradition and of the varieties of religious understanding within

---

[29] See Kuhn, *Structure of Scientific Revolutions*, p. 65.

[30] "Neither is the mind of the interpreter in control of what words of tradition reach him (sic), nor can one suitably describe what happens here as the progressive knowledge of what exists, so that an infinite intellect would contain everything that could ever speak out of the whole tradition." *Truth and Method*, p. 419.

specific traditions. These are not idle or abstract questions. They are questions concerned with the core of human experience. They both establish an understanding of the historical character of that experience, and explain the necessity of variety in individual and corporate historical experience. Hence, they establish the necessity of engaging in Philosophical Theology prior to undertaking the task of Systematic Theology.

Systematic Theology: Diachronic and Synchronic

Systematic Theology is reflection about the experience and claims of a particular religious tradition. It is systematic only to the extent that paradigms of reality are by necessity coherent models. In other words, Systematic Theology is not systematic because there exists some metaphysical or ultimate explanation to all of experience. Nor is Systematic Theology systematic because one addresses a particular set of issues in the theological agenda, e.g., God, humanity, salvation.

Since there are no indubitable logical proofs for the existence of any thing (either as an objective world of sense experience or as a subjective world of universals) independent of our individual consciousness of it and since causal explanation is always relative to a paradigm of reality and its internal coherence, there is no appeal that can legitimately be made either to an exhaustive systematic order that grounds experience in an ultimacy or to an ultimate causal order explaining experience. Such speculative judgments are the concern of Philosophical Theology, and they can be made only within the limits of the aporetic horizon of experience as faith.

Systematic Theology, in addition, is not the systematic addressing of issues of divinity, human fallibility, and divine liberation. One can productively employ such issues for identifying the constitutive ingredients of a religious tradition's faith claims, but no one set of questions defines a priori the agenda for Systematic Theology. Systematic Theology is descriptive. It is a posteriori not a priori.

Diachronic and Synchronic

The task of Systematic Theology is twofold. It consists, first, of a synchronic moment, reflecting the elements constituting what is taken to be the coherent reality claim of a particular religious community at a particular point in time. And second, it consists of a diachronic moment that situates the particular religious community in its broader historical tradition, compares and contrasts that particular understanding of faith with the faith claims of that broader tradition, and indicates within the particular religious community how the understanding of the faith has changed over time. Diachronic Systematic Theology includes, then, the insights of Scriptural studies as a constitutive ingredient of the investigation of, and response to, the tradition under investigation. Clearly, the diachronic moment is dependent upon the synchronic in Systematic Theology. Yet the diachronic moment can stand alone, e.g., as Biblical Theology or according to epochal divisions of a tradition, as that theological task responsible for the comparing and contrasting of the various historical articulations of religious faith both within a particular cultural heritage and among cultures.

It is important not to confuse the diachronic task with what has been called Historical Theology. The presupposition of Historical Theology, all too often, has been that there is some red thread of absolute truth uniting all of the formulations of Christian theology throughout history.[31] The aporetics of faith make the establishment of such a red thread, much less an absolute truth, impossible. Historical Theology in its traditional form has told us more about the presuppositions of its practitioners than it has about the truth of the Christian tradition.

The diachronic moment of Systematic Theology is not engaged in establishing the truth of a particular religious community or trajectory of tradition. Its task is descriptive and comparative.

The synchronic moment of Systematic Theology is also fundamentally descriptive. It consists of the systematic description of the religious claims of a particular faith community at a particular point in linear time. This involves the responsibility to sort out the different kinds of religious claims (e.g., in Christian Systematic Theology with respect to creation, fall, Christology, resurrection, sacraments, the Trinity, etc., or in Hinduism, maya, samsara, mokṣa, etc.) of a particular religious community. In addition, its task is that of arranging those religious claims in a systematic fashion that one can clearly see how the constituent parts of the faith claim are, or are not, related to one another.

Once one has thoroughly undertaken the diachronic and synchronic tasks of Systematic Theology, then one is in a position to engage a dialogue among various religious traditions (e.g., among traditions such as Christianity, Buddhism, Hinduism, Taoism, Islam). The task of comparative analysis among religious trajectories within a particular tradition is the re-

---

[31] Examples abound of this kind of approach to the diachronic task of theology. See, in addition to the philosophical formulation of Hegel, F.C. Bauer, Hermann, Ritschl, Harnack, and more recently Nygren's *Agape and Eros*.

sponsibility of diachronic Systematic Theology though subordinate to Philosophical Theology.

Descriptive Phenomenology

Systematic Theology, then, is a descriptive discipline. As such, Systematic Theology is phenomenological. Phenomenology has several meanings depending upon who is practicing it.[32] The classic formulation of Phenomenology is found in the work of Edmund Husserl. The starting point of Phenomenology is the *givenness* of phenomena (sensations and reflections) in experience. Husserl maintained that we must suspend all judgments about the "existence" of the phenomena (whether the phenomena truly exist independent of our perception or whether the phenomena are, for example, a mere product of the fantasy or of an optical illusion). Having "bracketed" the existence question, the task of Phenomenology, according to Husserl, is to describe, first, systematically and exhaustively how we experience the phenomena. In other words, before our ever making a judgment about what is fact and what is fantasy, we experience phenomena by means of a noetic-noematic structure of intentional consciousness. Intentional consciousness is always and already consciousness-of something. It is presupposed by any judgments made about the fact or fantasy of the experienced phenomena.

Judgments with respect to fact or fantasy are legitimate not on the basis of an appeal to the thing-in-itself behind the phenomena (for we can *never* arrive at it). Rather, judgments of fact or fantasy are made on the basis of consistency, coherence, and repeatability. What is important for Systematic Theology here is the recognition of the necessity of the epoché of the existence question and of the criteria (consistency, coherence, and repeatability) for adjudicating between "fact" and "fantasy." Phenomenology negates any absolute grounding of truth claims.

As much as Schubert Ogden's distinction between first order religious experience and second order theological reflection about that religious experience is phenomenological, Phenomenology problematizes Ogden's formulation. Ogden's schemata depends upon our being able to maintain a clear distinction between immediate experience and reflectively mediated experience. Phenomenology demonstrates, however, that such a distinction be-

---

[32] See the historical overview of the Phenomenological Movement by Herbert Spiegelberg, *The Phenomenological Movement: A Historical Introduction*, 2 vols., Second Edition (The Hague: Martinus Nijhoff, 1969). an invaluable review of books about the Phenomenological Movement is Hans-Georg Gadamer, "Die phänomenologische Bewegung" in *Philosophische Rundschau*, 11/1-2 (May 1963), 1-45.

tween immediate and mediated experience ultimately rests upon a dualism that is only subsequently imposed upon experience. The very givenness of phenomena is always and already paradoxically mediated. In short, there is no such thing as unmediated experience. It is not simply that we experience only within the horizon of an inherited language, already shaping our perceptions in the immediacy of experience, but we experience only within the context of a particular historical horizon of relationships, things, institutions, tasks, etc., that Husserl calls a "life-world."[33] It is a background of emotional response, understanding, and meaning from which we can never escape.[34] In other words, there is no such thing as "brute data" (or mere stimuli) uninterpreted and unmediated by a horizon of the affective, understanding, and meaning.[35]

Although there are difficulties in distinguishing between experience and reflection in the manner done by Ogden, the distinction remains helpful for describing and distinguishing the different kinds of activities going on in religion. Systematic theology is fundamentally descriptive. Its task is, first, to describe in a coherent and organized fashion the religious claims made by a believing community at a particular point in time (synchronic). Second, Systematic Theology engages in comparing and contrasting the systematically formulated claims of a religious community at any one point in time with the claims made within that community's tradition at other points in, and over a trajectory of, time (diachronic). Finally, Systematic Theology has the comparative task of setting the religious claims of one tradition over against those of other traditions in the dialogue of pluralism. In all of these activities, Systematic Theology is descriptive.

Hence, Systematic Theology is not normative. In other words, it is not the task of Systematic Theology to argue the truth of a religious community's faith claims. Nor is it the task of Systematic Theology to defend the truth of a particular religious tradition (or the formulations of that tradi-

---

[33] This notion of the "life-world" (*Lebenswelt*) is the specific concern of Husserl's 1934-1938 analysis in Part III of *The Crisis*. The life-world is what he had earlier in *Ideas* called the "background" of phenomenological experience. See Husserl's discussion of the theme of "background" (*Hintergrund*) in the 1913 text *Ideas*.

[34] See Martin Heidegger's analysis of "*Befindlichkeit*" in Sections 29-30 followed by his analysis of understanding (Section 31) and Interpretation (Section 32) prior to the analysis of Section 33 entitled "Assertion as a Derivative Mode of Interpretation" and Section 34 entitled "Being-there and Discourse. Language" in *Being and Time*, pp. 172-210. Discourse is taken to be equiprimordial with state-of-mind and understanding, and it is contrasted with mere assertion by Heidegger.

[35] See Kuhn, *Structure of Scientific Revolutions*, p. 125 and 196.

tion at any particular point in time) over against the claims of other religious traditions (or the claims made by other contemporaries or at some other point in a particular tradition). Systematic Theology has the important task alone of describing and arranging in systematic fashion the claims of a particular religious community in its historicality as an odyssey of faith.

The twofold synchronic and diachronic task of Systematic Theology presupposes the coherence of a religious paradigm as well as the aporetics of faith. In short, Systematic Theology presupposes the issues and questions of Philosophical Theology. Furthermore, Systematic Theology has a particular religious paradigm as the object of its investigation. Here is where it is appropriate to speak of method in theology and to stress the dynamic of correlation between the inherited tradition and present experience. Such a correlation is illuminating for understanding the diachronic dynamic of every living tradition. Finally, it is the task of Systematic Theology to engage the discussion among religious paradigms (both within the tradition of the primary religious paradigm of the particular Systematic Theology as well as among traditions) recognizing the historicality of all understanding and the role of paradigms and paradoxes in the social constructing of reality.

Practical Theology: Institutional Religion

The third moment of the discipline of theology is Practical Theology. Practical theology is procedural, instructional, prophetic, pastoral, and parenetic (though not necessarily in that order). Its concern is the interface between the life-world of the church as an institution and Philosophical and Systematic Theology of the tradition of that institution. The goal of Practical Theology is concerned both to prepare the leadership for a particular religious institution and to engage all the issues of praxis associated with a faith community. Although Practical Theology has generic elements appropriate to all religious traditions, this project will use Christianity for the purposes of describing the work of Practical Theology.

Procedural Practical Theology

What is meant by Procedural Practical Theology is the ritual and administrative functions of a particular religious community/denomination. Procedural Practical Theology is responsible for the on-going evaluation of the appropriateness and adequacy of the rituals of the community as well as the training of future leadership in the ritual calendar of the denomination. In addition, procedural Practical Theology is also responsible for the development of administrative models for the different sizes and kinds of congregations.

The ritual moment is central to the life of a local congregation and the vitality of a religious tradition in general. Ritual unites the worshipping community and situates it with respect to time and the life cycle of individuals. Procedural Practical Theology has the responsibility to formulate the purpose, and to articulate the range of meanings, in play in the ritual activity of the congregation. It also has the responsibility of preparing new rituals as well as evaluating the adequacy of old rituals for the articulating of the living faith of the worshipping community. This task is possible only with the aid of Philosophical and Systematic Theology.

Given the spectrum of types of congregations from rural to suburban, to large urban, to small inner-city, etc., a second important task of Procedural Practical Theology is the formulation of, and training of future clergy and laity in, a wide range of administrative models and procedures for the practical management of the institutional church. This includes everything from staffing issues, to computerization, to investment management, to building maintenance, to fund raising techniques, etc., necessary for the functioning of an institution in today's economy.

Instructional Practical Theology

The task of Instructional Practical Theology is the development of the educational curriculum and educational program of the church. Such skills range from defining the role of the pastor and laity as the vehicle for transmission of the tradition to the development and implementation of church school programing.

Since the pastor is a teacher, it is essential that s/he be trained not only in Philosophical and Systematic Theology which serve as the "knowledge" source of the tradition. It is equally important, if not more so, that the paster be trained in pedagogical techniques and skills. This ranges from small group dynamics to large classes. The pastor cannot be simply the dispenser of facts and figures, but s/he has the responsibility to engender and to foster the interest and enthusiasm of the congregation to learn for itself about the richness of its heritage. Essential for this purpose is not merely commitment to the faith of the tradition but an awareness of appropriate pedagogical techniques.

Instructional Practical Theology is also concerned with the development and evaluation of church school curricula. It, too, is heavily indebted to the work of Philosophical and Systematic Theology, and it must draw on the most effective curricular techniques. The future pastor, in particular, needs to become familiar with the wide spectrum of church school curricula. There needs to be an on-going interaction between theoreticians and practitioners in the continual review of the old, and development of new, curricula that the insights and information of Philosophical and Systematic Theology be effectively integrated into the practical ministry of the church.

Prophetic Practical Theology

The task of Prophetic Practical Theology is that of challenging the common assumptions and attitudes of the dominant paradigm shaping the perceptions and reality of the church. This task is informed by the hermeneutics of suspicion of Philosophical Theology and by observing the dynamic character of diachronic Systematic Theology where one clearly sees that common assumptions and attitudes have changed over time.[36] Prophetic Practical Theology builds, in particular, upon the ethics of Philosophical Theology to ensure that the church as an institution is not a blind perpetrator of oppression but is involved in the activity of both personal and social liberation.

Prophetic Practical Theology applies the insights of the "subversive" nature of Philosophical Theology to challenge the status quo. Its role is not simply change for the sake of change, but, rather, the demonstrating of the role of concealment that is necessary for the functioning of any community's paradigm. Prophetic Practical Theology points to what has been overlooked and taken for granted by the community's paradigm calling it to accountability for the consequences of its model of reality and of its concrete actions.

Pastoral Practical Theology

Pastoral Practical Theology is concerned with the concrete application of the hermeneutics of restoration in the life of the religious community. Its function is to demonstrate the community's debt to the actions and sufferings of others and to situate the community and individuals within the continuity of the tradition both historically and locally.

This responsibility requires, once again, the insights of Philosophical and Systematic Theology, but, in addition, the contributions of counseling models and techniques as well as awareness of community resources for the meeting of the social and psychological needs of the congregation. The future pastor needs supervised experience and training in prison, hospital, nursing home, shut-in, hospice, unemployment, welfare, and homeless envi-

---

[36] This is one insight that this project shares with George Lindbeck. See Lindbeck's *The Nature of Doctrine*, p. 105: "... what is essential to the church in one situation may not be in another. This awareness is intense among most contemporary theologians. It follows that what is doctrinally significant varies from age to age. What is vital in one context may become peripheral in another, and vice versa."

ronments and procedures both to process through her/his emotional and cognitive responses to such environments as well as to develop techniques for constructively responding to the needs of persons in such settings.

Pastoral Practical Theology is concerned with the wide range of counseling concerns and social needs which confront the pastor in her/his congregational life. In addition to encountering the various counseling models, Pastoral Practical Theology's task is to situate those models along with the insights of sociology within the context of faith reflectively developed by Philosophical and Systematic Theology.

Above all, Pastoral Practical Theology actualizes the continuing continuity of the tradition and the tradition's call to respond to the concrete needs of individuals and of the community. As such, it is part of the hermeneutics of restoration (and, therefore, indebted to the reflections of Philosophical Theology with respect to the hermeneutics of suspicion).

Parenetic Practical Theology

Always informed by the critically reflective work of Philosophical and Systematic Theology, Parenetic Practical Theology formulates the ethical injunctions of the religious community. This task is never engaged lightly, and must be informed, as well, by the sensitivities gained by Pastoral and Prophetic Theology. In short, Parenetic Practical Theology can never be engaged in abstractly, but is a most concrete application of the ethical norms of the tradition tempered by the concrete needs and issues of a particular faith community's context.

What is acknowledged by this task as a distinct activity of Practical Theology is that the Christian tradition has always articulated ethical standards that place the community in question and call it to accountability. This task is to be performed as a consequence of careful reflection, and is in no manner license to indiscriminately browbeat the community or individuals.

Practical Theology

This listing of the tasks and responsibilities is not meant to be exhaustive but rather suggestive. The charge of Practical Theology is the implementation of the work of Philosophical and Systematic Theology in the context of the institutional church and religious community by means of the insights of the appropriate disciplines concerned with the specific chore to be performed, e.g., management, pedagogy, psychology, sociology, and ethics.

Works Cited

Adler, Mortimer J., and Doren, Charles van. *How to Read a Book*. New York: Simon and Schuster, 1972 <1940>.

Ahlstrom, Sydney. *A Religious History of the American People*. New Haven: Yale University Press, 1972.

Allen, Paula Gunn. "Kochinnenako in Academe: Three Approaches to Interpreting a Keres Indian Tale." In *The Sacred Hoop: Recovering the Feminine in American Indian Traditions*. Boston: Beacon Press, 1986: 222-244.

Andresen, C. "The Integration of Platonism into Early Christian Theology." In *Studia Patristica*. Berlin: Akademie-Verlag, 1984: 399-413.

Anselm of Canterbury. *Anselm of Canterbury: Monologion, Proslogion, Debate with Guanilo, and a Meditation on Human Redemption*. Revised Edition. Ed. and trans. by Jasper Hopkins and Herbert Richardson. Vol. 1. Toronto: Edwin Mellen Press, 1975.

Apel, Karl-Otto, ed. *Hermeneutik und Ideologiekritik*. Frankfurt a.M.: Suhrkamp, 1971.

Aristotle. *The Basic Works of Aristotle*. Ed. by Richard McKeon. New York: Random House, 1968.

_____. *Metaphysics*. Trans. by Richard Hope. Ann Arbor, MI: University of Michigan Press, 1960.

Armstrong, A. H., ed. *Classical Mediterranean Spirituality: Egyptian, Greek, Roman*. New York: Crossroad Press, 1986.

_____. "Pagan and Christian Traditionalism in the First Three Centuries A.D." *Studia Patristica* XV (1984): 414-431.

Assel, Heinrich. "'Barth ist entlassen ...' Emanuel Hirschs Rolle im Fall Barth und seine Briefe an Wilhelm Stapel." *Zeitschrift für Theologie und Kirche* 91/4 (1994): 445-75.

Augustine. *Basic Writings of Saint Augustine*. Ed. by Whitney J. Oates. New York: Random House, 1948.

_____. *The City of God*. Ed. by Marcus Dods. New York: The Modern Library, 1950.

Ayer, Alfred Jules. *Language, Truth and Logic*. New York: Dover, 1952.

Barbour, Ian G. *Issues in Science and Religion*. Englewood Cliffs, NJ: Prentice-Hall, Inc., 1966.

Barth, Karl. *The Epistle to the Romans*. Trans. by Edwyn C. Hoskyns. Oxford: Oxford University Press, 1968.

_____. *Die Kirchliche Dogmatik*. München: Kaiser, 1935.

Barth, Karl. *Die protestantische Theologie im 19. Jahrhundert. Ihre Vorgeschichte und ihre Geschichte.* 5th ed. Zürich: Theologischer Verlag, 1985.

_____. *The Word of God and the Word of Man.* Trans. by Douglas Horton. Gloucester, MA: Peter Smith, 1978.

Barth, Paul. "Die stoische Theodizee bei Philo." *Philosophische Abhandlungen.* Berlin: Ernst Seigried Mittler und Sohn, 1906: 14-33.

Bayer, Oswald. "Theologie im Konflikt der Interpretationen. Ein Gespräch mit Paul Ricoeur." *Communio Viatorum (Praha)* 32/4 (1989): 223-31.

Beierwaltes, Werner. *Denken des Einen. Studien zur Neuplatonischen Philosophie und ihrer Wirkungsgeschichte.* Frankfurt a.M.: Vittorio Klostermann, 1985.

Benz, Ernst. *Indische Einflüsse auf die frühchristliche Theologie.* In *Akademie der Wissenschaften und der Literatur. Abhandlungen der geistes- und sozialwissenschaftlichen Klasse.* Wiesbaden: Franz Steiner Verlag GmbH, 1951.

Berggren, Douglas. "The Use and Abuse of Metaphor, I." *The Review of Metaphysics* XVI (December 1962): 237-58.

_____. "The Use and Abuse of Metaphor, II." *The Review of Metaphysics* XVI (March 1963): 450-72.

Bergson, Henri. *Time and Free Will.* New York: Harper & Row, 1960.

Biedermann, Alois Emanuel. "Die Aufklärung." *Zeitstimmen aus der Reformierten Kirche der Schweiz.* 6 (1864): 104-12, 113-27.

_____. *Christliche Dogmatik.* Zürich: Verlag von Orell, Füssli & Co., 1869.

_____. *Christliche Dogmatik.* 2d ed. Vol. 1. Berlin: Verlag Georg Reimer, 1884.

Birkner, Hans-Joachim. *Theologen des Protestantismus im 19. und 20. Jahrhundert.* Vol. 1. Stuttgart: Verlag W. Kohlhammer, 1978.

Bleicher, Joseph. *Contemporary Hermeneutics: Hermeneutics as Method, Philosophy and Critique.* London: Routledge and Kegan Paul, 1980.

Bloch, Ernst. *Das Prinzip Hoffnung.* Vols. 1-3. Frankfurt a.M.: Suhrkamp, 1982.

Bloom, Alan. *The Closing of the American Mind.* New York: Simon & Schuster, Inc., 1988.

Bohr, Neils. "Can Quantum Mechanical Description of Physical Reality be Considered Complete?" *The Physical Review* 48, second series (July-December 1935): 696-702.

Bonhoeffer, Dietrich. *The Cost of Discipleship.* Trans. by R.H. Fuller. New York: Touchstone Simon & Schuster Inc., 1995.

Braig, Carl. *Vom Sein. Abriß der Ontologie.* Freiburg im Breisgau: Herder'sche Verlagshandlung, 1896.

Brandenburger, Egon. *Fleisch und Geist. Paulus und die Dualistische Weisheit.* Neukirchen-Vluyn: Neukirchener Verlag, 1968.

Brentano, Robert. *Sources in Western Civilization - The Middle Ages.* New York: The Free Press of Glencoe, 1964.

Brightman, Edgar S. *An Introduction to Philosophy*. New York: Henry Holt and Co., 1925.

Brooke, John Hedley. *Science and Religion: Some Historical Perspectives*. New York: Cambridge University Press, 1991.

Brown, Frank Burch. "Transfiguration: Poetic Metaphor and Theological Reflection." *The Journal of Religion* 62/1 (1982): 39-56.

Brox, Norbert. "Die frühchristliche Debatte um die Seelenwanderung." *Internationale Zeitschrift für Theologie* 29/5 (1993): 427-30.

Buhle, Johann. *Geschichte der neuern Philosophie*. Göttingen: Johann Georg Rosenbusch's Witwe, 1800.

Bultmann, Rudolf. *Existence and Faith*. Trans. by Schubert M. Ogden. New York: World Publishing, Meridian, 1960.

————. *Die Geschichte der synoptischen Tradition*. 9th ed. Göttingen: Vandenhoeck & Ruprecht, 1979.

————. *Primitive Christianity in Its Contemporary Setting*. Trans. by R. H. Fuller. New York: Meridian, 1956.

————. *Theology of the New Testament*. Trans. by Kendrick Grobel. Scribner Studies in Contemporary Theology. New York: Scribner's, 1951.

Bushnell, Horace. "Language and Doctrine from Christ in Theology." In *Horace Bushnell: Selected Writings on Language, Religion, and American Culture*. Ed. by David L. Smith. Chico, CA: Scholars Press, 1984 <1851>: 59-67.

————. "Preliminary Dissertation on the Nature of Language as Related to Thought and Spirit." In *Horace Bushnell: Selected Writings on Language, Religion, and American Culture*. Ed. by David L. Smith. Chico, CA: Scholars Press, 1984 <1849>: 33-57.

————. "The Theory of Language." In *Horace Bushnell: Selected Writings on Language, Religion, and American Culture*. Ed. by David L. Smith. Chico, CA: Scholars Press, 1984 <1839>: 27-31.

Campbell, John Angus. "Scientific Revolution and the Grammar of Culture: The Case of Darwin's Origin." *The Quarterly Journal of Speech* 72 (November 1986): 351-76.

Capelle, Wilhelm. *Die griechische Philosophie II. Von den Sokratikern bis zur hellenistischen Philosophie*. Berlin: Walter de Gruyter & Co., 1971.

Cassirer, Ernst. *Die Philosophie der symbolischen Formen. Erster Teil: Die Sprache*. Darmstadt: Wissenschaftliche Buchgesellschaft, 1964.

————. *Vorlesungen über die Wissenschaft der Sprache*. Leipzig: Verlag von Gustav Mayer, 1966.

————. "Was ist Subjektivismus?" *Theoria* V (1939): 111-40.

————. *Wesen und Wirkung des Symbolbegriffs*. Darmstadt: Wissenschaftliche Buchgesellschaft, 1965.

Chadwick, Owen, ed. *Western Asceticism*. The Library of Christian Classics, Vol. 12. Philadelphia: Westminster Press, 1958.

Channing, William Ellery. "Unitarian Christianity Discourse at the Ordination of the Rev. Jared Sparks, Baltimore, 1819" *William Ellery Channing: Selected Writings*. Ed. by David Robinson. New York: Paulist Press, 1985: 70-102.

Chauncy, Charles. "Enthusiasm Described and Caution'd Against" *The Great Awakening: Documents Illustrating the Crisis and Its Consequences*. Ed. by Alan Heimert and Perry Miller. Indianapolis: The Bobbs-Merrill Co., Inc., 1967: 228-256.

_____. "Seasonable Thoughts on the State of Religion" *The Great Awakening: Documents Illustrating the Crisis and Its Consequences*. Ed. by Alan Heimert and Perry Miller. Indianapolis: The Bobbs-Merrill Co., Inc., 1967: 291-304.

Colpe, Carsten. *Die Religionsgeschichtliche Schule. Forschung zur Religion und Literatur des alten und neuen Testaments*. Göttingen: Vandenhoeck & Ruprecht, 1961.

Corssen, Peter. "Paulus und Porphyrios" in *Sokrates. Zeitschrift für das Gymnasialwesen* 73 (1919):18-30.

Darwin, Charles. *The Origin of Species by Means of Natural Selection or the Preservation of Favoured Races in the Struggle for Life*. London: Penguin Books, 1985 <1859>.

Davidson, Arnold I. "Symposium on Heidegger and Nazism: Questions Concerning Heidegger: Opening the Debate." *Critical Inquiry* 15 (Winter 1989): 407-26.

Davis, Edward B. "God, Man and Nature: The Problem of Creation in Cartesian Thought." *The Scottish Journal of Theology* 44/3 (1991): 325-49.

Derrida, Jacques. *Dissemination*. Trans. by Barbara Johnson. Chicago: University of Chicago Press, 1981.

_____. *Of Grammatology*. Trans. by Gayatri Chakravorty Spivak. Baltimore, MD: The Johns Hopkins University Press, 1980.

_____. *Margins of Philosophy*. Trans. by Alan Bass. Chicago: University of Chicago Press, 1982.

Descartes, René. *Meditations on First Philosophy in Which the Existence of God and the Distinction of the Soul from the Body Are Demonstrated*. Trans. by Donald A. Cress. Indianapolis: Hackett Publishing Co., Inc., 1983.

Dibelius, Martin. "Reitzenstein, R., Historia Monachorum und Historia Lausiaca." *Wochenschrift für klassische Philologie* 33 (1916):1037-42.

Dörrie, Heinrich. "Die platonische Theologie des Kelsos in ihrer Auseinandersetzung mit der christlichen Theologie auf Grund von Origenes c. Celsum 6,42ff." *Nachrichten der Akademie der Wissenschaften in Göttingen. Philologisch-historische Klasse*. Göttingen: Vandenhoeck & Ruprecht, 1967: 19-55.

_____. "Was ist 'spätantiker Platonismus'?" *Theologische Rundschau* 36/4 (1971): 285-302.

Duke, James. "Schleiermacher: On Hermeneutics." In Schleiermacher. *Hermeneutics: The Handwritten Manuscripts*. Trans. by James Duke and Jack Forstman. Missoula: Scholars Press, 1977: 1-14.

Edwards, Jonathan. *Religious Affections*. New Haven: Yale University Press, 1959.

Einstein, Albert, et al. "Can Quantum Mechanical Description of Physical Reality be Considered Complete?" *The Physical Review* 47, second series (April-June 1935): 777-780.

Eliade, Mircea. *The Myth of the Eternal Return or Cosmos and History*. Trans. by Willard R. Trask. Bollingen Series, Vol. 46. New York: Pantheon Books, 1965.

_____. *The Sacred and the Profane: The Nature of Religion*. Trans. by Willard R. Trask. New York: Harper and Row, Harper Torchbooks/The Cloister Library, 1961.

Emerson, Ralph Waldo. "The Transcendentalist." In *The Complete Essays and Other Writings of Ralph Waldo Emerson*, Ed. by Brooks Atkinson. New York: Modern Library, 1940: 87-103.

Epicurus. *The Essential Epicurus*. Trans. by Eugene O'Connor. Buffalo, N.Y.: Prometheus Books, 1993.

Farias, Victor. *Heidegger and Nazism*. Philadelphia: Temple University Press, 1989.

Ferry, Luc, and Renaut, Alain. *Antihumanistisches Denken*. Trans. by Ulrike Bokelmann. München: Carl Hanser Verlag, 1987.

Fetz, Reto Luzius. "Aristotelian and Whiteheadian Conceptions of Actuality: I." *Process Studies* 19/1 (1990): 15-27.

_____. "Aristotelian und Whiteheadian Conceptions of Actuality: II." *Process Studies* 19/3 (1990): 145-56.

Feuerbach, Ludwig. *The Essence of Christianity*. Trans. by George Eliot. New York: Harper and Row, Harper Torchbooks/Cloister Library, 1957.

Fichte, J. G. *Die Bestimmung des Menschen*. J.G. Fichte-Gesamtausgabe der Bayerischen Akademie der Wissenschaften I/6 (1981): 148-311.

_____. *Versuch einer Critik aller Offenbarung*. J.G. Fichte-Gesamtausgabe der Bayerischen Akademie der Wissenschaften I/1 (1964).

Flew, Antony, and Macintyre, Alasdair, eds. *New Essays in Philosophical Theology*. New York: The Macmillan Co., 1964.

Flynn, Bernard Charles. "From Finitude to the Absolute: Kant's Doctrine of Subjectivity." *Philosophy Today* XXIX/4/4 (1985): 284-301.

Franzen, Winfried. *Von der Existenzialontologie zur Seinsgeschichte: Eine Untersuchung über die Entwicklung der Philosophie Martin Heideggers*. Meisenheim am Glan: Verlag Anton Hain, 1975.

Frend, William H. C. *The Rise of Christianity*. Philadelphia: Fortress Press, 1984.

Freyer, Thomas. "Die Öffnung der Transzendenz. Thesen zum Logos der Theologie anhand der Philosophie" *Die Zeitschrift für Katholische Theologie* 114/2 (1992): 140-152.

Funk, Robert W. "Myth and the Literal Non-literal." In *Parables and Presence*. Philadelphia:: Fortress Press, 1982: 111-37.

Gadamer, Hans-Georg. *Die Idee des Guten zwischen Plato und Aristoteles*. Heidelberg: Carl Winter Universitätsverlag, 1978: 1-103.

Gadamer, Hans-Georg. "Die Phänomenologische Bewegung." *Philosophische Rundschau* 11/1-2 (1963): 1-45.

_____. *Philosophical Hermeneutics*. Trans. by David E. Linge. Berkeley, CA: University of California Press, 1976.

_____. "Rhetorik, Hermeneutik und Ideologiekritik." *Kleine Schriften I* (1967): 113-30.

_____. "On the Scope and Function of Hermeneutical Reflection." *Continuum* 8 (1970): 77-95.

_____. *Truth and Method*. Trans. by Garret Barden and John Cumming. New York: Seabury Press, Continuum, 1975.

_____. *Wahrheit und Methode*. 4th ed. Tübingen: J.C.B. Mohr (Paul Siebeck), 1975.

Geffcken, Johannes. *Der Ausgang des griechisch-römischen Heidentums*. Heidelberg: Carl Winters Universitätsbuchhandlung, 1920.

Gerrish, Brian A. *Grace and Gratitude: The Eucharistic Theology of John Calvin*. Minneapolis: Fortress Press, 1993.

_____. "The Nature of Doctrine" *Journal of Religion* 68/1 (1988): 87-92.

Gillispie, Charles Coulston. *Genesis and Geology*. New York: Harper and Row, Harper Torchbooks/Cloister Library, 1959.

Gingerich, Owen. "Hypothesis, Proof, and Censorship or How Galileo Changed the Rules of Science" *Colloquium: The Australian and New Zealand Theological Review* 25/2 (1993): 54-66.

Girard, René. *Violence and the Sacred*. Trans. by Patrick Gregory. Baltimore: Johns Hopkins University Press, 1977.

Goodwin, George L. *The Ontological Argument of Charles Hartshorne*. American Academy of Religion Dissertation Series. Missoula, MT: Scholars Press, 1978.

Gould, Stephen Jay. *Wonderful Life: The Burgess Shale and the Nature of History*. New York: W.W. Norton, 1989.

Grant, Robert M. "Neither Male Nor Female." *Biblical Research* 37 (1992): 5-14.

Gregor von Nyssa. *Die drei Tage zwischen Tod und Auferstehung unseres Herrn Jesus Christus*. Trans. by Hubertus R. Drobner. Leiden: E.J. Brill, 1982.

Guitton, Jean, Bogdanov, Grichka, and Bogdanov, Igor. *Gott und die Wissenschaft. Auf dem Weg zum Metarealismus*. Trans. by Eva Moldenhauer. München: Artemis & Winkler Verlag, 1993.

Habermas, Jürgen. "Der hermeneutische Ansatz." In *Zur Logik der Sozialwissenschaften*. 5te, erweiterte Auflage. Frankfurt a.M.: Suhrkamp Verlag, 1982: 270-366.

_____. *Knowledge and Human Interests*. Trans. by Jeremy J. Shapiro. Boston: Beacon Press, 1972.

_____. *Die neue Unübersichtlichkeit. Kleine politische Schriften V*. Frankfurt a. M.: Suhrkamp, 1985.

_____. *Philosophische Rundschau*. Beiheft 5 (1967).

Habermas, Jürgen. "On Systematically Distorted Communication." *Inquiry* 13 (1970): 205-18.

_____. *Theorie des kommunikativen Handelns*. Frankfurt a. M.: Suhrkamp, 1981.

_____. *Theory of Communicative Praxis*. Trans. by Thomas McCarthy. Boston: Beacon Press, 1984.

_____. "Towards a Theory of Communicative Competence." *Inquiry* 13 (1970): 360-75.

_____. "Der Universalitätsanspruch der Hermeneutik." Ed. by R. Bubner. In *Hermeneutik und Dialektik*. Tübingen: J.C.B. Mohr (Paul Siebeck), 1970.

Hamerton-Kelley, Robert. *The Gospel and the Sacred: The Poetics of Violence in Mark* Minneapolis: Fortress Press, 1994.

Hannay, Alastair. *Kierkegaard*. London: Routledge and K. Paul, 1981.

Harnack, Adolf von. *Lehrbuch der Dogmengeschichte* Vol. 1 Darmstadt: Wissenschaftliche Buchgesellschaft, 1964.

_____. "Über den Ursprung der Formel 'Glaube, Liebe, Hoffnung'" in *Preußische Jahrbücher* (April bis Juni 1916): 1-14.

Hartlich, Christian. "Historisch-kritische Methode in ihrer Anwendung auf Geschehnisaussagen der Hl. Schrift." *Zeitschrift für Theologie und Kirche* 75/4 (1978): 467-84.

_____, and Walter Sachs. *Der Ursprung des Mythosbegriffes in der modernen Bibelwissenschaft-Einführung*. Tübingen: J.C.B. Mohr (Paul Siebeck), 1952.

Hartshorne, Charles. *Man's Vision of God: And the Logic of Theism*. Hamden, CT: Archon Books, 1964.

Hegel, G. W. F. *The Phenomenology of the Mind*. Trans. by J. B. Baillie. New York: Harper Torchbooks, 1967.

_____. *Lectures on the Philosophy of World History: Introductions: Reason in History*. Trans. by H. B. Nisbet. Cambridge: Cambridge University Press, 1975.

_____. *Lectures on the Philosophy of Religion*. Ed. by Peter C. Hodgson. Vol. 1. *Introduction and the Concept of Religion*. Berkeley: University of California Press, 1984.

_____. *Phenomenology of Mind*. Trans. by J.B. Baillie. New York: Harper Torchbooks, 1967.

_____. *Phenomenology of Spirit*. Trans. by A. V. Miller. Oxford: Oxford University Press, 1977.

_____. *The Philosophy of History*. Trans. by J. Sibree. New York: Dover, 1956.

Heidegger, Martin. *Being and Time*. Trans. by John Macquarrie and Edward Robinson. New York: Harper and Row, 1962.

_____. *Discourse On Thinking*. Trans. by John M. Anderson, and E. Hans Freund. New York: Harper Torchbooks, 1966.

_____. *Hölderlins Hymne 'Andenken'* Frankfurt a.M.: Klostermann, 1982.

_____. *Hölderlins Hymne 'Der Ister'* Frankfurt a.M.: Klostermann, 1984.

Heidegger, Martin. "Die Idee der Philosophie und das Weltanschauungsproblem. Kriegsnotsemester 1919." In *Gesamtausgabe. Zur Bestimmung der Philosophie.* 56/57. Frankfurt a. M.: Vittorio Klostermann, 1987: 3-117.

---------. *An Introduction to Metaphysics.* Trans. by Ralph Manheim. Garden City, NY: Doubleday, Anchor, 1961.

---------. *Kant and the Problem of Metaphysics.* Trans. by James S. Churchill. Bloomington: Indiana University Press, 1962.

---------. *Kants These über das Sein.* Frankfurt a.M.: Vittorio Klostermann, 1963.

---------. Kant's Thesis About Being." Trans. by Ted Klein and William Pohl. In *Southwestern Journal of Philosophy* 4/3 (1973): 7-33.

---------. "Letter on Humanism." In *Philosophy in the Twentieth Century.* Vol. 3. Ed. by William Barrett and Henry D. Aiken. New York: Harper & Row, 1971: 192-224.

---------. "Logos (Heraklit, Fragment 50)." In *Vorträge und Aufsätze.* Pfullingen: Verlag Günther Neske, 1954: 207-29.

---------. *Nietzsche I & II.* Vols I & II. Pfullingen: Verlag Günther Neske, 1961.

---------. "Phänomenologie und Theologie." In *Wegmarken.* Frankfurt a.M.: Klostermanns, 1978: 45-67.

---------. "Phänomenologische Interpretation zu Aristoteles (Anzeige der hermeneutischen Situation)." *Dilthey-Jahrbuch* 6 (1989) <1922>: 235-274.

---------. *The Question Concerning Technology and Other Essays.* Trans. by William Lovitt. New York: Harper and Row, Harper Colophon, 1977.

---------. *Der Satz vom Grund.* Pfullingen: Neske, 1957.

---------. "The Self-Assertion of the German University and the Rectorate 1933/34: Facts and Thoughts." Trans. by Karsten Harries. *The Review of Metaphysics* XXXVIII (March 1985): 467-502.

---------. *Unterwegs zur Sprache.* Pfullingen: Neske, 1959.

---------. *On the Way to Language.* Trans. by Peter D. Hertz. New York: Harper & Row, 1971.

---------. *What is Called Thinking?* Trans. by J. Glenn Gray. New York: Harper and Row, Harper Torchbooks, 1972.

Hermann, Friedrich-Wilhelm von. "Augustinus und die phänomenologische Frage nach der Zeit." *Philosophisches Jahrbuch* 100/1 (1993): 96-113.

Hildenbrandt, Eberhard. *Versuch einer kritischen Analyse des Cours de linguistique generale von Ferdinand de Saussure.* Marburg: N.G. Elwert Verlag, 1972.

Hirsch, E. D., Jr. *The Aims of Interpretation.* Chicago: University of Chicago Press, 1976.

Hirsch, Emanuel. *Geschichte der neuern evangelischen Theologie im Zusammenhang mit den allgemeinen Bewegungen des europäischen Denkens.* 5 Vols. Gütersloh: C. Bertelsmann Verlag, 1949-54.

Hirsch, Emanuel. "Das Ringen der idealistischen Denker um eine neue, die Aufklärung überwindende Gestalt der philosophischen Aussagen über Gott. Dargestellt nach seinem Verhältnis zur reformatorischen Gotteserkenntnis." In *Christliche Wahrheit und neuzeitliches Denken. Zu Emanuel Hirschs Leben und Werk*. Ed. by Hans Martin Müller. Tübingen: Katzmann Verlag, 1984: 142-204.

Hofrichter, Peter. "Logoslehre und Gottesbild bei Apologeten, Modalisten und Gnostikern. Johanneische Christologie im Lichte ihrer frühesten Rezeption." In *Monotheismus und Christologie. Zur Gottesfrage im hellenistischen Judentum und im Urchristentum*. Ed. by Hans-Josef Klauch. Freiburg i. B.: Herder, 1992: 186-217.

Holte, Ragnar. "Logos Spermatikos. Christianity and Ancient Philosophy According to St. Justin's Apologies." Trans. by Tina Pierce. *Studia Theologica* 12 (1958): 109-168.

Hübner, Kurt. "Der Mythos, der Logos und das spezifisch Religiöse. Drei Elemente des christlichen Glaubens." In *Mythos und Rationalität*, Ed. by Hans Heinrich Schmid. Gütersloh: Gütersloher Verlagshaus Gerd Mohn, 1988: 27-43.

_____. *Die Wahrheit des Mythos*. München: Verlag C.H.Beck, 1985.

Hume, David. *Dialogues Concerning Natural Religion and the Posthumous Essays of the Immortality of the Soul and On Suicide*. Ed. by Richard H. Popkin. Indianapolis: Hackett Pub., Co., 1982.

_____. David Hume, "Of the Understanding" from "The Treatise of Human Nature" in *Hume Selections*. Ed. by Charles W. Hendel. New York: Charles Scribner's Sons, 1955.

Husserl, Edmund. *Cartesian Meditations: An Introduction to Phenomenology*. Trans. by Dorion Cairns. The Hague: Martinus Nijhoff, 1964.

_____. *The Crisis of European Sciences and Transcendental Phenomenology: An Introduction to Phenomenological Philosophy*. Trans. by David Carr. Northwestern University Studies in Phenomenology and Existential Philosophy. Evanston: Northwestern University Press, 1970.

_____. *Ideas: General Introduction to Pure Phenomenology*. Trans. by W. R. Boyce Gibson. New York: Collier, 1962.

_____. *V. Logische Untersuchung. Über intentionale Erlebnisse und ihre "Inhalte"*. Hamburg: Felix Meiner Verlag, 1975.

_____. *The Phenomenology of Internal Time-Consciousness*. Trans. by James S. Churchill. Bloomington: Indiana University Press, 1969.

_____. "Philosophy and the Crisis of European Man." In *Phenomenology and the Crisis of Philosophy*, Trans. by Quentin Lauer. New York: Harper and Row, Harper Torchbooks, 1965: 149-92.

_____. "Philosophy as Rigorous Science." In *Phenomenology and the Crisis of Philosophy*, Trans. by Quentin Lauer. New York: Harper and Row, Harper Torchbooks/Academy Library, 1965: 71-147.

_____. *Vorlesungen zur Phänomenologie des inneren Zeitbewußtseins*. 2. Auflage. Ed. by Martin Heidegger. Tübingen: Max Niemeyer Verlag, 1980.

Iamblichus. *On the Pythagorean Life*. Trans. by Gillian Clark. Translated Texts for Historians, Vol. 8. Liverpool: Liverpool University Press, 1989.

Inciarte, Fernando. "Der Begriff der Seele in der Philosophie des Aristoteles." Trans. by F. Dirlmeier. In *Seele. Ihre Wirklichkeit, ihr Verhältnis zum Leib und zur menschlichen Person*. Leiden: E.J. Brill, 1984: 46-65.

―――――. "Die Einheit der Aristotelischen Metaphysik." *Philosophisches Jahrbuch* 101/1 (1994): 1-21.

Inge, William Ralph. *The Philosophy of Plotinus. The Gifford Lectures at St. Andrews, 1917-1918*. 2 Vols. 2d ed. New York: Longmans, Green and Co., 1923.

Ivánka, Endre von. "Der 'Apex Mentis' (1950)." In *Platonismus in der Philosophie des Mittelalters*. Ed. by Werner Beierwaltes. Darmstadt: Wissenschaftliche Buchgesellschaft, 1969: 121-47.

Jäger, Alfred. *Gott. Nochmals Martin Heidegger*. Tübingen: J.C.B. Mohr (Paul Siebeck), 1978.

Jaspers, Karl, and Bultmann, Rudolf. *Myth and Christianity: An Inquiry Into the Possibility of Religion Without Myth*. New York: Noonday Press, 1958.

Johnston, William. *The Cloud of Unknowing and The Book of Privy Counseling*. Trans. by E. Alison Peers. 3d ed. Garden City, NY: Doubleday, Image, 1973.

Jonas, Hans. *Gnosis und spätantiker Geist*. Teil 2: *Von der Mythologie zur mystischen Philosophie*. Göttingen: Vandenhoeck & Ruprecht, 1954.

Jüngel, Eberhard. *Gott als Geheimnis der Welt: Zur Begründung der Theologie des Gekreuzigten im Streit zwischen Theismus und Atheismus*. Tübingen: J.C.B. Mohr (Paul Siebeck), 1978.

―――――. "Meine Theologie - Kurz Gefaßt." *Theologisches Jahrbuch* (Leipzig) (1988): 98-114.

Kant, Immanuel. *Critique of Pure Reason*. Ed. by Norman Kemp Smith. New York: St Martin's Press, 1929.

―――――. "Inaugural Dissertation." In *Kant's Inaugural Dissertation and Early Writings on Space*. Trans. by John Handyside. Westport, Conn.: Hyperion Press, Inc., 1979.

―――――. *Kritik der reinen Vernunft*. Hamburg: Felix Meiner Verlag, 1976.

―――――. *Kritik der Urteilskraft*. Hamburg: Felix Meiner Verlag, 1974.

―――――. *Religion Within the Limits of Reason Alone*. Trans. by Theodore M. Greene and Hoyt H. Hudson. New York: Harper and Row, Harper Torchbooks/Cloister Library, 1960.

Kappes, Michael. "'Natürliche Theologie' als innerprotestantisches und ökumenisches Problem? Die Kontroverse zwischen Eberhard Jüngel und Wolfhart Pannenberg und ihr ökumenischer Ertrag." *Catholica* 49/4 (1995): 276-309.

Kaufman, Peter. *Church, Book, and Bishop: Conflict and Authority in Early Latin Christianity*. Boulder, CO: Westview Press, Inc., 1996.

Kierkegaard, Søren. *Concluding Unscientific Postscript. Postscript to the Philosophical Fragments*. Trans. by David Swenson and Walter Lowrie. Princeton, NJ: Princeton University Press, 1968.

_____. *Fear and Trembling and Repetition*. Trans. Howard V. Hong and Edna H. Hong. Kierkegaard's Writings, Vol. 6. Princeton: Princeton University Press, 1983.

_____. *Philosophical Fragments or A Fragment of Philosophy*. Trans. by Hong and David Swenson. Princeton: Princeton University Press, 1969.

_____. *Repetition: An Essay in Experimental Psychology*. Trans. by Walter Lowrie. New York: Harper Torchbooks, 1964.

_____. *Stages on Life's Way*. Trans. Howard V. Hong and Edna H. Hong. Kierkegaard's Writings, Vol. 11. Princeton: Princeton University Press, 1988.

Kisiel, Theodor. "Das Entstehen des Begriffsfeldes 'Faktizität' im Frühwerk Heideggers." *Dilthey-Jahrbuch für Philosophie und Geschichte der Geisteswissenschaften* 4 (1986-87): 91-120.

_____. "Das Kriegsnotsemester 1919: Heideggers Durchbruch zur hermeneutischen Phänomenologie." *Philosophisches Jahrbuch* 99/1 (1992): 105-22.

Knowles, David. *Christian Monasticism*. New York: McGraw-Hill Book Co., 1977.

Kockelmans, Joseph J. "Heidegger on Metaphor and Metaphysics." *Tijdschrift voor Filosofie* 47/3 (1985): 415-50.

Köpf, Ulrich. *Die Anfänge der theologischen Wissenschaftstheorie im 13. Jahrhundert*. Tübingen: J.C.B. Mohr (Paul Siebeck), 1974.

_____. *Religiöse Erfahrung in der Theologie Bernhards von Clairvaux. Beiträge zur historischen Theologie*, 61. Tübingen: J.C.B. Mohr (Paul Siebeck), 1980.

Koschorke, Klaus. "Gnosis, Montanismus, Mönchtum. Zur Frage emanzipatorischer Bewegungen im Raum der Alten Kirche." *Evangelische Theologie* 53/2,3 (1993): 216-231.

Koyré, Alexander. "Galileo and Plato." *Journal of the History of Ideas* IV (1943): 400-28.

Kuhn, Thomas S. *The Structure of Scientific Revolutions*. 2d ed. Chicago: University of Chicago Press, 1962.

Langerbeck, Hermann. "Paulus und das Griechentum. Zum Problem des Verhältnisses der christlichen Botschaft zum antiken Erkenntnisideal." In *Aufsätze zur Gnosis. Aus dem Nachlaß herausgegeben von Hermann Dörries*. Göttingen: Vandenhoeck & Ruprecht, 1967: 83-145.

Leftow, Brian. "Aquinas on Time and Eternity." *New Scholasticism* 62/2-4 (1990): 387-429.

Lévinas, Emmanuel. "As if Consenting to Horror." *Critical Inquiry* 15/2 (1989): 485-488.

_____. "On the Trail of the Other." *Philosophy Today* 10/1 (1966): 34-45.

Lilie, Frank. "Heideggers Forderung nach einer Destruktion der Tradition." *Neue Zeitschrift für Systematische Theologie und Religionsphilosophie* 34/3 (1992): 315-325.

Lindau, Hans, ed. *Die Schriften zu J.G. Fichtes Atheismus-Streit*. München: Georg Müller, 1912.

Lindbeck, George A. *The Nature of Doctrine: Religion and Theology in a Post-liberal Age*. Philadelphia: Westminster Press, 1984.

Löwith, Karl. *Mein Leben in Deutschland vor und nach 1933: Ein Bericht*. Stuttgart: J.B. Metzlersche Verlagsbuchhandlung, 1986.

Lust, Johan. "A Gentle Breeze or a Roaring Thunderous Sound? I Kings XIX 12." *Vetus Testamentum* XXV (1975): 110-15.

Lyotard, Jean-Francious. *The Postmodern Condition*. Trans. by Geoff Bennington and Brian Massumi. Minneapolis: University of Minnesota Press, 1984.

Marcuse, Herbert. "Kritische Theorie zwischen 'Flaschenpost' und politischer Praxis." *Pflasterstrand* 209 (May 17 1985): 42-44.

Markus, Robert. *The End of Ancient Christianity*. Cambridge: Cambridge University Press, 1994.

Marqués, Alfonso García. "Der Begriff von 'Möglichkeit' nach 'Metaphysik' IX,3-4." *Philosophisches Jahrbuch* 100/2 (1993): 357-65.

McDermott, John M., S.J. "Dialectical Analogy: The Oscillating Center of Rahner's Thought." *Gregorianum* 75/4 (1994): 675-703.

McFague, Sallie. *Metaphorical Theology: Models of God in Religious Language*. Philadelphia: Fortress Press, 1988.

McGaughey, Douglas R. "Coming to Terms with Darwin and the 19th Century Paradigm Revolution" in *The Willamette Journal of the Liberal Arts*, 6 (Fall 1991), 65-90.

_____. "Husserl and Heidegger on Plato's Cave Allegory: A Study of Philosophical Influence." *International Philosophical Quarterly* XVI (September 1976): 331-48.

_____. "The Paradox of a Theologian - Weltanschauungen and Conviction: The Problem of Evil." *Explorations: Journal for Adventurous Thought* 4/2 (1986): 39-58.

_____. "Ricoeur's Metaphor and Narrative Theories as a Foundation for a Theory of Symbol." *Religious Studies* 24 (1988): 415-37.

_____. "On the Soteriological Significance of the Symbol of the Kingdom of God in the Language of the Historical Jesus." Ph.D. Diss. University of Chicago, 1983.

_____. "Through Myth to Imagination: On the Collapse of the Separation Between Myth and History." *Journal of the American Academy of Religion* LVI/1 (Spring, 1988): 51-76.

McGinn, Bernhard. *The Foundations of Mysticism*. Vol I of *The Presence of God: A History of Western Christian Mysticism*. New York: The Crossroad Publishing Co., 1992.

McKeever, Kerry. "How to Avoid Speaking About God. Poststructuralist Philosophers and Biblical Hermeneutics." *Literature and Theology: An Interdisciplinary Journal of Theory and Criticism* 6/3 (1992): 228-238.

McKinnon, Alastair. *Falsification and Belief*. The Hague: Mouton, 1970.

Meijering, E.P. "The Doctrine of the Will and of the Trinity in the Orations of Gregory of Nazianzus." *Nederlands Theologisch Tijdschrift* 27 (1973): 224-34.

_____. "Irenaeus' Relation to Philosophy in the Light of His Concept of Free Will." *Romanitas et Christianitas*. Amsterdam, North-Holland Publishing Co. (1973): 221-232.

_____. "Orthodoxy and Platonism in Athanasius." *Orthodoxy and Platonism in Athanasius: Synthesis or Antithesis?* Leiden: E.J. Brill, 1974: 114-99.

_____. "Wie platonisierten Christen? Zur Grenzziehung zwischen Platonismus, kirchlichem Credo und patristischer Theologie." *Vigiliae Christianae* 28 (1974): 15-28

Merleau-Ponty, Maurice. *Phenomenology of Perception*. Trans. by Colin Smith. New York: Humanities Press, 1970.

_____. *The Visible and the Invisible*. Trans. by Alphonso Lingis. Evanston: Northwestern University Press, 1968.

Meyer, Ben F. *Critical Realism and the New Testament*. Allison Park, Penn.: Pickwick Publications, 1989.

Miller, Patricia Cox. "In Praise of Nonsense." In *Classical Mediterranean Spirituality: Egyptian, Greek, Roman*. Ed. by A.H. Armstrong. New York: Crossroad Press, 1986: 481-505

Mitchell, Basil. *The Philosophy of Religion*. London: Oxford University Press, 1971.

Moltmann-Wendel, Elisabeth. "Zur Kreuzestheologie heute. Gibt es eine feministische Kreuzestheologie?" *Evangelische Theologie* 50/6 (1990): 546-57.

Motzkin, Gabriel. "Ehyeh' and the Future: 'God' and Heidegger's Concept of 'Becoming.'" In *Ocular Desire/Sehnsucht des Auges*. Ed. by Aharon R.E. Agus and Jan Assmann. Berlin: Akademie Verlag GmbH, 1994.

Mühl, Max. "Der λόγος ἐνδιάθετος und προφορικός von der älteren Stoa bis zur Synode von Sirmium 351." *Archiv für Begriffsgeschichte* (1962): 7-56.

Müller-Lauter, Wolfgang. "Nihilismus als Konsequenz des Idealismus: F.H. Jacobis Kritik an der Transzendentalphilosophie und ihre philosophiegeschichtlichen Folgen." In *Denken im Schatten des Nihilismus: Festschrift für Wilhelm Weischedel zum 70. Geburtstag*. Ed. by Alexander Schwan. Darmstadt: Wissenschaftliche Buchgesellschaft, 1975.

Müller, Friedrich Max. *Vorlesungen über die Wissenschaft der Sprache*. Leipzig: Verlag Gustav Mayer, 1866.

Müller, Hans Martin. *Christliche Wahrheit und neuzeitliches Denken. Zu Emanuel Hirschs Leben und Werk*. Tübingen: Katzmann Verlag, 1984.

Nietzsche, Friedrich. "Jenseits von Gut und Böse." In *Nietzsche's Werke*. Vol. 7. Leipzig: Alfred Kröner Verlag, 1910: 3-286.

_____. "Nietzsche's Lecture Notes on Rhetoric: A Translation." Trans. by Carole Blair. *Philosophy and Rhetoric* 16/2 (1983): 94-129.

Nietzsche, Friedrich. "On Truth and Lies in a Nonmoral Sense." In *Philosophy and Truth: Selections from Nietzsche's Notebooks of the Early 1870's*, Trans. by Daniel Breazeale. Atlantic Highlands, N.J.: Humanitis Press Inc., 1979: 79-97.

_____. *Thus Spoke Zarathustra*. Trans. by Walter Kaufmann. New York: The Viking Press, 1966.

_____. "Vom Nutzen und Nachteil der Historie." *Unzeitgemässe Betrachtungen*. Zweites Stück. *Werke*. Vol. 1. Frankfurt a.M.: Ullstein, 1980: 209-285.

Nigg, Walter. *Geschichte des religiösen Liberalismus. Entstehung, Blütezeit, Ausklang*. Zürich: Max Niehaus Verlag, 1937.

Nijenhuis, John. "'Ens' Described as 'Being or Existent.'" *American Catholic Philosophical Quarterly* 68/1 (Winter 1994): 1-14.

Noire, Ludwig. *Die Welt als Entwicklung des Geistes. Bausteine zu einer monistischen Weltanschauung*. Leipzig: Verlag von Veit & Comp., 1874.

Nygren, Anders. *Agape and Eros*. Trans. by Philip S. Watson. New York: Harper and Row, 1969.

_____. *Meaning and Method: Prolegomena to a Scientific Philosophy of Religion and a Scientific Theology*. Trans. by Philip S. Watson. Philadelphia: Fortress Press, 1972.

Ogden, Schubert M. *Christ Without Myth: A Study Based on the Theology of Rudolf Bultmann*. New York: Harper & Row, 1961.

_____. *The Reality of God and Other Essays*. New York: Harper and Row, 1966.

_____. "The Task of Philosophical Theology." In *The Future of Philosophical Theology*. Ed. by Robert Evans. Philadelphia: Westminster Press, 1971: 48-84.

_____. "What is Theology?" *The Journal of Religion* 52/1 (1972): 22-40.

Osborn, Eric. "Arguments for Faith in Clement of Alexandria." *Vigiliae Christianae* 48/1 (1994): 1-25.

Ott, Hugo. "Engelbert Krebs und Martin Heidegger 1915." In *Freiburger Diözesan-Archiv* 113 (1993): 239-48.

_____. "Martin Heidegger als Rektor der Universität Freiburg i.Br. 1933/34." *Zeitschrift des Breisgau-Geschichtsvereins* 102 (1983): 121-36.

_____. "Martin Heidegger und die Universität Freiburg nach 1945." *Historisches Jahrbuch* 105/1 (1985): 95-128.

_____. "Martin Heidegger und der Nationalsozialismus." In *Heidegger und die praktische Philosophie*. Ed. by Annemarie Gethmann-Siefert and Otto Pöggeler. Frankfurt a.M.: Suhrkamp Taschenbuch Wissenschaft, 1988): 64-77.

_____. *Martin Heidegger: Unterwegs zu seiner Biographie*. Frankfurt a. M.: Campus Verlag, 1988.

Otto, Rudolf. *The Idea of the Holy*. Trans. by John W. Harvey. New York: Oxford University Press, 1926.

Owens, Joseph. *The Doctrine of Being in the Aristotelian 'Metaphysics': A Study in the Greek Background of Mediaeval Thought*. 2nd Edition. Toronto, Canada: Pontifical Institute of Mediaeval Studies, 1963.

Palmer, Richard E. *Hermeneutics: Interpretation Theory in Schleiermacher, Dilthey, Heidegger, and Gadamer*. Northwestern University Studies in Phenomenology and Existential Philosophy. Evanston: Northwestern University Press, 1969.

Pannenberg, Wolfhart. *Jesus - God and Man*. Trans. by Lewis L. Wilkins and Duane A. Priebe. Philadelphia: The Westminster Press, 1974.

_____. *Theology and the Kingdom of God*. Philadelphia: The Westminster Press, 1969.

_____, ed. *Revelation as History*. In collaboration with Rolf Rendtorff, Trutz Rendtorff, and Ulrich Wilkens. Trans. by David Granskou. New York: Macmillan, 1969.

Paul, Jean. *Vorschule der Aesthetik*. In *Sämmtliche Werke*. Vols. 41-42. Berlin: S. Reimer, 1827 (1804).

Peacocke, Arthur R. *Creation and the World of Science*. Oxford: Oxford University Press, Clarendon, 1979.

Pearson, Birger A. "Philo and Gnosticism." *Aufstieg und Niedergang der Römischen Welt (ANRW)* II 21.1 (1984): 295-341.

Philo of Alexandria. "de Abrahamo." In *Philo von Alexandria. Die Werke in deutscher Übersetzung*. Ed. by Leopold Cohn, Isaak Heinemann, Maximilian Adler und Willy Theiler. 2d ed. Vol. 1. Berlin: Walter de Gruyter & Co., 1962: 93-152.

_____. "de gigantibus." Trans. by Hans Leisegang. In *Philo von Alexandria. Die Werke in deutscher Übersetzung*. Ed. by Leopold Cohn, Isaak Heinemann, Maximilian Adler und Willy Theiler. 2d ed. Vol. IV. Berlin: Walter de Gruyter & Co., 1962: 58-71

_____. "de opificio mundi." In *Philo von Alexandria. Die Werke in deutscher Übersetzung*. Ed. by Leopold Cohn, Isaak Heinemann, Maximilian Adler und Willy Theiler. 2d ed. Vol. I. Berlin: Walter de Gruyter & Co., 1962: 25-89.

_____. *quis rerum divinarum heres sit*. Trans. by Marguerite Harl. Paris: Éditions Du Cerf, 1966.

_____. "quod deus sit immutabilis." Trans. by Hans Leisegang. In *Philo von Alexandria. Die Werke in deutscher Übersetzung*. Ed. by Leopold Cohn, Isaak Heinemann, Maximilian Adler und Willy Theiler. 2d ed. Vol. IV. Berlin: Walter de Gruyter & Co., 1962: 72-110.

Plato. *The Collected Dialogues of Plato: Including the Letters*. Ed. by Edith Hamilton and Cairns Huntington. Bollingen Series LXXI. Princeton: Princeton University Press, 1973.

Plotinus. *The Six Enneads*. Trans. by Stephen MacKenna and B.S. Page. In *Great Books of the Western World*. Ed. by Mortimer J. Adler. Chicago: Encyclopaedia Britannica, Inc., 1952.

_____. *The Essential Plotinus: Representative Treatises from the Enneads*. Trans. by S. J. Elmer O'Brien. Indianapolis: Hackett Publishing Company, Inc., 1964.

Pöggeler, Otto. *Der Denkweg Martin Heideggers*. Pfullingen, 1983.

Pöggeler, Otto. "Hegel und die Anfänge der Nihilismus-Diskussion." *Man and World. An International Philosophical Review* 3 (September 1970): 163-99.

_____. "'Nihilist' und 'Nihilismus'" *Archiv für Begriffsgeschichte* XIX. Bonn: Bouvier Verlag Herbert Grundmann. (1975): 197-210.

Pohlenz, Max. *Die Stoa. Geschichte einer geistigen Bewegung*. Göttingen: Vandenhoeck & Ruprecht, 1992.

Poinsot, John. *Tractatus de signis: The Semiotic of John Poinsot*. Trans. by John N. Deely. Berkeley: University of California Press, 1985.

Praechter, Karl. "Christlich-neuplatonische Beziehungen." *Byzantinische Zeitschrift* 21 (1921): 1-27.

Price, R.M. "'Hellenization' and Logos Doctrine in Justin Martyr." *Vigilae Christianae* 42 (1988): 19-23.

Pseudo-Dionysius *Pseudo-Dionysius: The Complete Works*. Trans. by Colm Luibheid. New York: Paulist Press, 1987.

Rahner, Karl. *Hearer of the Word. Laying the Foundations for a Philosophy of Religion*. Translated by Joseph Donceel. New York: Continuum, 1994.

_____. *Hörer des Wortes. Zur Grundlegung einer Religionsphilosophie*. München: Verlag Kösel-Pustet, 1941.

Ramsey, Ian T. *Religious Language: An Empirical Placing of Theological Phrases*. New York: Macmillan, 1967.

Reardon, Bernard M. G. *Religious Thought in the Nineteenth Century*. Cambridge: Cambridge University Press, 1966.

Reitzenstein, Richard. "Die Entstehung der Formel 'Glaube, Liebe, Hoffnung'" in *Historische Zeitschrift* 116 (1916): 189-208.

_____. "Die Formel 'Glaube, Liebe, Hoffnung' bei Paulus" in *Nachrichten von der Königlichen Gesellschaft der Wissenschaften zu Göttingen. Philologisch-historische Klasse* (1916): 367-416.

_____. "Die Formel Glaube, Liebe, Hoffnung bei Paulus. Ein Nachwort" in *Nachrichten von der Königlichen Gesellschaft der Wissenschaften zu Göttingen. Philologisch-historische Klasse* (1917): 130-51.

_____. *Die hellenistischen Mysterienreligionen. Nach ihren Grundgedanken und Wirkungen*. Vortrag ursprünglich gehalten in dem Wissenschaftlichen Predigerverein für Elsass-Lothringen den 11. November 1909. Leipzig: Verlag von B.G. Teubner, 1920.

_____. *Historia Monachorum und Historia Lausiaca. Eine Studie zur Geschichte des Mönchtums und der frühchristlichen Begriffe Gnostiker und Pneumatiker*. Göttingen: Vandenhoeck und Ruprecht, 1916.

_____. "Iranischer Erlösungsglaube" in *Zeitschrift für die Neutestamentliche Wissenschaft und die Kunde der älteren Kirche* 20 (1921): 1-23.

Richards, Ivor A. *The Philosophy of Rhetoric*. New York: Oxford University Press, 1965.

Ricoeur, Paul. "Biblical Hermeneutics" *Semeia 4 (Paul Ricoeur on Biblical Hermeneutics)*. Ed. by John Dominic Crossan. Missoula: University of Montana, 1975: 29-148.

_____. "Erzählung, Metapher und Interpretationstheorie." *Zeitschrift für Theologie und Kirche* 84/2 (1987): 232-54.

_____. "The Hermeneutical Function of Distanciation." In *Hermeneutics and the Human Sciences*. Trans. by John B. Thompson. Cambridge: Cambridge University Press, 1981: 131-144.

_____. "Metaphor and the Main Problem of Hermeneutics." *New Literary History* VI (Autumn 1974): 95-110.

_____. "Narrated Time." Trans. by Robert Sweeney. *Philosophy Today* 29 (Winter 1985): 259-72.

_____. *Oneself as Another*. Trans. by Kathleen Blamey. Chicago: The University of Chicago Press, 1992.

_____. *The Rule of Metaphor: Multi-disciplinary Studies of the Creation of Meaning in Language*. Trans. by Robert Czerny, Kathleen McLaughlin, and John Costello. Toronto: University of Toronto Press, 1977.

_____. *Time and Narrative*. Trans. by Kathleen McLaughlin and David Pellauer. Vols. 1-3. Chicago: University of Chicago Press, 1984-1988.

Runia, David T. *Philo in Early Christian Literature*. Minneapolis: Fortress Press, 1993.

Sartre, Jean-Paul. *Being and Nothingness: An Essay on Phenomenological Ontology*. Trans. by Hazel E. Barnes. New York: Philosophical Library, 1956.

Saussure, Ferdinand de. *Course in General Linguistics*. Ed. by Charles Bally and Albert Sechehaye. Trans. by Wade Baskin. New York: McGraw-Hill, 1966.

Schleiermacher, Friedrich. *Brief Outline on the Study of Theology*. Trans. by Terrence N. Tice. Richmond: John Knox Press, 1970.

_____. *The Christian Faith*. Vols. 1-2. Ed. by H.R. Mackintosh and J.S. Stewart. New York: Harper and Row, Harper Torchbooks/Cloister Library, 1963.

_____. *Hermeneutics: The Handwritten Manuscripts*. Vol. 1. Trans. by James Duke and Jack Forstman. American Academy of Religion Texts and Translation Series. Missoula, MT: Scholars Press, 1977.

_____. *On Religion: Speeches to Its Cultured Despisers*. Trans. by John Oman. New York: Harper and Row, Harper Torchbooks/Cloister Library, 1986.

Schneeberger, Guido. *Nachlese zu Heidegger: Dokumente zu seinem Leben und Denken*. Bern, 1962.

Schner, George S. J. "Hume's Dialogues and the Redefinition of the Philosophy of Religion." *The Thomist* 55/1 (1991): 83-103.

Schütz, R. "Der Streit zwischen A. v. Harnack u. R. Reitzenstein über die Formel 'Glaube, Liebe, Hoffnung' 1. Kor. 13,13." *Theologische Literaturzeitung* 42 (1917): 454-57.

Schützeichel, Harald. "Kants Auffassung vom Ursprung des Bösen in seiner Schrift 'Die Religion innerhalb der Grenzen der bloßen Vernunft'" *RENOVATIO - Zeitschrift für das interdisziplinäre Gespräch* 46/1 (1990): 29-38.

Schwan, Alexander, ed. *Denken im Schatten des Nihilismus: Festschrift für Wilhelm Weischedel zum 70. Geburtstag.* Darmstadt: Wissenschaftliche Buchgesellschaft, 1975.

Schwartz, Sanford. "Hermeneutics and the Productive Imagination: Paul Ricoeur in the 1970s." *Journal of Religion* 63/3 (1983): 290-300.

Schweidler, Walter. *Die Überwindung der Metaphysik: Zu einem Ende der neuzeitlichen Philosophie.* Stuttgart: Ernst Klett Verlag - J.C. Cotta'sche Buchhandlung, 1987.

Schweitzer, Albert. *Die Mystik des Apostels Paulus.* Tübingen: J.C.B. Mohr (Paul Siebeck), 1981.

Sheehan, Thomas. "Heidegger and the Nazis." *New York Review of Books* 16 June 1988, 38-47.

_____. "Heidegger's 'Introduction to the Phenomenology of Religion,' 1920-21." *The Personalist*: 312-24.

_____. *Heidegger: The Man and the Thinker.* Chicago: Precedent Publishing, Inc., 1981.

Sokolowski, Robert. *The Formation of Husserl's Concept of Constitution.* The Hague: Martinus Nijhoff, 1964.

Speck, Josef. *Grundprobleme der großen Philosophen.* Göttingen: Vandenhoeck & Ruprecht, 1978.

Spiegelberg, Herbert. *The Phenomenological Movement: An Historical Introduction.* Vols. 1-2. 2d ed. Phaenomenologica: Collection Publiée sous le Patronage des Centres D'Archives-Husserl, Vol. 5. The Hague: Martinus Nijhoff, 1969.

Spranger, Eduard. "Zur Theorie des Verstehens und zur geisteswissenschaftlichen Psychologie." In *Festschrift Johannes Volkelt zum 70. Geburtstag.* München: C.H. Beck'sche Verlagsbuchhandlung Oskar Beck, 1918: 357-403.

Staudinger, Hugo. "Mythos und Geschichte. Überlegungen zur historisch-kritischen Exegese." *Forum Katholische Theologie* 7/3 (1991): 161-74.

Stegmüller, Wolfgang. *Metaphysik, Skepsis, Wissenschaft.* Berlin: Springer-Verlag, 1969.

Stepelevich, Lawrence S. "From Tübingen to Rome: The First Catholic Response to Hegel." *The Heythrop Journal* 32/4 (1991): 477-92.

Strolz, Walter. "Vom Sein zum Anderen. Extremer Humanismus im Denken von Emmanuel Lévinas." *Neue Zeitschrift für Systematische Theologie und Religionsphilosohie* 35/2 (1993): 176-197.

Taylor, Mark. *Erring, A Postmodern A/theology.* Chicago: The University of Chicago Press, 1984.

Tertulian, Nicolas. "Heidegger - oder: Die Bestätigung der Politik durch Seinsgeschichte. Ein Gang zu den Quellen. Was aus den Texten des Philosophen alles sprudelt." *Frankfurter Rundschau.* February 2, 1988.

Theunissen, Michael. *Hegels Lehre vom absoluten Geist als theologisch-politischer Traktat.* Berlin: Walter de Gruyter & Co., 1970.

Tibetan Book of the Dead. Ed. by W.Y. Evans-Wentz. London: Oxford University Press, 1969.

Tillich, Paul. *The Courage to Be.* New Haven: Yale University Press, 1969.

———. *Perspectives on 19th and 20th Century Protestant Theology.* New York: Harper & Row, 1967.

———. *The Shaking of the Foundations.* New York: Charles Scribner's Sons, 1948.

———. *Systematic Theology.* Vols. 1-3. Chicago: University of Chicago Press, 1967.

———. *Theology of Culture.* Ed. by Robert C. Kimball. New York: Oxford University Press, Galaxy, 1964.

Tracy, David. *The Analogical Imagination: Christian Theology and the Culture of Pluralism.* New York: Crossroads, 1989 (1981).

———. *Blessed Rage for Order: The New Pluralism in Theology.* New York: Seabury Press, Crossroads, 1975.

———. "Lindbeck's New Program for Theology: A Reflection." *The Thomist* 49 (1985): 460-72.

———. "Literary Theory and Return of the Forms for Naming and Thinking God in Theology." *The Journal of Religion* 74 (1994): 302-319.

Troeltsch, Ernst. *Der Historismus und seine Überwindung.* Aalen: Scientia Verlag, 1979.

Verbeke, Gerard. "The Meaning of Potency in Aristotle." In *Graceful Reason.* Ed. by Lloyd P. Gerson. Toronto: Pontifical Institute of Mediaeval Studies, 1983: 55-73.

Vogel, Cornelia J. de. "Platonism and Christianity: A Mere Antagonism or a Profound Common Ground?" *Vigiliae Christianae* 39 (1985): 1-62.

———. "The Problem of Philosophy and Christian Faith in Boethius' Consolatio." In *Romanitas et Christianitas.* Ed. by P. G. van der Nat, C. M. J. Sicking, W. den Boer, and J.C.M. van Winden. Amsterdam: North-Holland Publishing Company, 1973: 357-70.

Walker, Williston. *A History of the Christian Church.* New York: Charles Scribner's Sons, 1970.

Waszink, Jan Hendrik. "Bemerkungen zu Justins Lehre vom Logos Spermatikos." In *Mullus. Festschrift Theodor Klauser.* In *Jahrbuch für Antike und Christentum. Ergänzungsband 1.* Münster Westfalen: Aschendorffsche Verlagsbuchhandlung, 1964: 380-90.

Weischedel, Wilhelm. *Der Gott der Philosophen: Grundlegung einer philosophischen Theologie im Zeitalter des Nihilismus.* Vols. 1-2. München: Deutscher Taschenbuch Verlag, 1985.

Weiss, Wolfgang. "Glaube - Liebe - Hoffnung. Zu der Trias bei Paulus." *Zeitschrift für die Neutestamentliche Wissenschaft* 84/3/4 (1993): 196-217.

Welch, Claude. *God and Incarnation In Mid-Nineteenth Century German Theology: G. Thomasius, I.A. Forner, A.E. Biedermann.* New York: Oxford University Press, 1965.

──────. *Protestant Thought in the Nineteenth Century, 1799-1870.* Vol. 1 (New Haven: Yale University Press, 1972.

Wheelwright, Philip. *Metaphor and Reality.* Bloomington: Indiana University Press, 1968.

──────. "Semantics and Ontology." In *Metaphor and Symbol.* Butterworths. London, 1960: 1-9.

Whitehead, Alfred North. *Process and Reality: An Essay in Cosmology.* New York: The Free Press, 1969.

Widengren, Geo. "Die Religionsgeschichtliche Schule und der Iranische Erlösungsglaube." *Orientalistische Literaturzeitung* 58;11/12 (1963): 533-48.

Wiebe, Donald. "An Unholy Alliance? The Creationists' Quest for Scientific Legitimation." *The Toronto Journal of Theology* 4/2 (1988): 162-77.

Wiles, Maurice. "Eunomius: Hair-Slitting Dialectician or Defender of the Accessibility of Salvation?" In *The Making of Orthodoxy: Essays in Honour of Henry Chadwick*, edited by Rowan Williams, 157-72. Cambridge: Cambridge University Press, 1989.

──────. "In Defence of Arius." *Journal of Theological Studies* 13 (1962): 339-47.

Williams, Rowan. *Arius: Heresy and Tradition.* London: Darton, Longman and Todd, 1987.

Wimsatt, William K. Jr., and Beardsley, Monroe C. *The Verbal Icon: Studies in the Meaning of Poetry.* Lexington: The University Press of Kentucky, 1954.

Wittgenstein, Ludwig. *Philosophical Investigations.* Trans. by G. E. M. Anscombe. New York: Macmillan, 1958.

Wlosok, Antonie. *Laktanz und die Philosphische Gnosis.* Heidelberg: Carl Winter, Universitätsverlag, 1960.

Wolz-Gottwald, Eckard. "Oculus Triplex - Das dreifache Auge der Erkenntnis." *Internationale Katholische Zeitschrift Communio* 23/3 (1994): 248-60.

──────. "Die transzendentale Phänomenologie und die philosophische Mystik. Zum Durchbruch eines neuen Denkens im Spätwerk Edmund Husserls." *Philosophisches Jahrbuch* 101/1 (1994): 98-115.

Wyschogrod, Edith, ed. "On Deconstructing Theology: A Symposium on ERRING: A Postmodern A/theology." Authors Alphonso Lingis, Joseph Prabhu, Edith Wyschogrod, Thomas J.J. Altizer, and Mark C. Taylor. *Journal of the American Academy of Religion* LIV/3 (1986): 523-57.

Name Index

Abrams, M.H., 164n
Adler, Mortimer, 496
Ahlstrom, Sydney E., 164n, 214n
Anaxagoras, 383, 410
Andresen, Carl, 472n
Anselm of Canterbury, 6, 27, 105,
    131n, 132n, 135-136, 138
Apel, Karl-Otto, 96n
Aquinas, Thomas, 2n, 15, 25, 43n,
    91, 105, 384n, 446n
Aristotle, 8, 9, 15, 25, 27, 79n, 89n,
    131n, 132n, 139n, 200n,
    215, 219n, 229, 233, 238,
    239n, 264-265, 282, 317,
    331n, 359n, 384, 387f,
    387n, 392-393, 401-403,
    420n, 424, 447n, 459,
    462n, 466, 483
Arius, 184
Armstrong, Arthur H., 21, 21n, 22
Assel, Heinrich, 134n
Athanasius, 183, 186
Augustine of Hippo, 2n, 6, 9, 105,
    150, 196, 199, 384, 393f,
    397, 399, 402, 478, 478n,
    483
Austin, John L., 301
Ayer, Alfred Jules, 94n, 216-217,
    216n, 256, 332n, 467n
Balthasar, Hans Urs von, 476n
Barbour, Ian, 444n, 453n
Barth, Karl, 14, 26n, 36, 36n, 39n,
    61n, 134n, 137n, 189,
    255n, 476n, 478n
Barth, Paul, 30n, 149n
Bayer, Oswald, 103, 103n

Beardsley, Monroe C., 245n, 306-
    308, 350n, 475n
Beierwaltes, Werner, 466n
Benveniste, Émile, 199n
Benz, Ernst, 385n
Berggren, Douglas, 16n, 283, 286f,
    298, 309, 321
Bergson, Henri, 384n
Bernard of Clairvaux, 478
Biedermann, Alois Emanuel, 94n,
    144n, 474
Birkner, Hans-Joachim, 220n
Black, Max, 292
Blaire, Carol, 481n
Blanchot, Maurice, 143n
Bleicher, Josef, 122n
Bloch, Ernst, 231
Bloom, Alan, 108n
Boethius, 25
Bogdanov, Grichka, 71n, 281n
Bogdanov, Igor, 71n, 281n
Bohr, Neils, 119n, 136n
Bonaventura, 43n, 432
Bonhoeffer, Dietrich, 95n, 476n
Braig, Carl, 85n
Braithwaite, Richard B., 166
Brandenburger, Egon, 105n, 472n
Brentano, Robert, 21, 21n
Brightman, Edgar, 332f
Brooke, John Hedley, 188, 188n
Brown, Frank Burch, 83n
Brox, Norbert, 323n
Buber, Martin, 280
Buhle, Johann, 131n
Bultmann, Rudolf, 97-98, 97n, 476
Bushnell, Horace, 10, 164, 215, 478

Callistus, 23n
Calvin, John, 61n, 479
Campbell, John Angus, 27n
Capelle, Wilhelm, 137n
Cassian, John, 478
Cassirer, Ernst, 39n, 79n, 474
Chadwick, Owen, 196n
Chambers, Robert, 28n
Channing, William Ellery, 10, 94
Chauncy, Charles, 94, 449n
Chomsky, Noam, 179, 182
Clement of Alexandria, 14, 20n
Coelestius, 150
Coleridge, Samuel Taylor, 269
Collingwood, Robin G., 436
Colpe, Carsten, 488n
Copernicus, 444n, 445
Corssen, Peter, 488n
Crombie, I.M., 337n
Cyprian, 23n
Darwin, Charles, 27, 27n
Davidson, Donald, 143n
Davis, Edward B., 29n
Deely, John N., 28n
Derrida, Jacques, 5, 15n, 129, 143n, 149, 152, 155, 200n, 318, 340, 356, 481n
Descartes, 27, 30n, 110, 110n, 131, 131n, 136, 224n, 239, 332, 352n, 365, 383n, 408n, 420, 446n, 454, 465n, 482, 487
Dibelius, Martin, 488n
Diderot, Denis, 137n
Dilthey, Wilhelm, 11, 352n
Diogenes, 137n
Dörrie, Heinrich, 472n
Duke, James, 352n
Duke, James, 352n
Ebeling, Eberhard, 174n

Eckhart, Meister, 106
Edwards, Jonathan, 10, 32, 32n, 95, 449n, 478
Einstein, Albert, 119n, 136n
Eisler, 108n
Eliade, Mircea, 14, 243n, 374n, 480n, 497n, 500, 500n
Emerson, Ralph Waldo, 10
Epedocles, 383n
Epicurus, 281n
Erigena, John Scotus, 105, 478
Evagrius of Pontus, 478
Farias, Victor, 143n
Ferré, Frederick, 160, 166
Ferry, Luc 298n
Fetz, Reto Luzius, 201n, 466n
Feuerbach, Ludwig, 82n
Fichte, Johann G., 62n, 108n, 255n, 472n
Fish, Stanley, 172
Flew, Antony, 165, 256, 337n
Flynn, Bernard Charles, 383n, 465n
Franzen, Winfried, 143n
Frege, Gottlob, 301
Frend, William H.C., 23n, 117n
Freyer, Thomas, 434n, 435n
Funk, Robert, 415n
Gadamer, Hans-Georg, 4, 4n, 5, 17n, 37n, 86n, 87-88, 94n, 96, 114, 114n, 118, 121-122, 122n, 126-127, 143n, 192n, 200-202, 202n, 208, 234n, 230n, 274, 291, 304, 318, 350, 350n, 352n, 355, 357, 357n, 359-366, 368, 370, 373n, 374, 374n, 418-419, 450n, 467n, 502, 502n, 505n
Galileo, 25, 25n, 26n, 444n, 445
Geffcken, Johannes, 488n

Gerrish, Brian, 61n, 172n, 462n
Gillispie, Charles Coulston, 27n, 444n
Gingerich, Owen, 26n, 444n
Girard, René, 470n
Goodwin, George L., 132n
Gould, Jay, 208n
Grabbe, Christian D., 113n
Grant, Robert, 20n
Greeley, Andrew, 19
Gregor von Nyssa, 222n
Guitton, Jean, 71n, 281n
Habermas, Jürgen, 4n, 96, 122n, 143n, 205n, 335n, 499n
Hamerton-Kelly, Robert, 469
Hannay, Alastair, 231n
Hare, Richard M., 166, 337n
Harnack, Adolf von, 20, 20n, 488n
Hartlich, Christian, 49, 97n
Hartshorne, Charles, 114n, 132n, 157, 159
Hauerwas, Stanley, 13, 172
Hegel, Georg W.F., 11, 11n, 12n, 51, 51n, 77n, 352n, 386n, 492n
Heidegger, Martin, 5, 9, 14, 15n, 67n, 85, 85n, 87, 87n, 88, 89n, 95, 97, 102n, 107n, 108, 108n, 109n, 116n, 117n, 120n, 124n, 127, 129, 139, 139n, 200n, 201n, 205n, 215n, 243n, 244n, 297, 309, 344n, 353, 357n, 358-359, 362, 362n, 372, 377, 379n, 383n, 384, 393, 402, 403f, 405n, 411, 412n, 414f, 423f, 434, 454, 455n, 461n, 462n, 465n, 466, 483, 506n
Heisenberg, Werner, 334n

Heraclites, 145, 216
Herrmann, Friedrich-Wilhelm von, 393n, 394n
Hick, John, 174n
Hildenbrandt, Eberhard, 100n, 148n
Hirsch, Emanuel, 60n, 134n, 322n
Hirsch, Eric D., Jr., 350, 350n
Hofrichter, Peter, 185n
Hölderlin, 205n
Holte, Ragnar, 184n
Hübner, Kurt, 14, 494n, 500, 500n
Hugh of St. Victor, 33n, 344n, 432, 479n
Humboldt, Wilhelm von, 199n
Hume, David, frontispiece, 11n, 71n, 114n, 116, 122n, 132n, 155, 189n, 238, 241n, 340, 447n, 451, 458n, 459n, 465, 483
Huss, John, 478
Husserl, Edmund, 9, 26n, 116n, 117, 241n, 344n, 384, 397f, 402, 420, 421f, 426f, 426n, 429n, 431n, 434, 440n, 447n, 483, 505, 506, 506n
Iamblichus, 466n
Inciarte, Fernando, 420n, 446n, 462n
Inge, William Ralph, 386n
Ivánka, Endre von, 472n
Jackobson, Roman, 303
Jacobi, Friedrich Heinrich, 108n
Jäger, Alfred, 67n
Jaspers, Karl, 98n
Johnson, Barbara, 149
Johnston, William, 105
Jonas, Hans, 117n
Jüngel, Eberhard, 2n, 202n, 203n, 204
Justin Martyr, 105n

Kant, Immanuel, 9, 9n, 27, 62, 62n,
    74n, 102, 116, 122n, 131,
    352n, 374n, 380n, 384,
    395f, 402, 419, 419n,
    439n, 465, 483
Kappes, Michael, 2n
Kaufman, Peter, 23n, 34n
Kepler, Johannes, 26, 445
Kierkegaard, frontispiece, 39n, 51n,
    55f, 63n, 64n, 124n, 231n,
    243n, 461n
Kisiel, Theodore, 85n, 97n, 141n
Knowles, David, 25n
Kockelmann, Joseph, 139n, 200n
Köpf, Ulrich, 17n, 43n, 79n
Koschorke, Klaus, 20n, 21
Koselleck, Reinhart, 187
Koyré, Alexander, 25n, 448n
Kuhn, Thomas, 6, 7, 113n, 118-119,
    119n, 175n, 178, 180-182,
    240, 241f, 303, 336n, 357,
    360, 365, 420, 450-451,
    456, 502, 506n
Küng, Hans, 174n
Lacoue-Labarthe, 143n
Langerbeck, Hermann, 472n, 488n
Leftow, Brian, 384n
Leibniz, Gottfried Wilhelm von, 331
Lessing, Gotthold Ephraim, 454, 482
Lévinas, Emanuel, 9, 143n, 434f,
    434n
Lilie, Frank, 145n
Lindau, Hans, 108n
Lindbeck, George, 6, 13, 35n, 44n,
    101n, 172f, 255n, 462n,
    509n
Lonergan, Bernard, 35n, 157, 159,
    174n
Löwith, Karl, 143n
Lust, Johan, 356n

Luther, 479
Lyotard, Jean-Francois, 11, 11n
Marcuse, 143n
Markus, Robert, 24, 24n
Marqués, Alfonso García, 359n
Martin, Gottfried, 1n
Martin, Rex, 436n
Marx, Karl 11
McDermott, John M., S.J., 478n
McFague, Sallie, 3, 3n, 255n
McGaughey, Douglas, 18n, 27n, 97n,
    166n, 374n, 423n, 471n,
    474n, 495n
McGinn, Bernard, 17n, 105n, 472n
McKeever, Kerry, 150n
McKinnon, Alastair, 337n
Meijering, E.P., 472n
Merleau-Ponty, Maurice, 384n
Metz, Johannes-Baptist, 476n
Meyer, Ben F., 453n
Miller, Patricia Cox, 356n
Mitchell, Basil, 166, 337n
Moltmann, Jürgen, 476n
Moltmann-Wendel, Elizabeth, 255n
Motzkin, Gabriel, 81n
Mühl, Max, 184n, 185n
Müller, Friedrich Max, 320n
Müller, Hans, 134n
Müller-Lauter, Wolfgang, 108n
Murray, John Courtney, 184n
Natrop, Paul, 421
Newton, Isaac, 137, 138
Nicholas of Cusa, 478
Niebuhr, H. Richard, 10
Niebuhr, Reinhold, 10
Nietzsche, Friedrich W., 107n, 108,
    108n, 144n, 152, 243n,
    297, 318, 340, 343n, 352n,
    416, 418n, 456n, 481n
Nigg, Walter, 95n, 474n

Nijenhuis, John, 132n, 218n, 446n
Noire, Ludwig, 100n, 199n
Nolley, Kenneth, 179n
Nygren, Anders, 203n, 213, 213n
Occam, William of, 15
Ogden, Schubert, 6, 35n, 83, 88, 93,99n, 126, 157, 159, 202n, 203n, 207, 204, 490-491, 490n, 491n, 492n, 495, 505
Origen, 185n, 472n
Osborn, Eric, 472n
Ott, Hugo, 85n, 109n, 143n
Otto, Rudolf, 35n, 109, 109n
Owens, Joseph, 132n
Paley, William, 27
Palmer, Richard E., 369n
Pannenberg, Wolfhart, 2n, 14, 203n
Parker, Theodore, 10
Parmenides, 73, 131, 282, 293, 372
Paul, Jean, 320n, 481n
Peacocke, Arthur R., 120n
Pearson, Birger A., 184n
Peirce, Charles S., 10
Pfleiderer, Otto, 474
Philo of Alexandria, 30n, 79n, 105n, 149n, 184n, 447n
Plato, 6, 8, 9, 25, 45, 49n, 50, 71n, 73, 79n, 89n, 102, 114n, 146, 147n, 148, 149, 150, 218, 219n, 241, 282, 322, 356, 363, 384, 385f, 387n, 390n, 392, 401, 402, 403, 410, 419n, 420n, 424, 432, 433, 437n, 443n, 449n, 452, 458, 463n, 479n, 482
Plotinus, 9, 79n, 105n, 335n, 384, 386-387, 386n, 391f, 393, 401-402, 409-410, 417n, 482

Pöggeler, Otto, 108n, 143n
Pohlenz, Max, 14n, 20n, 21, 21n, 30n, 61n, 71n, 215n, 363n, 443n
Poinsot, John, 28n
Porphyry, 79n
Praechter, Karl, 472n
Price, R.M., 472n
Protagoras, frontispiece
Pseudo-Dionysius, 105, 478
Rahner, Karl, 8n, 99n, 174n
Ramsey, Ian, 161, 166, 337n
Reardon, Bernard M.G., 82n
Reitzenstein, Richard, 488n
Renaut, Alain, 298n
Richards, Ivor A., 270, 286, 298, 303, 307, 309
Ricoeur, Paul, 4, 4n, 8n, 9, 12n, 38n, 50, 50n, 74n, 76n, 83, 83n, 85, 87-88, 89n, 96, 102, 122, 157, 159, 169, 171n, 174n, 187, 187n, 199n, 205n, 228n, 241n, 244n, 255n, 285, 297f, 335n, 342, 342n, 345, 347n, 348n, 349, 350n, 351, 362n, 366n, 369, 373, 379n, 384, 400, 401, 405n, 407-408, 419, 435f, 440n, 443n, 450n, 454n, 456n, 462, 462n, 469n, 475n, 481n, 483, 484n, 497n
Rorty, Richard, 483
Rousseau, Jean Jacques, 137n
Runia, David, 447n, 459n, 472n
Sachs, Walter, 97n
Santayana, George, 6, 204
Sartre, Jean-Paul, 294, 298
Saussure, Ferdinand de, 100n, 148, 148n, 149, 151, 297, 199n

Schillebeeckx, Edward, 174n, 476n
Schleiermacher, Friedrich, 35n, 65, 65n, 109, 109n, 122n, 172n, 220n, 339n, 352n, 458n, 490, 495
Schneeberger, Guido, 143n
Schner, George, 189n
Schütz, R., 488n
Schützeichel, Harald, 63n, 122n
Schwan, Alexander, 108n
Schwartz, Sanford, 351n
Schweidler, Walter, 68n
Schweitzer, Albert, 185n
Seneca, 14n, 61n
Shakespeare, 446n
Sheehan, Thomas, 89n, 143n
Shelley, Percy Bysshe, 303
Socrates, 6, 13, 33, 48, 89, 181, 246, 282, 360, 363, 433, 457
Sokolowski, Robert, 433n
Speck, Josef, 447n
Spiegelberg, Herbert, 505n
Spranger, Eduard, frontispiece, 147n, 357n
Stanford, W. Bedell, 16n, 283, 287, 289
Stapel, Wilhelm, 134n
Staudinger, Hugo, 485-486, 485n, 486n
Stegmüller, Wolfgang, 113n
Stepelevich, Lawrence S., 11n
Stephen of Rome, 23n
St. John of the Cross, 106
Strauß, Levi, 297
Strawson, Peter F., 301
Strolz, Walter, 434n
Swidler, Leonard, 174n
Taylor, Mark C., 200
Tertulian, Nicolas, 143n
Tertullian of Carthage, 23

Theunissen, Michael, 51n
Tillich, Paul, 35n, 39n, 45n, 54, 54n, 79, 88, 92, 101, 112n, 126, 126n, 132n, 162n, 191, 192n, 231, 231n, 374, 476n, 482, 491
Tracy, David, 5, 19, 19n, 35n, 37n, 39n, 43n, 45n, 80, 80n, 83n, 84, 84n, 87-88, 90, 90n, 93, 113n, 126, 126n, 157f, 174n, 178n, 189n, 190n, 192n, 203n, 205n, 239n, 241n, 255n, 256-257, 335n, 337n, 350n 475n, 476n, 495n, 500n
Troeltsch, Ernst, 192n, 462, 474
Turbayne, Colin, 318
Turgenev, Ivan, 108n
Vaihinger, Hans, 335
Verbeke, Gerard, 455n
Vogel, Cornelia de, 105n, 472n
Walker, Williston, 29n, 496n
Waszink, Jan Hendrik, 184n
Weischedel, Wilhelm, 68n
Weiss, Wolfgang, 488n
Welch, Claude, 51n, 462
Wesley, John, 478
Wheelwright, Philip, 261, 269, 270f, 286, 290, 298, 307, 309 345n, 418n
Whitehead, Alfred North, 160, 234n, 241n
Widengren, Geo., 488n
Wiebe, Donald, 28n
Wiles, Maurice, 184n, 185n, 186n
Williams, Rowan, 184n
Wimsatt, William K., Jr., 245n, 350n, 475
Wittgenstein, Ludwig, 113n, 181, 182, 246, 457

Wlosok, Antonie, 105n, 472n
Wolz-Gottwald, Eckard, 33n, 432, 432n, 479n
Wycliffe, John, 478

Wyschogrod, Edith, 200n
Xenophanes, 131n, 383, 410
Zwingli, Ulrich, 467n, 478

Walter de Gruyter
Berlin • New York

INTERNATIONAL JOURNAL OF PRACTICAL THEOLOGY (IJPT)

Edited by: Don S.Browning - Rebecca Chopp - Duncan Forrester Wilhelm Gräb - Christian Grethlein - Ronald L. Grimes Maureen Junker-Kenny - Norbert Mette - Richard R. Osmer Hendrik J.C. Pieterse - Robert Schreiter - Friedrich Schweitzer Joon Kwan Un - Johannes A. van der Ven

Volume 1 (1997)
Two issues per year comprising a total of approx. 320 pages.
Complete volume DM 168.-/ öS 1.243,- / sFr 150,-;
Single issue DM 91.- / öS 673,- / sFr 83,- ISSN 1430-6921

The *International Journal of Practical Theology* is an academic journal. It is intended for practical theologians and teachers of religious education, scientists specializing in religion, and representatives of other cultural-scientific disciplines. The aim of the journal is to promote an international and interdisciplinary dialogue.

The journal contains contributions on an empirically descriptive and critically constructive theory of ecclesiastical and religious practice in society. Primarily, it deals with descriptions of religion as it is practised. Religion in this context can be understood in the broad sense of the word according to which all appreciative tendencies towards an ultimate view of oneself and of the world can be described as being religious. Thus the many different forms of religion as they are lived today are applied in a critically constructive manner to the normative self-image of churches, ecclesiastical groups and denominations. These contributions towards practical theology ultimately pursue the structure of practically orientated theories of ecclesiastical and ecclesiastically conveyed religious practice.

The contributions are in English or German. A summary (abstract) is given in the other language respectively to give the reader a general idea of the article.

Prices are subject to change

Walter de Gruyter & Co • Berlin • New York • Genthiner Straße 13 • D-10785 Berlin
Telefon: (030) 2 60 05-0 • Telefax: (030) 2 60 05-2 22
Unser Programm finden Sie im World Wide Web unter http://www.deGruyter.de

Walter de Gruyter
Berlin • New York

HANS MARTIN MÜLLER
Homiletik
Eine evangelische Predigtlehre

20,5 x 13,5 cm. XVII, 442 Seiten. 1996.
Kartoniert DM 58,- / öS 453,- / sFr 58,- ISBN 3-11-015074-3
Gebunden DM 88,- / öS 687,- / sFr 86,- ISBN 3-11-013186-2
de Gruyter Lehrbuch
Evang. Predigtlehre für Studenten und Vikare sowie für die Pfarrerfortbildung. Die Lehre von der Predigt wird aus der Sicht der evangelischen Theologie nach ihren historischen Voraussetzungen, ihrem systematischen Zusammenhang und ihren praktischen Konsequenzen dargestellt.
Der Autor war bis 1994 Ordinarius für Praktische Theologie an der Evangelisch-Theologischen Fakultät der Universität Tübingen.

MARTIN HONECKER
Grundriß der Sozialethik

20,5 x 13,5 cm. XXVI, 790 Seiten. 1995.
Kartoniert DM 78,- / öS 609,- / sFr 77,- ISBN 3-11-014474-3
Gebunden DM 118,- / öS 921,- / sFr 114,- ISBN 3-11-014889-7
de Gruyter Lehrbuch
Lehrbuch und Nachschlagewerk für das gesamte Gebiet der Sozialethik.
In einem zusammenfassenden Überblick werden zentrale Themen aus sechs Lebensbereichen dargestellt:
Leben und Gesundheit ("Medizinische Ethik") - Ehe, Familie und Sexualität - Natur und Umwelt - Politik und Staat - Wirtschaft - Kultur und Recht.
Einleitend werden die gängigen Modelle theologischer Weltdeutung (z.B. Zweireichelehre, Königsherrschaft Christi) diskutiert und am Ende wird die Aufgabe und Stellung der Kirche in der Gesellschaft erörtert.
Der Autor ist ordentlicher Professor für Sozialethik und Systematische Theologie an der Evangelisch-Theologischen Fakultät der Universität Bonn.

Preisänderungen vorbehalten

Walter de Gruyter & Co. • Berlin • New York • Genthiner Straße 13
D-10785 Berlin • Telefon: (030) 2 60 05-0 • Telefax: (030) 2 60 05-2 22

GENERAL THEOLOGICAL SEMINARY
NEW YORK

DATE DUE			

HIGHSMITH #45230   Printed in USA